ALSO BY BETTANY HUGHES

Helen of Troy: Goddess, Princess, Whore

THE HEMLOCK CUP

BETTANY HUGHES

THE HEMLOCK CUP

SOCRATES, ATHENS AND THE SEARCH FOR THE GOOD LIFE

ALFRED A. KNOPF

NEW YORK 2011

THIS IS A BORZOI BOOK
PUBLISHED BY ALFRED A. KNOPF

Copyright © 2010 by Bettany Hughes
All rights reserved. Published in the United States by Alfred A. Knopf,
a division of Random House, Inc.
www.aaknopf.com

Originally published in Great Britain in 2010 by Jonathan Cape,
an imprint of the Random House Group Limited, London.

Knopf, Borzoi Books, and the colophon are registered trademarks of Random House, Inc.

Library of Congress Cataloging-in-Publication Data
Hughes, Bettany.
The hemlock cup : Socrates, Athens and the search for the good life /
by Bettany Hughes.—1st U.S. ed.
p.   cm.
Includes bibliographical references.
ISBN 978-1-4000-4179-4 (alk. paper)
1. Socrates.   2. Philosophers—Greece—Athens—Biography.
3. Philosophers, Ancient—Biography.   4. Athens (Greece)—Biography.   I. Title.
B316.H84 2011
183'.2—dc22
[B]   2010045486

Jacket image: *Socrates,* engraving by Thomas Trotter after a drawing
by Peter Paul Rubens. Mary Evans Picture Library.
Jacket design by Jason Booher

Manufactured in the United States of America
Published February 10, 2011
Second Printing, March 2011

For

KE-SE-NE-WI-JA

xenwia and xenia

and therefore for my
friends, at home and abroad.

CONTENTS

ᕀᕀᕀᕀᕀᕀᕀᕀᕀᕀᕀ

ACT ONE – ATHENA'S CITY

ACT TWO – SOCRATES AS A YOUNG MAN

ACT THREE – SOCRATES THE SOLDIER

ACT FOUR – NEW GODS, NEW POSSIBILITIES: SOCRATES IN MIDDLE AGE

ACT FIVE – THE FIGHT GOES ON

ACT SIX – SOCRATES AND LOVE

ACT SEVEN – CUTTING DOWN
THE TALLEST CORN

ACT EIGHT – THE TRIAL AND DEATH
OF SOCRATES

Many wonders, many terrors, but none more wonderful or more terrible than a human being.

Sophocles, *Antigone*, 332

And what kind of person is more loved by the gods than the one who is most happy?

Xenophon, describing Socrates in his *Memorabilia*, 4.8.3

ACKNOWLEDGEMENTS

〇〇〇〇〇〇〇〇〇〇〇〇

I have referenced the works, both ancient and modern, upon which I have relied heavily or which might be of further interest to the reader. Although I would have loved Socrates to be Sokrates – and hence more Hellenic, I have in general chosen the more familiar, Latinised versions of the names of literary and historical figures and places.

The translations are my own or a collaborative effort between myself and my colleagues unless otherwise stated.

For help, humour, hospitality and the gift of *nous* my heartfelt thanks go to:

Julian Alexander, Anna Antoniou, Professor Mary Beard, Professor Lisa Bendall, Professor Sue Blundell, Richard Bradley, Professor John Camp, Professor Paul Cartledge, Sophia and Alex Constantidis, Professor Michael Cosmopoulos, Professor James Davidson, Dr Angelos Delivorrias, Professor Matthew Dickie, Dr Matt Edge, Kathy Elgin, Lucy Felmingham, Spiro and Millie Flamburiari (thank you for introducing me to the delights of Corcyra), Wing Commander John Foden (who, age 83, led me through the mountains of the Peloponnese), Dr Annelise Freisenbruch, Professor Betsy Gebhard, Dr Dimitris Grigoropoulos, Dr Angie Hobbs, Dr Dan Hogg, Ben Jackson, John, Jenny, Jane and Julia (for the houses), Professor Robin Lane-Fox, Bill Locke, Jack MacInnes, Peter Millett, John Morcom, Dr Alfonso Moreno, Professor Dirk Obbink, Justin Pollard, Jennifer Redfearn, Professor P. J. Rhodes, Laura Rizzotto, Sophia Roberts, Professor Charlotte Roueché, Dr Deborah Ruscillo, John Savage, Dr Michael Scott, Philip Sellars, Dr Victoria Solomonidis, Julietta Steinhauer, Dr Claire Stocks, Professor Barry Strauss, Professor Oliver Taplin, Lieutenant-Commander Alec Tilley, Dr Nicola Wardle, Olivia Williams. The staff of the Ashmolean and British Museums, the German Archaeological Institute, the Naples Museum and the Samos Epigraphical Museum, thank you for your patience. St. Hilda's College – my alma mater – always there for me. Professor Dirk Obbink – the treasures from the sands of Egypt have been patiently and generously revealed. Robin – you fired me to do all of this, when we meet or talk or I read a word of your work I remember why every single one of your tutorials was wildly inspirational. Never a dull moment. Matti and Nicholas Egon have been, as ever, wonderful. The world owes you much. Professor John Camp, your guided tours were exceptionally helpful, and illuminating for both me and my girls. Peter and Anna, you've let me impose on your hospitality so many times now, and Athens will not be the same without you. Pete, our road trips have been amongst the happiest days of my life. Sorrel and May Evans – thank you very much for reading out those Plato quotes at times of need. Adrian, thank you for living with a backview at a computer for the last five years. Ma and Pa, you made it possible.

Without the undinting support of all of the above this book simply would not have made it into print.

Ellah Allfrey and Dan Franklin sympathetically honed the text and saved me from both extreme colloquialism and self-indulgence, Tom Avery – the man with the most beautiful writing in the world, was charm personified despite my increasingly wild demands. Neil – thank you for the extension, Will for your good judgement, and Clara for your vivacity and vision. Julian Alexander, my literary agent, has been my rock and has become one of my dear friends, you have made my life better – and whenever I think of you I smile. Dr Alfonso Moreno, Dr Angie Hobbs, Professor Oliver Taplin, Professor Michael Cosmopoulos, Professor James Davidson, Professor Elizabeth Gebhard, Professor Matthew Dickie, Peter Millett, Dr Matt Edge have all been kind enough to read all or part of this text and save me from error and mania. Paul Cartledge has proved himself, once again, to be both the superior friend and scholar. He has met last-minute requests to look over this text – I blush to think how many times – with grace and generosity. He is one of the reasons I love antiquity with such a passion.

PREFACE

@@@@@@@@@@@@@

Those who are already wise no longer love wisdom — whether they are gods or men.
Similarly, those whose own ignorance has made them bad, rotten, evil, do not strive for
wisdom either. For no evil or ignorant person ever strives for wisdom.
What remains are those who suffer from ignorance, but still retain some sense and
understanding. They are conscious of knowing what they don't know.

Socrates, in Plato's *Lysis*, 218b, fourth century BC

PUT TWO AUTHORS TOGETHER IN A room and someone is bound to leave mildly depressed. The only exception seems to be when one of the pair is Peter Cook. Meeting a fellow writer in a bar, so the anecdote goes, he was asked whether he was penning a book. 'Yes, I'm not either . . .' came the soothing reply.

No such comfort for me. Sharing breakfast in an Edinburgh hotel with an award-winning novelist, just as I embarked on this book, the friendly chat came round to our next projects.

'Socrates! What a doughnut subject!' he exclaimed. 'Gloriously rich, with a whacking hole in the middle where the central character should be . . .' My smile fixed. Of course he is right: because as far as we know, Socrates wrote down not one word of philosophy. The idea of Socrates is immensely influential, and yet everything we know of him is hearsay. He is, historically, conspicuous by his absence. And thus for the past five years, as I've typed, I have had a spectral doughnut hovering over my shoulder.

But painters will tell you that the truest way to represent a shape is to deal with the space around it. The primary-source, autobiographical, historical Socrates is a lacuna; my hope is that by looking at the shape around the Socrates-sized hole, at the city in which he lived — Athens in the fifth century BC — I can begin to write not quite a life of Socrates, but a vivid sketch of Socrates in his landscape; a topography of the man in his times.

I have a warehouse full of unusual allies in this task — the earth-shifters, bulldozers, spades and trowels that have been picking over the Greek landscape in the last few years. The millennial year of 2000, the promise of a Greek Olympics in 2004, the new Acropolis Museum, a change in planning law – all these things have yielded huge amounts of material evidence from the fifth century BC. Socrates is an *eidolon* – the Greek word gives us idol, a ghost – who haunts a very real landscape. By exploring this physical landscape my hope is to flesh out this idol, and to imagine the life of one of the most provocative and provoking thinkers of all time.[1]

INTRODUCTION

@@@@@@@@@@@@

The unexamined life is not a life worth living for a human being.

Socrates, in Plato's *Apology*, 38a[1]

WE THINK THE WAY WE DO because Socrates thought the way he did. Socrates' belief that, as individuals, we need to question the world around us stands at the heart of what it means to live in 'modern times'. In the Socratic Dialogues, generated twenty-four centuries ago, we find the birth of *ethos* – ethics[2] – and the identification of the *psyche*.[3] 'The First Martyr' – the Greek *martys* means 'witness' – a witness to 'truth, virtue, justice' and 'freedom of speech', is commemorated as a bedrock of our civilisation.

Socrates stands at the beginning of our world – when democracy and liberty are first conceived as fundamental values of society. We need to understand him because he did not just pursue the meaning of life, but the meaning of *our own* lives.[4]

Socrates sees us coming. He worries that the pursuit of plenty will bring mindless materialism, that 'democracy' will become just a banner under which to fight. What is the point, he says, of warships and city walls and glittering statues if we are not happy? If we have lost sight of what is good? His is a question that is more pertinent now than ever. He asks: 'What is the right way to live?'

I am a stinging fly, sent to goad the city as though it were a huge, thoroughbred horse, which because of its size is rather sluggish and needs to be stirred.[5]

@@@@@

When Socrates comes into focus, in Greece in the fifth century BC, he is no didact: he wanders through the streets of Athens, *debating* the essence of what it means to be human. For the young men (and women) of the city he is irresistible: his relentless questioning appears to tap man's potential for self-knowledge. His 'ethics' programme centres on the search for the 'good life'. His, it was whispered – then and through the next 2,400 years – is a voice of incomparable *sophia*: of knowledge, skill, wisdom and truth.

The greater part of Socrates' life was spent out in public, in Athens, philosophising unrestricted. But when the philosopher was seventy, Athens turned against him. In March 399 BC the ageing citizen was tried in a religious court and found guilty of both primary and secondary charges: *'not duly acknowledging the city's gods and inventing new ones'* and *'corrupting the youth'*. The death sentence was passed: four weeks or so later Socrates killed himself by drinking the hemlock poison left for him by his jailer in his Athenian cell.

⚭⚭⚭⚭⚭

Socrates' arguments were perhaps just too incendiary, too dangerously charismatic. He believed that man had the potential to enjoy perfect happiness. A clue to the contemporary impact of his ideas is given by his pupil Plato. In the *Allegory of the Cave*,[6] with cool detail, Plato has Socrates describe a race of men who have been born in chains, and who, staring for ever at a cave wall, see only the shadows of creatures above them and believe these shadows to be reality. He then reveals the dismay and joy these captives feel when they are brought, blinking, into the light of the real world. The chained men represent those of humanity who have yet to hear or understand what Socrates has to say.

However, when it comes to wholeheartedly embracing the new, mankind displays a poor record. In a superstitious city, Socrates' spiritual and moral make-up was unconventional, troubling. He seems to have suffered from some form of epilepsy or 'petit mal' (hence his curious cataleptic seizures, when he stared into the distance for hours on end), which in a pious age was interpreted as a malign 'inner voice'.[7] His contemporary the playwright Aristophanes talks of the passionate men who go to hear him preach and turn their minds to fundamental issues rather than frivolities as having been 'Socratified'. And in his comedy *Clouds*,[8] Aristophanes jeers at Socrates' high-minded eccentricities, has him clamber into a raised bath and scramble around in the clouds to *'peer at the arse of the moon'*. Democracies need pragmatists, yet Socrates refuses to contain himself, to temper the power of principle. So *pheme* – rumour, gossip – starts to fly through Athena's city. As the robust philosopher is only too aware, a whispering campaign is the most pernicious and insidious of enemies.[9]

These people who have thrown scandal at me are genuinely dangerous. They've used envy and slander and they're difficult to deal with. I cannot possibly bring them into court to cross-question them or refute their charges. I have to defend myself as if I were boxing with shadows.[10]

Socratic thought and the living Socrates

@@@@@@@@@@@@

In all cities, it is easier to hurt a man than to help him.

Plato, Meno, 94e

In the Metropolitan Museum in New York hangs a painting of Socrates, just before death, by the great neoclassical painter Jacques-Louis David. Socrates — speaking slowly but determinedly, the hemlock about to run through his veins, a martyr to virtue and high principle — is surrounded by agitated disciples.[11] Crouched around his bed are those men such as Plato who will carry his words into literature and thus on into the very DNA of world civilisation.[12]

Now it is time for us to go away, for me to die and for you to live; but which of us is going to a better condition is not known to anyone except god.[13]

@@@@@

This is not a book of philosophic theory. I am a historian, not a philosopher, and cannot possibly better the work of those who have gone before me, who have squeezed ever-evolving interpretations out of Socrates' philosophical ideas; Plato, Aristotle, Diogenes the Cynic, Al-Kindi, Yehuda ha-Levi, Thomas Hobbes et al. — all these men have tussled with what Socrates' philosophy means. That is a bulging canon and one I would not presume to augment. But I can turn my eyes to the stones under my feet. I can see how Socrates' philosophy evolved in his time and his place.

For the purposes of this book, the joy of Socratic thought is that Socrates did not believe in or deal with abstracts. For him, morality stemmed from and emerged to deal with real problems in a real world. The characters he employs as porters for his ideas are often cobblers, bakers, priestesses, whores. Socrates continually emphasises that he is flesh and blood, and that it is as a flesh-and-blood man that he lived and understood life. It is one of the reasons his philosophy is so accessible to all of us. So bringing the humble, the archaeological and the physical back into the Socratic experience is appropriate. The totemic ideas that Socrates delivered were, put simply, as much to do with the religious ritual he had just witnessed down at his local harbour, with the pleasure of walking barefoot through Athens, with the death of a loved one, or the horror of living through a wasting-war, as they were with any kind of purely intellectual concept. Socrates' prime concern was with the world as lived. As this book weaves together the mongrel evidence for his life, where material remains are as valued as literary and documentary sources, a picture emerges of a world that is, for the first time, self-consciously trying to build a 'civilisation' that is based on a 'democracy'.[14]

Yet Socrates is not concerned just with our surroundings, but what is within us. '*He who orders us to know ourselves is bidding us to become acquainted with our soul.*'[15] Socrates is soulful. The philosopher believes open conversation an essential balm for the *psyche*. His method gets inner thoughts out into the public sphere, not as a monologue, but as a dialogue. For him this was cathartic – Plato uses the Greek word *katharsis*[16]– releasing 'bad things' from the spirit. Socrates is the first man for whom we have an extant record who explores how we should all live in the world, as the world was working out how to live with itself.

Truth is in fact a purification [katharsis] . . . and self-restraint and justice and courage and wisdom itself are a kind of purification.[17]

Socrates' philosophy is relevant to all of us, not least because it has been so tenacious. From Elizabeth I to Martin Luther King, from the Third Reich to twenty-first-century America, Socrates' example has been used to try to understand what society is, and what it should be. Socratic words filled the halls of Italian Renaissance humanists. The Jewish philosopher Yehuda ha-Levi in the eleventh century AD cites Socrates in a dialogue with King Khazar concerning the nature of Judaism. John Locke and Thomas Hobbes scatter their treatises of political theory with Socratic quotations.

Socrates was also a central influence in early Islam. Al-Kindi, the 'first' self-professed Arab philosopher, certainly the first Muslim philosopher, wrote extensive (long-lost) treatises on Socrates in the ninth century AD.[18] Socratic wisdoms were quoted in coloured stone, mortared into the very fabric of public buildings in Samarkand. The philosopher was nominated one of the Seven Pillars of Wisdom, his nickname 'The Source'. Socrates' inner voice was thought by medieval Muslims a sign that he was an angel in poor man's clothing. Throughout the Arab world from the eleventh century AD up until the present day he was said to refresh and nourish, '*like . . . the purest water in the midday heat*'.[19]

And yet why should we still care for him? Why commemorate this long-ago life? One good reason is because Socrates does that shocking thing – that thing we still crave – he implies there might be a way to be fulfilled on this earth. Socrates was magnetic because he counselled care of the soul. He believed that men can achieve true happiness only when they are at peace with themselves.[20] He suggested it is 'us', not 'them', who can make things better.

༄ༀༀༀ

Socrates, as I have said, is tantalisingly elusive. But what we do have in our favour is the physical setting of his 'not thereness'. If the play of fifth-century BC Athenian life was lovingly crafted by Plato, and Socrates was his inspiration, then the stage-set, Athens, is still available to all of us. All agree, when it comes to Socrates, that he was down-to-earth. His was a great mind supported by feet of clay. And it is those muddy footsteps that I will follow. So this is not a philosophical, but a topographical map of the man.

There are many reasons why Socrates' story demands to be told. It is, at its most basic, an electric courtroom drama. The men of Athens vote to exterminate Socrates. They think he is a threat. He thinks he can save the soul of the city. Is this mob-rule, a political conspiracy, or the perfect example of the rule of the majority? Is Socrates' story a tragedy or a useful staging post in the development of civilisation? Who is in the right?[21] The story of Socrates also incarnates the tension between the freedom of the individual and the regulation of the community. His refusal to compromise ends in his death. It is for this reason that he is hailed as humanity's first-recorded ideological martyr.

Socrates' life was spent in search of treasure, of an intimate understanding of humanity. And the combusting energy of that search drove him around the city of Athens. This book pursues the path he burned. His quest was to identify what place 'the good' might have in human society. We might not find that ultimate prize; Socrates himself was never sure that he had done so, and the only thing he seems to have been certain of was the futility of trying to find 'real' scientific explanations for everything in life. He thought it fruitless to stare at the skies and travel to the ends of the earth in order to catalogue the world, without learning to love it. Yet by inhabiting the Athens that raised him, we might just get a glimpse of the treasure-seeker: hot and cross sometimes, bad-tempered, self-absorbed, brilliant, dangerous, droll. Socrates never lost sight of his own temporality. The day he is condemned to death he declares: *I am, as Homer puts it, "not born of an oak or a rock", but of human parents.*[22] And so this books aims, physically, to inhabit Socrates' Athens – not just as recorded and as promoted, but as lived and experienced.

The city of Athens *is* Socrates. Nothing means more to Socrates than Athens, and, more importantly, than the Athenians within it. He tells one of his colleagues, Phaedrus, that his home, his world, is the city – a city full of people. For Socrates, people are his magnetic North: he *loved* them. Xenophon reports that his conversations *'were always about human concerns. He dealt with questions such as how people please and displease the gods, what is the essence / purpose of beauty and ugliness, justice and injustice, prudence and moderation, courage and cowardice.'*[23] All his philosophy is drawn to understanding the being of men and women around him. This understanding, this consciousness of one's own consciousness, is what Socrates calls the *psyche* – the life-breath or soul. And it is in the city of Athens, between the years 469 and 399 BC, that Socrates' soul flits.

My ambition is very simple: to re-enter the streets of Athens in real time. Not to revisit a Golden Age city, but to look at a real city-state that was forging a great political experiment and riveting a culture; a city that suffered war and plague as well as enjoying great triumphs. To inhabit a place that is at once absolutely recognisable and utterly strange. To breathe the air Socrates breathed. To meet democrats who pre-date democracy and philosophers who operate before the science of philosophy is born.

This history is pathos. Socrates' life and trial and death by hemlock are stories that Athens did not want fully told, but which we need to hear.

THE DRAMATIC STORY OF
SOCRATES – SOURCES
AND APPROACH

@@@@@@@@@@@@

*The words of Socrates survive and always will, although he wrote
nothing and left no work or testament.*

Dio Chrysostom, *On Socrates*, 54, first century AD

TRADITIONALLY WE MEET Socrates when a few of the key authors
from antiquity, in particular Plato and Xenophon (both pro-
Socrates) and Aristophanes (mixed), decide to open the door to
him: but in that doorway there is always the screen of the authors' opinions, their take on what they choose us to see. So, when we read the 'words'
of Socrates, it is hard to tell whether these are his or another's attitude,
another's philosophical enterprise.[1]

There is a second challenge. Plato, Aristophanes and Xenophon –
Socrates' immediate or close contemporaries, men who are the fathers of
Western philosophy, drama and chronicle – each deal with Socrates in a
notably theatrical way.

Plato writes as a dramatist, a frustrated playwright. In his work the
'character' of Socrates is – as all great theatrical characters are – essen-
tially charismatic, articulate and, to some extent, fabricated. The dramatic
persona is both amplified and collapsed, it is extra-articulate and two-
dimensional. Plato's Socratic Dialogues – crafted between twenty and forty
years after Socrates died – are brilliantly constructed, designed to engage.
Plato teases us and plays with us (he throws all the tricks of the enter-
tainer into his work), which of course leaves us with the possibility that
it is all just a fantasy. Xenophon is not much more help. Although more
down-to-earth and literal, his hard-fact histories are communicated via
animated, reported dialogue. Aristophanes, who satirises Socrates mercilessly, is not a biographer – he is a dramatist with a biting wit, he plays
to the gallery; he strives to make his audience howl with laughter. Spend
long enough with the Socratic texts from the fifth and fourth centuries BC
and you feel as though you have sat through a series of 'Socrates Shows'

— the TV docudrama, the West End, Hollywood and Broadway versions of a man's life.[2]

Yet these individuals, Socrates' contemporary biographers,[3] were not just showmen. They understood that drama can be an arterial route to truth. Socrates never wrote anything down, because, as he went about his philosophical business on the streets of fifth-century Athens, he believed in the honesty of joint-witnessing. For Plato to give Socrates a living voice in dialogue was as close as he could get to the original 'Socratic' experience.[4] The detail in Plato's work is conspicuous. We hear of the species of trees that shade Socrates, the birds he hears sing, the discomfort of the wooden benches he lies upon, the shoemakers he talks to, the hiccups he cures.

If this detail were utterly inappropriate, or fanciful, Plato would have been laughed out of the Academy he set up in around 387 BC, and out of history. Plato, along with Xenophon and Aristophanes, wrote for their fifth- and fourth-century BC peers — for men who were contemporaries of Socrates, many of whom were intimately involved in the philosopher's life and eye-witnesses to the events of the age. Downright lies just wouldn't have washed.[5]

Plato's memory matters. As a species, we remember and often we think in pictures, not words. Our visual memories are more acute than our aural.[6] In neuroscience these experiences are known as 'episodic memories' — vivid, patchy, but with a sensory quality that can be remarkably accurate. It is very likely that the physical setting that Plato provides for Socrates can be relied upon; the punchy, sensuous real-life scenarios he supplies are exactly the kinds of details that stick in the cortex. Add to that the fact that the Ancient Greeks invested in landscape in a way we can only begin to imagine: not only was visual stimulus, visual expression fundamental to society, but the world they saw was a place where spirits resided, a place full of signs and symbols. One begins to realise that the Platonic setting of ancient Athens was no mere convenient backdrop, but a four-dimensional landscape that Socrates, in real life as well as in Plato's imagination, almost certainly, vigorously occupied.[7]

Plato was perhaps over-compensating; doubtless some of those 'Socratic' sentiments were in fact his own — and so he gave us a virtual world, stocked with the real things that he and Socrates saw around them, copper-plating his own credibility as the historical Socrates' mouthpiece. But Plato's reputation now has archaeology on its side.[8] His philosophies work on many levels, but the hard facts they contain were certainly not all a lie. Archaeological digs — each year — are substantiating and backing up in precise detail the picture of fifth-century Athens that Plato so skilfully and energetically painted just after Socrates' death, 2,400 years ago. For the first time, for example, we can walk beside the narrow streets that lie under the new Acropolis Museum and across the Painted Stoa (a covered area or walkway) where Plato, as a young, impressionable man, sat and listened to Socrates speak. The ancient stones match Plato's ancient words.[9]

And so my attempt has been to re-create Socrates' world.[10] To follow the clues in Plato, Xenophon and Aristophanes to the physical reality of fifth-century Athens and therefore the physical reality of the story of Socrates' life. Through his dialogues Plato has given us the 'play' of Socrates' life, and described the most appropriate scenery before which the character of Socrates should enter. It is that scenery, that setting, that is now turning up in digs across the city.

The life of fifth-century Athens was itself, in essence, dramatic. Not only does Socrates' life span seventy of the busiest, most wonderful and tragic years in Athenian history, but the Athenians did, physically, construct a backdrop of democratic 'theatre' in which to play out their lives – democratic buildings, scenery, speeches, statues, props, music to help make their new democracy feel real.

Socrates will be best served not by Aristophanes' pantomime *Clouds*, but by a solid stage to stand on, from which he can speak audibly and directly to us, his audience. To this end I have used the latest sources – archaeological, topographical, textual – to construct a life for a man we can all benefit from getting to know a little better.[11]

DRAMATIS PERSONÆ

〰〰〰〰〰〰〰

Aristophanes

ARISTOPHANES IS THE OLDEST OF OUR sources for Socrates. A comic playwright, over his forty-year career he attacked everything from beetle-dung to apparently serious politics. These onslaughts earned him enemies: among them was Cleon, a hard-line demagogue who argued for the destruction of the entire male population of Mytilene in 427 BC and again at Scione in 423 BC. Cleon pursued Aristophanes in the courts, and in return was ridiculed repeatedly until his death at the Battle of Amphipolis in 422 BC. Aristophanes would continue making scabrous jibes at politicians at all levels, and mild satire of the Athenian people in general. Another target was Socrates himself, who was turned into a figure of fun in *Clouds*. Comic licence makes it hard to determine how serious this character assassination was: Plato suggests that Aristophanes helped fuel the public distrust of Socrates,[1] yet Aristophanes also features as an amiable dinner-companion of Socrates in Plato's *Symposium*, which is set after *Clouds* was first performed. Despite the violence of his satire, Aristophanes survived the deadly series of revolutions and politically motivated assassinations that characterised the final years of the Peloponnesian War in Athens.[2]

Aristophanes' career started with *The Banqueters* in 427 BC. He composed at least forty plays of which only eleven survive — we know the names of seventeen. *Clouds*, in which Socrates figures prominently, was produced in 423 BC. *Clouds* was not successful, finishing in last place at the City Dionysia festival. The poet-playwright's career continued until shortly before he died in 386 BC.

WORKS

Banqueters (427 BC); *Babylonians* (426); *Acharnians* (425); *Knights* (424); *Clouds* (423); *Wasps* (422); *Peace* (421); *Amphiaraus* (414); *Birds* (414); *Lysistrata* (411); *Women at the Thesmophoria* (411); a first *Plutus* (408); *Frogs* (405); *Ecclesiazusae* (391); a second *Plutus* (388); *Cocalus* and *Aiolosikon* (possible dates 387 BC and 386 BC[3]).

Xenophon

Xenophon's life was spent in warfare. Born near the beginning of the Peloponnesian War, probably in Erchia, a rural *deme* of Athens,[4] he would later write treatises on horsemanship from his estate near Olympia on the plains of the Peloponnese. Xenophon had probably served in the Athenian cavalry during the Peloponnesian War, and fought against the democratic insurgents in the Athenian civil war of 404/3 BC. After the democratic victory, Xenophon left Greece. He went to Anatolia to join the 'Ten Thousand', the Greek mercenary force supporting Cyrus the Younger's attempt to usurp the Persian throne. Cyrus was killed at Cunaxa (near Babylon) in 401 BC, and the five Greek generals in command of the Ten Thousand were themselves murdered soon after; Xenophon's star rose in their place, as he led the surviving Greeks on a dangerous and violent journey back to safety near Trapezus. It was during this period that Socrates was executed, and scholars are divided on how well the two men could have been acquainted.[5] Xenophon continued as a mercenary, first in Thrace and then for the Spartans in Anatolia and mainland Greece. Exiled by Athens, but protected by the Spartans, he was set up on an estate at Skillus, where he wrote most of his works. After the Spartan defeat at Leuctra, Xenophon was expelled from his estate and, though now reconciled with Athens, lived out the rest of his years near Corinth. His son Gryllus was killed fighting in the Athenian cavalry close to Mantinea in 362 BC.

XENOPHON'S WORKS MENTIONING SOCRATES, IN POSSIBLE ORDER OF COMPOSITION

Apology (composed after 384 BC?); *Memorabilia* (commenced); *Symposium* (before 371?); *Memorabilia* (completed); *Oeconomicus* (completed after 362).
Socrates also features in Xenophon's *Hellenica* (not completed before 359–355 BC), a history of Greek affairs from 411 to 362 BC.[6]

Plato

Plato was in his late twenties when Socrates was executed in 399 BC. He had probably known Socrates for all of his adult life.[7] Born some time around 428–423 BC, perhaps in Athens, into an aristocratic Athenian family, Plato was descended from Solon, who tradition claimed had brought democracy to the city.[8] Plato's uncle Critias headed the Thirty Tyrants, the murderous pro-Spartan faction that briefly controlled Athens after the end of the Peloponnesian War. Plato himself had been born in 428, not long after this war started. Growing up in the Athenian district of Cotyllus, he probably followed the normal educational path of a young aristocratic boy in poetry, music and gymnastics. He was a champion wrestler, almost certainly later serving in the Athenian military, presumably in the cavalry.[9] After Socrates' death, Plato's life was nomadic and eventful. He spent time in Megara, Egypt and southern Italy, associating with tyrants in Sicily and even being sold into (and immediately ransomed from) slavery on the island of Aegina in 388/7 BC. Shortly afterwards he seems to have established the Academy in Athens, one of the most significant intellectual institutions in the history of the world. There men such as Aristotle met; they were not taught as such, but engaged in the long conversations that characterise Plato's written output, and which Plato considered the necessary foundation-stone of all philosophical progress. Plato died in 348/7 BC.

It is important to remember that both Plato and Xenophon composed their works convinced that Athenians were wrong to vote for the death of Socrates.

PLATO'S DIALOGUES

The works are divided into three fluid and still-controversial periods: (a) early, (b) middle, (c) late. Perhaps *Lysis* was written while Socrates was still alive.

(a) *Hippias Minor; Ion; Crito; Euthyphro; Laches; Charmides; Lysis; Menexenus; Protagoras; Meno; Gorgias; Euthydemus*

(b) *Cratylus; Hippias Maior* (both perhaps early); *Phaedo; Symposium; Republic* (perhaps Book 1 is early); *Phaedrus* (perhaps late)

(c) *Parmenides; Theaetetus; Sophist; Politicus; Philebus; Timaeus; Critias; Laws;* (falsely attributed), *Plato Alcibiades 1.*

THE LIST OF DIALOGUES BELOW IS IN POSSIBLE ORDER OF *DRAMATIC DATE*

450 – *Parmenides;* 433/2 – *Protagoras;* 431–404 – *Republic, Gorgias;* 429 – *Charmides;* 424 – *Laches;* 422 – *Cratylus;* 418–416 – *Phaedrus;* 416 – *Symposium;* 413 – *Ion;* 409 – *Lysis;* 407 – *Euthydemus;* 402 – *Meno;* winter 402/1 – *Menexenus;* spring 399 – *Theaetetus;* 399 – *Euthyphro, Symposium* (frame), *Statesman;* May–June 399 – *Apology;* June–July 399 – *Crito, Phaedo*

ILLUSTRATIONS

@@@@@@@@@@@@

MAPS

INTEGRATED IMAGES

13.   Later cultures played on the possibilities of a sexual relationship   140
between Socrates and Alcibiades. This touched-up print was one
of a set made for a 1906 edition of the *De Figuris Veneris* (the
Manual of Classical Mythology); the images were first produced on
the Continent in the 1890s but titled 'Manchester 1884'. Of
course we hear from Plato that Socrates refused Alcibiades'
advances.

14.   The so-called *Mourning Athena* relief, commissioned around 460   147
BC. The artist is clearly endeavouring to portray the weight of
responsibility that comes with success. The relief is now beautifully displayed in the new Acropolis Museum, Athens.

15.   Athena's Silver Owl: the coin that became emblematic of both   159
Athens' wealth and of her control of the economy in the Eastern
Mediterranean for a substantial part of the fifth-century BC. The
silver to create this coinage came from silver-bearing seams of
lead in the mines of Laurion, south-east of Athens.

16.   The north-east corner of the Athenian Agora in 1931. By the   166
end of the first excavating season many of the key landmarks
of the marketplace of Socrates' day had been revealed. The fore-
ground column rests on foundation stones of Athens' great
'records office', the Metroon. Behind this are the foundations of
the monument of Eponymous Heroes and beyond that the steps
and altar stone of the Altar of Zeus Agoraios, where, it was
said, Socrates' father had prayed for his idiosyncratic son's future.

17.   A rare representation of a slave from the bottom of a drinking   203
cup. The man is shackled and is collecting rocks. *c.*490–480 BC.
Metal shackles from the early fourth century BC have been found
in the Athenian-run silver-mining district of Laurion.

18.   A stern Socrates rescues Alcibiades from the pitfalls and snares   227
of the world (in this case the arms of two beautiful young
women). Possibly the work of Lorenzo Bartolini (1777–1850) but
also attributed to Antonio Canova.

19.   Although Plato tells us that Socrates was not interested in the   235
physical aspects of erotic love, as this kylix indicates, this was
not an activity to which fifth-century Greeks were averse.

ising their mistake, set up a staue of the philosopher just in front
of this gateway to the city.

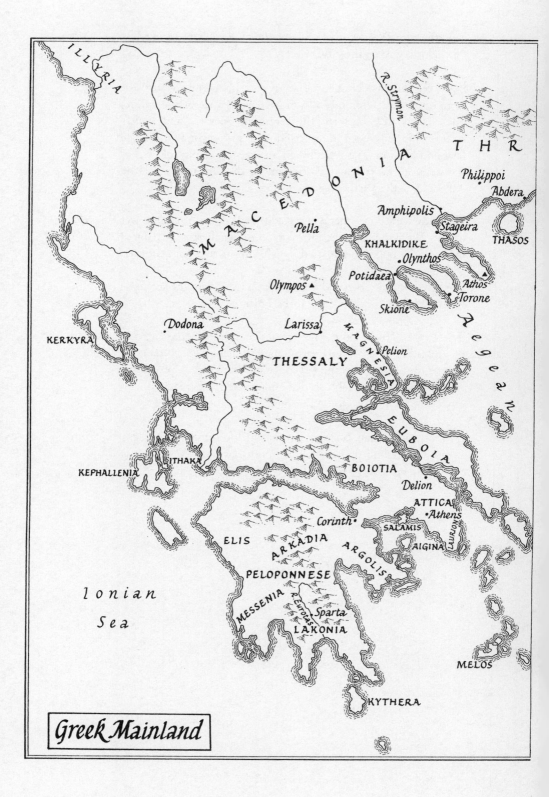

Greek Mainland

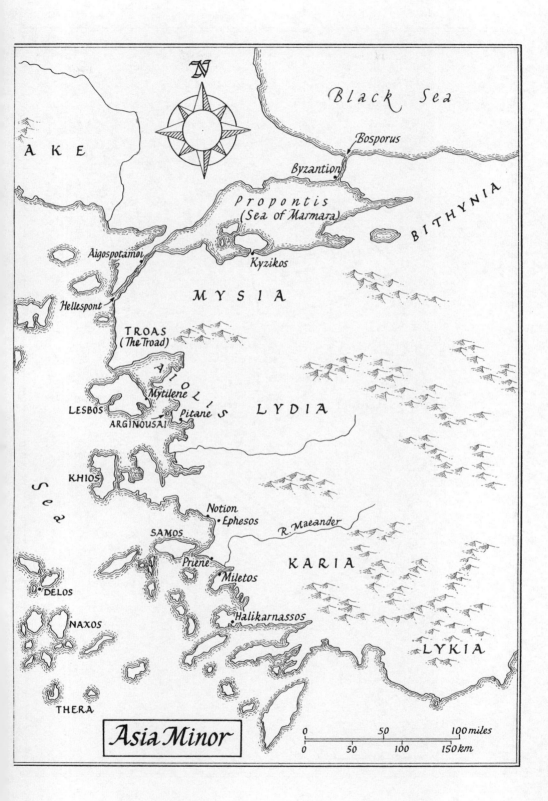

N

Black Sea

Bosporus

Byzantion

Propontis
(Sea of Marmara)

BITHYNIA

Aigospotamoi

Kyzikos

T H R A K E

M Y S I A

Hellespont

TROAS
(The Troad)

A I O L I S

Mytilene

LESBOS

Pitane

L Y D I A

ARGINOUSAI

KHIOS

Notion
Ephesos

R. Maeander

SAMOS

Priene

KARIA

Miletos

DELOS

Halikarnassos

NAXOS

LYKIA

Sea

THERA

Asia Minor

0   50   100 miles

0   50   100   150 km

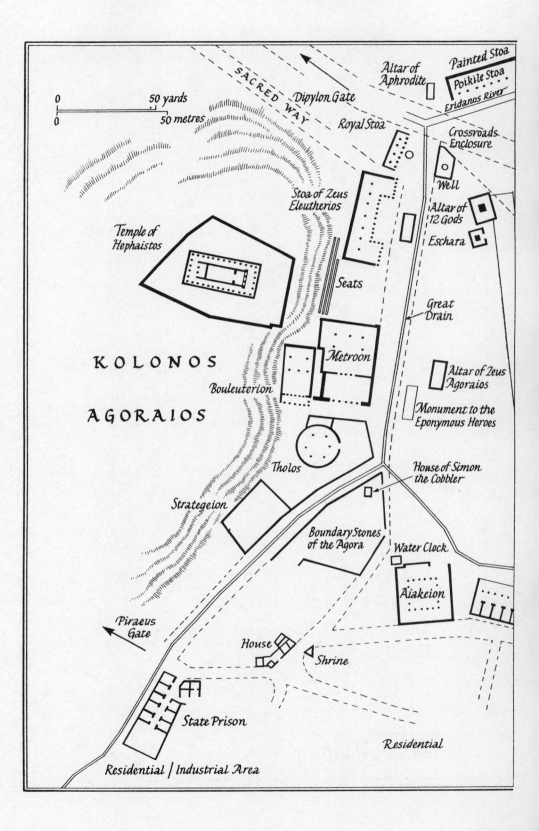

Sacred Way

Dipylon Gate

Altar of Aphrodite

Painted Stoa
Poikile Stoa
Eridanos River

Royal Stoa

Crossroads Enclosure

Well

Altar of 12 Gods

Eschara

0   50 yards
0   50 metres

Stoa of Zeus Eleutherios

Temple of Hephaistos

Seats

Great Drain

K O L O N O S

Metroon

Altar of Zeus Agoraios

A G O R A I O S

Bouleuterion

Monument to the Eponymous Heroes

Tholos

House of Simon the Cobbler

Strategeion

Boundary Stones of the Agora

Water Clock

Piraeus Gate

Aiakeion

House

Shrine

Residential

State Prison

Residential / Industrial Area

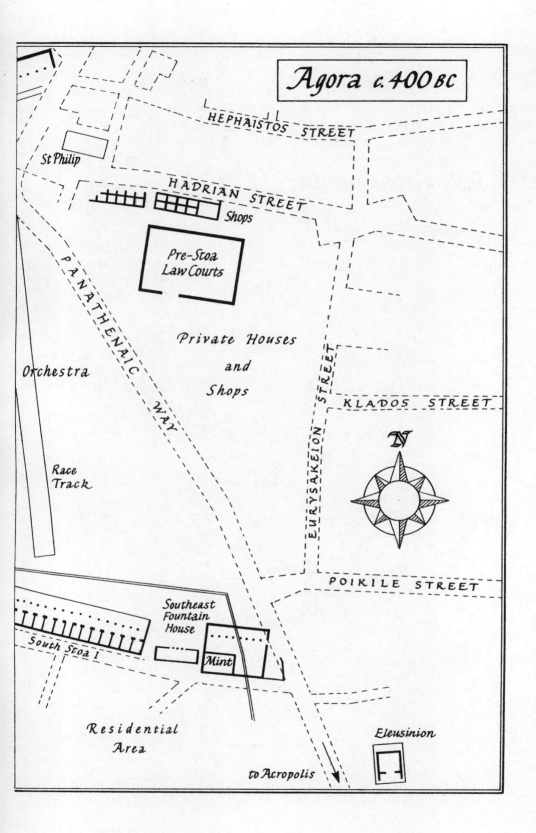

Agora c. 400 BC

HEPHAISTOS STREET

St Philip

HADRIAN STREET

Shops

Pre-Stoa
Law Courts

PANATHENAIC WAY

Orchestra

Private Houses
and
Shops

EURYSAKEION STREET

KLADOS STREET

N

Race
Track

POIKILE STREET

Southeast
Fountain
House

South Stoa I

Mint

Residential
Area

to Acropolis

Eleusinion

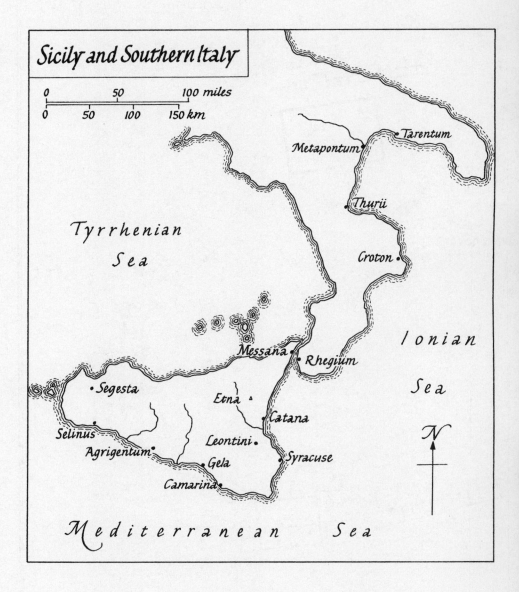

Sicily and Southern Italy

0   50   100 miles
0   50   100   150 km

Tyrrhenian
Sea

Metapontum
Tarentum

Thurii

Croton

Ionian
Sea

Messana
Rhegium

Segesta

Etna

Catana

Selinus
Leontini
Agrigentum
Gela
Syracuse
Camarina

N

Mediterranean   Sea

ACT ONE

∞∞∞∞∞∞∞∞∞∞∞∞

ATHENA'S CITY

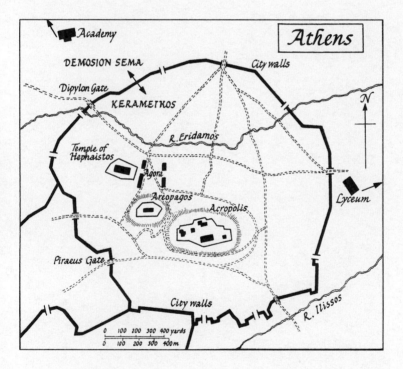

Athens

Academy
DEMOSION SEMA
City walls
Dipylon Gate
KERAMEIKOS
R. Eridanos
Temple of
Hephaistos
Agora
Areopagos
Acropolis
Lyceum
Piraeus Gate
City walls
R. Ilissos
N

0   100 200 300 400 yards
0   100 200 300 400m

1

THE WATER-CLOCK:
TIME TO BE JUDGED

@@@@@@@@@@@@

Athens, the Agora, 399 BC

How fitting is it to destroy an old man, a grey-headed man, beside the water-clock?

Aristophanes, *Acharnians*, 694[1]

IN MAY THE SUN RISES BRISKLY over Mount Penteli.

Five hundred men[2] are walking with purpose through the tight, packed-gravel lanes of Athens, past the modest mud-brick houses, around the gaudy public monuments: the communal baths, the Temple of Athena Nike, the new mint. Some of these public buildings are still wet with paint, few are more than fifty years old. At times the walking men have to pick their way across distasteful evidence of trauma — over derelict homes and past gaunt-hungry citizens. Unpleasant reminders of the catastrophes Athena's city has suffered during the last three decades: plague; foreign invasion; full-blown civil war; strife.

There are goats here, dogs, geese, cats, ducks; but hardly any women. Or at any rate there are few creatures classified as female; there are some shaven-headed slaves. These sub-human folk of Athens, male and female alike — 'man-footed things', 'living tools'[3] — have been about their business since well before dawn, preparing the food, mending the clothes, wiping the shit off the shoes of their masters.[4] At this time of day, the majority of Athens' other females, women-citizens, are moving back indoors. The night is their time. After dark, usually chaperoned, they are allowed out to gossip, to barter, to practise religious rites, and just before sunrise they

I

collect around the fountains to gather water. Now, with the sun climbing into the sky, it is appropriate to leave the streets. To be shut up at home during daylight hours is the only way for a respectable Athenian woman to behave.

But times have been hard. Once Athens could boast a stakeholder population of more than 200,000. Now, at the beginning of the fourth century BC, the number of adult men living in the city-state is one-tenth that number, closer to just 20,000. Since the outbreak of war with another Greek city-state, Sparta, in 431 BC, many tens of thousands of male citizens have died: in 404–3 BC alone up to 1,500 were killed, not by foreign but by Athenian hands – the death squads sponsored by rival factions during Athens' bitter civil war. Now women are forced to do that which their grandmothers would never have dreamed possible: bake their own bread, live in a bigamous marriage, sell ribbons on street corners. Rather than enter and exit the city through 30-foot-high monumental gates, decorated with bronze, the surviving females must stepping-stone across the stumpy remains of Athens' broken city walls; walls that were once the envy of all Greece.

A number of the men striding the street this late spring morning will be checking the precise time by the climb of the sun and the length of their shadow.[5] But these urgent Athenians are pulled not just to the brightening of the sky, but by the drip, drip of progress. The new mechanical water-clock that marks out time in this most adventurous of cities is soon to have its plug pulled. The judicial day is about to begin.[6]

All are making their way towards a court – the religious court of the *archon* – the magistrate of sacred affairs, a site that today is dissected by the jaunty-orange, rattling Athens metro and flanked by trinket and umbrella sellers.[7] This was, in the fifth century BC, a well-beaten path. Athens at that time was an exceedingly litigious place. In any one year up to 40,000 court cases might be heard. The Athenians loved a good legal brawl; their wrangles were a popular spectator sport. *Agon* – which translates as competition, struggle, set-to – is the Greek word often used. Gloves were off; *agon* is the root of our 'agony'. And today there would have been a particular frisson. The man Athenians have come to judge is considered a threat to society. His offence could be capital. It seems almost certain that this encounter will be agonising.

The Athenian jurors are here to try a stocky seventy-year-old, their fellow citizen – *Sokrates Alopekethen*, Socrates from the district of Alopeke. Socrates: not high-born, neither a decorated general, a prize-winning dramatist, nor a political hero, but still famous in his own lifetime. For the past thirty years men – particularly young men – have flocked to Athens from right across the eastern Mediterranean with the prime purpose of listening to him philosophise in the public spaces of the city. In decorated dining rooms, crowded back alleys and by the leafy banks of the city's rivers he could have been heard. He is a maverick; he did not found a school of philosophy, there was no individual aristocrat who funded his mission, it appears that he chose to write not a single word of philosophy down. And instead of polemic, instead of the great sweeps of rhetoric that have become so fashionable in Athenian society by the end of the fifth-century Golden Age, Socrates simply asks questions. His methods are, to put it mildly, unusual.

Yet the enquiring philosopher, now an old man, has become not just celebrated, but notorious. His eccentric methods, his unconventional lifestyle, his dogged interrogations, his troubling attraction to the young of the region have earned him as many enemies as friends. He walks to the court on this May morning accused of anti-Athenian activity, with undermining what it was that held the *polis* – the city-state – together. Today, those 500 Athenians will decide whether or not Socrates has corrupted the city's source of hope – their young men – and, even more worrying, denied its sublime security: the power of their traditional gods.

It's right for me to make my defence, Athenians, against the first of the false accusations made against me . . . 'Socrates does wrong and is too concerned with enquiring about what's in the heavens and below the earth and to make the weaker argument appear the stronger and to teach these same things to others.' [8]

How do you say that I corrupt the youth . . . ? Isn't it in fact clear according to the indictment you wrote that I do so by teaching the young not to believe in the gods that the city believes in but instead to believe in other new divinities? Aren't you claiming that it's by teaching that I corrupt them? [9]

The Athenian city has spent four generations dealing with clear and present danger in the form of invading forces and the military coups of enemies within. Socrates' crime is less tangible, but because of that, more pernicious – he is considered a bad, a dangerous influence. The citizens who make up the judge and jury (there was no hierarchy of judgement in the Athenian judicial system in Socrates' lifetime), hot-footing it through those narrow Athenian streets, have travelled from far and wide. Some started their journey in districts such as Cape Sounion, nearly 30 miles south-east of Athena's city, where the splendid temple of Poseidon still basilisk-eyes the boats that come in and out of Athens' harbours; others will have rolled off bed-pallets just five minutes away in what were little more than shacks on the bare rock,[10] beneath the Areopagus, where councils of Athenians have been meeting for close on 300 years. Rich and very poor alike, they are gathering here in this milky-dawn light because the Ancient Greeks believed something remarkable about men. They believed that each had been given, by the gods, an equal portion of *dike*, justice, and *aidos*, shame or concern for their fellow man.[11] If they put their minds to it, each true, mandated Greek could judge another fairly and wisely. This Hellenic hall-mark was proudly celebrated, in Athens' public spaces, by the commentators of the day:

> When I have chosen the best of my citizens I shall return; it is for them to judge this matter according to truth, since they have bound themselves by oath to say nothing contrary to justice.[12]

> On this hill the reverence and inborn fear of the citizens will hold them back from committing injustice by day and night alike, so long as they themselves do not pollute the Laws with evil streams: if you stain clear water with filth, you will never find a drink.[13]

So on that spring morning twenty-four centuries ago, the ordinary citizens of Athens, dirt-poor oxherds, smooth-palmed accountants, dark-tanned traders, were here to enact a unique, fifth-century form of direct democracy. Citizen to citizen, they were here to pass judgement on one of their own.

But today's court case did not, by any means, promise a cut-and-dried resolution. Because the one accused amongst them, who had also started to make his way to the court at dawn; who had also walked through the hub of Athens' democratic city as the city started to wake, a fellow citizen amongst the press of jurors; the man making his way to the dock today was, by any standards, an awkward customer to estimate: an extreme and disconcerting individual. Unsettling to look at, Socrates stood out in a crowd. He boasted, his contemporaries tell us, a pot-belly, thick lips, swivelling eyes, a pug nose and broad nostrils. Descriptions of his lifestyle suggest he possessed irrepressible energy and a wit that, even after one of his many nights of heavy drinking, struck home *'like the touch of a sting-ray.'*[14] In a city that made a cult of physical beauty[15] – which believed, in fact, that outward beauty was a sign of an inner nobility of spirit – Socrates was famously ugly. He had a rocking gait and he made it his business to power from one spot in the city to another, enlightening some, badgering others to engage in meaningful conversation. As one contemporary (according to Plato) – the man who had spent years as Socrates' love-interest – put it:

ALCIBIADES: When we hear any other person – quite an excellent orator, perhaps – pronouncing one of the usual discourses, no one, I venture to say, cares a jot; but as soon as we hear you, or your discourses in the mouth of another — though such person be ever so poor a speaker, and whether the hearer be a woman or a man or a youngster — we are all astounded and entranced. As for myself, gentlemen, were it not that I might appear to be absolutely tipsy, I would have affirmed on oath all the strange effects I personally have felt from his words, and still feel now. For when I hear him I am worse than any wild fanatic; I find my heart leaping and my tears gushing forth at the sound of his speech, and I see great numbers of people having the same experience. When I listened to Pericles and other skilled orators I thought them eloquent, but I never felt anything like this . . .[16]

Often Socrates out-foxed and floored his peers with his beguiling and relentless banter. But then, at other times, he would stand for hours, silent, stock-still, frozen. These 'trances' Socrates himself put down to his *daimonion semeion*, his 'divine sign'. Scholars still debate the cause of these odd seizures. Was this some kind of deep philosophic engagement? Were they signs of a medical condition such as catalepsy? Many at the time were more suspicious; they whispered, behind his back, that Socrates was possessed.

Whatever his disability — social, physical or psychological — the philosopher was clearly both unhampered and uninhibited, and for the previous fifty years had taken the concept of being an Athenian citizen to its upper limits.

Far from being an unworldly greybeard, we are told that Socrates spun through Athena's city like a tornado, drinking, carousing (though never out of control), talking, debating. Women, slaves, generals, purveyors of sweet and bitter perfumes — he involved all in his dialogues. Eccentric, grubby, his hair left uncombed, he famously stunned guests at a dinner party by turning up freshly bathed and oiled following an afternoon's session at the gymnasium — a display of personal hygiene that was way out of character.[17]

Socrates paddled in Athens' streams, he spent nights in her brothels, he worshipped the city's demanding inbred dynasties of gods as assiduously as, if not harder than, the next man. This is a dedication not to be underestimated, for there were as many as 2,000 separate religious cults, all clamouring for attention in Attica in the fifth century BC. Socrates fought for his city too. Strapping on linen and leather armour, sharpening his short, stabbing sword, he travelled hundreds of miles to defend Athens' interests. Although not one to join committees, or volunteer for jury service and neighbourhood watch, Socrates devoted limitless energy to making the *polis* work; in his own idiosyncratic way he was absolutely devoted to the political process. Those who did not participate usefully in Athenian life were labelled, in Greek, *idiotai* — laymen:[18] these idiots, Socrates had no time for. On that May morning, however dangerous he had come to seem, there was no doubt that democratic Athenians were judging one of their own.

The varied accounts of Socrates' life and philosophy make it clear: he was inspiring, exciting, maddening. He was brilliant and curiously naïve. He was impossible to ignore. Given that the philosopher was responsible for his own defence, this trial looked set to spark with verbal and intellectual fireworks.

MENO: *Socrates! Even before I met you they told me that in plain truth you are a perplexed man yourself and reduce others to perplexity. At this moment, I feel that you are exercising magic and witchcraft on me and positively laying me under your spell until I am just a mass of helplessness . . . My mind and my lips are literally numb, and I have nothing to reply to you. Yet, I have spoken about virtue hundreds of times and held forth on the subject in front of large audiences, and very well indeed, or so I thought. Now I can't even say what virtue is.*[19]

∽∾∽∾∽

Socrates might seem to us the North Star in Athens, the light by which others orientated themselves, but he was one in a galaxy. Walking through those jangling streets were many others who shone very bright. Here were familiar sun-worn faces, now familiar only as great names: the playwright Euripides, the historian Xenophon, the general-statesman Pericles (as well as his intriguing courtesan and soulmate, Aspasia – his 'partner' to her friends, his 'whore' to their enemies), the mane-haired, rippling aristocratic chancer Alcibiades, the witty Aristophanes, the 'father-of-history' Herodotus, the sculptor/designer Pheidias, whose genius had created the Parthenon, a young Plato. Fifth-century Athens supported a rare concentration of talent. It is for this reason that Socrates' lifetime is nominated a 'Golden Age'. Socrates witnessed the 'Greek Miracle' at first hand.

Yet on that spring morning in 399 BC, as the trickle of men into the law-court became a steady flow, Socrates' *alma mater*, his beloved Athens, and the men who had made this city world-class, who had witnessed the rise of their home-town to the status of superpower and had generated a civilisation to match, now wanted their troublesome philosopher shamed, and some wanted him dead.

This is how Socrates' story ends. But we are still at the beginning of a day that shook the world.

To understand the tenor of Socrates' trial, its flavour, its taste, its smell, its surface tensions and its undercurrents, we must stand in the classical Agora, look around us, and see what Socrates would have seen as he made his journey through the streets and on into the hallowed space of the law-courts. Above him, behind him if he travelled with his back to the rising sun, perched on the Acropolis rock, stood the great temple, the Parthenon, sacred to *Athena Parthenos* — Athena the Maiden. There, too, the Temple of *Athena Nike*, this time dedicated to Athena the goddess of victory. In the Agora itself were the training grounds where Athens' citizen-soldiers sweated day in, day out to ensure that they were fit to fight and to die for their city-state. All around were fine bronze and marble statues — so lifelike their rock-crystal eyes seemed to follow each and every passer-by. Their stone skin would have been thick with carnival-coloured paint. Analysis of the statues today reveals how gaudy they were — akin to theatrical scenery and props, designed to make an impression from afar. The air in the Agora would have been heavy with the scents of the market: spices from the East, saffron from the South, the tang of gold from the northern hills, the sweat of captured humans, shuffling slaves waiting to be sold on.

And the earth beneath Socrates was thick with the remains of Athenians past, men and women whose own triumphs and struggles had laid the ground for Socrates' progress.

Piecing together our story, on our own journey into Socrates' courtroom, we too should walk through the military, cultural and social landscape of Athens, as deep as it is broad, that the philosopher inhabited. We need to investigate the physical and psychological stage that had been set for Athenian greatness. To understand Socrates' thoughts, his life, and his death by hemlock poison, fifth-century Athens — Athena's City, the city that birthed *Sokrates Alopekethen* in 469 BC — must first come more sharply into focus.

2

ATHENA'S CITY

@@@@@@@@@@@@

Athens, 800–500 BC,
the Archaic period

For Athens I say forth a gracious prophecy —
The glory of the sunlight and the skies
Shall bid from earth arise
Warm burgeoning waves of new life and glad prosperity.

Aeschylus, *Eumenides*, 922–6[1]

THERE HAD BEEN A SETTLEMENT AT Athens since pre-history. Between around 2100 and 1000 BC, the time described by archaeologists as the Bronze Age, but thought of by the classical Greeks as 'The Age of Heroes',[2] men and women encamped on the Acropolis – the great lump of red-cretaceous limestone that improbably juts out of the Attic plain. Early Athenians lived and worshipped here. Eventually the prehistoric community started to sleep and eat in the shadow of the Acropolis as well as atop it. As time went on these lower settlements expanded, there was a degree of town-planning, a community with an identity was established. Athens could now call herself a *polis*, a city-state. The Acropolis itself, rising 230 feet above sea-level, believed to hold sacred powers, was predominantly a home for the god-tribe – when humans sheltered high on this geological fortress it usually meant that the city was under attack or in crisis.

Socrates' Athens was axiomatic: history began with geography. Greece in his time, Hellas (as it was and still is known), was a loose connection of close on 1,000 seperate *poleis* or city-states. These city-states – originally a coalition of neighbouring families and tribes who gathered together around

8

a central locale for self-protection – were isolated from much of Europe by mountains and from Asia Minor by the sea. Each Hellenic *polis* (with populations of anything from 1,000 to 30,000) was, typically, run as a republic. Kings had been all but lost with the downfall of the Bronze Age – the epoch immortalised by literary hero-leaders such as Menelaus, Agamemnon, Priam, Ajax. Philosophy and literature from across the period (found in the works of the poet Hesiod, the law-giver Solon, the historian Herodotus, the dramatist Sophocles, *inter alios*) indicate that all sense of society revolved around this *polis*, this collective whole. Morality meant the goodness of the community; loyalty to the city-state was paramount. Farmer-citizens, rather than following one military leader, together defended their *poleis* (their cities) – frequently against the hoplites (armed foot soldiers),[3] of another.

'*Man is a political animal.*' Pride bursts from Aristotle's voice. The Hellenic unit of society (*polis* is the root of our word 'political') fostered, without a shadow of a doubt, a sense of community and commonality. And within that *polis* there were men – embodied in the sturdy Farmer of Hesiod's *Works and Days* – who valued personal independence above (almost) everything, who fought hard against the smothering rule of aristocratic factions and despots, who made democracy a possibility. The poems of Hesiod show us that these Greeks had a fierce sense of self-reliance – if you were dependent on someone, or on the work of others, you were a *kolax* (a flatterer) or a *parasitos* (a parasite).[4] Hesiod's ideal Greek man works, works and works. He is industrious to a fault – he strives to better himself and the lives of his immediate neighbours.

Take fair measure from your neighbour and pay him back fairly, with the same measure, or better, if you can.[5]

The Greek – the Hellene – was loyal first and foremost to his city, and then to a loose notion of 'Greece', or rather 'Greekness'. A Hellene was Hellenic because he was Hellenic rather than barbaric; Greek rather than barbarian. Barbarians, in the eyes of the Greeks, were those who talked gibberish, who literally *bar-bar-bared* in their own language: Lydian, Persian, Thracian, Nubian, Goth, they came from all points of the compass.

The Greeks cheerfully demonised the way these 'others' ran their own affairs. They despised the monomaniacal autocracy of eastern super-kings, the slavish devotion to political orthodoxy, the dynasties of ruling classes of priests. They had to hate them, because these barbarians had become their enemies. Whereas once the whole eastern Mediterranean had been held together by the notion of *xenia* – an unspoken allegiance between the aristocrats of Greece, but also of Anatolia, Egypt, Macedonia – now dividing lines had been firmly traced: one, vertical, ran north and south, following

9

the Bosporus, the other stretched horizontally across the Balkans.[6] Mountain ranges – the Carpathians, the Julian Alps, the Dinaric Alps, the Pindus – divided Greece from the rest of Europe; the Aegean and Libyan Seas segregated Greek communities from those in Egypt and North Africa.

This Hellenic land-mass (with satellites on the western shore of what is now Turkey), whose population appears largely to have lost the power of literacy between about 1100 and 800 BC, no longer part of a tight network of trading routes, was, on the whole, left to its own devices. Jealousies between rival city-states festered. Citizen-soldiers, men who farmed in the spring and autumn and fought throughout the summer, now stood side by side and defended their home-town against that of their neighbour. The default position of the Greek *polis* through the Archaic period was to watch its own back.[7] The archaeological evidence tells us that city-states such as Athens were, in the hundred years running up to Socrates' birth, no strangers to warfare and conflict.

∽∾∽∾∽

In the mud, scree and debris that rises 15–20 feet above Socrates' Athens, up from the street level of 2,400 years ago, archaeologists discover, every year, new shards of the philosopher's city. In 2008 a sliver of a beautiful woman's stone face was excavated from the gravelly subsoil; within days her outstretched hand was also identified. In 2009 a marble horse's hind-leg was found just 30 inches below the surface; even more recently, limestone flowers have been unearthed. These amputated bits and pieces are remnants of the fine decoration that once rimmed the great Parthenon temple up on the Acropolis: classical stoneworks that were carved and hoisted into place when Socrates was still alive. Work on the Parthenon of Socrates' day was begun in 447 BC and completed in 432 BC. The woman, the horse, the flowers survived in place throughout antiquity, but were hacked at by offended Orthodox Christians, ground down for lime, and then blown apart in 1687 by a Venetian cannon.[8] The firepower was there to attack Ottoman Turks – the occupying power in Athens since 1458 – who by the seventeenth century were using the Parthenon as a mosque and an arms store.

The fragments that archaeologists are now carefully piecing back together have been doubly traumatised. Some of the earlier sculptures that have come to light were bruised by ancient Athens' bullying nemesis – the superpower that harried Greek lands through the sixth and fifth centuries BC: Persia. In 480 BC and again in 479 Persian forces breathed down the very necks of the Athenians; a Persian garrison occupied the Acropolis itself, and Persian forces smashed and burned all they could find there. Persians – powerful, ambitious,

10

greedy for land and human booty – had been the enemies of Athens for a hundred years. By 522 BC the Persian Empire stretched from the Balkans to the River Indus. The size of the Persians' geopolitical appetite can be measured by the words carved high into the rockface at Behistun beside the royal road to Babylon. In three languages, Akkadian, Old High Persian and Elamite, their ruler at this time, King Darius, thunders:

I am Darius the great King, the king of kings, the King of Persia, the king of all lands . . . so says Darius the King . . . these lands obeyed my rule. Whatever I told them to do, was done . . .[9]

A cousin of the next Persian leader, Xerxes – who invaded Athens just a decade before Socrates was born – was reported to have roared that he would *'complete the enslavement of all the Greeks'.*[10] It is impossible to understand Socrates' life without appreciating the bogeyman horror that the Persians represented to all Athenian citizens. Persian diabolics would come to be contrasted with Greek heroics. Socrates was a child when, at last, the Eastern threat appeared to have receded: after Persian forces had been conclusively defeated by a collection of Greek allies, Athenians, Corinthians, Spartans et al., at the Battles of Salamis and Plataea. 'Liberty' had become the watchword of all Athenians; a freedom not to be enslaved or oppressed by the *'dog-barbarians'* of the East. As Socrates grows up there is a sense, clearly, that a new age is dawning. The greatest despot in remembered history – Persia – has been thwarted, and the dream of people-power has become conscious. Socrates is born when the world is different. Because Athens is entertaining an extraordinary new ideology: democracy.

Demos-kratia
and a new town for a new democracy,
508–404 BC

@@@@@@@@@@@@@

May the people who hold the power in the polis maintain their office confidently: a system of rule that looks ahead and concerns itself with the welfare of the community.

Aeschylus, *Suppliant Women,* 698–700

When Socrates was growing up, we should try to imagine the flurry of papyrus sheets on workbenches and the fingers sketching in the dirt as draughtsmen and architects laid out plans for their new, newly democratic city. Stylus pens have been found deep in the earth all around the Agora. Project leaders would have been appointed, and slave-labourers briefed. Masonry blocks were laid one on the other to give a physical incarnation to the democratic ideology. A new, voguish, solid, round limestone building, the *Tholos* chamber, gave nightly dinners to fifty of those who served on the *Boule* – Athens' council. Five hundred ordinary men were picked by lot to meet here to administer the business of the Athenian Assembly for the space of one year.[11] In the sturdy, rectangular council chamber itself, the *bouleuterion*, and also in the Agora, business was prepared for the Assembly's citizen-politicians. The Assembly hovered like a stone cloud above the Agora – its home, known affectionately as the *Pnyx*, the 'packed-place', a natural, limestone-smooth auditorium where all Athenian citizens could decide how their *polis* should be run.

Greece already has a close-on-1,000-year-old written history at the moment we pick up Socrates' story – and in that history the powerful persecute the weak, might is right and tyrants lead men. Warlords and high priests dominate society. Ordinary men may have access to councils of peace and battle, but the final decision is never theirs.

Democracy is the most thrilling of developments. Now, for around 50,000 or 60,000 (the number varies, depending on population size through the fifth century BC) adult, male, Athenian citizens, not only could their voice be heard, but they could actively mould their society. You, your brother, your father, your son, could choose which issues were important to debate, which vital to legislate. The city built around Socrates was designed to keep democracy alive. Democratic Athenians did not serve the state, they *were* the state: its army, its executive, its judiciary.

∽∽∽∽∽

Demos had for much of its history been a dirty word. *Hoi polloi*, the people, the great unwashed, were something to be feared, to be mistrusted. But Socrates witnessed an extraordinary human development. Instead of kings and tyrants, instead of councils of elders and aristocrats, the *demos* – the people – were now in charge. Over a period of a hundred years a massive rupture had taken place in life on earth. Men in one city-state, Athens, had agreed, collectively, to rule themselves, and to be ruled in turn.[12]

The conditions for change were there in the place we now call Greece. Throughout the Archaic period, in the eighth and seventh centuries BC, Greece lay on the edge of things. Those unfortunate enough to live through 'interesting times'[13] were to be found on the other side of the Bosporus: Assyrians, Medes, Babylonians – all contained, as our story begins, within the vast Persian Empire. Many Greeks on Asia Minor's western seaboard lived under Persian rule. But mainland Greece had always been truculent geographically. Too many islands, too many shores; mountains too high to conquer easily. Greek colonists might be establishing settlements right across the eastern Mediterranean, but there is an admission that, in spirit, the Greek world has shrunk.[14] Men are no longer achieving that which the heroes of the Age of Heroes once did; they are not walking through palaces decorated with lapis lazuli from the Caucasus, not sitting on rock-crystal thrones, not boasting that they possess the most beautiful women in the world, that they are thalassocrats, 'rulers of the sea'. For centuries there has been a sense of waiting; of suspended animation. But Socrates has been born into a time and place where all that has changed.

In 594 BC the Athenian poet and law-giver Solon had already made bold attempts to make society work well. Sick of the filibustering influence of a network of aristocratic families, he instituted a series of reforms. He reduced the reach of those who had *pushed through to glut yourselves with many good things.*[15] He broadened Athens' power-base. Up on the cluster of polished limestone rocks – the *areios pagus* (hence Areopagus) – just in the shadow of the Acropolis, a broader-based council now sat whose role it was to protect the interests of the people. The men on the *areios pagus* were elevated, as close to the sacred inhabitants of the Acropolis as they were to mere mortals. Yet Athens' political reforms – founded on a Hellenic philosophical bedrock of justice and wisdom – paved the way for Athena's city to be stand-out progressive.

Some of the resulting laws from Solon's new political vision would play happily in any modern new-town development. Houses, walls, ditches, beehives and certain kinds of trees had to be an acceptable distance from your neighbour's property. You could not speak ill of the dead (or indeed the living). These reforms – which convey a sense both of solidarity and of self-determination – are a charming mix of the ultimately ideological and the extremely pedestrian. Solon was estimated a wise man, a *sophos*. He respected the common man's *timē* – his honour. But this revolution was circumscribed, this revolutionary was no democrat, he was an oligarch – a man who believed that the *oligoi*, the few, should maintain control, he had no desire '*to stir up the milk and lose the cream*':

> *This is how the demos can best follow its leaders*
> *if it is neither unleashed nor restrained too much*
> *For excess breeds hubris, when great prosperity comes*
> *to men of unsound mind.*[16]

Solon had no taste for tyrants, but he helped those who could help themselves. Even though the foundations of a new political order had been laid, political life was still dominated by the ambition of rival aristocrats. We can meet them today on the lavish grave *stelai* (stone blocks) they commissioned to outdo one another, monuments that would be ostentatiously raised along the roadsides of Athens. Between one and six feet high, these soft yellow stones are monolithic snapshots of the past. On the *stelai* in the Piraeus Museum well-bred, well-fed, well-formed men caress their peers; lavishly draped fathers crown sons with laurels. In the National Archaeological Museum six young, upper-class athletes on the base of a funerary monument play a game similar to hockey. The atmosphere is jovial, but the hunch of their carved backs gives away the deadly seriousness of the competition.[17] Without kings in Athens, the balance of power was constantly shifting between one family and another as they jostled to gain the upper hand.

It was during one particularly rancorous squabble, a scant ninety years after Solon's reforms, between the pro-Spartan Isagoras (an *aristos* with *kratos* – a high-born man with power) and the pro-*demos*, pro-Athenian Kleisthenes that, at the very end of the sixth century in Athens, a Rubicon was (prematurely) crossed.

Isagoras had invited the Spartan army, led by King Kleomenes, into Attica and then on into Athens to oust Kleisthenes – who had a particular taste for reform.[18] But Isagoras had miscalculated the mood of the moment. The Athenian people had got wind of Kleisthenes' more demotic tendencies and liked the sound of them. Returning from exile, Kleisthenes found he had a groundswell of support in his mother-city.

And thus, in 508 BC, the people of Athens did an extraordinary thing. Sheltering the Spartan king Kleomenes – ally of that bullish aristocrat Isagoras – the Acropolis was suddenly, violently occupied by *hoi polloi*, the common crowd. The *polloi* (the many) besieged the Spartan king for three days. Kleisthenes had little taste for making his personal struggle with Isagoras another tale for the *rhapsodes* – the tellers of epic tales who sang the deeds of great warrior men. His was a more pragmatic plan. Herodotus, the 'Father of History', records the moment – and you can hear the emotion in his voice as he does so, a mixture of horror and awe:

Then Kleisthenes took into his faction the common *people.*[19]

By storming the Acropolis with Kleisthenes' blessing and support, *ho demos*, 'I, the people', for the first time in recorded history, acted as one, as a political agent.[20]

And thus a thing that will be called *demos-kratia*, 'people-power', had been invented. The word was first used, as far as we know, in 464/3 BC, but quickly caught on. Wailing newborn boys, signs of the times, were baptised *Demokrates*.[21] Herodotus rolled the words around in his histories like a child tasting something new, something suspicious; the actors of Aeschylus' *Suppliant Women*, performed in 463 BC, beat out the concept in poetic metre: '*demou kratousa cheir*' – 'the demos' ruling hand'; '*to damion to ptolin kratunei*' – 'the people which rules the polis'.[22]

The impassioned, emotional way that the people dealt with this new creature in their midst, this female quality *demokratia* – literally, the power, the grip of the people – was to fetishise her. As with other, troubling, slippery, nebulous concepts (*nemesis* – retribution; *themis* – order or divine right; *peitho* – persuasion), she was personified as a woman. Law-courts were reformed in her name, territories seized. *Demokratia* became a concept that was potent, promiscuous and manipulated. Even immature, Democracy's name was taken in vain by orators keen to demonstrate that Athens bettered her non-democratic neighbours. Foreign policy became a series of ideological fixtures: Democrats vs Tyrants, Democrats vs Oligarchs. By 333 BC *Demokratia* was being worshipped as a goddess.[23] For a territory that had been living by aristocratic warrior codes for at least 2,000 years, the rate of change was exponential.

Democracy in Athens in the fifth century was – there is no doubt – a radical development. Every male Athenian over the age of eighteen could, by right, attend the *ecclesia*, the Assembly, which convened about once a month, usually on that raised, natural limestone auditorium close to the Acropolis, the Pnyx. Up here, where the sun beats hard and the clouds feel close, the active Athenian citizen had the chance to make direct decisions about his city-state's affairs and ethos: should Athens go to war? What is an acceptable rate of tax? What the best penalty for rape? High offices, influential positions, were held by ordinary men, selected at random, on a daily basis. We say a week is a long time in politics: for democratic Athenians, political life could be conceived and terminated in the span of one day.

Stage-set democracy

@@@@@@@@@@@@@@

Complicated systems were developed to ensure fairness in all things. Public officials, juries, state administrators were all chosen by lot. The selection process was closely scrutinised to prevent tampering or corruption. Public records were displayed on inscribed stone and inked papyrus notices across Athens – the workings of the democracy were expected to be transparent.

Old dynastic ties were weakened by law. Showy displays of wealth were frowned upon. Athens had built itself a robust and ground-breaking political system, and now architects put their minds to how they could create spaces and buildings and courtrooms and walkways that enabled a direct, participatory democracy to thrive. Socrates grew up inhabiting a purpose-built democratic landscape – the first of its kind in history. On his journey through the Agora and into the law-court, Socrates and those who had come to judge him were shadowed by dramatic, physical reminders of the brave democratic idea.

These buildings are still being excavated today. Twenty feet below street-level next to the cheap and cheerful tavernas at the bottom of Adrianou Street in central Athens, the massive Doric columns (so far the internal Ionic columns are squashed under a family business that refuses to budge) of the *Stoa Poikile* – the Painted Stoa – are rising back up out of the earth. At least 140 x 40 feet, this grand covered walkway would have been decorated with outsize painted wooden boards – each scene representing the defeat of Athens' enemies by honest-to-god Athenians. The Persians are thwarted at Marathon, Amazons are hacked down. Here ordinary citizens of Athens, just at the edge of the main political zone in the city, in the balm of the shade, were encouraged to walk and talk, to buttress the business of living in this radical democracy, with a cool packed-earth floor beneath them.

But there was a problem. Emphasis on the power of speech in this new democracy where every male citizen had, in theory at least, a voice also engendered a cult of personality and mass jealousy towards high-flyers. The democratic reformers, Solon, Kleisthenes and then later Ephialtes and Pericles, might have papered over the cracks in society, but the divisions between aristocrats and *hoi polloi*, between rich and poor, between the talented and the unexceptional, the 'few' and 'the many', had not been filled. Socrates' *polis* seemed robust, but was in truth a chimera, a morphing thing. As Socrates grew up, from babe-in-arms to toddler and then child, democracy too was finding its feet. Towards the end of the philosopher's life the democratic experiment would prove as divisive as it had originally been cohesive. Socrates lived through fragile, politically jumpy times.[24]

And there was one *polis*, 150 miles deep into the Greek mainland, the Peloponnese, which despised Athens' democratic revolution with a particularly fierce and bitter loathing. This city-state spotted the internal divisions within Athena's great city and chose to play them to her own advantage. Socrates was in fact fascinated by this polity and her extreme ideas, but in truth she was a *polis* that would prove to be both the philosopher's and Athens' nemesis. Her name was Sparta.

Sparta

@@@@@@@@@@@@

Socrates' story is a tale of two cities, of Sparta and Athens.

Three days' brisk walk south of Athens, a three-hour drive today, sat the *polis* of Sparta – in the region of Lakonia. Sparta was Athens' sometime ally and oft-time enemy.

During Socrates' lifetime the city-state of Sparta had legendary status. Protected by five mountain ranges and a shroud of secrecy, this was a place where another social revolution had taken place, but with rather different results. By the time of Socrates' birth, Sparta had become one of the most extreme city-states in the whole of Greece.

The Spartan landscape lulls one into a false sense of security. On a spring day it is fragrant with almond blossom, in the summer with oranges ripening in orange groves. The River Eurotas, high-reeded, fed by bubbling tributaries, winds through Sparta's river plain. Land here is flat and fertile – a rare commodity in Greece. The Tayegetan mountain range all around keeps its snow long into the summer. Stretching over 5,000 square miles, ancient Sparta was the largest city-state in Greece. But this was a Shangri-La with a rock-hard heart.

Sparta had trumped Athens in the political reform stakes. When the Athenian democratic experiment was still 200 years in the future, the Spartans revolutionised their society. As early as the seventh century BC Sparta had undergone a massive social and political head-shift. All land was shared equally amongst the *homoioi* – the equals – an elite group of super-citizens. These men had no profession other than to be crack soldiers; between the ages of seven and thirty all males lived together in a brutal military training camp called the *syssition*. Boys were raised in the *agoge* – the word means 'a herd' and they were indeed treated like animals. Given one cloak to wear all year round, taught to fend for themselves in the woods that still fringe the city, bare-footed, they had one sole purpose in their lives: to grow up to be perfect warriors. Spartan men were commemorated with a headstone only if they died in battle, Spartan women if they died in childbirth.

The Spartans believed that all Spartiate men (that is, all full, male Spartan citizens) should hold land and wealth equally. That all decisions should be made for the betterment of the city-state, and that the individual counted only as a healthy part of a supra-healthy whole. No Spartan adult worked – he devoted himself simply to being the 'perfect Spartan'. The *homoioi* (on average there were 8–9,000 of these 'equals' in the city-state at any one time) could afford to live so exclusively and with such unilateral focus because close to 725 BC the Spartans had enslaved another entire Greek people, the Messenians, to be their *heilotes* — more than just slave or servant, *helot* translates as 'captive'. It was by the sweat of this captive race of Greeks that the Spartans made their city-state great. Messenia had at one time owned wide and fertile territories. The Spartans deprived them of all land and all rights. The Messenians became a non-people, Messenia became an ex-city-state. These helots, once free men, lived and died only to serve their Spartan masters.

In Sparta, obedience was all. Citizens had to adhere to a curious set of rules. Coined money, moustaches and prostitution were banned. The 'national dish' was *melas zomos*, black broth — an unappetising stew made from boiled pig's blood and vinegar. Babies (we are told) were bathed in wine to toughen them up, girls were encouraged to train to fight and to eat the same rations as their brothers and boy cousins. Secret societies of Spartan youths, the *krypteia*, were sent out at night to kill and maim the under-class of helots at will. And secrecy was paramount in all things. Spartans were not allowed to talk about the workings or culture of their *polis*, and foreigners were frequently expelled.[25]

The Athenians decided to despise Sparta and all that it stood for. Although the two city-states, once described as 'yoke-fellows', had been allies against the Persians, and the only two *poleis* who refused to bring King Darius symbolic offerings of earth and water, as time went on the democracy recoiled from Spartan statecraft, which was totalitarian in tone. Athenian rhetoric, Athenian superiority and Athenian transparency came to be measured against Spartan secrecy and degeneracy.

There is a great difference between us and our opponents . . . Our city is open to the world, and we have no periodical deportations in order to prevent people observing or finding out secrets which might be of military advantage to the enemy. This is because we rely, not on secret weapons, but on our own real courage and loyalty. There is a difference too in our educational systems. The Spartans, from their earliest boyhood, are submitted to the most laborious training in 'courage'; we pass our lives without all these restrictions, and yet are just as ready to face the same dangers as they are.[26]

Ideologically, militarily, culturally, Sparta and Athens would, in hindsight, be certain to cross swords.

In Socrates' lifetime the climax of Spartan/Athenian rivalry would judder throughout the Greek world; it was a conflict responsible for decimating the Athenian population by the time of Socrates' trial. This trauma the Ancient Greeks simply called *stasis* — strife, discord — but we now label it 'the Peloponnesian War'. The war lasted a full generation, from 431 to

404 BC. Come the year of Socrates' death, it was Spartan brawn that had broken down Athens' city walls; Spartan fires that had torched the precious stretches of farmland outside the city walls. The war devastated the earth's very fertility, it caused the deaths of many hundreds of thousands. The territories that Socrates travelled through as a soldier were blackened with the back-fires of aggression. The young men that Socrates exercised with in the gym and with whom he debated – these were the children of strife, they grew up knowing nothing other than conflict.

And so when Socrates walked through the Agora to his trial in 399 BC he was surrounded by war damage and by a community that had been psychologically traumatised. When he was tried, Athens, which had once achieved so much, was a defeated society. The milk-and-honey promise of the democracy had curdled. Athenians were no longer champions of the world, they were the defeated. We can trace the disintegration of the *polis* in the woeful lines of Sophocles, Euripides and Aristophanes, Athens' playwrights, the men who documented Athens' trauma:

War will be men's business.[27]

So those men, who waxed so proud with bitter speech, are themselves in the mansions of the dead, all of them, and their city is enslaved.[28]

For here begins trouble's cycle, and, worse than that, relentless fate; . . . with trouble from an alien shore . . . as its result war and bloodshed and the ruin of my home; and many a Spartan maiden too is weeping bitter tears in her halls on the banks of the fair Eurotas, and many a mother whose sons are slain is smiting her grey head and tearing her cheeks, making her nails bloody in the furrowed gash.[29]

Although Socrates' professed concern was with the moral fundamentals of life, it was this tangled web of realpolitik and rival beliefs, of conflict and anxiety, that drew him to a religious court to defend himself against capital charges.

Yet war can stimulate as well as destroy. Before it drew to a close, the fifth century BC witnessed the most remarkable resilience and a breathtaking cultural efflorescence. Democracy in Socrates' day provoked rational thought, artistic experiment and wildly ambitious social and political schemes. During the fight with Sparta some of the most exquisite buildings – buildings that we consider to be the epitome of classical achievement – were constructed. Although maimed and denuded on that May morning in 399 BC, for much of Socrates' life Athens was a beautiful city. And the Athenian Agora in particular, Socrates' favoured stamping-ground, was one of the most exciting, if not *the* most vivacious and eye-opening of places to visit the length and breadth of the ancient world. The Agora, 37 acres of human endeavour, rimmed with boundary stones, was Socrates' second home. To appreciate why the philosopher enjoyed such influence and earned such hatred, we need to join him there once again as he travels, in 399 BC, to his show-trial.

3

SOCRATES IN THE AGORA

@@@@@@@@@@@@

The Agora, Athens'
marketplace, 451–399 BC

*But Socrates, moreover, was always out in public. In the morning he went to the
colonnades and the gymnasia, during the market he was seen there at the Agora, and for
the rest of the day he was constantly in whatever place he thought he would meet up with
the most people. And he talked quite a lot, and those who wished, could hear him.*

Xenophon, *Memorabilia*, 1.1.10[1]

THIS LATE SPRING DAY IN 399 BC, a time of year when marguerites,
the golden 'eyebrow of Zeus', grew around the sanctuaries of the
Agora (as they still do around their ruins),[2] Socrates wended his
way through the labyrinthine lanes and small passageways of Athens' marketplace.

The cheek-by-jowl dynamics of the district have just been brilliantly
revealed by a new excavation in the south-west corner of the ancient Agora.
'Fussing around', as the director of excavations put it, diggers uncovered
the rim of what at first seemed to be a giant *pithos* – a storage jar. But as
the earth was eased away, it became clear that this was in fact the edge of
a steep-sided well. Wells are good news for archaeologists, and for historians, because people throw objects into them, they drop things accidentally.
At the bottom of a well lies an unselfconscious snapshot of what life was
once like above ground.[3]

And this well has surprised the excavators. Until recently it was thought
that the Agora was a very 'public' place. The free-market, political hub and
adminstrative centre of the new democracy. But at the bottom of this

smooth terracotta shaft are all kinds of intimate objects: shopping lists, loom-weights, broken make-up boxes. This kind of mongrel debris implies that the little stone buildings that nustle up next to the grand public architecture of Athens' central marketplace were not just shops or storage rooms, as has long been suggested, but houses, living quarters. Homes for the ordinary men and the women of Socrates' Athens.

And so if we picture Socrates' journey to the law-court in 399 BC we should hear the hubbub of human habitation, and see a hundred pairs of eyes following his progress.

Padding barefoot, as he had done for most of his life, Socrates would have been drummed to court by a hectic beat; 500 jurymen on the move, many of them in their 'Sunday best' for a day in court, sporting leather sandals or sturdy footwear — on packed-gravel tracks; quite some sound. One doesn't imagine that Athenians were partial to hobnailed boots. But the rejected debris from the floor of one workshop on the fringes of the Agora — piles of iron tacks and ivory eyelets for laces — shows that many thousands of nails must have been hammered into leather by the cobblers of the city. And if the literary and archaeological sources really do intersect, then this particular, recently reinvestigated workshop was one in which Socrates, in happier days, spent a good deal of time, and made public a good deal of his philosophy.

Xenophon tells us that Socrates frequently stopped by here in the artisans' district at the Agora's limit because this was where youths and young men were allowed to meet to hear the philosopher's words — only over-eighteens had access actually *within* the boundary of the 37-acre Agora itself.[4] Athenian society was divided into strict age groups — strength was known to reside in youth, wisdom in age. Young men were Socrates' particular passion. Although later slander imagines him as some kind of philosopher-paedophile, the truth seems to have been simpler. Socrates sought out the company of the young men of Athens because he thought they had much to learn.

A writer called Diogenes Laertius, who carefully collated the *Lives and Opinions of Eminent Philosophers* (seriously researched, but written 600 years or so after Socrates' death), gives us the name of one particular fifth-century Athenian workshop owner who occupied that liminal zone where young men were allowed to hang out: Simon the Shoemaker. In the corner of the excavated, nail-strewn Agora workshop, the fragment of a drinking cup from the mid-fifth century BC has been discovered — one name is scratched in capitals on the base: '*SIMON*'. So it seems there was a Simon here at the time of Socrates, and he did make shoes.

Simon the Shoemaker was, according to Diogenes, an avid, early follower of Socrates; and excavators appear to have unearthed his very home. The philosopher would (we are told) spend hours on end at Simon's premises, riffing and chatting with the young men of the city, and after each debate the artisan would record the exchange. Eventually the cobbler collected enough material for thirty-three books, *The Dialogues of Simon.*[5] The anecdote, intimately connecting the philosopher and a shoemaker, is curious, but believable. Socrates went about his thinking-business in a completely unorthodox way – not philosophising in a formal school, or in the courts of kings and noblemen, but right in amongst *hoi polloi*. A cobbler's workshop-home would have seemed the most appropriate of places for unconventional Socrates to analyse the meaning and point of our everyday lives. And archaeology confirms that there was indeed a 'Shoe-maker' who lived and worked in the Agora when Socrates was at his productive peak as a philosopher, *c.*435–415 BC.[6] The 'Dialogues of Simon' have been lost to history, but later commentators throughout antiquity recorded that these debates, first heard within the warm-stoned, cottage-industries of Athens' jangling, cosmopolitan marketplace, dealt with many of Socrates' prime subjects: love, jealousy, the role of good in society.[7] Essential topics, zestily explored by Socrates day in, day out.

ᕤᕥᕤᕥᕤ

But when we are travelling through the Agora, in the late spring of 399 BC, Simon the Shoemaker is long dead.[8] Today Socrates has just one destination, the law-court. No roaming the Agora's nooks and crannies, asking unsuspecting passers-by their views on the best way to live, as was once the philosopher's wont. Soon this seventy-year-old man will be obliged to defend his case and his fundamental attitude to life in front of 500 judgemental Athenian democrats.

Ironic since for much of his life, the Agora has been where the philosopher has spoken freely – and for free. Stopping artisans and aristocrats alike, Socrates debated both the fripperies and the fundamentals of life. In a number of Plato's and Xenophon's chronicles he comes across as alarmingly unpredictable, leaping out at unsuspecting passers-by and startling them with a moral challenge. It was said that Xenophon first encountered Socrates in just such a manner. Walking as a young boy through the streets, Xenophon was approached by Socrates, who asked the lad where he could acquire a series of normal household goods. 'And what about a brave and virtuous man?' Socrates continued. When Xenophon was puzzled, Socrates suggested that the ingenu tag along for enlightenment.

Plutarch also recounts a tale of a visit that Socrates and his friends made to the Agora district where moneylenders set up their *trapezai* – banking tables – each morning. As the philosopher (surrounded as usual by a huddle of companions) walked southwards past the chipping-zone of the marble-workers he was struck by 'sublime inspiration' and suddenly dived off past a woodworking district while his colleagues took their normal route. The friends laughed at his abstraction, until they found themselves surrounded by a squealing, stinking herd of pigs, soon to be carved up into flesh and hide, their skins sent off down to be rinsed by the tanners at the Ilissos River just outside the city walls.[9]

Socrates had apparently, on this occasion, been enraptured by his own inner 'voice' – a kind of divine calling, a personal, private god; an idiosyncrasy that would attract suspicion and spark trouble as the years went by.[10] He called it his *daimonion* – his demon. This personal spirituality was very unorthodox in Socrates' day. The philosopher lived in a world where all religion was a matter for public consumption. In their demandingly poly-theistic spiritual landscape, Socrates and his colleagues were expected to pay their dues to a range of the gods most of the time. This worship took place mostly out in the open; it was a collective experience. A visit to the Agora would never *not* have involved some kind of act of worship.[11] Doubting the city's gods went beyond affront. Socrates' peers had dreamed up the atom,[12] but even they had a concept of something invisible beyond those indivisible particles – think perhaps of the sublime-spiritual world as being the quarks of Athenian existence, the building blocks of everything. Life itself was thought to be a religious experience.

෮෮෮෮෮

What do the gods want from us? What is beauty? What is love? Who is good? Who deserves power? What is virtue? What is knowledge? Where do we go when we die? Questions, questions. Plato depicts the maturing philoso-pher as so fascinated by human conversation that, far from charging for his ideas, Socrates declares he would subsidise passers-by so that they could listen to what he has to say:[13]

SOCRATES: *I fear that because of my love of people they think that I not only pour myself out copiously to anyone and everyone without payment, but that I would even pay something myself if anyone would listen to me.*[14]

As early as 430 BC, and quite possibly before, we know that this eager questioning was ruffling a few feathers in the city-state. A fragment of papyrus, copied out carefully by a Roman scholar and then by a Frankish scribe, and now held in a cardboard box in the warehouse of the Naples Museum, preserves a few lines of the Greek comic poet Callias.[15] Callias was a direct contemporary of Socrates. He noticed that which had begun to so bother the Athenians, that Socrates was not just a one-trick pony, but a consistent presence, and more than that: guru-like. A democratic citizen who was beginning to attract his own band of followers. Because Socrates' radical take on the issues of life was so refreshing, he gathered around him a coterie of disciples. One of Callias' characters moans that Socrates' methods made men dissatisfied and arrogant.

CHARACTER A: *Oh why this pride, why this disdainful eye?*

EURIPIDES (disguised as a woman): *I've every right to it; Socrates is why!*

We can picture the scene: followers of the philosopher prowling the busy marketplace, trying out the Socratic method on random passers-by; young men challenging their elders, the subservient challenging their betters – all following Socrates' principle that '*the unexamined life is not worth living . . .*'

But Callias was writing when Athens was in crisis – when the Peloponnesian War was brewing. By 432 BC hostilities between Sparta and Athens would be open. Whilst times were good, when the city-state was not at war, not crouching with its back against the wall, Socrates was a charismatic cause célèbre in Athens' marketplace, one of the many fine and stimulating attractions that the Agora had to offer.

◈◈◈◈◈

The prison complex was here in the Agora too, in the grubbiest quarter – the industrial zone; sweating bronze- and marble-workers hammered alongside those that a sprawling, polyglot, imperial city such as Athens had to keep temporarily under lock and key.[16] Manned by 'The Eleven', a not-to-be-messed-with law-enforcement body, with 300 public slaves to draw from as their heavies, the prisons contained men who awaited trial or execution.

If the trial of Socrates does not go well today, this prison is where he'll be heading.

It is a building the philosopher must have passed countless times. Socrates has lived, from birth, in and around Athena's busy city; apart from battle-missions and participation in a religious festival down South, he has barely left the place.[17] His presence in the Agora is nothing new; this is where for half a century he has plied his trade as an ideologist – a trader of word-ideas, unobstructed in the marketplace. He has watched and listened as Athenians created the first files on the subject of democracy. This is where, very recently, he has done his duty as an active, democratic Athenian citizen.

But today Socrates finds himself at the sharp end of democratic politics.

On this late spring morning the Agora of 399 BC is a changed place. Now, most of Athens' luminaries are gone. The great general Pericles is dead of the plague – or, some said, of a broken spirit; the playwrights Sophocles and Euripides have been taken too: dying just a few months apart, but only after Euripides, judged by many to be second only to Shakespeare in genius, has been hounded out of the city, and Sophocles has been charged with insanity. The free-thinkers whom Aristophanes and Callias mocked in their plays have been exiled or executed, their work burned.[18] The historian and general Xenophon, a fierce supporter of Socrates, is fighting as a mercenary in Persian lands. Socrates' one-time lover Alcibiades, already disgraced, now lies murdered, messily, by a contract killer. The master-architect Pheidias, responsible for the Parthenon and many of the city's beauties, has been (or so they said) poisoned.[19]

And now Socrates is charged with crimes that so offend Athens, that strike at its deepest sense of itself, that the penalty proposed is death.

So at that time of day when the early sun still rings haloes on human heads, Socrates is walking through the Agora to his judgement day.

4

THE STOA OF THE KING

⊚⊚⊚⊚⊚⊚⊚⊚⊚⊚⊚

Court of the religious Archon, Athens, March/April 399 BC

EUTHYPHRO: *Who has accused you?*

SOCRATES: *I don't really know the man very well myself. His name is Meletus, I believe — if you can recall a Meletus of Pitthus, lanky-haired, hooked-nose, with a sparse beard.*

EUTHYPHRO: *I can't, Socrates. But what's the charge he has brought against you?*

SOCRATES: *Charge? Rather a grand one, I think. It's no mean achieve-ment for a young man to have learned about these things. He says he knows how the young are led astray and who the people are who corrupt them.*

Plato, *Euthyphro*, 1b–c[1]

SOCRATES WAS TO BE TRIED IN a religious court some time close to May 399 BC — but he had been accused of crimes against the state a good four to six weeks beforehand. To hear the charges against him formally read, he had already had to make his way — through the Agora once again — to one of the most attractive new buildings in Athena's city.

The *Stoa Basileios* was discovered in the north-east corner of the Agora only in 1970. Work continued on the excavation site between 1982 and 1983 and has yet to be completed. It is a structure worth seeking out. Decorated with striking statues, supported by marble columns, this covered colonnade was, in Socrates' day, not only an elegant walkway where friends chatted in the cool of the shade; it was a building with a grave purpose. The *Stoa Basileios* was the home of the city's religious court. The title of the man who administered its cases was the *Archon Basileus*, 'King Archon'. He was, in effect, a high-ranking magistrate – one of nine who were selected by lot each year.[2] Kingship was a distant memory, but the use of the epithet *basileus* drove home to Athenians how fundamentally important were the piety trials that took place in this sheltered spot.

In Ancient Greece there was no separate word for religion. Spirits, gods and demigods were believed to be everywhere and in everything. Religion was not an optional extra, it was the known and the unknown world. Gods were around every corner – the people of Athens never knew when they would appear, in human form or perhaps in the guise of a swan, a ram, a rainbow, a swallow, a waterfall, a gust of wind. All life marched to the beat of the great gods' drums. The notion might seem oppressive to twenty-first-century tastes, but this was a rhythm that men prayed, fervently, would never be interrupted. Athenians were exhorted not to tamper with any ritual, or do away with '*any of the practices their ancestors had handed down to them, and not add anything to the customary ways*'.[3] Religion was at Athens' heart, it kept the citizen body alive.

Gods in the marketplace

@@@@@@@@@@@@@

The Agora of Socrates' day was thick with religious fervour. Stalls sold portable household shrines, and diminutive, messy sanctuaries would have been cluttered with offerings – the remains of burnt goat hair, dove's blood, the clay maquettes of diseased limbs, eyes, knees, genitalia, sacred flames that were never allowed to die. Greasy smoke hung in the air; Athens was, after all, a city occupied by many gods, all jealous for attention – forces that you neglected at your peril. Even the poorest would try to offer many deities some kind of sacrifice. Indeed, the longest extant inscription from the whole of Athens' classical history is a calendar of sacrifices set up in the marketplace. Every day but one was a festival in Socrates' city.[4]

Here there were shrines to Aphrodite, a Temple of Hephaestus, a colonnade named for Zeus the Liberator – *Zeus Eleutherios*. Statues commemorated the demigods and heroes who held a special place in Athens' heart. And in the north-eastern corner, close to the Archon's courtroom, stood the great Altar of the Twelve Gods: a massive stone block (the corner of which still survives) from which all distances in the known, Hellenic world were measured.

In the fifth century BC this was believed to be a world fat with threats. Earth – in the minds of Socrates' peers – was inhabited by spirits, typically malign, who resided in the swell of hills, the blister of a breaking wave, the mould in an ear of corn, the fetid breath of a dying man. Life was precarious. The Greeks did not need men to make it any harder for them by appearing to question and insult traditional gods. In Babylon or Egyptian Thebes or Macedonia the cities were orientated around the great might of a temporal leader. A king, pharaoh or emperor frequently appropriated to himself priestly powers, but it was his iron fist that ruled the state from inside tall palaces and golden gates. In Athens, though, it was the Acropolis with its cluster of temples, the home to many gods, that drew the eye. Proud democrats busied themselves in the Agora, the Areopagus, the Assembly and the warren of streets below. Even though kings and tyrants and despots had been done away with, there was no shadow of a doubt that in this odd new thing called a democracy, the Olympian gods still ruled. Life itself was thought to be a religious experience. Crimes against religion – such as those with which Socrates was charged – were fundamentally, desperately disturbing.

The gravitas of the Stoa's business was reflected in its marble and limestone dressings. Facing out onto the Agora, man-sized slabs, carved in wood and then stone, displayed the laws of Athens' political godfather, the celebrated poet and law-giver of the sixth century, Solon.[5] Inscribed laws such as these were a source of great pride for the Athenians – here was justice, literally, writ large. Recent excavations have shown how democracy was also built into the Stoa's fabric: along the north wall are stone benches for citizen-jurors.[6]

The intrinsic importance of the cases heard here – what could be of greater import than Athens' relationship with its gods? – meant this was a spot where passions ran high. But today, when Plato tells us that Socrates has bumped into an old acquaintance called Euthyphro, the atmosphere is temperate. Socrates has just come from the gym, following a languid chat with a young man called Theaetetus, stepping through the *Stoa Basileios*, past the mesmeric light and shade that the columns create. It is a relaxed scene; both men, in a rather world-weary way, have come to the Agora for legal reasons.

Socrates has been summoned to hear the serious charges against him:

SOCRATES: . . . *He [Meletus] must be a clever chap. Seeing my stupidity in corrupting his contemporaries, he goes off to accuse me to the State, as though he were running to his mother.*[7]

One can sense the irritation. An elderly man, a parent of both children and ideas, who has lived through regime change, war, plague, foreign invasion, is to be taken to court by three also-rans. We know their names: Anytus, Meletus and Lycon. Meletus was a poet, youngish, thirty-five or so. Anytus was a tanner, an industrialist and a politician who had become very popular with democrats (the democracy had been disbanded in 404 BC, and at the time of Socrates' trial was only recently restored; Anytus was in favour with the new regime). Lycon spoke on behalf of the orators of the city. We know very little about him other than that his son had been murdered by pro-Spartan oligarchs during the Athenian civil war. Without the later notoriety of Socrates' trial, it seems these are men with some clout, but who would, under normal circumstances, be only footnotes in history.[8]

The primary charge brought against Socrates was that he was impious. The fact that he corrupted the young was a secondary matter. He was believed to have corrupted Athenian youths *because* he tempted them away from the city's gods; he jarred the ritual tempo of society, he made young minds think independently. While chatting in the gymnasia, or in the dusty, noisy cottage-industries such as the workshop of Simon the Shoemaker, Socrates was accused of having sparked new, unorthodox thoughts in the youngsters' developing minds. For the Athenians, this was deadly serious.

And also make a law, by my order, that a man who is not capable of reverence and right shall be put to death, for he is a plague to the polis.[9]

Despite the inference of some excitable modern-day historians, there was no suggestion of foul play, or of sexual interference, in Socrates' '*corruption*' of Athens' young men. An Athenian court would have been the first to leap on such a weakness, if it had indeed been the case – in Athenian legislation a jury was *expected* to form an opinion of the defendant's moral character from his past reputation; courts *expected* prosecutors to shake a few skeletons out of the cupboard. Sexual misdemeanour crops up in a number of court cases from the period – as a crime, it is never once mentioned in the case of Socrates. And yet – perverse as ever – Socrates concedes that Meletus (although missing the point entirely) has some basis to his fears: that he has hit on something when he flags up the importance of the idea that young men are being targeted.

And he seems to me to be alone among the politicians to be starting in the right place. For he's right to care first and foremost that the young be as good as possible, just like a good farmer is likely to make the young plants his first concern, and after them he turns to the others.[10]

The young men of the city had a kind of totemic significance for Athens. Their heroisation is apparent in the statues that survive from the period. These were commodities that could not be tampered with. With charges that suggest the philosopher is perverting this golden youth, Socrates is in deep water.

〇〇〇〇〇

Socrates has arrived here today at the well-proportioned Stoa because, a few days earlier, as he walked through his beloved Athens, he was pulled up short. Meletus, buttressed by two summoners (a cross between town-criers and community police), informed Socrates he was in trouble. In a theatrically loud voice his 'crimes' were broadcast; a date was agreed upon (in this case, probably about four days hence) when Socrates and his prosecutor should visit one of the state-funded magistrates of one of the state-funded courts to thrash out the proposed case in a pre-trial examination. Given the lack of a formal communication system in Athens, this episode has a rather sinister ring to it. Meletus must have lain in wait for Socrates at one of his preferred haunts – the Agora, perhaps, one of the city's gymnasia or a favourite shrine – so that he could ambush the philosopher as he appeared round the corner.

Not that Socrates was a stranger to controversy or aggression on Athens' streets. By all accounts, his delight in needling men in order to prick closer to the truth, in his search for 'the good life', drove many to distraction. One later source describes how Athenians rained down blows on the philosopher, lashed out with clenched fists because of his interminable, irritating questions:

He said that the objects of his search were –

> *Whatever good or harm can befall man*
> *In his own house.*

And very often, while arguing and discussing points that arose, he was treated with great violence and beaten, and pulled about, and laughed at and ridiculed by the multitude. But he bore all this with great equanimity. So that once, when he had been kicked and roughed up, and had borne it all patiently, and someone expressed his surprise, he said, 'Suppose an ass had kicked me, would you have me bring an action against him?'[11]

What is good? How do we know that we know anything? Who is qualified to rule? What is love? Socrates was not a mollifying man. For more than fifty years he had dogged Athens with questions. He purported not to instruct, but to 'un-teach' men.

And here we can understand why Socrates' trial has such central importance – both for Athens and within world history. Come the year 399 BC, Socrates has, for the last forty (perhaps even the last fifty) years, encouraged those around him to think deeply, critically, about the meaning of life. He exhorts young men to do this, young women too, priests and priestesses, soldiers, seasoned citizens. He advocates thinking while men make shoes, row ships, break bread. He suggests that acquiescence to the status quo, to 'the way things are', is not just lazy, it is inhuman.

And while I have life and strength I shall never cease from the practice and teaching of philosophy, exhorting anyone whom I meet after my manner, and convincing him, saying: O my friend, why do you, who are a citizen of the great and mighty and wise city of Athens, care so much about laying up the greatest amount of money and honour and repu-tation, and so little about wisdom and truth and the greatest improvement of the soul, which you never regard or heed at all? Are you not ashamed of this? And if the person with whom I am arguing says: Yes, but I do care; I do not depart or let him go at once; I interrogate and examine and cross-examine him, and if I think that he has no virtue, but only says that he has, I reproach him with undervaluing the greater, and overvaluing the less. And this I should say to everyone whom I meet, young and old, citizen and alien, but especially to the citizens, inasmuch as they are my brethren.[12]

Despite the fact that the crimes now laid out in front of the philoso-pher are so serious they could incur the death penalty, Socrates does not appear over-bothered. For the next few days, if Plato has it right (and he was, at this stage in Socrates' life, an eye-witness in Athens), Socrates does not choose to exile himself from the city – which would have been a legal option.[13] Instead he has a chat in the gymnasium with some of these young men (those boys who, since birth, had known nothing other than war-years) and, only once sated with conversation, does he walk to the *Archon Basileus*, the 'King Magistrate', in the Stoa to make his plea.

The charges – that he has denied Athens' gods, introduced new ones and corrupted the city's young men – are read out once again. Socrates, we know, accepts that Meletus' accusation stands up, given the existing laws of the city.[14] This is a skirmish, an uncomfortable situation, which – like so many in his life – the philosopher is not going to duck.[15]

So some time in late March or early April the philosopher leaves the Archon's court. Now the well-oiled bureaucracy of complaint, of justice, is in train. One of the distinctive traits of democratic Athens was its obses-sion with posting public notices. Papyrus chits, graffiti, stone-carved *stelai* communicating new laws, fines, religious summons, would have been found everywhere in the city. Democratic decisions have to be shared with fellow democrats. And therefore a man handy with a paintbrush is given a job; the Agora – a witness to Socrates' ideas as he sat or strode up and down, asking one question after another – will now witness his defamation. Strapped to the railings outside the row of statues of 'Eponymous Heroes', possibly also painted on the white-plastered wall opposite, Socrates' crimes are set out in outsize red letters. Here is a rude accusation; his disruptive influence noted down, marked into the minds of his fellow Athenians, and ours.

In 1954 excavations uncovered white flakes deep in the ground in this south-east corner of the Agora: fragile fragments of marble-dust stucco. This find was not included in the excavation report, but just noted down on an inventory card. Recent investigation has, though, thrown further light.[16] The ghosts of letters on the flakes were once bold, ½ inch across, 2½ inches high. Freshly painted, ruddy, there would have been no missing the message they spelt out. One eye-witness, from antiquity, writing centuries after Socrates' death, said that shreds of his charges were still visible.[17]

The position of the red letters could not have been more significant. When the democracy was first established, the reformer Kleisthenes realised that he would have to break old loyalties in order to strengthen fidelity to the new mono-democratic Athenian city-state. Ancient Greece was a tribal society, but now millennia-old tribes had been effectively disbanded and ten new, manufactured tribes put in their place. It was one of those moments in history when men draw straight lines on the map – to try to obliterate the past.

The sociopolitical engineering was carefully thought through. Each tribe was given a hero. And each hero was given a fine, larger-than-life-sized statue in the heart of the Agora. This display of Eponymous Heroes was raised 15 feet above street level. At either end of the line-up giant flames burned. These bronze heroes had, at the time of Socrates' trial, reminded Athenians morning, noon and night of the radical power of the democracy for the last twenty-five years.[18] Here was street furniture with a message. Because beneath the statues, on wooden and plaster plaques, the charges of high-end criminals were etched. Ideal men, idols and condemned democratic sinners side by side. It was in the vicinity of the Eponymous Heroes – either directly beneath the figures or on the wall opposite – that Socrates' crimes were blazoned.

෨෨෨෨෨෨

When Socrates came to the law-court of the *Archon Basileus*, a century's worth of political crisis and political experimentation had come to a head. Athens had suffered the awful, abominable realities of *stasis* and civil war. Athenians were a brutalised polity. Twelve years before this trial, in 411 BC, a dreadful thing had happened, a nightmare that shook up courtroom dynamics.[19] The democracy itself had been overturned by an Athenian cell of aristocratic men. This was Athens' night of the long knives. Slaughter, torture, intimidation were companions of the political coup. Athenians spattered the streets with Athenian blood.

Reliving the horror of its memory-bright civil wars, once again Athens had attempted to institutionalise fairness.

When democrats repopulated the city squares from 410/9 BC, they were determined to do what they could to prevent cliques splitting the city apart a second time around. So now, to cauterise overt cronyism, the legally active in Athens on any one day – *dikastes* (the Athenian judge and jury) – have each been allotted to a different court that very dawn. The chance for tribal or political bloc-voting has been negated. Socrates' own situation in March/April 399 BC is another example of state-sponsored fairness. What now awaits Socrates is a pre-trial examination – more fluid than the trial proper will be. Chaired by the Archon, genuine questions and answers try to flush out vested interests, coercion, downright illegality. The pre-trial examination is a carefully orchestrated safeguard of fair play.

It is in democratic Athens that the *sycophant* is born: a man on the make who brings a trumped-up court case; someone who thinks he'll be able to score off the very presence of a justice system. *Sycophantai* were the fifth-century legal equivalent of ambulance-chasers; citizens who brought cases on flimsy charges so that they could be paid for attending court, and might possibly even net damages. And so steep fines have been introduced – if you don't succeed in getting any more than one-fifth of the votes, you have to pay the state back.[20]

But in the trial of Socrates, a fine for sycophancy seems unlikely. For whatever reason, Meletus has been moved to make an example of Socrates. The young poet does not even have to pay court fees, because by bringing Socrates to justice, he is thought to be furthering important state business, delivering a public service. At this stage in Athens, irreverence for the gods had to be prevented – no charge. Emotions and religious sensibilities were raw. Every living adult at the time of Socrates' trial has been traumatised. They would have seen their citizens limp home from attenuated foreign wars, would have heard their neighbours scream as they were exterminated for having the wrong kind of friends. These have been troubled times; dark days for the golden city. Athens needs its own catharsis, it needs someone to blame.

And so we might expect Socrates to be more than a little nervous about his impending trial.

Yet Xenophon reports that the old philosopher spends no time what-soever fussing about what he will say to the jury. He accepts in the pre-trial examination that the charges are just (if not justified), and looks forward to the trial proper with an academic interest. Here's the exchange between Socrates and a friend of his, Hermogenes, written in the form of a dramatic dialogue – as Plato might have set it down.

HERMOGENES: *Is it not necessary to consider, Socrates, something you can say to defend yourself?*

SOCRATES: *Do I not seem to you to have spent my whole life preparing my own defence?*

HERMOGENES: *How?*

SOCRATES: *By going through life doing nothing unjust. I think that is the greatest defence.*

HERMOGENES: *Do you not see how often the Athenian court is misled by a speech into putting to death one who has done no injustice, and how often one who has committed an injustice, has given a speech that moved the court to pity, or by speaking in a clever way, has been acquitted.*

SOCRATES: *Yes, by Zeus, and twice now I have attempted to think about my defence but my divinity opposes me.*[21]

For weeks now Socrates himself, his friends, Crito, Phaedo and Plato amongst them, priests, traders, scampering low-born children (here illegally; remember you had to be over eighteen, a fully-fledged citizen to show your face in the Agora[22]) coming and going at their liberty – they would all have had the chance to see what Socrates was said to have done, the crimes he needed to defend himself against. Written in deep red on a plaster wall, Socrates' full charges were set out:

Under oath Meletos the son of Meletos of Pitthos has brought a public action against Socrates the son of Sophroniskos of Alopeke and charged him with the following offences: Socrates is guilty of not acknowledging the gods acknowledged by the state and of introducing other new divinities. Furthermore he is guilty of corrupting the young. Penalty proposed: capital punishment.[23]

Shading their eyes to pick out the words as they headed for home, drinking in the cool of the evening air, Athenians must have tut-tutted at such a thing.

And now, in May, six to eight weeks on from the pre-trial, at the Archon's religious court, at the outset of the trial itself, with so many gathered in one place and with the sun climbing, the atmosphere would have been closer, fuggish, expectant. Socrates, we are given to understand, is walking unprepared into the packed courtroom. Even so, the philosopher must surely have read his publicly shaming charges, heard them whispered by the gossips of the city and bemoaned by his friends, and now he will hear them repeated again. The burning question Athens must have asked itself is: how will the philosopher choose to respond?

5

THE FIRST BLOOD SACRIFICE

☙☙☙☙☙☙☙☙☙☙☙

Religious law-court, Athens, May 399 BC

If you think that by killing people you'll put a stop to anyone criticising you because you don't live as you should, you're not thinking clearly . . . The best and easiest course is not to restrain others, but instead to do what you need to do to be as good as possible.

Plato, *Apology*, 39d[1]

ABLOOD SACRIFICE STARTED THE LEGALITIES in earnest. Today the oath stone is the only thing that feels secure in the boggy rectangle of the old religious court, the *Stoa Basileios*; archaeologists have to lay planks to cross safely. Marshy grass clumps around the few, marooned, listing, classical remains; a rude train from the leafy suburb of Kifissia to Piraeus rattles by at four-minute intervals. This block, a limestone table for sealing sacred oaths, was uncovered by the American School of Classical Studies at Athens, which undertakes excavations in this zone of central Athens.[2] It rests 20 feet below today's street level: overhead, tourists munch Greek salads above the masonry blocks and fallen columns here in the fashionable Plaka district — seemingly unaware of the drama that was once played out beneath them.

As Socrates watched in 399 BC, this cracked, worn, 6-foot-long altar-block may well have gleamed wet with blood and gore.

The theatre of justice had begun.

The *Archon Basileus*, the chief magistrate, his hair long and wreathed in myrtle,[3] his tunic unbelted, did the killing.[4] The oath sworn here was believed to be binding, its potency accentuated by the visceral nature of the sacrifice.

Goats, rams or oxen, their coats washed and scented, horns twinkling with gilt, were coaxed to the priests' blade. As they died, the animals' open veins coursed into a sacred bowl – here the magistrate plunged his hands. Wrist-deep in blood, now he was ready to oversee justice. But the oath-maker hadn't finished his gory business; the severed testicles of a sacrificed animal were then ground and squashed underfoot (a precursor of things to come: if he broke the oath, his own family would be emasculated). It was an ancient, unyielding custom: '*Whatever men first do wrong against the oath, let the brains of them and of their children flow to the ground like this wine,*' warns the *Iliad.*[5]

All jurors swore to do their duty: a synthetic strap of common purpose. One Greek said, '*The oath is what holds democracy together.*'[6] And what a mongrel democracy it was: farmers, old generals, cheesemakers, road-builders – all manner of men would have been here to judge Socrates; all Athenian citizens over the age of thirty, all chosen by lot. These were oaths taken in the presence of the gods themselves, their ritual aspect was central. And Meletus' own indictment of Socrates was itself an *antomosia,* a 'counter-oath-swearing' – a statement with the gods as his witness that what he said was true. We must never lose sight of how deeply pious, superstitious (one might say) Athens was. In the city that is often considered the catalyst of a rational, enlightened way of being, there was no doubt in the minds of the first democrats that spirits and magic were in the air. The sublime, inexplicable, potent world and its unpredictable, primeval, divine inhabitants were believed to be far more powerful than anything in the mortal coil. Spirits, dead heroes, gods, goddesses and demons were around every street corner in Athena's city.

And so the fact that Socrates stands accused of a religious crime, in a religious court, should remind us of the fundamental seriousness of this particular legal day.

☙❧☙❧

Since the early hours men have been preparing to judge Socrates. The eligible of the city have rolled themselves out of bed and trooped in to the Agora, busy even before dawn. In that blue-grey light, tribe by tribe, they have stood in line before a futuristic invention – the *kleroterion* – a random-selection machine. There were probably a number of these contraptions in the city; certainly one in the marketplace and at the entrance to the law-courts. Each tribe had its own machine, and the tribe members are here to find out if the day ahead of them is going to be one of justice; 6,000 have already made their names available for the annual selection by lot, and now a second selection from that list takes place.[7]

37

The *kleroterion* (really a proto-computer) is a neat bit of technology. Still available to marvel at in Athens – one in the Agora Museum, the other in the Epigraphic Museum – it randomised participation in democratic business. On the face of the hollow stone box there are carved slots, just big enough to take a metal disc on which is inscribed the name of an individual citizen. Down the left-hand side is a chute. Black and white marble counters would be sent down the chute (wood originally, now long gone), and when a black or white marble (we still don't know which) lined up with a bronze disc bearing your name and *deme* (the village district where you lived or where your family's name was registered), then you had been chosen for office on that day.

Selection for jury service was considered a thrill, a privilege, the mark of a democrat. A number of Athenians chose to be buried with their personal metal name-disc; so while we'll never know their faces, we know what these first democrats were called: Alexander, Draco, Georgios. Having been selected, there was still some administration to do: each juror would reach into an urn and pull out a ball marked with different letters. Depending on whether you got a 'lamda' (an L) or an 'omicron' (an O), you would end up serving that day in one particular courtroom. There was no chance of cheating – the moment your ball was inspected by a magistrate you were handed a coloured baton that corresponded with the paint daubed over the entrance to 'your' court, and this you had to show as you arrived.

And the engineering of democratic equity didn't stop at the *kleroterion* and tinted sticks.

Each tribe had its own entrance, its own machine, its own zone. Society might still be fiercely tribal, but families, friends, allies, conspirators were not allowed to sit together. Everyone suspected of a close connection, a vested interest that might cloud judgements, was given a place in separate stone blocks, lettered like our theatres and cinemas. It is no coincidence that Plato even refers to those listening to trials as '*the audience*'.[8]

Picture that audience. All middle-aged or old men, many settling down for the day with a cushion or reed-mat to stop their buttocks getting cold-stone sore. Each one has sworn to be impartial. No well-dressed, punctilious clerks organising things here. This is a direct democracy – individuals are actively, immediately involved in the administration and decision-making of their *polis*. You might have been a sheep-stinking farmer or a merchant of perfumed oils; in this land everyone was a politician. Each is to be paid three obols for his pains.[9] In the glory days of the Athenian democracy, money had not been a key motive. Sure, in the Assembly ideas could be formed, laws created; but it is in the law-courts that Athenian self-government could be put into play.[10] It was both a duty and a privilege to be here.[11]

But by the time of Socrates' trial so many citizen-judges of Athens have been killed, in defence of the city or by rival Athenian cliques. Today it is the disabled, the aged, the lucky few who have survived. The majority of the jurors are poor, they need the essential money that a day of justice will bring.

The minimum number of jurors allowed at a *graphe* – a public law-suit – is 500/501; Socrates' trial fell into this category. His crimes were believed to be of public concern; serious matters. By bringing Socrates to trial, Meletus was preventing religious outrage, he was doing Athens a favour. But, oddly, this was not a popular trial to attend. Juries could easily reach up to 1,000 or 2,000 men. Perhaps Athenians were already uneasy about what they might have to do – they came measured by the *hekaton* (hundred), not the *khilioi* (thousand).

The 500 jurors on that May morning, as always, are held in by a nominal security fence – a lattice of wood punctuated by gates – a symbolic ringing in of civilised practice. Because although events here were impassioned and powerful, law-courts were not particularly pretty places. Victorious prose-cutors could exact punishment then and there, beating their victims to a pulp.[12] The accounts of Socrates' trial describe jurors in an uproar, gurning and groaning when they hear something that displeases them.[13] Socrates himself complains that *thorubos* – tumult, baying, shouting, the acclamation of the rabble – disrupts the course of justice. But now, one presumes, there is just murmuring, as the chosen men – the ragbag judges – file in to take their place to enact the business of democracy. Once the entire panel is assembled and settled, the Archon motions for the wicker gate to be opened to admit prosecutor and defendant. Both stand on a *bema*, a raised platform. As the plaintiff and the to-be-judged appeared, all eyes must have swivelled immediately to stare, to check out their quarry.[14]

And here we have the worrying certainty of the world's first true democracy. If all citizen-men can judge their fellow citizens, then naturally men of all degrees can sit in judgement. Their decision will be representative. Every means possible has been thought of to prevent corruption. Alphabetical blocks of seats, secret ballots, random-selection machines. But still, the value of the judgement depends on those 500 odd men chosen to cram into the Stoa on that one day. As they shout and complain and applaud they will whip up and goad one another. They will bring their own neuroses, frustrations and back-biting, pre-judgements to bear.

Socrates has spent his life so far promoting the notion that every man should strive to be as good as he possibly can be. But he is to be judged before his advice has been institutionalised. As his darting eyes scan the courtroom – populated by men scrawny from hunger and disappointment, veterans scarred by war, tremblers scarred with shame, citizens who view him as an enemy of the state – one wonders with what degree of confidence he drew breath.

6

CHECKS, BALANCES AND MAGIC-MEN

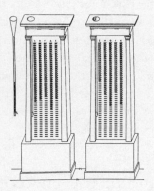

ⓔⓔⓔⓔⓔⓔⓔⓔⓔⓔⓔ

Athens, 462–399 BC

Do not be angry with me for speaking the truth; no man will survive who genuinely opposes you or any other crowd and prevents the occurrence of many unjust and illegal happenings in the city. A man who really fights for justice must lead a private, not a public life if he is to survive even for a short time.

Plato, *Apology*, 31e–32a[1]

OWN IN THE BASEMENT OF THE Agora Museum, where 250,000 ancient artefacts line up on shelves beautifully built in the 1950s, a number still kept in old olive-oil tins, there is an original fifth-century BC ballot box still in situ. This simple clay structure, looking for all the world like a marooned, subterranean chimney, is where Athenian men would toss their voting discs – *psēphos* (pebble – from the original tool of voting, a river pebble or stone). The ballots thrown in here around 399 BC were no longer river pebbles, but carefully designed. These were cutting-edge, newfangled things at the time of Socrates' trial. The size of finger cymbals, each has either a hollow or a filled stem. A hollow stem equals a condemnation, a solid stem an acquittal. If you hold the middle between your thumb and forefinger it is impossible to tell which way your vote has fallen (one side of the ballot box gathered together all the 'innocent', the other all the 'guilty' votes); this was an ancient secret ballot.

That surviving bit of archaeology in the Agora basement tells us something important about the psychology of democratic Athens. Despite the value of words in Athens, and their power of persuasion, Athenians knew they needed to try to keep rhetoric (not to mention vote-rigging and corruption) in check. Canny to the fact that their 'open' system was vulnerable to abuse, to intimidation, that gift of the gab or personal connections could carry enormous weight in a people-led system, Athena's children had spent a great deal of brain-time working out how to keep all procedures as fair, as fail-safe as humanly possible.[2]

Magic in the law-courts

@@@@@@@@@@@@

But even so, in a show-trial such as this one, the odds were stacked against a mortal like Socrates. Demons were also thought to be at work here in the courts.

In the Kerameikos Museum, a five-minute walk due north-west of the *Stoa Basileios*, there is a small figure of a man. He is made of lead, his hands have been tied behind his back, he has been buried in a lead coffin. On his right leg is scratched his name, and it is there again on the lid of the coffin: Mnesimachos.

Mnesimachos was the object of black magic — an aspect of the Athenian legal system that has typically been played down, since it does not fit very easily with a popular notion of Athens as a high-minded and enlightened quasi-utopia. On this miniature lead coffin lid other Athenians are remembered. These men may be the victims' friends — or his enemies who had brought him to trial. The coffin-lid curses cover all bases; at the end of the list is written, 'and anyone else who is either a legal advocate (*syndikos*) or a witness (*martys*) with him'.[3]

Elsewhere we find Athenian curse-tablets, folded up, pierced with a nail and left underwater — in wells and cisterns. Their messages seem to aim to disable those who attend the court:

Just as this lead is worthless and cold, so let that man and his deeds be worthless and cold, and for those men with him [also let] whatever they say and plot against me be worthless and cold.[4]

Figurines like these, along with the curse-tablets that turn up at all digs in the region of the law-courts (in central Athens and also in Piraeus and at the Kerameikos), show just how suspicious and superstitious a society Athens could be. Laying curses was once thought to be a habit of lower-grade Athenians, but the recent surge of archaeological activity in Athens paints a different picture. The frequency of the figurine and curse-tablet finds, and the names they bear, show that such sorcery was fairly standard procedure. A recent survey by the American School at Athens of all extant graffiti from excavations in the city shows that the bulk divides into two categories: the ABCs, where Athenians are learning to read and write, and the curses, where Athenians are perfecting ways of damning one another. Plato, in his *Republic*, refers to this kind of legal magic, the use of binding spells, produced through incantations:

They believe these things deliver us from evils in the other world, while terrible things await those who have neglected to incant and sacrifice.[5]

In the minds of many, magic was at work in other ways too in the legal system. Kleromancy, the quasi-supernatural power of randomness, was credited with guiding those balls in the *kleroterion* machines to their specific slots. The Athenians could not let the outcome of legal trials just rest on the power of a defendant's speech or the whim of the jury — darker forces had to be called into play.[6] And given how litigious a society Athens was — close on 40,000 legal cases, remember, in any one year — that is a lot of black magic to be in circulation.

With the help of the spirit world, Athens was a city that was used to condemning, to dispatching both the innocent and the guilty.

☙ ❦ ❧

The plug has been pulled on the water-clock in the Archon's court — all eyes are now on Meletus along with Anytus and Lycon (plus those Meletus has possibly brought with him, to chip in to substantiate his argument against Socrates). The team for the prosecution have precisely three hours to do their job.[7]

Before sunset on this one day, Athenians will decide whether or not a seventy-year-old philosopher is to live or die. It is not at all clear who will win this day in court.

There are no barristers or attorneys in the ancient Athenian legal system – Meletus, Anytus and Lycon have to mount the case for the prosecution, Socrates has to defend himself. What no one knows is whether Socrates' famous wit, his smart one-liners, his thinking mind, his self-belief, are going to provide sufficient ammunition to save his skin.

7

PERSUADE OR OBEY

⟨◎◎◎◎◎◎◎◎◎◎⟩

Religious court of the
Archon Basileus, 399 BC

*Well I am certainly wiser than this man. It is only too likely that neither of us has any
knowledge to boast of; but he thinks that he knows something which he does not know,
whereas I am quite conscious of my ignorance. At any rate it seems that I am wiser
than he is to this small extent, that I do not think that I know what I do not know.*

Socrates' defence at his trial, 399 BC, in Plato, *Apology*, 21d[1]

SOCRATES WAS IN COURT, IN ATHENS, in 399 BC on charges of
corrupting the young and denying the city's gods. Passions clearly ran
high and it was, by all accounts, a noisy trial. Time and again we are told
that during the court proceedings the philosopher was shouted down. His
cool, calm logic, even in the face of death, was clearly infuriating. But this kind
of vociferous attitude was a familiar refrain in Athena's democratic city.

Athenians were used to bellowing. Every month the frowsty roar of the
democratic Assembly up on the Pnyx rang through the city-state: 6,000 men
together in one place. Shoemakers next to aristocrats, fullers alongside
perfumiers, harbourmasters by slave merchants; all debating issues that
directly affected their lives. The Assembly was the living incarnation of the
democratic ideology. All here were equal under the law, each had the right
to rule and be ruled in turn. Heralds tried to keep order, but we're told
that at times the babble of these new democrats would reach to the skies.

The Pnyx was the name given to the natural rock auditorium just to
the west of the Acropolis and perched above the Agora. Men would congre-
gate here in the fresh dawn light to debate Athens' business: themes, topics

were selected by a rotating council of 500 men. The Council Chamber – the *bouleuterion* – back down in the Agora was where the issues of the day were selected; dinner was provided for fifty of the administrators in a strict rota system. Once the subject had been argued and counter-argued back up on the Pnyx, vote was by show of hands. Forensic research by one scholar has shown the exact square meterage ($0.65m^2$) on which each ancient Athenian could plant his feet or backside on that acoustically exciting hillside (and with 6,000 men there, the fit would have been snug) – contemporary Athens a panorama beneath him – to make his voice heard.[2]

Attendance at Assembly operated on a first-come, first-served basis. It was those men who decided to submit their names, locally or in the Agora itself, to put themselves forward for democratic duty, who made judgements on Athens' democratic life. Officials for particular jobs – and we are talking high office, not just clerical duties – were predominantly chosen by lot: the equivalent of having your head of state randomly selected for the duration of one year, and then the secretary of state picked afresh each twenty-four hours. All were working together, to ensure the *eudaimonia* – the blessedness, the health – of the city-state. All officials were (in theory at any rate) there to facilitate the popular will. The name for a citizen at this time was simply *polites*: city-person. Athens had delivered a social and political system that was exciting, empowering and head-spinningly radical. Policy was not in the gift of one king, it was dreamed up and enacted by 'the plebs'.

Gaining purchase here required a new kind of politician. In the past, the premier men of Greece spoke out to their community, but they were remembered, and lionised, for their heroic deeds. Now it was a way with words that counted. Arguments had to play to a mongrel audience. Although agricultural work would have kept many of the lower classes at home, there would have been lean, toothless men here, many battle-scarred or deformed by disease and malnutrition; but their vote still counted. In democratic Athens every citizen was a politician.

Yet many Athenians were, in fact, troubled by articulate people-power.[3] In a full democracy, citizen status and influence are not dependent upon social or economic standing or education or talent or virtue; the bigoted, the mildly crazed, the vindictive also have their say. A direct democracy is ideologically perfect and, in practice, flawed. Why believe that the outcome of a political process will be communal order and justice? Socrates had the kind of questing intelligence that challenged the value of absolute democracy. He was the child of a child-like political system. No one knew yet where this democratic experiment would lead. He was not complacent about the potential power of the emerging concept, not tired of it, not petrified of it. But he did what intelligent children do — he interrogated the situation he found himself in. Although some have, as a result, labelled Socrates an anti-democrat, he was in truth articulating the fears about the democracy of his day, fears that in their moments of doubt, secretly, subconsciously, and at times explicitly, made many Athenians quake.[4]

> THESEUS: ... *This state is not*
> *Subject to one man's will, but is a free city.*
> *The king here is the people, who by yearly office*
> *Govern in turn. We give no special power to wealth;*
> *The poor man's voice commands equal authority.*

> HERALD: ... *The city that I come from [Thebes] lives under*
> *command*
> *Of one man, not a rabble. None there has the power*
> *By loud-mouthed talk to twist the city this way and that*
> *For private profit — today popular, loved by all,*
> *Tomorrow, blaming the innocent for the harm he's done,*
> *Getting away with every crime, till finally*
> *The law-courts let him off scot-free! The common man!*
> *Incapable of plain reasoning, how can he guide*
> *A city in sound policy?*[5]

And Socrates — the man we credit as the champion of free speech and liberty — asked another, disconcerting question of democracy. Persuasive speech is all very well, but how much room does persuasion allow for goodness, for truth?[6]

Speaking freely in the law-courts

@@@@@@@@@@@@

But this is slavery, not to speak one's thoughts.

Euripides, *Phoenician Women*, 392

Freedom of speech was cardinal in Athens — and yet all clever democrats picked their words carefully. The silver-tongued did well in both the Assembly and the law-courts. The speeches of ordinary, nameless Athenians, many of which are only now being translated from scraps of papyrus, indicate just how canny these early democrats were. A few spoke their minds; most said that which they thought the crowd wanted to hear. Personal gain could be masked as moral purpose.[7] Herodotus' observation, that it is easier to persuade 30,000 to act than it is one, easier to deceive a multitude than one man, was a human truth of Athens' direct democracy.[8] It was a truth that Socrates was soon to suffer.

Pamphlets outlining the 'Art of Rhetoric' sold like hotcakes in the city. The number of copies of Aristotle's fourth-century *Art of Rhetoric* that are still turning up in the sands of Egypt are an indication of how popular such tracts had become for the layman. In the law-courts precise skills were required. Speeches had to be memorised, not read. The defendant or plain-tiff needed a clear voice, a dramatic delivery, a developed command of the Greek language (polysyllabic and complicated to speak) and he needed to be able to argue his case within precise time-limits.

The first to speak at Socrates' trial were his accusers, Meletus, Anytus and Lycon.[9] Meletus, remember, spoke on behalf of other poets,[10] whom Socrates had rubbed up the wrong way. The glitterati and their lackeys were turning against the irritating gadfly. Lycon was a representative of the orators, the men whom Socrates criticised for valuing style over content. Anytus was one of the city's entrepreneurs; Socrates, we hear, had had some kind of brief liaison with his son and had persuaded this young man to 'think' rather than to go into the family tanning business. Anytus was also a man who had lost much property during the civil wars – wars that saw oligarchs such as Critias, a pupil of Socrates', flourish. Who knows how long Anytus' rancour had been allowed to grow – perhaps even stretching back to those days when Socrates walked and talked with young men in the Ilissos district, while the tanners were restricted from using the clear water there to sluice down their bloodied skins. While the beautiful juveniles, the men with leisure and youth on their side, paddled in rivers and listened to Socrates and other sophists, Anytus' livelihood was degraded and threatened. As the philosopher and his friends enjoyed the cooling Ilissian waters, appreciated young boys in the gym, and thought, deeply, about the point of human life, a powerful subset of the business community was being snubbed.

In one of Plato's dialogues, Anytus and Socrates bump into one another in the back streets of Athens. The scene bristles with scarcely contained antagonism:

ANYTUS: Socrates, I consider you are too apt to speak ill of people. I, for one, if you will take my advice, would warn you to be careful: in most cities it is probably easier to do people harm than good, and particularly in this one.[11]

We don't know who wrote the speeches that promoted the arguments of the tanner, the poet and the orator on that spring morning; the prosecutors themselves, or one of the hired hands who sat at tables in the Agora and bashed out perfectly persuasive tracts, thanks to which men could save their own lives, prevent an abortion, claim their neighbour's garden was in fact theirs, et cetera, et cetera. Nor do we know what Meletus, Anytus and Lycon said (unless – always a possibility – their words are sitting on a scrap of papyrus in the storerooms of a museum in London, Paris, New York, Egypt or Athens, waiting to be translated and published; given that new fragments of new plays by Sophocles have recently been coming to light amongst the Oxyrhynchus Papyri collection, this is feasible). What is certain is that their orations against Socrates would have had to be to time.[12]

Because now that the trial-space in the Agora had filled, now that the charges against Socrates had been boomed out by a herald, a functionary of the court – after patiently waiting for the Archon's signal – had allowed the water-clock's regulating stream to start to flow: the sign that speakers could commence sharing their arguments with the 500-strong judge-and-jury.

We have a pretty good idea of what the Athenian water-clock or *klepsydra* in Socrates' trial looked like because the fractured remains of one *klepsydra* were found, in the 1930s, discarded down a well in central Athens. Two earthenware pots sit one above the other, and the water spouts from the larger into the smaller. This particular example releases water relatively quickly – it takes only around six minutes to drain. But the water-clocks in the bigger courts were commensurately larger, and we know that these earthenware pots were refilled time and again during the proceedings. It is a bottling of time that sits uneasily with Socrates' more fundamentally expansive approach to life. During his trial, Socrates points up the ludicrousness of making dead clock-time an arbiter in court:

SOCRATES: *If it were the law with us, as it is elsewhere, that trial for life should not last one, but many days, you would be convinced, but now it is not easy to dispel great slanders in a short time.*[13]

There is no real sense of hours passing by in this courtroom. ὥρᾱ only comes to mean 'hour' in the second half of the fourth century. Up until then the word implied both a season and a 'fitting or appointed time'. Socrates' lifespan has been rightly called the 'axial age'. Because this is a moment in human history when the old world starts to morph into the new. Athens still follows a primitive, bucolic calendar. Rituals and seasons mark out time. But new technology is starting to change things. The water-clock's slow leakage is inexorable.[14]

SOCRATES: Stop trembling. You should look away from some of your thoughts; and, having dismissed them, depart for a while. Then, go back to your brain; set it in motion again and weigh the issue.[15]

Socrates has agreed to abide by the rules of the court that has gathered to try him by the laws of Athens. And so he *has* to stand there, aged seventy, in his worn, woollen cloak and, like those around him in the court, within a prescribed length of time, strain to hear what it is his accusers have to say — because he, like all those in ancient Athenian courts, has to respond in his own defence.[16]

Agony in the law-courts

The adversarial nature of today's law-courts came directly from the Greek warrior tradition, where *agones* — competitions — were the prime means to prove you were a real man.[17]

The Athenian court was not about consensus — it was about winning. Defendants and accusers performed in a theatre. Emotional manipulation was an important part of the action: men would weep and beg, aristocrats would prostrate themselves at the feet of 'the people'. Of course the climax was not the roar of applause, but a judgement. And the courtroom-full of ordinary Athenians — think perhaps of a basketball court rammed to the gills — swayed by the tears, the wringing of hands, the fine words, these men could come to definitive, explicit, irreversible verdicts.

Despite their antipathy (and given what was at stake), the accusations raised by Meletus, Anytus and Lycon cannot have been world-class speeches, the kind of Ciceronian epics that have survived the millennia. Although we know that they stood up and addressed the assembled crowd in the allotted time, not one quote from the attacks appears to have survived. Yet it is not just the men's philippic skill that is in play here. Socrates knows, only too well, that he has something else to compete with. On this spring day, prejudice — pre-judgement — is clearly present in the courtroom; and so too is a force so powerful it was incarnated by the Greeks as a goddess:

SOCRATES: Those who persuaded you by using malice and slander, and some who persuaded others after they themselves had been persuaded — all are very hard to deal with. It isn't even possible to bring any of them up here and to question them, and in making my defence, it's absolutely necessary to shadow-box, as it were, and to ask questions when no one answers.[18]

Socrates is pointing up the dangers of 'slander', 'rumour', of 'word-of-mouth' judgements — all the stocks-in-trade of one acutely, intimidatingly powerful deity. A goddess beloved of democratic Athens called Peitho — Persuasion. Before Socrates has even opened his mouth, some in the court have already been persuaded. Slander, it appears, had swiftly flown on the breath of this, one of the most popular goddesses in democratic Athens. History has neglected her, but for the Athenians Peitho was a larger-than-life presence across the city, and a permanent fixture in the law-courts.

Well anyway, Athenians, that I'm not guilty according to Meletus' indictment doesn't seem to me to need much of a defence, and what I've said about it is enough. But what I was saying earlier — that there's a great deal of hatred directed at me and by many people, you may be sure that's true. And it's this that'll convict me, if indeed I'm going to be convicted — not Meletus nor even Anytus but the prejudice and ill will of most people. This is what's convicted many other good men and, I think, it'll do so in the future. And we needn't fear that it'll end with my case.[19]

The power of persuasion, in any democratic society, should not be underestimated.

8

PEITHO, THE
POWER OF PERSUASION

@@@@@@@@@@@@

Agora, Assembly,
law-courts, 469–399 BC

SOCRATES:. . . I don't know whether you have been convinced by my accusers,
gentlemen; but I myself was almost carried away by them, their arguments were so
persuasive. And yet hardly a word of what they said was true . . .

Socrates' defence, 399 BC, in Plato, *Apology*, 17a

I F YOU WALK ON THE SOUTH-WESTERN side of the Acropolis today,
on your right-hand side, before you start to mount the monumental
marble steps, there are the four walls of a home – a god-home.
   When every Athenian made his way up to the cult centre here, he knew
that he was visiting not a symbolic, but the actual, temporal seat of gods
and goddesses. Temples and sanctuaries were built as earthly lodgings for

the god-tribe. The experience on arrival must surely have been highly charged. Here you were, walking into the presence of what were believed to be the most powerful forces in heaven and on earth; entering a spiritually radioactive force-field.

This first house belonged to that of a powerful, wily goddess; the magnetic, effective creature called Peitho.[1] When you start to look, you find Persuasion/Peitho throughout the city-state. She hurries, ornamental chiton flapping, across funerary urns and drinking cups. She is commemorated in Pindar's ode *Olympian 13*, where prostitutes are nominated her servants. The art of persuasion has become so important in this new democracy – a place where ideas on the conduct of society, of justice, of war, of civilisation itself, must be sold to the Assembly – that Persuasion's divine incarnation was paid high honours. The pamphleteer Isocrates, writing in the late fourth century BC, claims that, by giving yearly sacrifices to Peitho, '*men aspire to share the power which the goddess possesses*'.[2]

Like Aphrodite, Eros and Nemesis, Peitho had a prehistoric pedigree. She was clumped with those deities who were believed to have emerged from the primordial night, a darkness that smothered the universe before humanity, before earth itself came into existence. Sappho describes her as Aphrodite's '*handmaiden bright as gold*',[3] and sometimes she is credited with a closer relationship to the goddess of love and passion – she is thought to be Aphrodite's daughter, or the daughter of Ate, fate.[4] Love and persuasion, a dangerous combination. Peitho is seductive, potent, undinting; sometimes she meddles where she shouldn't. But still the Athenians put their trust in her.

Democratic Athens in fact adored Peitho. With so many vested interests, such possibilities for freedom, how could the body-politic of Socrates' Athens possibly stick together? Peitho was thought to have an important job to do, not just to promote the ambitious, but to persuade Athenian men to think collectively, to encourage consensus for the common good. Athenians watched Peitho's glory played out in the theatres. Her priestesses were given special seats of honour in the Theatre of Dionysos.[5] (The persuasive nature of drink was as evident to the Greeks as it is to us.) Her chameleon qualities were turned into wooden cult-images or set in stone, by the most voguish sculptors of the day.[6] During one ritual a priestess would wash down a carving of Peitho's body and scatter doves' blood on her altar. Her name climaxed Aeschylus' Oresteian trilogy of tragedies.

ATHENA: *Holy Persuasion too I bless,*
Who softly strove with harsh denial,
Till Zeus the Pleader came to trial

And crowned Persuasion with success.
Now good shall strive with good; and we
And they shall share the victory.

CHORUS: *Let civil war, insatiate of ill,*
Never in Athens rage;
Let burning wrath, that murder must assuage,
Never take arms to spill,
In this my heritage,
The blood of man till dust has drunk its fill.
Let all together find
Joy in each other;
And each both love and hate with the same mind
As his blood-brother;
For this heals many hurts of mankind.

ATHENA: *These gracious words and promised deeds*
Adorn the path where wisdom leads . . .
. . . Let your state
Hold justice as her chiefest prize;
And land and city shall be great
And glorious in every part.[7]

The *Oresteia* trilogy was first performed in 458 BC when the democracy was a brave new idea. A decade when Persuasion, in a direct-democracy, seemed to be yielding splendid, life-enhancing results for the people of Athens. It is hard to read Aeschylus' lines without sadness, with the hindsight we have, knowing of the civil wars that did indeed rage, and of the ugly place where persuasion and circumstance would in fact take Athena's city. We should also note that Peitho, in ancient folklore, had a monstrous, bastard child – *pheme* is the name in Greek, which comes down to Latin as *fama* and to us as 'fame'. The derivation of the word is worth remembering. Fame in its original sense meant not notoriety but notoriety's life-spark – rumour. Through the fifth century, when talk was encouraged by democratic politics, talk's dark side, *pheme*, was welcomed as a new cult – worshipped with ever-increasing enthusiasm. In a tight-knit, free-to-go-as-it-pleased community like Athens, rumour and gossip salted many a conversation. Fame in Athens was, by the time of Socrates' trial, bringing as much pain as it was pleasure.

∽∽∽∽

Socrates had always been presciently ambiguous about *peitho* and *pheme*.

He seems to have recognised, and abhorred, the curious paradox that empty, persuasive words can often carry the greatest weight. Although many sophists invoked *peitho*, and came to sell their persuasive wares in the Agora, Socrates had strong reservations. Unlike many rhetoricians of Athens, the philosopher – as sold to us by Plato, Xenophon and later interpreters – was genuinely perturbed by degradation of the truth.

SOCRATES: *If you continue to delight in clever, idle arguments you'll be qualified to combat with the sophists but never know how to live with men.*[8]

His uncompromising quest was to distinguish the 'good' from the 'bad', the 'true' from the 'false'. At a time when compromise and spin were coming to have great value in Athens, Socrates, doggedly, infuriatingly, doesn't pursue popularity, he doesn't delight in managing with clever words to make black appear white – he is after something more solid, something with content as well as style.

SOCRATES: *And it's this [hatred] that'll convict me, if indeed I'm going to be convicted – not Meletus nor even Anytus but the prejudice and ill will of most people. This is what's convicted many other good men and, I think, it'll do so in the future. And we needn't fear that it'll end with my case.*[9]

Socrates was, transparently, a victim of rumour – of both *pheme* and *peitho*. Persuasive words in the court on that early summer's day will decide whether or not Socrates is to live or die.

But before we imagine how he met his end, we should investigate in what way and where the philosopher's life began.

ACT TWO

❀❀❀❀❀❀❀❀❀❀

SOCRATES AS A
YOUNG MAN

9

ALOPEKE: A PHILOSOPHER IS BORN

⚉⚉⚉⚉⚉⚉⚉⚉⚉⚉⚉

A *Deme* south-east of Athens, 469 BC

CRITO: *Either you shouldn't have children or you should share in their lives by nurturing and educating them completely.*

Plato, *Crito*, 45d[1]

SOCRATES: *Fellow citizens, why do you turn and scrape every stone to gather wealth, and, yet, take so little care of your own children, to whom one day you must relinquish it all?*

Socrates (attributed)[2]

A S IS OFTEN THE WAY WITH great men from history, we know precise and intimate details of their death, and very little about their birth. What we do know is that Socrates was born in the long shadow of the Acropolis — or to be more accurate, with the proud, 230-foot-high rock at eye level.[3] He was the son of Sophroniscus and Phaenarete, a man-child of the tribe of Antiochis and of the *deme*-district of Alopeke.[4] South-east of the city centre, Alopeke sits snug and high on the slopes of the foothills of Mount Hymettos.

The Acropolis, with its crusting of world-class buildings, is unavoidable today. Its profile, dominated by the Parthenon, has become an old friend; the Parthenon itself has come to represent, across the globe, a certain kind of civilisation. Of course Socrates' view would not have been ours; the classical Parthenon was not yet dreamed of; Socrates' Athens was innocent of the bold beauty to come. Instead he would have woken each morning to the silhouette of war-ruins – the Archaic Parthenon temple a jagged gash, toppled and burned by Persian battering-rams, Persian torches, Persian swords. But already there were whisperings that a phoenix would somehow rise from the ashes.

Even without the glory to be of the Parthenon, Socrates lived surrounded by the natural, cradling grandeur of the mountains that protected Athena's city. Lykabettos Hill, Mount Aigaleos to the west of Athens, Mount Parnes to the north and Mount Penteli to the north-east – all cloud-high. He would have seen traders nudging into Piraeus harbour, and the generous sweep of coastline, arcing down to southern Greece, becoming, just beyond Corinth, the Peloponnese. He would have as an old friend the mysterious white rock-formations of what is now called Philopappou Hill, where today lovers meet, but which was then a vital lookout point against invasion. Up here in Alopeke, the world – with all its possibilities, all its challenges – spreads out at your feet.

Here too, from Socrates' birthplace, you can see how geography gave Athenian history a kick-start. The story went that the goddess Athena and the sea-god Poseidon fought over the inland settlement – a special place. Surrounded by defensive mountains and lands rich in the raw materials of culture (marble, limestone, clay and silver), Athens is a kingfisher's whisper from the sea. Athenians have always benefited from maritime trade, but have little to fear from pirates. Their greatest exports were olives and expertise. So, the storytellers concluded – to give their daily way of life a sense of primordial, divine significance – Poseidon was rejected and wise Athena won out: the goddess was welcomed as a long-term resident of that great lump of red-veined Late Cretaceous limestone that we still call the 'High City': the Acropolis.

❧❧❧❧❧

When Socrates lived, Athens was still a tribal city, and, as discussed in previous chapters, society was ordered, emotionally and with a kind of loose apartheid system, into tribes. Each district, or *deme*, was assigned to a tribal group. Socrates was born as a man of the *deme* of Alopeke.[5] *Demes* were once villages, typically under the thumb of a local tribal warlord. But the reformer Kleisthenes recognised that tribal culture and democracy are inimical. If you owe loyalty to your tribe, you cannot owe it to your wider community. And so, in 508/7 BC, Kleisthenes introduced one of his most radical and sweeping initiatives. He smashed the old tribal system. No fool, he recognised that change is accepted most happily when it seems familiar. And so, in clusters or singly, villages were rebranded 'demes'. 'Tribes' stayed; they were just renamed and utterly reconfigured.

As cogent men have done through history, Kleisthenes ignored organic divisions in the demographic landscape and started to draw straight lines. On the face of it, to strengthen the army, he invented new teams of Athenians. Now the 'Ten Tribes of Athens' were drawn from across the Attic landscape.[6] At a stroke, nepotism, dynastic cliquery, the age-old superiority of age-old families were massively diminished. Of course, some tribal leaders must have been extremely disgruntled, but they would have been shouted down – these were exciting times, and suddenly so many more were empowered.

Fifty men from each tribe could come to represent their tribesmen's interests at a central council. And within those tribes each deme (in effect, a village government) could decide, by vote, who qualified as an Athenian citizen. Aristocratic and dynastic ties were immediately fractured. Now the demes – the name of course gives way to 'demos', the people – are compact units of grass-roots potency. All Athenian citizens feel empowered, and yet all citizens are umbilically linked to the mother-city, to Athena's city, Athens. Local festivals such as (to take just one example) the Rural Dionysia compound a sense of belonging. During the Rural Dionysia, which was held in the second half of the midwinter month of Poseideon, a large, stylised wooden phallus, garlanded with lilies and ivy, was paraded through the streets, a billy-goat was sacrificed, and locals competed in a dramatic contest (the level of contention at these drama contests is indicated by the fact that they could be represented pictorially as two fighting cocks). Aristophanes captures the sense of belonging that such deme-centred festivals fostered:

O Lord Dionysos, may my performance of this procession and this sacrifice be pleasing to you, and may I and my household with good fortune celebrate the Rural Dionysia, now that I'm released from campaigning;

> Revel mate, nocturnal rambler,
> Fornicator, pederast:
> After six years I greet you,
> As gladly I return to my deme,
> With a peace I made for myself,
> Released from bothers and battles . . .[7]

The city-wide festivals – such as the City Dionysia (where again a billy-goat, a *tragos*, was sacrificed, his name probably giving rise to the 'tragedies' that were performed during the drama competitions in honour of Dionysos) – ensured that one knew, ultimately, to whom one belonged: to the *deme and* to the democracy. In the *Republic*, Plato paints a busy picture of Athenians dashing about from one festival to another, drawn by the *craic*, by the crowd, by the knowledge that this behaviour would please the gods and their comrade-citizens.[8] The ten Eponymous Heroes – the ten 'team-leaders' who incarnated the brave new world – stood day and night as bronze statues in the heart of the Agora. This was the humming, consciously rebuilding, reconfiguring political landscape into which Socrates was born.

༖༖༖༖༖

Today Socrates' *deme*, Alopeke, still keeps an old-world village feel. Only a twenty-five-minute walk from the city centre, it has wild snapdragons growing on the verges. A few traditional mud-brick houses cling onto the hillside. They will be replaced soon, by developers keen to buy the 'air space' above such prime plots of real estate. Alopeke is not a rich district. After heavy rains, bearded men – a little shamefacedly – still scour the grassy banks in search of snails to flesh out the family meal. Many of the elderly Athenians and refugees here have reached the end of a line.

But at Socrates' birth this was a territory with much to look forward to.

In 469 BC Athens was a small place in a vast land-mass. Rich and strategically placed, the city had already attracted the unwelcome attention of the unforgiving Persian Empire. In late August 480 BC, 301 Spartans, at the front of a combined Greek force (6,000 or so), had held up King Xerxes and his army at the 'Hot Gates', the pass of Thermopylae, until all had fallen or fled – in the last instance the men fighting with bare hands and biting teeth. But then the Persian army advanced through Attica. They scorched the earth as they travelled, entrapping floundering civilians in their path in a net of soldiers, enslaving or slaughtering those they had caught. Towards the end of September[9] they reached the Acropolis itself and climbed up the archaic steps and red-limestone rock there, and then torched the place. Wooden structures roared and hissed to the ground, the archaic Temple of Athena toppled, split and ripped. Today you can still see the traumatised *kouroi* – beautiful, enigmatic statues of young boys – whose stone skin has been blistered, buckled and singed in the Persian inferno.

But there was the chance of a reprieve. In 483 BC slaves working under ground up to 4 miles deep through the rock in low hills to the south of Athens at Laurion had discovered a gift from the gods that demonstrated that the Athenians were 'favoured': the treasure, silver-bearing seams of lead. Overnight the city became cash-rich. This could have been a get-rich-quick opportunity – a chance for poor Athenian citizens to nudge their way out of poverty, for the well-to-do to become wealthier still. But one man, the general Themistocles, stood in front of the Athenian Assembly and proposed a far-sighted plan. Rather than enjoy the windfall then and there, he suggested something radical – that Athens should turn her face south, to the sea: she should become a sea-power, a 'thalassocrat', a ruler of the waves like those heroes of old that trim across the lines of Homer. And just as he was cogitating this grand plan, the Oracle at Delphi proved itself very obliging. A cryptic message told Athenians to put their trust in wooden walls. What walls? Where? the *demos* cried. The wooden fence around the sacred Acropolis, perhaps? No, says Themistocles; the Oracle refers to those walls which decorate the seas – the sap-curved timber of a fleet.

Despite initial scepticism, Themistocles' passion won the day. He commissioned 200 new triremes, first for flight, then to fight, and at a stroke turned landlubbers into 'seafaring men' (*thalassioi*).[10] The quavering Athenians certainly needed help. Xerxes' Persian force, glowering in the east, intent on invasion, was credited as being the most massive in human history: 1.7 million according to contemporary sources; 250,000 in a more sober modern estimate. Whichever number, this was an overwhelming body of soldiers – a seemingly unstoppable juggernaut. This was the army that had joined Europe and Asia by building a bridge across the Hellespont made of boats bound with clod-earth and brushwood. These were the men that had gouged a canal through the thick peninsula that points south into the Mediterranean and today bears the independent ecclesiastical state of Mount Athos. Some eye-witnesses stammered that the Persian leader, Xerxes, who commanded such monstrous, shape-shifting acts of the landscape, must be Zeus himself in disguise.[11]

The Persians could never be beaten with Greek brawn; Greek *nous*, however, might have a chance. And so early in autumn – the month of September for us, Pyanepsion in the Athenian calendar – the Persian forces, by now camped dangerously close on the fringes of Attica, were tempted into what would turn out to be the beginning of their military endgame.

The entire population of Athens – all, that is, except the priestesses, treasurers and trembling lingerers who had holed themselves up on the Acropolis (and were then slaughtered or burned alive as the Temple of Athena was torched) – had been evacuated to the Peloponnese or to the nearby island of Salamis. Well over 100,000 had been moved. Children were whimpering, women sweated with effort and fear. In this refugee crowd were many of the men who might have the chance to make Athens great: a teenage Pericles (almost certainly) was here, so too the dramatist Sophocles.

They were lines of snails in an electric storm. Families had with them some treasures, some grain. Their homes had been incinerated, everything was broken or looted. This was a sad, a debased moment. With the city of Athens still smouldering, all Athenians could do was watch and wait. The odds were heavily weighted against them. Enslavement, slaughter, rape seemed almost certain. Only if by some miracle — or, many must have thought, by the intervention of Athena herself — if the Greek plan worked, would they be able to take themselves and their families back to their cindered city.[12]

But that day Olympian deities, and particularly, it seemed, the gods of the wind, were listing towards the Athenian side. The straits of Salamis are a scant mile wide. If one climbs up the rocky white cliffs — where Xerxes himself sat to watch the battle — and stares down, the waters look little more than an inlet, a lake better suited to pleasure-boats. Salamis sits obstructively in between. However vast your head-count, at any one time, only a limited number of soldiers can fight here. The few Persian ships that entered were blown sideways. Fat, broadside bellies of the boats were presented to the Greeks. The warships started to cluster like leaves in a puddle. A frenzy of ramming followed. With the bottle-nosed metal bolt attached to the front of every ship, the Greeks splintered the guts of their enemies. Those men that didn't drown were skewered in the shallows. Screams echoed across the seas, the rocks slipped and shone with still-pulsing half-humans. Waters flushed with Greek and with Persian blood.

And then a sharp, sweet call cut through the air. The Greeks were celebrating their victory with a flute paean. A monumental statue would be set up in Delphi, 17½ feet high, holding the stern-post of a captured Persian warship. Blocks of stone would be inscribed and erected throughout the city, declaring that Western liberty could, and should, triumph over Eastern tyranny.

The defeat of such a gargantuan enemy ignited Athens. For seven long decades the Persians had been flexing their muscles, stealing Greek allies, marching through Greek lands, tempting Greeks to their side with the promise of riches beyond their wildest dreams.[13] And now overnight this attitudinal, radical little territory of Athens had become (by recalling exiles, empowering hoplite soldiers, training in new skills and — hands butchered with blisters and splinters — knocking out two triremes a week) the city of the invincible. The Athenians set about rebuilding their homes, and building up their reputation and their wondrous city-state.

Now Athens' name was spoken of in village squares across the diaspora. Spirits were flying high. In simple rooms throughout the city officials wrapped themselves in their best cloaks to travel to Asia Minor, Thrace and Egypt to bear the good news that Athens had taken on the job of uniting the eastern Mediterranean against its enemies. Because Athens was now a maritime power, she seemed like a natural leader against an enemy that invaded by sea and land. Two years on, Athenian pre-eminence was officially recognised on the sacred, Cycladic island of Delos. In the winter of 478 BC Athenians were declared leaders of (what we call) the 'Delian League'. Allied states paid tribute in thanks. Money started to pour into Athenian territory. Greek unity brightened the economic glow of the eastern Mediterranean. The defeat of the 'dog-barbarians from the East' had energised the city.

And just over ten years after the Salamis triumph, Socrates is born. If you subscribed to the common Greek belief that your name gave you your character, then you would know that this baby boy was *sos* – 'safe', 'very sound' (*sos* gives us our word *so*; this book is *so* long) and *kratos*, 'powerful', 'gripping'. *So-krates'* secure nomination was perhaps the heartfelt wish of a mother and father, Phaenarete and Sophroniscus, who had lived through brutal, troubled, bloody times. A mother and father who yearned for a more secure future for their boy-child.[14]

So as Socrates mewled in his crib, this was chisel-time in Athens. Building projects were in train the length and breadth of the city. In the year of his birth, the north citadel wall of the Acropolis was constructed; the *Peisianak-tios* (later the *Stoa Poikile* – the Painted Stoa) had its foundations laid on the edge of the Agora. The impressive harbour-complex of Piraeus was only twenty years old. Sculptors and stone-workers splintered and then smoothed limestone and marble to incarnate vital totems of the Greek world: plump, life-size toddlers prayed to a goddess of fertility, the goat-legged Pan-god was given his clambering cloven-hooves, ranks of hoplite stone soldiers marched to war and mourning young wives were draped on funeral pyres.

We are told that Socrates' father, limed, dusty, was one of the stone-masons in the hammering city.[15] A man kept busy and in pocket by the 'can-do' spirit of the day. Alopeke and its neighbouring districts – from that day to this – have a reputation as a zone where marble-masons live.[16] At the bottom of the hill the masons are still there, cottage-industry-compact, displaying their wares around the gates of the modern city's First Cemetery. Today their work is decorative – comforting the bereaved who want to do honour to the twenty-first-century dead with hand-carved sparkling stone. But in the fifth century BC, the stone-worker was the creature who would build brand-Athens.

So, Socrates' father, Sophroniscus, would have been in demand. The exquisite 'mourning Athena' relief was carved, the Klepsydra Fountain was sunk on the north-west slopes of the Acropolis, a bronze Athena Promachos was cast by master-artist Pheidias. The round dining-chamber, the *Tholos*, reminiscent of warrior-kings' tombs from the Age of Heroes, the Late Bronze Age, was erected in the Agora so that fifty councillors at a time could be given a square meal for their pains.[17] The population of Athens started to grow, and by the time of Socrates' death it would have increased fivefold. People flocked to the district. Modest, basic homes started to crowd the streets of Athens.

Illuminating the buildings came genius; a current of creativity that sped through the lanes and streets. Visual artists had the financial sponsors and the psychological support of a hopeful city. Two bronze 'tyrant slayers', Harmodios and Aristogeiton, became permanent inhabitants of the Agora; these statues which replaced originals stolen by Xerxes are the earliest examples of monumental political art from antiquity. Pheidias carved the exquisitely detailed Athena Lemnia, a forerunner to his massive gilded Athena in the Parthenon.

In modelling and sculpture, by what is the spectator most overcome? Is it not by the fairest and most magnificent statues, the ones which have achieved the limits of perfection in these matters? The Olympian Zeus, the Athena at Athens . . .[18]

The home-grown talent was matched by adventurers from the north and by craftsmen from the south and east. The master-painter Polygnotos arrived from Thasos and conjured up pounding horses and Amazons in the *Stoa Poikile*, the Painted Stoa, as did a rival painter, Agatharchos of Samos.[19] The philosopher Protagoras of Abdera was here; the sculptor Kresilas from Cydonia in north-west Crete worked in Athens; Democritus came from Thrace too – he whose mind gave the atom its name, a particle so tiny it is *a-tomos*, in-divisible. An extraordinary thing – to imagine and name something 2,500 years before it can be seen.[20] A bit of a local celebrity up north, 'in the streets of Athens,' Democritus would say, 'no one knows who I am!'[21] Aristotle from Stageira will travel this way too. Athens is an expanding pond crammed with big fish.

From infancy, Socrates would have glimpsed the capabilities of man and of the men around him.

⊚⊚⊚⊚⊚

And then when the boy Socrates was just two, an extraordinary thing. A celestial event that would be the talk of the town for years to come: a massive meteorite blazed through the sky and crashed to earth close to the Hellespont at a place called Aegospotami.[22] Some fields were burned – but, unusually, the Greeks did not all wail that this was the wrath of the gods. One of the rogue philosophers in Athena's city, Anaxagoras, would soon amuse others with his crazy theories – that the stars and planets were not heavenly creatures, but rock-hot masses. His belief seemed to have willed evidence out of the sky itself. The reformer-general-politician, Pericles, one of the rising stars of the new democratic city, started to take serious note of the theories – suddenly all sorts of wild, provocative ideas were a possibility.

So we should picture Socrates as a youngster. Riding on his mother's shoulders; being beaten for bad behaviour by his father (years later Plato has him referring to a truant running away from his pa);[23] at the age of three being listed on the 'he's-one-of-us' *phratries*[24] list – celebrating along with other three-year-olds at the festival of the Anthesteria. We see these Athenian minors on diminutive vases and cups in children's graves: pulling one another along in carts, pinging pebbles into pots, catching birds, playing with a stick and ball. Being children – for those who survived – and also becoming an essential part of the community.

At this time in history, death was something associated not with the old, but with the young. Socrates is one of the minority who weathers the illnesses that, in the fifth century BC, laid low three out of five children in Athens. The Persians stayed in the East, and young Socrates was not slaughtered, as so many from the generation before him had been, in a pitiless raid. His childhood was unusually calm. He and his *deme*-mates had time to play; jointed dolls were popular, as were *astragaloi*, knucklebones (discovered in a number of digs, jumbled on the earth as they would be on the mud floor of an Ancient Greek's hut), or, if you could afford them, dice, identical to those we use today – all favourite time-wasters for Athens' upcoming generation.

The boy Socrates would almost certainly have had an education. Typically the slave-tutor, the *paidagogos*, was a constant companion of young Athenians[25] – and, like the other sun-browned kids around him, Socrates would have watched as, down the lanes and footpaths, artisans and scientists, astrologers, painters, sculptors, quacks, slave-dealers and spice merchants all started to pace along arterial routes into the city, into the magnet that 'violet-crowned'[26] Athens had become.

So, for a Greek boy, an ordinary start to life in a place of quite extraordinary energy.

Yet if we believe our sources, there always seems to have been something that set Socrates slightly apart. It may just be hagiography, wishful thinking with hindsight, but the story goes that Socrates was somehow 'different' – savant-ish. His father went so far as to ask the Oracle at Delphi how he should deal with his eccentric son. The Oracle was laissez-faire: let the boy do *whatever came into his mind and not to constrain or divert his motivations but let them be*.[27] Heads down and keep out of trouble, the best way for a run-of-the-mill Athenian family to behave. All Sophroniscus had to do was to pray to Zeus of the Agora and the Muses: make sure he was keeping on the right side of the Olympians and their sidekicks. This was still an age – despite its democratic verve – when it paid not to attract too much attention to yourself. Those who became great and good frequently found themselves the victims of whispering campaigns; or, worse, were exiled from the city.

But 'safe' Socrates may have had less taste for anonymity and the status quo. Already, or so our existing sources tell us, an immature philosopher had started to interrogate the world he found himself in. Throughout his life he would make the question the thing. *'The only virtue is knowledge, the only evil ignorance.'*[28] *'An unexamined life is not worth living.'*[29] This lime-dusted, gently paced suburb of Alopeke was not, it seems, big enough for an enquiring mind. Socrates had to find his sparring partners.

The next we hear of him is pursuing knowledge – on the wrong side of the tracks, in Athens' downtown district, its suburbs of sin.

10

KERAMEIKOS – POTTERS AND
BEAUTIFUL BOYS

⊚⊚⊚⊚⊚⊚⊚⊚⊚⊚⊚

Outside Athens' city walls, 450 BC

Moreover Socrates was the first to call philosophy down from the sky.
Socrates autem primus philosophiam devocavit e caelo.

Cicero, *Tusculan Disputations*, 5.10

GOLDEN AGE ATHENS WAS SURROUNDED by antiquity's equivalent of a ring of steel: an encircling building programme of walls 3¾ miles long that buttressed the city, and then remarkably by 452 BC reached out for 15 miles to link Athens with its sister city – the downtown port district of Piraeus – the city-harbour that gave Athens an ocean-mouth.[1]

The building material used for construction was 'Persian rubble' – the remains of the city that the Persians had tried to destroy. The builders were ordinary men, women, children and slaves, all survivors who had staggered back home after the Persian nightmare had ended with the wake-up call of Salamis.[2] Athenians were fervent; they never wanted to suffer such carnage again. And so an ambitious construction programme began. Athens started to resemble the great cities of the Near East – Babylon, Nineveh – super-states protected by a defensive statement visible for miles around. Yet whereas Babylon's walls were blue-brick glazed, and Nineveh's carved with fantastical visions of paradisiacal gardens, it is clear that Athens' walls were put up in a hurry.[3] All kinds of debris ended up squashed in amongst the masonry blocks: chips of tombs, law decrees, broken pots.[4] Scrabbling to put something concrete between themselves and atrocity, the Athenians used what they could lay their hands on to keep Athens fortress-safe.

The protection offered by strong walls was written into the literature and psyche of the period. The philosopher Heraclitus from Ephesus in Asia Minor declared, *'The people should fight for the law as for their city wall.'* A study of the texts of the Old Testament drives home the horror of city walls tumbling down: *'I have wiped out many nations, devastating their fortress walls and towers. Their cities are now deserted; their streets are in silent ruin. There are no survivors to even tell what happened.'*[5] And Yahweh thunders, *'I will reduce the wicked to heaps of rubble.'*[6] The Athenians had no intention of enduring such a reduction and so they hand-lifted one block up onto another. The project was completed with all the subtlety of a juggernaut; houses, roadways, olive groves were swept aside. Athens saw that without a bullish defence system and permanent, controlled access to the port at Piraeus, she remained just another land-locked city-state, a beached sitting duck.

Because although Athens had become head of the Delian League, even though her boatyards were filled with the sleek 'wooden walls' of the Delphic Oracle, and despite the fact that she had brought a new word – 'democracy' – to the world and had sent the Persians packing, she was not universally loved.

CORINTH: *Keep it in mind that a tyrant city has been set up in Greece, and it has been set up against all of us alike; some of us it rules already, the rest it plans to add to its empire.*[7]

As well as the flattering epithet 'violet-crowned', at this time Athens garnered herself another: 'busybody Athens'. Without the common enemy of Persia as a clear and present danger, the city-states started to notice who amongst them had best picked themselves up and dusted themselves down. There was no doubt that Athens deserved that particular laurel. As well as mutterings from the Corinthians, the Spartans too (down in Lakonia in the Peloponnese) were none too happy with the reports that protective walls were rising from the Attic plain.[8] Sparta despised walls. Plutarch tells us that the Spartans boasted proudly that *'our young men are our city walls, their battlements the tips of our spears'.*[9] About 75 per cent of all Greek city-states had some form of enclosing wall by the time of Socrates' death. An extravagantly walled city takes on a mythic quality – it declares it can never be assailed. Athenians must have suspected that their building programme would antagonise the other superstate of the region, Sparta, but they had no intention of relenting. By 478 BC the city-wall fortifications were complete. Socrates was born outside the cordon of a truculently, hermetically sealed state.

∾∾∾∾∾

By the time Socrates was nineteen, Athens had been fully democratic for just twelve years.[10] So as the philosopher grew up, democracy too was beginning to ripen. Democracy was a strange, bold, radical experiment.[11] And, like all good experiments, it could yield the best results under stringent conditions. Athens hardly constituted an open society. The radical developments in the city were very recent, very raw. Its enemies were still only a morning's march away. The city built a cucumber-frame around its tender shoots. It became fiercely protective. Outside were foreigners, journeymen, the demi-monde. Inside were citizens, stakeholders. Golden Age Athens was truly a fortress city. Crenellated towers and battlements, at least 40 feet high, kept the haves apart from the have-nots.

Walk due north-west from the Acropolis today and one finds one of the most exciting ongoing Athenian archaeological digs – in that dangerous space *beyond* the mortar shield. The road to this, the Kerameikos district, still has a marginal feel. Moustachioed, toothless men play backgammon; there is an apologetic flea-market, where old magazines nestle up to older knives, but even the vendors recognise that most of what they sell is tat and abandon it to the dustmen when it rains.

It is this literally edgy district that can give us many clues to Socrates' life. Imagine approaching Athens not from the usual direction – via the writings of proud Athenians or self-confessed Atheno-philes – but instead from outside in. From afar the Acropolis, crowned with monumental temples and sanctuaries, dominated the skyline, as it does now. Closer in, the city's stench (no sewage system, no rubbish collection here) and its lime-polished patrolled defences (wide enough for troops to march along) would have announced that civilisation was close at hand. Here entry to the city was via a scrappy shantytown and through monumental double-gates.

The walls and the north-west Dipylon gate with its interior courtyard, 130 feet deep, covering in total 2,160 square yards – the largest gateway in the Ancient World, cut right across an ancient district. A fountain here was used to refresh and cleanse travellers before they entered the city. Named for the divinity Kerameus (his name means potter), this liminal area was colonised by eponymous craftsmen. The potmakers of the Kerameikos gave us the thing that, for many, defines the classical world: the Greek vase. We inadvertently honour their efforts, and Kerameus, each time we talk of 'ceramics'.

The Kerameikos must have been a gaudy, stinking, pulsating place: a place you came to celebrate both life and death. The River Eridanos flowed freely here; now reduced to a boggy, subterranean trickle. Tortoises amble purposefully above the ghost of the river.[12] Leaving the city, through its own door in the city walls, the river-water in Socrates' day was soiled and rank. But still the brown liquid stream was used to feed bathhouses, popular ones. The playwright Aristophanes declares, with a nudge and wink, a 'sausage-seller' (double entendre intended) here *sells sausages of mashed up dog and ass meat, knocks back the booze, and trades insults with the whores, slaking his thirst with the used, dirty water from the baths'.*[13]

When the young Socrates ambled through this district he would have found plenty of whores available to josh with: the Kerameikos supported scores of prostitutes, operating in what were often described in the Greek as 'factories' or 'fuck-factories'. Walking through the excavations today, you can still see their stalls. Tussock-grass and wild lupins grow here and all is open to the sky. But the squashed footprint of the buildings forces the imagination: rows of women, weaving clothes their day-job, busier still at night. A chunky silver medallion found in the corner of one of the rooms bears a plump 'laughter-loving' Aphrodite riding on a goat through a star-studded night sky, and is an honest indicator of the bawdy nature of the place 2,500 years ago.[14]

One fourth-century source describing Athens' red-light district tells us that *'women sunbathe with bare breasts, stripped for action in semi-circular ranks; and from among these women you can select whichever one you like: thin, fat, round, tall, short, young, old, middle-aged or past it'.*[15] Females of all hues too: many prostitutes were enslaved during military campaigns in Thrace, Syria and Asia Minor. These captives (not allowed into Athens itself) became an exotic fringe to the city. Women plucked and singed off their pubic hair to be ready to suit any sexual tastes. Men rocked up for a quick session 'in the sack'; or, as the Athenians would have put it, *'middle-of-the-day marriages'*. Male flesh was, of course, available. Aeschines describes boys lined up, *'sitting in stalls'*.[16] In years to come, it would be one of these stall-boys — a fallen aristocrat from Elis called Phaedo — who allowed Socrates to stroke his soft hair while the philosopher waited for death. Some prostitutes in the Kerameikos were brought so low even slaves could afford them: one obol a shag.

Love, sex, death, it was all here. From the twelfth century BC onward this had been a burial ground, and in Socrates' day the main thoroughfare was still lined as far as the eye could see with dressed stone graves – simple affairs, not the showy painted tombs that smelt of aristocratic power, but something more democratic. The dead were listed in tribal groups. A discrete 'political' cemetery housed public burials. But still the fallen of all degrees were honoured; orators celebrated the virtues of brave soldiers. Specially organised athletic games sent the dead off to Hades.

It is this noisy, pleasure-death-ground that Socrates, we are told, frequented as a young man. The Kerameikos is a key clue to his story and to the story of Athens' Golden Age. These visceral, vacillating lanes, nooks and crannies were his ethical nursery. This is a zone where man's basic needs, as well as his more elevated tastes, were catered for. Socrates makes it clear that his philosophy comes from observing, and living in, the good, bad and ugly place we humans call home. Despite what the world throws at us, his simple, infuriating, inspiring message is that however mongrel and challenging our surroundings, we should identify and embrace the good, the pleasant in life.

Tell me: do you agree that there is a kind of good which we would choose to possess, not from desire for its after-effects, but welcoming it for its own sake? As, for example, joy and such pleasures are harmless and nothing results from them afterwards save to have and to hold enjoyment.[17]

He used to praise leisure as the most valuable of possessions, as Xenophon tells us in his Symposium.[18]

Interestingly, as a young man, Socrates' enquiries seem to have been not just about the nature of goodness and happiness, but of a more scientific bent. In the Kerameikos the juvenile sage came to learn new things; he spent time, we are told, with the sophists, the professional thinkers who were drawn to Athens like iron filings to a magnet. Their studies were explosive: Was the world round or flat? (Socrates came to the conclusion it was round.) What was air made of? What was the point of the stars? These thinkers' investigations oriented around *phusis* – the function of nature.

SOCRATES: When I was young, Cebes, I was tremendously eager for the kind of wisdom which they call investigation of nature. I thought it was a glorious thing to know the causes of everything, why each thing comes into being and why it perishes and why it exists; . . . I prized my hopes very highly, and I seized the books very eagerly and read them as fast as I could, so that I might know as fast as I could about the best and the worst.[19]

Socrates would have been in good company during these al fresco seminars; for the well heeled in Athena's city, this was what the leisured boys of sixteen, seventeen, eighteen did. With two, possibly three slaves to every adult citizen, the young well-to-do Athenian did not have to trouble himself with too much work. Instead he spent his waking hours honing his body and mind.[20] All young citizen men (and particularly wealthy young men), outnumbered as they were by the population of slaves, had vast amounts of *schole* – leisure-time. It has been estimated that the young and middle-aged may well have spent three-quarters of their day at the gym. Here they prepared for competitions, for war, for being 'beautiful' and for their role in the city's many festivals.

At certain ages in Athens you could do certain things: Socrates, like all other healthy sons of citizens, had already been welcomed into Athenian society as a toddler at the Anthesteria festival. At seven he would have been allowed to read. At twelve to participate in religious rites, and then at eighteen – the real coming of age when beardless boys became bearded men – the number of festivals that he could attend increased exponentially.

The almost-daily religious festivals – the majority of which Socrates would have had the chance to participate in – gave Athens both a sense of security and a sense of purpose.[21] Its most splendid was the show-stopping Great Pan-Athenaea, a four-yearly fixture when outsiders were allowed into the city to marvel at Athenian greatness. Between the rival ten tribes of Attica, competition was fierce. It is the Great Pan-Athenaea that is represented on the Parthenon frieze. Foreigners carry honey-cakes, aristocrats parade along the street on horseback, their charges rearing and prancing; there are flute and lyre players; gods mix with men, young girls carry furniture in preparation for religious ritual to a high-priestess; and standing back to back with this priestess is none other than the *Archon Basileus* himself, the man who oversaw Socrates' trial. On the Parthenon's delicately carved marble the Archon, a stocky, well-honed figure, masterfully, tenderly folds a thick, heavy *peplos*, a new cloak for the premier goddess of the city – wise Athena.

There is no doubt that Socrates himself would have participated in the Pan-Athenaea. The celebrations lasted a week and spread right through the city. The festival route – the Pan-Athenaic Way – ran from the Dipylon Gate up to the Acropolis. Passing along it, one would have smelled the hot sweat of the athletes in the Agora running in full body armour and the hot breath of horses as they clattered past to cavalry and chariot events. In the harbour there were boat races, on the slopes of the Acropolis orchestral competitions, and up at the Pnyx recitations of Homer. Winning at the Pan-Athenaea was not just for honour, but for gain. First place in the chariot race for adult horses, for instance, earned you a whacking 140 amphoras of prize olive oil – approximately 7,850 pints. Winners flaunted their prizes during the florid parade in honour of Athena: the name of this procession – the *pompe*, initiated in the Kerameikos at the *Pompeion* – still suggests to us the ultimate in ceremonial greatness, a moment of pomp and circumstance.

Socrates grew up in a city that had become a master at *doing* things: yet this young man from Alopeke, at some point around 450 BC, appears to have decided to pursue not just the what, but the *why*.

One year when Pan-Athenaic carnival spirit was abroad in the air, there were two particularly respected visitors to the Kerameikos district: two great elder-statesman thinkers of the day, Parmenides and Zeno.[22] Pupil and master, lovers – all kinds of rumours circulated about these two travellers, footsore all the way from Magna Graecia, southern Italy. Theirs was a progressive idea: that our internal lives are as valuable as our corporeal existence. In all the pulsating, sweaty business of *living*, it seems that here Socrates, soaking up the eclectic experiences available to him, was quickened to the concept of *being*.

Parmenides was clearly a firebrand thinker, a man who burned his own path through society's undergrowth. Many credit him as the founder of all Western philosophy. The sophist wrote poetically, and in lush, descriptive terms. He conjures up luminous images to express his ideas: a divine chariot, driven by maidens – daughters of the sun, no less – and pulled by docile mares, which draws him down the path of truth. At the end of this path he will discover what it is 'to be'. His pupil Zeno developed philosophy further by establishing 'dialectics' – a method of testing the tenacity of an idea by taking it to its most ludicrous, paradoxical potential.

In this fledgling democracy, repeatedly throwing the rulebook out of the window – where new political structures, new built environments, new world orders are a possibility – maybe whole new ways of thinking, of living life itself, are a possibility too. Ideas such as these would have been eagerly discussed by the young men who gathered in the Kerameikos district. Over the outdoor braziers, and juggling too-hot fish from charred earthenware frying pans (one such was discovered during city-centre excavations in 2007 and is currently on display in the new Acropolis Museum), fundamentally illuminating ideas were played with. Socrates was born into very exciting times.

And one hot summer (the Great Pan-Athenaea took place in July/August), searing news.

Although the two alien philosophers Zeno and Parmenides were staying in this low-rent motel-strip of the ancient city, they had brought with them something priceless. A new book. Imagine the impact. The leather pannier opening, the papyrus unwrapped, the words, inked black with oak-gall and charcoal, marking out a fresh landscape of ideas.

Zeno and Parmenides once came to Athens for the Great Pan-Athenaea. Parmenides was a man of distinguished appearance. At that time he was well advanced in years, with his hair almost white. He may have been sixty-five years old and Zeno perhaps forty. They were staying with Pythodorus outside the walls of the Kerameikos. Socrates and a few others went there, anxious to hear a reading of the book Zeno had brought to Athens for the first time. Socrates was then quite young.[23]

Quite young – probably nineteen or so. His age was significant. Athens was not just a city divided by gender, tribe, wealth, but – and this is vitally important – by age-groups.

If the dating fits, then, during that same summer, as day slipped into night, Socrates' exact contemporaries (possibly even Socrates himself) would have been introduced to the citizen-body of Athens in all their naked glory down at the Kerameikos. The Athenian year ran from summer solstice to summer solstice. And round about the beginning of the New Year – in this case, the night before the Great Pan-Athenaea kicked off – boys became men by racing against one another from the altar of love in the Academy to an altar in the city.[24] These boys – all just eighteen or older, of an age one scholar describes, evocatively, as 'striplings'[25] – were stark naked, and each carried a torch.[26] It must have been a genuinely rousing sight – and we hear that many spectators gathered to give those young bottoms 'slaps of Kerameikos' as they went past.[27]

Their fathers had been slaughtered over the stretch of a half-century by the Persians, their mothers raped. And still they had not caved in. This new generation had much to live up to. Now the boy-children, Socrates' peers, healthy skin-oiled, flame-lit, pound along the Pan-Athenaic Way into Athena's city to show they are on their way to becoming men; and the Athenian horizon looks rosier.

৩৩৩৩৩

At the end of the Pan-Athenaea festival, there was a mass slaughter. Each and every city that owed tribute to Athens had to provide victims for sacrifice, and many hundreds of animals (mostly heifers) were killed. The bloodied cuts of meat were then processed down from the Acropolis to the Kerameikos, and the flesh cooked up in a massive feast for the people of Athens' *demes*. Socrates would certainly have participated in such communal activity. As the smell of roasting flesh met the night air, as travellers shared tales, as new perspectives on human life were explored, Athena's city was sated. The world and its wealth were coming to Athens because it was strong and confident and powerful.

It is a vivid scene. The stonemason's son, his suburban friends, the well-bred of Athens gathering to celebrate their city and to hear new ideas to add to their own fast-developing, novel world. In a cosmos dominated by irascible, anthropomorphic gods; gods who drank and argued and slept with each other's wives, together nature, *phusis* and democratic man suddenly appeared capable of producing her and his own mysteries and pleasures. A combination as powerful as that was unlikely to escape the notice of the authorities. The possibilities of the world – revealed by the brightest of sparks in this democratic city – might be fathomless. And in Athens one man, who was beginning to enjoy enormous influence, chose to open his doors to these new opinions, these new options and the radicals who propounded them.

Socrates was about to earn himself a taste of the high, as well as the good, life.

11

PERICLES: HIGH SOCIETY, AND DEMOCRACY AS HIGH THEATRE

@@@@@@@@@@@@@

Athens, 465–440 BC

[SOCRATES:] *Best of men, since you're Athenians, from the greatest city with the strongest reputation for wisdom and strength, aren't you ashamed that you care about having as much money, fame and honour as you can, whereas you don't care about, or even consider, wisdom, truth, and making your soul as good as possible?*

Plato, *Apology*, 29d–e[1]

Busts of *Pericles Chorlargeus* – Pericles of chorlargos – look odd. His helmet appears misshapen, strangely elongated and globular. Yet this is not some artist's aberration. In fact, the form corresponds to the unflattering jibes hurled at this statesman-general during his life-time: 'onion-head', 'squill-head' are hardly glamorous epithets.[2] But even through the taunts, it was whispered that under the great domed helmet of this most influential of Athenians hummed a notable life-force. Because within that bulbous, outsize helmet lay the very sharpest of minds.

Pericles was a strategist in both the ancient and the modern sense; he was a Greek *strategos* – a Greek general – and he was a man with muscular visions of what could be. When Socrates was nineteen or so and hanging out in the Kerameikos, Pericles was at the peak of his power, a reformer who shaped democratic Athens strategically, architecturally and intellectually.

Pericles came from good stock, inheriting from his mother the blue blood of the Alcmaeonid dynasty. His great-uncle was that key democratic reformer Kleisthenes. His family owned large rural estates. But this was a dynasty with skeletons in its cupboard. Pericles' own father had been banished under suspicion of 'medising' (fraternising with the Persians), and Pericles' childhood was part spent in exile. Expulsion was something of which the family seemed to make a habit. Further back, Pericles' archaic Athenian ancestors had been expelled from the city with a religious curse on their heads; it was said they had executed revolutionaries sheltering on sacred ground. To shed human blood on an altar was pollution so great that a Cretan soothsayer was called in to cleanse Athena's city – and to clear out the Alcmaeonids.[3] This was damaging superstition that allowed no quarter for pragmatism, and perhaps for that very reason, once he had real influence in the city, Pericles turned not to hardened, entrenched, superstitious tradition, but to new waves of thought.

Pericles comes into focus when Socrates is just six years old, in 463 BC. He lobbies on behalf of the Athenian people. He is instrumental in the reforms and purging of the Areopagus Council. By the time Socrates has come of age in the Athenian sense – after 451 – Pericles is campaigning in the Gulf of Corinth and has won enormous political respect. Chosen as Athens' General one season after another, he makes military achievements the basis of his power. This is the kind of man the democracy needs to give it backbone. And Pericles is not shy of reminding *hoi polloi* of the fact. His tongue was as sharp as his sword: he was an accomplished *rhetor* – a speaker.[4] For fifteen consecutive years from 443 BC (and twenty-two in all) he was re-elected as Athens' premier democrat.[5] Although he was not officially Athens' leader, think of him as the city's 'first citizen'. He had effective power because his lead was, almost always, followed in the Assembly. As *Strategos*, he could propose which motions were debated by the *demos*. He set the agenda for Athens' 'Golden Age'. His name, once again, seems prophetic. He is *peri-kles* – 'surrounded or rimmed with glory'.

Pericles, because of his position, his intelligence, and his known integrity, could respect the liberty of the people and at the same time hold them in check. It was he who led them, rather than they who led him, and, since he never sought power from any wrong motive, he was under no necessity of flattering them: in fact he was so highly respected that he was able to speak angrily to them and to contradict them. Certainly when he saw that they were going too far in a mood of over-confidence, he would bring back to them a sense of their dangers; and when they were discouraged for no good reason he would restore their confidence. So, in what was nominally a democracy, power was really in the hands of the first citizen.[6]

It could be easy to imagine Pericles doing what so many of his peers did, drinking a great deal, gossiping in the symposia. But he was not typical; head down, we are told, he made a beeline from his home to the Assembly, not allowing for any distractions, making democracy his business. He was both an intellectual, a theorist, and a man who *did*. His mind buzzed with political reform; he attacked the privileges of the Areopagus Council; in the late 450s he introduced payment for juries – now every man, even the very poorest, could afford to be a judge; in 451 he limited entry to the democracy by allowing only the children of parents who were both fully fledged citizens to become citizens themselves; throughout the 440s he encouraged and supported radical thinkers and made their ideas flesh in the stones of the city.[7]

Pericles was evidently a man who watched and listened to the world around him. He recognised that you cannot exercise your right as a democrat without being reimbursed for your trouble. And so by the end of his life soldiers, sailors, jurymen, councillors were padding their way, the majority by foot, a few of the rich on horseback, into the city-centre or down to Piraeus to ensure that their democratic power mattered. Thucydides credits Pericles with an acute understanding of what it takes to be a politician: '*to know what must be done and to be able to explain it; to love one's country and to be incorruptible.*'[8]

Athens, stage-set for democracy

When Socrates was in his early twenties, Pericles was the man who persuaded the *demos* to pour public money into the reconstruction of Athens' cult centre, the Acropolis; he oversaw the building of the Propylaia – a vast structure, a kind of glorified entrance hall to the Acropolis summit, the approach ramp rising, lined with Ionic columns and a ceiling of midnight-blue studded with golden stars – the first sight to meet those seeking access to Athena's earthly home;[9] he commissioned the new temple to Hephaestus overlooking the Agora, the worrying lair of Nemesis (the goddess of fate) on the wind-sweet site of Rhamnous, plus a temple to Athena above the Kolonos Hill. Pericles planned other buildings to herald a new Athens: each stone canopy served a spiritual function, replacing the god-homes destroyed by the Persians in 480/79 BC.[10] The Persians might have burned down the architecture of the Acropolis, but Pericles, on behalf of the Athenian democracy, would build it back higher.

And the splendification of Athens was not measured just in masonry. The modern-day pollution of central Athens is nothing compared to that in the Golden Age. On the south-east slopes of the Acropolis itself a foundry has recently been excavated. Massive clay channels here drained off the molten wax and other by-products of foundry-cast art. Temperatures of up to 950 degrees centigrade had to be stoked in the furnaces on these slopes – the Agora, the Parthenon itself, must have been regularly shrouded in clouds of charcoal-smuts. This was where those bronze sculptures, heroically naked, most funded by individual dynasties, were knocked out to satisfy both the city's renewed democratic sense of itself and aristocratic competitive instinct – visible proof that your family was capable of more great works than the next.

We should pause for a moment to imagine just how many created versions of the human form there were in Athena's city. Athens was a territory where the breathing population was watched by beautifully worked stone and metal men – idealised versions of humankind, an embodiment of the democratic Athenian's ambition. Sculptures – bronze, marble, wood – all dressed in real clothes as if they suffered hot and cold like any other human, lined the sanctuaries, the roads, the colonnades, the law-courts. Only a tiny fraction of the bronze statuary cast in Athens in the fifth century remains, so it can be easy to underestimate just what a packed, ever-expanding site-specific art gallery this city was, the public spaces populated by crowds of silent humans. Silent, but not muted. With a showman's urge to make their new attraction (in this case, the show city of democracy) as gaudy as any Persian king's court or Babylonian tyrant's processional way, the Athenians stage-set *demos-kratia*. Statues, monuments, temples, democratic courts were all painted and stained in Technicolor. The stark application and gloopy pigments used would shock most of us today, but these were designed to be seen under the bright Attic sun, and their gaudy glory to be remembered.

In 2007 archaeologists turned up in the earth of the Agora seashells pretty with cinnabar-red, lapis-blue and calchite-green mineral pigment. Winkled out of the ground, these craftsmen's paint pots were half-empty – their job, for some reason, interrupted. The majority of Athens' public buildings were painted or stained: recent analysis has shown that the Parthenon was gaudy with greens, blues, reds and gold. The Agora was where the backdrop of Athenian democracy was liveried. It was also where the fruits of the Athenian empire – exotic and home-grown – were enjoyed.

Scientists from the west coast of Asia Minor, rhetoricians from Sicily, philosophers from Thessaly and Macedonia made their way to Athena's city, all chatting, arguing, thinking: imagine the hubbub – the Athenians had a name for it, the *thorubos* – the buzz of opinion and dissent in the streets, the council chambers, the Assembly, and at those famous debauched-yet-refined symposia that Plato, Aristophanes, Xenophon et al. have immortalised, where wit and wine flowed, where poetry was sung and schemes of self-advancement were hatched.

Pericles also filled his city with billowing music. He commissioned the Odeion concert-hall in 440 BC and encouraged the production of new melodies for the city's parades: the sound of musicians practising would have been transported by Athens' soft winds through the central districts and even to its surrounding *demes*. The Odeion was splendid, with a vast conical roof, the largest covered building in the Greek world.[11] Later tradition alleged that it was an imitation of the tent of Xerxes, an architectural two fingers up to Persian might.[12] Pericles was taught by a certain Damon, who studied the effects of music on behaviour and character,[13] and the general promoted a soundtrack *'through which he harmonized the city'*.[14] According to Plutarch, Pericles reorchestrated the music in the Pan-Athenaea festival.[15] In the fifth century music was credited with medicinal qualities – Pericles was playing physick to his compatriots.

> *Here comes the squill-headed Zeus,*
> *Perikles, wearing the Odeion on his head,*
> *now that the ostrakon is past.*
>   Fragment of Kratinos[16]

No one could deny Pericles' piety, but he also entertained the abstracts of oddballs. This was an age when all kinds of astonishing ideas were abroad, outlandish notions from foreign thinkers; one, Thales, had guessed that all things come from water, another, Anaximander, stated: *'from the warmed-up water and earth emerged either fish or animals pretty fish-like: from these humans were created'*.[17] Then Anaxagoras of Clazomenae proposed that the sun was a red-hot rock, the moon a lump of earth. The thoughtful traveller from Asia Minor went further, having the audacity to suggest that consciousness rests not in the heart, but in the brain, and he introduced a concept of *nous* – 'mind' – a kind of super-presence that sets the world in motion:

It is the finest of all things and the purest, and it has knowledge concerning all things and the greatest power; and over everything that has souls, large or small, mind rules.[18]

Anaxagoras was allowed into Pericles' home – a man who, according to Socrates, *'filled him* [that is, Socrates himself] *with high thoughts and taught him the nature of the mind.'*[19] Pericles' sons associated with the philosopher

Protagoras. Socrates, already eagerly acquiring philosophic experience, may also have been welcomed.[20] All met at sponsored soirées: *phrontistai* – thinkers (and this is the Greek word used more frequently than 'philosophers') gathered to give practical advice on the well-being of this new, experimental society. Athenians recognised that democracy would be difficult to maintain, but they went out of their way to cherish and buttress the new ideology. These men inhabited the *phrontisteria*, the 'thinking shops' that Aristophanes would, thirty years later, mock so mercilessly. He ripped into the 'immoral logic' that they taught, and scorned the utterly ludicrous lines of enquiry that men such as Socrates followed.

STUDENT: *Chaerephon of Sphettus once asked Socrates whether he was of the opinion that gnats produced their hum by way of the mouth or – the other end.*

STREPSIADES: *Well, well, what did he say?*

STUDENT: *'The intestinal passage of the gnat,' he replied, 'is very narrow, and consequently the wind is forced to go straight through the back end. And the arse, being a hole forming the exit from this narrow passage, groans under the force of the wind.'*

STREPSIADES: *Like a trumpet, you mean. I must say that's a marvellous feat of intestinology. I can see getting acquitted in the Lawcourts is going to be child's play for a chap who knows all there is to know about gnat's guts.*[21]

But Pericles has set a precedent; in years to come we hear of 'open house' meetings elsewhere in the city: men gathering in the inner courtyards that were a feature of most mid-range Athenian homes. Here the premier educators of the day competed to see who would get to mould the city's future and its hope – its young men.[22]

Picture Socrates at these elevated gatherings, perhaps inside Pericles' home, perhaps in a neighbouring courtyard. Listening to what Anaxagoras has to say about a new meaning of life, *nous*; computing these notions, turning them over in his own, maturing mind.

I was delighted with this . . . It seemed somehow right that mind [nous] should be the cause of all things, and I thought that if this were the case then mind, in arranging all these things, would arrange each in the way that was best for it.[23]

Staring too up at the night sky, at that point in the earth's turn where thinking conditions in this region become more bearable. Although this would be a line of enquiry Socrates would later reject, in his early years mulling over with the great thinkers around him the secrets and purpose of the stars.

And he strongly advised them also to become familiar with astronomical measurement, however only to the point of being able to know the time-divisions of night, of the month, and of the year, for the sake of journeying and sailing and keeping watch.[24]

Yet Socrates at this stage was nothing more than a village boy, the son of artisans. It was intimidating surely to make his way into the circle of, possibly even the household of, the acolytes of, *the* most powerful man in all of Athens.

The domestics of democracy

But there is one thing it is important to remember about democratic Athens — just how cosy this city was. Here you would not find the 100-foot-wide avenues running to the palatial complex that will so impress in the city of Alexandria, or the equivalent of Nero's *Domus Aurea* in Rome. So far the archaeological record has not turned up an aristocratic 'district'. Men of all degrees walked through the winding streets, brushing shoulders with one another. Prostitutes could confidently ply their trade by slipping on customised little hobnail boots and casually strolling up and down the alleyways. In the dust their shoe-nails would spell out *akolouthei* — 'this way', or 'follow me'. Ordinary women, bread-sellers and washer-women joined aristocrats on their way to make dedications at sanctuaries or up on the Acropolis itself.[25] All life was here. Socrates, himself a great walker (we hear in one of the Platonic dialogues, the *Phaedrus*, that contemporaries thought walking a 'good way to think'), would have travelled through an Athenian landscape of surprising parity.

Because it seems, at least when Socrates was a young man, that the blue-blood dynasties, the 'old' Athenian families, had chosen not to cream off the benefits of democratic living; rich and poor democrats alike lived in homes that, from the outside at any rate, looked very similar. The excavations to build the new Acropolis Museum in Athens have revealed warrens of streets, modest, fifth-century BC terraced houses hugging right up close to the rock of the Acropolis. Twenty feet below the current city-level, visitors can now walk above the city of Pericles and Socrates, over a glass and Perspex sky: as though the hive of the modern city has been lifted to reveal a honeycomb of antiquity beneath. In one section of the dusty remains there is a neat drain from Socrates' day — touching somehow to imagine this bit of engineering quietly functioning, while the men and women around it got on with the business of being the world's first official democrats.

Their homes were simple, made of mud-brick, red-roof-tiled.[26] Socrates would have lived with his parents until he was thirty or so, in just such a house. Courtyards were where much of the bustle of being alive took place.

Very little fancy decoration here. Those expressive, brush-fine, pastel-shade fresco paintings from the fifth and fourth centuries BC that are still being excavated were kept mainly for the walls of graves (hence their survival) and of public spaces. Democrats – great and small – lived remarkably modestly.[27]

Personal satisfaction appears to have counted for little in the newly democratic city. In fact being 'private' was something that made the Athenians suspicious. Years later Socrates would fall foul of this anxiety; when he chose to expound his ideas behind closed doors within a tight aristocratic circle, democrats cried, Oligarch! Anti-democrat! It is telling that the only anecdote we have of individual aggrandisement when it came to interior decoration (scant archaeological evidence survives) gossips that Socrates' brash, larger-than-life, supremely aristocratic friend Alcibiades kidnapped a scene-painter (possibly Agatharcos of Samos) and forced him to make over his own house. Alcibiades also sponsored his personal sweatshop of goldsmiths. These were stereotypically audacious bits of posturing from a blue-blood who did not want to give up his aristocratic ways.

This was not Pericles' style at all. Despite his reputation in Old Comedy for an engulfing sexual licence, the Olympian's kicks, it seems, were satisfied not by personal wealth and domestic comfort, or by the obligingly varied knocking shops in the city, or even by the attentions of his courtesan-consort Aspasia (more of her later), but by the philosophical conversation of his protégés, by strategic military planning, by drama (as a young man he produced the playwright Aeschylus), and by the idea of what Athens could become.[28]

So we should imagine the modest home of Pericles – the man who is still a role-model for so many of our political leaders, the unofficial leader of Athens. Visitors striding in and out of his mud-brick and stone chambers. Slaves keeping the material world turning. Women everywhere in the house, apart from in the *andron* – the man's room. Unpretentious dinner services on the table, but new ideas all around. The invisible web of interconnecting possibilities, woven by the men who came and sat at Pericles' table, had sparkling ideas dropped into them like dew.

That Athenians employed ideas as a workhorse for civilisation was big news. This was an age when there were many gleaming examples of the wonders that man could achieve – Babylon's Prussian-blue and ochre-glazed Processional Way protected by glazed dragons and lions (standing until 1902 in the sands of modern-day Iraq); the pyramids at Giza, already 2,000 years old; the Apadana – the 'audience hall' at Persepolis, where Darius and Xerxes intimidated their subjects while guarded by massive carved dogs and winged bulls.[29] And although many other towns, particularly along the western coast of Asia Minor (modern-day Turkey), sponsored thinkers and scientists, Athens had something different: thoughts, ideas that were beginning to harmonise and to sound the timbre of an ideology, *demos-kratia* – the power of the people.

Listen to contemporary accounts of the excited reports of Athens' egalitarian attitudes from a Persian nobleman, Otanes:

The rule of the majority has a most beautiful name: equality under the law [isonomia] ... The holders of offices are selected by lot and are held accountable for their actions. All deliberations are in public. I predict – and suggest that we will give up monarchy and replace it with democracy. For in democracy all things are possible.[30]

Although Otanes' predictions of democracy in Persia are still to be fully realised, his final comment proved prescient. '*In a democracy all things are possible.*' Athens was focusing not just on making herself beautiful and fit for practice, her eyes were flicking elsewhere too. Pericles could not afford simply to indulge his time with humble-born, thinking men such as Socrates and Anaxagoras – scintillating as they might be – to play around with ground-breaking political experiments. Because he now had not only a city-state, but a burgeoning empire to run.

12

DELOS – AND THE BIRTH OF AN EMPIRE

The Cyclades, the Mediterranean basin, 478/7–454 BC

CALLICLES: *What do you mean?*

SOCRATES: *I mean that every man is his own ruler; or is there no need of one's ruling oneself, but only of ruling others?*

Plato, *Gorgias*, 491d[1]

THE ATHENIANS HAD SHOWN THEIR IMPERIAL hand early. Up until 477 BC, it had been the Spartans who bared their teeth at the Persians, controlling the loose alliance between like-minded Hellenic city-states that was formed to prevent another Thermopylae.

But then the Athenians became Hellenic protectors-in-chief. It was they who determined who should provide ships, who should offer up human muscle to serve the Hellenic vs Barbarian cause. It was the Athenians who collected tribute from those who couldn't run to oars and ramming prows. To all intents and purposes, 'tribute' was a protection tax, a way of paying for armaments and personnel that could be pooled for use against the Persians. That forced windfall was then stored 100 miles south-east of Athens, on the sacred island of Delos.

Delos will sound loud in Socrates' story. Even though it appears as just a speck on the map, this tiny 'floating' island at the centre of the Cyclades was always believed to have sacred powers. Since prehistory, men from across the eastern Mediterranean had gathered here. They left their calling cards: simple, angular, limestone human shapes, their surfaces tattooed with staring eyes, penises, abstract, organic patterns. And now that the Greeks felt strong enough to stand up to the bully-boys of the East, they made this charmed place the centre of their league of understanding. Delos was centrally placed between the great powers of the eastern Mediterranean, and yet the island was, in the eyes of the ancients, inhabited by an unusual number of divinities and demons. No one in their right mind would attack such a possessed territory.

And so, for a brief time at the beginning of Socrates' long life, while the Athenians were pre-eminent, the Persians quiet and other Greeks acquiescent, there was some degree of peace in the world.

Then in 465 a spat broke out in the northern territories. The honey-filled island of Thasos – just south of modern-day Kavala – owned mining rights on the mainland across a narrow stretch of water. Here the earth is porous: tombs are regularly sunk, and gold is frequently pulled out. Herodotus is ebullient in his excitement: '*The gold mines at Scapte Hyle yielded in all eighty talents a year . . . the islanders, without raising any tax on their own produce, enjoyed, from the mines and the mainland, a revenue of two hundred talents – and, in a particularly good year, of as much as three hundred. I have seen these mines myself; . . . A whole mountain has been turned upside down in the search for gold.*'[2]

Some of the most exquisite artefacts from antiquity are now emerging from the soil in this region: chandelier earrings, golden belt-buckles, tiny perfume bottles so heavy with gold and enamel they weigh in like a brick. A diadem made of gold and coloured with blue enamel – a wreath of wild metal flowers – shows what beauty could be created in these northern lands.[3] While being restored in 2008, this wreath was treated in the laboratory-workshops of the new Acropolis Museum. Testimony of its daintiness, as the door of the workshop was opened, a momentary, gentle breeze was sufficient to set the golden flower-heads dancing.

But jewels such as these attract thieves.

Athens, it seems, wanted a piece of the gold-and-honey action, and when Thasos defected from the League in protest in 465, the island community found itself blockaded. Athenian ships sailed one after another from the port of Piraeus. For two full years hoplite citizens whetted their swords and spears and stared across at the Thasian islanders – who were perturbed to discover that their enemies now spoke not Persian, but Greek. Athens was blatantly using League money to promote her own interests. By 463/2 BC Thasos had been decimated – it was forced to hand over its fleet, relinquish its mainland possessions, deliver up thirty talents (a crippling sum, the equivalent of circa £6 million in today's money) and raze its fortifications to the ground.[4] All this in spite of the fact that Thasos had secretly been promised help from the other supercity on the Greek mainland, Sparta.[5] Athens triumphantly took control of the mainland mines.[6] Climbing to the top of the ruined Byzantine castle that still crowns the island itself, looking out over a deep-blue sea, the air saturated with the scent of pine, it is disturbingly easy to imagine the picture-perfect setting, mired by human suffering and polluted by human greed.

But Athens was not sentimental. The hostilities with Persia rumbled on. Despite the Athenians' heavy-handedness, the Greeks knew they still needed to stand strong against Persian ambition. Athens registered the consensus of need — and harnessed it for her own purposes. For the League's 'further protection', she took matters into her own hands.

On the island of Delos there is a grand temple to Apollo, constructed to store the League's treasure-trove capital: money waiting to build new ships, to arm more men and to build back communities and lives when the Persians next attacked.[7] The temple was designed, in effect, as a League treasury, an independent building crammed with shared wealth.

Yet when one braves the curious weather-fronts and tides that swirl around this little isle that has always punched above its weight, where architecture clings to the mineral-rich rocks along with blasted vegetation, there is a surprise. Standing next to the Temple of Apollo's footprint, the sacred building feels oddly amputated. Here, there is something not ruined, but uncompleted. With good reason. In 454 BC slaves manhandling mortar blocks into position were ordered to down tools; the building work on Apollo's earthly home at Delos was peremptorily truncated. Athens wanted the Greek allies' material security closer to home. The treasury was moved, lock, stock and barrel, from neutral Delos to vested-interest Athens — and then quickly into Athena's lap, into the storage rooms of the Parthenon. We have a list of the capital harvest as accounted in 434/3 BC: 113 silver bowls, one gold bowl, three silver drinking horns, three silver cups, one silver lamp, one goblet, three large golden bowls, one golden statue of a woman, one silver basin, six Persian daggers, one gilt lyre, three ivory lyres, four wooden lyres, one inlaid ivory table, one silver-gilt mask, ten Milesian couches, six thrones, two silver-gilt nails, seventy shields.[8]

Now the Parthenon resembled less a sanctuary, and more a bank. Cities such as Neapolis (modern-day Kavala) on the mainland opposite Thasos contributed 1,000 drachmas a year to Athena in thanks for her protection. Money was baggage-trained from across the eastern Mediterranean straight to Athens. Athenian intention was clear.

Pericles and Socrates were maturing in a city that was rich in ideas, and was quickly becoming filthy rich.

Yet Socrates, remember, was a man who would ask whether we need warships and walls and glittering prizes in order to be happy. It was not clear whether a burgeoning empire and Socrates' philosophies were going to make for easy bedfellows.

13

PURPLE AMBITION

@@@@@@@@@@@@

The eastern Mediterranean,
465–415 BC

[PERICLES:] It is right and proper for you to support the imperial dignity of Athens. This is something in which you all take pride, and you cannot continue to enjoy the privileges unless you also shoulder the burdens of the empire.

Thucydides, 2.63.1[1]

SOCRATES: One mustn't be much concerned with living, but with living well . . .

Socrates to Crito, in Plato, *Crito*, 48b[2]

TODAY A JOURNEY TO THE NATIONAL Epigraphical Museum in Athens is a surprisingly risky one. Its entrance is up a side street — right next to the National Archaeological Museum. Although the authorities have managed to keep the neoclassical façade of the big museum clean, this side passage, with its grassy central spine, has become a favourite haunt for the city's drug addicts. The few visitors who venture in have to run a gauntlet of thin, angry self-exiles.

It is worth the effort. Just inside the building and to the left is a stop-still-in-your-tracks vast tribute stone. The inscribed rock stretches over 18 feet high. Carved across the surface of this megalith are the names of the cities who paid tribute to Athens between 454/3 BC and 440/39 BC.[3] Byzantium is there, as are Miletus, Mount Athos and settlements right along the Troad (the modern-day Biga Peninsula in northern Turkey). The inscriptions are tight, close. Not one inch of the stone surface has been left bare.

That tribute stone represents bags, barrels and chests of cash coming into Athens' coffers from her 'allies' in the League.

The discovery of all that silver at Laurion meant that the economic weather in the eastern Mediterranean was looking decidedly bright. Particularly for Athens. Because what goes out comes back in again, with interest. Tribute money was used to meet interest rates charged by the goddess Athena herself. When loans were taken from Athena's treasury on the top of the Acropolis – to fund the building of sacred statues, monuments or military action – the amounts, plus a hefty percentage, were repaid to Athena, now a divine usurer.

The surplus was poured back into the democratic state: jurors could be paid, theatre was subsidised, public buildings were refurbished, and for some councillors free meals were provided. In Socrates' lifetime more than 800 triremes were launched from Athenian-controlled harbours: the largest manned navy the world had ever known.

As Socrates grew up, tributes steadily accrued; from the Black Sea in the north – as far as Olbia (now in Ukraine); from Abydos in Asia Minor; from the east – way beyond Karia in Anatolia; from Dorus in the shadow of Mount Carmel in Palestine; and from the galaxy of islands throughout the western Aegean.[4]

Probably from the early 420s,[5] Athens required her allies to pay tribute in Athena's own coinage – the distinctive silver-owl – a measure that gave her dominance in international trade. Now allied city-states were forced to sell their goods directly to Athena (or her trading partners) in order to acquire the correct currency; no coincidence then that the Athenians, who produced their own wine and wool, preferred to drink the best Chian chianti and to wear fine fabrics made from the backs of the sheep of Miletus.[6] Resources – land, grain, gold, fish – had long tempted the ancients to roam wide through the eastern Mediterranean, but now Athens needed to satisfy more refined tastes too. Peacocks were imported to the city, lapis from Afghanistan and saffron from the volcanic island of Thera.

There was also coercion. If a territory attempted to secede from Athenian control it was punished, twice over: not only was it not given its liberty, but extra land was taken to be dedicated to 'Athena, Queen of Athens'. Erythrae in Ionia (on the western coast of modern-day Turkey) was strongarmed into taking on democracy.[7] A careful reading of all the texts and epigraphic evidence available does suggest that the population of the eastern Mediterranean was frequently inspired by the idea of coming under Athens' wing – even as a subject people, better to be a democrat than to live under oligarchs. But the pull of both poles (oligarch and democrat,

Spartan and Athenian) was strong; we will never know how many hundreds of thousands had their lives destroyed in the drag between. Socrates' lifespan witnesses an epoch of class struggle in its truest and purest form.

Thucydides writes about the state of affairs passionately, despairingly:

Practically the whole of the Hellenic World was convulsed, with rival parties in every state – democratic leaders trying to bring in the Athenians, the oligarchs trying to bring in the Spartans . . . in the various cities these revolutions were the cause of many calamities – as happens and always will happen while human nature is what it is, though there may be different degrees of savagery . . .[8]

And still the tributes came rolling in. Athens was able to beautify itself. Walls, monuments and life-sculptures were erected. Aphrodite's hoary, soot-blackened husband, Hephaestus, was given a new temple overlooking the Agora. In the city's spanking-new Odeion, citizens enjoyed public cultural performances and contests, male-voice choirs fifty to 1,000 strong competed here; new clothes were bought for performers and for the gods that their music honoured, and Athens' snaking walls crept four miles further south to Piraeus. Pericles' building programme was silhouetted on the Athenian skyline: the Propylaia, and perhaps too in his mind the glimmer of a plan for the Erechtheion – a kind of holy-hotel for many gods – famously buttressed by staunch caryatids.[9] And, above all, Athena's Parthenon: decorated green, blue, gold – dazzling like a peacock. Athena Parthenos, gilded and glowing with crystals and hippopotamus ivory, towered 39 feet high within the temple. Her gold clothes and accessories weighed 120 lbs, her skin gleamed, and on her outstretched palm perched a 6½-foot-high statue of Nike, the goddess of victory. In a pool of water below, Athena could glimpse her own splendid beauty; the reflected light's play rippled her skin; she seemed to live.

Travelling around Athens today it is still hard to escape the Parthenon. Gleaming at dawn, ghosting at twilight, it is always there: a double exposure on an old-fashioned photograph. Plutarch, writing 500 years after the Periclean building programme, marvels:

Though built in a short time they have lasted for a very long time . . . in its perfection, each looks even at the present time as if it were fresh and newly built . . . It is as if some ever-flowering life and un-ageing spirit had been infused into the creation of these works.[10]

Enduring spirit indeed. In the Byzantine era, from the mid-sixth century AD (the precise date has not been recorded), the Parthenon became no longer Athena's, but the 'Mother of God – The Lady of Athens" earthly home. Shadowed remnants of those days as an early Christian centre are still visible: carved on the columns of the Parthenon are the names of two Byzantine bishops

— it is still just possible to make them out — Theodosios, Marinos. In about AD 1175 the new Byzantine Archbishop of Athens, Michael Choniates, praised the city during his inaugural sermon within the booming interior of the Parthenon as 'the queen of cities', 'nurse of reason and virtue . . . exalted in fame not just for the monuments, but for virtue and wisdom of every description'. Choniates' new church was a particular delight to him: 'lovely', he declared. Three hundred years later it would be a Muslim leader's turn to eulogise. When Mehmet the Conqueror took over Byzantine lands he made a state visit to Athens in 1458. The Acropolis left him staggered; he was 'absolutely passionate' about the town. In 1687, while Venetian forces attacked the Turks who still held the territory, no fewer than 700 cannonballs were fired into the sides of the building (the pockmarks are still visible). Locals described rescuing the scraps of precious Arabic manuscripts that had been stored inside. For the first time in more than 2,000 years, Pericles' Parthenon had suffered a true body-blow, walls were cracked, columns collapsed, the roof fell in. At last it resembled a ruin, and from the mid-eighteenth century onwards, diplomats, tomb-raiders and adventurers did their bit to further decay. The Parthenon was chipped away at like an old Stilton.[11] The new Acropolis Museum is subtly, quietly doing what it can to gather back in from all corners of the globe the sculptural and architectural crumbs that have been removed.

But more of the Parthenon has lasted than we realise. Each time there is building work in the central area of Athens another fragment appears: a hand here, an arm there, a sliver of the side of a face, a stone spear. Archaeological teams are working week in, week out to reunite body-parts.[12]

The Parthenon has become a hallmark of the tenacity of 'Western' civilisation. For many it is a symbol of a certain set of values. But at the time of its construction there were those who raised their voices in protest. Is this really what a juvenile, wet-behind-the-ears political system should be focusing on? One sclerotic critic opined that Pericles was way out of order as he tarted up Athens with tribute money, dressing her up 'like a courtesan'. Around 443 BC the naysayer found himself ostracised.[13]

But Pericles knew of the value of nourishing a society that has confidence in itself, that is reminded day in, day out that it can achieve great things. Just listen to the General, in a grand finale of one of his speeches to the people of Athens, delivered to recorded history with a flourish by Thucydides:

Yet you must remember that you are citizens of a great city and that you were brought up in a way of life suited to her greatness; you must therefore be willing to face the greatest disasters and be determined never to sacrifice the glory that is yours.

. . . The brilliance of the present is the glory of the future stored up for ever in the *memory of man. It is for you to safeguard that future glory and to do nothing that now is dishonourable. Now, therefore, is the time to show your energy and to achieve both these objectives.*[14]

⟨⟨⟨⟨⟨⟩

Fine words. But Socrates was fully aware that Athenian democratic greatness had been built on war-blood and the sweat of another's brow, as well as on honest endeavour. Although we hear nothing of Socrates' philosophical opinions before c.420 BC, when he is forty or so, his ideas, passed on to us as Socrates' own by Plato, do seem to have been forged in a fiery, rough furnace. Socrates matured in a city-state that taught the lesson – for those who wanted to learn it – that the search for money, glory and power could bring compromise, heartache and trouble.

Through the 450s the Athenians were fighting aggressive wars on all fronts. Against the Persians on the one hand and the Spartans on the other, and against players in the theatre of power that was the eastern Mediterranean, who simply did not want to be bullied into being democrats. Between 459 and 454 BC they attempted to conquer no less a territory than Egypt itself; in 457/6 they besieged the nearby island of Aegina, which capitulated; in 456 Athenian soldiers destroyed the Spartan dockyards at Gytheion and captured the Corinthian territory of Chalcis in Aetolia. Uncompromising lessons for Socrates' youthful years.

Socrates was fully exposed to the casualties of ambition. In 449 BC his compatriot Cimon was killed on campaign – dying in Cyprus, probably from infected wounds – attempting to deal a crippling blow to Persian forces and holdings, in particular their worryingly effective navy, co-owned by the Phoenicians. Cyprus must have been a strange land to die in – with its many kings and its barren rocks, its adoration of the goddess Ishtar, a promoter of love and war since the Bronze Age. Accounts from the fifth century tell us that Cyprus had an edgy, threatening feel. But it was an island that the Greeks passionately wanted to 'liberate'.[15] The saturated heat of the Middle East blew a hot wind to Europe even then.

We do not know precisely when Socrates started to question the point of empire, the point of super-wealth. We do not know what he thought of Athens' early career as the region's premier usurer. But he was, it seems, underwhelmed. His attitude to empire was more than a little curmudgeonly. The questioning philosopher flicks his thumb at wars and walls and ships.[16] Others in the city had started to smell that bit sweeter, rubbed with rose oil imported from Syria, their bodies draped in linen from Corinth, their homes boasting the increasingly fine, black-figure dinnerware – so precious it was buried with its owners. Socrates, it seems, was stubbornly anti-material, anti both public and private grandstanding. He appears to have realised that great works might come of great strength – but they neither represent nor guarantee it.

O beloved Pan and all the gods of this place, grant to me that I be made beautiful within, in my soul, and that all external possessions match my inner state. Let me take wisdom for wealth; and may I have just the right amount of wealth that a self-restrained man can bear or endure.[17]

There was one city-state that seemed to share some of Socrates' reservations.

Laconic Sparta

Thucydides, the great historian and contemporary of Socrates, was prescient when he mused:

Suppose, for example, that the city of Sparta were to become deserted and that only the temples and foundations of buildings remained. I think that future generations would, as time passed, find it very difficult to believe that the place had really been as powerful as it was represented to be . . . If on the other hand the same thing were to happen to Athens, one would conjecture from what met the eye that the city had been twice as powerful as it actually is.[18]

If you walk through the modern city of Sparti today it is very hard to imagine this as one of the world's greatest and most fearsome civilisations. Ruins are diminutive and neglected, squashed between carelessly built 1960s condominiums, twentieth-century architecture on occasion brought tumbling down, as it was in Socrates' time, by regular earthquakes and tremors.

But there is good reason for the Spartan feel. The ancient society here believed passionately in the value of experiential over material delights. The Spartans did not regularly commission beautiful works of art; they banned coined money and perfumes. They did not write their own history, and did not believe in inscribing their laws. Unlike Athens, they mistrusted words – both spoken and written: the good Spartan, living as he did in the region of Lakonia, was expected to be 'Laconic'.

But Spartans did have a fiery zest for life. They sang obsessively, chanting sensual oral poetry; they worshipped their gods with an ecstatic devotion, often dancing late into the night; they even capered into battle (albeit with regular, choreographed steps), piping complicated, erotic rhythms on their haunting *auloi* – double-flutes. Girls as well as boys were allowed to train in the gymnasia (liberation unheard of in Athens); young women could spend heady evenings together by the banks of the River Eurotas, where they stroked one another with olive oil until they gleamed, while chanting of *'limb-loosening desire'* in the *'ambrosial night.'*[19]

Homer described Sparta as *'the land of beautiful women'* and lauded *'Lacedaemon's lovely hills.'*[20] The territory here at the heart of the Peloponnese is flat and fertile; in stony, mountainous Greece, Lakonia appeared Elysian. The wide River Eurotas, which dashes and then meanders through the Taygetan valley, is fed by snow-water from the top of the Taygetan mountain ranges, and in turn feeds Spartan lands. And it is in fact the riverbed and its environs that have yielded the latest clues to the extreme excellence of the Spartans.

In 2008 work was completed on an unpromising-looking rectangular stone structure – believed to date from the early fifth century BC. The building is a botched job, adapted and mucked about with over the years: but this DIY is revealing. It turns out this was a sanctuary with a long history, a spot overlooking the River Eurotas where dead heroes of the city were idolised.[21] Today the locale is uninspiring: nettles rim the site; to enter, one has to squeeze past a smashed-up car, and gawping Gypsy children fix on winsome smiles at the effort. But the Spartan authorities today are right to have preserved the remains, because the authorities back in Socrates' day would have kept this spot buzzing with activity. For the Spartans, dying well and living well were paramount. Soldiers, draped in their trademark red cloaks – red so as not to admit that blood might be spilt inside – could come back dead or alive as long as they were true to the Spartan ideals of absolute obedience and unstinting effort. At appointed days throughout the year, and particularly in late autumn after the campaigning season, these heroes would be fervently worshipped by the men and women of Sparta. With the Eurotas silver at sunset and the landscape behind a petrol-blue, with the clouds scudding down from the Taygetan mountain range that protects the city-state, it takes only a short moment of adjustment to imagine the passions that ran high here, the rigid sense of self-belief and specialness that the Spartan state enjoyed.

Supremely confident, the Spartans had no need of PR; unlike the Athenians, they did not glorify their own name or write themselves into history. And also unlike Athens, they mocked the need for city walls. Sparta was wall-less.

Back in Athens, Socrates would have heard reports of the glory of the

Spartan youths who emerged from their years of gruelling training; the Spartans' boast, you may remember, was that *'our young men are our walls, and our battlements the tips of their spears'.*[22]

He would have known that the supreme aim of this über-race was to achieve a 'beautiful death', one moment where you died well, in battle, cleanly, courageously. This, the *kalos thanatos*, was considered the epitome of Spartan achievement.

There is something horribly, magnetically enthralling about the single-minded purpose of Spartan life. Socrates matured at a time when Sparta was Athens' mortal enemy. Socrates himself – as a hoplite soldier – spent decades fighting against Sparta and her allies, yet he never seems to have despised his Peloponnesian cousins. Rather the opposite: he – and those associated with his circle – aped these extreme men.[23] Socrates admired the tight structure of their society. He approved of the Spartan drive to live life exceptionally well, to focus on the fundamentals rather than the fripperies of existence. Even though he preferred the laws of Athens, Plato has him concede that Sparta is *'well-governed'*.[24]

Socrates' penchant for straggly hair and irregular baths was very Spartan. Like the men of Sparta, he preferred to walk through his city-state shoeless. He is referred to as a *'Spartan hound'*[25] (like Spartan dogs, famed for their keen scenting abilities, Socrates could 'sniff out' the truth), and being *lakonomanea*, 'Sparta-mad'. One of the philosopher's closest friends, Cimon, calls his son *Lacedaimonius*. Socrates' fascination with Spartan mores will come to be mistaken for a love of their politics. Within two decades the philosopher and his circle will be denounced as lovers of Sparta – as 'laconophiles'.

Athena's city was troubled by Sparta for another reason too. There were many in Athens itself who secretly thought Sparta's adherence to the old, oligarchic way of doing things was laudable. For centuries – possibly for millennia – Greek society had promoted the idea that the powerful were powerful because they were the gods' chosen ones; they had not only a divine right to rule, but ruled because they boasted god-given gifts: status, courage, physical beauty, manly virtue. From the day of Socrates' birth to the minute of his death, many Athenians, either overtly or in private, hankered after the Spartans' sure sense of social order.

This tension between oligarchs and democrats, between aristocrats and the people, charged Athenian politics and culture, and infected its very atmosphere. And Socrates would be both an exemplar and a victim of Athens' great dilemma: in a true democracy, where power and responsibility are shared equally amongst all citizens, what is the place not just of the good, but of the very great?

And what about the city's tolerance — the 'forgiving nature of democracy'? Its 'don't care' about trifles? It utterly despises the things we took so seriously when we were founding our city, namely, that unless someone had a transcendently natural talent, he'd never become good unless he played the right games and followed a fine — a beautiful and a joyful — way of life from early childhood? Isn't it magnificent the way it tramples all this under-foot, by giving no thought to what someone was doing before he entered public life and by honouring him if only he professes to be the 'people's friend'?[26]

As time goes on, the ideology of Athens' brand of collectivism — *demokratia* — comes to be set against Sparta's own brand of high-achieving communalism, and so a fascination with Sparta is estimated anti-Athenian activity. And yet — despite the political temperature of the times — it is a half-Spartan boy, with a Spartan name and nursed at a Spartan breast, who will from here on in be Socrates' earthly love. A boy who will bring him much trouble. A boy called Alcibiades.

Born in 450 BC, Alcibiades was, following the death of his father Cleinias, an orphan by the age of four. But this child was not destined to be desti-tute — he would not end up abandoned (bone evidence from the period suggests this was not uncommon practice), for he had blue-blood, he was in fact a relative of the great General Pericles, and he was made a ward of this, the most powerful man in all Athena's city. He was wet-nursed by a Spartan woman — fashionable in those days, as Spartans were thought to be, physically, the lustiest of breeds — and, with Spartan relatives, Alcibi-ades was a character in the fifth-century BC play of democracy, with a foot in both the Montague and the Capulet camps. Raised in Pericles' halls from the age of seven, allowed to join the meetings of high minds that Pericles sponsored (thus enjoying an upbringing starkly unlike those of his seven-year-old Spartan cousins in the *agoge* down south), Alcibiades may well have first been met by Socrates as an indulged, mop-headed youngster, a beau-tiful boy.

Alcibiades appears one of those charmed individuals. He was, by all accounts, striking. Five hundred years after his death, authors such as Plutarch were still entranced by the idea of him — he was written of extensively throughout antiquity.[27] A Roman-period mosaic still on display in the Sparta Museum captures what men thought so lovely about him. Alcibiades is a latter-day Adonis — all flowing golden locks, a fine profile and with andro-gynously smooth skin.[28] He lisped sensuously, he loved women, girls, men, boys, dogs. He paraded through the Agora trailing a long purple cloak. A contrapunto character, he matured to be everything that Socrates was not: brash, feckless, loud-mouthed, debauched. Indeed, the relationship between the two men incarnates symptoms of both Golden Age Athens and Socratic thought; the struggle between personal liberty and social ambition; the relationship between the physical and the spiritual, between inner and outer beauty; the difficulty in identifying the true form of the good life.

Theirs was a testing, paradoxical match. But of all the long-lashed, bright-eyed, honed and eager young men of the Athenian city, it was Alcibiades — with his oligarchic, Spartan blush — who would endure as Socrates' favourite.

14

PADDLING IN THE RIVER, SWEATING IN THE GYM: SOCRATIC YOUTH

@@@@@@@@@@@@

The River Ilissos, 450–399 BC

He [Socrates] did not neglect his body, and he did not praise those who neglected theirs.

Xenophon, *Memorabilia*, 1. 2. 4[1]

How crusted with dirt most Athenians must have been; snotty-nosed kids, hormone-stinking teenagers, veterans with ulcerating wounds, men matt with the patina of pollution, droplets of sweat briefly cleaning grimy skin – all physical joys of living in the urban centres of the eastern Mediterranean. What pleasure then to be made clean.[2]

Socrates, from youth through to old age, was often to be found at the south-east face of the city walls, at the edge of the River Ilissos. Here he would talk with young men – paddle with them (as Plato has Phaedrus point out, the philosopher has the advantage as he always has bare feet) and, after a long walk, stretch out on a bank cushioned with grass, shaded by a spreading plane tree and a fragrant, flowering willow. Here there are chasteberry bushes and cult statues, the breeze is cool and cicadas fill the air with their almost unbearably heady percussion.

PHAEDRUS: *I am fortunate, it seems, in being barefoot; you are always so. It is easiest then for us to go along the brook with our feet in the water, and it is not unpleasant, especially at this time of the year and the day.*[3]

This pretty, pastoral stretch – running half a mile downstream – was a deeply ancient district, an area sacred since the Bronze Age. There were many sanctuaries here, many shrines. Religious processions regularly wound around the rocks and rivulets. One of Athens' most powerful and recondite festivals, the Great Eleusinian Mysteries, had its dress rehearsal by the banks of the river; priests of Eleusis (always from the same dynastic families), called in Greek the *mystagogos*, coached 'mystery' candidates in the *mysteria* on the banks of the Ilissos in March. These 'Lesser Mysteries' promised to open one of life's greatest secrets to their participants. All the best (and richest) families of Athens tried to ensure they could take part. Thanks to the Eleusinian Mysteries, an Athenian looked both forwards and back: back to a time when the best men, a select and privileged group, had power and also forward to an epoch when life after death seemed a possibility. This is a particularly fascinating aspect of Athens' new democracy – as men started to realise their mortal potential on earth, they were ever keener to believe that life continued beyond the grave. Socrates too (via Plato) hints that men who are good in this life can go on to enjoy a 'goodness' in a life beyond.

Death is one of two things. Either it is an annihilation and the dead have no consciousness, or, as we are told, it is a change, a migration of the soul from one place to another.[4]

Coming to the Ilissos must therefore have been a rich experience: typical of life in Athens, where a sensuous spirituality and a brisk belief in the sacred importance of the new democratic *polis* collided. Typical of Socrates' life as it is unfolding, where deep thought and a vigorous engagement in day-to-day life sit happily side by side. Water eddied and gurgled here, collecting in rockpools, gushing down through pint-sized chasms. Of course Socrates knew this spot like the back of his hand; familiar territory, he would have passed it regularly on the 25–30-minute route in – from his old *deme* of Alopeke to Athens' rammed city centre.

SOCRATES: *By Hera, it is a charming resting place* . . .

PHAEDRUS: *You are an amazing and most remarkable person. For you really do seem exactly like a stranger who is being guided about, and not like a native.*[5]

Often quoted as proof that Socrates had eyes only for urban matters and the city centre itself, this particular line in one of Plato's Dialogues is surely a character insight; Socrates drinks in the delights of the banks of the Ilissos, this habitual place, as if it is new to him. The clear-sighted are noted for looking on the world every day as if with new eyes.

In Socrates' day many gathered here at the side of Athens' other river. Even though the water's flow is now underground – the river was converted to a sewer in the 1950s – and the scrub is flanked by screaming arterial roads, young men still do so today. One wonders if these obliging individuals realise they are perpetuating a millennia-old tradition.

Lucky the lover who gets a workout when he arrives home
Sleeping all day with a beautiful boy.[6]

Socrates' Ilissos

@@@@@@@@@@@@

The banks of the Ilissos were indeed an area where some of the famous
'pick-up' points of classical Athens were situated – somewhere Socrates
(always full-blooded in his enjoyment of the physical pleasures of being
human) would have 'exercised himself'. At present, the area shows scarcely
any signs of Socrates' city. The most obvious 'classical' stones are in the
fifth century BC's future: the dizzyingly high temple columns erected by
Hadrian to honour a Roman Olympian Zeus and, of course, his imperial
self. But if you know where to look, there are hints of a more organic and
Hellenic classical past.

A careful exploration of the district short-circuits the investigator back
to a landscape that Socrates himself inhabited. Muffle out the noise of the
modern city, keep your eyes to the ground and it can seem possible to be
in two times at once. To the east of the Ilissos plunges a chasm where
honey-soaked cakes were once thrown. This was believed by Socrates' peers
to follow the route of the last waters of the Great Flood – sent by Zeus
and braved by the Greek Noah, Deucalion. Underneath a rocky outcrop,
still visible, are the foundation walls and the pebble floor of a court where
innocent and guilty manslaughterers and adulterers were tried.[7]

Light industry was here too. In a busy city there are many vested interests.
Free-flowing water and deep pools might equal rural idyll for some, but
industrialists also saw their opportunity, and just above the Sanctuary of
Herakles, as Socrates strolled here, tanners were moving in. Tanning is a
disgusting business involving human urine and much scraping of dead flesh.
Along with roughly cleaned skins, entire animal carcasses were imported to
the Athenian tanning yards. Some carcasses came from as far afield as the
Black Sea and Cyrene in North Africa – the smell here of decomposing
flesh must have been horrific. Socrates and his peers used leather extensively: for clothing, military equipment, agricultural implements and as hides
to cover seats and benches – the demand for leather goods was high; the
scale of production in this particular spot by the river banks intense. Hides
were pegged out on the ground and then treated with mulberry leaves or
urine to 'sweat' out or 'un-hair' the skin. Sometimes dog faeces were used

to 'purify' the leather. Surviving complaints from elsewhere in antiquity indicate just what a rank and stinking business this was (Roman citizens frequently brought legal cases against those tanners who polluted the air with their foul fumes). In Aristophanes' comedy *The Knights* a famous tanner (and politician) of the day, Cleon, is mocked as 'the dung-stirrer'.[8] A decree from 420 BC – recently discovered near the Lysikrates Monument – forbade tanners from rinsing their bloodied hides here above the spring, sacred to Kallirrhoe.[9] The fact that Byzantine and Ottoman tanners still productively, and profitably, manned the site 2,000 years after Socrates had been poisoned at the behest of the democratic Athenian state is an indication of how high tempers must have run when the fifth-century skin-merchants were put under the squeeze.

What is a great shame is that one of the key fifth-century BC attractions here, the 'bastards' gym – Kynosarges on the Ilissos' south bank – was cannibalised by the Emperor Valerian's rebuilding of the city walls from AD 254 (his defence against Teutonic tribes). Just beyond the perimeter walls, through the Diomeian Gate, Kynosarges was one of Socrates' haunts:

While he was on his way to the Kynosarges and getting near the Ilissos, he heard the voice of someone shouting, 'Socrates, Socrates!' When he turned around to find out where it was coming from, he saw Clinias, the son of Axiochus.[10]

Although the gym itself has been lost to time, the roadway that led to the area has recently been excavated. It is along this very track that Socrates would have walked to the Kynosarges district.[11] To get to the gym you would have had to cross the rills and rivulets of the Ilissos. Wooden planks bridged the fissured rocks and the man-made trenches that edged the running tracks. So we can imagine Socrates here, a young man, and then an older one, making his way towards one of the hubs of Athenian athletic activity, participating, spectating, indulging in the Greeks' particular fascination with the formation of the beautiful human body.

While the river here has hardly changed its course since the Bronze Age, and naturalised parakeets above and chamomile carpets beneath remind you that this would have been a corner of the city where you could exhale a little, now the running track is pounded by four-lane traffic and the exercise grounds are squashed beneath ugly commercial enterprises, the showrooms of a motorbike dealer and Eurobank. So if we are to walk with Socrates here, we must employ both the archaeological and literary sources available, and our imaginations.

The Kynosarges gym complex boasted a 200-yard course for sprinting, and there would have been the usual exercise grounds, plus perhaps a zone for military practice – although in fact the Kynosarges seems to have been less of a focus for military training than the other gymnasia of the city. Herakles was worshipped here – and as a result, years later, Spartan invaders were drawn to the place[12] (Herakles was Sparta's hero-in-chief). Before each exercise session libations would be poured to the semi-divine hero. In Socrates' day, even exercise was considered a religious experience. And keeping himself physically as well as mentally fit, emphasising that we are creatures of flesh and blood as well as of the spirit, would become one of Socrates' grounding principles. As a young man, he would have honed his body as well as his mind, and like the other young men around him, he would have spent many of his waking hours training to fight, in order to defend his city-state from invaders and to acquire new lands for his fellow citizens.

15

GYM-HARDENED
FIGHTING MEN

@@@@@@@@@@@@

The Academy, the Lyceum, 450–399 BC

*He was exceptionally handsome and exceptionally big, in that lovely season of life
when men pass out of the ranks of Boys and into the ranks of Men, blossoming most
pleasantly. Naked, wearing neither armour nor clothing, covered in nothing but oil,
he took a spear in one hand and in the other a sword . . .*

Plutarch, *Agesilaus*, 34.7[1]

P LATO TELLS US THAT SOCRATES VISITED Kynosarges later in his life,
so we don't know whether this was the space he used as a young
man (after all, it was his local), or whether his regular gym was
the (now more famous) Academy or Lyceum exercise grounds.

Plato certainly talks about the philosopher being doorstepped on the road between the Academy and the Lyceum, and that at the Lyceum itself in later life Socrates spoke, surrounded by an eager crowd.[2] Here Socrates sat in a dressing room (literally an 'un-dressing room'), there were a covered track, showers for athletes and a series of allegorical paintings around the walls. There was also a sense of *rus in urbe*; the fact that the Lyceum was dedicated to Apollo Lykeios – 'Wolfish' Apollo – indicates how bosky this part of Athens had once been.

This bucolic zone, where the men of Athens practised both physical and mental gymnastics, beautifully described in Aristophanes' play *Clouds*, had much in store; in the Academy, Plato would set up his school of philosophy, and in the Lyceum, Aristotle, his pupil, a rival. The modern world is populated by academics, academies and *lycées* thanks to these two institutions.

Now the Lyceum lies under the National Gardens. Originally designed in 1836 as a personal arboretum for Queen Amalia after the Greek War of Independence, its exotic plants have grown jungle-tall – a welcome relief in the city's midsummer heat. Toddlers in buggies are pushed along sandy paths to look at a city zoo that has seen better days; children – the sons and daughters of both shipping money and Albanian street-kids alike – play on swings: the overweight of the city jog, painfully, around the perimeter. It is a bit shabby and very pleasant here. But like the Academy, currently battling to be remembered beneath a pox of badly planned light-industrial units dealing in scrap metal, scrap plastic, wrought-iron gates, guarded by dogs and gypsy boys and hemmed in by the River Kephisos – today little more than a channel for (illegally dumped) industrial waste that flows in a toxic stream out to the Saronic Gulf – these once-idyllic spots could today scarcely inspire the purple (comic) poetry of Aristophanes:

RIGHT ARGUMENT: . . . *Spend your time in the gymnasium – get sleek and healthy. You don't want to be the sort of chap who's always in the Agora telling stories about other people's sex lives, or in the courts arguing about some piffling, quibbling, filthy little dispute. No, you'll run off to the Academy and relax under the sacred olive trees, a wreath of pure white flowers on your head, with a decent well-mannered companion or two; and you'll share the fragrance of leafy poplar and carefree convolvulus, and the joys of spring, when the plane tree whispers her love to the elm!*

If my sound advice you heed, if you follow where I lead,
You'll be healthy, you'll be strong and you'll be sleek;
You'll have muscles that are thick and a pretty little prick –
You'll be proud of your appearance and physique.[3]

~~~~~~

The fact that Socrates is happy to relax at Kynosarges, as well as the more upmarket Academy and Lyceum, tells us something significant about him. Kynosarges – 'White Bitch' gym – was designated for the half-castes of the city. As ever, Socrates does not just inhabit the 'showcase' venues of 'violet-crowned', 'show-city' Athens, but can also be found in its more mongrel spots.

The Kynosarges gym-goers were all bastard-citizens, metics with only one parent – either a mother or a father – who was a full Athenian citizen.[4] In 451 BC Pericles had passed a reform that limited access to Athenian citizenship. Athens was growing more popular and Pericles needed to keep the *demos'* power-base manageable; so only those born with both father *and* mother full Athenian citizens could be fully blown children of Athena. The democratic club was getting smaller. Coming to the gym and endeavouring to make yourself physically perfect, a honed fighting machine, was one important way that these second-class Athenians might prove themselves worthy of the mother city.

The highest hope of Socrates' peers, of young Athenian men, was to serve Athens by dying for her. Perceived as a military unit, Athenian eighteen-year-olds, called *ephebes*, from at least the fourth century BC onwards, swore an oath:

I shall not disgrace the sacred weapons [that I bear] nor shall I desert the comrade at my side, wherever I stand in the line. And I shall fight in defence of things sacred and non-sacred and I shall not hand down [to my descendants] a lessened fatherland, but one that is increased in size and strength both as far as [it] lies within me [to do this].[5]

This is an oath that Socrates too would have taken. The young men of Athens knew that their job was to defend Athenian interests and expand Athenian territories – and that they had to make their bodies both beautiful and in mint condition in order to do so. Although scant biographical evidence exists for Socrates' youth, we do know that he fought for Athens between 431 and 422 BC. He possibly started his soldiering career as early as 440 BC. There is no doubt that the young philosopher would have joined his compatriots in the gymnasia to train to fight; and no doubt that this was a sinew-stretching, macho business.

The young men who worked out in the gymnasia, unlike their Spartan cousins, did this not just to satisfy some kind of pugnacious militaristic ideal.[6] Thucydides is explicit. Young men in the Athenian gyms practise with arms because this is state-controlled, regulated activity – a million miles from the dagger-waving, brigand barbarity found elsewhere in Greece. Athens was militarised, but it was not indiscriminately bellicose.[7]

The Athenians were the first to give up the habit of carrying weapons and to adopt a way of living that was more relaxed and luxurious.[8]

However, there could be exceptions – in one tongue-in-cheek, hypothetical case a contemporary of Socrates, Antiphon, cites a sad instance in one of the city's exercise grounds, when there had been a fatality as a result of military javelin practice:

My young lad . . . was practising the javelin with his classmates and though he did indeed make the throw, he didn't exactly 'kill someone', not strictly speaking . . . The boy ran into the path of the javelin and put his body in its way . . . my son is not the perpetrator of an accident but the victim of one, in as much as he was prevented from hitting the target.[9]

Beautiful bodies – and Theseus, the most beautiful of all

@@@@@@@@@@@@@

Bastards they might be at the Kynosarges, but the trainee soldiers, the gymgoers (gymnasium comes from *gumnos*, the place where you exercise *naked*), were still eager to make themselves physically perfect. Socrates exercised regularly in the gym and we do him a disservice if we remember just the grey-haired condemned man by the water-clock and not the hirsute youngster, sweating, working out with his fellow Athenians.

SOCRATES: *I am a fiend for exercise.*[10]

At the gym and the wrestling grounds, oil, perfumes, fresh fruits, hair unctions were all used. Beauty was considered a quantifiable asset in the Greek city. As time went on, an increasing number of male beauty contests were hosted in the gymnasia. Courage, morality and physique were all judged as one psycho-physical parcel. Developing a beautiful body made you not just fit for posing, but fit to fight. Listen to Plutarch describing the merits of one particular young (Spartan) man:

. . . in that lovely season of life when men pass out of the ranks of Boys and into the ranks of Men, blossoming most pleasantly . . .[11]

The downy-chinned athletes at Kynosarges would have remembered the stories of how Theseus – Athens' special hero – himself arrived in Athens on this very spot; how, in a full-length chiton and with thick plaited hair, he was mistaken for a girl and had to ward off the amorous advances of the builders, heaving masonry blocks and cement to construct Apollo's temple here. (If the story was true, then Socrates himself as a young man would have bumped into Athens' founding father – since the classical Temple of Apollo was constructed in around 450 BC!)

∽∾∽∾∽

At this time in Athens images of muscle-rippling Theseus would have been hard to avoid. The replication of this master-hero became deeply fashionable. As the democracy gets more of a sense of itself, a place where individual men have the capacity and the right to act like kings, like gods, the irony (of course) is that the adoration of individuals, of 'the beautiful people', becomes ever more intense. And so the great deeds of that über-hero Theseus are replicated on the red-figure vases – both cheap tat and the highest quality, by the artisans of the Kerameikos; every year a festival, the Synoikia, celebrates in the month Hekatombaion (May/June) Attic unity and the new system of *demes*, *trittyes* and tribes (there were thirty *trittyes*, divisions of the population, in Attica. Each tribe was composed of one *trittys* from the coast, one from the city and one from inland) – and Theseus is invoked on the streets as part of the ritual; his domineering presence in Athens is enthusiastically celebrated. Even Theseus' 'bones' are rediscovered at Skyros and reburied in Athena's own soil.

All this because, in the minds of the Athenians, Theseus is perfect . . . He is muscular, ambitious, powerful, brave. With the new democracy that has, in theory, banished the personally ambitious and those squashing, wonder-boy aristocrats, Theseus is now Athens' 'virtual' role-model. This unambiguously macho warrior-hero – credited as the founder of the city – has a cocky aggression and drive to match Athens' own. A perfect young man of Athens, he loved his body, his city and his gargantuan ambition for both.

So it is not just 'wise' Athena, but Theseus ('steadfast in battle', 'brazen-breastplated' and 'protector of Athens' youth')[12] who succours the city in which Socrates matures. The Athenians' passionate belief in the value of their own mortal Theseuses – the belligerent, loyal, gorgeous young men of the city – will play out badly for Socrates. He comes to attract young, beautiful men around him as if he is their cult-leader; but Athens is jealous. As we shall see in the next chapter, Athena's city, boy-mad, sponsors her own cult of the young – and Socrates' Pied Piper-luring of the young men perturbs many in the juvenile, democratic city-state.

16

'GOLDEN AGE' ATHENS

@@@@@@@@@@@@@

The zones of Athens where young men are permitted, *c*.465–415 BC

CHREMES: *Then we all saw a handsome young man rush into the tribune, he was all pink and white like young Nicias.*

Aristophanes, *Ecclesiazusae*, 427–9[1]

WHETHER OR NOT YOU BELIEVE IN 'golden ages' per se, Golden Age Athens was so in actual terms. The hair of statues on the streets and public buildings of the city-state was, in Socrates' life-time, often highlighted in gilt and yellow paint. Bronze figurative statuary was so profuse that at one stage bronze humans must have appeared to clone them-selves around the city streets. (Some argue that these bronzes were cast from life, explaining their hauntingly realistic appearance.[2]) Detailed aspects of the human form (nipples, lips, teeth) were picked out in copper and silver. Ivory carvings were gilded. Luminous, gleaming rays of the sun reflected from their rock-crystal eyes: with their chryselephantine skin, their linen wraps, treated in oil until they gleamed, the statues of Socrates' day would have been lucent across the city.[3] The stage-set of Athens was littered with these perfect, permanently beautiful extras, a reminder of what humans could and should be.

And Athenian society also demanded a gold standard of physical perfection. The weak, the disabled were not welcome. We learn this from the bone evidence (very few humans with congenital disabilities are found in formal graves, suggesting that a number were exiled or abandoned),[4] but also from a few throwaway words in the Platonic Dialogues, at the moment when, in 399 BC, Socrates refuses to escape from his prison. His turn of phrase, his choice of analogy, suggests that the imperfect were frequently marked out in the city:

SOCRATES: [Imagining the Laws of Athens speaking to him] 'But you preferred neither Lacedaemon nor Crete, which you are always saying are well-governed, nor any other of the Greek states or foreign ones, but you went away from this city less than the lame and the blind and the other cripples.'[5]

☙☙☙☙☙

Athens: a city where the eyes have it. Visual references are stitched through the language – old women were called 'gauna', literally 'hot milk-skin'; you spoke not of being good, but of appearing good; the most precious possession in the city were the well-born, pulchritudinous young men, the kalos k'agathos – the 'noble in mind and appearance'. Not only was Socrates starting to develop a perturbingly robust internal life that belied his odd external appearance, but in that religious court, on that May morning of 399 BC, it will be the minds of this vital, peachy group that Socrates is accused of corrupting. The verb used is diaphtheirein, which can mean to destroy, corrupt, seduce or lead astray – politically as well as physically. An archaeological survey of Socrates' Athens drives home how precious these beautiful young men were to the psyche of the city-state. Images of them were tenderly, proudly replicated in civic, religious and military spaces; think of the Parthenon Marbles; boys on the cusp of becoming men lead sacrificial victims, they bear arms, they turn their faces to the sea and imagine the riches that lie beyond. The charge that Socrates had corrupted these paragons would have caused genuine distress.

One can still find these 'perfect Athenians', these 'beautiful young men', in the museums of modern-day Athens. Fit, less scarred than their fathers, less exhausted than their mothers. Good teeth. Muscles rock-hard. It is impossible not to be moved by their beauty. In the Kerameikos we just have their bones and their billets-doux, lovesick notes scratched onto terracotta by the potters of the Kerameikos: *'the boy is beautiful'*. In Socrates' day their names would also be daubed on notices in the centre of town and then cast in bronze. We are used to memorialising those who *fall* in battle; the Athenians commemorated their young men *before* they fought. Armies were levied from those over the age of eighteen. And these young hopefuls were then listed in public by their *deme* in massive age-group catalogues.[6] Laws were passed to try to ensure that the young were protected from malign influence – physical or psychological.

The orator Aeschines makes reference to the city's legislation on these matters:

First I will go over with you the laws laid down concerning the propriety of our Boys, then secondly those concerning Young Men, and thirdly, those concerning the other age-grades in turn.[7]

Being a young man in Athens brought with it an ecstatic belief that, if raised in an appropriately virile, legal, state-sanctioned way, you could bring security, wealth and great good to your *polis*.

Athens was alert to the possibilities of paedophilia, worried that beautiful boys might be preyed upon by older men. Middle-aged citizens (and, for the Athenians, 'middle-aged' meant in your twenties and thirties) had (by law) to train in the gymnasia with supervision. Trainers all had to be aged forty or above.[8]

CHORUS: I have not been seen frequenting the wrestling school intoxicated with success and trying to seduce young boys, but I took all my theatrical gear and returned straight home.[9]

And so Socrates would have matured in a culture that fetishised young men and their role in society, and then, as he grew older, chose actively to seek this group out as the favoured and favourite recipients of his philosophising. There is no doubt that, whether or not the emotion had a physical expression, Socrates loved young men. Eye-witnesses were happy to report his delectation of male youth. In one of the most charged sections of Plato's work, the philosopher describes the intense emotion that strikes Socrates on seeing the 'beautiful boy' Charmides enter the gym.

SOCRATES: . . . Charmides gave me such a look that I was helpless; and then all the men in the palaestra gathered round in a circle . . . I caught a glimpse inside [Charmides'] garment and burned with passion, there was nothing I could do . . .[10]

Our source – Plato – is, however, eager to point out that nothing inappropriate took place with Charmides (Plato's own uncle), and Socrates' pupil emphasises that the pair were chaperoned at all times.

But there is far more than just sexual innuendo in play here. Whatever

Socrates' actual interest, the idea that he was somehow captivating the strong young men in the gym with his endless, radical chat, diverting them from the path of good Athenian citizenship, was, to fifth- and fourth-century minds, very troubling. Young men across Greece were considered the flower of the city-state; its hope and its strength. And in Athens, metics and full citizens alike were the children of the empire. Young men were trained to speak persuasively (one of those who brought the charge against Socrates was a younger man, Meletus) in order to conform rather than rebel. They were not raised to challenge, but to buttress the status quo — that finely woven net of family, tribal, democratic and religious loyalties that held the city-state together — and so the anxiety about Socrates' influence over young men ran deep:

I certainly know there are young men you've seduced into believing you rather than their parents.[11]

Thus, in 399 BC, Socrates stood accused, despite the fact that, as he pointed out, it was probably the misuse of his own ideas by 'the young' that had got him into trouble (demonstrating perfectly that they were exactly the group that needed nurturing and guidance from worldly-wise men like himself) . . .

[SOCRATES] But in addition to this, the young who follow me around, doing so of their free will, who have complete leisure — the sons of the richest people — enjoy hearing people examined, and they often imitate me, and then try to examine others. And then, I imagine, they find an abundance of people who think they know something but know virtually nothing. That's why those who are examined by them get angry with me and not with them, and say that a certain Socrates completely pollutes the land and corrupts the youth.[12]

Polluting Athenian youth was a highly charged crime.[13] Little surprise that in Socrates' courtroom on that May morning we find fireworks.

◦◦◦◦◦◦

And there was in 399 BC another contributing factor to Socrates' fading popularity. Not only did he mess with the minds of young men, but he dared to associate with Athens' second-class citizens, with her women. Worse even than that, with one woman in particular, an individual who was thought dreadful in three ways: she was female, she was foreign and she was clever.

When he was still a relatively young man, in his early twenties, a teenage girl stepped off a boat at Piraeus harbour, someone whose life and reputation would become entwined with this ingenu philosopher. At this time, as word travelled around the eastern Mediterranean that Athens was creating a society and an economy quite remarkable, goods, essential and frivolous, poured into the rocky port of Piraeus in small independent boats or the sturdy trading vessels of rich men.[14] A cargo of great value was human booty. One day (calculations of the year vary, but 450 BC seems to be the most likely), it is almost certain that the feet that stumbled onto the new shore included those of a rather striking young lady. She was an adolescent from the city-state of Miletus in Asia Minor, a refugee who would make her mark on the city and would become intimately embroiled in Socrates' life and with the high-flyers of democratic Athens. A woman who would (according to Plato) end up as both the tutor and the confidante of the philosopher, as well as the victim of *pheme* – rumour, the source of many poisonous, sensational accounts, in fifth-century Athens and across the two and a half millennia that separate us from her.

She was a woman called Aspasia.

17

ASPASIA – *SOPHE KAI POLITIKE,* WISE AND POLITICALLY ASTUTE

@@@@@@@@@@@@

Piraeus harbour, *c.*470–411 BC

The resident aliens of Athens include not only Greeks from other states, but many Phrygians, Lydians, Syrians, and other assorted barbarians.[1]

WHEN ASPASIA STEPPED OFF THAT BOAT in Piraeus, she brought with her the whiff of Eastern spices and the whiff of trouble. She was a girl from Miletus, the natural harbour that lies low, just inland on the Turkish coast. It was a rich, busy little place, perfectly situated to trade both with ocean-edged civilisations and deep into the interior of Anatolia via the Maeander valley.

Miletus is a settlement with a profound history.[2] It is where the Mycenaean Greeks and the Hittites fell out a long time ago – its name is scratched into those clay tablets that bear Linear B, the Greek writing that pulled Europe forward from prehistory in around 1450 BC. As early as 1260 BC, this settlement in the Asian land-mass belonged to the Greeks. At its height its territories were larger than most other contemporary Greek *poleis.* But come the early fifth century BC, Miletus was back in Eastern hands – and in 494 BC the archaic city was razed to the ground and many thousands of Milesians were slaughtered. A year longer under the Persian yoke than the Athenians, Milesians must have watched, dismayed, powerless, as Athens, the new 'protector' of the eastern

Mediterranean, in 479 BC stepped in to take control over some of the Mile-sians' long-fought-for trade-routes and allies. Injury added to injury.

Today Miletus is plagued by gnats. Lying low in marshy mudflats, the ruins here can, at times, be immersed neck-deep in water. You may have to hitch-hike your way in and out of the ancient site, as the tourist buses are few and far between. But even so, the remaining stones chronicle a distant, impressive culture.

There has always been something a little special about Miletus. Inevitable perhaps. Stretching west from the Bati Mentes mountains, her foothills today bristle with olive trees, and the unfeasibly fertile Maeander valley is soft with fields of cotton. This was a valuable natural exit point westwards for the Persian Empire (which in the early fifth century spread from north of the Hindu Kush to southern Arabia), and a gentle segue east for Ionian Greeks. Sitting as it does on a cultural crossroads, Miletus nurtured an unlikely number of original thinkers: Thales, who identified water as a build-ing block of all life; Hippodamus, the architect who laid out the town of Piraeus; Anaximander, who voiced a notion of ecosystem and ecology – that the physical world is a finely balanced game between the weak and the strong and who set down the first map in the sixth century BC.[3] Many of those men who provided new ideas for Athens had started life in Miletus. And somehow, whether as a courtesan or the daughter of a noble, the young girl Aspasia has managed to get herself an education in this enlightening coastal city.

Triple-trouble in Athenian eyes, because Aspasia was not only from the East, not only educated, but was, of course, a female of the species. Women, in the fifth century BC, were generally objects of fear and revulsion. Aspasia would have been considered a 'leaky' being, someone who oozed pollution from her genitalia, her mouth, even her eyes. Hippocrates (the Greek medical expert from Cos whose lifespan almost exactly matches Socrates' own) explains that menstrual blood accumulates in the female body because this sex is organically porous. One of the reasons such a sump-residue gathers is because of women's 'sedentary' lifestyle.[4] At the moment of menstruation, women were thought to be infectious in all kinds of ways.

Aristotle elaborates. He explains that because the release of menstrual blood also impacts on the blood vessels in a woman's eyes, at her time of the month a glance from a female can infect the air in front of her – Aristotle's proof: this glance turns the surface of a mirror dark. He tells us that, whereas men are hot and dry, women are cold and clammy. Female bodies are a distasteful, deformed version of a man's. Their high-pitched voices are indicative of their 'unhinged' nature, while a man's vocal cords are, quite properly, lassoed to their testicles.[5] It is little surprise that Sophocles has one of his characters sniff, '*The best ornament of a woman is silence*.'[6] We know this because years later Aristotle avidly quotes the line.

This was a notion codified throughout Athenian culture. In 594 BC the reformer and law-giver Solon arranged (allegedly) that any woman walking the streets should be thought of as a prostitute.[7] Fathers could enslave children only when they were female and 'damaged goods' (girls who had lost their virginity), in which case they could be legally sold off as prostitutes. Respectable women of this period were expected to be seen and not to be heard.[8] Xenophon promotes the view in his book *Household Management*: '*So it is seemly for a woman to remain at home and not be out of doors; but for a man to stay inside, instead of devoting himself to outdoor pursuits, is disgraceful.*'[9] And again that women should '*see and hear as little as possible, and ask the fewest possible questions*'.[10] Censure barbed the Athenian argot: '*. . . It is not proper for girls to weave through the crowd.*'[11] Young women in particular were not to be trusted. The orator Hyperides points out that '*a woman who leaves the house ought to be at the stage in life where people who meet her ask not whose wife she is, but whose mother.*'[12] The truly good Athenian woman even trembled in the presence of her male relatives: '*He came there at night in a drunken state, broke down the doors, and entered the women's rooms: within were my sister and my nieces, whose lives have been so well-ordered that they are ashamed to be seen even by their kinsmen.*'[13]

So most Athenian women either were silent – or have since been silenced by their absence from the written record. Even if they were allowed to speak out in their day (unlikely), they have left us no account and so have escaped history. They are faceless; voiceless, textless, anonymous.

Not so Aspasia. She is one of the few women who have been written *in* to the story of Golden Age Athens.

Aspasia turns up in Greek comedies and orators' speeches, in Roman moral tales and Victorian operettas. In antiquity she is described as that 'dog-eyed concubine' (*pallaken kynopida*),[14] a woman-for-sale (*porne*).[15] She rarely features as anything less than lubricious, a voracious flirt. There's much double entendre; she will 'know' both young and old men in Athens. She needs little introduction, other than that 'we all know what she is like'. There is nothing at all to tell us that Aspasia was in fact debauched, but debauched she became. By the time that Clearchus of Soli was writing, 150 years after her birth, this young woman inhabits a disgusting, murky place. In his *Erotika*, Aspasia is listed alongside the man who tries to have sex with a statue, but has to make do with a slab of meat or an animal in season.[16]

Of course, we do not know that any of these wet-lipped accounts are true; in fact, the only intimidating thing we know about Aspasia for certain is that she was energetic, and clever.[17]

In the salons that Pericles sponsored, Aspasia was an attractive anomaly.

But before she ends up riffing with Socrates, before she shares dinner and a bed with the great statesman-general Pericles and, in the minds of the Athenians, tempts him to dark deeds, we need to take a step back. First Aspasia must make her mark in 'violet-crowned' Athens.

She arrives at the polyglot port of Piraeus in around 450 BC, perhaps in the 440s, apparently fatherless and on her own.[18] Aspasia is a representative of the influx of 'alien' population so disapproved of by a number of Athenians, as voiced by the conservative pamphleteer Isocrates: *They filled the public tombs with citizens, and the public registers with aliens.'* Miletus, after decades of Persian and then Athenian dominance, had tired of paying tribute to Athens and revolted, only to be retaken in 452 BC. These were difficult times for the city. Originally allies, then enemies, then subjects of Athens, the Greek inhabitants of Miletus had a somewhat schizophrenic relationship with Athena's city. There were both blood-ties and blood-feuds. By marriage, Aspasia was almost certainly related to Socrates' gaudy young companion Alcibiades.[19] So she had limped back across the Aegean, hoping to start a new life amongst one-time friends.

Yet Aspasia's chances of self-advancement were limited. The general Pericles, remember, had passed a law in 451 BC restricting entry to the democratic club. Now only the children of Athenian citizen fathers *and* mothers could themselves become citizens.[20] If Aspasia settled in the city, if she bore children, she was destined to be the mother only of a sub-class of *nothoi* – bastards.[21] The Academy and the Lyceum would be too good for her offspring; their only place of exercise would be the Kynosarges, the 'White Bitch' gym.

Despite her disadvantages, like a handful of other determined women at this time, Aspasia does seem to have been able to escape the tedious grind of weaving or sexual servicing, or both, that was the fate of most foreign females in Athens.[22] Metics such as she were not tenderly treated by the law, but from the 450s onwards an increasingly institutionalised option of *pallakia* – concubinage – emerged, where a woman could enjoy not the protection a wife commanded, but some kind of formal (contractual even) relationship with relatively high-born male citizens. By all accounts, malign and benign, Aspasia kept her wits about her. This was an opening that the young refugee seems to have quickly exploited. Although the bawdy renditions of her life suggest that much of what we know of Aspasia was made up, the fact that she attracts so much attention suggests there must have been something special about this girl from the East. Perhaps it was the Lydian rose-oil she used on her skin, the speed of her retorts, the intimate knowledge of new ideas she brought with her from Anatolia's shores. Because within a few years of arriving at Athens we find Aspasia — as a highly respected concubine-cum-companion — sitting at the very highest table, in Pericles' household.

There were plenty of *ménages à trois* in classical Athens. But Pericles' wife, whom he married in about 463 BC and who was the mother of his two sons, had been disposed of: divorced five or six years before Aspasia arrived. In Athens at this time divorce was relatively simple — effected by mutual consent or on the initiation of a third party. We don't know exactly how or when, but by 444 BC Aspasia had moved into Pericles' household. Pericles seems to have cared not a jot for the dynastic hurdle he had put in his own path. His focused sexual energy obliterated it. Aspasia became his consort, his intellectual sparring partner, his lover. For the last fifteen years of his life, until his death in 429 BC, Pericles was elected as 'chief democrat' every year — and Aspasia was with him at every turn. Contemporary sources recounted disapprovingly that the two would kiss in public every morning: they were savaged by comic playwrights, and no doubt slandered in the Agora:

> *Stasis and elderborn Time,*
> *mating with one another*
> *birthed a very great tyrant*
> *whom the gods call 'head-gatherer'.*
> *Shameless Lust bears him Hera-Aspasia,*
> *a dog-eyed concubine.*[23]

But despite the tongue-wagging through the streets of Athens, the General seems to have stuck by his unorthodox consort. Almost certainly Aspasia was with him to his death. How did she do it? How, in a city crammed with foreign, available women, with exotic beauties, did she manoeuvre herself to be the General's choice? How did she become one of those lucky ones who laced gold earrings through their ears, or wound around her neck ocean-fat pearls and cornelians the size of kidney-beans. (The democratic Athenians were not fond of ostentatious displays of wealth in public — jewellery was often worn in the privacy of your own home — but the scattering of fine golden and silver adornments dropped by chance and now reappearing up in digs across the city is telling.) And more than that, how did Aspasia manage to *influence* Athens' greatest general, to share with him in the 'brains-trust' evenings that he sponsored at home?

Although some cry 'There is no direct evidence' for all of this, for

Aspasia's active participation in the intellectual life of Athens (other than her confident appearance with Socrates in literature in Plato's Dialogues),[24] in male-dominated European societies to date there has never yet been one that did *not* sponsor talented, charismatic, intelligent women in private salons. In the courts of the Goths, the Caliphs, the Byzantines, the Carolingians, the Medici, the Rus, the Ottomans – they are always there. Aristotle remarks, with the sneer you expect to hear in his voice when it comes to women, '*Everyone honours the wise . . . [T]he Mytilenaeans [honour] Sappho, though she was a woman.*'[25] Aspasia might have been a trophy, a performing monkey even, but it is more likely than not that she was there, not just in Pericles' bed, but articulate and at his side.[26]

So now, in around 440 BC, picture the scene. In sharp-witted Pericles' halls there is a new perfume. Hetairas (high-class, often educated female consorts) in saffron-dyed, almost see-through drapes, some with faces whitened with white-lead and then rouged, cross in doorways. Aspasia, now Pericles' common-law wife, joins her husband as host. She is still a young woman, he is in his mid-fifties. Most Athenian wives are expected to absent themselves when male guests appear. If on occasion a wife is unfortunate enough to open a door when a man arrives unannounced she can, quite properly, be branded a scarlet woman, a tart.[27] But Aspasia's degraded, 'foreign' status has become her cloak of invisibility. She can go places, do things that citizen Athenian Greek women would never experience; she can say things that they would never be able to say.[28]

Not only does it seem that Aspasia has a voice, but we are given to understand that she speaks with the most exciting men of the day: Anaxagoras, Damon, Alcibiades and Socrates. She brings a new slant to the men's proceedings. When Socrates (via Plato in the *Republic*)[29] suggests that women are capable of virtue, it is perhaps Aspasia's example that he holds to the fore. He also quotes Pericles' consort on the topic of matchmakers and reliability, the value of telling the truth.[30]

The good matchmaker is an expert at joining people together – by giving true reports of their good qualities, but refusing to sing their praises falsely.[31]

While many of the key writers of the day – Xenophon, Aristotle, Hippocrates – scarcely acknowledged the existence of women, and if they did, mentioned them only in a suspicious or negative light, Socrates (if we can take some of Plato's scenarios at face value) seems to have been genuinely open to the possibility that women just might have something interesting to say. Plato's Aspasia, for instance, emphasises the emotional nature, the erotic nature of politics.[32] However much Plato employs Aspasia as a handy construct to get across his own message, read between the lines and it seems apparent that Socrates was indeed fascinated by her and her emotional view of the world. Aspasia arrived in Athens living off her wits. When she had nothing, she had to utilise *charis* – charm, an ability to click with those around her. Given what we know of Socrates' enquiring mind, his interest in Aspasia is in character. Offered a fresh furrow, a new (female) perspective on things, a different kind of life experience, he is more than happy to plough.

There's nothing like investigation. I will introduce Aspasia to you, and she will explain the whole matter [of good wives] to you with more knowledge than I possess.[33]

Plato's Socrates goes further, ironically citing Aspasia as his teacher in rhetoric.[34] They were, it seems, close – the philosopher's intellectual intimacy with this 'trumped-up whore'[35] was one reason his fellow citizens turned against him. Of her he said, '*I have an excellent mistress in the art of rhetoric – she who has made so many good speakers, and one who was the best among all the Hellenes, Pericles, the son of Xanthippus . . .'*[36] In one text Socrates credits Aspasia with composing Pericles' funeral speech,[37] and some modern historians of the ancient world still consider her to be the 'power behind Pericles' throne'.[38]

Socrates described Aspasia as possessing a perfect mind, as being the finest of politicians – and yet she has consistently been downgraded in the story of fifth-century Athens. At best she is described as Pericles' manipulative sidekick and the mistress of 'a house of procurement'. Plato, too, can be less than flattering. He talks of Aspasia *synkollosa*, 'gluing together' words. As you might expect, perhaps because she was unusually gabby, perhaps because of prejudice and blackballing, Aspasia is first written into the historical record not as a feisty and inspirational young woman, but as a troublemaker.

Aspasia's part in the revolt of Samos

@@@@@@@@@@@@@@

Aspasia's nemesis was the island of Samos. Samos nestles up to the coastline of Anatolia – from the coast road in Asia it feels within spitting distance; a dream island you want to reach out to, to make real. Recent sub-marine excavations in the area have revealed how busy this stretch of the coastline was in Socrates' day. In 2002 sponge-divers uncovered the wreck of a local trading vessel, packed with retsina and amphoras – the cargo is a reminder of the natural wealth of the region.[39] The blind marble 'eyes' of the boat, found on the seabed, would have stared out over the deeply wooded green hills of western Asia Minor and fruit hanging fat on the branches.

Destined by geography to be a footfall between Asia and Europe, Samos has always fiercely guarded its independence. Since the sixth century BC its main city had been ringed with a stone curtain wall – a protection that reached up to 5.2 metres in some places. But now that Athens was mother-henning it across the eastern Mediterranean, the Samians found they were being commanded to sign up to a democratic charter. The ruling oligarchs wanted none of it. And thus the island of Samos, 200 miles due east of Athens, was, between 440 and 439 BC, brutally suppressed for 'anti-democratic' activity.

Samos was a member of the Delian League, but entirely autonomous; she maintained her own fleet, she paid no tribute, she kept Athens at arm's length. And in 440 the island chose to bully the rich settlement of Miletus, Aspasia's home-town, a morning's row to the south. The acrid dispute between Samos and Miletus in fact concerned the city of Priene. Samos laid claim to Priene – a handily placed, pliable little settlement tradition-ally subject to its loftier neighbours, the Milesians, across a wide bay on the Anatolian western coast.

The Milesians could not defend themselves, but they *did* pay tribute to Athens and so, the argument went, Athens should now provide them with protection. Wiped clean by the Persians just fifty years before, then watching as Athenians efficiently picked off their territories and allies, the Milesians were in no state to fight their own battles. Early in 440 BC a delegation of desperate Milesian diplomats arrived at the Athenian Assembly, begging Athens for help. Pericles responded swiftly and decisively – fifty Athenian triremes were sent to teach the Samians a lesson.

It is a mark of Athens' confidence and sense of superiority in the eastern Mediterranean that Athenians felt justified when it came to the 'Samos Question' in fielding an indisputably interventionist foreign policy.[40] But it would mark the beginning of a lifetime of trouble. Pericles was proving that Athens could put her money where her mouth was; yet the General's critics didn't like the idea of making an enemy of a powerful entity such as Samos. And they chose to lash out, not at Pericles himself, but at his consort. The invasion of Samos, they said, had been sparked by Aspasia's love of her home-town. It was a dirty, foreign woman who had tempted Athenians across the waters to certain death.

Athenians were pulled in to this brutal conflict thanks to the sweet-nothings of a whore from Miletus.[41]

But Aspasia's accident of Milesian birth was not the real reason the Athenians were so jittery about involvement in Milesian affairs. An early fifth century oracle from Delphi shows that for mainland Greeks, intervention on behalf of the envied city-state was expected to bring nothing but evil. The underlying jealousies and tensions across the Greek world were rancorous and dengerously close to the surface. By involving his democratic citizens in this foreign expedition Pericles was re-opening a wound that was deep and fresh.

Then shall you, Miletus, the contriver of many evil deeds,
Yourself become a banquet and a splendid prize for many,
Your wives shall bathe the feet of many long-haired men;
And my temple at Didyma will be ripped from your hands and cared for by others.[42]

The Athenians might have been wrong to say it was Aspasia who pulled the trigger, to see in her clever little hands a smoking gun, but they were right to call the conflict that would follow 'brutal'.

ACT THREE

~~~~~~~~~

SOCRATES THE SOLDIER

18

SAMOS

@@@@@@@@@@@@

The island of Samos, 440–439 BC

With a sudden rush he turns to flight the rugged battalions
Of the enemy, and sustains the beating waves of assault.
And he who so falls among the champions and loses his sweet life,
So blessing with honour his city, his father, and all his people,
With wounds in his chest, where the spear that he was facing has transfixed
That massive guard of his shield, and gone through his breastplate as well,
Why, such a man is lamented alike by the young and the elders,
And all the city goes into mourning and grieves for his loss.
His tomb is pointed to with pride, and so are his children,
And his children's children, and afterward all the race that is his.

Tyrtaios, Spartan war poet, *c.*640 BC[1]

THE YEAR OF 440 BC WAS a dark one. Whether he was goaded by
Aspasia's pillow-talk or by realpolitik, Pericles, on behalf of the
Athenian people, as punishment for interfering with one of her
'allies', eradicated the Samian government and put an Athenian-style democracy in its place. An Athenian garrison was installed in the central city of
Samos to make sure the islanders accepted this regime change 'quietly'.
Hostages were roughly boated over to the nearby island of Lemnos. Athens
was suddenly looking, not like an ally, but an overlord. The Samians had
been taken unawares by the speed of Pericles' action, and they did not like
it. They turned to the Persians for help – Asia Minor was, after all, just a
short boat-ride away. The local Persian satrap Pissuthnes allowed the Samians
to raise a mercenary army – and suddenly Athens had not a squabble, but
a full-scale regional incident on her hands. The Samians reinvaded their

own home by night; local knowledge giving them the upper hand, they stormed the garrison and captured its soldiers. Retribution followed.[2] Athenian prisoners-of-war on the island had their faces branded with the shape of Athena's owl. A covert message went out to the Spartans and their allies in the 'Peloponnesian League' that this was Sparta's chance to provide support for those who wanted to challenge Athens' cocksure supremacy.

But, fearing those Athenian triremes, that supremely confident democratic Athenian army, no help came. The Samian walls, solid stone polygonal blocks faced with mud-bricks, in places reaching a whole house deep, with their extra fortifications, towers and a ditch, were considered impregnable.[3] So, Pericles besieged Samos for nine months. He sent one of his aristocratic generals, the tragic poet Sophocles, to ensure the loyalty of all Greeks in the region. Now the Samians were isolated; starving, in 439 BC they finally surrendered. In Sophocles' masterpiece *Oedipus the King*, written a decade later, we may hear a haunting memory of the atrocities there:

> *Oh Gods, Gods!*
> *Destroy all those who will not listen, will not obey*
> *Freeze the ground until they starve.*
> *Make their wives as barren as stone.*
> *Let this disease that shakes Thebes to its roots —*
> *Or any worse disease, if there is any worse than this —*
> *Waste them,*
> *Crush everything they have, everything they are.*[4]

Although Athens now had a new, intimidated ally, conveniently close to the coast of Asia Minor (and, usefully, a little further north, on the edge of the Bosporus, Byzantium followed suit, also declaring itself subject to Athenian 'protection'), the whole affair had made the eastern Mediterranean jumpy. Athens was earning her epithet 'busybody'. The military action on Samos had become one of the dominoes in the line of events that led to the Peloponnesian War. Foreseeing further trouble and needing to ensure that the morale of Athena's people was high, Pericles was reported to have given a great speech in Athens to honour the war dead.

'*For we cannot see the gods,*' he said, '*but we believe them to be immortal from the honours we pay them and the blessings we receive from them, and so it is with those who have given their lives for their country. They too gain immortality.*'[5]

But despite Pericles' best efforts at jingoism, the whisperers continued: they knew that Aspasia was a Milesian — obviously her pillow-talk, they hissed, had sharpened Pericles' sword: her alien patriotism had ensured the

Samians would have an example made of them. Aspasia is described by her (and Pericles') enemies as a 'Helen'; it was Pericles' lust for his clever courtesan that had created first the Samian atrocities and then the Peloponnesian War itself. Just as Helen drew men across the Aegean in her wake and sparked the war for Troy, so Aspasia would destroy Greek unity. Scared of the idea of her, democratic Athens never failed to remind contemporaries and history alike that Aspasia was an immigrant, an interloper of the wrong sex. It is in the bile that is poured out about this clever girl that we start to appreciate that this new democracy was not entirely comfortable with its cosmopolitan attitude, or in its own skin: canker spots were appearing.[6]

Socrates and Samos

@@@@@@@@@@@@

Socrates has an interesting footnote in the Samian affair.[7] He would have been twenty-nine when the campaign started, and there is every possibility that he sailed from Piraeus with one of Athens' contingents of forty, and then a further sixty, then forty again and then twenty more ships to fight there. This was a greedy punitive exercise. The sea battles were fierce, and Athens needed men such as Socrates, in his prime, to go to fight. All Athenian citizens between the ages of eighteen and thirty had to perform compulsory military service. In times of war any man up to the age of sixty could be called up. Although we have no direct textual evidence that Socrates sailed east in 441/0 BC, it would be decidedly odd if he had not. And so it is now that we can meet a Socrates familiar to the Athenians – Socrates the soldier.

We should imagine the philosopher dressed as young men are dressed on grave *stelai* in the Piraeus Museum today – the ideal hoplite of Athens. His breast would be cocooned within a bronze breastplate, and he would be wearing greaves on his legs, a helmet surmounted with a horsehair crest for protection and intimidation. Some specialist soldiers stabbed with the spear (up to 2.5 metres long) or were slingshot maestros; others, the peltasts, lined up tight in defence, threw javelins. But Socrates' weapon was his broadsword and massive *hoplon* – the round shield so weighty it is frequently shown in carvings resting on the thighs or shoulders for relief, the shield that gave the hoplites their name.[8]

Hoplites had to provide their own equipment, yet the philosopher's finances are a bit of a mystery. Clearly his beginnings were lowly. Socrates boasted that he never charged even half an obol, the equivalent of a penny – unlike other sophists in the city – for his thoughts. And yet somehow he had become wealthy enough to be a hoplite; to be a vertebra in the backbone of the Athenian city-state, a soldier who could afford to provide his own spear, helmet and *hoplon*. At this time in Athens there were about 14,000 of these, not uncomfortably well-off, lower-middle-ranking men.[9] Perhaps his stonemason father had benefited quite significantly from the Periclean building boom. One source connects Sophroniscus to the family of Aristeides the Just – a dynasty influential in Athens since before the Persian Wars. So the budding philosopher could have had 'good connections'. Maybe the father had a wit that prefigured that of his son; maybe he was paid well for his skill and his original ideas. Whatever the fiscal context, Socrates could afford to fight.

Alternatively, perhaps, Socrates was sponsored by one of those wealthy friends he had met in the aristocratic milieu of Athens' new 'think-tanks', and it is not impossible that his patron was Pericles himself – possibly the greaves he strapped on, the leather wristbands he shaped to fit around his thick arms, signified just how well in with the in-crowd Socrates had already become. He drank, ate and talked with those who would once have been called oligarchs – and now, of course, he had to stand shoulder to shoulder and fight with them too. Socrates was no mere oarsman, not just muscle to power-row triremes, a human-machine whose bones the fish would soon be scouring clean; he had also earned the right to be spear and hatchet fodder.[10]

And so if he had sailed to Samos as a hoplite passenger, a deck-boy, his lips and eyelashes stiff with wind, stinging, briny, he would have beached at the point of his – some would argue – first battlefield. The possibility of an involvement in Athens' Samian campaign reminds us that although Socrates loved Athens, and lived in the city-state most of his life, when we look at his life-story, and indeed the life of the Athenian democracy, we also have to set the compass north, south, east and west. Socrates' skill with a stabbing sword and an outsize *hoplon* shield would have been as important to his fellow citizens as any cleverness with philosophical words.

A contemporary of the philosopher's, Ion of Chios, is quoted as saying that without a doubt Socrates was at Samos in the company of another great thinker of the day, Archelaus, the pupil of Anaxagoras, a favourite of Pericles. Socrates could indeed have visited the island as a young man with the philosopher Archelaus in order to debate heavenly matters like the nature of cosmology[11] (comedians would mock Socrates for such airy-fairy interests later in life,[12] remembering that in his early days a wide-eyed Socrates '*had an extraordinary passion for that branch of learning that is called natural science*'[13]). Socrates might have come to Samos to learn, or he might simply have come here to kill. Because if he did travel to Samos as a soldier, he would have been required to shed blood. Pericles' orders to his Athenian troops were unyielding. The Athenians fighting in Samos exemplified perfectly Aristotle's summary, one hundred years later, of the purpose of all that intense military training back in the bosom of the city-state.

Military training . . . has three purposes:

1. To save ourselves from becoming subject to others.

2. To win for our own city a position of leadership, exercised for the benefit of others . . .

3. To exercise the rule of a master over those who deserve to be treated as slaves.[14]

The 'pax Atheniensis' had been short-lived. For the next thirty years Socrates, Aspasia, Euripides, Alcibiades, the young men in the gym, the traders in the Agora, the priestesses on the Acropolis will live through, or be destroyed by, one of the most pitiless wars that human history has known.

Isthmus, near Corinth, *c.*441–411 BC

⊚⊚⊚⊚⊚⊚⊚⊚⊚⊚⊚

You never left the city to go to a festival, except once to go to the Isthmus, nor to go to any other place except when you were serving in the army somewhere, nor did you ever make a trip abroad, as other people do, nor were you seized by a desire to know another city or other laws, but we and our city were enough for you.

Plato, *Crito*, 52b[15]

Yet it wasn't solely the promise of death that drew Socrates out of Athens. The one other time (as far as we know from existing evidence) that he may have left the city, as a young-to-middle-aged man, was to engage in a sweaty, agonising exertion of a different kind – participating (as an audience member more likely than as an athlete) in the Isthmian Games down south next to the Gulf of Corinth.[16]

Socrates would have left Athens on the Sacred Way. The road is still there, still called the *Hiera Hodos*. Although a drive along the Sacred Way today past out-of-town furniture emporia and oil refineries is not markedly spiritual, a sympathetic traveller can imagine Socrates and his fellow citizens making this pilgrimage. Socrates was a great walker. He talks about travelling 25-mile distances without a second thought. Walking and thinking seem to have been a true pleasure to him. And once the Sacred Way turns off to the old coast road, the bucolic nature of Ancient Greece feels closer. Here there are olive, fig and pomegranate groves. The air can be thick with birdsong, the wind, off the Aegean Sea, is always warm. And the mood of those taking this route would have been buoyant. Participation in the Isthmian Games, although taken deadly seriously, seems from ancient descriptions to have had a tinge of a holiday mood.[17]

How appropriate that religion and fighting, the two-speed engines driving the Athenian city-state, should be the only dynamos that could move the philosopher from his beloved home-town.[18]

Today when one visits the site of the Isthmian Games the place is quiet. A few after-hours students press their noses up to the metal perimeter fence, a child's swing creaks and a defunct alarm drones, but the most hectic activity inside is provided by bees and butterflies, which gorge themselves on the poppies that pretend to stretch down to the Saronic Gulf. Although the site is perched on the plateau of a low hill, the sea feels impossibly close here. Appropriate then that the sanctuary was sacred to the great sea-god Poseidon. In modern tourist terms, this lovely site is Olympia's poor cousin. And yet the ancient sporting competitions held here were as fierce, as symbolic and as significant as anything at Zeus' Olympian sanctuary site further west. Scheduled every other spring, these Isthmian Games were the warm-up competitions to the Olympic Games at Olympia and the Pythian Games at Delphi.

The fifth-century BC stone-flagged roads here – wagon-rutted still – are witness to just how busy the Isthmia became. The sanctuary itself was right at the edge of an arterial track that ran from Corinth to Athens. The Saronic Gulf today sits calm and grey, broken by lumbering cargo ships, but of course in the fifth century it would have been thrashing with commercial craft, bringing goods to and from the humming harbours that served the great mercantile city of Corinth.

And imagine the other sounds here 2,500 years ago when a man like Socrates competed. Musicians tuning up for the added-attraction music festival would slowly drown out the sound of the bees and the passing birds; the tang of fat cooking and spitting on the hearth would swamp the smell of fresh sweat. The sound of running water,[19] splashing into basins there to purify athletes and spectators alike, would soothe the nerves.

A participant had the choice of wrestling, boxing, discus, foot-races, chariot-racing, equestrian events and the pentathlon. The games were three days of physical devotion to the gods. Those who came celebrated with blessed feasts. They gorged on freshly sacrificed bulls. A circular pit that once contained gallons of water is now blocked with the old bones and the discarded votive offerings of the faithful. Terracotta body-parts, statuettes, jewellery, coins and pretty little vases have been left here by the Greeks, who would try all forms of bribery to keep their gods on side.

Socrates' trip to this busy sanctuary would, in all probability, have been a little marred. The vast archaic Temple of Poseidon that once dominated the site had burned down in 450 BC. Virtually everything inside was destroyed; just enough material survives to date the conflagration. The offerings of jars filled with olive oil would have acted like incendiary bombs – feeding the flames. Eventually the temple was rebuilt, but if Socrates had visited the Isthmus in his youth it was rubble, gaping, a blackened reminder of the unpredictable nature of human affairs.

In fact, although this sanctuary was not a conventional battlefield, the reason to be at the Isthmus did have something to do with welcoming decay and death. The Greeks were less concerned with dying than with dying well – were, in the case of the Spartans, desperate to achieve 'a beautiful death'. These games commemorated a mortal end: the death of a child-hero called Melikertes, who drowned at sea but whose body was brought back to shore by a kindly dolphin.[20] Priests wore black robes and crowned victors with wreaths of wild celery – the plant that was thought to grow so freely in the Underworld.

It is at the Isthmus that you get a good sense of how superstitious many fifth-century Greeks would have been. Dug out into the mud, 25 feet down into the earth, and under an overhang of the rock, are underground dining chambers. Up to twenty-two people could be accommodated here, reclining on baked-earth couches, eating food specially prepared by especially sacred kitchens. The haves and have-nots knew their place in religious ritual. Aristocrats from many city-states would have met at the site, and only some of the 'top brass' were allowed to dine in this special chamber. These games were Panhellenic, a useful chance to see how the other Greeks lived. All participants, whatever their origins, were watched over by the god Poseidon, in whose honour the games were held.[21]

Of course Poseidon knew that his mortal devotees – who stopped all aggression during the Isthmian Games, as they did during the Olympic Games while they met to compete – would soon use his watery highways to invade and colonise, to ship arms and to steal women, wealth and lives, as well as to trade. Man's theatrical dishonesty with himself in the name of tradition, of civilisation, is an aspect of humanity that Plato's works seem to reveal Socrates wished he could, somehow, change.

Since the god is good . . . He and he alone must be held responsible for good things, but responsibility for bad things must be looked for elsewhere and not attributed to the god.[22]

ᕫᕤᕫᕤᕫ

The bad things of life, whether initiated by gods or men, were about to become inescapable. What is certain is that around this time of his life, whether or not Socrates played an active part in the Samian campaign – whether or not he *personally* ran as an athlete at the Isthmus – the philosopher would swiftly be at the sharp end of aggressive Athenian imperial policy, because the hostilities sponsored by Pericles and his supporters would not end at Samos. In Athens men in the Assembly, the Agora, the symposia had started to talk, to say that the intervention on behalf of Miletus was a dangerous diplomatic precedent. Difficult to dip your toe in foreign waters and not get wet.

Samos, as it turned out, did not immediately spark Greece's equivalent of the First, Second and Cold Wars (decades of sclerotic fighting) – a Total War that was finally declared in 432 BC – but all over the Aegean ploughshares were being beaten into swords, shields polished, daggers sharpened. And the Greeks, once again, remembered their taste for laying the blame for epic conflicts at a woman's door.

And then the Megarians, garlic-stung . . . stole a couple of Aspasia's whores, and from that the onset of war broke forth . . .[23]

Not content to let the Samos affair rest, punitive comedy dragged Aspasia and her sexual power into an invented narrative concerning another real sequence of events, this time a domino-line of destruction that did indeed kick-start the great Peloponnesian conflict. The struggle that would make an indelible mark on the Athenian psyche, and indeed on the psyche of the West, had started to brew.

19

FLEXING MUSCLES

@@@@@@@@@@@@

Corcyra (Corfu) and Megara,
440–432 BC

Remember, too, that the reason why Athens has the greatest name in all the world is
because she has never given in to adversity, but has spent more life and labour in warfare
than any other state, thus winning the greatest power that has ever existed in history, such
a power that will be remembered for ever by posterity, even if now (since all things are
born to decay) there should come a time when we were forced to yield: yet still it will be
remembered that of all the Hellenic powers, we held the widest sway over the Hellenes,
that we stood firm in the greatest wars against their combined forces and against
individual states, that we lived in a city which had been perfectly equipped in every
direction and which was the greatest in Hellas.

Thucydides, 2.64.3[1]

CLAMBERING DOWN TO THE REMAINS OF Athens' Long Walls is
tricky. This archaeological site is the wrong side of the tracks. The
massive limestone blocks, laid between 459 and 457 BC, are now sand-
wiched between the railway, a dirty canal and an industrial plant bristling
with CCTV cameras. An arterial road moans overhead. Old fag packets
stick to the mortar.

The Long Walls, you will remember, were built two decades after the
city walls to connect Athens to its ocean-mouth, at Piraeus harbour.
Although five million tourists come to Athens every year, there are none at
this spot. The site is off-putting. These defensive stones don't reflect the
afterglow of the Athenian 'Golden Age', a time remembered as egalitarian,
free and high-minded. The walls tell us that Athens was indeed a fortress

city; that those who came in and out were strictly monitored and controlled. Socrates lived during some of the most volatile decades in Greek history. The city and its citizens needed protecting. The stone ring also guarded Athens' precious Piraeus harbour, Athens' bustling second city, the mini-state from which Athenian oarsmen rowed out to claim new territories in the name of *demokratia*.

Back in the dark days of Persian invasions there were only two city-states from the 700 or so in Hellas that, when commanded to by the Medes, refused to submit tributes of earth and water: they were Athens and Sparta. Both were united, both were torn apart by their extraordinary sense of themselves. Although separated by rivers, mountains and plains, the connec-tion between the two was intimate. When the Persians were amassing for the Battle of Marathon, it was an Athenian, Pheidippides, who had run the 153 miles, in under two days, to beg the Spartans to come to Athenian aid. But ever since, each culture had vied to prove that they had been dealt the stronger hand. And now that Athens had an ideology – a new thing called democracy – it was with democratic superiority that she took on Spartan supremacy.

The two city-states were spoiling for a fight. The port of Piraeus became extra-busy. A new section was hived off for the exclusive use of the Athenian navy – you can still peer down on its solidly built walls that today run under the throbbing peripheral road. Those surviving soldiers of the conflicts against Persia (Marathon, Salamis, Plataea), now in their seventies and eighties – the 'old courage' so lauded by Aristophanes – were asked by the young, gym-hard generation of citizens who had trained to fight day in, day out for their opinion on the best battle strategies. And Athens and Sparta quickly found reasons to become affronted by one another.

The result of this antipathy was a Total War that would engulf the rest of Socrates' life and, indeed, the whole of the region.

⌒⌒⌒⌒⌒

First the gentle harbours of Corcyra (modern-day Corfu) were bludgeoned.

One summer's morning in 433 BC the inhabitants of that island woke in the blue hour before dawn to a fearful sound: the rhythmic wash of warships at full speed. The Corinthians and the Corcyrans were thrashing it out for control of trade routes and territories – but Athens, a good 200-plus miles further to the east, looked to the future and saw what Corcyra would always be: a gateway for Magna Graecia to Northern Italy and the rest of Europe. Unlike any other city-state of the age, Corcyra had its own fleet of 120 warships. Envoys from the island had already reminded the Athenian Assembly of this: '*We possess a navy that is the greatest in all Hellas except for your own.*'² Persuasive words. In 433 BC Athens' politicians had made a defensive alliance with the Corcyrans. Up in the breezy debating chamber of the Pnyx, Athenian citizens had voted to ratchet up their presence in the far west. Distant but calculating, Athens then intervened on the side of the little, wealthy, well-placed island community.

When the Corinthians and Corcyrans came to clash, there would be thirty-three Athenian triremes in the fray. In a curious, edgy boxing match, around the rocks to the south of the island (called Sybota), which appear to bleed and bubble from the mainland into the sea, each city-state unfurled its sails and attempted to demonstrate that it was the most powerful in the ring. Of course the ripples from those grappling boats would spread wide. Worried that the Corinthians might use the fracas to galvanise their own allies against Athenian interests, the Athenian democrats took pre-emptive action. And, as ever with such conflicts, those with their fingers over the red button found that they needed to persuade themselves there were many reasons for aggression, many justifications for feeling threatened. On the seas outside Corcyra vindication was provided in the form of wooden boats from a small town just 30 miles west of Athens called Megara. Megara was an ally of Athens. Corinth was a powerful city-state, but even the strong need more firepower, and bobbing within its fleet were a number of Megarian ships.

Mediocre, modest Megara was to be a flashpoint; a signal flare that could not be ignored, a small place that determined a massive historical event.

Modern Megara has a rather listless landscape. On my last visit the liveliest event was a coach-outing of Greek widows led by a stern Orthodox priest. Megara lies in the no-man's-land in between the clamour of Athens and the embracing curves of the Corinthian gulf. It seems to have little going for it. Today Megara is where, they scoff in nearby cafés, 'men work for chicken-feed'. The land looks unpromisingly stony – in the fourth century BC Isocrates jibed that Megara 'farmed rocks'. But appearances can be deceiving, and somehow, through careful use of salt reserves, by keeping enough sheep alive, making cloth tunics popular with workers, by being en route (and having access to a gentle bay that provides easy docking for boats), by sending out ships of colonists to the Black Sea to found useful little colonies such as Byzantium, the Megarians came to mean something.

And within months of the Battle of Sybota in the blue seas around Corcyra, Athens started to bully them. The relationship between the two city-states was already not what could be described as warm. In 445 Megarians had massacred the Athenian garrison. The outrage had always rankled. Around 432 Pericles proposed a strange law.[3] He suggested that Megarian traders and shoppers should be banned from Athenian markets, and he wanted to prevent Megarian ships from docking in any harbour of any member of the Delian League. His proposal was accepted. This was a trade embargo, sanctions of a most debilitating kind, a political insult. None in the region could ignore the fact that Athens was *really* throwing its weight about now. The 'Megarian Decree' became an excuse for outright war.

Gangrenous gossip in Athens, as the Peloponnesian War proved itself to be a bad one, blamed Aspasia — once again. It was said that Aspasia ran a whorehouse, a sex-academy. When two of her prostitute-hostesses were abducted by Megarians, the dominatrix from Miletus got her gimpy general, Pericles, to retaliate — they said.

From this began the Great War in all Hellas — from three cock-sucking sluts.[4]

The blood of the eastern Mediterranean was up; that popular mythology should want to give the episode a sexual context and a female *casus belli* is sadly familiar.[5]

Those bloody, localised beginnings — nothing to do with a courtesan and her prostitutes — were symptomatic of the Peloponnesian War: a sense of aggrieved aggression; a sense that someone else wants what you want. An uneasy notion that the world was a greedy place and that even under that loose umbrella of 'Hellenism', your Greek neighbour was eyeing up your Greek land. Progress, overt success, is rarely a stranger to jealousy; as most wars do, the Peloponnesian War started as a pique, covetousness, fear, a frustration that turned into slaughter.[6]

Things started to escalate. The Athenians had already been flexing their muscles where the sun set in the far west (Corcyra) and towards the Peloponnese at Megara, and now it was the turn of the north. From one of the newly trim quays at Piraeus, Socrates would sail out for battle, his mission to subdue the northern territories of Greece. The course that the ship had set was for a pretty, birdsong-filled town named Potidaea; a town that would soon hear the percussion of an Athenian citizen army.[7]

❧❧❧❧❧

This was an age when war was endemic. And Athens in the late fifth century BC appeared to have a heightened taste for conflict. One year in two in the democratic Assembly, Athenian citizens voted in favour of military aggression. Young men had been training for years for this moment. Athenian soldiers had an active, and respected, part to play in the possibility of their democracy. These were not the shank-quivering quislings who had to be whipped into battle by Persian lackeys. Not the shock-haired Thracians who drank deep to their king as if it were still prehistory. Hoplites were firmly rooted in the Greek landscape and psyche. For centuries now, standing shoulder to shoulder, each man on the right had protected each man on the left with his *hoplon*, his distinctive round shield.[8] Already there was a sense of collective purpose in Hellas, but democratic politics bred extra confidence. Side by side in the Athenian Assembly, their stunning new Parthenon above them, their spanking-new fleet in the harbour below, Athenian citizens persuaded one another that they were capable of anything.

And now the rank and file of sinew and muscle that powered and turned the trireme ships also played its part. Not just slaves, but low-ranking citizens, bosuns and rowers forced these boats, which could reach up to nine knots and could change course 180 degrees in just one minute, to take a new word-idea, '*demos-kratia*', to new lands.[9] Athenian citizens – ordinary men – made Athenian expansion their business. Socrates witnessed this development at first hand. Because there was a consolidated body of stakeholding citizens at home, the Athenians were roused to embark on constant military action abroad. Twenty-four months would not pass when the Athenian Assembly did not, during Socrates' lifetime, vote for war. In the minds of the Greeks, this was a dawning age – an age when blood and the sword would be used not just for defence, but to build a brave, new, ideological world. These were high hopes (or rabble-rousing sentiments, if one takes a cynical view) that would be dashed. Socrates might aim to inspire men to live a 'good life' – '*never do injustice!*' – and other fellow Athenians might advocate social justice, but there would be inevitable casualties of creating a civilisation with virtue and democratic ambition at its core.[10]

What made war inevitable was the growth of Athenian power and the fear which this caused in Sparta.[11]

Athens had taunted austere, extreme Sparta. She had flaunted her high walls and her glittering monuments and her liberal ways, and now she would play a game of cat's-paw with the militarised *polis*. The Peloponnesian War, as its fifth-century chronicler Thucydides noted, and as Socrates continually iterates, speaks of the awkward, emotional business of living with others in the world. But the huge benefit to any biographer of Socrates is that when he becomes a fighter in the Peloponnesian War itself, we begin to get sharper textual clues to the nature of his life, his relationships, and to the man behind the philosophy.

SOCRATES: *Thus, I would have done a terrible thing, Athenians, if, when the commanders whom you elected to command me, stationed me, both at Potidaea and at Amphipolis and at Delium (or indeed, if I had stationed myself) and they remained and ran the risk of death; but when the god ordered — as I believed and understood to have been so ordered — to spend my life in philosophy and examining myself and others, then I were to desert my post through fear of death or indeed, any other concern. That would be terrible, and then someone might really bring me to court justly on the ground that I don't believe the gods exist, since I disobey the oracle, fear death, and think I'm wise when I'm not. In truth, the fear of death is nothing but thinking you're wise when you are not, for you think you know what you don't. For no one knows whether death happens to be the greatest of all goods for humanity, but people fear it because they're completely convinced it is the greatest of evils. And isn't this ignorance, after all, the most shameful kind: thinking you know what you don't.[12]*

It is also during Socrates' time as a soldier that we properly meet that other principal character in Socrates' life-story, the precocious, privileged child who is now a grown man, that flesh-and-blood counterpoint to frugal, Socratic existence. The charismatic individual who is partially responsible for bringing Socrates to trial, and arguably to his premature death; the force of nature that we last saw as a shock-headed boy in the courtyard of Pericles, the beautiful, dangerous aristocrat who bore a troublingly Laconic dynastic name: Alcibiades.

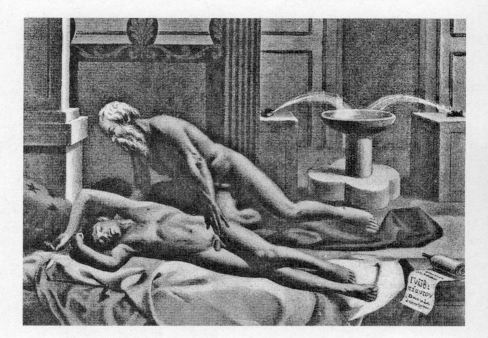

20

SOCRATES THE SOLDIER

@@@@@@@@@@@@

Potidaea, northern Greece, 432–429 BC

ALCIBIADES: Then if you care to hear of him in battle — for there also he must have his due — on the day of the fight in which I gained my prize for valour from our commanders, it was he, out of the whole army, who saved my life: I was wounded and he would not forsake me, but helped me to save both my armour and myself.

Plato, *Symposium*, 220d–e[1]

POTIDAEA, IN THE NORTH OF GREECE, just beneath Macedonia, is one of those ancient sites that it is only too easy to miss. Travelling south-east from Thessaloniki, you have to screech off the flyover and then track back on a sheer sliproad down to sea-level — to the canal hacked through the isthmus there in 1935. Now the site is umbrellaed by a six-lane motorway; a fast-food joint called Portes hems in the abandoned harbour.

Here there is a cannibalised architectural history. Medieval sea walls have swallowed up classical remains. A Roman temple to Poseidon lurches into the sea.[2] Pebbles mix with pottery shards on the beach. In the summer, butterflies follow their reflections in the crystal-clear water; but in the winter ice creeps its way from the shoreline.

This was a settlement that defined itself by its relation to the sea. When Corinthians arrived in the seventh century BC they took over the town at the neck of the peninsula and blessed it with the Doric version of their name for the sea-god Poseidon: Potidaea.

So the classical city of Potidaea was exposed on the edge of the Kassandra peninsula — then called Pallene, now named for the Macedonian king Kassandros. In the spring this 31-mile-long finger pointing into the Gulf of Thessalonica turns apple-green, a shade that signifies this is fertile territory well worth protecting.[3] Even unploughable coastal land here – a rock-filled, lunar landscape – is a refuge for the bees that produce some of the sweetest honey in Greece. From the highest point of the settlement it is possible to see the peaks of Mount Athos, the mountains of Olympus and Pelion.

Today the place seems untroubled. A fountain plays in the small town square; fishermen sit in a toadstool ring, mending their nets, smoking, joshing. Swallows dive over the sea, stinging the surface after an operatic arc to catch gnats. But in Socrates' day the inhabitants of Potidaea were trapped in paradise; the Athenians blocked the Isthmus, and every man, woman and child on the Kassandra peninsula was a prisoner.

By the beginning of the 430s this cheerful landscape had already begun to wear a frown.

The region was discontented. Pericles had stamped his mark on the surrounding territory and resentment had started to simmer. The foundations of the new Athenian-run towns of Brea in 445 BC and Amphipolis to the north in 437/6 BC could only mean one of two things: that the Athenians wished to expand their empire, or that they didn't trust the Greek inhabitants of the north to behave without Athens keeping a close eye on them. Neither motivation was flattering.

Then there was the problem of money. To rub salt into the wound, the annual levy demanded by Athens from city-states in the region was raised from six to fifteen talents.[4] The Athenians knew how a handover of cash can focus a troubled mind. To pre-empt a revolt Athens dispatched an ultimatum: pull down your walls, give over hostages, sever connections with the mother-city Corinth.

The Potidaeans desperately sent envoys to Athens and Sparta respectively. They asked the former to temper their actions and the latter to retaliate, should the Athenians become too heavy-handed. Athens' interventions in Samos and in the rich waters off Corcyra were fresh in everyone's minds. When it came to overseas interests, the Athenians were clearly forming a plan.

Unfortunately for Potidaea, although only a modest town it was useful to larger international interests. The nearby king of Macedon wanted to draw the Corinthians into this northern conflict to strengthen his own position against Athens. He fluffed up anxiety, joining the envoys that Potidaea had already sent to Corinth/Sparta with his own and demanding help from forces down south.

Now the military elite of the region were involved; the machinery of war was starting to turn. Thirty Athenian triremes left Piraeus, 1,000 hoplites – Socrates amongst them – started the journey north.[5] Word reached the jumpy inhabitants of Potidaea, and they knew that this wasn't simply cage-rattling. Here the earth is red-rich. Athenians were determined to protect (some would say to annex) these lands where iron keeps the hills green throughout the summers, where rival cities (Sparta, Corinth) and barbarian tribes were also battling to create empires. Anticipating casualties, a number of locals were evacuated to the nearby flagship new-town of Olynthos. And from roads way beyond Athens on the Peloponnese dust started to rise. Corinth dispatched 1,600 hoplites and 400 lightly armed troops to protect its threatened city-child.

The Greeks were at war — with one another.

Socrates at war

@@@@@@@@@@@@@

Greek encampments were untidy and relatively haphazard. Trees were cleared for firewood and rough shelters, soldiers would huddle under animal skins — one-man bivouacs. Those who could not afford tents companioned around camp fires.[6] The nights were chill at that time of year; the campaign fell some time between September and November in 432 BC. It was only the really wealthy who could afford a grand battleground-home. And one of the most beautiful men on campaign, Alcibiades, had a tent big enough for Socrates to share.

The two soldiers came from different tribes, but on this campaign they were mess-mates.[7] The democracy had thrown them together. They would have sat in the same theatre, drunk at the same *symposia*, perhaps trained together in the gymnasia or the Agora, and certainly sought one another out in the city; '*Hello there, Socrates. Where have you been? Not that I need ask, you've been chasing after that gorgeous Alcibiades.*'[8] We do not know how their relationship started, but we do know how far it went. They lay together, Alcibiades carping that nothing physical ever took place: '*I might as well have been sleeping with my father or an elder brother.*'[9] On campaign Pericles must have approved of this bit of mongrel billeting — social engineering if you like — the clever, classless philosopher shacked up with a muscular, aristocratic firebrand. They made an odd pair: Socrates just shy of forty and, we are told, still sporting his trademark thin cloak and bare feet.[10] Alcibiades twenty or so, a boy whose beauty '*flowered at each season of his growth in turn.*'[11]

Alcibiades was a long way from his family's homeland. This 'man beyond compare' was — so they said — a direct descendant of that sage old hero of the Trojan War, King Nestor. Nestor, the poets sang, lived on a beautiful bay at Pylos in the southern Peloponnese. 'Nestor's Palace' has now been excavated. Ranks of perfect *kylikes* – long-stemmed wine cups – have been found, 2,856 of them in one storeroom alone; a Linear B tablet from the Late Bronze Age shows that the court here ordered 375 gallons of wine to be drunk. It seems that the Bronze Age ruler of Pylos (Nestor or no) was a king who enjoyed his revels. And Nestor's many-times-great-grandson inherited his taste for the fermented grape.

If people told stories about Socrates, they could have filled books with the gossip that circulated about Alcibiades. This preening, irresistible-sounding specimen became a leader of the age. He encouraged Athenians to think it modish to start to drink in the morning; he turned his nose up at wrestling because it would mean rubbing up against plebs; he rejected flute-playing because it made your face pucker in an unattractive way. His beauty was breathtaking. '*He was hunted by many women of noble families,*' Xenophon tells us.[12] For many centuries after his death stories were still being told of his hot-headed exploits. It was rumoured, tongues clucking, that he had staged a murder and presented his friends with the corpse to test their loyalty and nerve.[13]

Oddly, despite Alcibiades' god-given gifts (his beauty, his strength, his dangerous charm), this was a man with everything – and nothing – to prove. Orphaned young (Athenians were thought of as 'orphans' when their fathers died, even if their mothers were still alive), he had been brought up by Pericles. He had the adoptee's liberty. He had no blood-father to resent. No excuse for curtailing his talents. Without the genetic anxiety of a natural parent to live up to, or to disappoint, anything was possible.

Plato has Socrates ask him, '*Are you willing, Alcibiades, to live having what you now do, or would you choose to die instantly unless you were permitted greater things? You would prefer to die . . . It appears to me that you would not . . . be willing to live, unless you could fill the mouths of all men with your name and power.*'[14]

The young man's know-no-bounds, excessive approach to life was written into history and into the urban myths of fifth-century Greece. But still, despite the debauchery, Alcibiades had blue blood. And for Socrates' peers, with the epic tales of Homer their roadmap to life, such a quality really counted for something: '*splendour running in the blood has much weight*', sang the poet Pindar.[15] And Alcibiades was certainly not shy of advertising this fact by surrounding himself with things splendid.

His shield was emblazoned with a picture of Eros hurling a thunder-bolt. At this stage in history Eros had yet to weaken into a soppy Cupid. The Greeks knew just how dangerous Eros really was. Naturally, Love and

Lust destroyed men. Eros brought the great and the weak alike to their knees. Socrates himself compared the kisses sponsored by Eros to the venom injected by a lethal scorpion.

'You are a fool,' said Socrates. 'Do you think that good-looking people inject nothing in the act of kissing, just because you can't see it? Don't you realise that this creature which they call the bloom of youth is even more dangerous than scorpions? Scorpions produce their effect by contact, but this needs no contact; if one looks at it, even from quite a distance, it can inject a kind of poison that drives one crazy. No; I advise you, Xenophon, when you see an attractive person, to take to your heels as fast as you can.'[16]

The gold and ivory of Alcibiades' fine armour must have flashed as the young man raged through that soft, pretty territory. One cannot imagine him having any trouble engaging, bloodily, with his enemies. By every account Alcibiades lived up to his name; he was a man of *alke*, strength, and *bia*, force. He was the kind of modern-day, all-Athenian hero to stir pride in Theseus' own, heroic heart.

But at Potidaea it was Socrates who saved Alcibiades, not vice versa.[17] The beautiful but inexperienced boy-man was – according to Plato – on the verge of extinction, the Athenian army having been attacked in a sudden, unexpected skirmish. Socrates, quick-witted, pulled the young lad out of the fray. And as befits the prince of self-promotion on the one hand and the master of understatement on the other, it was Alcibiades, not Socrates, who was awarded a suit of armour and crown by Athens – recognition of his conduct on the battlefield. Of course Alcibiades was honoured, for he was an aristocrat, and Socrates, a stonemason's son, was not.[18]

☙❧☙❧☙

Through the autumn, the massing of forces continued in the Pallene peninsula. By late September there were 3,000 Athenian hoplites in the region – close on 6 per cent of the entire male, adult citizen population, plus 600 Macedonian cavalry. Some of the smaller towns caved in, but not Potidaea. It resisted, and was caught in a firestorm. The first battle was over so quickly that only a fraction of the soldiers had the chance to fight; 300 from Potidaea or the south lost their lives, and 150 Athenian hoplites, including their general Callias, were killed.

Alcibiades was wounded either here or at one of the later skirmishes at Spartolus. But, luckily for him, according to Plato, Socrates was close by – and having scooped him plus his armour up (those showy, jauntily crafted bits of well-wrought metal that declared to the army of democrats that Alcibiades was just a bit special), Socrates incarnated the ethos of hoplite warfare: that you stand shield-to-shield, you are as strong as the mass you represent. Under a pale northern sun Socrates had kept the life in this golden teenage boy. Both lived to fight another day.

After the initial bouts of fighting with Athens and her allies, to save those who could still stand, the Potidaean community backed into its walled city and waited. The Athenians, Socrates included, bedded themselves down, ranging the benighted walls. The rituals of war continued. Potidaeans were allowed to bury their dead. The Athenians rigged up on the 'turning place' (the spot where a battle was lost or won) a trophy (derived from the Greek *trepein*, to turn). Trophies of this day and age were ghoulish scarecrows — often the stump of a tree dressed in the defeated's armour. A dead, point-less thing. As dead and as pointless, in this case, as the hopes of the Potidaean victims. Because the suffering wasn't over yet. Now new allied reinforcements came. Potidaea found herself besieged both by land and by sea — those trapped inside the city would have to wait for winter to come and go twice more before liberation; death by starvation or disease looked likely to be their first chance of relief.

21

DEMONS AND VIRTUES

@@@@@@@@@@@@

The Kassandra peninsula, northern Greece, 432–429 BC

*FRIEND: Where have you been now, Socrates? Ah, but of course you have been
in chase of Alcibiades and his youthful beauty! Well, only the other day, as I looked
at him, I thought him still handsome as a man — for a man he is, Socrates,
between you and me, and with quite a growth of beard.*

Plato, *Protagoras*, 309a[1]

IT WAS IN POTIDAEA THAT THE first, troubling, stories about Socrates
really began to fly.

Here, in the depth of winter, the middle-aged man (we hear from

Alcibiades back in Athens) stands shoeless, for five, ten, fifteen, twenty-four hours at a stretch. Rapt. Lost in his own mind. Staring blankly like the living dead; communicating with his *daimonion*, his inner demon. And then dawn appears and stills the sea: Socrates quietly says his prayers to the sun and carries on with the business of being a good democratic soldier in a foreign land.[2]

Socrates, Alcibiades and the citizen-army were in the north for two, possibly three years, and they did not waste their time. They burned the crops of those towns that seemed uneasy, and engaged in open warfare with the truculent settlement of Spartolus – here they lost all their generals and 430 men. The Athenian soldiers had walked through desiccated groves, sun-blasted, and they had hopped gingerly through a landscape so iced that the ground was iron-hard. They had watched, with amazement and no little suspicion, as Socrates strode through these same frosty landscapes with his trademark bare feet. Why, when you could afford shoes, might you choose to go without? Why put men like Simon the Cobbler, back in Athens, out of business? And what on earth was going on in the man from Alopeke's curious, spooky staring sessions – those hours when Socrates seemed to be talking to himself, wrestling with some kind of inner dialogue, not to mention inner demons?[3]

SOCRATES: *Be well assured, my dear friend Crito, that this is what I seem to hear, as the frenzied dervishes of Cybele seem to hear the flutes, and this sound of these words re-echoes within me and prevents my hearing any other words.*[4]

It is easy to imagine the questions slipping quickly through the camp. What is the superhumanity that this ugly soldier Socrates seems to enjoy? Who or what is his *daimonion*? How come he claims some kind of privi-leged, private access to the spirit world? Have you heard that he is one of that freaky circle who hang around with Pericles – the man who has brought us to this godforsaken, freezing place – one of the ones who says crazy things, like we all started as fish, and the sun is a red-hot rock. What an oddball, how peculiar.

But thus far, there was no persecution. Times were relatively good, Athens was still in that frame of mind where she believed she could do anything. The citizens had voted themselves into this war – in living memory they had beaten the Persians, and now they can beat the Spar-tans and their scumbag allies too. And look how badly it is going for those allies – the Potidaeans are really suffering, obviously the gods are not with them . . .

Because the fate of the Potidaeans had started to be shared in the tents of the army camp. Two annual cycles of self-imposed incarceration had

Pheidias Showing the Frieze of the Parthenon to His Friends by Sir Lawrence Alma-Tadema.
Pheidias is shown demonstrating his handiwork to Pericles and Aspasia amongst others.
During recent renovations of the Parthenon, the remnants of a stonemason's picnic-lunch
(fish and fowl bones) were discovered at this high level of construction.

An academic reconstruction of the kinds of colour schemes actually used by craftsmen of the sixth and fifth centuries BC to decorate the monuments and sculptures of Greek city-state. This particular statue came from a temple on the island of Aegina.

Socrates speaks to two students. An early thirteenth-century miniature now held by the Topkapi Museum, Istanbul. Illustration for the eleventh-century collection by Fatimid prince al-Mubashshir ibn Fatik, *Mukhtaral-Hikam*, 'The choicest maxims and best sayings'.

A romantic tradition has elevated Aspasia's influence in Athens, and over both Socrates and Pericles. This painting by Nicolas-André Monsiau was part product of the new vogue for 'salons'. Aspasia was hailed in certain circles in the early nineteenth century as the first salonière, as a woman who enjoyed an equal marriage with Pericles and who, quite rightly, had been free to choose whom she should love.

Athens' plague killed many tens of thousands. Scientific research over the last fifteen years suggests this was almost certainly a pandemic of the typhus virus. Michiel Sweerts, following Thucydides' eye-witness accounts, imagined its effects in this painting, *The Plague in Athens*.

A shoe-making workshop. The various processes of stretching and cutting the leather are shown here (note the knives on the wall and the bowl of water under the table). Socrates was said to have spent much time philosophising with the young men of the city in the workshop of Simon the Shoemaker at the fringes of the Agora.

The paintings around Athens would have been exquisite. None of these have survived but we get a good sense of the delicacy of the wor[k] from the well-preserved interior decorations of graves preserved in northern Greece — for example this lovely fourth-century dove currently on display in the Archaeological Museu[m] of Thessaloniki.

A cartoon version of Socrates' satirical treatment by Aristophanes in his comedy *Clouds*.

The Agora at its point of excavation in 1949 – the protecting presence of mountains around the city is clearly visible in this picture. This photograph was taken from the vantage point of the Hephaisteion.

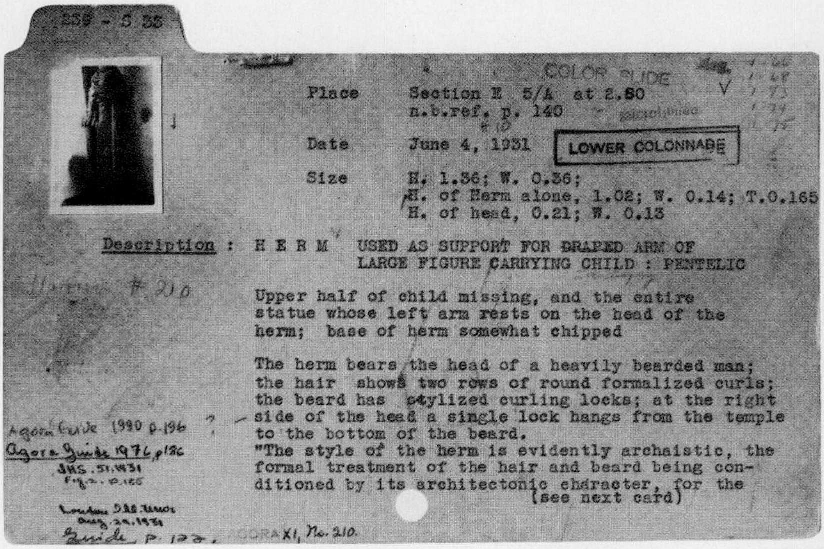

COLOR SLIDE

Place   Section E 5/A at 2.80
              n.b.ref. p. 140

LOWER COLONNADE

Date   June 4, 1931

Size   H. 1.36; W. 0.36;
           H. of Herm alone, 1.02; W. 0.14; T.0.165
           H. of head, 0.21; W. 0.13

Description : H E R M USED AS SUPPORT FOR DRAPED ARM OF
                   LARGE FIGURE CARRYING CHILD : PENTELIC

        Upper half of child missing, and the entire
        statue whose left arm rests on the head of the
        herm; base of herm somewhat chipped

        The herm bears the head of a heavily bearded man;
        the hair shows two rows of round formalized curls;
        the beard has stylized curling locks; at the right
        side of the head a single lock hangs from the temple
        to the bottom of the beard.
        "The style of the herm is evidently archaistic, the
        formal treatment of the hair and beard being con-
        ditioned by its architectonic character, for the
                                  (see next card)

Agora Guide 1990 p.196
Agora Guide 1976 p.186
JHS. 51.1931
Fig.2.p.185
London ILL News
Aug. 29. 1931
Guide p.123 AGORA XI, No. 210.

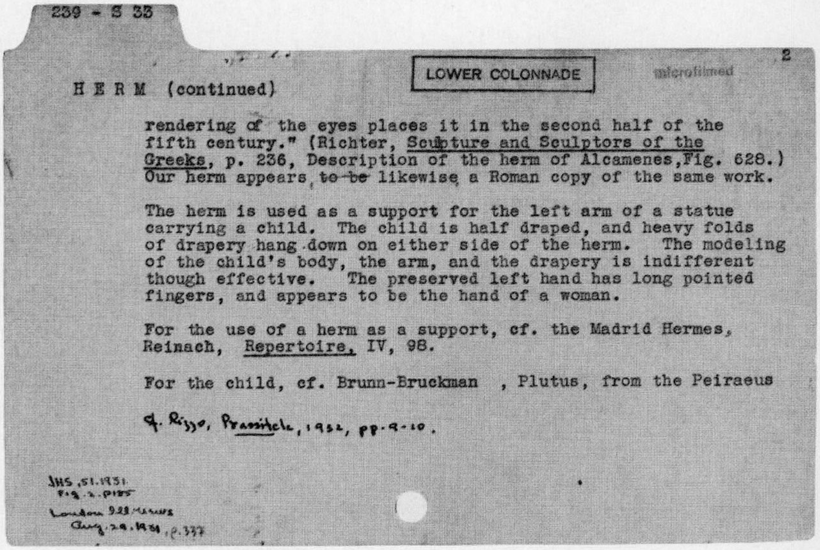

LOWER COLONNADE   microfilmed   2

H E R M (continued)

        rendering of the eyes places it in the second half of the
        fifth century." (Richter, Sculpture and Sculptors of the
        Greeks, p. 236, Description of the herm of Alcamenes,Fig. 628.)
        Our herm appears to be likewise a Roman copy of the same work.

        The herm is used as a support for the left arm of a statue
        carrying a child. The child is half draped, and heavy folds
        of drapery hang down on either side of the herm. The modeling
        of the child's body, the arm, and the drapery is indifferent
        though effective. The preserved left hand has long pointed
        fingers, and appears to be the hand of a woman.

        For the use of a herm as a support, cf. the Madrid Hermes,
        Reinach, Repertoire, IV, 98.

        For the child, cf. Brunn-Bruckman , Plutus, from the Peiraeus

        G. Rizzo, Prassitele, 1932, pp.9-10.

JHS. 51.1931
Fig.2.p.185
London ILL News
Aug. 29.1931. p.337

The index cards of the American School of Classical Studies at Athens
detailing the excavation of a herm. This herm is a Roman copy of a fifth-
century original. Herms would have been highly visible in Socrates' city
as boundary markers and totems of good fortune. The herms were shockingly devastated (it was whispered through the streets of the city-state,
by Alcibiades and his aristocratic crew) the night before the allied fleet
set sail to Sicily in 416 BC.

degraded and debauched an entire community. The new recruits coming up from Athens appeared to have infected the weak locals with a strange, pustular disease – a miasma that induced high fevers, sweats, racking coughs and a suppurating rash. More then 1,000 Athenian troops themselves succumbed to the infection while they waited to fight. Those trapped inside the besieged city were worst affected. They had no means of escape or of reaching new food supplies. The inhabitants who were not struck down by this alien illness could survive now only by eating human flesh – the Potidaeans had become cannibals.[5]

This is vindictive and shabby. Victorious Athena's crystal stare up on the Acropolis has a decidedly unpleasant glint.

⊚⊚⊚⊚⊚

So Socrates fought, and he stood and he waited and he thought. Already a recognised philosopher in the city, clearly this three-year-long campaign gave him new material. The Potidaeans were protecting themselves against rapacious Athenian interests. Did Socrates ever wonder what he was doing in someone else's back yard? As he fought and watched skulls smashing, guts spilled, the mortally wounded turning green and then black before their last breath escaped them – Greeks slaughtering Greeks, for honour and to grab land – did he wonder: Why? What is this for? The Athenians and the Spartans, one-time allies, men who spoke the same language, lived as neighbours, worshipped the same gods, now chose to emphasise their differences, to try to destroy one another.

He must over the years have observed the Spartans and their tight, effi-cient military machine: every single soldier a citizen, and a citizen who had been trained for one profession alone – to fight; to fight well, cleanly, swiftly, efficiently, to kill adroitly and to die a 'beautiful death'.[6] Did he contem-plate this facility and ask whether this was preferable to the demotic chaos of most inefficiently fought wars? Is this where the seeds of the respect that he undoubtedly felt for the über-specialist Spartan ethos were first sown?[7]

149

Socratic virtue

On each morning of battle Socrates would have heard the Corinthians clank and shuffle their camp into readiness for war. When Spartan troops were on the battlefield their advent was more sonorous, because this was a city-state that sacrificed to Eros before conflict, that encouraged its men to 'embrace death like a lover' and then played them into battle, singing and dancing as they had been taught to do from the age of seven. The Spartans rarely broke with tradition. They enjoyed doing what they were told. Spartiates believed that obedience was more important than freedom. '*At Sparta the most powerful men show utmost deference to the officials; they pride themselves on their humility, believing that, if they lead, the rest will follow along the path of eager obedience.*'[8] For the Spartans, virtue resided in unflinching compliance and the well-developed biceps of their citizen fighting machine. The passion for conflict was visceral, sensuous. Their very war music was erotic. But Socrates tells us that the body is the tomb of the soul, not its manifestation. Physical submission, for him, was of no interest as a moral goal. Although the philosopher admired the Spartans in some respects – he approved of their selfless communality, their pursuit of excellence in this life – he appeared to have a much more nuanced notion of what 'goodness' really is.

Socrates, so Plato and Xenophon tell us, spent years of his philosophical life propounding the need for virtue, *arete*. The orthodox notion of virtue at this time was a courageous, virile, manly concept. Young men were taught *arete* in the gymnasia, during military exercises. The virtue they possessed had to equip them, in literal and precise terms, for the cut-and-thrust of life in the fifth century. Although Socrates was, quite rightly, later lauded by Christians, his philosophy came before the 'turn-the-other-cheek' ethos was developed. In Greece at this time the *lex talionis* still operated: all is fair in love and war, and civilian men can all be slaughtered, women and children enslaved.

So *arete*, manly virtue, could, and did, lead to abominable acts. But Socrates played around with a rather different concept of 'goodness'. He thought of virtue in more subtle, multifaceted terms; for him, virtue was *sophrosune*, temperance, *dikaiosune*, justice, *hosiotes*, piety, and *andreia*, courage, all rolled together into one bigger ambition – *Sophia*, wisdom or knowledge.[9] His belief was that this was not pie-in-the-sky idealism, but a real option; a virtue that could withstand the vicissitudes of pleasure and pain, of anger, of frustration and jealousy, and be enjoyed by all. And this particular brand of *Sophia* – not pat answers, not wisdom-as-product, but a deeper and more connected mode of thinking – he eventually concurred, could, and should, be taught.[10]

Perhaps it is not too fanciful to suggest that, surrounded as he was both by great, human possibilities and by awful, disgusting, debasing human acts, he was trying to will a better, a newly virtuous kind of man out of the world. He was living *in extremis* and so he understood the value of moderation. Socrates was exposed to so much that was 'bad' that his search for 'the good' was ever more urgent.

In these wars of attrition men must have lain down at night wondering what carnage the next day would bring. Potidaea was just one in a line of diminishing, besmirching campaigns – orchestrated by Athena's city to protect her democratic interests. The ideology in play was discomforting. But at some point in this phase of his life, as he fought, as he lay in his tent with Alcibiades, the moonlight coming ghost-bright through the linen of the military awning, as he stood, frozen, a blank stare on his face but his mind whirring within, Socrates developed a new ideology, where the interests of 'the good' came before all other concerns.

⊱⊶⊷⊶⊷⊰

We don't know precisely how long Socrates and Alcibiades stayed in the north. The siege was finally lifted in 429 BC. Potidaean leaders – or what was left of them – gave up as it became clear that their Corinthian allies were insufficient, and that every last Potidaean, every mother, child and freshly bearded boy, would die unless they opened their city gates. The two soldiers may well have watched as the emaciated Potidaean men and women were, surprisingly, given permission to leave. They would have stumbled out, clutching the pathetic bundles that were to form the foundations for their future lives. All adult males with one garment, the women with two, and each with enough money to clear the war-zone. Were those tent-mates Socrates and Alcibiades blamed, as their field generals were, for the leniency that enabled the Potidaeans to depart? Back in the Athenian centre of oper-ations, men wanted blood, they wanted to hear that the vanquished city-state had been further humiliated. Perhaps those in the north were battle-weary – they did not want to hurt any more.

Our evidence for the Potidaea campaign is necessarily based on conjec-ture and literature. The battlefields around Potidaea have yet to be excavated, and many of the few extant remains in Potidaea itself were stolen from the village schoolhouse by the Nazis in 1941. But the campaign here became legendary almost as soon as it became historical. Because this unlikely pair,

Alcibiades and Socrates, were now characters in the soap opera of *popular* history. A hot-headed boy, the selfless, wiser, grizzled older man. Lovers whose passionate on-off affair would be played out against one of the most charismatic of city backdrops and against one of the most elongated and insidious wars in antiquity.

Stereotype or not, both friends would find it hard to shake off their given roles. Because it seems that from Potidaea onwards, Socrates' purpose was to identify the point of human lives, Alcibiades' to make or break them.

SOCRATES: *I questioned one man after another, always conscious of the anger and hatred that I provoked, which distressed and alarmed me. But necessity drove me on; the word of Apollo, I thought, must certainly be considered first.*[11]

At the very moment when a network of city-states were establishing themselves to form not just pockets of civilisation, but a new ideology for civilisation itself, and when civilisation was winning over subsistence, Socrates was asking whether Alcibiades – the embodiment of the Athenian ideal in so many ways, beautiful, strong, daring, pleasure-loving, charismatic, urbane – was also an embodiment of a flaw of civilised development, of our urge always to want more, to want that which we do not have.

For I go about doing nothing else than urging you, young and old, not to care for your persons or your property more than for the perfection of your souls, or even so much; and I tell you that virtue does not come from money, but from virtue comes money and all other good things to man, both to the individual and to the state.[12]

Socrates had cause for concern. Be careful what you wish for, they say. Athens had had a vision – that she could lead, perhaps even rule, the known world – but her hubris had been spotted by the gods on Mount Olympus. The Spartans had intensified their campaigns closer to the Athenian home. Their strategy was to tempt the Athenians out to pitched battle on the Attic plains, while their foot soldiers harried and destroyed the people and the crops of Attica. Led by King Archidamus, the debilitating invasions lasted between fifteen and forty days, and were repeated almost without exception year in, year out. Their effects were burned into the minds of Athenians, and onto the pages of their playwrights:

> *But now it seems the brutal god of war*
> *Stands at the gates*
> *With firebrand flaming blood*
> *To set this town ablaze.*
> *– O please don't let him!*
> *We share the sufferings of our kin . . .*

Your pain is our pain!
All round the city, lying like a
Low mist, are enemy shields
Like smoke that only needs one bloody spark
To blaze into the flame of battle.
A message for the War God to unleash
The Furies' Violence,
On sons of Oedipus.[13]

On the field, Socrates would have seen wounds both clean and unclean – he must have heard as men died quick and slow deaths. But nothing could prepare him for the charnel-house that Athens had become.

The home-town that Socrates and Alcibiades returned to in May 429 BC was changed into a sick city, a diseased thing in no mood to give anyone a hero's welcome.

22

THE PLAGUE

@@@@@@@@@@@@

Within Athens' city walls, 430–428 BC

If anyone feels secure, satisfied with what he thinks of as his established position in life, he is a fool. The forces that control our lives are as unpredictable as the behaviour of idiots. There is no such thing as certain happiness.

Euripides, *Trojan Women*, 1203–6

DAWN BREAKS IN ATHENS. THE STREETS are jolted out of the forget-fulness of night. Around the fountains and wells of the city there is a flock of human swallows. Capped women who have come to gather water, and to exchange news. Most of these will be low-born females and slave-girls. But there is a war on, all sorts of conventions slip at a time like this. Now is the one window for the women of the city to gossip – later in the day it will be the men who go to market to pick over the meagre supplies of food.[1]

Bad news spreads quickly in Athens. And today the word of mouth is particularly sour. Athenians – indiscriminately it seems, metics, women, men, priests – are being struck down by a curious curse. Their bodies are purple-stained, twisted in the agony of their death throes, their mouths gaping, their dying wish always water, water. The eyes burn, the tongue becomes bloodied, the skin breaks out in ulcers and the lungs constrict; it can take seven to nine days to die. Those few that survive are often blinded, incontinent. Contemporary Athenian sources describe men as possessed – they were, we can now deduce, simply brain-damaged. It is hard to say categorically what this affliction was – typhoid fever, Ebola, a new, mutant virus have been suggested – but the very latest analysis of tooth pulp from graves of the period makes typhus the most likely; and what is certain is that the

154

plague had a characteristic trait. Birds of prey and scavengers avoided the corpses. And even more monstrous, the dogs that did eat the diseased human body-parts perished too. This seemed to be an epidemic that had the power to jump from one species to another.[2]

The most terrible thing of all was the despair into which people fell when they realised that they had caught the plague; for they would immediately adopt an attitude of utter hope-lessness, and, by giving in in this way, would lose their powers of resistance. Terrible, too, was the sight of people dying like sheep through having caught the disease as a result of nursing others. This indeed caused more deaths than anything else.[3]

Contained in the city by military command, within a year the disease danced its way through the caged population of Athens and across the hot streets; 80,000 died. At a cautious estimate, at least one-third of the city was wiped out.

It had started in 431 BC. Pericles was implementing an ill-starred strategy. Spartans were harrying the Attic countryside, employing a scorched-earth policy. They sabotaged Athenian estates, indiscriminately. As a teenage boy, Pericles had watched Athens' city walls being raised to keep out the Persians, and he trusted in their strength. The General decided that the entire popu-lation of Athena's city-state should be pulled inside its ring of stone. And so from the 139 *demes* families dutifully travelled. Athens had already become crowded, and now it was crushed. Forced into the city, stumbling caravans of humans were trapped in 'suffocating shacks' in refugee camps that would swiftly resemble cemeteries. Livestock was sent to the nearby island of Euboea, and human stock was barricaded within the city walls. Socrates' grassy banks – home of his dawdling with young boys – were now deserted, the shrines and sanctuaries there unattended, the Dipylon Gate, like the other gates of the city, barred. Crops outside the city ripened unharvested, and were then torched.

The plague was subtle at first. But it left its mark. Sadly, those demo-cratic little houses of Athens, cheek-by-jowl (no villas protected by high-walled gardens as you find in the Roman period), were the perfect host for a visiting virus or bacterium. And now they were doubly, triply occupied – by city dwellers, by refugees and by a killer. As the disease spread the courtyards began to fill with bodies, and men, women and children desperately tried to find some relief from the searing heat of their internal cellular battle.

At first week by week, and then day by day, more and more Athenians needed to be buried. The eye-witness accounts make for unbearable reading.

Words indeed fail one when one tries to give a general picture of this disease; and as for the sufferings of individuals, they seemed almost beyond the capacity of human nature to endure.[4]

The bodies of the dying were heaped one on top of the other, and half-dead creatures could be seen staggering about the streets or flocking around the fountains in their desire for water. The sanctuaries in which they took up their quarters were full of the dead bodies of people who had died right there inside.[5]

Thucydides tells us that with the plague came degeneracy.

People had fewer inhibitions about self-indulgent behaviour they had previously repressed . . . The upshot was that they sought a life of swift and pleasurable gain, because they regarded their lives and their property as equally impermanent.[6]

Those citizens who, despite the outbreak of an ugly war, had behaved properly, had kept society running as it should, now remembered the animal in them. Running through the streets, feral, they looted and rutted. The carnage was surveyed by the fixed gaze of ideal Homeric heroes, the kinds of men Athenians were supposed to be, staring reproachfully from epic, decorated walls across the city.[7] The colours of Athens' painted-backdrop scenery – its statues and themed walkways and gaudy shrines – were still garishly bright. But the acts they witnessed were grubby. By the time Socrates and Alcibiades returned, the plague had been on the Athenian streets for two long years.

This horror-show was the home-town that Socrates and Alcibiades have re-entered.

The plague pits of Athens

The region of *Demosion Sema*, the public cemetery, in the north-west corner of Athens, is still, as it were, on the wrong side of the tracks. Traders as grubby as their suitcases sell twentieth-century debris. Here there are men who mend bikes and wicker chairs; many of the walls around about are covered with graffiti – some of it commissioned as an exercise in social inclusion, most not. There is much new development here: it is a district that sits somewhere between life and death. And just at the edge of this mongrel zone, construction workers preparing ground for the 1994 extension of the Athens metro made a gruesome discovery. Behind a metal fence is a half-dug building site. The concrete foundations are there to support something new, but they cover something very old. Because in Socrates' day this was a mass grave. Thucydides stated that during the plague years Athens had been infected by something supernatural, ghoulish, heaven-sent; he uses the same word that Socrates did to describe his own inner-demon, 'daimonion'.

And now one eleven-year-old girl, called Myrtis, has risen from this morass of the dead to throw light on Thucydides' ghoulish *daimonion*, on Athens' uninvited guest. She has been named by the scientists who resurrected her. In amongst the jumble of hastily buried bodies, thrown together into the ground in around 430/429 BC, Myrtis' skull was discovered. It is in a remarkably good state of preservation; the bone is smooth, the skull virtually intact, the teeth all present. In fact the remains are so robust, it is clear this young girl had a pronounced overbite, messy eye-teeth, a mouth that turned up slightly at the corner. Her face has been painstakingly reconstructed in a laboratory in Sweden, and she now gazes out surprised at a world that was two and a half millennia into her future. We can stare into Myrtis' face, but we cannot see the fear that must surely have been in her eyes as the world around her collapsed.[8]

Fetid, petrol-green water stagnates in the holes where steel girders and other twentieth-century detritus have been removed in the area where Myrtis was discovered. The digging was done quickly as the developers needed to move in. But now that weeds grow on the slag-piles of earth, archaeologists have made a good case to the authorities; there is so much more to discover, the site is safe for another half-decade. As well as the remains from the mass grave, those bodies and burial pots that have already been excavated nearby await further analysis, many stored in soft tissue paper in laboratories in America and Athens.[9]

The *Demosion Sema* was Athens' public burial ground. Extending for an entire mile from the Kerameikos towards Eleusis, this was the resting place for great Athenian men and for those who died in battle. The sixth-century law-giver Solon was (allegedly) buried here, so too tyrant slayers and philosophers. All lie in unmarked graves and, although large bone fragments do remain, it is hard to identify individuals from the burial sites because many of the skeletons have been cremated, burned at temperatures of up to 800 degrees Celsius. Under normal circumstances the Athenians would take more care, but at the time of the plague these too became more akin to mass graves.

In the presence of these grim, ashen human remains it is easy to envisage a gruesome calamity. Athenians were suddenly falling, not just in war, or from old age, but thanks to Spartan-enforced hunger and now too this groping pestilence. Yet still in the fifth century the Athenians tried to generate some beauty as men and women died. In the National Archaeological Museum there is a midden of funerary jars, beautiful, mournful things, expensively decorated, white-based domestic scenes picked out in soft-wash tints. Women say farewell to soldiers, they cradle babies, stroke pets. Children play in courtyards and young men shake hands. It is impossible to look at these vases and not be moved by the fine, fluid brush-strokes – those squirrel hairs and carefully mixed pigments capturing the fear and exquisite sweetness of still being alive.

What a paradoxical time this was for Athena's city.

Back in Athens, Socrates would have seen the aggression around him. He would have noticed the telltale clouds of smoke where Spartan forces – just half a mile away – were burning yet another grove of olive trees, yet another line of figs: 500, 700, some even 2,000 years old, these trees had witnessed the whole of Greek history. Planted before men had started to write and to understand the stars, they were now being turned to charcoal by Spartan spite.

This destruction burned deep into the psyche of the Athenians; listen to the street-talk, threats *'to turn cropland into sheepwalk'*.[10] On the stage, one of Aristophanes' characters cites those burning fields as the reason he despises the Spartans with such punitive fervour:

DICAEOPOLIS: I am ready to address the Athenians about the city while making comedy. For even comedy knows about what's right . . . I myself hate the Spartans vehemently; and may Poseidon, the god at Tainarum, send an earthquake and shake all their houses down on them; for I too have had vines cut down.[11]

We can imagine other degenerations that never made it into the record. The over-sweet smell of crops rotting outside the city walls. The stink of human excreta everywhere. Statues of deities and divinities in this period were washed and clothed, pampered as though they were much-loved flesh and blood. Not now; the garments of the city statues were sun-faded, dirty, bird-shat. The plagued Athenians were neglecting their gods, and their gods were forgetting them.

'Sleek' Athens – the city that, like Socrates, hated to be still – was now not just contained, it was mutilated.

Even so, Athens just about held itself together. As the enigmatic Hellenic sage from Ephesus, Heraclitus, had said right at the beginning of the fifth century, warfare and strife can be curiously stimulating. The following years were in fact some of the most productive for Socrates and the other creative and intellectual sparks of the day. Although the sheer number of those funerary vases tells of mass deaths, their very manufacture reminds us that men in Athens were still working, still creating world-class ornaments, still talking, still loving the beauty of the world. The Agora was still a thrilling home-from-home for Socrates. And at dawn, the birds familiar to Athenian ears – swifts, swallows, crag martins – still piped and sang.[12]

ACT FOUR

NEW GODS, NEW POSSIBILITIES: SOCRATES IN MIDDLE AGE

23

SILVER OWLS AND
A WISE OWL

@@@@@@@@@@@

The Agora, central Athens,
483–411 BC

Little Laureotic [silver] Owls
Shall always be flocking in
You shall find them all about you,
As the dainty brood increases,
Building nests within your purses
Hatching tiny silver pieces.

Aristophanes, *Birds*, 1106–8[1]

THE AGORA: A BUZZING HUB. THE heart, spine, liver, spleen and lungs of Athens; the engine – some would argue – of democracy, liberty, freedom of speech and the 'Greek Miracle'. The Agora derives from the Greek for 'to gather together for trade or politics' and gives its name to the word *agoreuein*, 'speak in public'. It is nominated as a place to converse, to debate, to exchange ideas – the market gave traction to the democracy, and words fuelled it. Possibilities unimaginable a generation before were made flesh here.

Travelling along the Agora's central axis, the 'Sacred Way', from north-east to south-west, Socrates, returning from his campaigns in the north, would have passed through a melange of scents. Fish, carrion and sesame stalls. Wool, friction-hot off the loom. The corpses of birds laid out on musky, wet clay tables. Sleeveless tunics sold alongside hopeless slaves.[2]

Five hundred years before Socrates' day, in 'Dark Age' Greece, the Agora had been a graveyard: excavators still turn up the skulls and bones of 3,000-year-dead early Athenians, 20 feet or so below the surface.[3] But come the fifth century, the Agora had been rejuvenated. Political innovation and a degree of military success had given the Athenians enormous self-confidence. Fountains had been tapped, plane trees were planted. Offerings were made to the immortals on fragrant altars. Pyramids of figs, opiates, spices, aromatic oils from the East and saffron from the Cyclades were for sale. The zest of newly excavated minerals, newly minted silver coins, was in the air, the taste of unusually seasoned stews, cooked on outdoor stoves, on the tongue.

Socrates knew the Agora as the home not of the dead, but of life. Musical recitals were held here, soldiers drilled, books sold, dramas performed, sculptures shaped and smoothed. Speech-writers sat at tables to scratch out words on papyrus and tree-bark so that less articulate men could defend themselves, or prosecute others in the law-courts. And administrators, chosen by lot, met to standardise the business of democratic living. Roses were boiled down for perfume, bones for glue. Around Hephaestus' Temple[4] were more carbon-stinking foundries, mass-producing arrowheads, spear tips and even lead slingshots blazoning the slogan 'Take that'. In one zone, where the choral and dance displays were practised vigorously, un-ignorably, we hear from Socrates that, at a (high) price, you could purchase pamphlets peddling the very latest doctrines and ideas.[5] In the Agora, everything was for sale. Athenian silver kept the market chiming with commerce and with ideas.

Silver Owls

◎◎◎◎◎◎◎◎◎◎◎◎

The spoil of the latest Agora excavations is still being treated backstage at the Agora Museum in Athens. Here a young archaeologist lovingly eases apart a fused hoard of 400 tetradrachms – the silver coinage produced by the Athenian state and known as its 'Silver Owls'.[6] The coins had been buried together in a time of crisis, either during the Persian invasion or the Peloponnesian Wars. But their safekeeping devalued them – these silver pieces, squirrelled away out of the sight of enemies, have been warped and buckled in vicious fires. The stash is worth at least £250,000 in today's money: their loss would have been felt keenly by their owners. Stamped with the distinctive wide-staring, wise owl of Athena or with the goddess' own head – helmeted, ready, as ever, for conflict – the coins have suffered so much heat that their surfaces have been almost wiped clean. But the single foreign coins dropped by chance throughout the Agora have fared better. Here there is well-preserved evidence that Socrates' fellow Athenians did not just barter; there was a thriving cash economy driven by Athens that stretched right across the eastern Mediterranean. Unlike secretive Sparta, Athens positively encouraged external influence – and external cash – within her walls. Each city in the classical period minted its own distinctive coinage. Metal discs (gold, silver, bronze, some decorated with turtles and dolphins, others with griffins and ducks, or beautiful Helen and her twin brothers, the Dioscuri – from Corinth, Persia, Aigina, Macedonia), all were weighed and exchanged in Socrates' regular stamping ground, the Agora.[7]

And the people of Athens, in fits and spurts throughout Socrates' lifetime, were getting visibly richer. Although the democracy did not encourage conspicuous consumption, the archaeology tells us that life was looking up. The paint on pots is laid on more thickly, the gold of earrings dangles heavier, wine comes from ever further-flung locations. Yet Socrates goes against the grain; as the years go by, he becomes even more theatrically shabby.

I loathe that poverty-stricken windbag Socrates who contemplates everything in the world but does not know where his next meal is coming from.[8]

Socrates bothered Athens because, in this money-loving state, he was demonstrably unmaterialistic. From the Bronze Age onwards the silver mines of Laurion in the southern corner of Attic territory had given the *polis* something special. Come the fifth century and activity in the mine had increased tenfold. Every day 20,000 slaves were sent 4 miles into the dark earth to gouge out silver-bearing lead ore. The glittering harvest was driven along dirt-tracks back to the Mother City. By the middle of the fifth century Athens could boast a cash reserve of 6,000 talents.[9] This is the equivalent of more than £45,200,000 or $64,200,000 in today's money. Yet in this markedly material world Socrates preached a form of fundamentalism – a return to absolute values rather than the pursuit of self-advancement at any price. He typically wore no shoes and thin clothes. All year round he sported the same, worn woollen cloak. Contemporaries roared with laugher at his parlous sartorial state:

That dog Socrates. How dare he preach when he only has one coat to boast of, come rain or shine![10]

Unlike the other sophists of the age who were coining it in with their public philosophising, Socrates refused to amass wealth. And, worst of all, when he debated and conversed in the public spaces of the city, he suggested to young Athenian men, the flowers of Athens, that their future might lie not in imperialist ambitions and rows of fine colonnades, but in a more satisfying life – a life that revolved around the good, rather than the great.

Socrates didn't come to buy and sell in the crowded marketplace. When he walked past the merchants' tables, set up and down each day,[11] he just talked, he came to trade ideas. The philosopher must have been every seller's nightmare. In his ragged cloak – we're told – he mocked those who sought out gewgaws for themselves. *'How many things I don't need!'*[12] he says as he marches along, striding on bare feet through the irrelevant market stalls. Socrates is not blind to beauty, to craftsmanship, to epicurean pleasures, he is certainly no killjoy, but he wants to start back at the beginning; his intention is to trade the material of the human mind.[13]

But Socrates himself was clearly the opposite of this type of person – he was a man of the people, and a lover of mankind. For he took in many enthusiastic followers, both citizens and foreigners, and never charged anyone any fee for his companionship, but rather gave of his goods unstintingly to everybody. Some of them received small portions from him as a gift, sold them to others for much money, and were not men of the people as he was; for they refused to speak with those who could not give them money.[14]

Socrates' ambition is to find the *psyche*, humanity's soul, its spirit. If the Agora is a blast-furnace for civilisation, then Socrates believes there must be bellows at work, pumping a life-breath into all these flames. As he strides through the marketplace, through conversation with those around him, he tries to wrestle the answer to the ground:

Then the wise or temperate man, and he only, will know himself, and be able to examine what he knows or does not know, and to see what others know and think that they know and do really know; and what they do not know, and fancy that they know, when they do not. No other person will be able to do this. And this is wisdom and temperance and self-knowledge – for a man to know what he knows, and what he does not know. That is your meaning?

Yes, he said.[15]

It is an invigorating, a terrifying search.

While Socrates' contemporary Protagoras declares at this time, *'Man is the measure of all things'*, the exciting, the difficult, the inconvenient truth of Socrates' philosophy is its plangent suggestion that 'man's relationship with man' and 'man's relationship with the world around him' is the measure of all things. In addition his opinion seems to be that this relationship can never work unless each of us is as 'individually good' as we can be. The philosopher, in amongst the traders and tanners and soldiers and sailors who thronged the Agora, explores the unique capacity of man to be conscious of things, and to be conscious of being conscious of things. He does it as a real man, in a real historical place, in real terms. The Roman statesman Cicero makes a perceptive comment about Socrates' ideas:

He applied it [philosophy] to ordinary life, directing his enquiries to virtues and vices, and in general to the study of good and evil.[16]

But there were others in the Agora at this time who saw in the trading of words a less high-minded opportunity. These were the sophists. Rather than simply view philosophical exploration as a route to enlightenment, some also exploited words as a means of personal enrichment. Socrates was (Plato vehemently declared) not a sophist, but because his business was words and the ideas behind them, he came to be tarred by his contemporaries and by history with the brush of sophistry.

24

HOT AIR IN THE AGORA

@@@@@@@@@@@@

Sophistry, 426–416 BC

SOCRATES: Stop trembling. You should look away from some of your thoughts; and, having dismissed them, depart for a while. Then, go back to your brain; set it in motion again and weigh the issue.

Socrates in Aristophanes, *Clouds*, 807–10[1]

IN THESE SCABROUS, TAINTED DAYS, WHEN life continued, but the Spartans breathed down the Athenians' necks, Athens remembered an old, new friend. Words had been the fairy godmother of the democracy;

word-ideas; *demos-kratia* (people-power), *eleutheria* (liberty), *parrhesia* (freedom of speech) had been chiselled into architecture and broadcast on ocean currents around the Mediterranean; words had promoted the aspirations of democrats in assemblies and law-courts, and then made public the decisions that a democratic assembly chose to take. By the mid-fourth century, Athens was described as a '*City of Words*'.[2] Rhetors ruled, and words on the streets of Socrates' city seemed to give comfort, to suggest that the Athenian democracy was still a logical, a solid thing.

ᘒᘒᘒᘒᘒ

Walking through the bleached bones of ancient sites, it is easy to forget how hectic they once were. Not just with smells and colours, but in the case of Athens, with a massive barrage of information. Stone *stele* blocks, the length of roadways, at crossroads, outside sanctuaries, like stained teeth jutting from the ground, were laced with ideas. As stonemasons gouged out the hopes and fears and codes of society, granite, marble and limestone sparks would have flown. The public spaces bristled with urgent, talkative *stelai* like newly filled graveyards.[3]

Here the workings of the world's first democracy were inscribed. Two jigsaw-puzzle pieces of marble, each half a foot square, discovered near the Agora and dating from *c.*500 BC, have just been reunited in the National Epigraphical Museum in Athens. Although the remains are very battered, the precise wording is just about visible. The fragment '*DE*' has been joined with '*MOS*' to give us the earliest extant hard evidence of *DEMOS*, 'the people', as an active political body.[4]

Democratric Athens strove for transparency. Decisions from the sublime to the ridiculous were published on *stele* noticeboards. Chipped out of stone and then emphasised with red paint, these could deal with issues as lofty as the state of public finances (newly restored inscriptions have just been installed in the new Acropolis Museum, covered in carefully calculated lines, these aimed to prevent backhanders, political sweeteners, and to name and shame those suspected of sequestering public funds).[5] Elsewhere the correct pricing for offal for sale to citizens and foreigners has been immortalised. In the Piraeus Museum a 3-foot-high block declares that the market inspectors have passed the quality of tripe on a particular stall down by the harbour; the feet, head, brains, womb, breast, liver and lungs of pork and goat-meat have all been diligently listed: the stone inventory then was matter-of-factly, democratically put on public display.[6]

Athens' word-fetish was unusual. In a democracy ideas have to be shared, outcomes agreed, and that consensus then made public. A dictatorship has little need for written confirmation, no taste for the brouhaha of village squares. And whereas earlier cultures – the Hittites, for example, the super-power of the Bronze Age who controlled much of modern-day Turkey, Palestine, the southern Black Sea shore and northern Iraq – wrote every-thing down on tablets so numerous they were stored in a central temple-archive the size of four football pitches, and in Lower Egypt Ramesses II built his power into the very cliff-face at Abu Simbel, in Athens the decisions of the democracy were declared, but in order to communi-cate the will of the *demos*, not simply as a means of control.

The walls of Athenian houses and public buildings would also be daubed with painted letters, white and red.[7] Scraps of papyri notices rolled off hawkers' stalls. Books were coming to be objects of desire. A *biblion* (a papyrus sheet, typically the length of an armspan and coiled around a central dowl, the *omphalos*) was designed to be portable and user-friendly. Some of these books were small enough for the ancients to fold them up in their fists, or tuck them into their clothes. When Socrates bumps into one colleague, Phaedrus, the Athenian has a suspicious bulge in his tunic – as it turns out, a book.[8] Twenty years later, we hear of bundles of papyrus rolls stacked up on book stalls and in the Agora's warehouses.[9] In the *Metroon*, a stocky public library, scores of scribes bent over papyrus sheets and wax tablets, day in, day out, recording the 'office' copies of democratic business. Here too the 'personal effects' of Athenians – letters, contracts, writs – were stored. Because of systematic military activity in the Agora area, not to mention a climate that rots papyrus within a matter of weeks, this fund of knowledge is no longer available to us. The majority of the rich papyri of Athens represent portable history that, sadly, will never make the journey down time, although one recent discovery in an Oxford University collec-tion of Egyptian papyri from the Greek-run town of Oxyrhynchus can go some way to help us to visualise Athens as a city of words: a place where notices were pinned to public buildings, to walkways and outside private homes.[10]

The water-table in Egypt is lower than it is elsewhere in the eastern Mediterranean, and as a result much organic material has survived in the sands there – evidence lost everywhere else in the world. So if we want to get an impression of the written landscape of Athens, oddly it is to evidence from Egypt that we must turn. This particular piece of papyrus in the Oxford collection, just under a foot long, half a foot wide, has emerged from a dig in the necropolis city of Saqqara, which once served ancient

Memphis. The papyrus rectangle is a notice – one that was pinned up on the tent of Alexander the Great's chief commanding officer and then discarded once its message no longer applied. The neatly, swiftly made, confident ink characters in perfect Ancient Greek read:

ROYAL ORDER OF THE MAIN GENERAL OF THE MACEDONIAN ARMY
BY ORDER OF PUCHESTOS
DO NOT COME IN. OUT OF BOUNDS TO SOLDIERS.
RITUAL IN PRACTICE[11]

In that royal tent in Memphis priests were clearly at work and did not want to be disturbed. Although they have not survived, Athens' streets would have been full of such messages. The Athenians set a precedent for keeping *hoi polloi* up to speed with what was going on behind closed doors. *'Keep out'*, *'Occupied'*, *'Out to lunch, back in a short time'*, *'Ritual in progress'*. All these day-to-day messages would have formed part of Socrates' Athenian landscape.

But words in Athens could also have a sinister ring. Those whom the democracy disliked found their names scratched onto broken pottery shards – *ostraka* – gathered together by officials in giant pots and then systematically counted. The unfortunate man whose name appeared most frequently on these *ostraka* was ostracised, exiled from the city for ten years. Kleisthenes had instituted the system – originally to rid the city of would-be tyrants. But quickly ostracism came to be a handy way of eliminating the unsuccessful, or unpopularly successful, individuals. The piles of scratched *ostraka* in the Agora Museum in Athens are hard evidence of lives ruined; *'Kallias'* is ostracised in *c.*450 BC, *'Hyperbolus'* in 417–15 BC and another *'Sokrates'*, *'Sokrates Anargyrasios'*, in 443 BC. Tens of thousands of these *ostraka* have been discovered – many in the same hand, suggesting that votes were sometimes rigged. Resourceful law-breakers in Athens clearly offered a service whereby they could effect block-vote ostracism.[12]

Socrates was wary of the written word. His anxiety was that it could neither account for itself nor answer back. Words were everywhere in Athena's city, but Socrates, unusually, did not set his own down on papyrus with an inky flourish. In a city filled with authors of every kind, he was anxious about the impact of writing without the accountability of face-to-face contact. *'I cannot help feeling, Phaedrus, that writing is unfortunately like painting; for the creations of the painter have the appearance of life, and yet if you ask them a question they preserve a solemn silence.'*[13]

For the first time in recorded history, words, and in particular written

words, started to count as much as deeds. Socrates lived through an information revolution. By the time of his trial, a huge swathe of Athenians
right down to the artisan class had become literate. Every excavating season
wheelbarrow-loads of written material are rescued from the levels of Classical Athens. It was in Athens in the fifth century BC that the written word
– which gives all of us so much – took flight. Athens declared its authority
not just with fine monuments, but with strings of letters.

∽∽∽∽∽

Now, from 429 BC onwards, that democratic life was not looking so rosy,
perhaps words could warm things up a little again. So the Athenians
employed wily words as protection against their pain. Words, both oral and
inscribed, became a commodity. Wordsmiths, sophists, peddled a new kind
of product in Athens' Agora. Pindar refers to 'sophistes'[14] as early as 478 BC.[15]
But these pay-by-the-hour philosophers would wait another fifty years before
they really flooded the Athenian market. It was during the Peloponnesian
War, when the purpose of life must suddenly have seemed a little less clear,
that the services of sophists, in effect travelling wisdom-merchants, apparently became indispensable.[16]

Sophists filled Athenian streets with their saleable advice on how to
write or to speak the best *lines*. These travelling educators – who typically
charged pretty steep fees for their services – claimed, no less, that being
able to talk your way out of any situation would ensure your survival. During
festivals, fine speakers would deliver grand, extended lectures for the enjoyment of the Athenian public: words as mass entertainment.[17]

Socrates loved the spoken word – but in honest, bite-sized chunks. By
all accounts the philosopher was very wary of the great sophistic exercises
where high-flying rhetoric and grand oratory could persuade men to do
almost anything.[18] As he says, mischievously, with lengthy rhetoric it is so
easy at the end to forget what the point of the whole thing was at the
beginning, quipping that in a long speech you lose your initial notion; or,
more saliently, the audience does, and so can be duped by the power of
language alone.[19] For Socrates, the Athenian democracy was best served by
dialogue, not by bombast.

When persons who are unworthy of education approach philosophy and make an alliance
with her who is a rank above them, what sort of ideas and opinions are likely to be gener-
ated? Will they not truly deserve to be called sophisms, having nothing in them genuine, or
worthy of or akin to true wisdom?[20]

But the philosopher's tastes were unfashionable. Schooled in the epic, the Athenians of this period seemed to delight in a show-stopping rhetorical tour de force. And where you have an audience, you have a commercial opportunity. Sophists travelled long miles to exploit Athens' market.[21] Gorgias of Sicily stunned Athenian audiences with his *Encomium of Helen* – a defence of the indefensible *femme fatale*. It was said that thousands came, and paid, to hear him lecture in the Agora.[22] His work was a self-fulfilling prophecy – one line in the *Encomium* declares that speech has an addictive, chemical power:

The effect of speech upon the condition of the soul is comparable to the power of drugs over the nature of bodies.[23]

Athens in the late fifth century became a land of bluff: worshipping (literally) at the shrine of the goddess of persuasion. Suddenly arguments mattered less than the amplified skill of the arguer. Every male citizen over the age of eighteen had the vote – and that citizen needed to be persuaded to vote in the right way. The Athenians wanted to hear the benefits of their city and their culture talked up. A law was passed that encouraged citizens *me mnesikakein*, 'not to remember the bad things'.[24]

But Socrates' approach was rather different. Socrates was a blot on the puff-filled, near-perfect city-state that Attic ambition was contriving to build. He encouraged men to humility rather than arrogance, to honesty rather than self-delusion. Even though the Athenians were living through one of the most debilitating wars in the history of the world, his fellow citizens endeavoured to keep their city band-box bright. There is a sense throughout these decades that the Athenian show must go on. But with all the sensitivity of a blunderbuss, Socrates discouraged his peers from fooling themselves.

Wisdom is wealth. Do we need anything more, Phaedrus? For me that prayer is enough.[25]

Wealth is the parent of luxury and indolence.[26]

Socrates' candour has been described as 'relentless'. Perhaps he suffered from the curse of the clear-sighted: to imagine that those around him would judge the world with corresponding clarity. His ideas were designed to stimulate, to provoke – and we all know how irritating, how needling that gadfly, that conscience-pricking gnat can be. Socrates appeared to challenge the great cobweb of spirituality and spirits of Olympian gods and demons that wrapped themselves around Athens and through its streets, by suggesting that it was not divine influence but men who can make mankind good. His words were doubtless threatening; the difficulty with proposing immense moral individualism is that each individual is under pressure to be immensely moral.

Bodily exercise, when compulsory, does no harm to the body; but knowledge which is acquired under compulsion obtains no hold on the mind.[27]

In the first place, are they not free; and is not the city full of freedom and frankness — a man may say and do what he likes?

'Tis said so, he replied.

And where freedom is, the individual is clearly able to order for himself his own life as he pleases?

Clearly.

Then in this kind of State there will be the greatest variety of human natures?

There will.

This, then, seems likely to be the fairest of States, being an embroidered robe which is spangled with every sort of flower. And just as women and children think a variety of colours to be of all things most charming, so there are many men to whom this State, which is spangled with the manners and characters of mankind, will appear to be the fairest of States.[28]

And there was an added issue. In a world that believed in magic, Socrates was thought to have the power of a *goēs* – a sorcerer. As he walked through the lanes, gymnasia and green spaces of Athens, crowds of the young followed him as though he were pulling them by an invisible thread. Plato tries, throughout his Dialogues, to dissociate Socrates from the kind of cheapskate street-magic that many sophist-sorcerers used to entrance their listeners. But nonetheless he allows Socrates' friends and acquaintances, through the Dialogues, to assert that Socrates' words are, somehow, spell-binding.

ALCIBIADES: . . . *If you chose to listen to Socrates' discourses you would feel them at first to be quite ridiculous; on the outside they are clothed with such absurd words and phrases — all, of course, the hide of a mocking satyr. His talk is of pack-asses, smiths, cobblers and tanners, and he seems always to be using the same terms for the same things; so that anyone inexpert and thoughtless might laugh his speeches to scorn. But when these are opened and you obtain a fresh view of them, by getting inside, first of all you will discover that they are the only speeches that have any sense in them; and secondly, that none are so divine, so rich in images of virtue, so largely — nay, so completely — intent on all things proper for the study as such as would attain both grace and worth.*[29]

For whatever reason, Socrates, throughout the 420s BC, became a big draw. Perhaps it was simply that here was an ordinary man who did not just satiate with honeyed lies, but who plumped up the soul. Socrates was not happy just to consolidate the Athenians' sense of themselves: he did not only want to talk *about* the world, he wanted to change it. All around him were forging the trappings of civilisation – but this philosopher seems to have been interested in forging the civilisation of inner lives.

SOCRATES: *If anyone, whether young or old, wishes to hear me speaking and pursuing my mission, I have never objected, nor do I converse only when I am paid and not other-wise, but I offer myself alike to rich and poor; I ask questions, and whoever wishes may answer and hear what I say.*[30]

In a sibling dialogue (to Xenophon's *Symposium*), the *Hippias Minor*, another Socratic characteristic is revealed that would have troubled the Athenians:

I go astray, up and down, and never hold the same opinion.[31]

And again in Plato's *Euthyphro*: '*In any case, I was thinking while you were talking and I put this question to myself . . .*'[32] Socrates has moved on to the next strain of thought in his head while we are all still struggling with the first – infuriating and fascinating in equal measure. The philosopher chews away at ideologies. He does not spit them out, verbally, like half-sucked acid drops. And he also proposes an unusually feminine idea for this macho society – true consensus: '*Isn't it when we disagree and aren't able to come to a sufficient answer that we become enemies to each other, whenever we do, I and you and everyone else?*'[33]

This was a land at war, decimated by plague. Athens wanted action, not theories; heroes, not nay-sayers; answers, not questions.

ᘐᘐᘐᘐ

Stellar in intellect, Socrates was also, we are told, infuriating. Unlike the sophists, who gave the audience what they wanted, Socrates wrong-footed *hoi polloi*. There is something of the Lord of Misrule about him. The apparent open-season of conversation in the Agora seems to goad the philosopher into pushing the boundaries of good taste.

The iconic superheroes of Athens – Themistocles, Pericles, Miltiades and his son Cimon – are described by Socrates as '*pastry-cooks, flatterers of the ignorant multitude.*'[34] 'Ironic' and 'irony' (derived from *eironeia* in Ancient Greek) are words first applied to Socrates. To be the first ironic man on earth was not necessarily an enviable position.[35]

. . . And he on hearing this gave a great guffaw and laughed sardonically and said, 'Ye gods! Here we have the well-known irony of Socrates, and I knew it and predicted that when it came to replying you would refuse and dissemble and do anything rather than answer any question that anyone asked you.'[36]

There are many ways to translate *eironeia*; it is a nuanced expression to describe a tricky concept. In Aristophanes' comedies it meant a downright lie, in Plato more of an intended simulation. For Aristotle, irony was a concealed superiority – the opposite of boasting. Ancient authors tussled with this new, spikily playful notion.[37] But all were clear that, while fascinating to witness, irony could wrong-foot the ordinary man. Ironic Socrates had the ability to make honest democrats look like fools. To have been closeted in a debate with Socrates must, in many ways, have been an uncomfortable experience; sitting in the Agora, or gym, or at a drinking session with friends and discovering you've been seated next to a laser-sharp barrister, an odd-looking man who elegantly slices through your woolliness and lights up your inadequacies. Socrates was a philosopher who, over dinner, made others pink and shiny with embarrassment:[38]

Thrasymachus produced an amount of sweat that was a wonder to behold, since it was summer – and then I saw what I had never seen before, Thrasymachus blushing.[39]

His enemies said that by employing irony Socrates dissembled, that he covered up his true feelings, that he mocked Athenians as he appeared to indulge them, laughing at the *demos* from behind his sturdy, hairy hands. But his friends and admirers were roused, aroused by his ironic smile, his cleverness, his just-out-of-reachness. Of all the attractions on offer in the Agora, Socrates was coming to be (particularly for the impressionable population of the young) one of the most eagerly sought out. A fact that, later, would be used against him:

So what gives one a deal of happiness is not to park next to Socrates and waffle all day long, neglecting all great culture, music and the best of the tragedian's works. It's sheer madness to waste your time with lofty, pompous, idle words, with words for idle speculation! That's the sign of a man who's lost his mind![40]

※※※※※

On the fringes of the Agora men today still cluster when it looks like there could be the chance to make a fast buck, or a rumpus is brewing. It might be a gambler or an illusionist, throwing dice, hiding ping-pong balls in tumblers, a makeshift cardboard-box gaming table quickly kicked aside when the local police cruise by. Or it might be a row, a debate that's attracted attention; a small crowd (even in the twenty-first century still mainly of men), worry-beads clacking, can cluster together so fast, setting the world to rights. Nearby students gather, buying up past-their-expiry-date spray cans from the flea-market so that they can protest on the streets. They are, in one sense, all Socrates' children. The fact that they talk about politics, and challenge one another's opinions – not to mention the status quo – is what Socrates would have wanted them to do.

SOCRATES: I am one of the few Athenians – not to say the only one – who undertakes the real political craft and practice of politics.[41]

Socrates took the democratic experience to its logical conclusion. Not just gassing in the Assembly or orchestrating himself onto committees, but walking through the streets and lanes, talking to other Ancient Greeks about their political experience. Absolutely of his time, he is also of ours. He realised that the more we learn to do in and with the world, the more we need to learn about ourselves. The more sophistication and complication there is around us, the more important it is to be sure of what is going on within us.

SOCRATES: So the command that we should know ourselves means that we should know our souls.[42]

And so for Socrates the Agora was the home of our conscious selves, of our souls.[43] Socrates believed humanity *was* society. He said he would travel to the ends of the earth just for human company. His credo was that we cannot be wise and utterly alone. The further we quest for knowledge, the more human companionship we need. Ignorance is evil, knowledge is good. If we know (or admit) what is good, we will enact it. And we do that not by shutting ourselves away from the world, but by engaging with it, by taking it on, warts and all.

◦◦◦◦◦◦

So Socrates speaks in the Agora, but he sticks out like a sore thumb.

He did not believe himself to be a sophist. He was not there to teach, not there in the market to sell wisdom; and anyway, he declared that he knew nothing – how can a man who has no knowledge cite knowledge as his stock-in-trade? Socrates argued that only God can be a sophist, only God can be truly wise. He would perhaps be happier with the title we give him – a *philo-sophos*, someone who loves, who *yearns* for wisdom. Unfortunately for Socrates, *Homo sapiens* has always been very good at rewriting history. The one man who counselled against empty, clever words was remembered as, and punished as, one of the most prominent ancient sophists of all.

This confounded Socrates, they say; this villainous misleader of youth! And then if somebody asks them, 'Why, what evil does he practise or teach?' they do not know, and cannot tell; but in order that they may not appear to be at a loss, they repeat the ready-made charges which are used against all philosophers about teaching things up in the clouds and under the earth, and having no gods, and making the worse appear the better cause; for they do not like to confess that their pretence of knowledge has been detected — which is the truth: and as they are numerous and ambitious and energetic, and are all in battle array and have persuasive tongues, they have filled your ears with their loud and inveterate calumnies.[44]

Socrates' stock-in-trade was words. Yet words would prove both his weapon and his executioner.

SOCRATES: You might think written words spoke as if they had intelligence, but if you question them, wishing to know about their sayings, they always say only one and the same thing. And every word, when it is written, is bandied about, alike among those who understand and those who have no interest in it, and it knows not to whom to speak or not to speak; when ill-treated or unjustly reviled it always needs its father to help it; for it has no power to protect or help itself.[45]

25

DEMOCRACY, LIBERTY AND FREEDOM OF SPEECH

@@@@@@@@@@@@@

Piraeus harbour and across Attica, 420 BC

Free men have free tongues.

Sophocles, Frag. 297aR

No longer will men keep a curb on their tongues; for the people are set free to utter their thoughts at will, now that the yoke of power has been broken.

Aeschylus, *Persians,* 592–4[1]

PHAEDRA: *My friends, it is this very purpose that is bringing about my death, that I may not be detected bringing shame to my husband or to the children I gave birth to but rather that they may live in glorious Athens as free men, free of speech and flourishing.*

Euripides, *Hippolytus,* 419–23[2]

AROUND 420 BC THE SMELL OF freshly cut Aleppo pine, oak and, perhaps, silver fir would have filled the boatyards of Piraeus harbour. A new vessel was being made. This was an expensive enterprise: 200 slaves were here, fifty or so skilled boat-builders. The raw materials had been sourced from Magna Graecia, Macedonia, Phoenicia, Syria. It would take at least three months to complete, the labour was intensive, but the craft's launching was eagerly anticipated. Because this boat was named *Parrhesia.*[3] The Greek *parrhesia* translates as 'freedom of speech'.

The wood was not sawn, but split and adzed. The peg-holes were slightly

177

misaligned so that driving in the connectors neatly pulled the planks together; much of the wood used had a natural curve, a genetic twist that gave the belly of the boat great strength. The floating skin was built up element by element, oak ribs inserted as the planking progressed, all nailed down with bronze or copper nails.[4] Each boat was given a pair of bright-painted marble eyes and a ramming bronze snout. Contemporaries talk about these vessels intimately, as if they lived and breathed. When divers today find these marble eyes on the sea-bed, they describe the uncanny feeling that they are being watched.

Constructed on the open ground between the shipyards of Kantharos and Zea, the building blocks of Athens' navy were then stored in the stone ship-sheds at Zea – themselves inspiring architectural enterprises. These triremes were not mere boats, they were the very vessels of democracy itself. Warships like these had defeated Eastern tyranny, they had carried Athenian soldiers right across the Aegean to claim new lands in the name of *demoskratia*. The choice of names for each craft was given much careful consideration. The fact that in Socrates' lifetime one new boat was named *Parrhesia* should not be underestimated.

Freedom of expression was the great innovation of the new democracy. The fact was, all citizens could now not just speak in the Assembly, but vote in it too – and more than that, ordinary men could dictate and nuance which issues were voted upon. Assemblies of men had been important in Homer's *Iliad*.

. . . Agamemnon sent the criers round to call the people in assembly; so they called them and the people gathered thereon.[5]

. . . but here men stood or sat and nodded or murmured at the outpourings of the great and the good. Witness the Homeric fantasy art almost certainly imitating pre-classical life in a scene on Achilles' god-forged shield:

Meanwhile the people were gathered in assembly, for there was a quarrel, and two men were wrangling about the blood-money for a man who had been killed, the one saying before the people that he had paid damages in full, and the other that he had not been paid. Each was trying to make his own case good, and the people took sides, each man backing the side that he had taken; but the heralds kept them back, and the elders sat on their seats of stone in a solemn circle, holding the staves which the heralds had put into their hands. Then they rose and each in his turn gave judgement, and there were two talents laid down, to be given to him whose judgement should be deemed the fairest.[6]

The nuance of *parrhesia*, freedom of speech, is that Athenians did not simply have equality of speaking abilities (*isegoria*), but could speak their minds, they could openly criticise the regime. The Greek is perhaps better translated as 'the ability to speak frankly' – it is a peculiarly Athenian attribute, and is lionised by Athenian authors. Its counterbalance was *diabolē* – slander. Diogenes the Cynic, a successor of Socrates', declared that *parrhesia* was the most beautiful of all things in humanity.[7]

Socrates too chewed over the subject. For him, freedom of speech was the mark of a citizen, a privilege not available to foreigners.[8] It was a privilege he enthusiastically employed. Socrates seems to have been most active in Athens from his forties onwards, and during this time, both publicly in the streets and privately in the homes of the well-to-do, he explored the relationship between man and his soul. He did this, it seems from the evidence that has survived, without any interference from civic or religious authorities. The city might be entrenched in a bloody war, but it still honoured its assumed role as an intellectual playground for natives and exotic guests. Athens still had principles. She still vaunted liberty. Between 460 and 416 BC she was still remarkably tolerant. One of her dearest-held tenets was that free democrats should, where possible, enjoy freedom of expression.

But not everyone welcomed this phenomenon unreservedly; as the years went by people started to speak freely not just in the Assembly, but in the Agora, the gymnasia, the temples, their own homes. The ideological flame of *parrhesia* was fanned by Athens' jumbled street layout: in the narrow walkways, from unshuttered windows and through the open courtyards and squares of Athena's city free-talk sparked. This was fine in theory, but in a tight-knit community freedom of speech can quickly degenerate into gossip and then to slander. And slander was against the law.

Athens was one of the first polities to allow freedom of speech – and immediately it had to deal with the conundrum of who had freedom to offend.

'*Who wishes to speak?*'[9] calls the steward in the Assembly during one of Aristophanes' most popular comedies. Yet his is not a celebration of *parrhesia*, but a parody. In another of Aristophanes' dramas, *women* are being encouraged to speak out when they have taken over the city. The playwright is making a cutting point: in this upside-down world of the democracy, any awful creature can have a voice.

The phrase 'freedom of speech' is so caught up in our own twenty-first-century heads with a notion of rights that we can lose the meaning of the word in Socrates' day. Here it was something more like 'saying everything', sharing. In the Athenian Assembly the order of the day was: make sacrifice; enact religious ritual; offer the chance to speak frankly – in that order.

When the sacrificial victim has been carried round, and the herald has uttered the ancestral prayers, once the purification is complete, he commands the presiding officers to take the initial votes on matters to do with religious affairs, he deals with heralds and embassies, and then with secular matters; after that the herald asks, 'Who wishes to speak of those above fifty years of age?' When they have all spoken, he then invites anyone who is entitled to and who wishes to speak for the rest of the Athenians to speak up.[10]

Socrates in the *Protagoras* describes the scene in detail: '*carpenter, bronze worker, shoemaker, merchant, shop-owner, rich, poor, noble, lowly born*' can all stand up and deliberate on the governance of the city.[11] But only within limits, only if they speak respectfully, with *aidos* – the Greek word means a sense of shame, a 'knowing-your-placeness'. In one Greek text, Zeus thunders, 'He without *aidos* is a disease to the city.'[12]

But Socrates dares to take Zeus on. He brings to the city a new kind of discomfiting free-talk. In the *Protagoras*, Socrates seems to be generating a system of free speech – 'dialogue' – which is not controlled by 'shame' and convention, but by a pattern; by strict Q and A. The Greeks were anxious that 'free' (as in 'footloose and fancy-free') words would break down society. Socrates, employing his Socratic method (*elenchus* in Greek – 'question and answer', 'logical debate', 'investigation'), develops a system to contain free words: he is ahead of his time.[13] Yet the proof of the value of free speech is in the eating, and Socrates' Athens was still a giant *krater*, a mixing bowl into which all kinds of ingredients were being thrown. The Athenians were not sure that they enjoyed this novel taste, they were not entirely convinced that the confection they had created was good.

In Athens *parrhesia* was truly, and worryingly, a new way of doing things. Aristotle's estimation of what a democracy was – '*whatever seems best to the many, what the majority decides is what is final and this constitutes justice*' . . . '*to live as one wishes*' [14] – could be interpreted in two ways: either this was extreme civil liberty, or it was a political madness that heralded anarchy. Socrates sits firmly in the eye of that particular storm.

<hr />

The most intense flurry of discussions about *parrhesia*, this peculiar attribute of Athens, began, as so much did, with reference to the defeat of the Persians in 480/79 BC. The Athens that Socrates grew up in was decorated with the fifth-century equivalent of billboards, bronze and stone declarations. These proud street signs declared that the West was now *free* from Persian tyranny. That Greek men were, at last, *free* to express themselves as true Greeks, not as quavering subjects of a Persian tyrant. Similar sentiments were projected in the most powerful of Greek dramas:

From East to West the Asian race
No more will own our Persian sway,
Nor on the king's compulsion pay
Tribute, nor bow to earth their face . . .

Now fear no more shall bridle speech;
Uncurbed, the common tongue shall prate
Of freedom; for the yoke of state
Lies broken on the bloody beach.[15]

Also during Socrates' lifetime, in the salty landscape of Athens harbour, in 425 BC,[16] another boat had been built. It too needed to be strong because it carried yet another heavy burden; the name of this vessel was *Eleutheria* – Liberty.

෧෬ඏ෮෯

To get to Socrates' courtroom, many jurors would have passed through an attractive walkway called the *Stoa Zeus Eleutherios*. Here an emotional concept was writ large. We are used to statues of Liberty; but the Athenians got there first, they built Liberty colonnades. The Stoa of *Zeus Eleutherios* – Zeus of Freedom, Zeus the Liberator – was created in thanks for the victory at Salamis against the Persians.[17] Sauntering through, shaded from the sun, good Athenian citizens were at liberty not to be slaves; not to be ruled by a despot. There are other dedicated sites at Marathon and Rhamnous, where Athenians gave thanks for their delivery from Persian might. This was a society that honoured freedom in a *palpable* way.

But – crowd-pleaser as it is – Socrates does not concern himself with liberty. Instead he focuses his energies on identifying virtue. He argues that only the pursuit of a virtuous life brings exquisite happiness. Total liberty is a chimera; happiness accepts, even delights in the certainty of compromise. Plato's Socrates goes further, he suggests that tyranny is spawned by the liberty of all in the *demos*. Here he is the first to suggest that liberty is an illusion fostered by the great to keep the many happy.

Come then, tell me, dear friend, how tyranny arises. That it is an outgrowth of democracy is fairly plain.[18]

This was a man born into the most fervently patriotic of 'liberty' moments. In defeating the Persians, the Athenians had committed to freedom to a quite lunatic degree. They had shaken off the yoke of the greatest superpower of the day. They had declared that Greeks shall never be slaves to the East. They had chanced their wit and belief in self-determination against despotism and brawn. Wondrously the gamble had paid off. To do so they had to work themselves into a fever-pitch of self-belief. When one man suggested accepting Persian terms of peace soon after the Battle of Salamis, he and then his wife and children were mobbed and stoned to death.[19] But there is one thing that Socrates does that is very troubling to the Athenians. Nowhere does he challenge the need for liberty itself – yet, rather than vaunt the liberty of the city, he champions an inner, spiritual liberty.

Such is the good and true City or State, and 'the good' and man is of the same pattern; and if this is right every other is wrong; and the evil is one which affects not only the ordering of the State, but also the regulation of the individual soul.[20]

Then when any one of the citizens experiences any good or evil, the whole State will make his case their own, and will either rejoice or sorrow with him?

Yes, he said, that is what will happen in a well-ordered State.[21]

In these collective times individual liberty, rather than the liberty of the city-state, was both a novel and an awkward concept for fifth-century Athenians. And they were uncomfortable with Socrates' unconventional views for a very precise reason.

In democratic Athens, at least one in three, possibly one in two, of the population were of slave status. These creatures were hardly classified as human – some described them as 'living tools', for others they were simply the 'man-footed thing'. Athena's city was particularly reliant on foreign slaves because the law-giver Solon had passed a decree that no Athenian would be forced to work for another. Owning slaves, rather than being owned, was a hallmark of the free Athenian. So slaves gave Athenians an unusually robust sense of their own peculiarly elevated standing. Fetching your water, cooking your food, polishing your jewellery, writing your letters, mopping your brow, stitching your wounds, praising your poetry – in a thousand ways every day the slave system reinforced the fact that the 'free Athenian' was someone a bit special. Work by archaeologists to the south-east of Athens at Laurion between 1998 and 2008 tells us that this situation was not accepted with total equanimity.

The Laurion district (particularly around what is now called Thorikos) is an odd, listless place. Today the striped towers of a nationalised electricity company, DEH, loom over the bay. Gleaming white boulders and iron-red earth combine to give the landscape a planetary feel. The caves are colourful with minerals. Up until 1923 silver was extracted from the seams here; lead, manganese and cadmium are still harvested.

Up in the hills today there survive forgotten spoil heaps from Athens' classical mines — those that were grim with industry when Socrates was alive. Venture too far down clefts in the rock and you'll find yourself in an abandoned mine-shaft. The landscape today is deserted; scrabbling through the pines here you can be alone for days on end, but in the fifth century this region would have teemed with slaves and their masters. At night these 'human machines' went back to guarded village-camps. The slave population was, in effect, sterilised, for men and women were not allowed to breed and were billeted separately. A rising, broken, square stone structure overlooking one of the slave camps is identified by some archaeologists as a watch tower — little surprise. This was a manufactured human settlement with the potential to be more than a touch restless.

But it was vital that the humans here be kept liberty-less, because it was the muscle and sweat of these men and women that kept commerce chiming back in Athena's city. Socrates' suggestion that all men, whatever their background, might possess an equal capacity for personal liberty was extremely inconvenient. It was Athens' slave population that produced for Athenians the coin to spend in the Agora, and their broken lives that gave free citizens, and men such as Socrates, the time to talk, and to freely express themselves there.

అ అ అ అ అ

As well as the new ideals of democratic life, which were being made flesh down in the boatyards at Piraeus, in the form of the boats *Parrhesia* and *Eleutheria*, new democratic religious rituals were also being initiated here. Athens was demonstrably proving that she was big enough to tolerate new forms of religious expression. And Socrates, we are told, was an eye-witness to their spectacular, sacred inauguration.

26

THE GOOD LIFE –
AFTER DARK

@@@@@@@@@@@@

Piraeus harbour,
432–428 BC

'Do you mean to say,' interposed Adeimantus, 'that you haven't heard that there is to be a torchlight race this evening on horseback in honour of the goddess?'

'On horseback?' said I [Socrates]. 'That is a new idea. Will they carry torches and pass them along to one another as they race with the horses, or how do you mean?'

'That's about it,' said Polemarchus, 'and, besides, there is to be a night festival which will be worth seeing. For after dinner we will get up and go out and see the sights and meet a lot of the lads there and have a good talk . . .'

Plato, *Republic*, 327c–328a[1]

TORCHLIGHT ON THE SEA'S SURFACE IS magical. Pockets of flame dance from one ripple-crest to another, linked by a spider-line of fire. And around 2,440-odd years ago just such a spectacle was laid on in the Piraeus district in honour of a newcomer to the city. Worshipping a new goddess – the barbarian Bendis – sometime around 429/428 BC, many Athenians, Socrates apparently amongst them, came down to watch the premiere of this black-and-gold light show. A new festival for Bendis was being inaugurated by Athenian citizens down in the harbour-town of Piraeus.[2] This was a significant intro-duction to the neighbourhood – the *demos* must have authorised payment for a swell welcoming party. There were horseback torch relay-races to honour the interloper divinity, a visitor from the wilds of Thrace. As Plato's colloquial account shows, this was an attraction worth leaving the dinner-table for.

Greece has a long history of worshipping gods from the East. Zeus himself first appeared as a small bronze from Sumeria (made in the third millennium BC) before there was any mention of him in records west of the Bosporus. Dionysos too danced, swung and lurched his way over from Central Asia at just about the moment that written records in what we now call Greece began. But in the fifth century BC, a full thousand years later, in Socrates' day, the community of gods on Mount Olympus was a little more settled. There was, indeed, an Olympian establishment. The arrival of a new divinity, relatively infrequent, never failed to cause a stir. Bendis was a newcomer whom the Athenians wanted to make particularly welcome. Her worship had been accepted by democratic vote in the Assembly. Not only would she protect and nourish the sizeable population of Thracian immigrants who worked in Piraeus, but she might bring onside the warring tribes of Thrace themselves – fierce soldiers whom Athens did not want to find buttressing a Spartan army.

The night festival must have been thrilling. Greek torches were half-human size: made of pine or cedar, their scent was pungent, the flames burned bright and long. Bendis was a huntress like Artemis; she prized speed, and a keen sense of competition. So down in this humming harbour-town, with its mongrel population and a 'where-there's-muck-there's-brass' mentality, an edgy carnival was promised. No one knew what to expect. Women priestesses had been chosen to administer the cult, and citizens and aliens alike played an official ritual role.[3]

Much was made by Socrates' biographers of the fact that Socrates did not travel around the Mediterranean as his sophist contemporaries did, sightseeing, lecturing. But he had little need to travel out of Athens; the world came to him. Bendis' acceptance was as much to do with political survival as it was with spiritual enlightenment. The Athenians knew, with war-cries all around, that the goodwill of the wild men of Thrace was more than useful.[4] There were many immigrants in the Piraeus district, a sizeable community of Thracians amongst them; and now they had a charismatic, ritual crowd-puller to call their own; a sense of belonging. Simple marks in stone, a decree, tell us that the goddess' heady celebrations ran all night.

Night and day, before, during and after the Peloponnesian War, there is no doubt that Socrates revelled in the many and various Athenian festivals – and valued them. These events were vital: a way that stakeholders got together, on the streets, and enjoyed what it meant to be a community. Socrates, quite rightly, opines that that these aren't just blind traditions, entrenched ways of being that stumble along in the train of orthodoxy, but feel-good experiences. Reasons to live. Their predictable presence is part of what constitutes the good life.

Festivals, singing, shared celebrations of all kinds — these are initiated by Eros, and they give life itself a sweetness and a sense.[5]

Perhaps because Socrates was accused of impiety, Plato, writing with hindsight, emphasises the number of times the philosopher throws himself into the worship of Athens' various gods. The fact that Plato cites Bendis might well be a pointed reminder (given the accusations against Socrates during his trial) that Athens, and not just Socrates, was open-minded enough to embrace new divinities. The philosopher's dying words, according to Plato, remember another divine hero new to the city, the healer Asclepius. Even if the mention of Bendis is all a ploy on the part of Plato, there is no reason whatsoever to believe that Socrates disrespected the city's traditional gods — whether they were newcomers or established cohabitants of Athena's city.[6]

❧❧❧❧❧

Socrates, war-blasted, would have seen during the Peloponnesian War what happened when the religious idols of a city were burned. When the patchwork of materials that made up the earthly incarnation of a god or a goddess — the wood, the marble, the paint, the chryselephantine ivory, the rock-crystal eyes, the gold hair filaments — melted, twisted, buckled, warped and blackened in the flames. Greek religion was patched and glued together like the images of its living gods. There were many thousands of ways to worship the lustful, greedy, fickle god-tribe. Although conventionally pious, Socrates, it appears, searched for something more essential, something stiller and more stable. A creed is precisely what he was feeling his way towards.[7]

Is not this the reason, Euthyphro, why I am being indicted, that when people tell such stories about the gods I find it hard to accept them? Do you really believe that these things happened and that there was a war among the gods, and fearful enmities and battles and other things of the sort, such as we are told by the poets?[8]

These were incendiary thoughts. While we might think of religion as a convenient means for corralling morality, for the Greeks it was where morality — a social code — began. Odysseus' Cyclops is godless, which is why he eats men.[9] In the *Laws*, religion guarantees that the judiciousness of the citizens is the foundation and the mortar of political life. And at a time when there was only one day in the year that was *not* designated a festival,[10] to be perceived by your fellow Athenians to be doubting the gods was dangerous indeed. And yet Socrates goes one step further — according to Plato, he does not deny the gods, but he does claim something even more shocking: to be as wise as they are, to know their very minds.

27

DELPHI, THE ORACLE

@@@@@@@@@@@@@

Delphi, north of the Gulf of Corinth, c.440–420 BC

SOCRATES: And don't interrupt me with your jeering, Athenians, not even if I seem to you to be bragging. The story I'm about to tell you [about myself] isn't mine, but I refer you to a speaker you trust. About my wisdom, if it really is wisdom, and what sort of wisdom it is, I'll produce as a witness Apollo the Delphic god.

Plato, *Apology*, 20e[1]

To KNOW YOUR FUTURE IN THE FIFTH century BC you had two choices: travel by road or boat. Boat was quicker. Your destination: the sacred harbour of Kirrha.[2]

Kirrha was the tollgate, the mouth of the single most important sacred site in the whole of Greece. It was the coastal station for Delphi – and in the Greek mind, Delphi sheltered the *omphalos*, the very navel of the earth. At the beginning of time Zeus had sent two eagles flying, one to the East, one to the West, and, so the story went, where they met marked the earth's geographical and spiritual centre-point. The stories originated back to before Greek civilisation – to the very beginning of the Bronze Age, as do the archaeological remains that tell us that, come Socrates' day, Delphi had been a significant religious site for more than 2,000 years. Still visited through the Late Bronze Age, the Greek 'Dark Ages', it flourished from the Archaic period and by the fifth century BC had gained a phenomenal international reputation. It drew men from across the known world. To get to the sacred mountain and the nerve-centre of Delphi itself, you had to dock at Kirrha, and climb.

Today the beaches on this side of the Corinthian Gulf are lively with runaway towels and beach-grilled fish. In Socrates' day this shoreline was ten times busier.

Worshippers had to buy meat, new clothes, food, dedications, souvenirs while they waited for Delphi's divine pronouncements. We know the region was economically strong because it minted its own silver coins. Kirrha was in fact so profitable – all those pilgrims wanting to know their future – that it attracted unwelcome attention.

In the so-called 'Sacred Wars', back in the Archaic age (close on 120 years before Socrates' birth), *c.*595–585 BC, the population of Kirrha was intimidated by a local league of cities; this 'Amphictyonic League' was purely and simply jealous of the Kirrhans' religio-tourism economy. The League (supported by Athens, Solon reportedly deciding on the strategy himself) stationed soldiers at Kirrha's gates. Kirrha was said to have held out against its rivals for ten years, until the city's own water supply turned enemy – poisoned with hellebore by the troops outside the walls. The toxic effects – delirium, diarrhoea, muscle-cramps, asphyxia, convulsions and heart-attacks – were infamous. The plant, they said, grew at the Gates of Hades itself, but was, and still is, abundant in the region – a boat-ride away above Antikyra. The men at the local *kafenion* still recall how, as children, their mothers rubbed their gums with hellebore roots (these must have been tiny doses; hellebore is medicinal in small quantities) to alleviate toothache. These locals do not, however, tell the story of the hellebore of antiquity that was mashed into the water-pipes and wells, whose invisible alkaloids struck down first children and the old, then pregnant women, the sick and finally Kirrha's young men: biological warfare that offended the Greeks' 'rule of honour'. The poisoning of Kirrha was a blot on Hellenic memory, and elders codified that such calculating evil should never happen again. This was one of the events that gave Athenian soldiers such as Socrates the code of honour to which they were expected to adhere.

Traces of former glories in Kirrha are few and far between. There is the odd fifth-century masonry block on the beach that fishermen use to stand on, children to jump off. All that is left of the harbour is a play-ground's worth of knee-high stone stumps; the remains of docking bays – surrounded now by rabbit-chewed earth, not sea.

But in Socrates' time this spot would have been jangling. The Kirrhans might have lost their independence in the 'Sacred Wars' – Delphic priests controlled the place now – but no one could take away their strategic loca-tion. Special rules applied to those who made their pilgrimage here on the way to Delphi. Boats bringing ambassadors and the faithful were allowed to dock for the duration of their visit to the sanctuary. The *theoroi* and diplomats had semi-permanent lodgings. Offerings were made. Rituals of all ethnic hues from Asia Minor, North Africa and right across the eastern Mediterranean quickened the shore.

It must have been a convenient place to size up your rivals and allies. To gossip. To be enlightened ('Who'd have thought the Thebans made their libations in that order . . . ?') or to buttress bigotry, because the Corinthian Gulf is a salmon-flick of water that connected the prickly city-states of Greece with the wider world. This was a polyglot landing. Business deals were struck, at Kirrha and in the Delphic hills above, treaties discussed — yet the heart of the experience was, without a shadow of doubt, spiritual. At Delphi the gods opened their mouths to men.

And (so we are told) a certain Chaerephon, a friend of Socrates, came to Delphi to enquire who was the wisest of all mankind. In some versions of the story, it was Socrates himself who made the journey.

∽∽∽∽∽

Chaerephon has come down to us in history as a rather quixotic individual; agitated, emaciated, *'impetuous in everything he did'*.[3] You can perhaps imagine him, beaded with sweat, flushed, a man on a mission; taking a ride in a cart, or making the long march up through the foothills where Delphi itself was hidden, tucked into the cleft of the mountains known as 'The Shining Ones'.

He would have journeyed through a landscape of incident. Dramas such as those of Oedipus and Jocasta were thought to have been played out here.[4] Travellers to Delphi carried with them the epic stories they had first heard told around campfires and then in the newfangled tragedies written to instruct Athenian citizens of the terrible ways of the world. Delphi is not a soothing, but an imposing, an exciting place. At sunrise and sunset the ring of rock that is Mount Parnassus beckons with flesh-pink veins. But during the heat of the day the mountain stands granite-stern: a giant reflector, beating Apollo's sun rays back down onto his own sanctuary.

Delphi, its columns and treasuries, its walkways polished shiny-wet by human traffic, feels as though it is a stone site simply borrowed from the mountains; that the earth will soon reclaim its own.[5]

Before you could even consider a visit to Apollo's oracle here you had to purify yourself with holy water from the Kastalian spring. You can still scoop out the sweet silver-ice trickle, but will find yourself with few companions other than stragglers from an unusually eager tourist group, filling up a bottle for the coach journey home (perhaps in the hope that it still — as it was believed to in the fifth century — brings the muse).

And then Chaerephon would have had to push through the hordes on the Sacred Way, gawping at the material might of civilisations crammed into and onto the state treasuries that lined this thoroughfare. Finds from twentieth-century excavations — for instance, a life-size silver bull, 7½ feet long, three layers of silver sheet pasted over a wooden core — still take our breath away. During one battle amidst the 'Sacred Wars', exquisite ivory statues of Apollo and Artemis were burned.[6] Both lay buried under the Sacred Way until 1939, when they were stumbled upon by the unsuspecting excavation team and brought, blinking and black, back into the light, their gold headdresses, earrings and necklaces untarnished. Through the carnage these charcoal-dark immortals still wear their enigmatic smiles.

But in comparison with the other treasures on show at Delphi these were nothing. Who could miss the monumental highlights that became legend sooner than they became history: the colossal sphinx, atop a 40-foot-high column, dedicated by the islanders of Naxos as proof of their might in the sixth century; a giant statue of Apollo; friezes of Amazons and Trojan war heroes in red, blue and bronze against a royal-blue back-ground; the Cnidian Clubhouse (a kind of sacred embassy building), gaudy with paintings by the master artist from Thasos, Polygnotos — he who also decorated the Painted Stoa back in Athens. Croesus of Lydia, consulting the oracle before he attacked the Persians, dedicated at Delphi a solid gold lion, rampant on 117 blocks of fine, white gold.

A journey through the site today is so denuded in comparison. The lime-stone paving stones are polished smooth by human footsteps, and the views — clouds that scud through the plain below, eagles that perch on the highest peaks, twisting valleys that tempt you to imagine what life is like just out of sight — are still heart-stoppingly magnificent. But there is none of the brouhaha that would once have been here. Instead of broken walls, imagine a kaleido-scope of colours on the painted marble surfaces, the greasy smoke of sacrifice — and everywhere the butter-yellow reflection of gilt, silver, gold.

A Lydian tyrant built the first-ever treasury at Delphi. Whatever the political persuasion of the city-state as time went on, these flamboyant treasure-stores, bank-deposits in effect, maintained the same trouble-making, virile, 'look-at-me-and-tremble' feel. The Athenians dedicated their own treasury after victory over the Persians at the Battle of Marathon of 490 BC. Here many oiled and gilded muscles were being flexed.

And so Chaerephon would have made his way to the oracle dazzled by the sparkle and gleam of loot. One-tenth of military booty was expected to be dedicated at a sanctuary, and much of it came to Delphi. Hoplite shields, necklaces, thrones, sections of whole throne-rooms, crystals, spears, teams of golden horses, bangles grabbed from the suppliant arms of the vanquished, were all displayed here.

It must have been an emotional journey for every single pilgrim. Here you were surrounded by both your *polis'* great victories and its great humiliations. And although it was Athenians, the Alcmaeonid family, who had completed Apollo's brash temple (*'a marvel to see,'* says Pindar[7]) in the sixth century, Athena's people were by no means immune from public disgrace in the sanctuary. On the hill above the commemorative Stoa of the Athenians, the limestone equivalent of a two-finger salute, stood the Treasury of Brasidas and the Acanthians, built after the allied Spartan victory against the Athenians at Amphipolis (422 BC). A battle that Socrates himself would soon suffer. Each island, each city-state, each alliance that visited this sacred place wanted others to remember that power was fleeting, that the powerful would have their day.

But still, in happier times the atmosphere in Apollo's sanctuary must have been charged, expectant. All ages came and men of all degrees. The prettiest girls would trek out here to dedicate locks of hair. Heads of state bowed to ask for advice in foreign affairs – although after the oracle had given a number of wrong answers during the Persian Wars the footfall of official delegations dwindled a little. Overwhelmingly popular were personal questions. From the trembling 'Whom should I marry?' to complex character profiles; hence Chaerephon's question, 'Is Socrates the wisest man of all?'

But Socrates' friend would get his answer only if he penetrated the inner sanctum of Apollo's temple where the Pythia – the voice of the oracle – resided. So on he walked, up past the monstrous altar dedicated by the people of Chios, which, during the Pythian Games held here every five years, would have run with the blood of a hundred sacrificed bulls. Past the dripping sound of Apollo's own sacred spring, the Kassiotis, that ran into the sanctuary itself and gurgled on towards the slope that led inside.

The smell of roasting flesh must have penetrated the interior, just as it sharpened the air outside. Not only pilgrims but all priests had to make sacrifice to the god before approaching the sanctuary. Scrubbed and beautified animals, coy with garlands of flowers or ribbons, their horns gilded, would be led to the knife, concealed in a 'blameless' maiden's basket under barley-cakes. A sprinkling of water or oats ensured the animal nodded its head at the right moment – meeting the Delphic oracle's own injunction, *'That animal which willingly nods over the holy water, that one, I say you may justly sacrifice.'*[8] For tight-stomached country men the atmosphere must have smelled Elysian.

And from the holy of holies, the *adyton*, where the Pythia herself sat, other olfactory tendrils would reach out to the nostrils: the ever-burning hearth, the laurel leaves and barley scattered on the flames. And – as has only just been scientifically identified by an international team of geologists – the hallucinogenic vapours seeping out of the ground.[9] After years of scepticism, the most recent geological surveys have shown that two faults meet right under the current Temple of Apollo. Through a fracture in the limestone, hydrocarbon gases, including ethylene, may well have escaped in antiquity.

It was over these that the Pythia, an old woman dressed in a young virgin's clothes, would sit and would babble out the Oracle – ramblings turned into hexameter verse by a priest so that the Oracle could be delivered. And here at Delphi, a place that bannered itself with aphorisms – *Meden Agan*, 'Nothing in Excess'; *Gnothi Seauton*, 'Know Yourself' – and that set a moral tone for the eastern Mediterranean (advising, for example, that murder requires atonement), there came a stark retort that would quickly be spoken of across Attica and throughout the Athenian Empire. When Chaerephon asked, 'Is there any man wiser than Socrates?'

The answer came back:

'No.'

28

GNOTHI SEAUTON –
KNOW YOURSELF

@@@@@@@@@@@@

Delphi and Athens

Is there anybody wiser than Socrates?

No.

*Whatever does the god mean? Whatever is his riddle? For I know that
I am not wise, not extremely wise, not even moderately wise. So whatever does
he mean by saying that I am the wisest?*

Plato, *Apology*, 21a–b

*When one of his pupils, Chaerephon, enquired of him in front of a large crowd at
Delphi the reply came back: Apollo answered that no man was more free than I, or more
just, or more prudent. Socrates adds, Apollo did not compare me to a god. He did,
however, judge that I far excelled the rest of mankind.*

Xenophon, *Apology*, 14–16[1]

CHAEREPHON HAD TO TAKE HIS MESSAGE back to his mentor.
Unlikely that he'd have chosen an overland route – after all, there
was a war on, and the journey from Delphi in Central Greece back
250 miles south to Athens would have taken him through tracts of enemy
territory.[2] So it would be on to the shore at Kirrha, boarding a small boat
that would take the weighty news back to Athens. A time-bomb nudging
its way in through Piraeus harbour.

KNOW YOURSELF and NOTHING IN EXCESS were the maxims '*useful for the life of men'* built into the fabric of the Delphi complex. Exactly where, and when, depends on whom you believe. Pausanias describes them appearing in the forecourt of the Temple of Apollo.[3] Others tell us they were carved into the Propylaia,[4] on the temple front or on doorposts,[5] on a column or (most likely) across the temple wall.[6]

But for many Greeks, the incised homilies were as inflexible as the stone into which they were carved. For the Greeks (and remember, of course, Delphi served Greeks of all shades, and men of all ilks), this meant 'KNOW YOUR PLACE', do not get above yourself. Do not push your luck. It is, in its fifth-century context, a limiting phrase. Socrates' peers were a population that 'knew' its place, which, day in, day out, participated in rituals and invocations and athletic competitions that confirmed the status quo.

But this was not, it seems, how Socrates interpreted the maxim.

To move the world, first move yourself.

The philosopher's understanding of the command is paradoxical. It is perturbing at both its polar ends. Know that you have great limits – but do not be content to be told who you are. Know who you are inside. Know yourself through your relations with others. Understand yourself by loving those around you. Know that you know nothing.

When the democracy was feeling strong, such unsettling notions could be confidently batted about in the Agora. But times change. Athens from the 430s onwards was much more thin-skinned.

Whether it had been Chaerephon's 'impetuous' charisma, his money (Delphi was not beyond the odd bribe) or Socrates' notoriety that inspired the oracle (or history's myth-makers) to such an answer, the stark response would, almost certainly, be the beginning of the end for Socrates.[7] Delphi was believed to hold all the answers to all the questions in the world. When enemies wanted to invade Greece, they checked their battle plans with Delphi's God; when Themistocles had asked how Athens should be saved, it was to Delphi that he put the question.'[8] And cheeky Socrates wasted the great god Apollo's breath; by confirming that he was Athens' premier smart-arse he had committed hubris of the highest order.

> For in all cities the story of the citizens of Erechtheus makes the rounds,
> Apollo,
> How they made your dwelling in divine Pytho
> A marvel to see.[9]

The 'citizens of Erechtheus' were Athenians. Pytho was an early name for Delphi. Athena's city felt she had a privileged connection to the sacred site of the Delphic Oracle. It was Athenian *nous* and Athenian cash that had helped to construct Apollo's great temple there. The suggestion that Socrates should enjoy some kind of favoured position with the great glittering super-god Apollo, that he be the wisest of all Athenian democrats, of all Greeks — as wise as a god even — would have seemed, to many, to be sheer blasphemy.

29

ARISTOCRATS, DEMOCRATS AND THE REALITIES OF WAR

@@@@@@@@@@@

The Agora, *c.*426 BC

*For a sharp . . . saw . . . gobbling . . . of the whole . . . sharpening the flashing iron. And
. . . the helmets . . . are shaking their purple-dyed crests, and for the wearers of the breast-
plates the weavers are striking up the wise shuttle's songs, that wake up those who are asleep.*

And he is gluing together the chariot's rail . . .

Newly discovered fragment of Sophocles, first published 2007[1]

TWO RECENT ARCHAEOLOGICAL DISCOVERIES HELP TO flesh out the
picture of life – physical and emotional – in and around Athens'
city walls during the Peloponnesian War: a picture where Socrates
is always there, just to the fore of the crowd throughout the mid-420s BC.
They also hint at the social and political environment of the day. One is
a tiny scrap of papyrus. To see it we must leave the eastern Mediterranean
and travel back to a wet England, where the fragment is kept in a storeroom behind the Sackler Library, Oxford.

Beaumont Street in Oxford might not be the obvious place to get a
sense of the scent-rich Athenian Agora of 2,440 years ago. But at the back
of the splendid Ashmolean Museum are some particularly redolent biscuit
boxes. Ginger Nuts, Huntley & Palmer; rows of tarnished silver-grey tins.
Some boxes have not been opened since they were deposited in the vaults
in 1906. Ninety-nine per cent of the material here is still waiting to be
studied. Lying inside are the contents of an Egyptian rubbish dump – and
remnants of Socrates' life. Here are Athenian words that were recopied over

the centuries by Greek scribes based in Oxyrhynchus (the Greek translates as 'The Town of the Sharp-Nosed Fish'). With the multi-spectral technology that usually peers through gas and particles in space, we can now find traces of words describing Socrates' city. The scanner highlights the original characters – frequently invisible to the human eye – that were inked onto each page. We hear from the speech-writers who sat in the Agora selling their words; we hear from letter-composers, angry wives, angrier husbands, issuers of summonses, evidence of indictments.[2] A lost gospel excluded from our New Testament is possibly here, a version of Euripides' *Medea* where she does *not* kill her children, but I am interested in Fragment 4807.

Fragment 4807 is a new find, unread for 1,900 years, the lost section of a play by Sophocles. The shred of papyrus itself is 4 inches long and 2¾ inches tall. Now preserved in between two plates of glass, the fragment is badly damaged. The fibres of the papyrus plant itself are clearly visible, the two columns of lines split by a great gash in the text.

The lines belong to a play called the *Epigonoi* (The Progeny). They describe an ancient city preparing for war. Although the scene is set in Thebes, Sophocles was an Athenian (and a general), and there can be no doubt, since the play was composed in the late fifth century BC, that the author was drawing on his own experience of the atmosphere and activities in Athens during the ghastly attrition of the Peloponnesian War. Listen again:

For a sharp . . . saw . . . gobbling . . . of the whole . . . sharpening the flashing iron. And . . . the helmets . . . are shaking their purple-dyed crests, and for the wearers of the breast-plates the weavers are striking up the wise shuttle's songs, that wake up those who are asleep.

And he is gluing together the chariot's rail . . .[3]

The gaps in the text are where the papyrus is torn or has rotted away. With those missing millimetres of the fragment have, almost certainly for ever, gone the words that Sophocles set down, that men such as Socrates, Plato and Aristotle would have heard under a bright Mediterranean sun.

The Agora, which once produced books, gold jewellery, marble statues that were the envy of all Greece, was now focusing its energies on glue for chariots and whetstones for swords. The inhabitants of the city were kept awake not just by the possibilities of their world as they lay under the stars, but by the whine of the weaver's loom as it wove protection for men who would soon be dead.

☙☙☙☙☙

The second find from Athens' city-centre is the exquisitely carved head of a horse. The broken piece of statuary, two-thirds life-size, has recently been restored in the new Acropolis Museum. The marble horse's nostrils flare, his eyes roll and his mane is wind-ruffled. The curator in charge of his recent restorative grooming speaks animatedly of the personal character of this animal: and he is right. The carving is clearly a portrait – the immortalisation of a much-loved, much-prized individual aristocrat's warhorse.

The Athenians were fervently proud of their horse stock and horsemen. Those who sponsored winning teams at the Panhellenic games – Olympia, Corinth, Delphi, Nemea – were given free meals for life. It is a press of mounted cavalry that leads the procession around the Parthenon frieze. By the time of Socrates' trial, the central spine of the Agora was a racetrack, with water-troughs at various intervals where sweat-flecked, steam-snorting horses could quench their thirst.[4] In the 450s a census of the wealthiest 'democrats' in Athens had led to the formation of a 'democratic' cavalry. In reality these were old-style aristocrats legitimising a traditionally aristocratic pursuit. Alcibiades, who used his horses for self-aggrandisement when they won no fewer than seven Olympic chariot-races in a row, was one such. The Athenian cavalry trained in the Agora; their favourite spot was just outside the Royal Stoa, at the crossroads where busts of the god Hermes, his erect penis a symbol of fortune, spectated with blind eyes. Xenophon gives us a great sense of the dynamic spectacle of the horses and their men here at exercise:[5]

As for the processions, I think they would be most pleasing to both the gods and the spectators if they included a gala ride in the Agora. The starting point would be the Herms; and the cavalry would ride around saluting the gods at their shrines and statues . . . When the circuit is completed and the cavalcade is again near the Herms, the next thing to do, I think, is to gallop at top speed, tribe by tribe, to the Eleusinion.[6]

It is a utopian picture of blue-bloods; a demonstration of high-born refinements and the superiority and swagger of a cavalry that still marched all democratic Athenians into battle.

Put together, the finds speak of the class divisions that remained, just below the surface, in Socrates' city. Democratic Athens never ceased to be an entity that was populated by aristocrats and oligarchs, as well as democrats. The papyrus also communicates both the aspirations and the daily grind of the *demos* (being able to vote for war, and then having to fight in it), of people who have for centuries been an underclass. Socrates, whose life spanned both social sets, would find, towards the end of his three-score years and ten, that his 'double-agenting' disturbed, and then envenomed, his fellow citizens. He was slowly proving himself to be out of kilter in many ways in Athens. He held unorthodox views on the power of persuasive speech, he shunned the material wealth that empire brought, his lines of communication to the gods were suspiciously direct. Yes, he fought, but unlike his comrades, he seemed to question whether military might was the greatest goal for a man, whether battle brought good.

Then without determining as yet whether war does good or harm, thus much we may affirm, that now we have discovered war to be derived from causes which are also the causes of almost all the evils in States, private as well as public.[7]

Both discoveries — the warhorse and the papyrus fragment describing the fierce preparation for military campaigns — also remind us that throughout the second half of Socrates' life the Peloponnesian War was a cancer shadow in the back of all Athenians' minds: an awful reference point for every day.

After the plague had bludgeoned Athens there was a brief respite, a couple of years when the invasions of Attica slowed down. But aggression, inevitably perhaps, resumed. Soon those Athenians travelling from the Agora to worship on the Acropolis, or returning from council duty, or having just cast their vote in a law-court or the Assembly, turning their eyes north and west, would see new flames — not the pine torches of Eleusinian initiates or priestesses of the cult of Bendis, but something wider, darker, at a distance. These were beards of fire on the horizon: the Spartans starting to scorch the earth around them once more. The clouds above the land darkened from cream to a smoky yellow, as if their enemies were pissing into the milky sky. And then the mountains around turned a charcoal-black.

In the city Athens' citizens might have been trying to forget the war as they continued to commission plays and sculptures, as they debated with sophists and paid respects to their many gods, but the war had not forgotten them.

Foul breath – Mytilene, Corcyra and the Agora, 427 BC

᠙᠙᠙᠙᠙᠙᠙᠙᠙᠙᠙᠙

The casualties of Athens' war with Sparta were not just the foot soldiers. Pericles, the official elected as one of the ten generals every year for fifteen years, had died in *c*.429 BC. Blamed for masterminding a policy that welcomed plague into Athens, he was heavily fined and then stripped of his office. His own family – like so many in the city – had been thinned out by the disease; his sons from his first marriage were amongst the first to die. Whether it was physical or psychological damage that killed the General, we shall probably never know.

What is certain is that he represented a corporate malaise in the city-state.

Communities around the eastern Mediterranean had started to notice that Athens was faltering. The cities of Asia Minor and its offshore islands in particular, many still oligarchic, started to get restless. One such, Mytilene – the first city of the island of Lesbos – decided to chance her luck and sent envoys to Sparta and to Olympia asking for military aid, reminding her would-be Laconic saviours that *Athens had been ruined by the plague and the costs of the war.*

Athens was appalled by Mytilene's gall. Hands shot up in the Assembly once more, and the Athenian democrats who had survived battle and pathogens voted for unstinting aggression. Mytilene was besieged, and then starved into submission. But still the Assembly, urged on by hardline orators, raged. In 427 BC democratic Athenians voted to wipe the hubristic rebels – man, woman and child – off the face of the earth. A trireme was to be sent eastwards, its instructions to cut the breath out of all who stood there. The boat was dispatched, bristling with arms, but then overnight the democrats slept uneasily. They dreamed of the brutality of the decision they had made. The next day as they walked to the Pnyx at dawn, with the clarity of the early-morning air around them, they realised what a horror they had unleashed. One man, Diodotus, stood up and persuaded another course, with words that have great purchase: why slaughter, he said, when this will send such a malign signal out to the rest of the world, and why maim when Mytilenean resources – manpower, boats, cash – could be so useful to us? A second trireme was sent out from Piraeus, its rowers fed superfoods (barley-cakes soaked in honey and fortified wine) so that they had the strength of heroes; they had to overtake the first trireme, packed with assassins, even though it had almost a day's advantage.

Thrashing through the Aegean surf, the second trireme arrived just in time. The orders were reversed. Women wept with relief, men lived to see another day. Both the mob-passion and the flexibility of this fledgling democracy had been proved at a stroke. But Athens' act of mercy would become far from typical. In the Assembly a motion was passed that Athens' allies should be forced to 'love' the *demos*: a love-affair that saw Athena developing into an oppressive and domineering partner. Little surprise that when recording the 'free cities' in league with Athens, there was sometimes a slip of the stonemason's chisel; instead of 'our allies' on inscriptions, the Athenians started to refer to 'those cities that we rule'.

⁂

Mercy had been shown at Mytilene. Corcyra (modern-day Corfu) would not be so lucky. Oligarchs on the island had gained the upper hand. Athens decided that, after all, they did need to make an example of those who stirred up trouble. Corcyra had tempted Athens into conflict with Corinth and Sparta back in 433 BC, and now it was causing trouble again. The *oligoi*, the 'few', rather than the Athenian-sponsored democrats, had taken back the reins of power. But, hearing Athenian reinforcements were on their way, these insurgents headed for the hills. Men and women both retreated to Mount Istone, the sky-scraping rock that towers dark above the island's subtropical green. The Athenians claimed they would be relatively lenient to all those from the captured garrison, as long as not one man attempted flight. The insurgents were shipped over to the islet of Ptychia – a stop-off before being put on trial in Athens. But agents (some say democratic Corcyrans, some say Athenians) infiltrated the concentration camp, tempting the prisoners with promises of boats waiting in bays and an open, night-black sea ahead; an escape plan was formulated. Some oligarchs made a dash for it and were immediately executed. A number of survivors still cowered in their island prison, sticking to their side of the bargain. But the Athenians were tested, and did not honour the promise they had made. Two-by-two these prisoners were roped together and brought out in blocks of twenty. The Corcyrans thought they were being transferred, but in fact waiting for them were rows of enemy hoplites – mainly democratic Corcyrans with a grudge – who speared them as they ran. Whips kept the prisoners moving on and into the blades. Sixty or so were torn to pieces. The remaining Corcyrans refused to come out of their barracks – so the democrats used them for target practice, shooting arrows into the garrison, hurling down roof tiles. Many of the rebels decided to take their own lives, slitting their own throats or hanging themselves with shreds of clothes and bed-linen. At least 1,000 died.[8]

An ideological struggle was turning into a very dirty war.

⁂

War, promoted by the democracy, was depriving many of their liberty and their lives. Between 425 and 421 BC Athens' Agora corralled not just slave-labour, but another kind of captive. Socrates would have seen, as he came to talk around the market-stalls, a dejected reminder of Athens' imperialism: a great huddle of almost 300 Spartans, prisoners-of-war.[9]

These drooping captives were treated by the Athenians like the attractions in a freak show. Many citizens came to gawp and point. Because these Spartans – and remember, Spartan boys were trained from the age of seven never to surrender, never to give up, to fight their way through to a beautiful death – had caved in.

Just months before, the men had been trapped in a Spartan garrison, on the small island of Sphacteria opposite the bay of Pylos. The rock here was scrubby, exposed. No chance of agriculture or animal husbandry; birds and a few small rodents were the men's only companions. Sparta's allied fleet had been withdrawn and, realising these men would die (they did represent, after all, 10 per cent of the Spartan army), the Spartan authorities sued for peace. Athens refused. The fighting continued, with the marooned Spartans somehow clinging on, eating berries, bugs, rats. And then, disaster. Incompetents in the group managed to start a fire in the dry scrub, and in effect the Spartans smoked themselves out. Dashing to escape the flames, they were picked off by Athenian arrows – usually sneered at by the Spartans as 'spindles' because they believed a technological trick like this, that killed at a distance, was feeble, womanish. But now, rather than remain target practice, the survivors surrendered. Hangdog, they were route-marched back to Athens.

And suddenly the Spartiates had a very masculate sword hanging over their heads. The Athenian Assembly had sent a curt message to the Spartan council. If so much as a single Spartan step was taken into Attic territory, the miserable soldiers now hunched in the Agora would be summarily executed. The news chilled the council of Spartan *ephors*; instead of a 'beautiful death', the greatest warriors in the world risked being dispatched, in shackles, like beasts in an abattoir.

One of the Spartan prisoner-of-war's shields is still in the Agora Museum. It is massive, more than 3 feet in diameter, the bronze now a gentle green, but – warped and battered – this is clearly a piece of kit that has been put through the mill. And punched onto the surface of the *hoplon* shield is a simple triumphant message: 'FROM THE SPARTANS, FROM PYLOS'. It is a war trophy that the Spartans believed the world would never see.

Tempted, perhaps, by this show of weakness, the Athenians renewed their aggression against Sparta, and Socrates found himself back on the road again – fighting for a city-state he loved, and for an ideal he might or might not wholeheartedly believe in.

ACT FIVE
THE FIGHT GOES ON

30

THE PELOPONNESIAN WAR, PHASE TWO – A MESSY SIEGE

◉◉◉◉◉◉◉◉◉◉◉

Delion, 424 BC

SOCRATES: Wars and revolutions and battles are due simply and solely to the body and its desires. All wars are undertaken for the acquisition of wealth; and the reason why we have to acquire wealth is the body, because we are slaves in its service.

Plato, *Phaedo*, 66c–d[1]

SOCRATES: Courage is inseparable from wisdom.

Plato, *Laches*, 1996[2]

SOCRATES COULD NOT JUST BE WISE. His city needed him to kill.
Democracy forces a confidence. It forces a belief in collective power. When the elite stood next to the masses, hoplites next to *thetes*, clamouring and heckling under the open sky, up would shoot an amalgam of hands to register their vote, some palms soft from indolence, some hard from labour. This tightly knit citizen-body could encourage itself to go to fight again and again and again. And now democratic Athens had cash to add to credo. As more satellite societies came under its wing, as more insular people became part of a mental mainland, money meant that Athena was honoured with a permanent army. Her people could keep on building ships that could keep on travelling out on ram-raid expeditions.

Potidaea might have spawned the horror of cannibalism, Pericles might have entrapped his people in their own city with a pandemic pathogen, tens of thousands might already have died, but Athens was far from ready to give up the fight with Sparta. Two days' slow march north of Athens, in 424 BC, Socrates was about to walk onto his bloodiest battlefield.

⣿⣿⣿⣿⣿

When the Athens underground was being renovated in 1995, one rather beautiful stone *stele* was dug up.[3] On it we see rows of finely carved horses, a Boeotian footsoldier being trampled, and we read about the aristocratic cavalry who made their way into battle in Tanagra, possibly Delion too. Here is the paradox of the Athenians: the foot soldiers of a democracy, who vote for a war and then have to go out to fight in it – they now lie unmemorialised, while the aristocrats, who stick to many of their old oligarchic ways, still have the resources to commemorate themselves as heroes. Even despite the democratic revolution, the 'cream' that Solon anxiously spoke of (worrying that it might be skimmed from Athenian society during political reforms) was certainly still there; not only that, but it had a way of rising to the top.

On the way to Delion, Alcibiades rode, Socrates walked.

The philosopher was no longer a young man; now he was grizzled, forty-five or so. The hoplites, the men whom Socrates marched alongside, ranged between eighteen and sixty. These were the democratic politicians who would lead from the front; those who would be barged and stifled and skewered, who would attempt, by holding together, not to degenerate into a mindful frenzy. You can still see their salvation in a number of Greece's museums.[4] Here are bronze greaves, perfectly moulded to shins and knees, and the rough helmets that have been beaten out of ploughshares; here are shields' metal skins, pockmarked and warped from punitive impact and the storms of arrowheads that once rained down – on the battle sites that now seem so tranquil.

Today, Dhilesi, the site of the Battle of Delion, feels not just calm, but more than a little backwaterish. Refuse collectors haven't bothered to come, roads remain untarmacked. Not many tourists travel here – and, for that very reason, the Hellenism of the place is uninterrupted. The stretch of blue water between the mainland and the island of Euboea throws its snow-headed mountains into relief. This is a Greece worth fighting for. And in 424 BC this was a Greece, as yet, inconclusively claimed.

The columns of soldiers who marched out of Athens, heading here on paths dust-hard at the end of a long summer, were, literally, ideological. They carried with them a word idea, *demos-kratia*, democracy, that had been in existence for a scant forty years. Their instructions were to take Boeotian territories, and to take the Boeotian people from under the oligarchs' noses; to make Delion a pro-democratic base from which Athens could hoover up other territories, other cultures, other 'less democratic' political systems. On the face of it, the motivation was high-minded. But in reality this was a war-game. By breaking the Boeotian alliance to Sparta, the Athenians would eradicate the Peloponnesian War's northern front, which was, really, too close for comfort.

By the time Socrates arrived here in Delion six years had passed since he last saw active service. And now he was stepping out with 7,000 men – a full hoplite force of Athens. Alongside the soldiers were as many as 20,000 civilians: camp-followers, construction workers, corpse-gatherers, all there to secure a tactical victory. Each hoplite's batman had packed his provisions: a bag of flour, jars of wine and water, snacks (salted fish was a favourite) wrapped in fig leaves, sleeping mats, spare leather straps, shovels, hoes, axes, scythes to destroy enemy crops, money to buy spare food or your way out of a ransom demand.[5] This was a satellite-city on the move, nomadic, marching to protect the mother ship.

But Athens' plan[6] – to bring democracy to the north – would fail, and 1,000 hoplites, along with 1,000 unarmed men, would die. Socrates was one of the few foot soldiers to survive.

Delion was supposed to be a surprise attack, but Boeotia was well supplied with spies and, learning of the Athenian advance, managed to make herself ready for the onslaught. The Athenians arrived in two deployments, yet failed to coordinate and were separated by a vital twenty-four hours and 15 miles. Then they added insult to incompetence. The Athenian idealists, it seems, made a dreadful religious gaffe. News of their faux-pas had filtered through the clouds around Mount Olympus to affront winged Nike, the goddess of victory – and suddenly it was not at all clear that Athens was going to win this battle that it had picked. Athenian troops had elected to fortify themselves in Delion's Temple of Apollo and to use a sacred spring as the camp sluice. As locals heard of their total lack of respect for the gods and disregard for centuries of combat-convention, their gorge rose. Outrage sharpened the claws of pragmatism.

Socrates and his peers would have prayed to their gods, made a libation and then, with a sudden clanking, the battle began. But immediately there was another unforeseen challenge. When it came to the fighting, the Boeotian enemy was configured in an unusual way; on the battlefield the Theban hoplites were twenty-five rather than the normal eight men deep. There was confusion, and at one point fighters were so close they could not see who it was that they were puncturing, throttling, grinding down. The casualties from this friendly-fire were significant. This was a matted mass of men stabbing out wildly at any flesh they could reach. The sun might have been bright in the sky, but sweat, dust, blood, snot, the deafening hum of their helmets and metal skull-shields blinded and disorientated the warrior-democrats.

Athena's brave soldiers start to turn and flee.

And then the enemy cavalry pursued them. Charging down the hill, stumbling, chests heaving, the Athenians ran for their lives, discarding their heavy, chafing armour as they went – into the woods, to the foothills of Mount Parnes and eventually, thankfully, under a cloak of darkness as the sun set. This is difficult territory to escape into. The ravines here are scrubby and crumpled. Now shadowed by pylons and plasterworks, this wrong-footing landscape once sheltered and exposed soldiers in equal measure. The area has never been fully excavated; as you walk you still crunch over millennia-old pottery shards, and somewhere down here are the broken bones of a battlefield.

But Socrates, through this carnage and chaos, was one of the few who survived. He remained calm. Men were drawn to him in the pandemonium. He led (so Plato tells us) a small group to safety – amongst them a character called Laches, a successful general who would go on to have a Platonic dialogue named for him.[7] All through this – we are told – Socrates' beautiful companion Alcibiades watched from the vantage of horseback, glimpsing busy soldier Socrates through the heat and dust. Socrates' beautiful boy '*happened to be there*'[8] when he spotted the philosopher and his band – a good indication of how confused, how random, how utterly unplanned battle in antiquity could be. An indication too of how ill-suited horseback fighting was in this hilly terrain – the cavalry's distant impotence at Potidaea would be remembered, sorely, for years to come. Yet through this jangling, ugly maelstrom something stands out: Socrates' determination. He was a man strong enough to fight when challenged, he was unflustered by the difficulties of the day, he is portrayed to us as having about him a peculiar serenity.

ALCIBIADES: *Here indeed I had an even finer view of Socrates than at Potidaea – or personally I had less reason for alarm, as I was mounted; and I noticed first how far he outdid Laches in collectedness, and next I felt – to use a phrase of yours, Aristophanes – how there he stepped along, as his wont is in our streets, 'strutting like a proud marsh-goose, with ever a sidelong glance', turning a calm sidelong look on friend and foe alike, and convincing anyone even from afar that whoever cares to touch this person will find he can put up a stout enough defence.*[9]

In the Platonic dialogue *Protagoras*,[10] Socrates offers good advice: we need to know what it is that we are scared of; courage is knowledge of what is and what is not truly to be feared. Our inability to distinguish between the two, between real and perceived threat, is of course what every terrorist, then and now, plays upon.

Still, the prospect was not looking good. The Athenian troops were scattered, so many soldiers were wounded that a victory was impossible; one group grimly held on in their base in the Temple of Apollo. The Athenians had lost and yet, by still occupying Apollo's sacred home, they were blasphemous even in defeat. And so the Thebans and the other Boeotians, in collusion with the Spartans, refused to let the Athenians collect their dead. The corpses lay there for seventeen days, starting to rot.

It must have been a hellish scene. Bodies beginning to swell, stink and burst. The great and the nameless lying twisted together – Pericles' nephew was one of the young men who slowly putrefied on these coastal killing fields. The Boeotians had already stripped the bodies of their armour, so the Athenians' flesh must have been fed on by dogs and flies. But still the surviving soldiers, Socrates' peers, cowered, braving it out in the temple.[11]

These cocky invaders had to be shifted; and so the Boeotians resorted to diabolic ingenuity – chemical warfare – sending pitch and sulphur shooting into the garrison-temple itself. The Athenians were now about to be assaulted from the skies by something that resembled a thunderbolt-rage of Zeus. A crude wooden siege-breaker, 20 feet tall, was raised next to the walls. Delion was recaptured with this noxious flame-thrower, and it is easy to imagine the stench of burning sulphur in the air, burnt hair in the nostrils, the taste of roasting human flesh on the tongue, the sinking pit of defeat in the democrats' stomachs.

These were hardly the glory days.

After seven days it is difficult to move decomposing bodies from one place to another, but at Delion the bodies had now lain, unburied, for two and a half weeks.

As Socrates looked at the mould blooming on the skin of these once-humans, did he wonder whether this was all there was? Whether all that glittering chat, those beautifully crafted words and manufactured things back in Athens, whether it all came down to that gamey, dropping flesh? And although Socrates stood against the lex talionis – the typical way of proceeding, when all male soldiers were put to the sword, all women and children were seized, all booty, human and otherwise, that could be packed on carts or dragged behind the army train – it was this slaughter in cold blood that he now witnessed.[12]

Socrates lived, and his bravery and clear-headed tenacity at Delion were noted.[13] His peers, and as a result history, remembered Socrates as a courageous man.

For, as a rule, people will not lay a finger on those who show such a calm fortitude in war.[14]

But even if Socrates had acquitted himself well, the return to Athens must have been subdued; this was a dishonourable defeat.

Socrates limped back to Athens with the ragtag remains of the Athenian army. Here in the mother city, life jogged along. Athena might have taken some body-blows, but she was still standing. More than standing, in fact, she was still earning her various epithets: 'busybody', 'violet-crowned', 'sleek and oily'. She was still self-consciously promoting herself as the brightest and best in the region. The story of the 'Greatest City on Earth' still looked set to run for quite some time; and, increasingly, Socrates was finding himself central to the Athenian drama.

31

BRICKBATS AND BOUQUETS

◎◎◎◎◎◎◎◎◎◎◎◎

Theatre of Dionysos, Athens, 423 BC

A bold rascal, a fine speaker, impudent, shameless, a braggart, and adept at stringing lies, and an old stager at quibbles, a complete table of laws, a thorough rattle, a fox to slip through any hole, supple as a leather strap, slippery as an eel, an artful fellow, a blusterer, a villain, a knave with one hundred faces, cunning, intolerable, a gluttonous dog.

Aristophanes, *Clouds*, 445–51

SOCRATES: *But what do we care about what most people think, Crito?* . . .

CRITO: *But surely you see, Socrates, that it's necessary to care about what most people think. The circumstances we're in now make it clear that most people are able to do not just the smallest evils but virtually the greatest if someone's been slandered when they're around.*

Plato, *Crito*, 44c and 44d[1]

CLUTCHING A METAL THEATRE TOKEN, EVEN in March, is a sweaty business. The discs of bronze – the size of a fat ten-pence piece and worth a day's wages for the Athenian poor – mark the palms: on a really hot day they leave fingers sticky-wet. Just one more odour to waft on the pungent Athenian breeze.

Little matter since the crowds entering the Theatre of Dionysos on the slopes of the Acropolis rock were hardly at their freshest. As one of Athens' key religious expressions, the preparation for theatrical contests in the city-state was intense, at times frenzied. Drama had (probably) started as a religious ritual in the sanctuary of Eleusis centuries before, and had made its way into the villages of Attica and then on into the Athenian Agora. The re-defining of the City or Great Dionysia festival in around 500 BC has been seen as an expression of democratic fervour, a means for Athenian citizens to explore the potential of this new kind of socio-political way of being. Drama's movement to a purpose-built theatre was a departure during Socrates' lifetime; Athenian playwrights – Aeschylus, Sophocles, Euripides – gave plays their trademark form, with a chorus and leading actors, but the theatre never lost its intensely religious undertones. The build-up to Greek drama, for example, was bestial. Men dressed in ritual costume led sacrificial animals through the streets. Military leaders, the great and good of the city, sprinkled piglet's gore across the theatre-space. Given that the whole event was sacred to the god Dionysos, once the blood had flowed, so did the wine: all night. Most theatrical productions must have been watched with distinctly sore heads.

And pre-show manners were hardly something to write home about. Finding one's seat in the open-air auditorium could resemble a stampede.

. . . People would rush for seats and even occupy places during the night before the performance, there were shoving matches, battles and beatings.[2]

Democrats clumped together in tribal formation. Priests and high-ranking officials had their own seats towards the front, but such favouritism was not popular. In the middle of the fourth century BC when Demosthenes invited ambassadors from Philip of Macedon's court to the theatre in Athens, giving them ringside positions with plump cushions and a purple throw on top, the anger was audible: *'people hissed at the disgrace'*.[3] So to beat the rush, men often arrived at the theatre half a day or so before the performance.

[SOCRATES TO CRITOBOULOS:] As it is, I've known you to get up very early in the morning and walk a very long way to see a comedy and eagerly urge me to go along and see it with you.[4]

Socrates grew up with theatre beating its juvenating rhythm out to his city. In 472 BC, three years before the philosopher was born, Aeschylus had been inspired to exalt Athenian victory at Salamis with *The Persians*. When Socrates was fourteen, Euripides first competed in the Great Dionysia festival, and it was said that in later life the two became as thick as thieves, Socrates furnishing the playwright with inspiration and ideas:

> *The Phrygians, that's a new play by Euripides;*
> *Actually, Socrates puts on the firewood.*
> *Again he says:*
> *. . . Euripidean [tragedies?], nailed up by Socrates . . .*

And Aristophanes says in the Clouds;
He's the chap who writes tragedies for Euripides,
Those wordy, clever ones.[5]

When Socrates was around twenty, at the foot of the Acropolis, drama was given a permanent home: a wooden theatre auditorium was consecrated to Dionysos, the greedy god who demanded festivals across one whole third of the Athenian year.[6] Dionysos was a god for the 'whole' of democratic Athens — for everyone in this shiny, new-look city. As one scholar puts it: 'A master of illusions, he produces drunkenness and madness; he destroys the barriers between man and animal, male and female, young and old, free and slave, city and country, man and god.'[7] Dionysos was known as '*main-omenos Dionysos*'[8] — raving Dionysos — but also as *Psilax* — he who gave men's minds wings.

Theatre was a consecrated act in fifth-century BC Athens, an entertainment that brought Athenians closer to the gods; it was also the right and the responsibility of those in the democratic state. That theatre token, fingered by so many democratic Athenians queuing for the day-long entertainments (comic and tragic), marked you out as a stakeholder in one of the most adventurous cities ever known. Sitting together in the sunlight, Athena's democrats explored complicated, awkward, inspiring ideas together. The rich were obliged to pay for choruses (chorus members, like the actors, were themselves Athenian citizens) and specific aspects of the production. In Socrates' day tragedy was fresh, raw, an idea with the celerity of novelty. As with so much in Athenian society, the drama festival was also an *agon*, a competition. Plays were performed just once. Every dramatist, every producer was fiercely competitive — winning here, in front of your peers, really mattered.

To call Greek drama an 'art-form' is somewhat anachronistic. The Greeks (unlike many modern-day bureaucrats) didn't distinguish drama as 'art' — something separate from 'society', 'politics', 'life'. Theatre was fundamental to democratic Athenian business. Aristophanes via one of the characters in his comedies declares, '*Poetry makes people better in their societies.*'[9] Members of the chorus were exempt from military service. A fund was set up to support those too poor to buy their own tickets.

Now tourists, on their way from the Plaka shopping district up to the Acropolis, wander a little listlessly through the Theatre of Dionysos. Tour guides give a good impression of the 'what' and the 'how', but not the 'why'. Yet in the fifth century this was a place where Athenian democrats came to understand the very world they lived in. The contrast with the press of men here 2,500 years ago, eager to hear what, in this land of free speech, an Athenian would dare to say next – the rock of the Acropolis and the gods who lived there his witnesses – could not be starker.

> Ignorant men do not know what they hold in their hands
> until they have flung it away.
> To him who is in fear everything rustles.
> For somehow this is tyranny's disease, to trust no friends.
> Words are the physicians of the diseased mind.[10]

Athenian theatre dealt with the very stuff of life.

The original theatre audiences here were tenderised – the theatre was a space where emotions were intentionally heightened. All manner of tricks and tropes were used to ensure that the democratic Athenians, – 10,000, 15,000, 20,000 of them – were deeply moved by what they saw before them. Primal, shared musical nights were the stem-cells of Greek theatre. Drama had evolved from ritual song and dance. Playwrights were also poets; actors learned to sing haunting refrains and to fill the theatres with abstract, choral sounds. Euripides et al. composed their own music: melodic, monophonic rhythms that beat out the heart of the matter. Refrains from oboes (*auloi*) and cymbals represented *ethos* – sensibility itself. A theatre performance guaranteed all kinds of assaults on your senses, on your sentiments. And so the fact that Socrates turned up as a character in the plays of Aristophanes, one of the most ingenious and waspish playwrights of the day, was significant. Scrutiny of this new art-form was intense. Socrates' appearance on the comic stage in Aristophanes' play *Clouds*, where he was parodied mercilessly, mattered.[11] We learn of the impact that the theatre had on Socrates' contemporaries from one of Plato's Dialogues, when Socrates bumps into a rhapsode, a professional 'reciter' called Ion:

SOCRATES: *And are you aware that your rhapsodies produce these same effects on most of the spectators too?*

ION: *Yes, absolutely aware: for I look down on them from the platform and see them at such moments, crying and turning awestruck eyes upon me and yielding to the amazement of my tale. For I have to pay the closest attention to them; since, if I set them crying, I shall laugh because of all the money I take, but if they laugh, I myself shall cry because of the money I lose.*[12]

Athens' plays might be matchless in their honesty, with their forensic analysis of the extremes of the human condition, their investigation of human flaws, but they wrapped the experience in a lusty, feel-good mantle. Plays were where you came to process information, to learn to form an opinion of the

world around you, and to love your *polis*. Although there is frequently criticism in the dialogue of overweening ambition, of cliques, of tall poppies, an
imaginary, theatrical Athens is often a place that is high-minded and fair, in
direct contrast to the bad-boys of Greece: Corinth, Sparta, Thebes. The experience of theatre was meant to be one that re-affirmed Athens' robust sense
of *demos*-solidarity. The very front row was reserved for the sons of men killed
in war. As a showy prelude to the drama, these fatherless young men paraded
through the theatre dressed in state-sponsored armour. Each war orphan then
took a binding oath to protect and preserve the city. And when the tributes
had been collected from amongst Athens' 'allies', these goods (to all intents
and purposes, taxes) were processed in public, before an admiring Athenian
crowd, at the opening of the Great Dionysia competition. The March end-
of-year returns in Athens' treasury were an explicitly theatrical affair. Theatre
in Socrates' day was a heady and patriotic experience.

Although women and foreigners were almost certainly not allowed in
to see the comedies and tragedies, children may well have been, possibly
even as judges of the competition[13] – an impressionable age to sit and watch
a charismatic version of real life played out in front of you.[14]

It is into this highly charged atmosphere, in 423 BC, in front of citizen-
democrats and the next generation of Athenians that an unlovable,
buffoon-make-believe version of Socrates is flung.[15]

෨෨෨෨෨෨

Picture Socrates in 423 BC, in late March or early April, bustling up to
Dionysos' theatre at the base of the vast Acropolis rock. Taking his seat in
his tribal block, buying the snacks – figs and nuts and chickpeas – to munch
during the show, settling down for an experience that was devised to change,
to some degree, how he, and the men around him, thought about the world.
But today would be a little different. Because it was Socrates himself who
would provide the entertainment. A young buck (aged twenty-two or so)
called Aristophanes has written all about the gobby philosopher and his
peculiar ways. The title of this thinly veiled slander is *Clouds*. In his summation of Socrates, the author certainly did not pull his punches.

*A bold rascal, a fine speaker, impudent, shameless, a braggart, and adept at stringing
lies, and an old stager at quibbles, a complete table of laws, a thorough rattle, a fox to slip
through any hole, supple as a leather strap, slippery as an eel, an artful fellow, a blusterer,
a villain, a knave with one hundred faces, cunning, intolerable, a gluttonous dog.*[16]

Clearly, to spark such intemperate smears, Socrates was already known
in Athens: a big character in the city. And a big name too. The kind of

name worth inventing words for. Nine years later, in another of his plays, *Birds*, Aristophanes describes Socrates' followers as like the *Lakono-manes* — those who are Spartan-mad. These are people who have aped Socrates, they are *esokratun*, they are Socratised.[17] The year 423 is the year of *Clouds*, but also, more importantly, the year that the winning drama is Cratinus' *Wine-flask*, a play lost to us now, but in which Socrates was *also* mocked; clearly in 423 it pleased the Athenian crowds to lambast the philosopher.[18]

> CHORUS [*in the form of Clouds*]:
> *Hail, grey-headed hunter of phrases artistic!*
> *Hail, Socrates, master of twaddle!*
> *Out of all the specialists cosmologistic*
> *We love for the brains in his noddle*
> *Only Prodicus; you we admire none the less*
> *For the way that you swagger and cuss,*
> *And never wear shoes, and don't care how you dress,*
> *And solemnly discourse of us.*

STREPSIADES [*in raptures*]: *How fantastic! How divine!*
SOCRATES: *Yes, these are the only truly divine beings — all the rest is just a lot of fairy tales.*
STREPSIADES: *What on earth! You mean you don't believe in Zeus?*[19]

So what, one wonders, had turned the tide? Socrates had spent a period of eight years fighting for his country. In many ways he had followed the conventional path for a good Athenian citizen — but clearly he had started to irritate people. It could just be simply that he had been a fixture in the Agora for too long, asking his annoying, soul-searching questions. But the plot-line of *Clouds* offers other clues.

Clouds

⊚⊚⊚⊚⊚⊚⊚⊚⊚⊚⊚

In a nutshell, *Clouds* is a little like a restoration comedy: a story of town and country. Our lead, the middle-aged, bumbling bumpkin Strepsiades, is lured into the city by his urbane missus. His son runs up debts; Strepsiades decides that Socrates' popular philosophy establishment, the 'Thinking

Foundation', will sort the boy out, will show him how to wangle himself out of tricky situations. But it is the father who ends up in the crammer. Strepsiades watches (for our amusement) as Socrates is shat on by lizards while gawping at the heavens, measuring with great solemnity the distance a flea can jump and then *peering at the arse of the moon*.

Clouds is not stellar – and it wasn't judged so. Aristophanes won third (last) prize when the show was first presented. But with the phlegm of youth – remember, he would have been twenty-two or so at the time – the playwright set out to make his comedy that bit edgier. *Clouds* had an unperformed, more savage, iteration, and now recent, gruesome historical events were recalled as part of the drama.

In about 454 BC a group of Pythagoreans had gathered together as per usual in their meeting house in Croton, one of the Greek cities in Magna Graecia, southern Italy. Their conversation would perhaps have been about the stars, mathematics, the nature of the universe, the nature of society, the nature of love. This think-tank engaged with the world around them in the most vigorous of ways. But others were there too, in the shadows. As the radical group of thinkers settled down to business, the door was barred – from the outside – and a torch put to the tinder. All the Pythagoreans within were burned alive.

In his new version of *Clouds*, Aristophanes imagines a similar, awful fate for Socrates and the others in his 'Thinkery'.

SOCRATES [*coughing in the smoke*]: *Help, I'm going to suffocate!*

CHAEREPHON [*still inside*]: *Help, I'm being prematurely cremated!*

STREPSIADES [*descending the ladder, followed by his slave* XANTHIAS]: *No more than you deserved; people who cock snooks at the gods and argue about the arse of the moon must pay for it. [Kicks* SOCRATES *on the bum.] Get them! Stone them! Revenge! Revenge for the injured gods! Remember what they did! Revenge.* [20]

This time, Socrates and his companions escape. But the scene, even if it had a happy ending, was ugly.

And how did Socrates react to such public blackballing? Well, with equanimity, we're led to believe. Aristophanes, after all, appears (from Plato's *Symposium*) to have been an acquaintance of his; friend, not foe. The two would drink together, sharpen their wits on one another. Was this perhaps a feisty, testy tale written with a kind of wry affection? According to a later anecdote, after Socrates had watched himself on the stage 'peering at the arse of the moon,' he stood up and bowed to the crowd. He smiled. What a society, where men can be parodied, in public, in front of anyone who is anyone, as well as those who appear to be nothing, and laugh at their own trouble.

Of course comedy is where Socrates belongs. Where else could he be? The ugly, pot-bellied eccentric. The wrong-footing genius; the stonemason's son who understands how fragile and foolish mortal life is, and yet at the same time how sublime. The soldier commended for his bravery who stands, like a snowman in the middle of a winter campaign, caught in one of his embarrassing staring fits. All the other characters in Socrates' story – Alcibiades, Pericles, Aspasia – could appear in tragedy, in epic drama. Socrates, unique, world-class as he is, is at the same time a queer middle-aged man with feet of clay. A curiously comforting, curiously unsettling pilot-passenger in the leaky lifeboat. A man easy to mock.

At the time of this production of Aristophanes' *Clouds*, many experimental thinkers were being lambasted and lampooned in Athenian theatre – yet tolerated too. But theatre was, after all, a religious experience. The ideas floated here had surprising weight. And times would change, once – in the future, at the beginning of a new century – Socrates was isolated, his fellow radicals persecuted and exiled, and his city-state the loser in one too many battles, the roar of Athens' crowd would be sharper, the laughter hollow.

In good democratic style, at this juncture maybe Aristophanes was simply trying to ensure that a man who walked strong and tall in this democratic city did not get a swollen head. But he still made it clear that Socrates could act very *un*-democratically when he meddled with young men's minds. The children sitting in the Theatre of Dionysos had been given something distinctly unpleasant to lodge in their cortical memory. At the time of Socrates' trial these youngsters will be grown men, just thirty, old enough to vote, old enough to be judges in a law-court. As Socrates strode off at the end of the day's entertainment, home to his mother's house in Alopeke, with his waddling gait, his darting eyes, his hairy hands, perhaps they giggled and sneered at him behind his back. Come 399 BC, and Socrates' trial in a religious court, the philosopher was certain that this appearance in the theatre had been immensely damaging.

First, then, it's right for me to make my defence, Athenians, against the first of the false accusations made against me and against my first accusers, and then against the later ones and the later accusers . . .

But the earlier ones worry me more, men, who, having got hold of many of you when you were children, convinced you with accusations against me that weren't any truer than the ones I now face. They said that there's a certain Socrates, a wise man, who thinks about what's in the heavens and who has investigated all the things below the earth and who makes the weaker argument appear to be the stronger. Those who spread this rumour, Athenians, are the accusers that worry me. For the people who hear such things believe that those who enquire about such topics also don't believe in the gods. There are lots of these accusers and they've been at it for a long time already, telling you these things when you were still at an age when you were most apt to believe them, when some of you were children and others were adolescents and they made their case when absolutely no one presented a defence. But the most unreasonable part of all is that it is impossible to know and say their names, except one, who happens to be a certain writer of comedies . . .

For you yourselves saw these things in the comedy by Aristophanes; Socrates being carried around there, saying that he is walking on air and all kinds of other nonsense that I don't understand at all.[21]

Trial by media has been, and always will be, of peculiar potency.

Yet one aspect that Aristophanes never mocks is Socrates' courage. This is a war veteran after all – a decorated one. A man who does not deny the value of war in a warring age.[22] And a man who – despite being mocked by his city – will, within months of Aristophanes' premiere of *Clouds*, have to risk his life for her once more.

32

AMPHIPOLIS

⊙⊙⊙⊙⊙⊙⊙⊙⊙⊙⊙

North-eastern Greece, 424–422 BC

SOCRATES: *The envious person grows lean with the fatness of their neighbour.*

Plato, *Phaedo,* 66c

BEHIND ATHENS' CITY WALLS TRAGEDIANS AND comedians may have continued to write, musicians to compose, and philosophers to debate – but beyond that ring of stone, hostilities dragged on.

Delion's humiliation of the city-state had given Athens' enemies renewed vim. In 424 BC word reached Athens that the Spartans and their allies were fingering Athenian possessions in the north-east of Hellas. So Socrates was back on the road northwards once more, marching (possibly sailing) as part of the Athenian army – to a landscape so different from that around Athens that even today it seems outlandish that a city 200 miles to the south should consider it right to claim it as its own.

This is the road today to Turkey, and the further east one travels, the more apparent is the fallout of the disastrous exchange of population in 1923. Still remembered as the '*Katastrofi*', 'The Catastrophe', formalised as the Treaty of Lausanne in July 1923, 390,000 Muslims were forcibly taken from Greece to Turkey and 1,300,000 Christians from Turkey to Greece. The small towns stretched along the coast from here to the Bosporus still have a temporary, refugee feel about them. But they shelter within an abundant, confident landscape.

Here the hills never seem to stop; all are shaggy with trees, the earth beneath rich in minerals. Amphipolis was a new town, founded only in 437 BC, but it sat on top of a prehistoric settlement. The Athenians had attempted to establish a colony here in 465; it was disastrous, and 10,000 colonists were killed. So strategically placed, the settlement's Thracian name was 'Nine Ways'; it would be from here in just under 100 years' time that Alexander the Great would set out to conquer the whole of Asia.

To get to the most likely site of Socrates' next battle at Amphipolis you still cross the Strymon (in his day 'well-bridged') River. Now the river banks are married and marred by a rusty and rattling metal crossing. But the river itself keeps its ancient scale – it is broad, banked by reeds – a life-support system that must be defended. The Strymon, in fact, was the mother of Amphipolis – the settlement had been built by Athens only thirteen years before in order to provide an effective crossing point, and to control trade: planks from those trees, gold from those hills. This is what Socrates had been sent out to defend.

In 424 BC the historian Thucydides had already tried to do his patriotic duty in this region. The Spartan commander Brasidas, backed by a motley crew of Peloponnesian hoplites and helots in hoplite armour, had made a surprise sortie here. A message was sent to Thucydides, who was manning and maintaining seven triremes back on that honey-rich island of Thasos (the place that had witnessed the stirrings of Athens' imperial ambition), to say that the Athenian general had to come, and fast. It took Thucydides half a day to arrive. He had a vested interest here, the ownership of a number of gold-mining concessions in the fertile landscape. Thucydides should have been the perfect man for the job. But his tardiness, and Spartan brio, worked against him. Brasidas, under the cover of a raging storm, had forced his way into the city. Not long inside, he had already persuaded the men of Amphipolis to give up their settlement without so much as raising a sword. He promised safe passage to those who wanted to leave, and no sequestering or looting of the property of those Amphipolitans who decided to stay. Suddenly, with their fair play and diplomatic niceties, it was the Spartan-side who appeared to hold the moral high ground in this unpleasant war. When news filtered back to Athens that Thucydides had failed to secure Amphipolis and had also allowed Brasidas to appear the benign liberator, the general was swiftly recalled to the mother-city and put on trial. Thucydides was found guilty. Amphipolis would be the last live military action that the key historian of the Peloponnesian War would ever see. Thucydides' humiliating failure earned him lifelong exile. The general and his family lived out the rest of their lives in Thrace. It was in this northern, rugged territory that Thucydides produced his *History of the Peloponnesian War*, one of the greatest factual works of all antiquity.

Spartan forces were now installed in the Amphipolis garrison. On and off over the next two years the two enemies taunted one another, nibbling away at territories, treating the natives of the region like pawns in their own realm-wide game of chess. But the Athenians had no intention of letting a rich settlement such as Amphipolis slip from their grasp. The army's instruction was to recapture Amphipolis at all costs. Socrates was one of the soldiers asked to effect this victory. After a year of mutually agreed armistice, in 422 BC the Athenians were back. The site of Socrates' fiercest fighting is now a scrubby, low mound, where today cars engage on the crossroads between Thessaloniki and Drama.

This time as Socrates fought, he did so alongside Thracians. Thracians were a fickle bunch, barbaric fighters in both the true and the received sense of the word. Greek was not their native tongue; instead these men had their own bar-bar-baring language. They also committed atrocities on and off the battlefield. The rumours flew that they ate babies, that they never allowed their enemies to bury their dead. Frequently they hired themselves out to the highest bidder.[1] Socrates' immediate experience of war here was almost certainly an ugly one. Rather than the picture-perfect elegance of hoplites on the black-figure vases that litter the graves and archaeological layers of fifth-century Greece, we should turn to the bone evidence of the period, where eye-sockets are pierced with arrows, shin-bones sliced with axes, teeth smashed back into skulls. The fine vases may perhaps be the image that democratic Athens would prefer us to remember, but the bones too are the reality of fifth-century democratic politics.

❧❧❧❧❧

When last at the Amphipolis site in 2006, I arrived at 2.30 p.m. to see the museum's key-holder disappearing in a puff of blue diesel smoke. I mooched around, sulky. My children followed suit, and then started to spot pottery churned over by a farmer's plough – the remnants of a war and a settlement and of the settlement the war destroyed. Arrowheads, javelin heads and meat-hooks on occasion emerge from the earth here – a reminder of the up-close-and-personal, literally gut-wrenching mode of warfare that Socrates executed on behalf of the *polis*. At Amphipolis the philosopher was one of the fortunate few who emerged unscathed and unmaimed.

Two years after the town had first been taken by their laconic enemies, the Athenians, led by Cleon, tried to attack the Spartan garrison. The Athenian general manoeuvred his troops into position, but when the Spartans failed to emerge from within Amphipolis' barricades, he presumed they could not be tempted out to fight. Given that the Spartans were well drilled for this kind of head-on collision, the situation seemed unusual. Cleon turned tail, retreating so that he could formulate another plan. But the Spartan forces were following behind him. Hoplites, trained in the foothills of the Taygetan mountains and on the Eurotan plain, were proving themselves adept at this kind of guerrilla warfare. What followed was a one-sided massacre: 300 horses, brought in by the aristocratic Athenian cavalry, screamed and slipped in the gore. The Spartans routed their Attic cousins; 600 Athenian hoplites died that day, but as few as seven Spartans.[2] Brasidas, leading from the front, was mortally wounded, although he lived long enough to be told that he had successfully seen off the Athenian threat.

Developed, specifically, as an outpost of Athenian power, as a taxing point for rich raw materials, Amphipolis was now occupied by Spartan heavies and fireside stories of Spartan 'do-gooding'. Brasidas was clearly a charismatic man; after his death locals celebrated him, every year, with games and sacrifices. A monument was erected, posthumously he was honoured as the 'founder' of Amphipolis itself and lauded as the 'liberator of Hellas'. Even more galling for Athenians than the strategic loss of the city was the fact that the local population appeared to welcome the Spartans with open arms. Athens was plangently failing in its mission to 'force' other Greeks to love the *demos*. The democratic superpower was not wanted here; Amphipolis represents a moral as well as a military setback.

The capture of Amphipolis caused great alarm at Athens . . . The cities subject to Athens . . . eagerly embraced the idea of a change, made overtures to Brasidas, begging him to march on their territory, and vied with each other in being the first to revolt.[3]

The chirpy birdsong in the trees that now grow over the site of the battle is a useful corrective. This was a defeat for Athens, yes, but a victory for the Spartans. Since the Athenians wrote our history of Greece, their account is naturally biased. We are used to reading about the fifth century BC from the Athenian point of view. Make this the Athenian War rather than the Peloponnesian War and Amphipolis becomes a great, a significant victory: a victory of the oppressed against their oppressors. Sparta had won affection once more, Athens had lost another cash-cow.

೧೦೧೦೧೦

The year 422 was a busy one. After the defeats at Amphipolis, the remaining Athenians moved, with the other hoplite troops, against the rebellious settlements of Scione, Mende and Torone. Mende caved in after only two days of resistance – and the Athenian troops pillaged the town. At Scione the male inhabitants were executed. And now it was the turn of Torone. Coastal Torone is strategically situated; during the Second World War the Germans used its bay as a naval base. Today it is sleepy. A Byzantine fortress is all that visibly stands from earlier fortifications. But the orders were harsh here too and in 423/2 BC the lilting landscape would have been bruised and broken. Here all women and children were captured and enslaved, all men were marched back to Athens as prisoners-of-war.[4] One by one, cities in the region were bullied and beaten into submission.

❧❧❧❧❧

In Potidaea, where the bid for democracy forced besieged men to eat one another; in Delion, where the gods were ignored, and yet the world did not fall apart; in Scione and Torone, where young children, grabbing at their mother's skirts, stumbling, were driven down south to be slaves, Socrates developed his ideas.[5] And his respect for the Spartans possibly developed too — those extreme southerners who devised their entire society so that life on earth could be as Spartanly perfect as possible, so that *eunomia* (good order) could hold sway. The Spartans were men who lived vigorously in the mortal world, but who had no fear of death: an attitude that Socrates would take with him to his own grave.[6]

Come 422 and Cleon lies dead, the Spartan Brasidas lies dead, and the maimed and dying and fleeing warriors bear very little relation to the fallen heroes of the hoplite code. After this campaigning season the towns of Scione, Mende, Torone have been bled dry. The landscape is scored by an army's tracks. Athens' army lumbered through the 420s with strength, but little grace. The Spartans matched Athenian audacity with tenacity and dynamism. Cities were beginning to empty because the countryside was full of fighting men. The Hellenic hoplites were the armadillo skin of Greece — its distinctive character, its greatest organ — but no longer a thing of beauty.

Salient then that Socrates has no interest in skin-deep strength. He endeavours to poke through to the soft flesh beneath the superficial layer. The man who asserted that 'one must never do injustice' has blood on his hands. He could just remain an ugly soldier in an ugly war. And yet the philosopher brings back into Athena's city not only bad memories, but beautiful ideas. He exemplifies his own belief that the best way to deal with life's horrors and its troubles is to live it to the full: to find the good in the world.

The demeaning military actions in the territories north of Athens were the kinds of campaigns that men drank to forget. But one particular night back in Athens in 416 BC (or so Plato would have us believe), Socrates drank to remember. This long, warm, companionable feast is the basis of one of Plato's most brilliant examples of philosophical theatre – his dialogue the *Symposium*. Hoplite shields, swords and breastplates have been put aside. Fine dinnerware has been spread out on rugs. With some deep in their cups, amidst carousing, Socrates goaded his compatriots to remember, to debate and to identify the meaning not just of hate and revenge and might and despair, but of virtue, of moderation and, above all, of erotic love.

ACT SIX

SOCRATES
AND LOVE

33

SOCRATES IN THE
SYMPOSIUM

@@@@@@@@@@@@

Domestic dwelling, Athens, 416 BC

SOCRATES: . . . savouries, perfumes, incense, prostitutes, pastries . . .

Plato, *Republic*, 2.373a[1]

WINE WAS A SERIOUS BUSINESS IN Athens. During excavations of Athens' city-centre a well was found bunged up with terra-cotta debris, the mess clearly derived from great drinking binges. Deep inside were pitchers and black-glazed drinking cups, along with amphoras that told of the origins of some of the booze on offer. Here there was honeyed wine from the windy island of Lesbos – *alma mater* of the poetess Sappho – and here too a vintage from Corinth, on the coast road that ran down to the Peloponnese, and, sweet as nectar, wine from remote Thasos – the island so irresistible to Athenians – and Dionysos himself was said to have blessed it.

So, around 416 BC, according to Plato, we find Socrates entertaining democratic daytime Athens with perceptive, withering philosophical insights, and then in select company consuming the crushed fruits of empire as the sun sets.

Dinner defined the Golden Age citizen. He was the true inheritor of Athens' greatness, who could lie on a couch, listen to flute-girls, flirt with young boys and eat delicacies grown by another's hand. It is often said that Socrates was anti-material because he refused payment for his work – but he did accept dinner: and the *symposium* was up there with the finest gifts that

229

any could give a man. This was, traditionally, how the aristocrats of the day strengthened their blue-blood bonds. How they kept themselves sleek in a landscape that could feel stony and barren. It was a gift, however, that lacked some finesse. *Symposia* were bawdy, and however high-minded the conversation, the evening often ended crudely. Drinking games such as the popular *kottabos* (where a cup is balanced on a stick in the middle of the room and the assembled company attempts to knock it off with their wine-dregs) could only operate with slaves on hand to clear up the citizens' mess. Socrates debauched with the best of them, and his presence at the *symposia* shows that his tastes were discreetly, plangently Athenian.

The argot of Golden Age Athens was money and food. In Attic comedy men often joked about the honesty of an empty belly, and poets fantasised about the wealth – and feasts – in store, should the Persian Empire ever be conquered,

> *While trees on the hill will shed at our will, not leaves but giblets of kid*
> *And deciduous bushes drop fricasseed thrushes and succulent gobbets of squid.*[2]

In preparation for the *symposium* (literally, the 'drinking together'), slaves would cook relatively wholesome food throughout the day (none of the excesses of Roman banquets here, although the Athenians did have a soft spot for pastries – in fact, fried fish, lentil soup, sausages and raisins were more likely to be on the menu than flambéed peacock). Male guests, eleven or so, were typically wreathed for the occasion: myrtle, rose, wild celery could all be worn. A hymn was sung, usually to *Zeus Soter*, Zeus the Saviour, and the *symposiarch* – the colleague elected by his fellow diners to be in charge – would decide how many units of watered-down wine (often three parts water to one part wine) should be drunk that night.

At Socrates' *symposium* – reports Plato – the agreement was that the guests themselves should decide how much to drink, a hint that even within closed aristocratic circles democracy was in action. But although this detail does copper-plate Socrates' democratic credentials, Plato's point was not heavy-handed. The *symposia* were far more than just a chance to imbibe and consume; they were the unofficial gatherings that kept the world turning. These were evenings (sometimes longer: a *symposium* could run for thirty-six hours) that enabled small groups of men to get together behind closed doors. Since the Late Bronze Age these drinking events had been *the* way in which the elite of society shared experience and advice, where the young bloods were properly educated. At a *symposium* in democratic Athens, things might now be done a little differently, but just by being there aristocrats could relive those days when they called the shots; and they could talk about *Demokratia* behind her back. Years later, in the Archon's courtroom, there is no doubt that Socrates' ready association with these exclusive groups would be held against him.

Symposia were claustrophobic affairs. To appreciate their scale it is best to leave Athens and drive five hours north to the magical little hill of Olynthos, back in fact to the district where Socrates had been fighting around 424 BC. Olynthos, 20 miles north of Potidaea, 120 miles south-west of Amphipolis, was laid out on a Hippodamian-style grid (Hippodamus being the Milesian architect who had also designed Athens' Piraeus district so neatly) – part of the region's redevelopment programme after the fierce fighting of 432 BC. Olynthos' appearance resembled Athenian mores, if not its constitution; this was a town led by an oligarchy, one that resisted Athens' offer of democracy, but it still looked to the future: to a time when urban planning would make life better.

Because vast sections of fifth-century Athens lie smothered and inaccessible under the modern city, Olynthos – recently re-excavated – offers us a more complete glimpse of the built environment that Socrates would have enjoyed. There is a down-the-rabbit-hole feel to the architectural remains at Olynthos today, as if you are marching through some giant golden board game. The footprint of the town's layout has been raised, four blocks of stone high, and what is striking (apart from the odd tree that has established itself as a rare umbrella of shade) is the regularity of the place: little boxes on the hillside where fifth-century Greeks settled down to the business of promoting Greek civilisation.

One house at Olynthos has been particularly well preserved; and fortunately for archaeologists and historians one room here is in particularly good nick – it is the men's room, the *andron*. In a sense there are no women's quarters in Ancient Greek homes – the whole domestic space was a woman's turf:[3] apart, that is, from the *andron*. The *andron* was an area for men only. Most were built with doors to the outer street so that women didn't have to sully the atmosphere by passing through to reach the rest of the house. Serving slave-girls, flute-girls and hetairai were, of course, an exception.

Although Athenian houses of this period were notably simple, the one room where you were likely to find internal decoration was the *andron*: this was, after all, a place of pleasure. At Olynthos the mosaics from two of the *andrones* still exist. Charming, if slightly crude, things, made up of river pebbles, they show Bellerophon mounted on Pegasus, killing the Chimaera, and Nereids frolicking with sea-horses. Stone-slab seats, wide enough for two lean Greeks to recline side by side, edge the room. Wooden couches were often brought in to sit on top of these platforms. Here songs were sung, toasts were made, poetry was composed and the talk was of politics – the things of import to the *polis*. At the time when the *Symposium* is set, there is a war on: battle-weary men, deep in their cups, were also here to lick the wounds and extend the bonds made during the fighting.

Socrates' nights on a low couch tell us about far more than his preference for good wine and tasty, slave-prepared food. Not everyone went to *symposia*. Some of those 'born to rule' kept themselves above such things. Pericles, we are told, strode straight from the Agora to the *Boule* (the council) without stopping to waste his time with chat and networks.[4] The 'Olympian' had better things to do than shoot the breeze and stir up aristocrats. But Socrates was a philosopher who enjoyed hanging out with the top drawer of society as well as with its artisans and dogsbodies.

Plato's *Symposium* may be pure fantasy, but it is at once a brilliant psychological drama and an acute picture of precisely the kind of event that could, and did, happen on many a fifth-century Athenian night.[5]

The *Symposium* party is being thrown in January or February 416 BC by a group of well-heeled businessmen. One of the symposiasts, Agathon, Socrates' host for the evening, has won a prize for tragedy at a prestigious dramatic festival.[6] Drama is so hard to write and produce well that winning really meant (and means) something. We should imagine that spirits are high. There are songs, discussions, party games.

There appear to be many great minds round this table: Aristophanes, whose waspish pen would help to bring Socrates closer to hemlock, lay on one bench, and together with Agathon burned the tallow low with Socrates and his companions.[7] Plato paints strong, black-outlined characters here. Alcibiades bursts in, more debauched than normal; Socrates is more self-deprecatory and enigmatic; the host, Agathon, is preternaturally beautiful (his soft white skin is tenderly described); and a kind of mystery guest – a woman no less – is part of the dialogue too: Diotima, the thoughtful, articulate priestess whose ideas are, in Plato's *Symposium*, reported by Socrates.

Many *symposia* were, doubtless, dreary. Others must have sparkled. Aristotle, Xenophon, Euripides – all these men spent time wreathed with laurels and lying on the symposiasts' couch. These high-octane experiences must surely have given Socrates food for thought. And at this particular *symposium*, the guests appear on fine form.[8] Alcibiades teases Socrates about his delight in self-denial; there is discussion of Socrates' oddness, of the fact that much that he says has an ambiguous 'dream-like quality'. His ugliness is mocked. But then something rather interesting happens. Socrates is compared to one of the cult statues of the city — wooden and coarse on the outside, but a structure that opens up to reveal a thing of great beauty within:

ALCIBIADES: ... *If you chose to listen to Socrates' discourses you would feel them at first to be quite ridiculous; on the outside they are clothed with such absurd words and phrases — all, of course, the hide of a mocking satyr. His talk is of pack-asses, smiths, cobblers and tanners, and he seems always to be using the same terms for the same things; so that anyone inexpert and thoughtless might laugh his speeches to scorn. But when these are opened and you obtain a fresh view of them, by getting inside, first of all you will discover that they are the only speeches that have any sense in them; and secondly, that none are so divine, so rich in images of virtue, so largely — no, so completely — intent, they are relevant to most or rather to all things worth considering for someone who strives to be beautiful and good.*[9]

Beauty at the time of Socrates

Beauty in Athens at this time was seriously considered to be the sign of a brilliant and noble spirit; a gift of the gods. Those laudable qualities that justified privilege and dominance were believed, naturally, to have been given an appropriately attractive shell. And all those heroically naked paragons around the city itself (both the living, breathing men in the gymnasia and the bronze and marble statues) reflected the visual experience of Athens — this was a land where men stripped to exercise, to bathe, to talk, to worship their gods, to work in the fields. The goddess Athena was honoured by a city-wide *kallisteion*, an all-male beauty contest at the time of the Pan-Athenaea. The winning beauty was handsomely rewarded with more than one hundred amphoras of sacred olive oil. In Socrates' Athens the 'body-beautiful' also signified a beautiful mind.[10] Being beautiful meant that you possessed a moral beauty; *kalon* in Greek means 'fine' and 'praiseworthy' as well as 'fit'.

And so the notion proposed here, that inner beauty can sometimes be contained within a hoary shell, is radical. In the Socratic canon itself, an entire dialogue, the *Hippias Major*, is devoted to a discussion of the definition of 'the beautiful'. Socrates suggests that beauty is not just to do with the line of your leg, the proportion of your nose, the gleam of your skin, but with the state of your soul:

By means of beauty, all beautiful things become beautiful.[11]

If you weren't yourself beautiful, your inner beauty, your virtue could catalyse great things; a man '*moving towards the goal of the erotic suddenly glimpses a "beautiful" which is of wondrous essence, precisely that for which he had previously given such pains, the pure being, imperishable and divine, the "idea of the beautiful".*'[12] These are left-field thoughts for Greek society; an internal character differs from, but is as potent as, external show. Beauty is an attitude, a psychological goal, not just a set of vital statistics.

In classical Athenian terms, Socrates' appearance was utterly dysfunctional, repellent. As soon as figurines of Socrates were commissioned, they were moulded in the form of a satyr. Satirical Socrates seemed to care not two hoots.

My eyes are more beautiful than yours, because yours only look straight ahead, whereas mine bulge out and look to the sides as well.[13]

⧫⧫⧫⧫⧫

Socrates takes the affectionate jibes at the *symposium* on the chin. Once again he wrong-foots Athenian standards and the mono-allure of *kleos* (fame, celebrity, being talked about). Here, in Agathon's friendly soirée with its spiky guests, the philosopher proves how odd he is: he resists sexual advances; despite drinking all night he talks cogently; he is happy not to fit into the good Athenian stereotype of being *kalos k'agathos* — beautiful on the outside and noble on the inside — he's a *satyr* and that's the end of it. After the *symposium* he does not even need access to one of the many hangover cures available in Athens, and bounces off the following day for a full philosophising session, plus a quick trip to the gym.

But the important thing to note is that he is still *there*. Unlike those unfortunate Pythagoreans who shut themselves up in a 'Thinkery' in Croton to philosophise (and were then burned alive), Socrates both refuses to cut himself off from the real world and yet has, so far, despite his lambasting in the Theatre of Dionysos, managed to escape persecution. His relationship with the other guests at the *Symposium* is immediate, comradely, corporeal, concrete, flirtatious, fond. It is in the *Symposium* that you get the sense of a man who thought it important to live life to the full, who refused to bend with the political wind.

Perhaps no surprise then that Socrates also allows for the pursuit of pleasure in his 'good life'. Of course, this quest cannot be excessive, harmful, selfish, degenerate, but Socratic 'good' does not deny the place of delight — hedonism even — in human lives. In Plato's *Gorgias*, Socrates himself declares that his two loves in life are *'philosophy and Alcibiades'*.[14] He judges his own face to be that of a sensualist.[15] Alcibiades is not to be rejected just because he is flawed. Alcibiades' love is visible, it is *'obvious'*.[16] But Socrates is attracted to him precisely because he is extrovert, charming. No one can accuse Socrates of asceticism; drinking, chatting, eating around a low dinner-table on a warm Athenian night, once again he proves himself a philosopher of the people, someone who did not divorce the physical from the meta-physical.[17]

And what the *Symposium* reveals most cogently about Socrates is what he thinks of the power of love in the real, messy human world that we all occupy.

34

THE TROUBLE WITH LOVE

@@@@@@@@@@@@

Fifth century BC and beyond

SOCRATES: Love is the one thing I understand.

Plato, *Symposium*, 177d

EVERYONE KNEW THAT EROS WAS OFTEN an uninvited – but antici-pated – guest at *symposia*. The rutting, squelching, hot, pounding business of physical love was much more evident in Athenian society than in our own. Vase-painters were obsessed with the activities, for example, of prostitutes – which they covered from every angle.

But whereas many evenings in fifth-century Athens ended (and some-times began) with sex, Socrates seemed to be determined not to be a slave to his passions. He was ecstatic, sensuous, but not necessarily interested in the jiggery-pokery of sexual union. This abstinence is something we seem to find easier to imagine in the ecstasies of early Christians, not the pagans, but self-denial is certainly there in the character of Socrates as sold to us by Plato and Xenophon.

'*But to tell you the truth, gentlemen,*' *he continued,* '*By Heaven! It does look to me — to speak confidentially — as if he had also kissed Cleinias; and there is nothing more terribly potent than this at kindling the fires of passion. For it is insatiable and holds out seductive hopes. For this reason I maintain that one who intends to possess the power of self-control must refrain from kissing those in the bloom of beauty*'.[1]

'*Socrates,*' *said Euthydemus,* '*I think you mean that he who is at the mercy of the bodily pleasures has no concern whatever with virtue in any form.*'

'*Yes, Euthydemus; for how can an incontinent man be any better than the dullest beast? How can he who fails to consider the things that matter most, and strives by every means to do the things that are most pleasant, be better than the stupidest of creatures? No, only the self-controlled have power to consider the things that matter most, and, sorting them out after their kind, by word and deed alike to prefer the good and reject the evil.*[2]

A number of the vases depicting the imaginative, adventurous business of symposiast sex are now squirrelled away in locked rooms and cabinets in museums around the world: the Secretum at the British Museum, the Gabinetta Secreta in the Naples Archaeological Museum, a whole extension behind the Corinth Museum. The objects were stored here by nineteenth-century excavators who considered them offensive and 'anti-Hellenic'. Those first-draft democrats of the fifth century would have been politely puzzled. What better way to express the health of your community than with sex? This society was extremely priapic. Herms (busts of the god Hermes) on street corners boasted fine erections, their penises carved onto the shafts of the columns that supported them. Girls on vases take it in every orifice. Athenian sex seems to have been gymnastic and athletic – in the Greek sense of the words – a great deal of flesh on show and all very *athlon* (contest-driven), all aiming for much satisfaction, high prizes. The Gabinetta Secreta and the Secretum are packed because the Greeks cheerfully filled their own lives with so much erotica.

But despite Socrates' undoubted belief in the power of love, tribadic, gasping, physical love for its own sake was not for him.[3] In Xenophon's *Symposium* a slave-boy and slave-girl tenderly re-enact Psyche's seduction by Eros. All in the room are stimulated to go home and make love to their wives. Socrates goes for a walk.

[SOCRATES:] Of course, you don't suppose that lust provokes men to beget children when the streets and stews are full of means to satisfy the sexual urge . . .[4]

Instead he suggests that love means more than a moment in the sack. That real love makes you richer:

SOCRATES: *The man who is attracted only by his beloved's appearance is like one who has rented a farm; his aim is not to increase its value but to gain from it as much of a harvest as he can for himself. On the other hand, the man whose goal is friendship is more like one possessing a farm of his own.*[5]

The stories that Socrates shares around the drinking couches of the *symposia* are not stories of sex, but stories of love. *Ta erotika* in his book means 'the good things' or 'what leads us to the good things and good spiritedness'. And the philosopher does not pull his punches. He criticises one of the most powerful men of the day – a man who will then go on to bring civil war and tyranny back to Athens – for being obsessed with plain, burning, fluid-exchange sex. Critias was the name of this influential, reactionary, oligarchic individual.[6] A relation of Plato and an aspiring tragedian with a darkly tragic bent, he moved in Socrates' circle. Critias was hot for a younger man called Euthydemus. Socrates did not approve.

Critias seems to have the feelings of a pig: he can no more keep away from Euthydemus than pigs can help rubbing themselves against stones.[7]

Critias was furious. After the event he tried to gag Socrates, to stop him talking to anyone under thirty. Critias despised the self-righteous philosopher.[8] This tells us as much about Socrates as it does about Critias. Often criticised by modern authors for being more than a little reactionary and 'educating' some of the most oppressive oligarchs of the day, this spat over Euthydemus exemplifies that in fact Socrates was troubled by Critias and his crowd. Just because the philosopher drank with them and they listened to him did not make him their role-model; we should never confuse a catholic taste in friends and acquaintances with evidence of indoctrination or sectarian cliquery.

Socrates was perfectly at ease in the *symposia*, but in the minds of others he sits there a little uncomfortably. He was not after all an aristocrat – and neither the democrats nor the oligarchs of the city would forget that he had broken convention by dining late into the night with the great and the good.

The philosopher was perhaps that troubling mix: a demotic high-flyer. The Athenians cherished those who were 'first in wealth and breeding'. They believed the beautiful *kaloi k'agathoi* were fit to rule. Socrates was not quite fully the ascetic, not fully the democrat, not fully the oligarch – and he was ubiquitous. A few years from now, when Athens has suffered so much and yet Socrates still swaggers through the Agora with his infuriating sense of purpose and his beatific attitude, perhaps he was just too vexatious, exasperating; a gadfly that needed swatting. Already we know from the plays of Aristophanes that the philosopher was beginning to rub his fellow citizens up the wrong way. And there is another, sadder possibility. Perhaps towards the end of the fifth century BC Athens was simply tired of him. The conversations about Socrates, once excited, indulgent, were now tetchy, damning. Those who have an extended stretch in the saddle are often wearied of; as time passes the tallest poppies are frequently cut down.

And Socrates should perhaps have chosen a little more carefully the men he decided to insult, thought twice before taking on and cutting down to size a character such as Critias, one of the high-flyers of the day.

One street proverb from the period should have sounded a warning bell in Socrates' ears:

I hate a drinking companion with a memory.[9]

35

OH, TELL ME THE TRUTH ABOUT LOVE

@@@@@@@@@@@@

Athens, 416 BC

*Wisdom is a most beautiful thing, and love is of the beautiful; and therefore
love is also a philosopher or lover of wisdom, and being a lover of wisdom is in
a mean between the wise and the ignorant ... Such, my dear Socrates, is the
nature of the Spirit of Love.*

Plato, *Symposium*, 204b[1]

I N SOME SENSES THE *SYMPOSIUM* IS the most urgent of all Plato's works
– the narrative trips over itself to arrive on the page, the dining room
in a back street of Athens is a factory for beautiful ideas, ideas of
beauty, beautiful things. Even the silences sparkle.

At this dinner party, set more than 2,400 years ago, Love is the night's
theme. The *Symposium* can still be read as one of the greatest stories of love
in Western literature. The only subject in the world that Socrates believes
himself to be the unsurpassed master of is love.[2] '*I cannot remember a time
when I was not in love with someone.*'[3] Socrates loves his fellow men with an over-
powering eroticism, and because he believes he can look into their eyes and
understand a little about himself as he does so, we are taught that it is
through our relationship with the world around us that we can become
whole. Socrates sees the massive power of love.[4] We too are just beginning
to unpick the complex, psychophysical parcel that love is. Socrates makes
our relationships with one another his life's work.

Socratic love is enormously powerful, it turns the world upside down.
What the philosopher knows is that we love love-stories, and our love is

often a love-story played out. But nowhere does he mock. Socrates' love is literal: the point of life is to love it. He is erotic. He states that if Eros passes you by in life, you are a nonentity. All those aspects of love he approves of, as good-life glue for society, since 'festivals, sacrifices, dances' are motivated by Eros. And, more than that, love is a guide — a passion for what is good and a horror for what is degrading.[5]

And the genuinely heart-warming revelation of Socrates in the *Symposium* is that dedication to love is not a selfish pursuit. The point of love is not gratification, but symbiosis. And love, desire, ambition, hope, concord, enthusiasm, drive whatever you want to call it — if tended, if not allowed to burn itself out, plays a long game. His love is not flash-in-the-pan passionate. In Socrates' eyes, it is honesty and a pursuit of knowledge rather than ignorance that leads to loveliness in life. For him, love has a purpose. It is the life-force, the desire to do, to be, to think. It is the thing that makes us *feel* great about our world, and therefore makes us *be* great in it. Socrates describes these 'good' dynamos as *ta erotika* — the things of love.

SOCRATES: *Those who are already wise no longer love wisdom, whether they are gods or men. Neither do those who are so ignorant that they are bad, for no bad and stupid person loves wisdom. There remain only those who have this bad thing, ignorance, but have not yet been made ignorant or stupid by it. They are conscious of not knowing what they don't know.*[6]

Socrates and women

Socrates has positioned love, goodness and companionship squarely at the centre of his idea of a well-functioning society. But still the philosopher needs to sort out what to do about women. The nobility of love between men is possible to imagine — but between a man and a woman? Given that the first created woman was nominated by Hesiod the *kalon-kakon*, the beautiful-evil thing, this is going to take quite some untangling. Unlike so many men of his day, Socrates does not choose just to ignore the female of the species. And since he is keen on those who really know about a subject rather than just pretend knowledge, he turns to the figure of a woman for illumination.

They praise in such splendid fashion that ... they bewitch our souls ... [E]very time I listen fascinated [by their praise of me], I am exalted and imagine myself to have become all at once taller and nobler and more handsome ... owing to the persuasive eloquence of the speaker.[7]

And so into the theatrical setting of the *symposium* enters a female character: the priestess Diotima.

Diotima is, I am sure, used to some extent as a mouthpiece for Platonic ideals – voicing ways to build the perfect society. (She is one character who is a free and equal participant in Plato's *Symposium*, and, atypically, she is a woman.) It is useful to have a woman here in Socrates' *symposium* because the discussion is so much about the male/female act of fertilisation and then the female business of gestation and parturition. There are complex discussions of how what we would describe as 'heterosexuals' and 'homosexuals' give 'birth to beauty', through children and through accounts of virtue, respectively – the former via pregnancy of the body, the latter via pregnancy of the soul. Relationships with beauty and beautiful things can lead to a bigger and better kind of beauty. You can see why Socrates lends himself so well to Judaeo-Christian and Islamic philosophy; positively seeking out good here on earth brings about the good of mankind and the good of the hereafter. Unfortunate, perhaps, that Socrates' respect for the opinions and standing of this priestess character did not also prove tenacious within the later iterations of the monotheistic religions that supplanted paganism, nor unassailable within Golden Age Athens itself. Because the character of Diotima tells us much about the value of women both then and now.

36

DIOTIMA – A VERY SOCIAL PRIESTESS

◎◎◎◎◎◎◎◎◎◎◎◎◎

Naples and Athens,
Fifth century BC and beyond

Look at what people usually do — all women in particular, they dedicate the first thing that comes to hand, they swear to offer sacrifice, and promise to found shrines for gods and spirits and children of god.

Plato, *Laws*, 909e–910[1]

This counterfeit coin, woman, to curse the human race.

Euripides, *Hippolytus*, 616–17[2]

ONE OF THE FEW REMAINING IMAGES of Socrates and Diotima is lost in the vast Naples Archaeological Museum: literally. I turned up there one blisteringly wet October afternoon to examine the little bronze plaque (originally used to decorate furniture in some well-to-do household). It was not on show, so a curator took me backstage, to the fabulously functional, creaking, gargantuan storerooms where much of the finest art from an entire antiquity is kept under lock and key.

Past racks of frescoes from Pompeii, dulled with dust, past one-armed goddesses, downwards in stainless-steel lifts with mobster-manqué security guards and over to a padlocked metal locker. We peered into an old plastic crate, the bottom of which was scattered with metal objects, many wrapped in brown paper and string and simply labelled. But Diotima wasn't there. Loaned to an exhibition, she was playing hide-and-seek somewhere with her philosopher-companion.

A stern bust of Socrates was on show in the public galleries, as was a finely tessellated mosaic – the pieces so numerous that no one has yet counted them. But the intricacy of the philosopher's relationships, particularly with the women around him, was not obvious. Nor was this furniture-decoration, priestess-loving Socrates, a Socrates the public wanted to see. But in fact the character of Diotima is a close ally when it comes to trying to understand both what Socrates thought and who he was.

Diotima was a priestess. A priestess from Mantinea.[3] It is difficult to tell how accurately she is represented in Plato. It could quite possibly be that she is fictional. But then again, no one in Plato's Dialogues is entirely made up, apart from the mysterious 'Eleaic Stranger', so it would be slightly odd for Plato to fabricate her entirely. And then, too, there is the fact that Diotima's demeanour, her life skills, are very believable. She talks in public – as priestesses were allowed to;[4] she represents herself as a kind of messenger (priestesses from the Oracle at Delphi and those in charge of the sacred mysteries at Eleusis were also the message-carriers of the gods). And (in some aspects) Diotima is believable as a woman. When ruminating on love, she looks for a productive middle way – she thinks that it is love that inspires humankind; desire forces us to want to be better: better philosophers, better lovers, better humans.

This, when once beheld, will outshine your gold and your clothing, your beautiful boys and young men, whose aspect now so astounds you and makes you and many another, at the sight and constant society of your darlings, ready to do without either food or drink if that were in any way possible, and only gaze upon them and have their company. But tell me, what would happen if one of you had the fortune to look upon essential beauty entire, pure and unalloyed; not infected with the flesh and colour of humanity, and ever so much more of mortal trash? What if he could behold the divine beauty itself in its unique form?[5]

Sometimes described as an anomaly, in fact Diotima reminds us that priestesses were a highly visible part of the Athens where Socrates lived, worked and loved.[6] These women were not just arranging antiquity's equivalent of flowers on the altar – they were responsible for the smooth running of ritual and religion, and therefore of life itself. The Athenians thought their good fortune came only from their good relationship with assorted spirits and Olympian deities and it was all down to the women of the city to keep this relationship sweet. One fragment from a lost play by Euripides – performed, in Athens, during the Peloponnesian War – makes that poetically clear:

And in divine affairs — I think this of the first importance —
we have the greatest part. For at the oracles of Phoibos
women expound Apollo's will. At the holy seat of Dodona
by the sacred oak the female race conveys
the thoughts of Zeus to all Greeks who desire it.
As for the holy rituals performed for the Fates
and the nameless goddesses, these are not holy
in men's hands; but among women they flourish,
every one of them. Thus in holy service woman
plays the righteous role.[7]

So the women in Socrates' day didn't just drift around at home: many of the best-born were busy priestesses. Virgin, wife, old maid alike — these women had practical duties. If they were well heeled, they would be expected to fund the building of cisterns, porticos, temples. They supplied oil for gyms and animals for sacrifice.[8] Priestesses could be temple key-holders — a big job given that these sanctuaries doubled up as banks, a safe depository for the community's wealth.[9] The temple keys themselves were enormous things, more like the starter-handles of early-twentieth-century cars, and on a number of carved *stelai* we see women confidently wielding them.

And then, often at night, the female religious leaders were joined by their devoted followers: mature women or girls bearing the finest of baskets — willow-woven, bronze, gilded, silver — which contained the most precious, the most mysterious of things. Banish the image of women just balancing water on their heads after another back-breaking trip to the well; these creatures had the honour of bearing the holiest of liquids.

This is not to deny that some of the all-female activities ring a little discordantly in twenty-first-century ears: the Thesmophoria, for example. This festival's origins stretch back to the Stone Age. Married women (no men were allowed) congregated to indulge in rites that were largely obscene and extreme. The worshippers would insult one another and expose themselves, they would carry phallic objects. Slaughtering a large number of piglets or puppies, they threw the corpses into a chasm, and then days later dug up the gamey, half-decayed remains as an offering for the goddess Demeter.

Little surprise, perhaps, that some Athenian men should seem a bit nervous of their womenfolk.

So think back. The sound of young women's voices, praising in the temples and sanctuaries, carried on the air, their figures stone-silhouetted against the sky, their names carved on *stelai* and statue plinths and grave monuments across the city – these were clearly a force to be reckoned with. In the British Museum there is a 3-foot-high gold sceptre, and a golden necklace heavy with flowers, with fruits waiting to burst, nestling next to the heads of horned women. The provenance is shrouded in the treasure-seeking, tomb-raiding ambiguity of the 1870s, when the artefacts were acquired – but one sensible reading is that these belonged to the priestesses of a cult of the goddess Hera.[10] Some of the religiously significant women in Athens wore necklaces of dried figs, a sign of their fertility, while others were chosen for their 'god-given' beauty. We know this from their names: *Kallisto*, Most Beautiful; *Megiste*, Most Great; *Chrysis*, Golden; *Theodote*, God-Given;[11] *Aristonoe*, Best.[12]

At night women's ritual activity increased exponentially. It was thought appropriate that women should operate most vigorously not in the brightness of day, but in the gloom. In the all-female Haloa, a festival associated with wine, fertility and libido, it seems that women 'tended' fake phalli (not surprising to learn perhaps that the festival was particularly popular with prostitutes). Young girls sang from door to door in honour of the 'great Mother' (the oldest fertility goddess), accompanied by the dark and, so they thought, the priapic god Pan.[13] Young and old processed at night to praise another newcomer to the city, the god Sabazios, a 'dodgy' easterner from Phrygia.[14] Young devotees of Aphrodite carried 'unspeakable offerings in baskets' through the Acropolis at night. Dread forces, the 'nameless goddesses' – awful creatures like the *Eumenides*, the 'Kindly Ones,' more honestly known as the *Erinyes*, the 'Furies' – were escorted back into the earth at night by women thankful, one imagines, for the comfort of the flaming torches they carried. In women-only rites, young dogs were sacrificed after sunset and flung into flame-lit crevasses to appease the goddess of the Underworld, Hekate. The *Adonia*, where females mourned with Aphrodite the loss of the beautiful boy Adonis, involved a night-time ritual, a mock-funeral procession, much wailing and no little drinking. Deeper into the war, the grief of these Adonis-worshippers was thought to be a terrible omen for Athens.[15]

Although our literary sources tell us that respectable women in classical Athens should stay indoors, women who walked hand-in-hand with the gods in fact glinted and scintillated as, carrying the golden sceptres and staffs of their priesthood, they officiated at civic rituals, filling the air with unearthly ululating sounds. They spoke out, and their hands flashed as they killed and carved the sacrificial meat.

As soon as I turned seven I was a child hand-maiden, up on the Acropolis,
then, I ground sacred grain; when I was ten I shed
my saffron robe for the Foundress, being a bear at the Brauronia;
And once, when I was a beautiful maiden, I carried sacred baskets,
wearing a necklace of dried figs.[16]

This list appears in a cool, serious passage in the middle of Aristophanes' play *Lysistrata*. It is presented as an explanation as to why women's voices, in Athens, needed to be heard. In the Socratic Dialogues of Plato we have the only other extant example of Athenian women, through conversations with the philosopher, being given a high-level platform. Socrates is rare in the philosophical canon. This unusual, thoughtful man, and his disciple Plato, who were in reality surrounded by women active in the maintenance of Golden Age, democratic Athens, however briefly, give women a voice.

37

LITTLE BEARS

ல௸௸௸௸௸௸

Brauron, north of Athens

Women so beautiful it hurt your eyes to see them.

Herodotus, *The Histories* [adapted], 5.18

A ND WHAT OF THE OTHER FEMALE citizens: the girls, the maidens, the widows of Athens?
Every four years, Socrates would have seen, walking through the Agora and along the Sacred Way, diminutive lines of temporary exiles. Their destination was Brauron, a two-day hike east of Athens; for many this must have seemed a long road, because the majority of these pilgrims were young children. Eight-, nine-, ten-year-old girls from good families were regularly sent out to this religious sanctuary from Athena's city, to live for three, four, five years, as 'wild animals'.

Little Bears, *arktoi*, they were called. Dedicated to the virgin huntress goddess Artemis, they wore animal skins and headdresses, and on occasion saffron-yellow dresses. Vase fragments from the site show naked maidens running away from pursuing bears – a rite the girls themselves possibly endured with real wild beasts. Sometimes the girls raced in short chitons, sometimes naked. Plato approved: in his ideal city-state, as in Sparta, young women were encouraged to compete nude in foot-racing and athletics.[1] The purpose of the exercise at Brauron was to run the animal out of the child. Their time in this religious boarding school appeased the coiled, virgin goddess Artemis – the chaste huntress whose arrows could strike women down in childbirth. The Little Bears' days were filled with dances. They learned the jobs a good Athenian wife would be expected to accomplish – in their sanctuary-home you can still see the dormitories where (one imagines, worn out) they slept.

What remains of the temple complex is peaceful now. Today the only sound of water is the leak of pipes, and the ghost of a stream, irrigating nearby fields. In its heyday, in the mid–fifth century BC, as recent excavations have shown, a monumental fountain, 60 feet long, was installed here to channel the sacred water. Lichen-covered rocks are a protection and a backdrop, a reminder of the primeval wash of this sanctuary's devotion. But we should also remember that in some ways this sacred zone would have resembled an outpost of the rag-trade; when women died in childbirth their clothes were dedicated here; draped, hung and stored around the sanctuary; a limp gift to pitiless Artemis, to whom, probably just a few years from now, the girls would be calling out during the dreadful pangs of labour.[2] Votaries still come here to pray for help in childbirth from a distant relative of those goddesses, the Virgin Mary, in the pretty little Byzantine church on the edge of the site.

During the Peloponnesian War Brauron's satellite sanctuary up on the Acropolis was extended. Athens had a gimlet-eye focused on Brauron in political terms – useful strategic territory, but as the Athenian population was effectively being thinned out by the dragging conflict, it was also essential that the girls – the reproductive future of the community – were kept secure. In Brauron itself, the youngsters, it was hoped, would chasten the beast within them and learn to appreciate the grinding reality of being an Athenian wife. Subdued, de-spirited, around the age of twelve the youngsters would then be dressed in modest clothes and marched back to Athens to find a husband.

⌾⌾⌾⌾⌾

Socrates – in a straightforwardly pragmatic way – seemed to think the female of the species could be used in society a little more imaginatively.[3]

SOCRATES: Is there anyone to whom you commit more affairs of importance than to your wife?

CRITOBULUS: No.

SOCRATES: Is there anyone to whom you talk less?

CRITOBULUS: Few or none, I confess.

SOCRATES: And you married her when she was a mere child and had seen and heard almost nothing?[4]

During the city's difficult war-days the philosopher suggested that a group of women, relatives of one of his friends, become gainfully employed in the wool-working business.[5] And in the *Republic*, the character of Socrates discusses the value of giving women the same education as men, and access to all functions and professions.[6] While Plato opines in his *Laws* that women are '*accustomed to an underground and shadowy existence*,' and again Xenophon writes that they are '*brought up under the most cramping restrictions, raised from childhood to see and hear as little as possible, and to ask only the fewest possible questions*',[7] perhaps Socrates, who was happy to stare right through convention, realised that raising 50-plus per cent of the population as etiolated creatures was a waste.

And when, during the *Symposium* (Xenophon's this time, not Plato's) Socrates is watching a slave-girl performing complicated circus tricks for the amusement of the assembled company (juggling, contorting, diving through crossed swords), he chips in:

SOCRATES: *A woman's nature is not at all inferior to a man's — except in that it lacks understanding* [reasoning, effectiveness] *and strength. So if any of you has a wife, let him confidently set about teaching her whatever he would like to have her know.*[8]

Although of course, with a distance of 2,400 years and given the provocative, sexually charged circumstances, it is difficult to tell whether or not Xenophon gives the philosopher this line with an ironic smile.

Socrates first and then Plato (even to some extent Aristotle) may well have watched all the precise, well-handled busyness of women in society — doing those important jobs listed by Aristophanes — and thought 'What a waste!' These are creatures that could be even more productive . . . there are other ways they can add to society.

Listen to further conversations in Plato's *Republic*:

Many women, it is true, are better than many men in many things.[9]

If, then, we are to use the women for the same things as the men, we must also teach them the same things.[10]

Socrates was, above all, fascinated by the business of being human. And in the human genus, he happily includes both women and men. He was, as a result, humane; Xenophon has Socrates comment as he visits the prostitute Theodote:

. . . There are many attractive servant girls, and they show absolutely no sign of neglect . . .[11]

Take off those rose-tinted glasses: the philosopher is no campaigner for a classical-age, sexual revolution, he also refers to women as horses, as slaves. No proto-feminist here; but Socrates does have the courage to look beyond the orthodox. And the significant women who crop up in the literary accounts of his life far outnumber those who appear alongside other 'great men' of this period. His name is also linked to that of real, historical women — and not just in a sexual or moral scandal (which is how women typically make their way into the historical record), but as an inspiration; witness this antique inscription on the tombstone of a young woman:

She was the splendour of Greece, and possessed the beauty of Helen, the virtue of Thirma, the pen of Aristippus, the soul of Socrates and the tongue of Homer.[12]

Socrates and wives, midwives and war-widows

⊚⊚⊚⊚⊚⊚⊚⊚⊚⊚⊚⊚

Socrates' mother, we are told, became a midwife.[13] Socrates may have been conceived in a city showered with talents, but he was not born with a silver spoon in his mouth. Phaenarete was a *'well-built woman'*,[14] with a stocky set suited to her physically demanding job. Between the ages of eighteen and thirty, while the philosopher lived at home (the standard arrangement in Athens at this time), Socrates would have watched his mother preparing for and practising her difficult, essential business. Not a precious upbringing; he might have seen Phaenarete preparing herbs – *pharmaka* – drugs, useful little things. Pennyroyal to catalyse contractions; cardamom concoctions to fumigate the womb through a long reed; pomegranate pessaries. He would have heard what happened when births went wrong and child, or mother, or both, died. He would have known that some Athenian parents chose to expose their newborn to the elements if she was a girl-child.

In the National Archaeological Museum in Athens there is a useful cabinet that gathers together images of women who gave birth, or helped. These are often crude objects, social records rather than aspirational *objets d'art*. Many are still unpublished by scholars: this is an aspect of Greek history that early collectors had little interest in celebrating. In one particularly rough group of figures two headscarved women, one woman cradled in the other's lap, sit while a baby appears from beneath the full skirts. They are not gorgeous things, but as terracotta mementoes they work. They remind us what a lusty, messy business giving birth really is.

But nonetheless, the midwife (*maia* in Greek) ensured that a community survived. At the point of birth the midwife and her companions howled with joy to the heavens. If the child was a boy an olive-wreath would be pinned to the doorway; if a girl, a tuft of wool – a prophecy of the woven goods that, as an Athenian female, she would spend much of her life producing. Many babies died in classical antiquity, between 10 and 30 per cent, and others were exposed to die: also the midwife's job.

If you take what he says at face value, Socrates' family background (stonemason father, midwife mother) — at the coal-face of civilisation, knocking out citizens, knocking up monuments to house them — had an enormous impact.[15]

SOCRATES: *My art of midwifery is in general like that of midwives. The only difference is that my patients are men, not women. My concern is not with the body but with the soul that is in labour. The highest point of my art is the power to prove by every test whether the offspring of a young man's thought is a false phantom or is something alive and real. I am so much like the midwife that I cannot myself give birth to wisdom. The common reproach is true, that, although I question others, I can bring nothing to light because there is no wisdom in me. This is because God constrains me to serve as a midwife, but has debarred me from giving birth.*[16]

Socrates would have been under no illusions. He would have known what a bloody, churning, searing, dangerous, wonderful business it is, coming into this world. His mother must have come home tainted with the sweet-acrid smell of childbirth and stillbirths. She would also have come home polluted for at least five days, by her presence during the parturition. Childbirth was one of the many ways that women were thought to generate *miasma*, pollution, in the Ancient World.

And yet, despite knowing all of this, despite a childhood listening to *rhapsodes* (epic-poetry reciters) charm year in, year out around village camp fires with stories of demonic, intemperate, sex-crazed women — Helen, Klytemnestra, Medea, schemers who brought down the Age of Heroes — despite being nudged, sweaty-seated, faces red from the glowing embers, by his fellow boy-Athenians, the next-generation citizens; despite spending the majority of his waking hours at men-only gymnasia, or fighting shoulder-to-shoulder with only males, walking through the streets in which, during daylight hours, respectable women were conspicuous by their absence — despite all this, Socrates' attitude to the female of the species appears unconventional and relatively welcoming.

∽∾∽∾∽

For Diotima was not the only female character with whom Socrates had a rather unorthodox literary relationship — his conversations with Aspasia had (apparently) been more than a little unusual. Plato, who reports this in his dialogue *Menexenus*, is, one suspects, mildly uncomfortable with Socrates' deference to Pericles' fancy-woman. In the Dialogue, the two have had a memory contest to see who could recall more of a speech — Socrates his own words, and Aspasia Pericles' famous funerary speech, which she was rumoured to have written.

SOCRATES: *But I was listening only yesterday to Aspasia going through a funeral speech for these very people. For she had heard the report you mention, that the Athenians are going to select the speaker; and thereupon she rehearsed to me the speech in the form it should take, extemporising in part, while other parts of it she had previously prepared, as I imagine, at the time when she was composing the funeral oration which Pericles delivered; and from this she patched together sundry fragments.*

MENEXENUS: *Could you repeat from memory that speech of Aspasia?*

SOCRATES: *Yes, if I am not mistaken; for I learnt it, to be sure, from her as she went along . . .* [17]

This is more than just a parlour game. Those with bardic memory at this stage of human development were the repository of all civilisation's information. Wise men were wise because they had impressive recall. Homer's epics, a touchstone for Ancient Greek life, were put onto the brain's hard-drive and reproduced in public squares, on street corners, in private homes. A retentive mind was considered a great gift of the gods. It is fascinating that Aspasia is credited with such a gift.

Of course men had always been jealous of Aspasia; that interloper who benefited from Athenian *nous*, who wormed her way into the arms of their great Pericles and then 'weakened his limbs', as many Athenians saw it. That perfumed, jewel-spattered whore. A recent archaeological discovery suggests they might just have had some small justification. One of the heavy baubles dedicated up at the Parthenon to the goddess Athena – a gold tiara – is inscribed as the gift of Aspasia. Only an extremely wealthy person would have been able to afford such a fine offering. [18] Even in a democracy men, and women, had ways of showing that they were, or had been, special.

In 438–436 BC the xenophobia directed at Aspasia came to a head. She was in court on charges of impiety – it could possibly have been her reported conversations with Socrates, and the other more radical philosophers of the day, that got her into such trouble. [19] At the same time Pheidias was accused of embezzling public funds and Anaxagoras of denying the gods. Aspasia was – we are told by hostile sources – saved through the intervention of Pericles, who wept and moped around with more care for her fate than his own. She might have been saved from condemnation by the courts, but the parodying of this episode by Athenian playwrights suggests that Socrates' association with Aspasia would not play out well for the philosopher.

What the characters of Diotima (and Aspasia) and Socrates do seem to have shared was a passionate belief in the potential of relationships. The Platonic Dialogues make it clear that relationships make our world better. Mutual commitment is wrapped in and gives birth to love. This love can bind marriages, cities, states, religions. Aphrodite does not just sponsor the poison-tipped arrows of *Eros*, but the lint-gauze of *Harmonia*. Heterosexual love can forge a path to virtue. And there is no doubt that when it came to real, human relationships Socrates could speak from experience. Because some time in the philosopher's early to mid-thirties (Plato suggests thirty to thirty-five, and Aristotle recommends thirty-seven as the prime age to get hitched), he married.

Once a suitable partner had been selected for *Sokrates Alopekethen*, a series of customs, social and religious – unchanged for generations – would have been set in train. An Athenian wedding's primary purpose was to legitimise the sexual union, the '*gamos*', between a man and a woman. Groom and father of the bride-to-be sealed the pact with a firm handshake. Socrates and his 'intended' would have performed a series of pre-nuptial sacrifices, often with the accompaniment of marriage hymns and incense for Aphrodite. They would have purified themselves in the waters of the city – the sacred spring of Kallirrhoe or at the banks of Eridanos. Clean, rendered 'extra' fertile by the sacred waters, both man and girl-woman (most brides were fourteen or so) would have then doused themselves with perfume – myrrh was a favourite – both were garlanded and the bride was veiled.

After entering the bride's family home, sweet with herbs and ribbons, a curious symposium would begin. Men down one side, women the other, wedding cakes made of sesame seeds were eaten, the sacrificed animals were roasted for the feast, there were bawdy songs (as with Greek weddings today, this whole process could last for three days) and then at last the bride's father 'presented' his daughter to the groom. She would have lifted her veil, and now Socrates had a wife. The union was then witnessed by more citizens of Athens as the wedding procession wound its way, noisily, through the city's back streets to Socrates' family home.

Like the other newly-weds of his day, the philosopher would have been showered by his mother with a hail-storm of nuts, figs, dates, coins to ensure the prosperity and fertility of his union. Like them too he may have trooped over to the Sanctuary of Aphrodite Ourania to deposit one silver drachma in the stone wedding-themed slot machine recently identified and now on display in the new Acropolis Museum – a payment to ensure Aphrodite's blessing for the nuptials. And on his wedding night Socrates' way would be torch-lit to bed by his mother, his new wife's new mother-in-law.[20]

Remembering his years in the company of beautiful boys, in particular Alcibiades, all golden hair, gym-hardened muscles, a knowing light in their eyes, it can be easy to forget that Socrates had a wife. But he did, Xanthippe, a woman who has come down to us in the literature of antiquity as a termagant, a nagging shrew.

38

XANTHIPPE

❦❦❦❦❦❦❦❦❦❦❦

District of Alopeke, Socrates and Xanthippe *c.*420 BC

*Socrates is said to have had an exceeding antipathy towards almost all
women, either because he had a natural disinclination to their society, or because
he had had two wives at the same time (since that was permitted by a decree
passed by the Athenians) and they made wedlock hateful to him.*

Aulus Gellius, *Attic Nights*, 15.20.6[1]

W AR WAS PLAYING ITS STATISTICAL GAME in Athens. Almost a
decade into the Peloponnesian conflict and the male Athenian
population was horribly reduced; plague and battle had killed

one-third, maybe as many as one-half of the men in the city-state. Over the last eight years the city had come to resemble Sparta more closely than it could have liked. In Sparta the city streets were filled with women; all men between the ages of seven and thirty were away training in their military camp. And now Athena's city had a new, similar imparity – because so many men had been hacked down by Spartan swords.

And so some of Athens' women had multiple partners. Aspasia is one example. Although we hear little of her fate after Pericles' death we know that she quickly became the consort of a sheep-dealer. Not only were there re-marriages, but bigamy was both legal and becoming increasingly popular. Different women were allowed to bear more than one man's child. Looked at another way, well-bred women were allowed to be both a wife and a mistress at the same time. Some sources would have us believe that Socrates also married bigamously.[2]

Socrates and Euripides are amongst a number of fifth-century Athenian men who, it was reported, were allowed by the circumstances of the war to become bigamists. There are two possibilities here. One is that the stories of Socrates' bigamy took hold because they conveniently emphasise his oddness, his eccentricity. (Useful too for a quick bit of misogyny. Xanthippe is shrewish because, tediously, she not only has a poor eccentric for a husband, but also has to host an even younger model – a girl called Myrto – in her household.) The other is that the stories were true.

Socrates' two young women were said to squabble furiously (Socrates was in his late forties by this time, Xanthippe probably only just twenty), and when Socrates guffaws at their backbiting, they 'would pull him apart . . . saying he was a most foul man with snub nostrils, receding brow, hairy shoulders and bandy legs.'[3] In one episode that has given great delight to cartoonists and engravers down the centuries, Xanthippe, raging after one argument with her maddening philosopher spouse, pours the contents of a bedpan over Socrates' head; 'I always knew that rain would follow thunder,'[4] sighs the philosopher, resignedly mopping his brow.

But maybe this farcical situation, these pantomime gags told down time, held more than a kernel of truth. Athens at this time must have been reminiscent of Kabul 2002–10: ragged, war-torn, veiled women in the streets with no husbands, brothers or sons. Athenians were nothing if not pragmatic. The city needed repopulating. In fact the *lack* of a decree allowing for bigamy, rather than its presence, would have been odd.[5] And we hear from Plato that Socrates was, at the end of his life, visited in jail by his three children: Lamprokles – a *meirakion*, a 'young chap'; and Sophroniskos and Menexenos, *paidia* – small children. In terms of keeping Athens' population stable, this was a bigamous arrangement that seems to have done the job.

The age difference of Socrates' offspring could indeed be explained by two wives. The mixed messages given out by the sources in antiquity about Socrates' marital status could be because bigamy sits a little uneasily along-side many dreams of moral goodness. And we should remember that writers in the fifth century were typically bored by a man's married affairs – which is why in all 100,000 words of Plato's Dialogues, Xanthippe gets only two mentions.[6]

Still, Xanthippe (who must have been relatively high-born with a name like that, *Xanthippe*, Golden-Horsey; Pericles' blue-blood father, for example, was called *Xanthippos*), it seems, was no pariah, she did have some friends. One of Socrates' followers (and incidentally one of Plato's rivals) was a man called Aeschines. Aeschines' work was widely circulated up until the end of the second century AD, and then it fell out of favour. It was said that his own dialogues were in fact derived closely from Socrates', which had been passed on to him by Xanthippe in gratitude for Aeschines' friend-ship after the philosopher had been killed. Interestingly, Aeschines' portrayal of Aspasia also seems to be an unusually sympathetic and subtle one.

Aspasia began a discussion with Xenophon himself. 'I put a question to you, Xenophon,' she says, 'if your neighbour has a better horse than yours, would you prefer your own horse or his?' 'His,' Xenophon replies. 'Suppose he has a better farm than you have, which farm, I should like to know, would you prefer?' 'Beyond all doubt,' Xenophon jumps in, 'whichever is the best.' 'Suppose he has a better wife than you have, would you prefer his wife?' Well, on this Xenophon was silent.[7]

It is almost certainly from Aeschines' work that the Roman-period author Plutarch gets the notion that both Pericles and Socrates were drawn to Aspasia because she was both *sophe*, wise, and *politike*, canny, wised-up and astute. Our loss of Aeschines as an uncorrupted source for the fifth century is immensely frustrating. But reading between the lines the author does give us some useful clues to the temper of Socrates' city and life. Aeschines' close connection with Xanthippe suggests that she was more than just a nag.

Socrates, we are told, dealt with Xanthippe not atypically. He talks about 'handling' her as though she were a spirited horse. He appears happy to let her fend for herself, feeling no pressure to bring home household funds. Even with the scanty evidence available to us (his putative relationships with Diotima and Aspasia, the suggestion that he allows Xanthippe to berate him in public, his belief that women should have a concrete role in society), his heart, one feels, lies with the men around him.

And it is from his interaction with the man who stole Socrates' heart, Alcibiades, that we learn both a great deal about the philosopher's relationship to his city and how, towards the end of the fifth century BC, that city was beginning to fracture from within.

39

ALCIBIADES: VIOLET-CROWNED, PUNCH-DRUNK

@@@@@@@@@@@@

Athens, 416 BC

*If only wisdom were like water which always flows from a full cup
into an empty one when we connect them with a piece of yarn — well, then
I would consider it the greatest prize to have the chance to sit down next to
you. I would soon be overflowing with your wonderful wisdom.*

Plato, *Symposium*, 175d–e[1]

IT IS IN THE *SYMPOSIUM* THAT we meet again the other leading player
in Socrates' story — Alcibiades.

Alcibiades has burst into that immortalised dinner gathering on a
hot night. He is more than a little drunk, his head is wreathed in violets
(how could Socrates resist his violet-cream-perfumed golden locks — a heart-
turning double-sweetness?). But he is beauty with a forked tongue.

SOCRATES: *I beg you, Agathon . . . protect me from this man!*[2]

So why did those pretty flowers ring Alcibiades' head? In Athens, young
men who worshipped Demeter and Dionysos wore just such a gentle, pungent
crown. Was the aristrocrat preparing himself for a hard night of drinking?
Centuries later Pliny would advise men to wreath themselves in violets to
dispel the fug of wine-fumes or of a wine-fuelled headache. The plant —
actually a purple gillyflower — still grows profusely in Athens today and is
a favourite decoration at parties that involve serious boozing.

Or is Plato reminding us that Athens herself has an epithet, 'violet-crowned'? He is perhaps giving us Alcibiades as Athens: beautiful, louche, supremely confident, sensuous, redolent, flawed, war-hungry – and visibly wilting.

⌒⌒⌒⌒⌒

Alcibiades is one of those enchanting, magnetic historical characters who always seem to take things just that bit too far. He clearly drove men and women to distraction. The only extant evidence we have for a woman initiating her own divorce in this period concerns Alcibiades' wife Hipparete. She leaves Alcibiades in protest at the number of prostitutes he brings back to the house, and moves in with her brother Callias. The long-suffering woman goes to register the divorce with the Archon (on her own) and is seized shortly afterwards by Alcibiades and dragged – one presumes ignominiously – back to their old home.

Within a few months the pair are separated.

That brilliant, glowing, selfish party-animal Alcibiades illuminates the cracks in the 'liberty and equality' of the radical new state. His behaviour began to prove that Athenian democracy, deep down, was a sham and always had been. Whereas others in the city had, as the fifth century progressed, suggested something a little more egalitarian in their dress, Alcibiades seemed to delight in his deep-purple cloak, the colour of 'congealed blood'. He might put up with democracy, but he refused to bury his aristocratic privileges and pretensions. This purple was so highly prized, a signifier of kings since prehistory, that it was banned by most cults in Attica. The cult par excellence, however, the Eleusinian Mysteries, prescribed that their sacred officials should wear the *phoinikis* – a purple wrap. When Andocides was cursed for his part in Alcibiades' alleged profanation of the Eleusinian Mysteries, we're told that the priests thunderclapped their purple cloaks at him.[3]

Like Athens, Alcibiades was an attention-seeker of monstrous proportions, loudly confident. In 416 he entered seven chariots at the Olympic games, and three came in poll positions, first, second and fourth. His victory ode was written by none other than Euripides himself:

Victory shines like a star, but yours eclipses all victories.[4]

Paintings of the conquering hero (commissioned by Alcibiades himself) and his horses were executed by the master-painter Aristophon for the Propylaia, at the entrance to the Acropolis: work so impressive that men started to whisper that Alcibiades styled himself 'tyrant'. Again like Athena's city itself, Alcibiades' achievements were immense, his use of funds generated

259

by the rosy economy of a material democracy inspiring. But such showy confidence sparked jealousy. Men disapproved of Alcibiades and other city-states were clearly starting to disapprove of flash, look-at-me Athens.

Mind you, don't forget that Athenians were brought up on the epics. From the cradle they were entranced with tales of a time when, in the Age of Heroes, Achilles, Ajax, Odysseus et al. were giants of men and coloured the earth with their heroic deeds. For some, a character such as Alcibiades appeared to have brought heroism back to earth. His extreme gorgeousness could be interpreted as a sign of his quasi-divinity – his beauty a gift given directly by the gods.

This much is clear. Suppose that there were men whose bodily physique showed the same superiority as is shown by the statues of the gods, then all would agree that the rest of mankind would deserve to be their slaves.[5]

The passions this larger-than-life character aroused were violent. Alcibiades was handsome, brash, materialistic, ambitious, feckless, power-hungry, decadent – and yet Socrates did not condemn the boy, he was fascinated by him. Alcibiades was the Athens that Socrates was struggling to live with. Socrates was drawn to all that was heady and worldly and meritocratic about the 'Queen of Cities' (and he was himself famously 'hedonistic'), but he smelled its weakness, he feared for the future of a thing that was driven by individual ambition and was called, all too conveniently, a democracy.

Alcibiades, boasting (thinly disguised) that even he, even *he* with his luxuriant charms, could not seduce Socrates, framed his time with Socrates as a love-story. This should be a great fable. The meeting of the perfect mind with the perfect body. In the *Symposium*, Alcibiades protests that he wants to be a better man and that only Socratic magic can work to achieve this end. Again he is like Athena's city herself – full of potential, successful, but still seeking a position on a moral compass:

Nothing is more important to me than becoming the best man I can be, and no one can help me more than you to reach that aim . . .[6]

And tonight Alcibiades sits with Socrates while the party rocks, and lies with him when it is over. Alcibiades recalls another night the two lay close together, around the time of the Potidaean campaign. Socrates has only a thin cloak, but he is wrapped in Alcibiades' rich mantle. Excited by his words – as Alcibiades says – still energised even by the memory of what was said (*'I can feel it at this moment even as I'm speaking'*[7]), the lusty, lusting young warrior is determined to have his curious bedfellow.

We have all been there: the dark, the whispers, the unseen skin pricks connecting flesh to flesh. Yet Socrates chose to love Alcibiades with his heart, not his body. He wanted to live in an Athens that could deny itself, as well as indulge. And so in Plato's *Symposium*, Socrates turns the advances of Alcibiades down. The power of love, Aphrodite's tricky gift to man, was of great fascination for Socrates. He recognised the trouble love caused, when sexual desire drove you mad (*mania* is a Greek word that can mean a kind of erotic frenzy) . . .

'By Herakles!' said Xenophon, 'What awesome power you attribute to a kiss!'

'And this amazes you?' said Socrates. 'Don't you know,' he said, 'that scorpions, even though they are no bigger than a half-obol's size, when they merely touch one's mouth wear humans down with gut-wrenching pains and deprive them of their good sense?'

'Yes, by god,' said Xenophon. 'The reason is that scorpions have some poison in their bite.'

'You foolish one!' said Socrates. 'Don't you think that beautiful boys also have some poison in their love, which you don't see? Don't you know that this beast, which they call "the beautiful boy in the prime of his youth", is so much more dangerous than scorpions because scorpions at least have to touch whereas this beast can poison from a distance? . . . But I advise you, Xenophon, whenever you see some beautiful boy, to flee with all speed.'[8]

And of course Socrates' philosophy cannot but bear relevance to eroticism and sex. In this Greek world the physical and the spiritual were two breaths in the same whisper. An older man made love to a younger to instil virtue in him. This was the 'good' love that could be complemented by 'bad' physical love. Plato allows Socrates' philosophy to be heavy with his sexual overlay. And even 'bad' love has a greater purpose. For Socrates sex is a means to an end – a way of producing beautiful men and (since the advice is given by Diotima in the *Symposium*) beautiful women too. To populate and promote a beautiful city. Socrates might not choose to have sex with Alcibiades, but he never denied the power, or purpose or pleasure of sex itself.[9]

Enchanting, illuminating and thought-provoking as the scenes in Plato's theatrical *Symposium* are, the real life of its characters was grubbier.

ᖇᖇᖇᖇᖇ

Despite all this talk of love and affection, outside the warm walls of the historical *symposia* things had not been going well for the Athenians. Following the debacle of Delion and Amphipolis there had been a three-year peace between Athens and Sparta. But then in the summer of 418 the Spartans beat the Argives (Athenian allies) and Athenian forces at Mantinea. Mantinea sits in a wide floodplain 100 miles south of Athens. Alcibiades, by this time voted Athenian General, had persuaded Argos, Mantinea and Elis (all democratic cities at this stage) to join together as comrades in the

Peloponnese. Sparta read this, correctly, as a threat and decided to take action. Troops began to mass, glaring at each other from their respective camps. Initially the Spartans had tried to burn Mantinea's crops, and then threatened to divert their river so that the city-state's fields would be drowned under flood-water. Both then proceeded to play at push-me-pull-you, each side trying to use the vagaries of the dramatic landscape in the area to their own military advantage.

On the final day of fighting, under the glowering shadow of the Lyrkian mountains, it was superior Spartan strategy that resulted in the deaths of more than 1,000 allied troops, many Athenians amongst them. Messengers ran gloomily back to the mother-city, retracing the route that the Athenian Pheidippides had taken all those years ago to try to ensure Spartan aid at the Battle of Marathon, when Sparta and Athens were still friendly. With their back to the Tegean valley, not a thing of beauty, glacially eradicated, farmers still building here in mud-brick as they have done for 4,000 years, while leaves raced themselves through the sky, back to a city-state where men were beginning to lose their sense of purpose. The rousing words of Pericles, when Athens was broadcast as '*the leader and envy of all Greece*,' were wearing decidedly thin. From the time when Plato's *Symposium* is set, 416 BC, onwards, Athens was fragile and fractious. Men voted to ostracise one another from the city. The tension between aristocrats and democrats was rising. In years to come the *demos* would remember, darkly, the rumours of these highfalutin evenings when men such as Socrates and Alcibiades drank and ate well and talked of love while an enemy breathed down Athena's neck.

And it was the affront of words spoken behind closed doors, or in intimate conversations — the exchanges that give us Plato's Dialogues, that would come to make Socrates both one of the world's most tenacious and most widely read philosophers — and that would turn the tide of contemporary opinion against him.

At the end of the *Symposium*, Alcibiades lurches off, wine-swollen, to carry on with his Bacchic revels. He is a satire of himself — or, as Socrates puts it, *to satyrikon*, a satyr-play. His drive is to love the fug of the crowd, to be loved by it; no doubt to reach a heady climax on this hot spring night. In history, Alcibiades is, around the time of the setting of the *Symposium*, sailing dangerously close to the wind. He enjoys increasing influence in the Assembly with his grand talk and even grander gestures, but already men are anxious about his degree of influence and jealous of his degrees of success. In 416 BC he comes close to being ostracised. And in the *Symposium* he shatters the dining party's spell; while bright talk and a searching exploration of the nature of love have kept the *andron* alight, he pollutes the high-octane atmosphere by bringing in something (to Greek minds) grubby, and obvious. A prostitute: a flute-girl. There is a dark double entendre here. When Athens' walls are eventually pulled down, the democracy destroyed, Spartans trampling through Athenian homes, it will be the city's flute-girls – sick perhaps of having been the musically talented sex-slaves to Athenian democrats all their adult lives – who raise a victory cry, who herald the end of 'Golden Age' Athens. It is men like Alcibiades, implies Plato, who are killing Athens with the wrong kind of love.

Demon drink

Tomb-raiders know how to take all the best goods. In the basement of one Greek museum sits a beautiful, huge drinking bowl rescued from the illegal antiquities trade. Delicate vines lace around the edge, men lie close to one another, intimate and trusting, but in the centre of the cup is a petrol-blue monster, a Gorgon who grimaces and through her gaping teeth lolls her engorged tongue out at the viewer, at the drinker, the symposiast. Painted close to the year that Socrates died from hemlock poison, the cup is reminding us what horrors excessive love of our fellow men – lulled by wine, by a false sense of security and joint purpose, loose-tongued, seen to be having too good a time – can lead to. Around the *symposia* foul-breathed rumour *pheme* would do her withering work, and out of the intense, charged gatherings could come ideas of pure evil.

If Plato was giving us Alcibiades as Athens, then his metaphor was horribly accurate. Alcibiades, beautiful young Alcibiades, had become greedy, belli-cose and corrupt. He was driven not by virtue or by *nous*, but by his primal appetites. The young aristocrat thought he wanted to learn from Socrates, but instead he chose to sway off drunkenly into the night. Like Athens he was drinking, partying, living and dying too hard.

Socrates had seen how easily citizens slid into barbarity; how in hard times men preferred hard talk. His exhortation to his fellow Athenians to moderation, to thinking before leaping, seemed to be falling on deaf ears.

SOCRATES: *Then it is impossible to be happy if one is not temperate and good.*
ALCIBIADES: *Impossible.*

SOCRATES: *So it is the bad men who are wretched.*

ALCIBIADES: *Yes, very.*

SOCRATES: *And hence it is not he who has made himself rich that is relieved of wretchedness, but he who has made himself temperate.*

ALCIBIADES: *Apparently.*[10]

ACT SEVEN

〰〰〰〰〰〰

CUTTING DOWN THE TALLEST CORN

40

MELOS

〰〰〰〰〰〰〰〰〰〰

416 BC

SOCRATES: If you think that by killing people you'll put a stop to anyone criticising you because you don't live as you should, you're not thinking clearly.

Plato, *Apology*, 39d[1]

Geography has a lot to answer for. Some territories are blessed, others are burdened with supplying the raw materials of human civilisation. The island of Melos is one such. It is a tiny island whose geological composition has proved both a bonus and a curse.

Ringing the Cyclades, a swirling volcanic archipelago in the heart of the Aegean Sea, Melos has, since the age of prehistory, been civilisation's paintbox. Geophysical activity means that the rocks weep sulphur, kaolin and gypsum. In the north of the island the beaches are still littered with treacle-black volcanic glass – obsidian – which has been in demand across the known world since the Stone Age. Melos was long on Athens' radar. Finds at Laurion show that Bronze Age Attic Greeks traded their metals for the razor-sharp knives, the arrowheads, the surgeon's scalpels that obsidian so usefully becomes. In ancient times Melos' exports were essential. Now the island thrives on selling barite to force-ripen cherry tomatoes for the global salad market.

Melos is an odd, beautiful, slightly perturbing place. Children digging on the beach find the sand gets hotter and then dangerously hot as they approach the earth's crust. Steam jets suddenly bubble the skin as one swims in its coves. The world-famous Venus de Milo was found, gawky, half-submerged in a cave covered with unremarkable scrub by a (surprised) farmer hoeing his patch at the beginning of the season in 1820. And today on a deserted hillside site, smothered with wildflowers and droning with diligent bees, massive Doric blocks of stone, dark gore-red, shield human settlements that are no longer there.

This ancient place feels like a ghost town, for good reason.

In 416 BC the Melians made the political mistake of asserting that they were happy to continue their '700-year' independence and not join the Delian League. For more than a decade Athenians had been pressing the islanders to secede. Back in 425 BC Athens had assessed Melos for tribute; the Melians had refused to pay up. Clearly, Melian independence was a thorn in Athens' flesh. And now that the Peloponnesian War had dragged on for years, the Athenians needed all the cash they could lay their hands on. With Alcibiades and his coterie to all intents and purposes in charge of the Assembly, the small island and the mainland superpower entered a heated debate. Melos, don't forget, was at a disadvantage by this stage. Athenians had become highly skilled at argument. The Assembly was no stranger to grand oratory – and already the historian Thucydides was commenting on the dangers of these rabble-rousing situations. Witness his report of one of Cleon's speeches in the Assembly.

In speechifying competitions of this sort the prizes go to the spin-doctors and the state is the loser. The blame is yours, for stupidly encouraging these competitive displays . . . If something is to be done in the future, you weigh it up by hearing a good speech on the subject, and as for the past, you judge it not from your own first-hand, eye-witness experience but from what you hear in some clever bit of rhetoric . . . You all want to be the first to make a speech, and if you can't do that, you try to sit there looking as though you are one step ahead of the speaker . . . you demand changes to the conditions under which you live, and yet have a very dim understanding of the reality of those conditions: you are very slaves to the pleasure of the ear, and more like the audience of a paid public speaker than the council of a city.[2]

Athens' most persuasive and hard-line negotiators were sent across the water to make the Melians see sense. Theatricalised it may be, but the following exchange between the men of Melos and the Athenian envoys is one of the most sobering in world literature. The author, Thucydides, may have invented it for dramatic effect, but the point of drama is that it can communicate that awful moment when attitudes harden, when love is lost, when men decide to hate one another. Stinging from defeat at the Battle of Mantinea in 418 BC, and irked by the fact that Melos had been friendly to the Spartans, on hearing that the Melians still insisted on their independence, and – one suspects – remembering Melos' staggering natural resources, angry voices in the Athenian Assembly up on the Pnyx (Alcibiades almost certainly amongst them) proposed a violent motion: this was going to be gunboat diplomacy.[3]

A massive force was mobilised: 2,500 hoplites all told, 320 archers, twenty crack-squad cavalrymen – all boarding boats whose prows would be pointing south.[4]

Any Melian – a shepherd, a miner, a baker looking out on the pearly northern horizon one day in May – would have seen a worrying, and then a horrifying, stain: thirty-eight triremes (Athens' own as well as boats offered up or sequestered from Athenian allies), 3,000 soldiers bearing down. Frothing through the deep water and then nudging their way into Melos' natural harbour.

Because the Athenians did not want a plucky anomaly in the heart of the Mediterranean, they were determined the Melians would admit that they were a subject state in Athens' empire. Melian oligarchs and magistrates refused to allow the Athenians to present their case to the full community – and there were not that many of them: 1,600 or so in total in an island only 15 miles long and 10 miles wide. Why such censorship? To prevent mass panic spreading, perhaps? Believing they could avert atrocity and come to some mutually beneficial deal? In case the banner of democracy would be too easily planted?

Thucydides gives us his version of the conversation that followed. The Melians admit it will be difficult to contend with Athenian power, but say that they will 'put their trust in the gods', they will 'try to save themselves'. The Athenian reply is chilling.

Of the gods we believe and of mankind we know, that by a necessary law of their nature they rule wherever and whatever they can. And it is not as if we were the first to make this law, or to act upon it when made: we found it in existence before us, and shall leave it to exist for ever among those who come after us; all we do is to make use of it, knowing that you or anybody else, with the same power as ours, would do precisely the same as us.[5]

The Athenians declare 'Might Rules'. They need no other excuse for unprovoked aggression than the size of their army.

Whether or not Thucydides was writing up this exchange to express his own sensitivity to moral debates has been and always will be debated. But what is certain is the disgusting brutality of the outcome. For a number of months the Melians were besieged. Melos would be a hard nut to crack because the island has and had great advantages. As the rim of an extinct volcano, it is a natural fortress; fresh water runs into the citadel (a number of the cafés and houses in the modern village still have their own wells) and a giant's march of jagged volcanic rocks protects the island's highest point, Mount Halakas. But the rocks' colour, that of dried blood, would appear to have been prophetic.

Through a hard winter the Melians held out. Then disease, starvation, fear swirled in the air around those who were left. In 415 BC, forced back right to the crow's nest of the island on top of a plug of unexploded magma, the islanders capitulated. Their soot-blackened oil lamps, mirrors, hair-pins and scythes – still being turned up by archaeologists – were left in their households for one last time.[6] The remains, sitting quietly now in Melos' municipal museum, are pathetic shards of ordinary human lives abandoned.

The Athenians were ruthless. This would be a blood-bath. Their orders were to slay every man standing, and to enslave every woman and child.

We can only imagine the carnage, because it seems not one single man survived to leave us their account.[7]

41

VENUS DE MILO ABUSED

֍֎֍֎֍֎֍֎֍֎֍֎

Athens, 415 BC

TALTHYBIUS: *Come, child; I pity your mother, but time is up.*
No more embracing now.
You must climb to the topmost fringe of your father's towers,
Where the sentence says you must leave your life behind.
Take him. — A job like this
Is fit for a man without feeling or decency;
I'm not brutal enough.

HECUBA: *O little child, son of my dear lost son,*
Your life is ravished from us by murderers.
What will become of us? What can I do for you?
Only to beat the head and bruise the breast —
This we can give; no more.
Lost city, lost child: what climax of suffering
Lacks now? Have we not reached
In headlong plunge the abyss of pain?

Euripides, *Women of Troy*, lines 782–98, written in 416/415 BC
around the time of the Melos massacre[1]

THE ATHENIANS HAD A NEW ISLAND; and they had blood dripping from their hands. Alcibiades held the Melians' faces and rubbed them in the dirt. He took one of the bereaved Melian women, enjoyed her and left her pregnant with a son.[2]

Alcibiades, who carries his villainy to such unheard-of lengths that, after recommending that the people of Melos be sold into slavery, he purchased a woman from among the prisoners and has since had a son by her . . . a child . . . sprung from parents who are each other's deadliest enemies, and of his nearest kin the one has committed and the other has suffered the most terrible of wrongs.[3]

And it is at this point that we see Socrates' city beginning to fracture irreparably. There is no doubt that the massacre at Melos worried the Athenians. That same year Euripides wrote his throat-tighteningly powerful tragedy *Women of Troy*. He would have applied to the Chief Archon for permission to write in the July or August before the massacre, but then clearly adapted his script during the winter of 416/15 as the Melians were suffering their abominable trauma. The scene is set back in the Age of Heroes, when Troy has fallen and the Greeks are wreaking their vengeance on the Trojan population – *Women of Troy* picks up where Homer's *Iliad* Book 24 leaves off. But the resonance is a contemporary one, and Euripides' point is clear. In many ways, the men who have been speared and sliced and clubbed and hacked to death in atrocities such as Melos are the lucky ones. It is the women – who have in front of them a long life of exile, enslavement, rape, forced separation from their children – who are the most dehumanised victims of war. It is these women who will be shipped to an alien city, Athens, or sold in the Athenian Agora to travel yet further afield. Socrates would certainly have passed these casualties of his friend Alcibiades' high-handed policy as he made his habitual journey through the marketplace. Mothers and children side by side, orphans, childless mothers all staring out at Athena's city with wary eyes. The actors who wore masks and became the 'abused women' of Euripides' and Sophocles' tragedies in the Theatre of Dionysos might well have passed them too – the spoiled life that their dramatic art imitated.

One Melian man escaped the carnage – because at the time of the massacre he was hiding as a resident alien in Athens itself. A philosopher, known as Diagoras of Melos, he had been attracted to Athena's city in happier days when the eastern Mediterranean was at relative peace, when thought and moral exploration were currencies valued as highly as talents of tribute silver and prisoners-of-war.

Diagoras was not exterminated by an Athenian trireme, yet it was Athenian paranoia that would cut him down. Because within two years of the Melian massacre the Assembly had called for his assassination without trial, and Diagoras had fled the city-state with a price on his head. For centuries we have not known precisely the nature of his crime, other than that, like Socrates', it was not for his deeds, but '*his words*'.[4] But a recent thrilling discovery may now make that clear.

42

PRIEST OF NONSENSE: PLAYING WITH FIRE

@@@@@@@@@@@@

Derveni, northern Greece, and Athens, 414 BC

*Anaxagoras was justly imprisoned for his impiety regarding the
sun and moon; you banished Protagoras fairly and appropriately for asking
whether the gods exist or not; you were wise to promise a reward for the person who
would kill Diagoras, since he mocked Eleusis and the ineffable mysteries; but who can
say that there is a book or an argument about the gods by Socrates that is contrary to
law? As you cannot show us one, Anytus, even if you cite a myriad of sophists
who have been ruined you still do not convict Socrates.*[1]

Libanius, *Apology*, 154–5

O N THE E75 FROM ATHENS TO Thessaloniki the long vehicles juggernaut past. Searching out excavations on the motorway verge at
Derveni has to be at once one of the most unrestful and one of
the most rewarding of journeys. Widening the road here between 1961 and
1963, workers' pickaxes struck a completely unexpected find: a series of fabulously rich aristocrats' tombs. Burial chamber A11 is now protected by
concrete walls and canopied with scrubby earth. There is a lot of litter.
The husband-and-wife curators (key-holders who seem a little surprised
that visitors might have an interest in their charge) struggle to lift the metal-
grille gate because this grave has so few visitors.

When you clamber down to find the sarcophagus, still in situ, it takes
a good minute or so for your eyes to adjust to the blackness inside.

The riches within, when first discovered in May 1962, physically took
the breath away. Archaeologists' reports tell us that as the coffin lid was

removed, the excavators gasped and cried out. Inside the tomb were two finely cast golden urns each 2 feet high; here too rock-crystal vases; golden diadems and necklaces with gold tendrils cotton-fine; perfume still sweet. Although his name was nowhere to be found, it was clear that this was the grave of a wealthy and cultured aristocrat. A man who collected not just material riches, but also intellectual delights. Because here there were gems relevant to Socrates' story, but jewels so fine they almost blew away in the dust: here there were the charred ghosts of words.

On the stone-block lid of this coffin at Derveni, 2,400 years ago, tightly rolled papyri had been burned. These clearly contained sentiments that, for some reason, meant a great deal to their owner – and they were also incriminating, which is why they were burned with him when he died. Chanting (raised by the professional mourners and the female relatives allowed out of their homes as a special concession to this funerary ritual) would have been punctuated by the crackling from the flames that were believed to take the spirit of the cremated aristocrat aloft. The flesh of the owner has long gone – but this enforced, fiery desiccation saved something extraordinary from that anonymous aristocrat's funeral pyre. The rolled papyri – we now realise – represent the oldest book to have survived in all of European history.

At first glance, the remains of this book look like the end of a bonfire – the newspaper leftovers that remain after they have fed the blaze – and initially excavators were dismissive of the scraps. But then a bit of a phrase in Attic Greek was spotted and, as archaeologists from the region of Thessaloniki gently separated the 200 fragments and prised apart the charred rolls that resembled nothing less than charcoal briquettes, the ghostly remains of beautiful, finely scribed Greek letters started to appear.

The stories dealt with here are highly coloured. They describe how Zeus rapes his mother and then eats the severed penis of the god of the sea. None questions that these stories are true – but the author also sees in them an allegory: a suggestion that *phusis*, nature, and *bios*, life (as we know it), emerged from some kind of primal vortex. There is magic in the words: the goddess 'HERA' is equated with 'AIR' (AER in Greek), and so forth. In essence what we have at Derveni is an entirely new way of looking at the world; touch-paper at the moment it is lit. The burnt poems are a tortured, complicated attempt to square cutting-edge and revolutionary scientific thought with the presence of the old gods; as has been said, it is like devout nineteenth-century Christians trying to justify evolution by reading the Bible as an allegory for genetic development.[2]

This is hermetic evidence that opens up Socrates' world.

Given those who were active in Athens at this time, and their recorded fates, it could well be Diagoras of Melos (or one of his close circle) who wrote those beautiful, complicated words discovered burnt beside a motorway at Derveni. The authorities were clearly troubled by the ideas contained within the mystical verses – but in a land without orthodoxy, there was no mechanism for prosecuting 'heretics' or 'free-thinkers'. 'Heresy' comes from the Greek verb 'to take, to make a choice' and 'blasphemy' in Greek meant 'speaking ill'. In Socrates' day, heresy was meaningless. And so instead, in 414 BC, the author of the works, Diagoras (if it was indeed he), was charged with a crime that would be a precursor of Socrates' own. He was charged with not recognising the city's deities and branded *a-theos*, an atheist, a man away from the gods.[3] The Assembly put a price on his head. The culprit was wanted back in Athena's city, dead or alive. Now Diagoras, like those fellow islanders who fled from the massacring swords of the Athenians,[4] was a fugitive from the democratic decisions of the world's first democracy.

Aristophanes jokes about Diagoras' persecution a year or so after the event in his play the *Birds*, but the language chills. Undesirables will be strung up like songbirds (the playwright fantasises); those who are trapped no longer have wings to fly. He beats out the message in his harsh, funny poetry:

CHORUS LEADER: On this particular day, you know, we hear it again proclaimed that whoever of you kills Diagoras the Melian shall get a talent.[5]

INFORMER: It's wings I want, wings![6]

The birth of atheism and heresy

In democratic Athens there was no religious dogma, no equivalent of the Bible. There was no credo, no 'I believe', no creed. Socrates lived at a time when many gods and goddesses were jealous for attention. Each constantly vied for more gifts, more sacrifices, more devotees than the next. The city-states were just small enough to allow their citizens to scurry around from one shrine and sanctuary to another and get home before sunset. The acts of belief, rather than faith itself, were what was important.

Although, inevitably, there were powerful religious dynasties within the sanctuaries, there was no priestly class to preserve and promote an orthodoxy for the pantheon of Hellenic gods. Men could interpret religious texts as they liked. The boundaries of blasphemy were blurred. The freedom of expression encouraged by the democracy facilitated both philosophical and spiritual enlightenment, and then witch-hunts.

For much of his early life it must have seemed to the philosopher and his coterie that Socrates had been born at the right time. Pericles might have created and ruled an empire with a fist of iron – but he was also a man who believed in the expansion of the mind. He wasn't afraid of the shocking, original ideas that deep thinkers brought behind Athens' walls. Pericles had experienced at first hand where bigotry leads: his own mother lived with a religious curse on the family. Her tribe, the Alcmaeonids, were accused of pro-Persian sympathies after the Battle of Marathon – and leading members were ostracised. Pericles had spent his adolescent years in exile. Perhaps these circumstances combined to give the General an unusual sense of the power of the future. For most Greeks, the future was a Frankenstein of the gods; it was in the past that security lay. Pericles seems to have appreciated that living in the past, rather than living with it, can hinder human development. And so he cultivated a forward-thinking culture. Yet Socrates, and the other great thinkers of the day – Diagoras, Anaxagoras, Protagoras et al. – as has been discussed earlier, operated at a time when freedom meant a very particular thing: not freedom of the individual, but freedom of the community, freedom of the state. And as with present-day societies and governments, that state could not decide whether or not freedom of speech, freedom of thought gave one freedom to offend.

While Athens started out its democratic life remarkably tolerant (after all, Socrates was allowed to operate without inhibition for more than half a century), eventually new thought became nefarious. There had always been an undercurrent to Athens' apparent open-mindedness. When Socrates was growing up, Anaxagoras proposed that the sun was not Helios in fiery form, but a red-hot stone. The Assembly, intrigued and horrified by his suggestion, passed a decree that declared astronomy sacrilegious, and forbade its study. The ubiquity of religious belief skewed much of the free-thinking of the day. And then men started to gossip: had political tyranny in fact been replaced by tyranny of the mind? Athens was trying to shore itself up, to build and build, to support military blockades and masonry blocks with sweat and mortar, to set in stone the laws of an empire; and yet the sophists and Socrates appeared happy, at an atomic level, to deconstruct things.[7]

The Derveni papyrus went to the grave with its owner. Other texts were ripped from the hands of the living. A Roman tradition tells us that Protagoras' life-work, *On the Gods*, was burned in public. Heralds called for every last copy to be jettisoned from homes, the conflagration filling the Agora with smuts and smoke. Only the first sentence of that work now survives, passed down in whispered oral memory: '*About the gods I cannot say either that they are or that they are not, nor how they are constituted in shape; for there is much which prevents knowledge, the unclarity of the subject and the shortness of life.*'[8] Incendiary stuff; thinking they had obliterated his ideas from history, Athenians then voted to exile Protagoras from their city. If the stories are true, then book-burning begins in Athens as soon as 'the book', as a popular art-form, arrives in the city-state.

Those boys, Socrates included, who hung out around the walls of the Kerameikos and bartered for new information from the travelling sophists were aware that they were handling dangerous goods. Just as Euripides charts in the *Bacchae* his gruesome (both figuratively and actually), heart-splitting tragedy, rationalism goes so far, and then the instinct to destroy starts to shadow the light.

TEIRESIAS: I do not countenance or imagine the powers of heaven to be subtle. The faith we inherited from our fathers, as old as time itself, shall not be cast down by reason, no! Even though it were the very subtlest invention of wit and sophistication. Maybe some one will say, I have no respect for my grey hair in going to dance with ivy round my head; not so, for the god did not define whether old or young should dance, but from each and every one of us he claims a universal homage, and scorns calculating niceties in the way he is worshipped.[9]

Of course there will be many radical thinkers we have never heard of; many ideas that were burned or knocked back before they could even make it into the historical record. This period has been billed as the dawn of enlightenment: but it was also an age that, for the first time, labelled men atheists; that democratically sponsored censorship. Intellectual progress was made here which remained unmatched for the next 1,500 years. But shamed by their defeats in war, confused by the freedom their own political system gave them, the Athenians from around 415 BC onwards chose oppression over liberal thinking. After c.415 BC there was no further need for ostracism – because now the state could harry and censor at will. Socrates' death came at the end of more than a decade of intellectual and political persecutions. We must never forget that although Socrates is the most famous victim of Athenian oppression, there would have been scores – perhaps hundreds – more like him whose names have escaped the historical record. Athens' story, and therefore the story of the intellectual development of mankind, could have been very different. The Athenian experiment was starting to calcify.

∽∽∽∽∽

But as is the way with these things, the persecutions within the city and the slaughter on Melos, that colourful little volcanic island, seem to have given the Athenians an appetite for more aggressive expansion. The aristocrats in the Assembly, used to outdoing one another with feats of military might, stood together once more and looked out to sea. Amongst them stood Alcibiades. Always the showman, in 415 – a year after the Melian affair, after Plato's *Symposium* is located in fifth-century chronology, and after the aristocrat had wiped the floor with his rivals in the Olympic Games – Alcibiades ordered himself up a theatrical backdrop of truly epic proportions. Now his sights were set on an even bigger prize: Sicily.

For more than fifteen years now Alcibiades had been wading knee-deep in the blood of Greeks and barbarians alike. He had been charming the people of Athens with his heroic feats, and earning the jealousy and hatred of men the length and breadth of the city-state. The Furies had their eye on him, but he was not finished yet. The Athenian force as instructed by the Athenian Assembly preparing to invade, of all places, Sicily was building up to be *'the most expensive and splendid fitted out by a single polis up to that time'*.[10]

Yet this was a splendid sight destined to suffer terrible hardship. There are many mournful artefacts in Athens' National Archaeological Museum, but one of its saddest has to be a grave *stele* tucked away next to a doorway on the ground floor.[11] The 4-foot-high piece of stone was found in the Piraeus port area. The design is original, and beautiful. A young man – a tiny figure – sits in a windswept, empty landscape. We have his name, inscribed, 'Demokleides son of Demetrios'. Demokleides cradles his head in his hands, his helmet lies behind him. Beyond stretches a beautiful boat, a deep, wide sea. The death that this young soldier mourns is his own – one of the many Athenians killed for the city-state in a naval battle. Athens' triremes, those 'wooden walls' that the Oracle at Delphi had predicted would keep Athens safe, were slowly morphing into water-borne coffins. And the seas around Sicily would soon be their graveyard.

43

SICILY

@@@@@@@@@@@@

416/15 BC

CHORUS: . . . Over the streets of the central city
A shriek of death rose like a grip at the throat;
And trembling children clutched at their mothers' skirts;
And War went forth from his secret lair;
And the work of the virgin Pallas was accomplished.

Men sank in blood while their dead hands clasped the altar;
The head half-raised from the pillow
Defenceless rolled from severed neck;
And beside the dead the victor's lust
Planted the seed of a son for Hellas
Watered with tears of Troy's despair . . .

Euripides, *Women of Troy*, lines 555–67, produced
two months before the invasion of Sicily[1]

IN SEPTEMBER, IN ATHENS, THE MOON appears to be the colour of a
blood-orange. Winds start to whip dust off the ground.

And back in 416, in early autumn, at a time of year that already feels unsettled, the Athenian Assembly began to debate a crazy, megalomaniac plan. Athens was forever short of grain. Aerial spy photos from the Second World War have revealed the ghosts of agricultural terraces from antiquity – thin shelves on hillsides all around the city where men have tried to coax food out of the stony, unhelpful earth.[2] Unlike Sparta, Athens could not boast swathes of flat, fertile land. But the Athenian people needed to be fed.

A policy of land-grab, thinly disguised under the banner of democratic enlightenment, had long been in play in the city-state. The result was a peculiarly Athenian phenomenon called *clerouchia*, or cleruchy. These settlements – a refined, aggressive form of the Greek colony – had been established across the Mediterranean basin. An Athenian force would turn up in a new territory (the island of Euboea, literally 'well-oxed', is an excellent example) and claim the fertile farmland in the name of the democratic experiment. Each time troops from the mother-city appeared, natives would be forced off their land. Athenian administration generated 50,000 refugees from Euboea alone, at least 500,000 in total; homeless men, women and children, trudging through the eastern Mediterranean, fearfully searching for a new yard of earth they could call their own. On Euboea, Athenian forts manned by democratic-soldiers and guarding the Euboean farmland of Athenian absentee landlords await excavation. Today the few remaining masonry blocks cling to the rock faces and the promontories are easy to miss. But once one begins to trace the footprint of these buildings, their scale is apparent. These garrisons were well staffed – the ground is thick with pottery, the discarded cooking pots of generations of Athenian-paid soldiers who lived here to stand guard over Athens' newly acquired land. The sites on Euboea, when fully excavated, will tell us a good deal about the demanding nature of the democratic experiment.

And of course Athenian imperialism-by-any-other-name had as much to do with aristocratic ambition as it did with demotic provision. Athens' old oligarchs, its cavalry class, would stand on hills and look out to sea – here was an opportunity for aristocratic competition; land-grabs and head-counts that proved you were capable of strategic marvels, worthy descendants of your ancestor Theseus.

And so in 416 BC we can perhaps imagine the stellar aristocrat Alcibiades standing one night on a high point in Athens and looking out across the crowded cityscape beyond the Acropolis to Piraeus bay and the dimpled lapping of the sea. This is still, and was then, a spiriting view. What other lands lay beyond that horizon? Persia seemed unconquerable, the Egyptian expedition of 459/4 had failed spectacularly – so what about the place where the sun sets, corn-yellow at this time of year, what about the west?[3]

In the choppy waters between the toe of Italy and the north coast of Africa there is a lush, large island: Sicily. And that autumn, as its wheat and barley and oats started to ripen in the fields, the Athenians put Sicily at the head of their list.

The Sicilian campaign was launched.

Today Piraeus harbour is still busy – up until the year 2000 it thronged with people – but now it has been dragged into the modern age and mechanised. Containers have done away with the need for porters, the Olympics clean-up has removed the illegal immigrants who used to sell pirate sunglasses and CDs as you waited to embark. Cars take travellers into the bowels of 200-foot-long ships – and then on to the Greek islands. Apart from those scurrying onto boats, there are scarcely any people.

The scene in spring of 415 BC – the eve of the send-off of the boats – would have been very different. Sanctuaries around the port were full of the trinkets of worshippers. The harbour walls were, we are told by Thucydides, edged with eager onlookers. Citizens, metics, foreigners, allies – Thucydides gives us the impression that anyone who could walk or ride made the pilgrimage down to the port. It would have been odd if Socrates were not here. Particularly given that the plan had been masterminded by his one-time soulmate, the dashing Alcibiades. This was Athenian democracy in action. A force of citizen-soldiers voted to war by their own fathers, brothers, and by their own show of hands in a democratic assembly; an exhibition of democratic might. Gold and silver vessels were at the ready to pour libations of wine into the sea, and each and every soldier had made a particular effort with his armour so that 'it looked more like a demonstration of the power and greatness of Athens, than an expeditionary force against the enemy'.[4]

Symptomatic of the aristocratic one-upmanship that was so rife in Athens, ship-owners had carved particularly flamboyant figureheads on their ships, and the boats were carnival-bright. Cavalrymen and their horses – spooked doubtless by the noise and water all around – were clattering into the storage areas of some of the boats. The Sicilian expedition (to all intents and purposes Alcibiades' vanity project, an expression of aristocratic power) was set to leave Piraeus on a swell of manufactured brio. Trumpets were being sounded and throats cleared to sing a communal hymn of high praise.

But there was a problem. Athens and its stolidly conventional religious cycle could not be interrupted. This was the month when the women of the city worshipped Adonis. In a (to us slightly bizarre) manufactured replay of Adonis' life, women planted small rows of vegetables and left them unwatered. They watched these wither and die, and then mourned their terrible loss. This was the death of promise, of a beautiful boy, it was what city-state and mother alike feared; it was the world all wrong, but the world as it really was. As a climax to the ritual, an effigy of the divine Adonis – a creature thought bigger, shinier, the epitome of what humanity wanted to be – would be wrapped and thrown into the sea.[5]

And on that autumn night the rites could not be interrupted, for such an irregularity might offend the gods, and so women's voices had been rising in the air all night, shouting, screaming, wailing. Athens is a vast auditorium, and the horseshoe of mountains keeps clamour in, the limestone of the Acropolis acts as a giant sounding board. Hollering and shouts of fear still, in the noisy modern city, hang in the air like low cloud.

As females tore their faces and shrieked at the loss of male youths, it could not be a good omen. However, 134 ships, 5,100 hoplites, 700 slingers, thirty horsemen, thirty horses and thirty cargo ships were ready for the off. Huge crowds came down to the shore to wave them goodbye, torches were lit and carried along Piraeus quayside, libations were poured; the acrid, sweet smell of a civilisation on the move was in the air.

⦚⦚⦚⦚⦚

But those in the know in the crowd were subdued. The night before, a sickening thing had happened in the city. As Athens slept someone (or, it was whispered, something) had stalked through the streets. Over life-size marble carvings of bearded, half-smiling men at every junction in the city – in the Agora outside the Royal Stoa, at the edge of the public burial ground, beneath the shrine of Aphrodite and Peitho – herms, their erect phalluses proof that they brought good luck and strength to the city, had been horribly mutilated.

Muffled by cloth, metal had eaten into these smooth, cool, strong, stone men. With such a disturbance the dogs of the city must have set one another barking. But perhaps the human shadows that glided from place to place seemed just too intimidating to interrupt, because the peculiar mutilations were not stopped, no one was arrested. The strange, hideous sacrilege was allowed to continue unabated. On the ground now were shards of marble, chips of paint, splinters of desecration. Many of the herms of the city had had their noses – and, in some cases, their penises – smashed off.

Not even the most wily soothsayer or a Pythia priestess could interpret this as a good omen. Sculptures whose spirits ensured a fair journey were now weak, broken shadows of themselves. The jaws of the departing soldiers who knew of the scandal took a rather grim set.

But then things picked up. The sailing was smooth. Allied fleets that had already assembled in Corcyra made the crossing without mishap. Nicias, the senior officer in charge of the Athenian fleet, although in ill health before he left, seemed to be coping well. There was no massed force waiting to bludgeon the allied Athenian troops (all 25,000 of them) to death. The Spartan allies of the Sicilians were conspicuous by their absence. The landings went smoothly, the pastures and foliage, particularly lush on this side of the island, were meadow-sweet. And maybe sick of slaughter, maybe sensing the need not to repeat another Melos, the Athenians did two very odd things. They treated the campaign a little like a scouting mission, property developers making their way up the coast.

And they did not attack: this, it seemed, was going to be a well-mannered invasion. They had the best men with them and a fair wind behind. Instead of punishing the local populations, they started to fan out along Sicily's eastern seaboard. There was no complacency, this was of course a tricky operation, but still . . . The Athenian hoplites and their aristocratic leaders seemed to have at last recaptured some of that heroic vigour that immortalises them still in the Parthenon Marbles and around the sides of masterfully painted pots.

Then *pheme*, gossip, fouled the air with her bad breath. As the ships had been ploughing their way west, tongues had started to wag back in the mother-city. Someone had heard something at one of those infamous *symposia* that made for juicy gossip. Golden-haired Alcibiades, that provoking, beautiful, privileged boy, that adorant of the eccentric old Socrates, that lisping lover of oligarchs and Spartans, had mocked the gods. And not just a roadside-shrine god, but the goddess Demeter herself, the female whose sacred, mysterious rites at Eleusis promised you both an afterlife and acceptance into the 'haves' of Athenian society. They gossiped that he had held his own version of the Eleusinian Mysteries within the privacy of his own home, and even worse, it was muttered, it was none other than Alcibiades and his motley over-privileged crew which had rampaged through the city the night before the fleet set sail and destroyed the herms – the very totems of Athenian security abroad.

What a cocksure fool, they started to say, what an oily, blasphemous, dangerous streak of lightning. We'll recall him, we'll charge him, we – the emasculates who are left in the city along with women, children, the sick, the other grey-hairs – we'll show that we still have fire in our bellies.

And so the message was sent that Alcibiades must return to face trial.

Alcibiades heard the news and replied with the most spectacular two-finger salute. Why on earth should he slink back to the city, charged with a capital crime: sacrilege and treason? Thucydides tells us that after Sicily the General had been planning to take Carthage too – and from that victory the whole of the African continent, not to mention Spain and beyond, would be spread out before him. Fearless Alcibiades was on track to conquer the world, so he would hardly want to trot back, meekly, to have his wrists slapped – or worse. And maybe, just maybe, this slight flicked him on the raw. The golden boy could do wrong after all. Wounded pride has a way of festering. And so Alcibiades did a wonderfully audacious thing: he slipped away at night. Where he ended up shocked everyone.

He appeared to be setting sail for home. His ship was docked in Thurii (a new-town colony of Athens, founded 446–443 BC and settled by a number of Greek luminaries, the historian Herodotus amongst them). And then Alcibiades vanished. Thurii, like many settlements at this time, nurtured anti- as well as pro-Athenian elements and clearly someone there had been persuaded, or had been paid sufficiently handsomely, to cover his tracks. Alcibiades was next heard of in the bosom of Athens' arch-enemy, first in Elis and then in the wall-less city-state of none other than Sparta.

The Athenians were wild with rage – and we have found hard evidence of their anger. Reused in the Agora as rough building material there is a stone block about 3 feet high,[6] and on it is etched Alcibiades' shame. This block denounces the aristocrat as an enemy of the democracy; it was displayed, haughtily, up on the Acropolis. Alcibiades' property and that of his immediate clique was confiscated. His estates, even twenty-two of his gowns, were auctioned off. His name was cursed by priests in sanctuaries and in public arenas such as the Agora. Any Athenian who thought of making contact with him would become eternally polluted.[7] He was condemned to death. It would appear that Alcibiades had burned every one of his bridges.

Socrates' influence had, apparently, rubbed off on his protégé, although hardly with results that the philosopher would condone. Why do the obvious? Why blindly follow an orthodox path? If the action you are taking feels good, then why not turn convention on its head and pursue your course? Socrates had taught the young in the Agora, and soldiers, and dinner-mates, that men need to think for themselves. Well, no one could accuse Alcibiades of conformity. He was individual to his core.

Now the Athenians needed to be very worried. They had a bitter, well-informed, charismatic traitor in the heart of their enemy's camp. By doubting Alcibiades they had lost the one man who was guaranteed to fire up democratic soldiers to fight a pitiless battle in a foreign land. Careless!

Alcibiades wasted no time. He swaggered with his new-found rebel-power – he managed to intimidate both his countrymen and the Spartans at the same time. The smart aristocrat warned Sparta that Athens' ambitions to take over the Peloponnese were unlimited. Their women would be impregnated by Athenian cock, their boy warriors forced to march to war under an Athenian yoke. Go to Sicily, he said, my hoplites are all over the place, they haven't packed half enough forces; send out your diplomats, your *proxenoi* – tell the rest of the Aegean that ballsy, busybody Athens is stumbling; and get yourself into a crow's-nest position above the city-state itself: go just north of Athens, to the Attic town of Decelea.

∾∾∾∾∾

Back in Athens, panic joined gossip in the lanes and courtyards, in the Agora and Assembly. Religious paranoia escalated. The herms had been defiled, the sacred mysteries mocked. The flower of the city, the Athenian youth, was abroad – tempted out by a man who (or so the tongues wagged) despised Athena and her democrats. A man who had endeavoured to pollute the city from within, but had fled to Laconian lands (so he was not mired by the dirt that he had scattered through Athenian streets and sanctuaries). Informers set to work. The early toleration of the democratic state was forgotten. Citizens were tortured and executed. Fundamentalists clamoured that religious radicals should be put to death without trial. The priests of the mysteries of Eleusis helped coordinate the witch-hunt. Almost a hundred years later Aristotle would also be on the run from the Eleusinian elite. In 322 BC the priesthood brought charges of impiety against the fourth-century philosopher; fearing for his life, he left Athens, remarking pointedly that he would not let the Athenians *sin against philosophy a second time*.[8] Those thinkers who had been playing around with religious ideas were the first to come under suspicion. This was when Diagoras of Melos fled the city with a price on his head.

And while the Athenians, spring-trapped within their own walls, let anxiety and paranoia foment and take the place of religious and intellectual exploration, Alcibiades walked wide in the city of Sparta that had no boundaries. This was the man, remember, with a Spartan name, a Spartan wet-nurse – in many ways it must have felt as though he had come home. The Athenians raged. Athena's city was now fighting on three fronts: against Sparta, against a rejuvenating Persia and against the enemy within.

An inspired system, which had harnessed the competitive instincts of the aristocrats for the benefit of the people, had turned into a regime that drove some of its greatest talent into the arms of the enemy. Maybe it does not always work, to rule and be ruled in turn. Jealousy was a new god in Athens. Jealousy now ruled the Golden City.

44

RIVERS OF BLOOD

⊚⊚⊚⊚⊚⊚⊚⊚⊚⊚⊚

Sicily, 414–413 BC

*[The Sicilians] took particular measures to lead
the Athenians into dread, noxious conditions.*

*This was the greatest Hellenic action that took place during this war,
and, in my opinion, the greatest action that we know of in Hellenic history —
to the victors the most brilliant of successes, to the vanquished the most calamitous of
defeats; for they were utterly and entirely defeated; their sufferings were on an
enormous scale; their losses were, as they say, total; army, navy, everything was
destroyed, and, out of many, only few returned. So ended the events in Sicily.*

Thucydides, finale of Book 7, *History of the Peloponnesian War*, 7.87[1]

MEANWHILE SICILY, ONCE AN ISLAND THAT most Greeks thought
of as a distant, western outpost of civilisation, had become a
killing field. The Athenians had overreached themselves.

The general Nicias, tense with the pain of kidney disease, asked to be
recalled. He sent a message for reinforcements. He was told to stay put,
and the reinforcements that arrived were sizeable but pitifully insufficient.
Three years into the campaign, and city-states up and down Greece had
begun to sense which way the military wind was blowing; now more and
more were joining Sparta rather than Athens as allies. Nicias made the decision to return home. But then an unexpected omen: on the night of 27
August 413 BC the bright full moon was suddenly, fully eclipsed. Nicias was
a deeply religious man. He sought the advice of a soothsayer, who hedged
his bets. Don't depart yet, the augur said. Lie low in the harbour for a few
weeks — now is clearly not the time to sail. Nicias concurred. His enemies

heard they had a sitting duck in Syracuse and launched a blistering attack. In a set-piece naval battle in the harbour of Syracuse the Athenians were resoundingly defeated, their triremes captured or burned.

But 40,000 survivors were still on dry land and Nicias tried to march them to safety. These men had watched their transport home vaporised – their sense of entrapment must have been suffocating. And the Sicilians not only had local knowledge, but paddocks full of fresh horses. In a terrible drawn-out game of cat-and-mouse the Syracusans and their Spartan allies stalked Athenians down, charging, then slaughtering, and then withdrawing. After eight days of marching the men were delirious with thirst and hunger.

Then they arrived in a steep valley. The Sicilian horsemen drove them to the riverbed of the wide Assinarus River. Desperate for water, the broken Athenians fell on the muddy pools. Allied Syracusan forces above and around them were closing in, but the Athenians needed to drink before they died. Many were butchered as they knelt to cup the water, others drowned in the crush. Their fellow soldiers lay slaughtered all around them, their blood spilling into the stream, but still the Athenians gulped to satisfy their thirst. One by one they were cut down, or staggered into their own spears. That armour which had been polished so extra-shiny bright for the showy departure from Piraeus two long years before was now dull and mired.

One source tells us that 18,000 men were killed in a single afternoon.[2]

And we must not forget what it means to be slain by a classical Greek sword. Pornographically graphic descriptions of ways for men to die in battle are riven through the corpus of Ancient Greek literature, and none of this is horror-fantasy. Witness Euripides:

He drew back his left foot but kept his eyes closely on the pit of the other's stomach from a distance; then advancing his right foot, he plunged the weapon through his navel and fixed it in his spine. Down fell Polyneikes, dripping with blood, ribs and belly contracting in his agony.[3]

Xenophon reports simply that a maimed Arkadian *'reached the camp in flight, wounded deep in his belly and holding his intestines in his hands, he told all that had happened.'*[4]

A stone inscription tells us the Athenians had voted in the Assembly to force their allies to *'love the demos of the Athenians'.*[5] In Sicily it became clear that this love was, blatantly, unreciprocated.

There were a few survivors, 7,000 or so Athenians, and their fate was, if anything, even more gruesome. The Syracusans had always had a love of the playwright Euripides. And so Athenian soldiers were marched to a natural quarry just outside Syracuse, where they were forced to barter verses of Euripides for the chance of freedom. Today you can still enter, as the site has become a national park, gently planted; the quarry itself has cathedral-esque proportions, flocks of white doves roost at its height and fill the space with a low, rumbling coo. Given no food or water, crushed so tight they could not lie down, the Athenian interlopers were forced to recite lines of their own premier dramatist until they dropped from exhaustion or were felled. The torture was calculating. Sicilian demagogues remembered Melos and called for no clemency.

All in all, after the Sicilian debacle, close on 50,000 Athenian troops and their allies were missing, all presumed dead; 216 triremes were lost.

The wailing women, mourning Adonis, whose cries had cankered the air that night back in Athens twenty-four moons ago, were suddenly believed prescient. Effigies of the dead boy-god, corpse-stiff like the corpses in the quarry at Syracuse, had been carried to the coast. The Athenian women had buried beautiful figurine boys in the Aegean Sea in order to safeguard real men. But now those flesh-and-blood heroes were coming home across the waves in body-bags.

The Athenian dream had been that the Sicilian campaigners would return from their western adventure wealthy and bathed in glory; a whole new land-mass would be waiting, arms open to welcome Athenian democrats and their families. As it was, a handful of traumatised hoplites limped back, amputated, violated, covered in shame.[6] Socrates himself — as represented by Plato in the dialogue *Ion*, set just at the end of the Sicilian disaster in 413 BC — comments that the Athenians were now desperate for personnel. Their citizen population was mortally reduced: they would even recruit generals from the ranks of foreigners. It is a passing remark that has recently been backed up by inscriptional evidence.[7]

SOCRATES: My splendid Ion, you know Apollodorus of Cyzicus, don't you?

ION: And what sort of person might he be?

SOCRATES: He's someone whom the Athenians have often elected as their general, foreigner though he is; and Athens also appoints to generalships and the other posts Phanosthenes of Andros and Heraclides of Clazomenae, even though they are foreigners, because they have demonstrated their merit.[8]

As those tattered remains of an army began to pull into the port of Piraeus, the frightened men of Athens needed to impugn, they needed scapegoats. The Athenians would remember Socrates' curious fascination with the Spartans. Well, now the Spartans had become their devils, and anyone associated with them the devil's incubus.

FIRST HERALD: Founder of the most renowned City of the Sky, do you not know what great honour you have won among men, and how many of them you have who are passionate lovers of this country? Before you founded this city, in those days all men were Spartan-mad, all hairy, hungry and dirty, Socrates-y and carrying clubbed sticks.[9] . . .

CHORUS: *And near the Shadefeet there lies*
a lake where unwashed
Socrates charms up men's souls.[10]

And while the Athenians slept uneasy in their beds, flailing around in nights of long nightmares, arms reaching out to try to find someone to blame, Alcibiades was busy.

Aristophanes said of Socrates' one-time-lover:

> *Better not bring up a lion inside your city,*
> *But if you must, then humour all his moods.*[11]

A tricky, half-wild, half-domesticated rogue lion, with plenty of bite left, was precisely what Athens did not need roaming at the edge of its territories right now.

Alcibiades' hubris boded well neither for Athena's city nor for his brother-in-arms, Socrates.

45

DECELEA – CLOSING DOWN
THE MINES

⦿⦿⦿⦿⦿⦿⦿⦿⦿⦿⦿

Decelea, 414–404 BC

Freedom is delicious to eat and hard to digest.

Jean-Jacques Rousseau, *Considerations on the Government
of Poland and on its Proposed Reformation* (1772)

ECELEA, 13 MILES NORTH-WEST OF Athens, was, in the Greek mind,
a troublesome place. In particular it was a place where, through
remembered time, friction between Athens and Sparta had sparked.
The Greeks spoke of it often. This was the site of one of the most
unpleasant episodes in mythical history. The legendary Helen, princess of
Sparta, was said to have been dancing naked with other maidens down by
the banks of Sparta's River Eurotas. She was a child, twelve, ten, even as
young as eight, some said.[1] The old man Theseus, a hero-king of Athens,
and now about seventy, spied her and was so enraptured by her that he had
to have her. She became the summation of all earthly desire. Theseus,
wheezing, sprang a trap, kidnapped the beautiful girl and carried her away
to the hilltop fort of Aphidna near Decelea. But his lust had blinded him.
He forgot, perhaps, that Helen had divine twin brothers, Castor and Pollux:
toned, fist-flailing warriors who would have none of this affront. Riding
out to retrieve their too-desirable sister – a scene that gallops across some
of the earliest Greek vases – they found the people of Decelea as outraged
as themselves by Helen's abduction. The old men of the city helped the
twins get Helen back, leading them to Theseus' hideout at Aphidna while
he was off pursuing more skirt in the form of Persephone. Spartans never

forgot the Deceleans' kindness. In all the years they sent out those blis-tering raids to the Attic countryside, Decelea was left alone. Now, in 413 BC, thanks to honey-tongued Alcibiades, it was Spartan warriors who occupied the hill once more.

Twenty-four centuries later the place still smacks of regime change. This is where the Greek monarchy last made its summer residence. In the coup of 1967 the mini-Versailles here was abandoned. Now it moulders in a limbo. The swimming pool is empty of water and full of graffiti, a 2-foot-high roaring marble lion has a mouth that has long since gaped dry, the stables are derelict, there are sheep-turds on the lawns.

But in its heyday the aristocrats of Europe stretched out here because the cool and pine of the mountain air brings welcome relief from the city fug. As you drive across the arterial road today, leaving behind jerry-built blocks selling fridges and cheap furniture, the freshening of the air and the smell of the humus suddenly strike. Back in the fifth century, Decelea's elevation meant this was a perfect lookout from which to guard Athens to the south-east, to keep an eye out for invading Thebans (or other Boeotians) to the north.

In 414 the Athenians had riled the Spartans. They commissioned a series of seaborne summer raids on grain supplies that had already been gathered in from across Lakonia and from the lands of Spartan allies. The smell of wasted, roasting fodder sparked Spartan ire. Alcibiades – back in the suck-ling home of his memory – gave good advice.[2] He knew that the Athenians had so come to depend on the fruits of their empire that they needed to be cut off from them. He reminded his hosts of that first assault on Decelea, when Spartan heroes had once rescued the honour of a child-Helen from the ravages of the old Athenian King Theseus. Spartan warriors oriented themselves there once again. The known world's crack fighters determined to take Decelea from under the Athenians' noses.

Cleverly they waited until winter. These were men, remember, who from their earliest memory had been trained to endure dreadful extremes: weeks out in the cold, survival all year round in nothing but a summer cloak. While the Athenian garrison guards shivered, Spartans tensed their muscles for the attack.

The Spartans first ringed the settlement and then stormed it. Their success was absolute. A slightly later source, that arch-conservative Isocrates, writing in the fourth century BC, exaggerated when he said that 10,000 men died here, but clearly there was mass slaughter at Decelea.

And now the Spartans had a permanent base in Attica just 13 miles from Athens' walls. They could do more than just intimidate, than just burn vines and olives. From this vantage point they could disrupt the flow of trade, they could intercept communications. Here they started systematically to catalogue the loot they had taken from Attic territories and commandeered local farmers, forcing them to feed Spartan rather than Athenian mouths.

King Agis commanded. In 412/11, Miletus, Aspasia's home-town, revolted and went Spartan.[3] As the months yawned into years, Agis persuaded allies to provide 100 new triremes and now in 408 or 407 BC his *Navarch*, his admiral-in-chief, Lysander, could begin to harry the Athenians from the sea too. Sparta had always been timid around the sea, but now she had taken a leaf out of Athens' book and was embracing naval technology with all the verve of a fresh convert. Without ruling the waves, democratic Athenians could guarantee the safety of neither their own city-state nor their empire.

This was not something the ruling democrats could cover up or sweet-talk away. The people of Athens smelled disintegration, and then, shockingly, devastatingly, more than 20,000 of their slaves in clusters or singly revolted and deserted.[4] A number of these one-time 'human-tools', these 'man-footed things', ended up throwing their lot in with the Spartans at Decelea. The majority of the women and men should have been down in those coastal mines at Laurion, harvesting Athens' cash-crop. But instead they chose to serve masters whose mission was to humiliate and to destroy Athena's city.

It is a two-day walk from Laurion (south-east of Athens) to Decelea (in the north). But the alacrity with which the slaves joined Spartan ranks suggests this was a distance the ex-slaves covered in half that time. These rebels had lived their lives as subhumans. Men and women had been kept separately. The cramped boxes close to the Laurion minefields were all that they had ever called home. When the Spartan slave population revolted, it was said that they wanted to *'eat the Spartans even raw'*.[5] We have no first-hand accounts of those who cut themselves loose from Athenian shackles, but every reason to believe the hatred of their masters was as prodigious, as dangerous.

In terms of sheer muscle and man-power, the foundations of democratic Athenian society had been removed. Without their slaves, the Athenians would no longer be able to scrape silver out of the earth, no longer stimulate the market, no longer sustain their position as 'the envy of all Greece'. Now the Spartans really had Athens in their sights. Always scorning coined money (coinage was banned in the Spartan state), the Spartans must have rubbed their hands with glee at the thought that they had cauterised the

Local men
(up to 100 were
employed in the
first excavating
season of 1931)
remove spoil
from the Agora –
this waste was
sent out to be
dumped along
the Sacred Way
leading to Eleusis.

Pot menders at work in 1937.

The diggers who helped to expose a Bronze Age Mycenaean chamber tomb
beneath the Agora in 1939.

Athena – the goddess both of war and of reason and wisdom. In this depiction from 460 BC, Athena's spear is resting on her shoulder, her shield on her thigh; it is the writing tablet in her hand that holds the goddess rapt, a stylus held up to her mouth. The technology and popularity of writing exponentially increased during Socrates' lifetime.

Two young girls (aged somewhere between five and ten) hold hands and join in a group dance in honour of the goddess Artemis. Dating from the first half of the fifth century BC, this fragment has recently been discovered down a well in the south-east stoa area of the Agora.

A 'Little Bear' from the Sanctuary at Brauron. These Athenians were sent out of the city for a year to 'run' the wild animal out of them. The young girls are often shown cradling pets.

A young child is welcomed in to society during the Athenian Festival of Anthesteria, a ritual that honoured the god Dionysos. A celebration of the rebirth of nature and of the dead, the Anthesteria also reminded the community of the vital power of children. Once a child had reached the age of three and was then further honoured at the feast of Choes, its name was entered on to the phratry list – it was now officially part of the Athenian citizen community.

Socrates in Prison by Nicolai Abraham Abildgaard. Socrates, alone with his two daimonia—his inner 'demons'. He hears only the voice of the good spirit because the bad daimonion's mouth is covered up. The Athenians were very troubled by Socrates' expressions of a kind of private piety as represented here.

Socrates, glaring, sitting on a bench, appeared on the walls of a private house in Ephesus in the first century AD and also on the walls of Pompeii.

The Death of Socrates by Jacques-Louis David. Neo-classical and Romantic painters frequently heroised the moment of Socrates' hemlock-drinking. Current scientific research suggests the form of hemlock the philosopher imbibed may well have ensured a relatively dignified death – which nonetheless included paralysis and suffocation.

production of Athena's Silver Owls: coins that were a symbol of both high-minded achievement and imperial might.

With the Thebans at their backs and an impoverished Athens ahead of them, it looked as though Sparta's favourite hero, Herakles, had broken the back of his thirteenth labour — that soon Athena's city would be his.

46

TIME OF TERROR

@@@@@@@@@@@@

Athens, 412–406 BC

Remember, democracy never lasts long. It soon wastes, exhausts and murders itself.
There is never a democracy that did not commit suicide.

John Adams, letter, 15 April 1814

AND WHAT OF ALCIBIADES? WOULD THIS not be the time for him to wield his killer-blow against the city that had so publicly disowned him?

Yet, like all jilted lovers, the '*adored tyrant of Athens*'[1] would not cut loose, not be rejected so easily.

Always a little 'weak about the trousers', Alcibiades was said to have been busy during his time in Sparta, particularly in the balmy district where the two Spartan kings lived. Magoula, as it was known then and still is today, feels privileged. In amongst the banana and orange groves are the homes of rich men. The tributaries of the Eurotas River, high-reeded, gurgle through the fields, and jasmine spills over well-built walls. The remains of Roman baths, abandoned in olive groves, remind one that this was once a place of relaxation and sensual pleasure. And it was here that Alcibiades seduced the Spartan wife of King Agis while the cuckold was away on campaign.[2] The love-match had spawned a child – and court gossips recalled that years later this wife, Timaea, still whispered into the ear of her golden-haired babe, 'Alcibiades, Alcibiades.' Agis, furious, had ordered Alcibiades' execution – but of course the lustful Athenian had no intention of accepting termination, all because of a few moments of heterosexual pleasure. And so, bribing and dodging his way out of a Spartan death-penalty, he was on the road again – travelling back, not to Athens, but to where he smelled the money: to the east, to Persia.

His timing was good. Two generations after their defeats at Salamis and Plataea, the grandchildren of those shamed Persian kings were growing in confidence once more. The Persian emperor and his familiars supervised a long game of inter-state chess – manipulating the pieces so that now it was Athens, now the Spartans, who had the upper hand. Soon, they reasoned, these two, already weakened after twenty years of conflict, would pick away at one another's defences so successfully that the Persians would be able to stride across their lands, and the lands of their allies, without so much as a sword being raised. Sparta and Athens had become two old cats in a bag, whose only option was to scratch one another to death.

And so it should come as little surprise to hear that by 412 BC we find Alcibiades in Asia Minor, acting as a double-agent-cum-advisor for the Persian Viceroy Tissaphernes.

For three years Alcibiades hedonised in Sardis – 'medising', soaking up the opulence of the Persian court and the ways of the 'Medes'. His massive charisma was appreciated. '*Even those who feared and envied him could not help delighting in his company.*'³ He became Tissaphernes' closest friend; Persian pleasure gardens were named after him. But Alcibiades was restless in the East. He had abandoned the black-broth – the pigs'-blood-based national dish – in Sparta, and you sense he was itching to return to his home-town Athens, although strictly on his terms. He had friends and relatives and men who owed him one in the city, and the runaway made it clear to them that he was still a player in the Athenian game. Making use of the network of spies and messengers that stitched together the eastern Mediterranean and the Near East, Alcibiades got word out to Athens. Promising the allegiance and support of the Persians, he started his own whispering campaign. Tough times call for tough measures, he said. The Spartan wolf is at our gates. We need finance and leadership and control, if we are to win. He offered to broker a deal – Persian gold would come into Athens if broader democratic ambitions were pushed out.

Alcibiades knew that Athens' bullion was running dry. The closure of the Laurion mines meant that Silver Owls were no longer being produced from Attic soil, and many of Athens' 'allies' were failing to deliver their tribute to the mother-city. Money was still dribbling in, but now there were moths rather than rubies in the Parthenon bank. A couple of years later, around 407/6 BC, the Athenians would be forced to melt down some of their golden statues for ready cash. Even glittering Athena Parthenos, that proud wonder of the ancient world who once surveyed an Athenian Empire broad and long, was turned into gold coin.⁴

So Alcibiades encouraged a brief oligarchic revolt in Samos, and, explicitly or unwittingly, set in train a series of events that would spell the beginning of the end of Athens. The details of this moment in history are still mysterious – almost certainly because they were planned covertly.

The general Assembly was persuaded that Athens' situation was desperate. A committee of thirty (all, as it turned out, renowned oligarchs) were chosen to consider Athens' options. Due to present their findings to the Assembly up on the Pnyx, there was a last-minute change of venue. An unfamiliar meeting space was arranged for what would turn out to be a momentous decision – the extinction of the democracy for the first time in almost a hundred years. The citizens of Athens were instead invited to a sanctuary of Poseidon Hippios in the *deme* of Kolonos, a mile or so outside the city walls. The location was designed to befuddle; a local sanctuary with distinct aristocratic connotations (it is aristocrats who have *hippoi*, 'horses', after all), it had neither the timbre of those great democratic debating grounds – the Agora, the Odeion, the Pnyx, the Theatre of Dionysos – nor, importantly, space enough to fit everyone in. The Spartans were only a few miles away at Decelea. Where the Pnyx had natural fortifications. It seemed the sanctuary-meeting place was going to be protected by oligarchic heavies. Any democrat here at Kolonos must have felt distinctly exposed.

The uneasy crowd gathered. It was clear that not everyone was welcome here, and that there was a danger of being trapped in the sanctuary, should you want to get out fast. In the 'narrow space', as Thucydides describes it, a series of reforms were pushed through. The democracy voted itself out of existence and voted in a new kind of constitution. A self-selected council of 400 was to replace the 500 citizens who once queued up to be chosen for office by lot in *demes* across Attica. The Athenian citizen-body would be restricted to 5,000, and only men who could carry hoplite arms. Athens had become a democratically elected oligarchy. The blue-blood horsemen who travelled home past their traditional exercise grounds at the herms' crossroads opposite the *Stoa Basileios* now wore sardonic smiles.

Within a few days the council was dissolved. Someone – it is still not clear who precisely was the driving force behind this sociopolitical unrest – had achieved a very clever bloodless coup. The democracy had not been bypassed, but instead coerced into renouncing itself. Heavily armed highborn men ostentatiously hung out in the streets, escorted by the 120 so-called 'Hellenic Youths' (early pre-echoes of the 'Hitler Youth') to check there was no trouble.[5] Democrats were intimidated into staying indoors, lying low and keeping quiet.

Thucydides tells us that '*no one dared to speak out against them, fear was every-*

where, and it was clear that the conspiracy was widespread; and if anyone did . . . straight-away, in some convenient way he was a dead man.'[6]

Immediately the new system was open to abuse. The 5,000 'citizen-body' never materialised. Instead, for four months, the Four Hundred ruled, and tried to tidy up the city by exterminating their enemies. The sanctuary of Poseidon Hippios was set down in popular memory as a place where *ate*, fate, was played out to its dreadful conclusion. Kolonos Hill today still has a slightly uncertain feel – it struggles to be an urban park – and it is not a place to visit after dark. Red graffiti on the wall yells 'COPS! MURDERERS!' as a protest against the shooting of a student by police in Athens in December 2008. Mature pines and olives cushion the jag of cheaply built apartment blocks, but there are syringes under park benches and rubbish in the bushes. The place is listless. Pointedly, when Sophocles wrote his final Oedipus tragedy in 401 BC (which he would not live to see performed), he tried to turn back the clock and hymned Kolonos as an idyllic grove – whose sanctity a blind, imperfect Oedipus violates.

But the Athenians were not fooled. Kolonos came to be remembered as the *locus* of the beginning of 'the troubles'. The council of the Four Hundred had sufficient money to pay assassins to work swiftly and effectively. *Demokratia* had suddenly become treason, the *'demos'* was once again a dirty word. There were summary executions, Athena's city was staggering into civil war. All pretence of freedom of expression was dropped. By 411 BC the Four Hundred had the bit between their teeth and believed they were on a winning streak. They decided they could manage without Alcibiades, who twisted and turned once again. The democrats in the fleet in Samos were horrified by what had happened back in the mother-city. Alcibiades smelled an opportunity, sympathised, and they voted him their general. Now to all intents and purposes, the exile had his very own private Athenian navy.

And meanwhile the new, prematurely confident oligarchic Athens was not doing well. The 400 had secured neither Persian money nor Spartan appeasement. Spartan troops took over the breadbasket that is Euboea and then slowly started to pick off cities potentially friendly to Athens: Byzantium in 410, and from 407 many more as the satrap of Asia Minor, Prince Cyrus, decided to put his money behind Sparta's cause. When it was clear that the Council of 400 – still meeting regularly in the *bouleuterion* in the Agora – wouldn't work, the Athenians tried a new way to restrict the full democracy, instituting a property qualification for full citizenship.[7]

These were all lame gestures. The club of the great and the good had become just too small to allow Athens to revolutionise its political system effectively overnight.

Throughout the fifth century, fighting on many sides — against Persians, and then Persians and Spartans, and then Spartans, and then Spartans and Persians once more — the Athenians had managed to lose sight of, or perhaps more accurately gloss over, internal disputes, and were able to pretend that they presented a united front. They exiled or ostracised those who caused trouble, they shouted loudly together in the Assembly — they persuaded themselves that they were as one. But now cracks within the city-state were widening.

It is in 411 that Thucydides' narrative ends. He was of course (following his disgrace at Amphipolis) in exile in Thrace. His health broken, within a few years he would be dead. From 411 BC onwards it is also almost as though the true father of history cannot bear to write about Athens anymore.

The Four Hundred were in power, the democracy had been lost, but some men of Athens remembered that Alcibiades was in fact only two days' sailing away in the region of Samos with the pro-democrats Thrasybulus and Thrasyllus. Alcibiades, despite his treachery, despite his hubris and quicksilver politics, had a totemic reputation for many Athenians. He might not have demonstrated the pure 'nobility of spirit' that was thought to come with the beauty of an aristocrat, but he still had the vigour, the driving ambition that incarnated democratic Athenian verve. And — this is of key importance — he had the loyalty of a water-borne army.[8] Athenian *hoi polloi* were quickened once again to the idea that this quasi-legendary figure might be able to save them.

And indeed it was Alcibiades, Socrates' couch-mate, who pulled off a temporary reversal of fortunes, earning great victories for Athens and at last bringing good news back into the Agora. In one sense this was all a great confidence trick. Alcibiades appeared to have the ear of the Persians, and so the Athenian people rolled over to his side. Flurries of triremes on the white-flecked Aegean — Spartan, Athenian, Persian — had been thrashing it out for control of sea and land. Alcibiades had lived in and around Asia Minor and his local knowledge helped to effect a string of victories. With his triumph at the Battle of Kyzikos in 410, Alcibiades grappled back some self-respect for Athena's city. By setting up a kind of customs house at Byzantium, charging 10 per cent to all trading traffic that sailed through the Hellespont, he also brought some hard cash back to the city-state.[9] The *demos*, loyal to Alcibiades, who flattered and charmed them with deeds and coin, began to drift back to the Assembly. By 410/9 the old-style democracy had been restored, proving how remarkably resilient this word-idea in fact was — and how vindictive. The horsemen of the Four Hundred were not smiling now. There were reprisals the length and breadth of the city.

CHORUS: *And if things don't go well, if these good men*
All fail, and Athens comes to grief, why then
Discerning folk will murmur (let us hope):
'She's hanged herself — but what a splendid rope'.[10.]

When Socrates was young, the smell of destroyed carcasses in Athens came from the meat markets in the Agora, the tripe stalls on Piraeus harbour front or the dead animals prepared for tanning; now it was human flesh, first of democrats and then of oligarchs, that was making the air above Athena's city rank.

Aristophanes' *Frogs*, written when the city was a daily host to such barbarity, again captures the mood of the moment — where salvation no longer seems to lie in the future, but somewhere in a romanticised past:

But remember these men also, your own kinsmen, sire and son,
Who have oftimes fought beside you, spilt their blood on many seas;
Grant for that one fault the pardon which they crave you on their knees.
You whom nature made for wisdom, let your vengeance fall to sleep;
Greet as kinsmen and Athenians, burghers true to win and keep,
Whosoe'er will brave the storms and fight for Athens at your side![11]

Athenian society's underlying belief in the power of the 'old' way of doing things bubbled to the surface at a time of crisis. The reformed democracy of 410 set to inscribing the resumed democratic laws in stone. But what was being set down there was not a brave new world. The hard evidence, a surviving a carved stone *stele*, demonstrates that the public statements in Athens now have, literally, a more draconian feel. *'The Athenians shall be governed in the ancestral ways, using the laws, weights and measures of Solon and also the regulations of Draco which had previously been in force.'*[12] It was to a conventional past that a traumatised people turned to find strength.

Alcibiades, the prodigal son

With the democracy restored and a number of oligarchic troublemakers executed, for a short time, in domestic affairs at least, Athens seemed to be temporarily robust. In 407, as a conquering hero once again, opportunist

Alcibiades was recalled to Athens. Greeted at Piraeus with all the pomp and affection befitting one who had that vital Greek virtue *kleos* – fame, the worth to be sung of as the heroes of old – he went straight to the Pnyx to flex his well-exercised rhetorical muscles. At this moment Alcibiades was truly the prodigal son returned. The *stele* incarnating his disgrace was up-ended, dragged down from the Acropolis and thrown into the sea. In his play the *Frogs*, Aristophanes says the Athenians '*pine for him, they hate him, but they wish to have him back*'.[13]

Alcibiades led the procession heading towards the Eleusinian Mysteries – by necessity rerouted for a number of years to skirt those areas of Attic land under Spartan occupation – cocking a snook at the Spartan garrison at Decelea. The returning hero was followed by a gaggle of eager, sycophantic ('sycophant' in the modern, not Attic Greek, sense) citizens, welcoming their lost-boy home. The Athenians, delirious with relief that something at last seemed to be going their way, forgetting his treachery and the disgrace he had brought to their doors, lauded Alcibiades loudly. Plutarch later said of him, with a sniff, that he '*so demagogued the humbler and the poorer classes that they yearned – lusted even – for him to rule over them like a dictator.*'[14]

But it was the briefest of honeymoon periods. Four months in total. Within a number of weeks Alcibiades' deputy Antiochus lost the sea-battle at Notion and, with particularly bitter-sweet contrast, other Athenian generals won the significant sea-battle of Arginusae. Alcibiades had rolled his last dice; he flounced back to Persia and then north to Thrace and the Hellespont. The Athenian Empire had become so sprawling, so big, so weak that it was localising again, and many Greeks gave up all pretence of fighting under an ideological banner. Alcibiades was resurrected amongst the malcontents of the north as a warlord. The Dark Ages were back, a time when powerful men carved up territories on the map for purely personal gain.

Like a bad penny, Alcibiades would turn up once more in Athenian affairs; but his offer of help would be rejected. Now he was in his mid-forties, bald, perhaps looking seedy, a good deal of his glamour had finally worn off. His end was certainly ignominious; not epic, not heroic, not golden. He had lived his life for glory – and had earned many enemies in the process. Deciding to give up on Hellenic interests altogether, he travelled east again, anticipating a new alliance with the grand King of Susa, Artaxerxes. En route – with his beautiful courtesan-consort Timandra – he slept one night in a small town in Phrygia. In the early hours a scraping sound woke him. Assassins (to this day we don't know whose) were setting his lodgings alight. Alcibiades stumbled out, sword in hand, choking, but was lynched at a distance with javelins and spears. His whore was spared –

but only to wash and bury, or burn, Alcibiades' body, which had by now been decapitated.

∽∽∽∽∽

And what of Socrates through all this turmoil and political heartache? How did he react to the messy, exiled death of the man he had once loved as dearly as philosophy itself? Well, Plato has us believe that, as ever, he wasted not a moment worrying about the casualties or minutiae of the power politics of the day. His concern, purely and simply, was now what it had always been – to encourage the young men of the city to learn how to be good.[15] And the philosopher achieves this as he has always done, by wandering through the hot, still inspiring streets and sanctuaries of his city-state.

SOCRATES: *The locusts seem to be looking down upon us as they sing and talk with each other in the heat. Now if they should see us not conversing at midday, but, like most people, dozing, lulled to sleep by their song because of our mental indolence, they would quite justly laugh at us, thinking that some slaves had come to their resort and were slumbering about the fountain at noon like sheep. But if they see us conversing and sailing past them unmoved by the charm of their Siren voices, perhaps they will be pleased and give us the gift which the gods bestowed on them to give men.*[16]

Despite all this retrogressive pain, Socrates was still looking to the future; he was still coaching the young men of Athens in their job of being thinking men. And he did so in one of the most trim of all Athens' locations, a wrestling ground, a *palaestra*.

SOCRATES: *What is this place? And what do you do here?*

[The young men reply:] It is a newly-built wrestling ground; but in fact we spend much of our time talking and debating – would you like to come to join us?[17]

An entire Platonic Dialogue, the *Lysis* (subtitled 'On Friendship'), is set here. The date is 409 BC. Socrates, putatively aged about sixty, describes to us two conversations he has with a handsome young man, Lysis, and his friend Menexenus. Their discussions focus on the motivations for personal affection, and on the nature of friendship. It is a charming and practical work.

Hence anyone who deals wisely in love-matters, my friend, does not praise his beloved until he prevails, for fear of what the future may have in store for him. And besides, these handsome boys, when so praised and extolled, become full of pride and haughtiness: do you not think so?

I do, he said.

And then, the haughtier they are, the harder grows the task of capturing them?[18]

Excitingly for scholars of Plato's work, recent excavations that preceded the 2004 Olympics and that extended earlier archaeological work between 1924 and 1925, and between 1960 to 1981, have confirmed the exact geography of Socrates' opening lines.

SOCRATES: *I was walking straight from the Academy to the Lyceum, by the road which skirts the outside of the walls — just under the wall, and had reached the little gate where you'll find the spring of Panops [of Hermes the 'all-seeing'], when I chanced upon Hippothales, the son of Hieronymos, Ktesippos the Paeaniain, and some more young men, standing together in a group . . .*

Come and join us, he said.

Where do you mean? I asked; and who do you mean by 'us'?

Here, he said, pointing out to me an enclosure with a door open. We pass our time here, he went on; not only us, but others besides, — a great many, and handsome.[19]

It is still possible to peer down at these excavations in the north-eastern corner of the city today. Hefty stone blocks mark the parameters of the gateway and the boundary of the old wrestling ground. The traces of the spring of Panops are now visible. The work has also uncovered a new cemetery in the area, created during the Peloponnesian War to deal with the increasing number of corpses that Athens produced in those dull decades of its Golden Age history. Touching little artefacts have emerged from the graves: a child's golden bracelet and finger ring, a young man's voting disc.[20] Moving to think that this spot may well have been precisely where Socrates delivered lines so thoughtful and universal that they still chime today:

May not the truth be that, as we were saying, desire is the cause of friendship; for that which desires is dear to that which is desired at the time of desire?[21]

And the real Lysis himself has left us an unexpected archaeological treat. In the newly refurbished Archaeological Museum down in Piraeus district, in between the shafts of light that come sea-bright through the blinds, stands a fine funerary urn.[22] It is made of solid stone, creamy, finely carved. Chiselled into its front face is a tender scene. An elderly man sits while a woman stands behind him. The man is old, but poised — he extends his hand in farewell. His name is Lysis, son of Demokrates. He is bidding farewell to his own son, Timokleides, who has, prematurely, been taken from the world. The mourning Lysis is the same bright lad that Socrates chatted with one warm day at the wrestling ground. He is in more ways than one 'the son of Demokrates'. Young, confident, like the democracy itself, he has lived to suffer disappointment and great loss. His fifth-century story can still be read in the stones underneath modern Athens' feet.

We can map with increasing certainty Socrates' peregrinations (and those of his peers) around Athens during those final spasms of the Peloponnesian War. Yet the philosopher is still a challenge for history writers, for he does not fit into an easy political narrative. He is not a campaigner. He does not die for the sake of democracy. He does not seize power with the oligarchs, exterminate his enemies and debauch on victory. Instead, while all around him are losing their heads, their principles and their lives, he apparently relaxes in the gymnasia and at the wrestling grounds and, with the next generation of young Athenian men, debates the nature of friendship and looks to the future.

But there is a strong hint in one of the lines given to Socrates by Plato that this devoted entanglement with the young, the not fully mature, spells disaster.

SOCRATES: The young who follow me around, doing so of their free will, who have complete leisure — the sons of the richest people — enjoy hearing people examined, and they often imitate me, and then try to examine others. And then, I imagine, they find an abundance of people who think they know something but know virtually nothing. That's why those who are examined by them get angry with me and not with them, and say that a certain Socrates completely pollutes the land and corrupts the youth. And when anyone asks them what I do and what I teach . . . I think they wouldn't want to say what's true, that they're plainly pretending to know, and in fact, they know nothing.[23]

When the democracy was developing and expanding, it was bullish, confident it could cope with Socrates' eternal questions. It could even handle (albeit reluctantly) the precocious self-belief of his young protégés — immature men who started to interrogate those around them before they had learned how to answer questions themselves. It turned a blind eye to the fact that Socrates meandered through the city and talked, and talked; he never pulled his weight in an overtly democratic way; he did not put himself forward for jury service, or for high office. But now, after two decades of battle, after plague, after five years of civil strife, this high-handed, apparently self-indulgent questioning must have seemed intolerable. Socrates' association with a particular 'young man' would also have been to the fore of Athenian minds. Alcibiades, that glaringly ebullient latter-day Theseus, was now dead, and a disgrace to the city. He was as despised as he had once been loved. How could the Athenians possibly *not* remember that Socrates had shared Alcibiades' tent, his couch, his well-turned drinking cup? Who was to say the philosopher did not also share half-Spartan Alcibiades' superiority, his dangerous, knife-wielding aristocratic friends, his oligarchic leanings, his part-Spartan heart?

And then, three years after his debate with the young men at the wrestling grounds, an unusual thing happened: Socrates himself, who all his life had shunned 'conventional' politics (the Assembly, the law-courts, the *Boulê*) suddenly seemed to change tack. In the late summer of 406 BC we find him back in the Agora – not wandering around and provoking his fellow-citizens, not sharing ideas with those forty or fifty years his junior, but acting more conventionally, as a member of a *prytany*, the inner circle of the democratic *Boule* council itself. At last, with just seven years to live, Socrates was acting like a good-to-honest, conventional Athenian democrat.

47

ARGINUSAE – STANDING OUT IN THE CROWD

The Assembly, Athens, 406 BC

SOCRATES: Because I'm not just now but in fact I've always been the sort of person who's persuaded by nothing but the reason that appears to me to be best when I've considered it . . . Consider then: doesn't it seem to you to be correct that one shouldn't respect all the opinions people have but some and not others, nor the opinions of all people, but some and not others? What do you say? Is this right or not?

CRITO: It's right.

SOCRATES: Then should we respect the good ones but not the bad ones?

CRITO: Yes.

SOCRATES: Aren't the good ones the opinions of the wise, and the bad ones the opinions of the foolish?

CRITO: Of course.

Plato, *Crito*, 46b–7a[1]

A SCANT SEVEN YEARS BEFORE HIS own capital trial Socrates stood in the company of another group of men, 6,000 or so this time. He had put himself forward for selection by lot (a system of which he took a rather dim view) to judge on the *Boule* council in the melodramatic case of the Battle of Arginusae.[2]

In 406 BC the Spartans looked set to take over the western seaboard of Turkey and had their eyes set on the strategic city of Methymna on the island of Lesbos – the Athenians' only chance to thwart them was a battle around a small group of islets close by, the Arginusae. Athens was much attenuated come 406 BC, but the city drafted in all men, citizens, freed slaves, whoever was strong enough to hold a weapon to fight. Eight of the ten generals elected by the Assembly were prepared to command the campaign. A battle force was set. It made the two-day journey east under a scorching August sun. Two generals from the board of ten were besieged in the region at Mytilene, and so those eight remaining men had a size-able, strategic burden to carry.

The land here, deserted today apart from the odd visit by extreme swimmers who enjoy the challenge of the currents in this spot, is curiously unprepossessing. And in 406 BC, around the tricky rocks of Arginusae, 120 Spartan triremes and 155 Athenian swung into their ugly seaborne dance: ramming and burning, throat-slitting and heart-piercing until one side could stand it no more.

The battle was a close call, but, just, a victory for Athens. And then a summer storm came. Storms in this region split open the sky. At a distance of 10 miles the rains scurf up the sea's surface, and close at hand the rain-drops travel so fast they are immediately blinding. The foul conditions back in 406 BC (or this was the official story at any rate) prevented the generals from picking up the bodies of the dead and wounded. Today a storm of this magnitude washes up fag-ends and cuttlefish right along the shoreline. In 406 BC it left shreds of battle, of humans. But the hours and days that followed the battle were so intemperate these scraps could not be retrieved. Uncollected, this meant that mutilated corpses could not be given a proper burial; their souls were lost, condemned. Two of the Athenian generals realised the implication of their failings and melted away into the Eastern Mediterranean. Six returned home, expecting perhaps a heroes' welcome – there had been mitigating circumstances after all. Jittery and bad-tempered with worry, the Athenian *demos* did not receive the homecomers as they might have expected.

Instead of garlands and laurels, the six generals still standing found themselves on trial. Athens, fleet of foot as ever, had arranged a hearing in the Assembly the men charged, collectively, with anti-democratic activity. As it so happened, Socrates was presiding officer for the day – serving with the *prytany*, the committee of the council.[3] He had volunteered himself for service, back in the assembly of his local *deme*, Alopeke.[4] His selection as overseer was a chance one; just the way the lottery machine chose to allo-cate democratic jobs that day. We do not know why Socrates volunteered himself, the man who famously left that kind of politicking to others.

Payment for *prytany* duty was around 5 obols for the day – perhaps he simply needed the money.[5] But his motivation could also have been more high-minded. He realised perhaps that Athens needed practical help to keep the body-politic together; that for once the philosopher's role was to be not the wound, but the bandage. So, that late-summer morning in 406 BC, just as they would do in the near future at the philosopher's trial, citizens were hurrying, at dawn with Socrates himself among them, to pass judgement on their fellow democrats.

As presiding officer in the Assembly, Socrates had gone through that theatre of democracy that enabled ordinary men to prosecute one another or to declare them innocent. He had sworn an oath in Theseus' Sanctuary that his counsel would be *'for the best advantage of the state'*. He would have made a sacrifice to *Demokratia*. He had stood up in front of the council members to declare himself fit for practice – giving the names of his mother and father, his grandparents, declaring that he honoured their names and the family cult, that he was not a pauper and that he had seen military service. He had eaten dinners (simple fare – the dinner services still being dug up here are not at all fancy[6]) in the round dining hall, the *Tholos*, by now more than fifty years old; he might have stayed the night there, he would have debated Assembly business with a press of the *demos* listening to him from behind railings, and he would have plunged his hands into the baskets of cold pebbles, some black, some white, so that he could vote 'for' or 'against'.[7]

We should not underestimate the significance of Socrates' decision to be a politician for a day, either in his own narrative or in the story of the dog days of Athens. The man who spent no time in his life busying himself with the practical, explicit business of being a democrat had now put himself forward for selection. He admitted that Athens needed him, and he needed to make his voice heard in the city. After years of brutalisation something had changed, – Athena must have been visibly stumbling.

This case of the disgraced generals was going to be tried under the operatic canopy of a Greek sky. The Pnyx was the location – that creamy, rocky slope where up to 6,000 men could sit or stand comfortably side by side. And so piglets were sacrificed, invocations and curses were sent up to the gods, the Assembly men were now ritually pure. The fact that the disgraced generals from Arginusae were to be tried together – and by so many accusers – did not look good. No precedent in Athenian law allowed for group trials. This smacked of a kangaroo court. It seemed the generals' guilt was a foregone conclusion. Socrates (a lone voice, or so Xenophon and Plato would have us believe) refused to go along with the ugly mood of the crowd. They shouted that he would be indicted for treason, but Socrates did not budge. The laws of Athens stated that men should be tried individually, and Socrates was sticking to the letter of the law. There was a stalemate; in the darkening sky that shadowed so quickly at this time of the year, the show of Athenian hands could not be counted clearly. The trial of the hangdog generals was postponed, and in the revolving-door arrangement of the democracy, tomorrow would bring another day, and another amateur politician to supervise proceedings. There was a promise of separate trials.[8] Socrates was off the case.

Athens had voted and agreed, but somehow, thanks to a bit of parliamentary ducking and diving, the Assembly was now told that this mandate was invalid; the progressive democracy had become a mob that preferred illegality to frustration. Their blood was up. Agitators infiltrated the court, their heads shaved as if they were in mourning. They produced a witness, a man who said he survived by clinging on to debris from the Arginusae wreckage – a bran tub of all things – and wailed that these generals did not even collect the men, dead, half-dead, dying, bobbing and gasping in the water, who had proved themselves *most brave in the service of the country*.[9]

We do not have the name of the man who took over from Socrates; but what we know is that he did not have the philosopher's qualms. The next day all six surviving generals in Athens were jointly tried, condemned to death and executed.[10] Their means of death, hemlock poison.

The generals had been voted into their posts, and into their graves, in a matter of weeks by the democratic Assembly. Socrates, who always questioned whether 'democracy' was indeed an automatic route to 'the good', seemed in the case of Arginusae to have grounds for concern.

Loose ends

One of the unfortunate dead – one of the six generals summarily executed – was Aspasia and Pericles' son, Pericles II. Pericles' two legitimate sons by his first marriage had died in the plague; Pericles II had been made a citizen by special decree. For a short time in his life he was accepted as a valid member of the Athenian democratic body. But now Athenian policy had managed to eradicate the genetic remnant of that union that had irritated them so all those years ago – a remnant of a great, an exemplary man and a seductive, beautiful woman from the East.

By the time her son died, Aspasia had long been lost to history.

But recent evidence has brought her back. Excavations in Piraeus during the laying of a new road turned up a number of artefacts in the rescue archaeology, amongst them one of the curse-tablets so favoured of fifth-century Athens. Someone had gouged Aspasia's name out of lead and buried their curses in the Piraeus district. A grave *stele* mentioning her family was recently discovered here too – in the home of prostitutes, of liminal foreigners and their families.[11] Centuries after her death one man reports seeing Aspasia's tomb in the harbour district.[12] And there is the chance that a piece of figurative statuary now copied in the Vatican guarded her grave. Rather matronly, stodgy and sensible-looking, if this stone bust is indeed Aspasia, it is hard to credit that she caused the Peloponnesian War thanks to her looks and the lust of her nymphomaniac dancing girls. But that was what the mob persuaded themselves they wanted to believe. Once this slander was on the streets, it was nurtured until it became popular history – and was then quoted as fact. Like most goddesses, the goddess of persuasion, Peitho, and Pheme, the goddess of rumour, could be irrevocably unkind.

We commemorate Aspasia as a bright, self-made woman, but the Athenians never accepted this foreign courtesan. The democracy recognised the benefits of a cosmopolitan city, but shied away from endorsing and buttressing it. The Athenians, who had for a few decades proved themselves to be the most radical and liberal thinkers, who had embraced revolutionary, ground-breaking intellects from across the known world, gradually allowed the flaws of human nature – jealousy, self-delusion, greed, hubris, gossip, fear – to keep their democracy a flicker rather than a forest-fire in history. As a *demos*, a crowd, they made their judgement of Aspasia just as they did in the case of Arginusae.

Xenophon records his distaste for the Athenian gannets up on the Pnyx. '*The crowd,*' he simply says, '*forced its will by thorubos.*'[13]

This is sometimes dismissed as the snobbish slight of an aristocrat, but anyone who has lived in the real world should be able to taste Xenophon's fear in their own mouths. *Homo sapiens*, time and again, craves the anonymity of the herd. All of civilisation's darkest hours have been bayed on by men who want scapegoats, who want the finger of blame to turn in any direction, as long as it is away from their own face. Loose, jealous tongues are the bane of history. *Thorubos* can mean a buzz, a jangle of minds stimulated by one another, or it can mean the clatter of prejudice, where individuals choose to follow herd opinion. We call these shames abominable, but the complicity of the crowd is a distinctly human affair.

So how could it not be that one peculiar, uncompromising man, who refused to go with the flow, who refused to vote to kill to make a community feel better about itself, would not soon have a taste of society's own medicine?

SOCRATES: You pay attention to and concentrate on this one thing; if what I say is just or not. This is the virtue of a judge; the virtue of a speaker is to tell the truth.[14]

Just over six years later that same crowd would prove that men like Socrates could not thwart them with his high-minded talk. If a crowd, a court, an all-powerful democracy wanted to dispose of someone, with truth on their side or no, they had the power to do so.

48

TALL POPPIES, CUT CORN

࿇࿇࿇࿇࿇࿇࿇࿇࿇࿇

Athens, 405–404 BC

By cutting the tops of the tallest ears of corn he [Periander, advising Thrasybulus]
meant he must always put out of the way the citizens that overtop the rest.

Aristotle, *Politics*, 5.10[1]

I T WAS NOW EASIER TO DESTROY those that the democracy had built
up, that the people had once loved. Those who flowered too tall and
too bright were regularly being cut down. The *demos* had always been
ambivalent about their leading lights. Was a visionary, high-achieving man
an asset, or did his very specialness, his head-above-the-crowdness make him
anti-democratic?[2]

Athenian drama is riddled with scenarios that explore this theme:

> OEDIPUS: *O power —*
> *wealth and empire, skill outrunning skill*
> *in the rivalry and battlefields of life,*
> *what spite and envy follows after you!*
>
> CHORUS: *Who could behold his fame without envious eyes?*
> *Now in what a sea of overwhelming troubles he lies!*[3]

Greek theatre is frequently cited as a civilising influence, an altogether
good thing. A space where people could meet their fears together: joint-
witnessing. But we mustn't forget these were gatherings that could fan the
flames of prejudice and resentment and jealousy, as well as of good judgement.

Socrates had been lambasted on-stage when there was still hope in the city. When in 423 BC Aristophanes had described him as a *'rascal, a braggart, a liar'*, when other playwrights had mocked his *'one ragged cloak'*, his *'shoeless disciples'*, there was still a chance that Athens could triumph in her foreign and internal struggles. The Dionysia itself may have been reduced from five days to three for the duration of the Peloponnesian War, but at least it was there. Approaching the year of Socrates' death, Athens was ground down, jaded, wrecked, exhausted, febrile. Euripides' *Women of Troy* and *Hecuba* talk not just about the sickening, fetid brutality of war, but of the dull, wasteful messiness of it.

Woe, woe is me! What words, or cries, or lamentations can I utter? Ah me! For the sorrows of my closing years! For slavery too cruel to endure, to bear! Woe, woe is me! What champion do I have? Family and city — where are they?[4]

And it was in these dark days, when the searing joviality of Aristophanes' *Clouds*, the genial colours of an April day in 423, with pigs' blood and wine and dancing, would still have been viable if distorted memories, that Socrates was judged. He was judged when hope had waned. When at least one-half, possibly three-quarters of the Athenian population had died. When the city's greatest enemies had broken down Athenian walls, pissed on their thresholds, outlawed democracy — when the roar of the crowd suddenly showed a sharper edge.

It is not [my accusers] but the envy and detraction of the world, which has been the death of many good men, and will probably be the death of many more; there is no danger of my being the last of them.[5]

In the latest tragedies written — Euripides' *Phoenician Women*, composed just ten years before Socrates' trial, is a prime example — the picture is clouded. Now the city is a place compromised by war. Families are ruined, both tribal ties and individual ambition tear apart the city-state. We watch the last great works of Euripides and hear fifth-century Athenians weep.

Your pain is our pain![6]

Outside the Theatre of Dionysos where these plays are performed are the visible, physical casualties of war. The hunger-drawn middle-aged men. Women who cannot spawn new little humans to support them, and who have lost the sons they once gave birth to. These are fixtures of all war-zones: outlaws with no families, no role. We hear of one such after Socrates has died, in the fourth century BC. An older woman who is suspected of not being a citizen because she is reduced to working as a wet-nurse and a ribbon-seller: jobs normally fit only for slaves and metics. Her son Euxitheus declares with aching under-statement that many crones like her are forced to work as nurses, wool-workers, grape-pickers. 'We do not live in the way that we'd like,' he sighs.[7]

By the end of the fifth century BC the mood in Athens had become uniformly ugly. Grain supplies were getting low. Brother could not trust brother. A recently discovered letter written by a contemporary of Socrates, etched onto a foil-fine piece of lead and long lost in the Black Sea, sees a banker called Pasion, himself an ex-slave, instructing a lawyer to effect retribution in Athens:

I, Pasion, write with instructions to Dikaiarchos to punish and pursue Satyrion and Nikostratos . . . since they are wronging and plotting against me, and [against] Glauketes and Aiantodoros, and are plotting also that . . .[8]

One can imagine the atmosphere: Athenians all looking over their shoulders to see who would be the next to stab them in the back. A weary whisper must have stolen through the cramped streets – someone must be responsible for all this suffering, for the degeneration of a city that was once in the ascendant. And the people of Athens lashed out at what they could hear and see: at the sophists, the clever men who, at one time, had, with flowery words and tricks of rhetoric, with the goddess Persuasion at their sides, glorified Athens to the wider world and within its walls. Much like the financiers in the first decade of the twenty-first century, these specialists traded in clever, invisible assets that seemed powerful, but that none outside their circle fully understood. There was a time when the delight of good argument, the cosy glow of inspiring words, had seemed to protect Athens: to give Athenians a great sense of themselves, to publicise their undeniable cleverness and self-confidence throughout the Eastern Mediterranean, to make anything seem possible. In the new inclusive political system, ordinary men needed their fancy words to survive the bear-pit of the law-courts, the fracas of the Assembly. The influx of foreigners, of foreign ideas, was, briefly, intensely exciting for Athens. Some sophists managed to grow fat on the democrats' willingness and need to pay for words. At the outset of the democracy great orators had been adulated and the city-state had fallen in love with the art of rhetoric. But now men realised that the slickest speakers were running rings around them: if you could argue black was white, then it was only the most persuasive argument – not the most sound, the most logical, the best – that would win the day. Democrats realised that men could be tricked into doing dreadful, as well as noble, things. Smooth talk was recognised as spin, and it lost its charm.

Throughout Socrates' life, men had flocked to hear word-merchants talk in the Agora. Now mobs banged on their doors late at night demanding the expulsion of these self-same sophists from the city. Athens was no longer a state you wanted to arrive at, it was a place from which you tried to escape.

∾∾∾∾∾

Aristophanes' comedies, always surgically sharp, speak even more bitterly now of men like Socrates. The philosopher is not just a figure of fun, he is unpatriotic, devaluing the work of the great tragedians with his '*hair-splitting twaddle*.'⁹ There were not many intellectuals left in Athens by the turn of the century and there was the sense that those who were there had their backs against the wall.

Alcibiades was exiled, Nicias dead, Pericles just bones in the earth. The democratic mob, and for once this is what it was, had terminated the lives of the successful generals of Arginusae – eight men who had originally been picked as the brightest sparks that remained in a dulled city-state. Athens simply had no great men to lead it, and the bellies of the people were growing big with hunger. But the appetite for war was undiminished and Athens, it seems, still had the stomach to fight.

The next theatre of engagement between the old enemies Sparta and Athens would be on the stretch of water that now sits between Europe and Asia, the Hellespont, and in particular a spot that still demarcates the division between East and West – a place called Aegospotami on the European side of the mouth of the Bosporus. The landscape here is listless and unfriendly. Nearby are the modern-day battlegrounds of Gallipoli, where other young soldiers were slaughtered in their thousands during the First World War. It is inhospitable territory – land you have to know well if you are to survive.

This is the region that had become Alcibiades' home patch; the Chersonese peninsula, where he had been given estates and fortified tagging posts. To all intents and purposes he had morphed into a Thracian warlord. The harshness of his life was written in the landscape around him. Learning of the planned battle at Aegospotami, Alcibiades, thundering up to the generals like a former-day knight in shining armour, just got near enough to offer advice – it is crazy, he said, to beach Athenian ships on those exposed hills that seem to grow only rock and low scrub, where the Spartans could spike them. But a 'privateer'¹⁰ now rather than a true Athenian, his golden touch seemed cheap, fake. Alcibiades' words were summarily dismissed. In some ways, if Athenians were going to go down, perhaps it was to their credit that they did not throw out a desperate lifeline to the rackety, trashy, charismatic athlete-aristocrat, who had played fast and loose with their affections so many times.

And now not only did the Athenians anchor their ships where they were vulnerable, but they left them unattended while going out into alien territory to forage for supplies. They had not a chance of victory, particularly given that Sparta had two phosphorescently luminous young male characters on her side. The Spartan general Lysander was on the attack, and as he ploughed through the sea, it was said that the twin brothers of Helen, the divine Dioscuri, came rushing to the aid of Spartans abroad once more. Athens was once a thalassocracy – a power that ruled the seas. But now the Spartans, landlocked for so long, had learned to adapt. And it was their warrior-citizens, along with those fit underclasses called *helots* (slaves) and *mothakes* (bastards) who were forcing the oars of triremes to power-surf through the Aegean at spine-tingling speeds. Now it was the Spartans who had control of coasts and waterways and beaching points, of naval strategy.

At Aegospotami, Athenian ships scattered, and all but two were taken captive. All Athenian citizens on board, at least 1,000 of them, were lined up and executed. Spartan Lysander had won. Athens surrendered. The region that had witnessed a heavenly shower of meteorites when Socrates was just two years old, a line from the heavens that encouraged Athenians and visitors to Athens to debate the scientific nature of the universe, had now trailblazed the death of the Athenian Empire.

Spartan administrators lost no time in broadcasting their city-state's triumph. In Delos a decree was issued, written in the distinctively bucolic Spartan dialect, stating, laconically, that the Delians had their freedom, their sanctuaries and their funds once more – never again would this be an Athenian offshore bank.

And in the navel of the world itself, in Delphi, the Spartan commander Lysander was commemorated with a gaudy monument. As you walked up the rousing Sacred Way, with the plain of Kirrha on your left, Mount Parnassus to your right and behind you, this hubristic memorial would have been impossible to miss. Right next to the Athenian show-off zone, with its eponymous heroes, by a statue of Miltiades (the victor at the Battle of Marathon) now stood a new, Spartan plinth boasting thirty-eight bronze statues precisely commissioned by Laconic overlords. Here there were Zeus, Apollo and Artemis, here too those helpful twin brothers Castor and Pollux, and there was Lysander, being crowned by the god who had lost the battle for the Acropolis and for Athens, Poseidon. But Poseidon had won the ultimate victory. He now adored these Spartans, who had, at last, seen sense and floated their boats and their chances on his briny battle-plain: together gods and god-fearing Spartans had brought that busybody superpower Athens down. Athena, on this occasion, was nowhere to be seen.

After the disastrous naval defeat at Aegospotami all of Athens' allies deserted her, with the exception of idealistic Samos, once so troublesome but now staunchly democratic. The Athenians, desperate to remember their few friends, commissioned a beautiful relief of the two goddesses Athena and Hera (protectress of Samos) warmly shaking hands; the Samians — whose restlessness all those years back in 440 BC helped to spark the zero-sum Peloponnesian War — were now given Athenian citizenship.

Athens had been great, but one wondered, this year, who would want its citizenship? Outside the city walls were camped those two Spartan kings. The Spartan fleet, warming to its new sea-legs, ringed the harbour of Piraeus. The 150 ships prevented grain supplies getting through to the Athenian people — and there were many Athenians inside the city as Lysander had swept through all the nearby territories, ordering the children of Athena to go and hide in the skirts of their wise, war-loving goddess. In 404 BC the Athenians, with the Spartans at their gates and confidently billeting themselves in those once-beloved, once-thriving places, the *gymnasia* and wrestling grounds,[11] were hopelessly besieged, hungry and weak with a certain fear of what they had coming to them:

They could see no future for themselves except to suffer what they had made others suffer, people of small states whom they had injured not in retaliation for anything they had done but out of arrogance of power and for no reason except that they were in the Spartan alliance . . . and so though numbers of people in the city were dying of starvation, there was no talk of peace.[12]

We hear that while all in the city were wailing and pulling their hair, gnawing at wood to beat the pangs of starvation, Socrates was typically phlegmatic in the face of disaster, typically out of step with those around him:

SOCRATES: *During the siege, while others pitied themselves, I lived no worse than when the city was happiest.*[13]

But we have reached the endgame. Sparta had Athens surrounded. Athens no longer commanded the treasured asset she had fought for seventy-odd years before — *eleutheria*, freedom. Socrates and his fellow Athenians found that if they wanted to live, they had no choice but to vote out their own democracy, and vote in a Laconophile oligarchy instead.

Hearing that democratic Athens was at last defeated, a tsunami of resentment and hate raced towards Attica. The Thebans and Corinthians (Sparta's allies) wanted to slaughter and maim, to turn rich, cultured Athenian territory into land for sheep. But the Spartans were less emotional.

Calmly they demanded four things: the reduction of Athens' fleet to twelve ships; the disbanding of the democracy — and the smashing down of those city walls that they so resented, and in whose shadow they had fought for so long. And then those words that have come to have such a familiar ring, in modern as well as ancient societies: the edicts of the powerful instructing subject nations how they will now think, who will now be their friends and their common foes; the Spartans made one final demand and the statement was blunt, unambiguous: either you are with us or against us.

Athens to have the same enemies and the same friends as Sparta has and to follow Spartan leadership in any expedition Sparta might make either by land or sea.[14]

It was done. Athena's city no longer belonged to Socrates and his fellow Athenians. Now she belonged to Sparta. Those who had been subject-states controlled by Athens stretched their arms wide and welcomed this change of regime.

Brick by brick, block by block, Athens' proud city walls were tumbled to the ground.

And so, Xenophon tells us, the flute-girls, the prostitutes around the city walls, quickly changed sides, dancing in the embers of the Athenian Empire.

They believed this day to be the beginning of freedom for the Greeks.[15]

THIRTY TYRANTS

@@@@@@@@@@@@

Athens, 404 BC

They tore people from their children, parents and wives, . . . and did not allow them to receive the lawful and customary burial rights, considering their own might-is-right authority to be more powerful than the punishments of gods.

Lysias, Speech 12, *Against Eratosthenes*, 12.96

FOR MORE THAN TWO YEARS SPARTAN-controlled populations across the Aegean had had to live under the rule of pro-Spartan juntas, 'the rule of ten' – and now the Athenians too were about to taste that experience.

Lysander supported a group of just thirty men who were to have command of Athena's city. These were all Athenian citizens, but had to have had oligarchic or pro-Spartan leanings. The interim body of 'over-seers' was given a Spartan name, the *ephors*. We have to imagine that this 'Thirty' were not selected because of their holistic, democratic views or their support of fair-handed moderation. Critias, an uncle of Plato and an arch-conservative, the man whom Socrates had condemned as a rutting pig thanks to his sexual appetites, masterminded the operation. Socrates' other favourite, Charmides (he whom Socrates described, on spotting him in the gym, as being *'perfectly beautiful'*), was one of the Ten that the Spartans backed to keep the Piraeus district subdued, and under a form of Spartan system of control. Other members of Socrates' circle were part of the narrative of the restriction of people-power in this chapter of Athens' history.

But there was nothing symposiastic, dreamy, genial-boozy, butter-warmed about these men. Three per tribe, the Thirty had been legally elected, but they were in charge of an abused, traumatised city; and a Spartan 'big brother' watched over all. Much Athenian property was seized, and wealthy men, in particular foreign men, were targeted.

The Thirty instituted a reign of terror, purging the city of their personal and political enemies. The business started by oligarchs back in 411 BC, when death squads had roamed the streets, was being seen through to its awful conclusion.

These new rulers of Athens held power for just twelve months, but they steadily thinned the Athenian population; over one hundred men a month were 'disappeared'. Apart from the back-street massacres, the stiflings in beds, the snatching of children from the 'wrong' families, all the incidental displacements in the city must have been so distasteful, so heart-rending. The *Tholos* — that attractive roundhouse created to feed democrats while they worked all hours to make the democracy robust — was taken over by the Thirty in 403 BC as their headquarters. From their base there in the Agora's circular, visibly egalitarian building (architecture of deep symbolic importance), the Thirty sent out their orders of intimidation and murder. The awful irony cannot have been lost on those Athenians who had seen the *Tholos* raised as a triumphant hurrah for liberty and equality.

From 404 through to 403 BC, Athens was stifled in an endless nightmare. Fists and wooden clubs pounded on doors. Citizens turned slaughterers to avoid their own messy deaths. To appreciate the horror of this long night, it is important to recall just how small Athens had become. A city of 100,000 Athenians plus 200,000 slaves had been reduced, through disease, the Peloponnesian War and civil strife, to a core of 60,000 or so.

Only 30,000 of those were men, and just 10,000 lived within the walls of Athens itself. This was Balkan-village atrocity. Neighbours turned on neighbours, sometimes brother against brother.

In the year of the Thirty, between 1,000 and 1,500 Athenians died. We know about the citizen deaths; there may have been many thousands more – anonymous corpses. Metics, slaves, the inhabitants of Piraeus were also purged. Vigilantes were around every corner. We have one unusually vivid eye-witness account of the attacks.[1] One Lysias (a 'leading citizen', originally from Thurii, Sicily, who was himself a prominent speech writer and whose father had been a friend of Pericles) tells us the details of his narrow escape. Arrested, he made a dash for the back door. His brother, Polemarchos, was not so lucky. As with all coups, loot seems to arouse as much passion as politics. The golden earrings were ripped from Polemarchos' wife's ears; his relations were raped and their goods stolen. Also confiscated by the state were the contents of his brother's factory in Piraeus: 700 shields, plus gold, silver and 120 slave workers. The democracy had always disapproved of shows of wealth. Men who did well in the unusually buoyant economy of the mid-to-late fifth century, in the spirit of communal achievement, stashed capital away in their homes. Well, now this opulence was being ripped from private hands, not by egalitarian idealists but by jealous aristocrats and oligarchs; by men who had perhaps secretly always thought it a disgrace that ordinary, non-aristocratic, Athenians should be allowed to succeed.

The actions across the city were carefully orchestrated. To kill their rivals, to cut down the tall poppies, the Thirty adapted the various means of death already available in Athens. Men could be thrown into pits alive, they could be strapped with metal restrainers by their necks, legs and arms onto wooden boards; but what the Thirty brought to a fine art was death by hemlock.[2]

The recipe for a fatal hemlock dose had only just been perfected. Herbalists had worked out that less than a quarter of an ounce was needed to kill. There were ways of making the murder weapon extra-effective, or 'quick and easy' as the contemporary sources have it: if the plant was skinned, ground in a pestle and mortar and then sieved, its poison became particularly efficacious.

Aristophanes jokes about the situation.[3] Death by domestic implement: the ludicrousness of us carefully, steadily working out mundane ways in which we can more easily force others to die. In 405 BC this was a new-fangled bit of terminal chemistry. And by 404/3 BC drinking hemlock became a 'habitual' order. Men were forced to die in their own homes, and many were denied a burial. Athena's city had become a ghoulish morgue, the stuff of nightmares.

The Thirty were established, and many of the Athenians died drinking hemlock, and many went into exile.[4]

Socrates too was intimidated. Critias had clearly not forgotten that Socrates had criticised his pig-like libido all those years ago around Agathon's dinner table, and decided to cut him off from his *raison d'être* – the company of the young. The philosopher was told that he could no longer associate with men under the age of thirty.[5] Socrates' old drinking companions had become war criminals. This fact was frequently used to debase the philosopher's reputation, guilt by association. But Xenophon, that pragmatic writer, came up with the most obvious and natural explanation, one that is typically overlooked. Xenophon says: we cannot blame Socrates for the evil of others, this is not the philosopher's fault – people let themselves down, they change.

'But,' the accuser added, 'Critias and Alcibiades became intimates of Socrates, and the two of them did the city the most grievous wrongs. Critias became the biggest thief and the most violent and murderous of all those in the Oligarchy, while Alcibiades became, for his part, the most irresponsible and high-handed and violent of all those in the democracy.'[6]

And I know that Alcibiades and Critias, too, were temperate while they were with Socrates, not because they were afraid of being charged a fee or struck by Socrates, but because they believed at that time that this was the best action to be taking.

Then, perhaps many of those who claim to be philosophers might say that the just man could never become unjust, nor the temperate man rash and high-handed, nor was it possible that a person who learned anything that could be learned might ever un-learn it. But this is not what I understand to be the case about these matters.[7]

Friends, companions can surprise with their actions – and can suddenly seem strangers. Scholars often chide Socrates for the reactionary outcome of some of his pupils. But there is a tendency to over-promote the absolute tenacity of morality teaching. Socrates, who mingled with all manner of men, cannot be blamed for associating with individuals who went on to disappoint in later life.[8]

Now a list was drawn up, 3,000 citizens of whom the Thirty approved, and all others in Athens were disarmed. Socrates (and it is unclear why, given Critias' antipathy towards him) was on the 'approved' list.[9] One of the Thirty, Theramenes, protested against the new, restrictive policy; he was executed, poisoned with hemlock after being dragged from the railings of an altar by Athens' heavies, 'the Eleven'.[10] Theramenes' body should have been wrapped in a shroud with the word 'persecution' woven into the fabric. His death signified the empty ethical shell that Athens had become; democracy, liberty and freedom of speech, always qualified, now had no place. Theramenes was no democrat – and yet even he could not speak out. It was becoming crystal-clear what would happen to anyone who exercised their right to *isegoria*, 'equal right of expression'. Now, by day and night, a number of Athens' aghast citizens crept out of the city, exiling themselves from within the walls, broken now, that had protected them since birth.

Seven, fourteen, at least twenty-one harvests had been gathered since the beginning of the Peloponnesian War. But the dark days for Athenian democracy were about to become darker still. Although the Thirty had initially free rein to murder and rob and intimidate, a democratic Resistance started to form. Democrats who had melted away from the city began to regroup outside the city walls, in quite some number. The Thirty heard tell of the scale of partisan involvement and started to flee, most ending up 15 miles to the north-west of Athens in Eleusis. The oligarchs had prepared this bolt-hole, theoretically, but in practice the town did not welcome them. So they and their henchmen took Eleusis by force. The Thirty then went on to trick the male Eleusinian citizens into nailing their colours to the mast, declaring whether or not they were democrats. The Eleusinians were forced to walk out through a gateway – a kind of census, ostensibly to plan an effective garrison for the town. Waiting outside the gates were cavalry and the Thirty's lackeys. The oligarch Eleusinians walked free, the democrat Eleusinians were seized, bound and transported to Athens. Xenophon finished the gruesome story in his *Hellenica*; the retelling is stagey in its cold-heartedness.

Critias, he says, had already '*begun to show this lust for putting people to death*'.[11]

On the rocky, sun-drenched slopes beneath the Acropolis it was not Persian whips nor a heroic code of honour that drove the captured men to their deaths – it was an open, democratic vote. In a crammed Odeion, Critias raised his voice loud:

My friends, we are organising this government in your interests as well as in our own. It is right that, just as you share in the privileges, so you should share in the dangers. And so, in order that you may have the same hopes and same fears as we have, you must now pass the death sentence on these men of Eleusis who have been captured.[12]

Given that the space – which once hosted the aspirational music of Damon et al., whose concerts were thought to provide a medical balm for the democratic mind – was now blatantly a place weighted in the oligarchs' favour, papered with Spartan racketeers and with Spartan-sponsored soldiers standing at the entrance gates, it was clear which way the vote was going to fall.

Elsewhere, from previously oligarchic strongholds in Thebes and Megara, which, surprisingly, gave a number of democrats shelter, steady streams of men climbed up to where the pine starts to sweeten the air, to the security of a place called Phyle. Phyle lies 3 miles north-east of Athens and offers excellent natural protection. A high promontory, it affords stunning views in the summer across the plains of Attica. In winter the clouds and mists wrap Phyle in its own veil of security. Amongst the renegade group camped up here was the man who had already made one journey north looking for a better place: Socrates' Delphic envoy and treasured friend Chaerephon. On one of those bright, clear days of winter, the Thirty tried to flush the democrats out from their democratic den, but then the sky whitened and snow started to fall. We hear of the impact:

The fighters could no longer see one another, let alone their enemy.[13]

So the pro-Spartans returned home, frustrated, empty-handed.

Still in Athens, the Thirty wanted Socrates' hands bloodied along with their own. The philosopher was instructed to go to Salamis, that long, low island which kick-started the story of Athenian liberty from Persia, and was ordered to arrest a once-democratic general called Leon so he could be murdered in cold blood. Socrates refused.

SOCRATES: *The Thirty summoned me and four others to the Tholos and ordered us to bring Leon from Salamis to be put to death. They often ordered many others to do such things, since they wanted to implicate as many as possible in their causes. At that time I made it clear once again, not by talk but by action, that I didn't care at all about death — if I'm not being too blunt to say it — but it mattered everything that I do nothing unjust or impious, which matters very much to me. For though it had plenty of power, that government didn't frighten me into doing anything that's wrong.*[14]

Enraged by his intransigence, the philosopher was now marked out by the Thirty as an enemy of the State. The death squads were, we are told, coming for Socrates next. It is one of history's great what-ifs. If a back-door murderer had been dispatched by Critias and his mob to deal with this troublesome, recalcitrant philosopher then and there, we would have no martyr to liberty, and we might well have lost Socrates from history. On this occasion, Socrates escaped by the skin of his teeth. Because the wind-blown democrats up on Phyle decided to try to claim their city back. Coming home through Piraeus, they met the Thirty in battle. Critias and Charmides were killed. It was said that on Critias' tombstone was carved the figure of a fierce woman 'Oligarchy' physically torching the anthropo-morphised lady *Demokratia*. While the denuded oligarchy withdrew to the city centre to lick their wounds and plan their next move, the 3,000 citi-zens who remained deposed them. Now a new board of ten, one per tribe, was elected. The Spartans were brought in to attempt to get the city back into some kind of order. Spartan diplomacy between those Athenians who had all stood together in the Assembly as one, as a single mass of 6,000, but who were now bitterly opposed to each other, meant that the oligarchs were allowed to live with their mysteries in Eleusis and all democratic exiles were recalled.

One of those who came back into Athena's city, a chip the size of Crete on his shoulder, was a one-time tanner, now owner of a tanning factory, called Anytus. Anytus would be one of the men who would bring Socrates to trial.

And in 401 BC, when Spartans and Spartan swords were occupied else-where in the region, at a safe distance, the returned democrats stormed Eleusis and slaughtered the remaining oligarchs. Were they defending them-selves, their families, an ideology? One wonders. But this was a time when there were many different reasons for hands to ball into fists. What is certain is that Athenians, whether reluctantly or with gusto, had developed a taste for spilling Athenian blood.

Socrates, throughout these dark days, remained intransigent. Was this one of his most irritating acts – the moment when it became clear to his compatriots that he really meant it when he said he did not want to be involved in politics? That all that otherworldliness was not just a pose? Socrates had not raised his voice to condemn the slaughter on Melos in 416 BC and now he did not – on record – condemn the slaughterers who had been busy on the streets of his home-town. Because although Socrates stood up to the oligarchs, he did not formally denounce them, he did not flee the city along with democratic friends such as Chaerephon, holing up, planning a revolution from the north. He did what he had done through plague and siege and war and peace: he stayed and walked around the streets of Athens, and he talked.

The delightful thrill of being with a man who was resolutely happy to plough his own furrow, even if what he did shocked those around him, was starting to wear decidedly thin.

Three years passed. These had been terrible times. Socrates had grown old in a city which since his birth had memorialised the extraordinary fact that Athena's children had beaten back Persian might. But now there was shame; the Athenians could not match the muscle of their fellow Greeks, the Spartans, and they could not beat the enemy within. They could not maintain their empire, they could not employ the ideology of democracy as a convenient panacea, they could not control their own internecine strife. Socrates took the sting of this disgrace.

And so it was that, a scant five years after the Spartans had broken down Athenian walls, just four years after the democracy had been suppressed out of existence, and with the memories of slaughter and political executions still keen in the minds of the Athenian crowd, their wounds still suppurating, Socrates felt the hand of the poet Meletus on his shoulder, and he was called to court by the Athenian people.

ACT EIGHT

THE TRIAL AND DEATH OF SOCRATES

50

THE SCAPEGOAT

෧෧෧෧෧෧෧෧෧෧෧

Religious court of the
Archon Basileus, 399 BC

*He was the first person who really talked about human life; and he was also the first
philosopher who was condemned to death and executed.*

Diogenes Laertius,
The Lives and Opinions of Eminent Philosophers, Socrates, V[1]

So WE ARRIVE AT THAT MAY morning in 399 BC. Socrates stands in
front of 500 of the few remaining Athenian citizens and is charged
with disrespect for the city's gods, with introducing new divinities and
with the corruption of the young. We cannot imagine the philosopher in
a religious court on that day in 399 BC without recalling the heady, dreadful
history that has been played out in the streets, the theatres and the homes
all around the law-court. And knowing that bloody, disrupted history, we
should be shocked by the apparent coolness with which Socrates treats his
own trial.[2]

The philosopher is insouciant, apathetic. Standing there in the packed
courtroom in his shabby clothes (no flaxen linen for him, although this
would have been available), woven, almost certainly, in one of the *gynaikeia*
of the city,[3] the master of words appears diffident, as if he has no taste for
this particular drama, as if he perceives it all to be a sham.

His naïvety is distasteful — it seems to mask some kind of misplaced
superiority. Athens has prided itself on its legal system, on its ability to
bring men to justice in front of their peers. But Socrates confesses that he
has had no time for such legalities. Not only that, but the Athenians also

know that he has cast aspersions on the lot-selection system itself – the very apparatus that has been the envy of the known world and has kept the democracy a democracy for so long.

'But, by god,' the accuser said, 'he made his companions despise the established law, saying that it was foolish to establish the rulers of the city by lot, and that no one would want to make use of a captain chosen by lot, or a builder, or a flute-player, or any other arts, any of which do far less damage when their practitioners make a mistake than do those who make a mistake about affairs of the city.' And such arguments, the accuser said, raised up young men to look down on the established constitution, and made them violent.[4]

In the heads of the Greeks, this disdain was doubly offensive. They believed it was the power of the gods that had guided those white and black balls in the *kleroterion* to their slot. Nothing happened during this age and in this land without the gods' say-so. The *kleroterion* machine was not just an agent of random selection, but of potent kleromancy – a divine, magical process that should not be mocked.

And then, despite the fact that Socrates has spent more than sixty years in Athenian society, the philosopher, in Plato's version of events, informs the court of a peculiar anomaly:

The fact is that this is the first time I have come before the court, even though I am seventy years old. I am therefore an utter foreigner as far as courtroom speaking goes. So now I make what I think is a fair request of you: disregard my manner of speaking. Pardon me as I speak in that manner in which I have been raised, just as you would if I really were a foreigner.[5]

Gallingly, this cocky philosopher doesn't seem to take the privilege of a fair trial seriously.[6] The man who is accused of poisoning democracy with words has the chance to use words in self-defence, yet he acts the dolt, the innocent. He refuses to play word-games. Socrates' professed ignorance of typical democratic activity might have been endearing to start off with, but by this stage in his life, and with the troubled back-story of Athens, it has become intensely infuriating.[7] Here were clod-footed *deme*-men, who for the first time in human history had been given the chance to be proactive politicians, and someone like Socrates cracks a gag about not knowing how to vote when he serves a term on the *Boule*, the council.[8] Here were men who had lost fathers, brothers, sons in the recent civil wars when oligarch death-squads had roamed Athena's city. Athena's citizen-children – who since the age of three have been earning their stripes to become mechanics in the engine-room of democracy – have traipsed to court this morning to keep their democracy clean.

And Socrates seems to be laughing at them.

For certain, there was much this philosopher did that sparked real pain in the hearts of democrats. Athens liked things cut and dried, as black and white as the balls in the *kleroterion* machine. Actions were either 'good' or 'bad', gods were either officially introduced to the city or they were the demons of Athens' enemies. This nebulous, knowing, exploratory, open-ended questioning that Socrates insisted on pursuing was just too troubling. It is perhaps because of this sense of discomfort, this aggravating, literally eccentric attitude, and not because of any 'crimes' he committed, that Athens' antipathy towards Socrates mushroomed. Every juror here, don't forget, has seen an empire won and lost, has crouched trembling in his mud-brick home as brother kills brother, has put all trust in this brilliant and burning new idea of 'democracy', and has watched as the hope of a commonly run city-state has wasted into personal ambition, blood-lust, arrogance, cynicism, tyranny. The gods are clearly enraged. Athena despises her own children. The milk-and-honey moment of the democracy has curdled. Athens has been brutalised.

Yet Socrates keeps about him an air of optimism, a sense of proportion, a moral certainty, an infuriating otherworldliness.

Meletus, Anytus and Lycon accuse Socrates of two abstract but fundamentally serious crimes:

Under oath Meletos the son of Meletos of Pitthos has brought a public action against Socrates the son of Sophroniskos of Alopeke and charged him with the following offences: Socrates is guilty of not acknowledging the gods acknowledged by the state and of introducing other new divinities. Furthermore he is guilty of corrupting the young. Penalty proposed: capital punishment.[9]

Perhaps we should not be surprised that a city-state that we laud for its commitment to democracy, liberty and freedom of speech chooses to punish a maverick in their midst.

The verdict of the court is not directly recorded, but Plato has given us his version of Socrates' response:

Many things contribute to my not being angry at what's happened — that you voted against me — and the result was not unexpected by me, but I was much more surprised by the total number of votes on each side. For I didn't think it would be such a small majority. I thought it would be much larger. Now it seems, if only thirty votes had gone the other way, I'd have been acquitted ... So the gentleman [Meletus] asks that the penalty be death. Well, what shall I propose for you as a counter-penalty? Isn't it clear that it should be what I deserve? So, what would that be, what do I deserve to suffer or to pay for not having led an inactive life and for not caring about what most people care for — making money, managing my affairs, being a general or a political leader and any of the different offices and factions in the city? I believe that I was really too good to go down that path and survive. I didn't go where I would have been no help at all to you or to me, but went, instead, to each one of you in private to do the greatest good. As I say, I went there, undertaking to persuade each of you not to care about your possessions before you care about how you will be the best and wisest you can be, nor to care about what the city has, before you care about the city itself, and to care about other things in just the same way. Being this sort of person, what do I deserve to suffer? Something good, Athenians![10]

The Athenians disagree. In the courtroom that May day, 399 BC, the jurors of Athens find Socrates guilty as charged.

51

AN APOLOGY

@@@@@@@@@@@@@

Athens' religious courtroom, May 399 BC

SOCRATES: I'll be judged the way a doctor would be, when prosecuted by a manufacturer of sweet-treats before a jury of young children.

Plato, Gorgias, 521e[1]

SOCRATES IS GUILTY.

But his punishment is not yet set.

Socrates' accusers have spoken, and now the water-clock has been filled afresh to give the defendant his modest allotted time to put across his point of view. At last Socrates stands on the *bema* (the speaking plat-form), as he very self-consciously has *not* done throughout his time as a citizen in the Assembly. This trial was of the type known as *agones timetoi* — assessed trials; the court recognised that a level of guilt was in question and therefore the punishment should be equally calibrated. It was up to the man in the dock to suggest his own penalty. The philosopher who delighted in picking an argument now has to argue his way out of a death sentence.

Socrates has listened to the case against him — a fundamentally serious one, corruption of the young and denial of the city's gods — in the religious court of Athens. Eye-witnesses (Plato himself was at the trial) tell us the place was a bear-pit that day: much heckling, jangling, scolding.

Once the hubbub has died down, Socrates has the chance to speak.

It is worth waiting to hear what the philosopher has to say: this is, after all, the man who has been accused not for his deeds, but for his words. And by all accounts, his clever command of the human tongue was exquisitely painful. Alcibiades once breathed that Socrates' moderated voice and way with words was like that of *'the music of Marsyas [a satyr fond of rivers]*[2] *who only had to put his flute to his lips to bewitch mankind'.*[3]

Now Socrates can outfox the sly gentlemen who have trapped him here.

But the speech that Socrates makes in response to his conviction (as recorded by Plato)[4] is short and to the point. He states that he has lived his life for the benefit of Athens; he deserves reward, not punishment.

SOCRATES: I'm not a clever speaker at all – unless they call a clever speaker one who tells the truth. If this is what they mean, I'd agree that I'm an orator, though not the way they are. As I say, they've said almost nothing that's true. But you'll hear only the truth from me, and yet not, by god, Athenians, in beautifully crafted language like theirs, carefully arranged with words and phrases. Instead, you'll hear things said by me without any planning, in words as they occur to me – for I assume that what I say is just – and none of you should expect anything else.[5]

In Plato's *Phaedrus*, Socrates says that the danger of written words is that they can't answer back. And of course the doubly dangerous thing about speaking in public is that anyone can. Because now Socrates suggests an incendiary thing.

And so the man proposes the penalty of death. Well then, what shall I propose as an alternative? . . . Now what is fitting for a poor man who is your benefactor? . . . There is nothing, men of Athens, so fitting as that such a man be given his meals in the prytaneum . . . For he [an Olympic victor] makes you seem to be happy, while I make you happy in reality . . . So if I must propose a penalty in accordance with my deserts, I propose maintenance in the prytaneum.[6]

Commemorate me as if I were an Olympic hero, he says. Honour me as you do the very greatest in the city. Give me the hearty spread that you dish out to the *prytany* council. Free dinners in perpetuity at the state's expense, in recognition of the good I have done – naturally that is what I deserve.

We can still feel the heat of the crowd's rage in the court of the *Archon Basileus* as they shout Socrates down. The citizen-jurors hold the philosopher's life in their hands, and yet he mocks them.

'I beg of you gentlemen,' says Socrates, *'let me speak without interruption. He [Chaerephon] asked the god whether there was anyone in the world wiser than I, and the Pythia responded that in fact there was no one.'*[7]

Socrates has already taunted the men – shifting on their jurors' stone seats – with the suggestion that he is the wisest man in the world.

And, men of Athens, do not interrupt me with noise, even if I seem to you to be boasting; for the word which I speak is not mine, but the speaker to whom I shall refer it is a person of weight. For of my wisdom – if it is wisdom at all – and of its nature, I will offer you the god of Delphi as a witness.[8]

Well, once he went to Delphi and made so bold as to ask the oracle this question; and, gentlemen, don't make a disturbance at what I say; for he asked if there were anyone wiser than I. Now the Pythia replied that there was no one wiser. And about these things his brother here will bear you witness, since Chaerephon is dead.[9]

Unusually moderate in an age of extremes, at his trial Socrates seems to have forgotten entirely the meaning of the word 'humility'.

Is he abhorrently arrogant? Has he lost his mind? Is this radicalism or (what we would call) hubris? First Socrates suggests his punishment should be free dinners for life, then he reminds the court he is the wisest man on earth. Has he forgotten what his fellow Athenians have recently been through? Or is he genuinely apologetic – in the Greek sense of *apologia* – defensive? If he believes that Apollo gave him a mission to bring wisdom to the world, does he think that a reminder of his 'special calling' will be the perfect defence against this ridiculous charge that he is 'impious'? Or is Socrates, with his reference to Apollo and the Delphic Oracle, actually suggesting that the god is in all of us, that we are all capable of god-like activity? All his life the philosopher has claimed that if we look deeply into ourselves we will realise what depths we humans have. Perhaps Socrates was desperately reiterating his belief to a court that wanted to see him extinguished.

In a democracy, men are meant to be allowed to speak out. But at his trial in 399 BC Socrates speaks too big, literally. *Megalegoria* is the word used by Xenophon. Socrates does not play ball. He does not charm, or incite. He does not whip the crowd up to a favourable fever-pitch. Instead he is belligerent – 'full of big talk'. Whatever form this *megalegoria* took, Socrates wasn't meant to behave in this way. He was expected to observe the finely orchestrated dances of public speaking, where the audience is led – but knows it – and is comfortable about being navigated along in a barque of persuasive words.[10]

He was meant to weep and wail, to bring his family in tearing their cheeks, to prostrate himself, begging for mercy; he was supposed to incarnate the highly emotional timbre of a traumatised, volatile city, of 399 BC, of after-shock Athens.

Already raucous, now the crowd in the courtroom bays at him. Socrates has made many men laugh in his time, he has charmed them, enthralled them, seduced them, befuddled them, he has changed their lives – but now he cannot even raise a smile.

Perhaps only now does Socrates realise that for once he is not going to be the tenacious one, the one who is *not* carried off by plague or stasis, by a Spartan sword or an insurgent's knife. And so, instead of his flippant request for dinners, the philosopher proposes a serious alternative. A fine: 30 minas – the equivalent of close on nine years' labour for an average Athenian, or enough to pay 6,000 Athenian men to come to court in order to act as jurors for one day.

His offer is rejected. The court is in no mood to play games, let alone consider leniency. The only penalty now on offer is death.[11]

Too little time to fight for a life

SOCRATES: The man of the law-courts is always in a hurry when he is talking; he has to speak with one eye on the water-clock. Besides, he can't make his speeches on any subject he likes, he has his adversary standing over him . . . Such conditions make him keen and highly-strung, skilled in flattering the master and working his way into favour; but cause his soul to be diminished and warped.

Plato, *Theaetetus*, 172d–173a[12]

The pissing stream of the water-clock has drooped.

Those who spoke last know their time is up. Now for the vote. This is the city, remember, that is never still. There is no pause for reflection. The crowd is asked to give its verdict immediately.

And for Socrates, the fact that his entire life could be judged on just a few hours of well-spun words, by a mongrel crowd of men – a day of democracy in action – exposed one of the great shortcomings of Athens' glorious experiment.

If it were the law with us, as it is elsewhere, that a trial for life should not last one, but many days, you would be convinced, but now it is not easy to dispel great slanders in a short time.[13]

Throughout that one, heated, epoch-forming twelve-hour stretch, each juror has had charge of two discs of metal. One with the axle solid, the other hollow. They have been fingering them perhaps throughout the speeches, cooling them in the folds of their clothes, warming them in their hands, and now they have to choose which one to drop. A pierced axle is a vote for Socrates' death, a solid axle for his innocence. The first few discs of metal thud on the terracotta-and-earth base in the ballot box, then as the box fills, the bronze clamours for attention, chiming out the decision of the troubled democracy.[14]

The first majority that decides Socrates to be guilty has been slender; but now the margin is far more substantial. These Athenian democrats want closure on the situation. Whereas 220 had voted for him and 280 against in the first mandate, now only 160 choose to acquit the philosopher and 340 vote for his death. Originally, it seems, the Athenians remembered that, in 403 BC, they had sworn an oath of *amnestia*, amnesty. A promise officially to forget the 'bad', the anti-democratic offences of the past. But Socrates' hubris, his worrying religious unorthodoxy was too much to bear. If, in that initial round casting, just thirty men had chosen to vote with a different-coloured pebble or a different bronze disc (because a tied vote always fell in favour of the defendant), if Socrates had not become a martyr, a *cause-célèbre*, then the history of philosophy, the value-system of the West, and of the East, might have been immeasurably different.

⟨∽⟨∽⟨∽⟩

The Athenians were as fearful of what they could not see as they were in awe of that which they could. Imagine a miasma seeping through the court. Criminals, 'honourless' and infected men were not allowed to speak in the Assembly. It was thought that their very presence, and in particular their dirty words, would pollute the common good.[15] And yet now, in full view, breath-on-cheek close, is this man who, it seems, is on the hit-list of the gods, spitting out a series of home truths. The Athenians may have accused Socrates of being beloved of the sophists, but a bit of sweet sophistry would have softened those verbal blows. Yet Socrates' case is proved in the manner of his defence. He does not attempt to sway the crowd with his cleverness. He just tells the truth. He is, he says, naked before them.

In his apology the philosopher continuously stresses that he speaks the truth — that his accusers run from it. He compares his adherence to the gods, his sacrifice for what he loves and his preference for death over a bad life to the choices that Achilles once made. Achilles and Socrates? How in heaven's name could the philosopher compare himself to this Hero of Heroes? How could he (or perhaps his biographer Plato, given that all these words are Plato's) introduce a Homeric hero into the rhetoric at this make-or-break juncture? The hard-toned, sinew-sweet, love-locked war-machine that was Achilles set up against a dirty, smelly (probably), rolling, pug-

337

faced, daydreaming stonemason's son? Yet there is some logic in Socrates' self-pairing with Achilles' self-serving might. Both men, despite appearances, share one vital thing. They are true to themselves. They know themselves. They are who they are, not who society wants them to be.[16]

You get the sense that the Athenians really did not know what to do with this obdurate, annoying, wonderful man, impossible to pigeonhole, neither true democrat nor dyed-in-the-wool oligarch, neither golden hero nor twisted villain. Socrates has dined in Periclean circles, but has criticised imperial ambitions. He cautions virtue, but never once spoke out against the outrages in Mytilene, Corcyra, Melos. He loves young men, he gives voice to young women. He worships, fervently, with his fellow democrats, but also enjoys a strange, private kind of piety. In the good days Athens could cope with the philosopher; Socrates was, above all, an irritant – a gadfly on the flesh of Athena's people. But now the city is swarming with flies and bloodsuckers – actual and allegorical – it seems less troublesome to have him dead than alive.[17]

The minuscule cash-surplus generated within the city-state (any trickle of income from Athens' attenuated empire had by now dried up) was used to pay the jurors for this day in court. The functionaries of the democracy have had to sit in judgement on the man who is both the summation of democracy and its nemesis.

And so, their decision made, the judges file out of the courtroom. Not, as they have done for centuries, only at *boulutonde*, the time when the cows come home, but because the clock has run dry. And the tally of metal discs in the ballot box shows no ambiguity. Socrates is condemned. The only journey that remains for him is terminal – to Athens' jail and then to his death.

SOCRATES: . . . *But surely it is possible – and indeed one ought to say a prayer to the gods that the journey from here to there will be a happy one. That's what I pray and may it turn out to be so.*[18]

Athens, though, is going to make the philosopher attend his death. Because the Delian festival of Apollo has begun, this is a month of ritual purity. The beautiful sun god with his enigmatic smile now commands all attention in the city. Socrates can wait. Athens, still religious to the core, is preoccupied.

52

TWILIGHT AND
DELOS AT DAWN

⊚⊚⊚⊚⊚⊚⊚⊚⊚⊚⊚

Delos, the Cyclades, 399 BC

ἄιδεις ὥσπερ εἰς Δῆλον πλέων

You sing as if you were sailing to Delos.

Zenobius, 2.73[1]

As happy as sailing to Delos.

Popular Attic Greek proverb

T HE DAY BEFORE SOCRATES' TRIAL, ATHENS would have breathed
in the smell of crushed stalks and bruised petals.[2] The philosopher
is now condemned. But he is going to be forced to wait to die.
Because it so happens that his trial fell on the day in the year when Athenians started to celebrate an ancient festival on the small Cycladic island of
Delos.[3]

The story behind the festival is still told today: the Athenian hero
Theseus — as a young man, before he has raped Helen and chased Persephone, before he has, as a ghostly apparition, led the triumphant troops
of Athens at Marathon — was sent by his father, the King of Athens, to
slay the Minotaur on the island of Crete. Theseus brings with him to that
'wide and lovely' island the usual tribute: seven young boys and seven
maidens. But his plan is to end the humdrum human sacrifice with which
the Athenians have had to put up, year in, year out. His aim is to kill an

339

abhorrence, a man-monster. What better way to earn your stripes as a trainee hero?

Theseus does manage to slaughter the beast, but only with the help of King Minos' daughter, dancing Ariadne. They love, but Theseus is not polite. He leaves the princess, heart-broken, on Naxos. When he sails back home, preoccupied with his own marvellousness, he also forgets to change his sails from black to white, and so his father Aegeus, thinking his son dead, hurls himself into the sea (the 'Aegean' Sea still bears his name). But what Theseus does find time for is a little stop-off at Delos, Apollo's birthplace. The sun god was born of a difficult labour – nine days; Hera, jealous of this creature (Zeus' love-child by Leto), accidentally-on-purpose forgot to let Eileithyia, the goddess of parturition, and an aide to women in labour, know that Leto was about to give birth.[4] But when at last the god-child arrived wailing into the world (in some versions with his twin sister Artemis), the island – which had until then been unfixed, a wandering womb on the sea – became rooted.

The Athenians commemorate Theseus' selfish heroics in grand style. They send to Delos a modern chorus in (so they told themselves) the *very* boat that Theseus himself had used.[5] Lovingly cared for in dry-dock throughout the year, possibly near the sanctuary at Brauron where those young Athenian girls grew up as little bears, the boat is kitted out as a barque fit for heroes.[6] As the priest of Apollo garlands this legendary vessel, crowning the stern-post with a laurel wreath and making sacrifices to ensure the safety of its journey, the city enters a period of purity. This is a time when no executions are allowed. And so Socrates has to sit and wait. Meanwhile the gaudy boat with its cheerful cargo sails out of the harbour at Piraeus. It is a sacred journey, and as the devout Athenians turn their faces to the south-east, they know that powerful divinities must be appeased. The boat's passengers sing, keeping the world turning with superstition and cant.

Approaching the island of Delos today, it still feels as if the gods of wind and rain protect the place. The gneiss rock, coarse-grained, metamorphic – layered with quartz and ferromagnesium – is unwelcoming. But many city-states have left their mark here, claiming a stake in the pooling, prehistoric sanctity of the island. Rain drips off the bared gums of rows of snarling lions, installed by pious Naxians just before 600 BC. Massive statuary, a Hellenistic row of engorged 6-foot-high penises, still brave it out against the elements. City-states had their own boarding houses next to the ritual sites. By reviving the Delian festival some time around 427 BC the Athenians made the triangular connection between Athens, Delos and Theseus even stronger. They wanted to remember the good old days, when the treasure houses were full, when heroes stole women, when a small, favoured city ran the known world's most productive and energetic territories.

The theatre of purity at Delos was considered essential. Come the Roman period, all visitors were required to be spotless of hand and soul and, at the sanctuaries of Zeus Kynthios and Athena Kynthia, to wear white.[7] Delos' sanctity stretches back until before recorded time. For the prehistoric populations of the eastern Mediterranean, this speck on a map was no less than a magical island. The dances that Theseus was credited with perpetuating here, as he sailed fecklessly back to Athens, the abandoned princess Ariadne behind him, a hopelessly anticipant father in front, stemmed from the rich and deep Minoan culture.[8] These were dances of youths and maidens of intense importance. Human sacrifice almost certainly took place on the island of Crete.[9] It could be that teenage boys and girls beat out their path to adulthood with the stamp and sway of the communal dance, and that some dances ended with a victim being killed.[10]

In Socrates' day the dances on Delos still had this charged, edgy feel and took place at night. Lamps and torches were lit, the undulating movement of the dancers catching and escaping the tallow-light as they wove between one another. There were sacred games too, established, as the pious Athenians loyally repeated, by Theseus himself.

Delos might be a sacred island, but it too had suffered during the pitiless Peloponnesian War. In 422 BC, the Athenians had expelled the entire population – restoring them again on the advice of Apollo at Delphi in 421 BC, furious, presumably, that *his* birthplace should be treated with such high-handed disdain. Dumped marble found in an old cistern shows that after the Spartan victory of 404 BC the lands were rented out, interest was taken on sanctuary money, fishing rights were claimed – and all by a new Spartan overlord. And the massive roofless temple to Apollo, abandoned in 454 BC, half-built, when the Athenians withdrew Delian League money back to the Parthenon, still stood, an aborted enterprise that spoke loudly of Athens' glorious hubris.[11] But now, briefly, Athenians had the upper hand once more. Their commemoration of that brave, lusty, straightforward founder-hero Theseus must have had even more resonance in 399 BC. There must have been even less patience for complicated flies in the ointment such as Socrates.

The purified pilgrims are cutting their way back to Athens through the surf. They are leaving behind an island where no pollution is allowed – the elderly, the sick, the disturbed are evacuated by Athenian decree. Eugenics has given this place a brittle, make-believe perfection. The Athenians have spent close on a month celebrating a young hero who rescued the flowers of the city-state from pernicious foreign influence. The boat's load – the elderly spectators, the *theoroi*, the young bloods – are pure again. When they land on Attic soil, men like Socrates can start to die once more.

෨෨෨෨෨

The pastoral Ilissos of Socrates' day – the site of his ramblings with young men – had had a prophetic relevance to the philosopher's fate. In one corner next to the river bank was an enclosure where Theseus' father (so the story-tellers had it) dashed to the ground a poisoned cup of wolfbane, prepared by the wicked Medea for her handsome stepson. But Socrates had no king-father to protect him. While the Athenian hero Theseus was paid the highest of honours, Athens' anti-hero, Socrates, would be forced to drink hemlock in a small Athenian cell.

53

SOCRATES BOUND

@@@@@@@@@@@@

Athens' prison, the Agora,
June 399 BC

SOCRATES: *Then we agree that the question is whether it is right for me to try to escape from here without the permission of the Athenians, or not right. And if it appears to be right, let us try it, and if not, let us give it up.*

Plato, *Crito*, 48b–c[1]

SOCRATES TRAVELLED ONLY 300 yards or so from his courtroom to the prison; it was the last time he walked freely.

Imprisonment per se was not devised as a punishment in classical Athens, but it cannot have been remotely pleasant.[2] Socrates was, almost certainly, shackled with iron fetters. Other prisoners talk about the 'physical abuse' and 'physical suffering' that came with fifth-century BC prison life. *Desmoterion*, the word for 'prison' at this time in Greece, means 'a binding down place'.[3] Inmates were often strapped to the ground in wooden stocks; Herodotus tells us of a foreign prisoner in Sparta who was so desperate to break free that he hacked off a section of his own foot and slipped out of his restraint – an agonising contraption known simply as 'the wood'.[4]

Athena was used to punishing. Exile from your city, outlawing, debilitating fines, death – these were all penalties. A scrubby area outside the walls appears to have been used as a death zone. Plato tells a story that brings the unpleasant realities of the fifth century BC more sharply into focus.[5] Circling the North Long Wall, a young man called Leontius walks past bodies on the ground next to an executioner. The Greek terms used suggest that these almost-corpses are in their final death throes – men

343

strapped to boards and left to die. An executioner watches over them. They have already been exiled from the city, they know they have already lost all chance of a good burial and therefore a good afterlife, and now theirs will not be a death that can in any way be described as 'beautiful'.

Greek law has little time for prison sentences; it is too inefficient, too expensive, too odd to make someone suffer by locking them up. The prison was really a holding bay for the dysfunctional, the innocent, the framed, the unlucky. Socrates' jail would have been patrolled and serviced by 'the Eleven', a law-enforcement body — our police, judiciary and prison medics rolled into one. But there is no concept here of jail *sentences*. Little surprise then that the jail-block that contained Socrates resembles a simple storage room. The footprint of the prison can still be traced in the Agora and, although it is roped off from the public, some children still play on the low walls that mark the perimeter.[6] I was last there on a wet Tuesday and most tourists seemed unimpressed by the diminutive ruins; even the stray dogs that lounge in the modern city's public places pass listlessly by, no useful shelter here.

Yet the view from the *Stoa Basileios* up towards the prison zone, which would have been Socrates' panorama as he left the court, is magnificent today, as it would have been in his day. There is the Parthenon, there the rock of the Areopagus, and under a sky butter-yellow at the time of year of Socrates' incarceration, and at the magic hour, the hour before sunset, precisely when the philosopher was condemned and then released from his day in court to prison, just over 2,400 years ago — there is the Acropolis, that gory stone that looks like some kind of petrified, god-sized brain. A giant divine system for thinking; a *nous* that Athenians for 1,000 years have already been boring into, pock-marking with niches and tunnels and caves and staircases and offering-pits — to try to understand what was going on inside, to try to placate, and approach, the meaning of life.

It is almost certainly this that was the last view Socrates had of the city in which he had lived and loved and talked for seventy years. It might have been his last glimpse of the outside world, but this would not be his last day on earth.

Because of the ritual delay, the Delian festivities, Socrates has a full month of life ahead of him. When he walks in through the guarded doors of the prison his purpose is to wait. And according to Plato, Socrates chooses to sit, chained, and carry on within his prison walls that which he has always done outside — talk with friends and strangers. It is in the prison that Plato situates entire Socratic Dialogues such as the *Crito*.

The atmosphere of the philosopher's cell is, according to Plato, positively convivial. Although Socrates is closely guarded, his companions seem to have formed a good relationship with the prison authorities:

SOCRATES: I am surprised that the prison warden was willing to let you in.

CRITO: He is used to me by now, Socrates, because I come here so often, and besides I have done him a favour.[7]

The prison officials and their senior command, the Eleven, were not a body of men to be messed with. These Athenians could take the law into their own hands. If they caught a common criminal in the act and he confessed his guilt, they had the right to execute without trial. Accompanied by public slaves (possibly Scythians) armed with whips, cudgels, bows and daggers, they made arrests, confiscated property, supervised the torture of slaves (slaves' evidence was thought admissible in fifth-century Athens only if obtained under torture). Employed extensively as vigilantes and assassins by the Thirty, the Eleven were little loved. By turn they slept in another two-storey building next to their charges in the prison complex.[8]

Oppressive as this sounds, Socrates seems to have found the company of his jailors – perhaps members of the Eleven, perhaps just prison-running slaves – counter-intuitively congenial.

Socrates has, Plato tells us, bided his time doing little things in jail: turning Aesop's Fables into lyric verse, a sweet task. Making jottings. It is the only evidence we have that Socrates ever wrote anything down.[9] His musings during this period do not betray an agitated man. The philosopher might have been calm, but his friends were not. Because now, four weeks on from Socrates' trial, probably in early June, Theseus' ship has been spotted off Cape Sounion – twenty-nine days after it left Athens.[10] When the visitors to Delos land, Socrates must die. But in Socrates' drama, as written, imagined, related by Plato, at this point there is suddenly a chink of hope.

CRITO: . . . I only wish I myself were not so sleepless and sorrowful. But I have been wondering at you for some time, seeing how sweetly you sleep.[11]

Crito, one of his oldest friends, learning of the return of the ship from Delos, is (Plato tells us) in the prison trying to persuade Socrates to escape. Contacts across the eastern Mediterranean have been alerted and are ready to protect this renowned philosopher; foreigners have helped raise money to realise an escape plan. Here there is a hint of the old-boy network, aristocrats, gearing up for action to save a beautiful thing from the bile of the mob (networks are rarely formed of peasants). Across the entire region they appear to have agreed to collude in Socrates' escape. At a modest price, Socrates' 'vanishing' is presented by Crito as a very real possibility.

CRITO: It is not even a large sum of money which we should pay to some men who are willing to save you and get you away from here . . . Do not be troubled by what you said in court, that if you went away you would not know what to do with yourself. For in many other places, wherever you go, they will welcome you.[12]

The reply that comes back is elegant but immutable. All his life Socrates has lived by Athenian laws. How could he possibly now turn his back on them?

SOCRATES *[quoting the Laws and Commonwealth of Athens as if they are talking to him]: Are you not intending by this thing you are trying to do, to destroy us, the Laws, and the entire state, so far as you can? Or do you think that state can exist and not be overturned, in which the decisions reached by the courts have no force but are made invalid and annulled by private persons?*[13]

As befits Socrates' idiosyncratic character, escape is simply not an option.

If I am condemned now, it will clearly be my privilege to suffer a death that is adjudged by those who have superintended this matter to be not only the easiest but also the least irksome to one's friends.[14]

How, in any case, do you escape from a city that sleeps lightly? Bribery, violence, subterfuge, all of these things might have been essential. This is not Socrates' style. But then again, maybe the jailers had given Crito a nod and a wink. Perhaps the hushed conversation as Socrates slept implied some complicity with the escape plan. Possibly Athens is already regretting her decision. Maybe Socrates could have slipped away with very little fuss, while the Eleven turned a blind eye. Remember the democracy called back the ship that was beating through the water to massacre the Mytilenaeans: Athena might have heaved a sigh of relief if Socrates had escaped – no one could then accuse the democracy of a blood-lust that matched that of the oligarchs, and the Spartans, and the juntas of the Thirty.

But in any case, Socrates is having none of it. He does not want to suffer what Homer describes as the 'creeping humiliations' of old age. Arguing that it seems ludicrous for an old man to be scared of dying, and that naturally, as always, he has to do what is right, and obey the Laws of Athens, Socrates stays.

SOCRATES: *Ought we in no way to do wrong intentionally, or should we do wrong in some ways but not others? Or, as we often agreed in former times, is it never right or honourable to do wrong? Or have all those former conclusions of ours been overturned in these few days, and have we old men, seriously conversing with each other, failed all along to see that we were no better than children? Or is not what we used to say most certainly true, whether the world agree or not? And whether we must endure still more grievous sufferings than these, or lighter ones, is not wrongdoing inevitably an evil and a disgrace to the wrongdoer? Do we believe this or not?*

CRITO: *We do.*

SOCRATES: *Then we ought not to do wrong at all.*[15]

And so when a messenger brings news that the Delian ship has indeed landed, Socrates is to be found, not scrambling across some rocky Attic landscape on his way to a waiting boat, but sitting quietly, in his cell, in the Agora. The Eleven give Socrates' jailor the instruction to start making preparations for his death.

Execution in Athens would normally (for slaves and common criminals) entail a 'bloodless crucifixion'. Bloodless to prevent pollution. But it was still a hideous way to die. With the victim strapped to a board by his arms, legs and neck, the iron noose was slowly pulled tighter and tighter until he was garrotted. But for Socrates hemlock was in store.[16]

Killing the philosopher

The hemlock (the 'poison hemlock' variety almost certainly, although 'water hemlock', also poisonous, would have been available at this time) was ground up with a pestle and mortar. Opium might have been added to lessen the severity of the venom's symptoms – convulsions and muscle cramp. The opium poppy had been used extensively in Greece as a medicine and a duller of pain since the Bronze Age; carbonised seeds have been found in archaeological digs, residues of laudanum in massive cooking pots in Mycenaean graves. The poppy juice was put onto linen and held against wounds; it was given to sick and teething babies; it was used, in overdose, to assassinate kings. And now, in post-democratic Athens, it is used in the preparation of killing draughts.

The Thirty, remember, had recently favoured hemlock poisoning. The sound of the stone against stone, releasing the alkaloids of the plant, must surely have been a sinister grinding, a familiar, throat-tightening sound.[17] Aristophanes jokes, darkly, about the death-bringing, hemlock-grinding pestle and mortar in his *Frogs*:

DIONYSOS: . . . *Just give me the directions, my quickest route down to Hades, and don't give me one that's too hot or too cold.*

HERAKLES: *Let me see, which one shall I give you first? Hmm. Well, there's one via rope and bench: you hang yourself.*

DIONYSOS: *Stop it, that way's too stifling.*

HERAKLES: *Well, there's a shortcut that's well-beaten – in a mortar.*

DIONYSOS: You mean hemlock?

HERAKLES: Exactly.

DIONYSOS: That's a chill and wintry way! It quickly freezes your shins as hard as ice.[18]

I have ground up hemlock and it releases a nose-wrinkling sour smell. It also sparks a pain above your eyes and across the brain. I have never known, though, whether this is psychosomatic. Because I know, from Plato, what hemlock can do.

Hemlock was a pricey plant back then, twelve drachmas per dose. Under Athenian law, criminals were responsible for the costs of their own punishment, so hemlock poisoning was a death only available to the rich, or those with rich friends.[19] All most men needed was a small measure – a solution that would fit into an eye-bath; a number of modest phials of just such dimensions survive (there are two rows of them in the Agora Museum). Black-glazed, rough-cast, they are straightforward, functional objects. Although Romantic painters like to imagine the damned Socrates drinking deep in his cups, this is a dose you would have had to have necked to toss down.

The Eleven have come to Socrates before dawn – they must now prepare the philosopher for his last day on earth. There are fixed procedures that have to be adhered to, traditions that should be upheld. Socrates' wife, Xanthippe, and the couple's young child, Menexenos, come into the cold, stone room. For days Xanthippe has been doing what the females of a prisoner's family had to do: keeping the prisoner fed and watered (some prisoners died during incarceration because their families neglected them), arranging for slaves to clean out the cool, stone cell. But now, as it is clear that in just a few hours Socrates will be dead, Xanthippe does what is expected of good Greek wives, she wails – she raises her hands to the heavens, beats her forehead and with rigid nails scours her cheeks.

Yet Plato tells us that Socrates sends away this howling second-class citizen. Seized upon as an example of his coldness, of his misogyny, this is surely a last display of unorthodoxy: not for him the moaning press of women, brought in for centuries by the well-to-do, primarily to display aristocratic might, the size of the dynasty's entourage, the number of grateful dependants – Socrates wants an *un*traditional death. Perhaps – given that the philosopher seemed sensitive to what went on in the minds of others, and that everything written about him suggests that he had an odd but affectionate disposition – maybe, just maybe, this was a display of tenderness.

And then, to save women from the job – unconventional, self-reliant to the last – Socrates washes himself in the prison's cistern. In one room in Athens' Agora, excavated in 1931, in the prison-complex (possibly the room in which Socrates bathed himself), a giant *pithos* stands, half-buried, cool for holding water, and a small basin. The water flow that rinsed the early-summer prison grime off the philosopher would surely have been more like a squaddies' shower. Socrates, of course, had a reputation for never bathing himself properly.[20]

The job is done. When his body is rigid, once it is dead, it will no longer need dousing. Unlike those other Greeks – witness Electra and Antigone, whose hearts were broken because their brother's body lay outside the city walls, and unwashed – Socrates continues his atypical interest not in the corporeal superstructure, but in the soul within. It is the moment of transition that Socrates anticipates, not death itself. The fate of his physical body seems irrelevant. He has watched those pounding plays of absolute tragedy so popular throughout the fifth century BC. Works of art that drove home the horror of lying unburied. And yet, if his questions at the point of death reflect those he has asked during life, it is what lies beyond the decaying, the turning to worms and bone, that occupies this man's mind.

So Socrates is now ready to meet death. Family and friends are allowed back in, they are distraught. But Socrates is apparently serene.

And from now until the dying of the light the philosopher will talk, talk, talk.

He is as moderately sensual with his male companions as he has been throughout his life:

He stroked my head and gathered up the hair on the nape of my neck in his hand – he was in the habit of playing with my hair sometimes – and said, 'Tomorrow, Phaedo, maybe you will cut off this lovely hair.'[21]

Socrates recalls the Homeric heroes, reminding history, and those around him, how all Athenians were basted in an epic past. He quotes Homer, choosing lines that bring home to his friends that he is a mere mortal man, neither a hero nor a creature of '*oak and rock*'. The earth – that troublesome, beautiful orb which, as an ingenu philosopher, he argued was round – is turning. The sun is starting to sink, and at sunset Socrates must die.

And now it is time. The philosopher takes the cup, and looks, as is his manner, 'directly' at the jailor who has brought it to him. He asks if he should tip out a little libation. A dusty pool of hemlock. He prays.

Some in this period made the hemlock poison more palatable with herbs – dill was one recorded. Whatever the taste, this was a lethal brew. As planned, the philosopher serves himself the drug – the state likes it this way. Self-administration of the fatal dose will clear the body-politic of any miasma. This is not murder, it is state-sponsored suicide. The Athenians abhorred a messy death. The oozing, viscous, cloying and clinging liquids of the body deeply troubled the Greeks. This is why they strangled men to death, and although some varieties of hemlock can cause you to spew bile, to froth at the mouth, to piss and shit uncontrollably, poison hemlock is not one of them. Water hemlock attacks the central nervous system, but poison hemlock attacks the peripheral nervous system.[22] If it was indeed poison hemlock that Socrates took, we can understand why he thanks Athens for giving him an 'easy' death.[23]

Socrates, throughout his life, has watched the dreadful dying of men and boys, women and children. He was there when humans slipped easily into barbarity and murdered countrymen, neighbours, family and friends. Dying in old age, surrounded by his best-loved, lying on a bed is, approximately, his fate.[24] It is not a bad end to a good life. His lack of interest in whether his body is buried or burned is palpable. It is the moment of passing that has always fascinated him. Perhaps this is why he covers his face as he dies, to experience this greatest of all journeys alone.

It is the effects of poison hemlock that the prison official of Plato's *Phaedo* seems to demonstrate to Socrates' companions.

And passing upwards in this way, he showed us that he was growing cold and rigid. And then again he touched him and said that when it reached his heart, he would be gone. The chill had now reached the region about the groin . . .[25]

Poison hemlock does indeed attack the extremities first, often damaging the peripheral nerve, a massive single cell, up to 4 feet long, that runs from the spine to the toes. There is a terminal seizure as the brain is starved of oxygen. This would normally be a violent spasm, but by this stage all muscles are paralysed, so they cannot convulse.

So at that time of day when everyone else is scurrying home, when the market stalls in the Agora are being cleaned of their wares, unsold slaves taken back to their shackles for the night, slugged lettuce leaves and soiled spice abandoned, when little boys scour the dust frantically searching for the thing they have lost, without which a welcome home means a beating, Socrates is being terminated.

But before he dies he says an odd thing.

And uncovering his face, which had been covered, he said — and these were his last words — 'Crito, we owe a cock to Asclepius. Pay it and do not neglect it.'[26]

Socrates invokes an unusual god. Asclepius, the god of healing, was a newish divine arrival in the city of Athens.[27] In 420/19 BC, as men across the Eastern Mediterranean licked the wounds delivered by the Peloponnesian Wars, a sanctuary had been built in Socrates' city to the great healer — a divinity already popular in the Peloponnese, the homeland of Athens' enemies. The sanctuary site on the slopes of the Acropolis is now being restored. The air here is sharp with marble-dust, the columns have an unfamiliar (to us), temporary fresh-cut-white perfection, the earth is mud-wet where new foundations for Asclepius' temple are being relaid. Socrates, twenty-four centuries ago, would have watched all this fuss happening the first time round as Asclepius' sanctuary was being established; today we can watch the diverting arrival of a new home for the healing god, precisely as he did.

Socrates (and in this way he was *like* the citizens of Athens, rather than *unlike* them) seems to have put his faith in Asclepius. He was clearly becoming a popular deity; stone *stelai*, now in the National Archaeological Museum, show the faithful driving their pigs up to his altar for sacrifice. His daughter Hygieia is at the ready, helping out her clever, medical father with poultices and wraps. In the new sanctuary at Athens, sitting under a pleasant portico with the sound of sacred water running from a fountain, patients, calmed, lulled would wait to be healed by the appearance of the divinity in their dreams. Over-familiar with so many deaths on the battlefield, so much collateral damage, all those stinking plague bodies where choruses once danced and men drank wine, the Athenians were flinging out a life-line – trying to persuade a premier healing spirit to be their friend.

[SOCRATES:] *'Crito, we owe a cock to Asclepius; make this offering to him and do not forget.' 'It shall be done,' said Crito, 'tell us if there is anything else.' But there was no answer.*[28]

Socrates' invocation to Asclepius has promoted a great deal of scholarly ink. Is Plato trying to show how pious Socrates really is? That in fact Athens too has accepted new gods? Is he reminding the people of Athens that they themselves, in the sanctuary of Asclepius, are visited by divinities in their dreams – that Socrates' *daimonion* is not really so weird? Is it a last moment of Socratic irony; the philosopher gives thanks to the health god for relieving him of the sickness of being alive? Or could the answer be more simple, more basic? Socrates, thanks to the effects of the poison, is slowly suffocating to death as he speaks; who better to cry out for at this time than the god of healing? Socrates was used to meeting spirits in his dreams; perhaps Asclepius would come to his aid at this time of need. Asclepius' sanctuary sits cheek-by-jowl with the Theatre of Dionysos and has a bird's-eye view of all that goes on there; maybe this was the chance for the new divine neighbour of Dionysos to physick the wounds inflicted twenty years ago in Athenian drama, when Socrates was mocked on-stage in 423 BC in front of 20,000 Athenians as a dangerous nutter, a threat to society.

And there is another thing. In many myths, Asclepius was said to be able to raise men from the dead. Maybe Socrates was not quite so phlegmatic about leaving this mortal coil after all. Perhaps he wanted another chance to bustle around like a beautiful nurse in a recovery clinic, tempting the world to a better idea of itself; to ensure the extension of his soulful life. Whatever his last conscious thought, Socrates lies there, twitching, lungs constricting, mind absolutely alert, his face wrapped in a cloth. All eyes must have been upon him, but no one saw the very moment when his *psyche* – his soul, his spirit – slipped from that ugly, satirical, unforgettable face.

But after a little while he moved; the attendant uncovered him; his eyes were fixed. And Crito, when he saw it, closed his mouth and eyes.[29]

The now-dead hand of democracy has done its work. Socrates' fearful, unseen *daimonion* is sealed up inside the shell of his lifeless flesh, gristle, bone and skin.[30] The philosopher is destroyed.

SOCRATES: *I hope that there is something in store for the dead, and, as has been said of old, something better for the good than for the wicked.*[31]

I think it was no coincidence that Socrates was killed in May/June – the ancient month of Thargelion. Every year at this time, in an obscure ritual known as the Thargelia, two people – either male and female, or representing the male and the female by wearing a necklace of black and green figs respectively – were exiled from the city as scapegoats. Flogged outside the city walls, their expulsion was a symbolic gesture. The Athenians believed their sacrifice would prevent pollution and stasis from seeping through the city-state. The death of Socrates, in this propitious month, could be justified as a further gift to the gods.[32] When Socrates was a boy and playing around with incendiary ideas outside the city walls in the Kerameikos he was encouraged and patronised, and when he was trading his ideas in the Agora and Athenian life was sweet he could be tolerated, but now that things had gone bad, his enemies believed that he had brought pollution within the city. His was a miasma that had to be tidied up, obliterated. Socrates suffocated to death when the poppies in the city would have been blood-red. The dying democracy had ensured that one of the tallest of all Athenian poppies was cut down.

SOCRATES: *I go to die and you to live, who knows which is the better journey.*[33]

54

FLIGHT FROM THE WORLD

⊚⊚⊚⊚⊚⊚⊚⊚⊚⊚⊚

Beyond the city walls, 399 BC and beyond

ALCIBIADES: *There is no one like him and I do not think there ever was or will be . . . you will never find anyone else like Socrates or any ideas like his ideas. Not today, not in days gone by.*

Plato, *Symposium*, 221c–d

No EXTANT EVIDENCE TELLS US WHERE Socrates' body was taken. In such circumstances after one day lying in state the corpse would typically be released to his family for burial. Women would have helped to lower his corpse into a coffin, and with their shorn hair, their scratched cheeks and chests red with thumping would have wailed his way to Hades.[1] But in contemporary sources we hear neither of Socrates' body nor of his wife and children again. The most tangible remnant of Socrates was a small piece of papyrus, the affidavit that detailed the charge against him, kept available for inspection in the public registry. And so rather than Plato, or Xenophon, the first human hand to record the outcome of the philosopher's trial would have been a literate slave.[2] A Persian perhaps, a man who sat within the shade of the Metroon in the heart of the Agora, recording day in, day out the business of this once-great democracy.[3] Socrates would have known that this is how he would be inked into history. The power of the written word – a potency that Socrates mistrusted until the last – had, in one sense, and in the physical landscape at least, the final say.

⊚⊚⊚⊚⊚

We are told by later traditions that the Athenian citizens, very quickly, realised that they had done wrong.[4] Athena's children instituted a period of mourning for the murdered philosopher, closing the gymnasia and training grounds. Socrates' prosecutors were banished, Meletus was put to death. And down at the Kerameikos district, where Socrates had started his journey into philosophy, a bronze statue of the man from Alopeke was erected. Unashamedly prominent, it was set outside the Pompeion, where young men gathered and sacred artefacts were kept for use in *pompe* — religious processions. This was where Socrates himself had gone over half a century before, to join in the Great Pan-Athenaic procession, and to listen to the foreign philosophers Zeno and Parmenides bringing their ideas into the city-state. And so Athens memorialised Socrates as he wanted to live: at the edge of the city walls, a place that drank and swore and fucked; where soldiers were commemorated and women wove — but also a place that invited in new ideas, that welcomed men whose job it was to open minds. And most of all, a place where young people gathered, where heads could be turned to look to a better future.

Socrates thrived in a democracy — because this was a state that gave ordinary men voice, that tolerated new ideas. He was silenced, on the face of it, because democratic Athens could stand much criticism, but not criticism of the value of *demos-kratia* itself, and not by men who suggested it was neither walls nor fine buildings nor warships that made a democrat great, but the soul within him.[5]

Unpack that state of affairs a little. The democracy — the power of the *demos*, the people — was small, face to face, made up of men who knew one another, whose inspiration, animation, fear, genius, jealousy, frustration and prejudice rubbed off between citizens as they jostled together in the streets, at the Assembly, on battleships, by brothels, outside the law-courts. Socrates' single most plangent message, that there can be no good, even in a democracy, if each individual is not as good as he can possibly be, is also beautifully exemplified in his death sentence. Athens might have been right to insist on Socrates' conviction (to the letter of the law, this was state-sponsored suicide and his ideas could indeed, on the face of it, pose a threat to the robust orthodoxy of democratic Athens), but, in a Socratic system, he too was right to die as he did.[6] Socrates would never have escaped, because this would not have been a 'good', or a *sophon*, a wise, thing to do.

In short true virtue exists only with wisdom, whether pleasures and fears and other things of that sort are added or taken away.[7]

When Socrates died, Athens was bleeding. Its city walls were broken down; confidence, talent, self-esteem seeped through the gap. Plato, sick to the stomach at the prospect of Socrates' death, melted away to Megara, exiled or, sensibly, keeping a low profile while the political heat in Athens was high.[8] Xenophon, one of Socrates' closest supporters, had been away (since 401 BC) in Persian territory (modern-day Iraq and across Asia Minor and the Middle East), fighting as a mercenary. Socrates had advised him not to take up the commission. At the moment that Socrates was executed, Xenophon – now in Spartan service and leading Spartan troops – had just reached Greek territory on the Black Sea. Meno, the man once so impressed by the philosopher that he was struck dumb, betrayed the Greeks into the hands of the Persians. This was a time of despair and shame. The world had been turned upside down. Socrates was both an agent and a casualty of this turmoil. He exemplified the paradoxical brilliance and the brutality of his 'Golden Age'.

Man is mortal
Socrates is a man
Therefore Socrates is mortal[9]

Socrates was indeed a mortal man, in a mortal world, but his spirit – because we still write about it, read about it, debate it today – was undimmed.

The fifth century BC had rough charisma. Poets, story-makers and politicians have always recognised this fact. There is something alluringly immediate about Golden Age Greece. Ordinary people were, for the first time, long-running players in the theatre of power. Philosophers could love wisdom as a viable profession; strategists – the *strategoi*, the generals – had to live out their fantasies face to helmeted face with their enemies. Men fought on the plains of war that they had engineered. You got what you saw, and you lived what you got.

Golden Ages are comforting; we love the thought that in the dim and distant past we achieved absolute perfection, and that if as a species we did it once, we can do so again.[10] We want ancient Athens to satisfy our yearning for a fair, ordered, beautiful society. We want to believe that ideologies such as 'democracy', 'liberty', 'freedom of speech' have, at some time, achieved a perfect form. But – even though Athens was unique, wonderful – that is laying too great a burden on both Athena's city and on history.

Socrates knew the shiny democracy as an infant, an adolescent and in middle age. He watched it flourish, diversify, dull, die and, briefly, revive. He never let the democratic ideal become complacent. He died obeying its laws. He was both the product and the casualty of direct democracy. His death reminds us to care about the world we live in, to respect it, to challenge it, but above all to remember *ta erotika* – the 'things of love', the things that drive us to pursue the good.[11]

CODA

THE TOMB OF SOCRATES –
THE TOWER OF THE WINDS

⊚⊚⊚⊚⊚⊚⊚⊚⊚⊚⊚

*SOCRATES: For no one knows whether death happens to be the
greatest of all goods for humanity, but people fear it because they're
completely convinced it is the greatest of evils.*

Plato, *Apology*, 29a–b[1]

SOME WILL TELL YOU THERE IS still a mausoleum for Socrates right
in the heart of Athens. Many visitors continue to pay their respects
to the philosopher here; eighteenth-century watercolours show Grand

357

Tour eagers bowing their heads at the place as if in prayer. It is folly. The 'Tomb of Socrates' is in fact a huge time-machine, the Horologion of Kyrrhestos, probably built by the astronomer Andronikos from Macedonia in the first century BC.

This chunky, confident, octagonal tower (much approved of by the Roman architect Vitruvius and listed in his catalogue of classical excellence *De Architectura*) decorated with flying, bearded figures was designed to house one of those relatively newfangled measures of human life – a water-clock.

When I last visited the Horologion it was being renovated. The bronze weathervane that showed the direction of the winds was under reconstruction, the sun-clock was absent, the vigorous carved figures under the parapet needed more than a little expert attention. Inside, scaffolding poles and bags of mortar lay abandoned – there was, it seemed, no urgency to shore up this tower, which has already stood for 2,000 years. But somewhere in the Horologion there was a leak – and nature's own water-clock was drumming drip by drip, marking out the span of all our mortal lives.

In a sense this is Socrates' true tomb – the trap of calibrated time, the false friend, some would say, of which Socrates was acutely, atypically, aware. The tyrant time that civilisation brings, that allows us to do so much and stops us from doing more.

Socrates despised the artificial constraints that time-counting puts on human affairs, he raged against the ludicrous notion that the volume of a terracotta water-clock should determine how long a man is given to argue for his life. But he had a powerful sense of one measure of time – a lifespan. For him it was vital for each and every living individual to think how well man spent his time on earth.

So in some ways the 'House of the Winds' is not an inappropriate memorial for Socrates. It is muscular, odd, ferocious – an eccentric, anachronistic folly, plonked as it is at the top of Athens' Roman forum. And yet it has endured. Socrates' name lives on in the great civilisations of both East and West. Although traditionally we focus on his trial and death, he was actually a survivor. By 399 BC, many men in Athens were destroyed or were shadows of their former selves. As Socrates chooses not to escape, chooses to take the hemlock and obey the laws of his city, as he jokes with his friends, no one could describe him as a destroyed man. All democratic Athenians were architects of Athenian democracy, and Socrates was one of the few who lived to see its demolition, and its rebirth. He lived through much.

As has that Horologion. Just two generations after Socrates' death, Aristotle declares democracy dead. For him the hierarchical warrior-greatness of the *Iliad* is still the way to run things; an opinion enthusiastically taken up by Aristotle's protégé Alexander the Great. Democracy has a very light hold on history. In antiquity it lasted just over 180 years. The Horologion in the centre of Athens saw many political systems, many civilisations come and go: republics, empires, tyrannies, monarchies – but not until the twentienth century did it live through a democracy once again. All faiths passed by here too: pagans, Byzantine Christians, Frankish Christians, Muslims. In the Ottoman period the 'Tomb of Socrates' was used as a *tekke*, where whirling dervishes would free their own souls, to the delight of European visitors.

And for 400 years the 'Tomb of Socrates' stood opposite one of Athens' great madrasas, the Islamic school where the faithful learned to praise Allah, and also to praise Socrates. Because, remember, Socrates does not just belong to a Western tradition. The mystic and philosopher Ibn 'Arabi approved of the Socratic maxim 'I know that I do not know'. Al-Razi, the prolific writer, produced more than 200 books and modelled himself closely on Socrates. The madrasa in Athens, continuously – for 200 years – employed the Socratic method of question and counter-question.

When Islamic culture made Greece its home throughout the Ottoman period, locals elevated Socratic influence. They believed that the Parthenon was 'Plato's Academy' – the place from which the 'divine' pupil of Socrates would share his pearls of knowledge. They imagined Plato sitting in the marble throne in the apse, considering the decoration of the east wall.[2]

Sometimes in history it is helpful to put the cart before the horse. When we see how enthusiastically Islam embraced Socrates as 'The Source of Wisdom', we are reminded both that the philosopher's own, fifth-century life was orientated east before the chart was reset west, and that Plutarch was prophetic when he described Socrates: '*Not as a citizen of Athens, or a citizen of Greece, but a citizen of the world.*'[3]

Socrates escapes the compass. His ideas were peddled by caliphs as avidly as they were in the courtyards of Renaissance princes. The humanist philosopher Marsilio Ficino self-consciously replicated Socratic-style seminars in Florence, but so too did the scholars of Coptic Alexandria. One of the oldest surviving copies of Plato – from the tenth century AD – sits in the library of the Carouine Mosque behind the souk in Fez; its edges are crumbling, like fine biscuit, but the internal pages are yesterday-bright. Plato (in Arabic 'Aflatones') is still a very popular Islamic name; as popular as the name Socrates still is in the US and Europe. Whether we approve of Socrates or not, whether we believe Athens was or was not justified in contriving his death, we must remember him. Because he is part of our heritage and because our lives can only be better if we keep pursuing knowledge, and 'the good'. We are indeed ignorant if we pretend that we already have all the answers to life on earth.

SOCRATES: For no one knows whether death happens to be the greatest of all goods for humanity, but people fear it because they're completely convinced that it's the greatest of evils. And isn't this ignorance, after all, the most shameful kind: thinking you know what people don't?[4]

> *I know that I do not know.*
> Ibn 'Arabi – following ninth century AD Islamic Hadith

Socrates is a strange hero. His life interrupts the predictable beat of world civilisation, a rhythm that pumps out wars and tyrants, experiments, certainties, old solutions to new problems. We strive for answers, for closure; but all Socrates does is ask questions. His notorious slogan is stimulating and troubling in equal measure: '*The unexamined life is not worth living.*'

Socrates' debates between duty and desire, between politics and personality, between sex and sophistication, between the power of men and the capabilities of women, between principle and pragmatism, still inform our lives today. He embraced paradox; he delighted in the essence of what it is to be human, in the extremes of the human life as lived. The heady, paradoxical, essential, extreme world of fifth-century Greece provided the flashpoint for his ideas.

Within five years of Socrates' death, Athens had allied herself with her one-time enemy, Persia – with the topsy-turvy outcome that in 394 BC it was an Athenian general, Konon, who led the Persians to victory over the Spartan fleet. A sea-power for just ten years, Sparta was land-locked once more, and now a shadow of her former self. Never again in her history could she claim to rival Athenian *nous* with Spartan brawn. Limestone block by limestone block, it was the Persians who helped the Athenians rebuild their totemic fortifications, the walls that the Spartans had eagerly destroyed in 404 BC. Socrates' lifespan marked the beginning and an end of an idea – the idealistic vision of an autonomous, tolerant, democratic Athenian city-state.

AFTERWORD

✎✎✎✎✎✎✎✎✎✎

The gods have put sweat between us and virtue.

Plato, *Republic*, 364

WHEREAS THE PORTRAITS THAT WENT UP of Socrates ten or twenty years after he died cast him in Silenus mode – as the plain, portly, peculiar anti-hero – as the years go by the philosopher becomes a bit over-refined, more of a gentleman-scholar. In Naples he leans on his staff, hand on hip, the very incarnation of the leisured conversationalist. In the British Museum there is a glistening marble statuette, based on that commissioned by one of the finest sculptors of the time, Lysippus of Sicyon. There again is the fashionable, classical contrapposto pose: his hair is fluffier, his paunch is sucked in, he modestly holds his himation drapes in place: this is the acceptable face of radical philosophy.[1]

Socrates has been tidied up. The smell of sweat and blood, the fried fish of Piraeus quayside have been scrubbed off him.

But perhaps the most telling Socratic image of all was dug up in the philosopher's prison. We'll never be sure exactly who this foot-high figure is. The location and proportion, though, suggest this is Socrates himself – an offering left by someone who mourned his forced death. Half his face has been chipped or rubbed off. Only his torso survives – but what a body, robust, firm-set, hairy. Unlike the fantasy heroes that lined most Athenian streets, this man is very human.

And whether it is Socrates or an idol Socrates, Socrates' ghost, his *eidolon* that we follow, the idea of Socrates is an ethical one. He argues that the soul – the *psyche* – is all-important. That *eudaimonia* (a kind of good karma, realising all your potential as a human being) is more important than jewels, baths, designer clothes, warships, dogma. He focuses our minds on how we

361

should live, how we should flourish. He throws down a gauntlet; it is not 'them', but 'us' who are responsible for the world's happiness. You, and you alone, can hurt yourself by being unvirtuous. Vice is self-inflicted ignorance.

SOCRATES: Writing, Phaedrus, has this strange quality, and is very like painting; for the creatures of painting stand like living beings, but if one asks them a question, they preserve a solemn silence. And so it is with written words; you might think they spoke as if they had intelligence, but if you question them, wishing to know about their sayings, they always say only one and the same thing. And every word, when it is written, is bandied about, alike among those who understand and those who have no interest in it, and it knows not to whom to speak or not to speak; when ill-treated or unjustly reviled it always needs its father to help it; for it has no power to protect or help itself.[2]

Because Socrates generated not a single written word from his philosophising, we can never claim truly to have found him. His life and work will never be a tablet of stone. Socrates is recondite. And he is essential. He reminds us to keep debating the meaning of life, to keep questioning, to keep speaking to one another, to keep looking for answers. However you value him, you cannot argue with the central tenet of his philosophy. Because he beseeches mankind not to be thought-less.

APPENDIX ONE

HONOURING APHRODITE

@@@@@@@@@@@@

Acropolis rock and Agora, 469–399 BC

Do you not see what a great goddess Aphrodite is? She, whom you can neither name nor measure, how great she is by nature, from how great a thing she comes through. She nourishes you and me and all the mortals. And as proof, so that you might not only comprehend this in words, I will show you by deed, the strength of the goddess.

On the one hand, earth desires rain when the dry barren ground is in need of moisture on account of drought; and on the other hand, the revered sky, when it is filled with rain by Aphrodite, desires that it fall on the earth; and when the two mingle into the same thing, they beget everything for us, and at the same time, they nurture everything through which the mortal race lives and grows.

Fragment from a lost play by Euripides[1]

BECAUSE THE PARTHENON DOMINATES ATHENS' SKYLINE, it is easy to imagine that Athena allowed few other goddesses elbow-room in her golden city. But swathes of the Acropolis rock – the very foundation of Athena's peacock-blue and green and gold shrine – were sacred to Aphrodite.[2]

Gouged out of the red limestone of the Acropolis itself are tiny pocks – little stone larders prepared for the offerings of the faithful in Athens. These niches were sacred to the goddess of love. Here, throughout the year, men and women would come to placate and honour Aphrodite and her son Eros: they left small cakes, marble replicas of genitalia (now kept modestly under lock and key in the storerooms of the Agora Museum) and terra-cotta figurines for the goddess. When I last visited, despite the fact that the area was cordoned off to the public, someone was coming week in, week out to leave a fresh-cut pomegranate for the erotic spirits of the place.

Two fifth-century BC inscriptions have survived next to the crumbling niches. They are so eroded now as to be almost invisible to the human eye – best to feel them out with your fingers:

FOR APHRODITE ... FOR EROS

At night, pairs of two or four virgins (aged seven to eleven years old) would pick their way down to these niches. These were the Arrhephoroi, distinguished children selected by the *Archon Basileus* of Athens for religious service. Imagine a high-class 'Myrtis', the little eleven-year-old plague victim whose face has recently been re-created by a team of international scientists. Housed east of the Erechtheion, the Acropolis would be their home for almost a year.[3] Both sacred and juvenile, these were children allowed to play with childish things; up on the complex was a courtyard for ball games. One can easily imagine the jointed dolls – which now sit unloved in the glass cases of museums – being dangled on knees and clutched tight up here, with the jangle of Athens and the wide reach of the Attic countryside stretched out beneath. The girls probably spent the bulk of their days tending to the needs of Athena Polias (it might be them peeping out from the skirts of the priestess on the Parthenon friezes), and then one night of the year the priestess summoned them, presented them with a basket of *arrheta* – secret things – which they were instructed to transport to the niches.[4]

But not for them the monumental sloping stairway through the Propylaia. They travelled down through the very bedrock of the Acropolis itself. Their staircase was a vulva-like cleft in the north citadel, which, following earthquake damage in the thirteenth century BC, had been scooped out by the pious Late Bronze Age inhabitants of the Acropolis and still emerges discreetly at niche-level. Slowly, slowly, with their precious load (what could these unspeakable offerings be? genitalia? – but these were common at the time, nothing to be covered up – a sacred dew for Athena's sacred olive tree perhaps?), they climbed down deep inside the cold rock.

Now the passageway is dank and smells appropriately (given that the dove was Aphrodite's familiar) of the guano of a colony of collared doves. Here the girls emerged. The rituals they engaged in at the niches themselves are unrecorded, although it seems that at the end of the nocturnal rites the maidens returned to the Acropolis – to be replaced by next year's fresh-faced votaries.

And Aphrodite did not just walk the Athenian streets at night. She was there too at the grand entrance to the Acropolis complex. Today tourists shuffle past the polished stones oblivious to their significance – happy only that they will soon be reaching the summit. For this was where Aphrodite Pandemos (Aphrodite of all the people) was worshipped together with the goddess Peitho – Persuasion.[5] The fifth-century Athenians knew only too well that they inhabited a fragile city-state. Where there were so many polit-ical players, each with a vested interest, how could they possibly stop the body politic from fracturing? Aphrodite's stock-in-trade – love, desire, communality – were all vital in a political system that had suddenly given each citizen equal rights.

And so Aphrodite's unions were not all thought to be sexual. When we think of the goddess of love, we should banish the voluptuous Venus figure that inhabits many imaginations. As well as bodies, the goddess of love also joined hearts and minds. And for this reason the flow of the faithful to her shrine was steady. At the very least the love goddess has eight altars in and around Attica, including one – as recent excavations have shown – in the heart of the Agora itself.[6] Damaged by the Persians, this love-zone in the Athenians' marketplace kept functioning through the Peloponnesian and civil wars. The epistyle of her temple at the edge of the Acropolis was discovered in 1968, and on it an inscription. '*This to you, O great August Aphrodite Pandemos we honour you with our twenty gifts.*'[7] In the summer, at the festival of Aphrodisia, thimblefuls of the blood from the breasts of sacred doves were spilled onto her altar here.

And in the Agora itself more sacrifices were regularly made to the goddess of unions.[8] Between 1980 and 1982 the American School of Clas-sical Studies at Athens unearthed a wide altar, just at the northern limit of the Pan-Athenaic Way, a stone's throw from the court of the *Archon Basileus* and within spitting distance of the Altar of the Twelve Gods (the Centre-point of Athens), and here were burned offerings of sheep and goats, because horned creatures were the animals most sacred to the goddess of desire. As Socrates walked through the Agora – particularly on the fourth days of the month[9] – he would have seen, month in, month out, these habitual, desperate measures to keep these goddesses on-side.[10]

Did the banality of such practices trouble Socrates? Did he look at priestesses catching thimblefuls of blood or at priests faffing around with the slippery tongue of a goat and think, quietly: why are we going through such futile gestures? Love and harmony are vital, but can we really ensure them only by sending burnt offerings to the sky, or by sending out children to scramble around on rock staircases at night?

If you read between the lines of Plato's Dialogues, it seems that Socrates offers an alternative when it comes to the matter of love.

DIOTIMA: [*The*] *right way of approaching or being initiated into the mysteries of love* [*is*] *to begin with examples of beauty in this world, and using them as steps to ascend continually with that absolute beauty as one's aim, from one instance of physicial beauty to two and from two to all, then from physical beauty to moral beauty, and from moral beauty to the beauty of knowledge, until from knowledge of various kinds one arrives at the supreme knowledge whose sole object is that absolute beauty, and knows at last what absolute beauty is.*[11]

Socrates sees in the power of human wisdom, of will, the potential to hold together societies, however disparate. For him, love = virtue = knowledge = social cohesion and happiness. Socrates sought some kind of universal union in human affairs. He invokes the wise men who '*claim that community and friendship, orderliness, self-control, and justice hold together heaven and earth, and gods and men, and that is why they call this universe a world order*'.[12] He goes on to argue that *nous* – mind – encourages the heavens to move in an orderly way, just as *nous* brings order and health to the human body.[13] Socrates' life-work was to encourage men to find a way to live together and be good. But he does not simply see Harmonia dripping out of the neck of a dove as a gift of Aphrodite.

◈◈◈◈◈

Unfortunately for those on the wrong side of her clever little tongue, Peitho's (Persuasion's) force could be malevolent. But she did have her good days. The great goddess Aphrodite was, remember, family. Aphrodite added passion to Peitho's persuading power. The goddess of love could herself persuade Peitho to persuade men to act harmoniously, to seek concord. Peitho's goddess-mistress-mother Aphrodite was thought capable of promoting an important sensation in the democracy – *harmonia/homonoia*, harmony/union: qualities vital to the variegated political entity that was fifth-century Athens.

Kleisthenes himself recognised the potency of the Aphrodite-Peitho combination. When he advanced his reforms and set Athens on the road to democracy, around 507 BC, he cast Athena on the front of his triobol coins and on the obverse a female Janus — a woman with two faces — the potent Aphrodite-Peitho, Love and Persuasion, hybrid.[14]

Socrates too promoted the unifying power of love within human society. Aphrodite was one of the goddesses that he worshipped with most reverence. In fact the philosopher suggested that it is only when you look for your own goodness in others, and find it — in other words, allow yourself to love others — that you yourself can be a truly good person:

As the effluence of beauty enters him through the eyes, he is warmed; the effluence moistens the germ of the feathers, and as he grows warm, the parts from which the feathers grow, which were before hard and choked . . . become soft . . . as nourishment streams upon him.

Love is the one thing in the world I understand.

I cannot remember a time in my life when I was not in love with someone.[15]

APPENDIX TWO

MYSTERIA – THE ELEUSINIAN MYSTERIES

@@@@@@@@@@@@

GREEK RELIGION MADE A LOT OF NOISE.
Just imagine one of the most secretive of rituals, the procession out of Athens from the Sacred Gate along the Sacred Way to Eleusis. Beginning in the Kerameikos, and striding the 14 miles to Demeter's lauded sanctuary, thousands, perhaps tens of thousands (Herodotus tells us there were 30,000 in one parade) of Athenians would travel – each in search of enlightenment. Aeschylus had journeyed here, Sophocles, Herodotus and Aristophanes. Centuries later Plutarch and Pausanias too will be Eleusinian *mystoi*, initiates. Participants would cry out to the spirit of Iacchus (almost certainly a mutated form of the god of drink, Dionysos) a haunting chant that could be heard for many miles around. They carried with them blazing pine torches. A clanging gong marked their search for Kore, Demeter's daughter. The spirits of the Underworld were believed to accompany the initiates along the way.

As with the cult of Bendis down at Piraeus, these votaries are doing something that is less than normal in Greek religion. They are part of a travelling cult. The Eleusinian cult in particular is concerned with individuals; it speaks to each man and woman about the possibilities of a mystical, eternal life. The rituals have their own name, they are *mysteria*, mysteries. The word comes from the Greek and means 'with mouth, and/or eyes closed'. And indeed these were rituals that should be neither spoken of nor seen by non-initiates. In the museum at the Eleusis site there is a large bronze cinerary urn, packed with the semi-burnt remains of a woman. We don't know her name,[1] just that she requested to be buried at Eleusis' sacred site, so that she could take her secrets not just to her grave, but into the very clods of Demeter's earth itself.

To be an Eleusinian initiate, you had to be Greek-speaking, pure (untainted by a blood-crime, a murder) and it helped if you were rich.[2] The tight cabal of Eleusinian worshippers frequently comprised self-made businessmen. Although the cavalcade itself was fairly egalitarian, with rich and poor alike – even some slaves – walking (although a few well-bred women managed to ride in wagons or on a donkey, the jangle of tack adding to the noise of the procession), all was controlled by a powerfully influential dynasty of Eleusinian priests. In years to come these priests would be central to the persecutions of 'radical' thinkers in Athens: men, like Socrates, who believed in challenging the status quo.

Eleusis is writ large in Socrates' drama.[3] We have no hard evidence that the philosopher himself was an initiate – although the ecstatic language of Plato's works suggests that perhaps this pupil, possibly even Socrates himself, had experienced the Mysteries. The heady, primitive atmosphere of the worship at Eleusis, its development of the importance of the individual and the fact that Eleusinian influence could be seen all around the city meant that Socrates' story was played out as an Eleusinian backdrop waited in the scene-dock. The Sacred Way ran from the Kerameikos through the Agora and on up to the Eleusis sanctuary (as it still does today). It was along this sacred, arterial track that as an initiate, Socrates would have stepped every single year of his life. The Archon who conducted his trial was the high-priest of the Eleusinian cult. In years to come, when Alcibiades mucks about with and mocks the Eleusinian Mysteries, he brings a death penalty onto his own head and infects Socrates with the disgrace. Eleusis was, in a sense, the spiritual touchstone of Athens. Not of the whole city-state, but of those who had really made it in the world.

The Mysteries were one of the most anticipated and drawn out of Athenian festivals.[4] In spring – the month of Anthesterion (March) – the Lesser Mysteries, a dress-rehearsal for the main event, were celebrated near the banks of the River Ilissos, in the region that Socrates himself frequented. Candidates were coached, in secret, by the Eleusinian priests. In the year of Socrates' death (399 BC) these Lesser Mysteries would have been in full swing in that no-man's-land time for the philosopher, probably April, between his abrupt meeting with Meletus in the Agora and his trial itself in the *Archon Basileus'* law-courts.

Five moons later, in the calendar month of Boedromion (around September), sacrifices and processions through the heart of Athens – the start of the Greater Mysteries – prepared the faithful for the pilgrimage to the Sanctuary itself. The build-up to the excursion was long and demanding; initiates had to purify themselves, were obliged to carry ritual objects from the Eleusinian shrine in Athens back to Demeter's sanctuary, and libations and sacrifices were demanded. Secret chants were learned – if the students mocked these they could be executed.

The site of Eleusis is currently being re-excavated and is slowly yielding its secrets. Today we are asked to contemplate the grimy, once primary-coloured monuments to heavy industry that lie between Eleusis and the Aegean Sea beyond. But in Socrates' day this would have been an idyllic spot. The land was rich and fertile – hence its connection to the goddess of grain, Demeter. The limestone bedrock erodes to form a natural auditorium. A building called the *telesterion*, developed within this space in the fifth century BC, has now been identified. Windowless, punctuated by columns, this vast area was where many thousands of the faithful gathered together. Initiates could not reveal what went on in here, on pain of death. On these earth-made benches, men and women would sit to watch scenes played out in front of them. These religious stories constitute the earliest form of Western drama. What the initiates saw was said to leave them '*shivering, and trembling with sweat and amazement*'. Apparitions (early theatrical tricks) produced '*every kind of terror*'.[5]

The burning torches were both an enactment of Demeter's desperate search for her daughter and a symbol of light that was extinguished and then returned again. Walking together, in orange light and then pitch-dark, initiates were encouraged to confront their fears. This is a story where terrible things happen: a girl is raped, a mother loses her child, the pain of brutality spurs the goddess to dreadful vengeance – parching the earth of water, draining it of food, bleaching out life until all is barren and dying. But then Kore is found. The climax of the Mysteries was heady, joyful. At the point of reunion on the ritual 'stage' men and women in the 'audience' perhaps engaged in the sexual act. The rituals inspired collective terror and then collective relief.

The popularity of the cult in the fifth and fourth centuries BC shows that this was an epoch when ordinary, mortal men were questioning the ordin-ariness of their lives. If individuals could have potency in the polit-ical arena, if they could vote when warships were launched and against whom, then row these very warships themselves, if their lives were that valuable, might the value not extend beyond the grave? Socrates lived through a time when life itself meant more, when man's potential on earth was being explored, when an afterlife became something that was not to be feared, but desirable.[6]

The rites at Eleusis speak volumes about the subtle play of power, old and new, in Athens.[7] Despite the new democratic, equable structure of the state, there were those who wanted to keep things 'a little bit special', to find ways of distinguishing the haves from the have-nots.

Socrates ate and drank with aristocrats, he slept with them, and yet he was not automatically welcomed into their ranks. He walked for days on end with the ordinary people of Athens through the Agora and streets, he fought alongside them, and yet he would not always just join them in their popular expression of communal spirituality. Socrates, like the Eleusinians, looked to the possibility of a life after this one, but unlike them, his was a personal, internal experience. This delight in privacy made many in Athens suspicious of the remotely clever philosopher. It certainly helped to bring about the demand for his death.

Platone narra nel Teeteto, che Socrate fia ftato di nafo fimo, e da lui il confer ma Ammonio. Polemone dice Socrate effer ftato luffuriofo, perche hà conc aua quella fuperficie, che è frà'l nafo, e la barba . Plauto introduce nel fuo Rudente, Labrace affai luffuriofo, e cattiuo, e dice effer ftato, caluo fimo, e ventruto. Ruellio Francefe fù di nafo fimo, e luffuriofo. Sono ancora molti di parere, che Horatio Cocles, non perche haueffe perduto vn'occhio nella

Year	Life of Socrates	Life of Alcibiades	Life of Plato	Life of Pericles
470/469	Birth of Socrates			
467				
466				
465				
463/2				Pericles participates in unsucce prosecution of Kimon
462/1				Pericles joins Ephialtes in the on the Areopagus
461				Pericles rises to power in Athe
460				
459/8				
458				
457				
456				
454/3				Pericles campaigns in the Gul Corinth
451/0				Periclean legislation to restric Athenian citizenship to those two Athenian parents
before 450				
450		Birth of Alcibiades		

Life of Xenophon	History	Culture	Year	Constructions, sculptures and statues
			c.470	Repairs of Opisthodomos? Construction of the north citadel wall of the Acropolis
			470–460	Construction of the Peisianaktios (later known as *Stoa Poïkile*)
			465–60-455/50	Bronze Athena (Promakhos) by Pheidias
		Aeschylus, *Laius, Oedipus, Seven against Thebes, Sphinx*		
	Hellenic victory over Persia at Eurymedon River			
	Athens blockades Thasos. Artaxerxes I reigns 465–425 BC			Construction of the *Tholos*
		Aeschylus, *Suppliants, Aigyptioi, Danaids, Amymone*		
	Radical democracy established at Athens. Athens abandons alliance with Sparta against Persia. Reduction of the Areopagus. Kimon ostracised			
	First Peloponnesian War			Construction of the wall of Kimon. Construction of the south citadel wall of the Acropolis, pre-Erechtheion. Reconstructed Klepsydra Fountain (north-west slope of Acropolis) constructed
			460–450	Mourning Athena relief
	Athens' expedition to Egypt			
	Cincinnatus appointed dictator of Rome and defeats the Aequi	Aeschylus, *Oresteia, Agamemnon, Libation-bearers, Proteus, Eumenides*		Building of Long Walls connecting port of Piraeus to Athens begins. Erection of the statue of Athena Promachos.
	Zeugitae eligible for archonship			
		Death of Aeschylus		
	Greeks in Egypt defeated by Persian satrap Megabyzus. Treasury of the Delian League moved to Athens			
	Kimon returns from ostracism			
				Agora planted with plane-trees
	Expedition to Cyprus Death of Kimon	Birth of Aristophanes. Dramatic date of Plato, *Parmenides* (Aug)		Academy rearranged

Year	Life of Socrates	Life of Alcibiades	Life of Plato	Life of Pericles
450s				Pericles proposes dikasts should paid
449				Pericles proposes building programme
449				
447/6				Pericles commands the expeditic put down the revolt in Euboea
445				
443/2				Pericles elected one of Athens' egoi
442				
441				Pericles supports Athens' interve in the conflict between Samos a Miletos
440	Socrates serves in Samian campaign?			
438				
437/6				
435				
c.434				
433				
432	Siege of Potidea by Athens begins: Socrates serves there			
431	Outbreak of Peloponnesian War Sparta invades Attica			Pericles gives his funeral oratic Pericles persuades hoplite farm move inside the city walls

Life of Xenophon	History	Culture	Year	Constructions, sculptures and statues
				Construction of the Desmoterion Poros building Square stone bases socketed to hold temporary wooden posts on the Pan-Athenaic Way installed — starting posts for races House of Simon House of Menon Houses C and D (house/workshops east of the Street of Marble Workers) Construction of the Synestrion
			after 450	Strategelon
			450–445	Temple of Athena Nike authorised
	Peace of Callias — end of war with Persia			
			449–444	Construction of Hephaisteion on Kolonos Agoraios
	Renewed hostilites with Sparta			
	Revolt of Megabyzus, Persian satrap of Syria Battle of Coronea	Death of the poet Pindar		Building of Parthenon begins Workshop Construction of Parthenon terrace Periclean add-on to south citadel wall
	End of First Peloponnesian War Thirty-year peace treaty between Athens and Sparta sworn	Prometheus Bound		
	Thucydides, son of Melesias, ostracised			Public baths
		Sophocles, Antigone		Parthenon frieze carved
	Revolt of Samos			
	Athens besieges Samos. Legislation prohibits certain kinds of comic abuse			Odeion of Pericles
	Pheidias leaves Athens after being accused of embezzlement	Euripides, Alcestis		Statue of Athena by Pheidias dedicated in Parthenon
			437–42	Construction of Propylaia on Acropolis (never finished). Architect: Mnesikles Athena Nike bastion remodelled Artemis Brauronia sanctuary remodelled
	Comic-abuse legislation repealled Founding of Amphipolis			Athens waterworks, public project
	Athens condudes defensive pact with Corcyra			Construction of Erechtheion (finished 395)
				Demeter and Kore sanctuary, precinct wall and entrance?
	Treaty between Athens and Corcyra			
	Revolt of Potidea	Dramatic date of Plato's Protagoras, Alcibiades (Second Alcibiades)		Parthenon completed
		Euripides, Medea. Thucydides begins to write his History of the Peloponnesian War		

Year	Life of Socrates	Life of Alcibiades	Life of Plato	Life of Pericles
430	Chaerephon possibly journeys to Delphi to ask the oracle if anyone is wiser than his friend Socrates			*Demos* fines Pericles and removes him from office
429	Socrates returns to Athens from Potidaea			Pericles re-elected Death of Pericles
428				
427			Birth of Plato	
426				
425				
424	Athenians invade Boeotia: Socrates present at Athenian defeat at Delion			
423				
422	Socrates serves at Battle of Amphipolis, where Brasidas and Cleon are both killed			
421				
421–416/15				
420				
418/7				
417				

Life of Xenophon	History	Culture	Year	Constructions, sculptures and statues
of Xenophon	Plague in Athens	Euripides, *The Children of Herakles*		Temple of Ares Chalkotheke precinct Great steps west of the Parthenon Stone funeral reliefs reappear in Athens Construction of South Stoa Ilissos temple
			420s	Shrine of Athena Hygiela
	Surrender of Potidaea	Dramatic date of Plato, *Charmides* (May)		
	Island of Lesbos, led by the city of Mytilene, rebels against Athens	Euripides, *Hippolytus*		
			427–425/4	Building of Temple of Nike on Acropolis (second phase)
	Capture of Mytilene by Athens and execution of rebels			
	Earthquake in Athens – affects buildings in Kerameikos			
	Athenians capture Sphacteria and Pylos	Euripides, *Andromache* Aristophanes, *Achamians*		Erection of the Eponymoi Construction of the Stoa of the Hermes Diateichisma
			425–400	Construciton of the Stoa of Zeus Eleutheorios Rebuilding of the Sanctuary of The Twelve Gods Old *Bouleuterion* changed into *Metroon* and archive room Construction of the New *Bouleuferion* Construction of the Argyrokopeion Votive offerings left at the Crossroads enclosure Law-courts in Agora Dionysos Eleuthereus theatre remodelled South-west fountain house and aqueduct *Tholos* repaired Apollo Patroos sanctuary cleared? Sanctuary of the Nyph. precinct wall? Tritopatreion, precinct wall Pompeion I
	Xerxes II, King of Persia, assassinated and succeeded by Darius II Spartan general Brasidas takes Amphipolis in northern Greece	Death of Herodotus Aristophanes, *Knights*. Dramatic date of Plato, *Laches* (winter)		
	One-year armistice between Athens and Sparta	Aristophanes' *Clouds* performed at Athens. Euripides, *Hecabe, Suppliant Women* Ameipsias, *Konnos*		
		Dramatic date of Xenophon, *Symposium* Dramatic date of Plato, *Cratylus* Aristophanes, *Wasps*		
	Peace of Nikias	Aristophanes' *Peace* performed at Athens		
		Dramatic date of Plato. *Critophon, Greater Hippias, Lesser Hippias*		Bronze cult statues of Hephaistos and Athena by Alkamenes
				Asklepieion founded and equipped on Acropolis south slope
	Athenian-Argive force defeated at Mantinea by Sparta	Dramatic date of Plato. *Phaedrus*		Neleion remodelled
		Euripides, *Heracles, Electra*		

Year	Life of Socrates	Life of Alcibiades	Life of Plato	Life of Pericles
416	Birth of Socrates' son Lamprokles			
415		Alcibiades commands expedition to Sicily Alcibiades accused of involvement in religioius scandals; recalled from Sicily for trial; flees to Sparta		
414				
413				
412		Alcibiades involved in Sparta's decision to concentrate on the Aegean rather than the Hellespont, flees to Tissaphernes	Appointed general of Athenian fleet at Samos	
411				
410	Birth of Socrates' son Sophroniskos	Athenian fleet under Alcibiades defeats Spartans at Battle of Cyzicus		
409/8				
408				
407		Alcibiades returns from exile Cleared of religious charges		
406	Athenians defeat Spartan fleet at Arginusae: Socrates opposes subsequent charges against Athenian generals for failure to rescue survivors		Alcibiades retires to Thrace	Possibly present at the trial of t generals?
406/5				
405		Approach to the Athenians before Aegospotami rebuffed Takes refuge with Phamabazus		
404	Socrates ordered to arrest Leon of Salamis; refuses Socrates tries to save Theramenes?	Assassination of Alcibiades	Plato's uncle Critias is part of 'the Thirty' and Charmides one of the Peiraeus Ten.	
403				
402	Socrates' son Menexenos born			
401				
c.400				
399	Trial and execution of Socrates			

Life of Xenophon	History	Culture	Year	Constructions, sculptures and statues
		Dramatic date of Plato, *Symposium*		
	Mutilation of the herms and profanation of the Mysteries in Athens Massacre at Melos by the Athenians Athenian expedition to Sicily	Euripides, *The Trojan Women* Dramatic date of Plato, *Eryxias*	415–400	Nike temple parapet
		Aristophanes, *Birds*		
	Athenian army in Sicily defeated	Dramatic date of Plato, *Ion*		
		Island of Chios rebels against Athens	Euripides, *Ion Iphigenia among the Taurians, Helen, Cyclops*	
	Oligarchic revolution in Athens and Council of 400 established	Aristophanes, *Lysistrata, Women at the Thesmophoria*		
	Demokratia reinstituted			Sculptural decoration of Temple of Athena Nike completed
			410–400	Two projecting wings added to the *Stoa Basileios* (to display new copies of the law code)
ed in cavalry action in Ionia?		Euripides, *Phoenician Women* Dramatic date of Plato, *Lysis* (early spring) Sophocles, *Philoctetes*		Work restarts on the Erechtheion
		Euripides, *Orestes*		
		Dramatic date of Plato, *Euthydemus*		
	Dionysus I becomes Tyrant of Syracuse Athenian defeat at Notion			
		Euripides, *Iphigenia in Aulis, Bacchae* Death of Euripides Death of Sophocles		Erechtheion finished
	Death of Darius II of Persia: succeeded by Artaxerxes II Battle of Aegospotami: Athenian fleet defeated by Sparta Piraeus blockaded and Athens besieged by Sparta	Aristophanes' *Frogs* performed at Athens		
hon fights the democratic ents during the civil war	Athens surrenders to Spartans and rule of 'the Thirty' imposed Dekeleian War			Spartan forces compel Athens to destroy the Long Walls Pnyx meeting place remodelled
	Fall of 'the Thirty': democracy restored in Athens Amnesty decree passed by Athenian Assembly			
		Dramatic date of Plato, *Meno*		
hon joins expedition of the ousand to Asia		Sophocles, *Oedipus at Colonus* staged Dramatic date of Plato, *Menexenus* (winter)		
command of survivors; leads o Byzantium				Construction of the Mint Asklepeion, stoa building South and east branches of the Great Drain
hon becomes a Spartan ary		Dramatic date of Plato's *Theaetetus, Euthyphro* (spring); *Sophist, Statesman* (May–June), *Apology, Crito, Phaedo* (June–July)		

TEXT ACKNOWLEDGEMENTS

❦❦❦❦❦❦❦❦❦❦❦

Grateful acknowledgement is made for permission to reproduce material from the following translations: D. Allen, from 'A Schedule of Boundaries: An Exploration Launched from the Water-Clock of Athenian Time' (1996), *Greece & Rome* (43.2), Cambridge University Press; J. Barnes, from S. Everson (trans. and ed.), *Aristotle: The Politics and the Constitution of Athens* (1996), Cambridge University Press; D. Barrett, from *Aristophanes: The Frogs and Other Plays* (1964), Penguin; S. Berg and D. Clay, from *Oedipus the King: The Greek Tragedy in New Translations* (1978), Oxford University Press; S. Blundell, from page 1 of S. Blundell and M. Williamson (eds.), *The Sacred Feminine in Ancient Greece* (1998), Routledge; T. C. Brickhouse and N. D. Smith, from *The Trial and Execution of Socrates: Sources and Controversies* (2002), Oxford University Press; C. L. Brownson, reprinted by permission of the publishers and trustees of the Loeb Classical Library from *Xenophon: Volume I*, Loeb Classical Library Volume 88, translated by C. L. Brownson, Cambridge, MA: Harvard University Press © 1918, by the President and Fellows of Harvard College. Loeb Classical Library ® is a registered trademark of the President and Fellows of Harvard College; C. L. Brownson, reprinted by permission of the publishers and trustees of the Loeb Classical Library from *Xenophon: Volume III*, Loeb Classical Library Volume 90, translated by C. L. Brownson, Cambridge, MA: Harvard University Press © 1922, by the President and Fellows of Harvard College. Loeb Classical Library ® is a registered trademark of the President and Fellows of Harvard College; R. G. Bury, reprinted by permission of the publishers and trustees of the Loeb Classical Library from *Plato: Volume IX*, Loeb Classical Library Volume 234, translated by R. G. Bury, Cambridge, MA: Harvard University Press © 1929, by the President and Fellows of Harvard College. Loeb Classical Library ® is a registered trademark of the President and Fellows of Harvard College; S. Butler, *Iliad* from Perseus Digital Library (http://www.perseus.tufts.edu); E. P. Coleridge, from W. J. Oates and E. O'Neill Jr. (eds.), *Euripides: The Complete Greek Drama in Two Volumes. Vol. I, Hecuba* (1938), Random House (USA); F. M. Cornford, from E. Hamilton and H. Cairns (eds.), *The Collected Dialogues of Plato* (1973), Princeton University Press; H. G. Dakyns, from *The Works of Xenophon* (1890), Macmillan; J. Davidson, from *The Greeks and Greek Love: A Radical Reappraisal of Homosexuality in Ancient Greece* (2007), Weidenfeld & Nicolson, an imprint of The Orion Publishing Group, London, © Orion Publishing/Random House, New York; J. M. Dent, from *Thucydides: The Peloponnesian War* (1910), Penguin (for E. P. Dutton); J. Elsner, from *Roman Eyes: Visuality and Subjectivity in Art and Text* (2007), Princeton University Press; H. G. Evelyn-White, reprinted by permission of the publishers and the Trustees of the Loeb Classical Library from *Hesiod*, Loeb Classical Library Volume 57, translated by H. G. Evelyn-White, Cambridge, MA.: Harvard

Plato: *Symposium*, from J. M. Cooper (ed.), *Plato: Complete Works* (1997), Hackett; G. Norlin, reprinted by permission of the publishers and the Trustees of the Loeb Classical Library from *Isocrates: Volume II*, Loeb Classical Library Volume 209, translated by G. Norlin, Cambridge, MA: Harvard University Press, © 1929, by the President and Fellows of Harvard College. Loeb Classical Library ® is a registered trademark of the President and Fellows of Harvard College; E. O'Neill, from *Aristophanes: The Complete Greek Drama, Vol. 2* (1938), Random House (USA); B. Perrin, reprinted by permission of the publishers and the Trustees of the Loeb Classical Library from *Plutarch: Volume IV*, Loeb Classical Library Volume 80, translated by B. Perrin, Cambridge, MA: Harvard University Press, © 1916, by the President and Fellows of Harvard College. Loeb Classical Library ® is a registered trademark of the President and Fellows of Harvard College; S. Pomeroy, from *Xenophon, Oeconomicus: A Social and Historical Commentary* (1994), Clarendon Press; K. A. Raaflaub and J. Ober, from K. A. Raaflaub, J. Ober, R.W. Wallace (eds.), *Origins of Democracy* (2007), University of California Press, © 2007 by the Regents of the University of California; C. D. C. Reeve, from *Plato on Love* (2006), Hackett; P. J. Rhodes, from *Aristotle: The Athenian Constitution* (2002), Penguin; B. B. Rogers, reprinted by permission of the publishers and the Trustees of the Loeb Classical Library from *Aristophanes: Volume II*, Loeb Classical Library Volume 179, translated by B. B. Rogers, Cambridge, MA: Harvard University Press, © 1924, by the President and Fellows of Harvard College. Loeb Classical Library ® is a registered trademark of the President and Fellows of Harvard College; C. Rolfe, reprinted by permission of the publishers and the Trustees of the Loeb Classical Library from *Gellius: Volume III*, Loeb Classical Library Volume 212, translated by C. Rolfe, Cambridge, MA: Harvard University Press, © 1927, by the President and Fellows of Harvard College. Loeb Classical Library ® is a registered trademark of the President and Fellows of Harvard College; L. J. Samons (and quoting P. Harding), from *What's Wrong with Democracy? From Athenian Practice to American Worship* (2004), University of California Press, © 2004 by the Regents of the University of California; T. J. Saunders, from *Early Socratic Dialogues* (1987), Penguin; T. J. Saunders, from *Plato: The Laws* (1975), Penguin; I. Scott-Kilvert, from *Plutarch: The Rise and Fall of Athens: Nine Greek Lives* (1960), Penguin; A. De Sélincourt, from *The Histories: Herodotus* (1954), Penguin; P. Shorey, reprinted by permission of the publishers and the Trustees of the Loeb Classical Library from *Plato: Volume V*, Loeb Classical Library Volume 237, translated by P. Shorey, Cambridge, MA: Harvard University Press, © 1929, by the President and Fellows of Harvard College. Loeb Classical Library ® is a registered trademark of the President and Fellows of Harvard College; T. A. Sinclair (revised by T. J. Saunders), from *Aristotle: The Politics* (1981), Penguin; C. F. Smith, reprinted by permission of the publishers and the Trustees of the Loeb Classical Library from *Thucydides: Volume I*, Loeb Classical Library Volume 108, translated by C. F. Smith, Cambridge, MA: Harvard University Press, © 1919 (revised 1928), by the President and Fellows of Harvard College. Loeb Classical Library ® is a registered trademark of the President and Fellows of Harvard College; C. F. Smith, reprinted by permission of the publishers and the Trustees of the Loeb Classical Library from *Thucydides: Volume III*, Loeb Classical Library Volume 110, translated by C. F. Smith, Cambridge, MA: Harvard University Press, © 1921, by the President and Fellows of Harvard College. Loeb Classical Library ® is a registered trademark of the President and Fellows of Harvard College; H. W. Smyth, reprinted by permission of the publishers and the Trustees of the Loeb Classical Library from *Aeschylus: Volume I*, Loeb

Classical Library Volume 145, translated by H. W. Smyth, Cambridge, MA: Harvard University Press, © 1922, by the President and Fellows of Harvard College. Loeb Classical Library ® is a registered trademark of the President and Fellows of Harvard College; A. H. Sommerstein, from *Aristophanes: Lysistrata, The Acharnians, The Clouds* (1973), Penguin; A. H. Sommerstein, from *Aristophanes: Birds* (1987), Aris & Phillips, an imprint of Oxbow Books; J. D. Sosin, from 'The New Letter from Pasion' (2008) in *Zeitschrift für Papyrologie und Epigraphik* 165: 105–108; R. K. Sprague, from *The Older Sophists* (2001), Hackett; C. A. Stocks, from Haase (ed.), *L. Annaei Senecae ludus de morte Claudii, Epigrammata super exilio* (1902), Lipsiae: in aedibus B. G. Teubneri; G. Theodoridis, from http://www.poetryin translation.com/PITBR/Greek/FrogsActIIScenelll.htm; H. Tredennick, from *The Last Days of Socrates* (1954), Penguin; H. Tredennick, from E. Hamilton and H. Cairns (eds.), *The Collected Dialogues of Plato* (1973), Princeton University Press; H. Tredennick and R. Waterfield, from *Xenophon. Conversations of Socrates* (1990), Penguin; P. Vellacott, from *Three Plays: Hippolytus, Iphigenia in Tauris, Alcestis. Euripides* (1953), Penguin; P. Vellacott, from *Aeschylus: The Oresteian Trilogy: Agamemnon, The Choephori, The Eumenides* (1956), Penguin; P. Vellacott, from *Aeschylus: Prometheus Bound; The Suppliants; Seven Against Thebes; The Persians* (1961), Penguin; P. Vellacott, from *Euripides. Orestes and Other Plays* (1972), Penguin; P. Vellacott, from Euripides. *The Bacchae and Other Plays* (1973), Penguin; R. Warner, from *Xenophon: A History of My Times* (1966), Penguin; R. Warner, from *History of the Peloponnesian War: Thucydides* (1972), Penguin; R. Waterfield, from *Plato: Republic* (1993), Oxford University Press A. Wilson, Euripides' *Phoenician Women*, from The Classics Pages (classicspage.com/phoenissae.htm); P. Woodruff, from *On Justice, Power and Human Nature: The Essence of Thucydides' History of the Peloponnesian War* (1993), Hackett; C. D. Yonge, from *The Lives and Opinions of Eminent Philosophers* (1853), Henry G. Bohn; D. J. Zeyl, Plato: *Gorgias*, from J. M. Cooper (ed.), *Plato: Complete Works* (1997), Hackett; unless otherwise indicated, all Scripture quotations are taken from the Holy Bible, New Living Translation, copyright © 1996, 2004, 2007 by the Tyndale House Foundation. Used by permission of Tyndale House Publishers, Inc., Carol Stream, Illinois 60188. All rights reserved.

Grateful acknowledgement is made for permission to reproduce material from the following publications: E. Bloch in 'Hemlock Poisoning and the Death of the Socrates. Did Plato Tell the Truth?' (2002), in T. C. Brickhouse and N. D. Smith, *The Trial and Execution of Socrates: Sources and Controversies* (2002), Oxford University Press; R. Janko from 'Socrates the Freethinker' in Ahbel-Rappe and Kamtekar (eds.), *A Companion to Socrates* (2006), Blackwell Publishing; H. Kahn (2006), 'Socrates and Hedonism' in L. Judson and V. Karasmanis (eds.), *Remembering Socrates: Philosophical Essays* (2006), Clarendon Press; Meier, from *Athens: A Portrait of the City in its Golden Age* (1999), John Murray; L. E. Navia, from *Socrates: A Life Examined* (2007), Prometheus; J. Ober, from Xin Liu Gale 'Historical Studies and Postmodernism: Rereading Aspacia of Miletus' (2000), *College English* (62.3), © 2000 by the National Council of Teachers of English. Reprinted with permission; P. J. Rhodes, from *A History of the Classical Greek World 478–323 BC* (2005), Blackwell; A.W. Saxonhouse, from *Free Speech and Democracy in Ancient Athens* (2006), Cambridge University Press; R. Waterfield, from *Why Socrates Died: Dispelling the Myths* (2009), Faber and Faber; J. A. Zahm, from *Women in Science* (1913), Appleton.

IMAGE
ACKNOWLEDGEMENTS

෧෧෧෧෧෧෧෧෧෧෧෧

INTEGRATED IMAGES

All maps drawn and lettered by Reginald Piggott. 1. Portrait Herm of Socrates © Corbis images; 2. Excavations of Athens' Agora, taken from *Agora Excavations 1931–2006: A Pictorial History*, Craig Mauzy (The American School of Classical Studies at Athens, 2006). Courtesy of the Trustees of the American School of Classical Studies at Athens; 3. A reconstruction of the Kleroterion, taken from M. L. Lang, *The Athenian Citizen: Democracy in the Athenian Agora*, rev. J. McK. Camp II (Princeton, 2004), figs. 27–29. Courtesy of the Trustees of the American School of Classical Studies at Athens; 4. Women gathered at the Fountains of Athens, Image no. AN0175173001 Attic; Archaic Greek; The Antimenes Painter © The Trustees of the British Museum; 5. Boiotian Terracotta Figurine © Getty images; 6. Early fifth-century Attic cup by Foundry Painter, courtesy of Berlin Staatliche Museum; 7. Eugene Vanderpool, Professor of Archaeology of the American School 1947–1971, taken from *Agora Excavations 1931–2006: A Pictorial History*, Craig Mauzy (The American School of Classical Studies at Athens, 2006). Courtesy of the Trustees the American School of Classical Studies at Athens; 8. The 'tyrant-slayers' Harmodios and Aristogeiton, courtesy of The Naples Museo Nazionale Archeologico; 9. Sculpture of a young Athenian man, taken from *Athens: The City Beneath the City: Antiquities from the Metropolitan Railway Excavations*, (Kapon Editions, 2000). Courtesy the Greek Ministry of Culture; 10. A portrait herm, possibly depicting Aspasia, currently held by the Vatican, courtesy of the Vatican Museums; 11. Socrates is imagined dancing to Aspasia's tune in this French cartoon of 1842. Photograph © 2010 Museum of Fine Arts, Boston; 12. Two hoplite soldiers, named Chairedemos and Lykeas, on a funerary relief. Courtesy Archaeological Museum of Piraeus © Hellenic Ministry of Culture and Tourism/Archaeological Receipts Fund; 13. Socrates and Alcibiades, drawing by Paul Avril, engraved by T. Fillon, for a 1906 Paris edition of F. K. Forberg's *Manuel d'érotologie classique*; 14. Mourning Athena, courtesy of the Acropolis Museum, Athens © Hellenic Ministry of Culture and Tourism/Archaeological Receipts Fund; 15. Athena's Silver Owl © Money Museum, Zurich; 16. The north-east corner of the Agora, taken from *Agora Excavations 1931–2006: A Pictorial History*, Craig Mauzy (The American School of Classical Studies at Athens, 2006). Courtesy of the Trustees of the American School of Classical Studies at Athens; 17. Drinking-cup, courtesy National Museum of Antiquities, Leiden; 18. Socrates summons Alcibiades, courtesy Kunsthalle Bremen; 19. Kylix, Musée du Louvre, Paris; 20. Grave stele, Athens, National Archaeological Museum © Hellenic

PLATE SECTIONS

courtesy Archaeological Museum of Brauron © Hellenic Ministry of Culture and Tourism/Archaeological Receipts Fund; 17. Attic Red-Figure Chous, Athens, National Archaeological Museum, Vlastos Serpieris Collection, BS 319 © Hellenic Ministry of Culture and Tourism/Archaeological Receipts Fund; 18. Nicolai Abraham Abilgaard, *Socrates in Prison*, courtesy New Carlsberg Glyptotek, Copenhagen; 19. Socrates sitting on a bench © Art Resource; 20. Jacques-Louis David, *The Death of Socrates* © Metropolitan Museum of Art, New York.

The author and the publishers have made every effort to trace the holders of copyright in illustrations and quotations. Any inadvertent omissions or errors may be corrected in future editions.

NOTES

PREFACE

1 Socrates is not just a whetstone for scholars, not just an inspiration. He is a key witness to the Golden Age of Athens in the fifth century. For millennia, scholars have wanted to sharpen their wits on his portly legacy. There is a void where Socrates' personal testimony should be, a void the waters of interpretation have rushed to fill. Around the empty, Socrates-sized space that is the philosopher, all kinds of worlds have been constructed: ethical, legal, spiritual; but only a handful deal with the one thing we do have, the *physical* setting of his not-thereness.

INTRODUCTION

1 Trans. Brickhouse and Smith (2002).

2 Socrates spent his lifespan in pursuit of an individual morality. See e.g. Rudebusch (1999) on Socrates' pursuit of both pleasure and virtue as the chief good.

3 *Psyche* is an Ancient Greek word meaning life-force or breath. It is also the Greek for butterfly.

4 '*Socrates is the first to show that life at all times and in all parts, in all that we suffer and do, always admits philosophy.*' Plutarch, *An seni respublica gerenda sit*, 796e.

5 Plato, *Apology*, 30e.

6 Plato, *Republic*, VII, 514a–20a.

7 Although some later Christian commentators saw in this the development of a new kind of internal faith.

8 Produced in 423 BC and then possibly rewritten in 418 BC. The lost comedy of Ameipsias, the *Konnos*, also lampoons Socrates.

9 '*Do as I tell you and keep away from the gossip of people. For Pheme [Rumour] is an evil thing, by nature, she's a light weight to lift up, yes very easy, but heavy to carry, and hard to put down again. Pheme [Rumour] never disappears entirely once many people have bigged her up/indulged her. In fact, she really is like some sort of goddess.*' Hesiod, *Works and Days*, 760ff. (Greek didactic poem, eighth or seventh century BC).

10 Plato, *Apology*, 18d.

11 Socrates could have been crucified for his crimes (although this was perhaps a punishment reserved for 'sub-citizens', e.g., slaves) – hemlock was thought a kinder death. But excruciating death can be measured by degrees, and poison was only a few degrees kinder than crucifixion. David's painting is romantic in many ways.

12 Plato was a classical author vigorously studied in Baghdad's 'House of Wisdom'. Muslim families still call their children Aflatonion.

13 Plato, *Apology*, 42a.

14 We fondly imagine that democracy is ancient Athens' greatest legacy, but in fact democracy has consistently been rejected throughout Western history. Plato's ideas (he can be viewed as an anti-democrat) – and therefore perhaps Socrates' – proved far more tenacious. Socrates' disciples in the Ancient World included: Antisthenes, the Cynic philosophers such as Diogenes of Sinope, Plato, Xenophon, Euclides, Aristippus. The following of Plato's Dialogues are linked in their discussion of Socrates: *Theaetetus-Euthyphro-Apology-Crito-Phaedo*. In territories both pagan and monotheistic, both Eastern and Western, Socrates' ideas have informed how humans have lived. The value of his methods is having something of a revival: the Socratic method and Socratic counselling are recognised as having absolute worth. They are becoming fashionable once more in schools and colleges. See links from: www.Socraticmethod.net.

15 Plato, *Alcibiades*, 1, 130e.

16 Plato, *Sophist*, 227d.

17 Plato, *Phaedo*, 69b–c. Trans. H. N. Fowler (1914) [LCL].

18 We still have their titles: *On the Virtue of Socrates; Socrates' Pronouncements; Of Socrates' Death* – to name but a few.

19 To understand Socrates' place in Islam, works by Ilai Alon are hugely helpful, e.g., *Socrates Arabus: Life and Teachings* (Jerusalem, 1995).

20 'Know yourself.' 'What counts most is not to live, but to live right.' A summary of Socrates' aims is provided eloquently by Louis E. Navia: 'Self-knowledge, the key that unlocks the door to virtue, is accessible only within a person's own soul. The path that leads to it is narrow, rugged and steep. This is why most people do not choose to strive in so uninviting a direction. Their intellectual inertia and spiritual barrenness prevent them from doing so. Here is a source of their guilt, that is, in the abandonment of what Socrates viewed as the only solution to the riddle of human existence. This abandonment becomes even more reprehensible when it involves the rejection of the opportunity furnished by the presence of someone like Socrates.' Navia (2007), 234.

21 Plato himself debates the conflict between legalistic and true justice.

22 Plato, *Apology*, 34d.

23 Xenophon, *Memorabilia*, 1.1.16.

THE DRAMATIC STORY OF SOCRATES

1 The fact that Socrates has, as advocates, the mischievous, assiduous trio of Plato, Aristophanes and Xenophon no doubt has resulted in an inflation of the Socratic tradition – but archaeology backs up the importance of the key moments of his life-story, and goes partway to explain Socrates' preoccupations with particular issues of the challenging world in which he lived.

2 Theatre gives us a version of the external world and the internal worlds of imagination, of thought, of emotion that is comprehensible. More than that, that is believable.

And more than *that*, that moves us in some way. The challenge of a playwright is to transfer ideas, emotions to an audience and to create a make-believe experience that we also comprehend as the real world. See Chapter 31, 'Brickbats and bouquets'.

3 'Biography' as we understand it today does not exist in this period – the works dealing with Socrates are therefore 'ancient-style' biographies.

4 Writers are often tempted to understand Socrates' trial and death in hard political terms. It is indeed exciting to try to unpick our extant textual sources and work out who was in whose faction, what political undercurrents were in play. I have tried to take Socrates' story one stage further back. Political squabbles are emotional – and the one thing that Plato is certainly trying to do is to convey the emotional complexity of how a city such as Athens dealt with a man like Socrates.

5 But throughout this book where a particular line of Plato is ambiguous, tricky or contested, or where later interpolation is an issue, I have either omitted it or flagged up the difficulty in hand. Where ideas are clearly Plato's and not Socrates' own, I have made note – but I have not censored. Following scholarly convention, the Socrates in this book is the character depicted in Plato's 'early' or 'sceptical' dialogues (*Apology, Charmides, Crito, Euthydemus, Euthyphro, Gorgias, Hippias Major, Ion, Laches, Lysis, Menexenus, Meno, Protagoras* and *Republic 1*, with the exception of *Theaetetus*).

6 Many thanks to Professor Patrick Haggard, Institute of Cognitive Neuroscience, University College London, for his confirmation of my initial enquiry and for his help with these points.

7 For an overview, see the websites of the Greek Archaeological Service. Specific sites dealing with places and events relevant to Socrates' life are marked in the map section of this book.

8 And similar details crop up in the texts antipathetic to Socrates.

9 The Socrates I have chosen to guide us around the fifth century BC is, in the main, the dramatic/historic character offered to us by contemporary eye-witnesses. I am using this 'phantom-Socrates', this 'Socrates-sized shape', to transport us through the city of Athens.

10 Socrates is a man of Athens. But his own travels through the eastern Mediterranean, and key events that impacted directly on his life, are located in a geographical area that encompasses perfectly all the hot and the high spots of the fifth century BC. Using history and archaeology in the field, I have attempted to visit every site connected to Socrates' life and to pin down what it is that gives *cause* to his ideas, and what throws them into *context*. This book follows the coordinates that Socrates himself would have used.

11 And I believe we have to listen to Socrates now. Socrates lived in a brutal world – but he saw its potential. As is ours, his was a time of change. Just as the warrior ethos, the 'might is right', the 'harm enemies, help friends' modus operandi of prehistoric and archaic Greece was being replaced by something more consensual, more discursive, more intelligent, so now – when we are sliding back in to a new age of warring – we need to remind ourselves why Socrates' analysis of life matters. Socrates offered a roadmap for humanity that was coming out of the Greek 'Dark Ages': we should follow his path as we approach a future that again looks stormy.

DRAMATIS PERSONÆ

1 E.g., Plato, *Apology*, 18b–c, 19d; Dover (1996), 164.

2 Dover (1996), 164.

3 For discussion of dates see Meineck (1998), p.xvi, fn. 16: 'An inscription (IG ii2 2318.196) gives Araros a Dionysia victory in 387; if the hypothesis to Plutus is correct that after 388 Aristophanes produced Cocalus and Aiolosikon through Araros, we can assign victory with Cocalus to Aristophanes in 387.' The hypothesis referred to is Hyp. 4 Arist. Wealth, Hyp. 3 in the recent OCT. P. Meineck, *Aristophanes I: Clouds, Wasps, Birds*, (Hackett 1998).

4 It has been suggested that Erchia was near the modern Spata, about 10 miles outside Athens, in the Mesogeia (Macleod [2008], 7; Pomeroy [1994], 1 with bibl.). Nb *Deme* affiliation was hereditary, he may not have lived here.

5 Nails (2005), §2.1 *s.v.* 'Xenophon' suggests that Xenophon could not have known Socrates well, because Xenophon lived in Erchia, which was not a simple journey to Athens; Macleod (2008), 7–8, argues that Xenophon's family would have spent a lot of their time within the city walls, to avoid the constant raiding by the Spartan forces based at nearby Decelea.

6 Following Macleod (2008), 13–16 at 16.

7 428/427 are the dates usually suggested for Plato's birth (see, e.g., Szlezák in the New Pauly), but D. Nails considers it more likely that Plato was born in 424/423 (see Nails, *The People of Plato*, [2002], 245–6).

8 Press (2007), 15: 'Plato's connection with Socrates was not more than eight years.' A similar length of acquaintanceship is implied by Szlezák (2000), IX, *s.v.* 'Platon (1)', col. 1095: 'Erst mit 20 J. schloß er sich mit Sokrates an.' [Plato did not associate with Socrates until he was 20.] Nails (2005), *s.v.* 'Socrates', §2.1 *s.v.* 'Plato': 'Plato ... had probably known the old man most of his life.'

9 Press (2007), 15; Szlezák, ibid., col. 1095.

CHAPTER ONE
The water-clock: time to be judged

1 Trans. D. Allen (1996).

2 It has been suggested that the introduction of 501 jurors occurred a few years later in the fourth century BC. See Thomas C. Brickhouse and Nicholas D. Smith (eds.) (2002) *The Trial and Execution of Socrates: Sources and Controversies* (Oxford: OUP).

3 Herodotus, 1.155, 156; 3.25, 29, 59; 4.203, 204; 6.9, 17, 94; 8.126; and Aristotle, *Politics*, 1.4 1253b23. Cf. Hunt (2002), 42 n.13.

4 The appearance of slaves in this period is subject to debate. Pseudo-Xenophon, *Constitution of the Athenians*, 1.10, describes them as indistinguishable from regular citizens. Some slaves would undoubtedly have been well dressed, but the majority must have been easy to mark out, not least because most were of non-Greek origin and the female slaves may well have had cropped hair. Cf. Deighton (1995), 56; Osborne (2004), 18; Gray (2007), 192; Patterson (2007), 156.

5 Aristophanes, *Ecclesiazousae*, 652; Menander, Frag. 364 K.

6 Water-clocks were installed elsewhere in external locations, but significantly, the first large stone *klepsydra* was situated on the outside wall of the north-west face of the Heliaia (a court of judgement in the centre of the Agora).

7 Recent analysis suggests this is possibly where Socrates was tried. Alternatively his court-room could have been in the open air at the Areopagus (unlikely given the kind of scene-setting presented to us by Plato), which had originally been established to deal with issues that 'polluted' the city; or in the Heliaia, 'Sun-Court' or 'Sun-Area' — yet to be excavated, but possibly in the south-west end of the Agora. (The Heliaia was in the form of a rectangular peribolos, with four walls open to the sky.) Law-courts dating from the late fifth century BC have almost certainly been identified in the north-east corner of the Agora under the reconstructed Stoa of Attalos. See, e.g., R. Townsend, *Athenian Agora XXVII. The East Side of the Agora: The Remains beneath the Stoa of Attalos* (1995).

8 Plato, *Apology*, 18b; 19b. Trans. Brickhouse and Smith (2002).

9 Plato, *Apology*, 26b. Trans. Brickhouse and Smith (2002).

10 Athenian housing was notoriously small and cramped, even for wealthy citizens. Most would be flat-roofed (some two-storey) with a wooden framework, mud-brick walls and earth floors; the larger would probably have had a small courtyard. Aristophanes (*Wasps*, 125–32) describes the old man Philokleon trying to escape from one such house, desperate to make his trip to the law-courts whilst his slaves tried to keep him indoors. Cf. Tucker (1907), 29; Jones, Sackett and Graham (1973), 75–114; Deighton (1995), 15, 18; and MacDowell (1971), 148 on Aristophanes.

11 Plato, *Protagoras* esp. 322–4. Interesting that this Protagoras is a non-Athenian.

12 Athena in Aeschylus, *Eumenides*, 487–9.

13 Athena in Aeschylus, *Eumenides*, 690–5.

14 Plato, *Meno*, 80a.

15 Possessing 'the beauty of Helen' and 'the soul of Socrates' was a flattering epithet on a woman's tombstone of the fourth century BC.

16 Plato, *Symposium*, 215d–e. Trans. W. R. M. Lamb (1925) [LCL].

17 Plato, *Symposium*, 174a.

18 Pericles' *Funeral Speech*, Thucydides, 2.64.

19 Plato, *Meno*, 80a–b. Trans. W. K. C. Guthrie (1956).

CHAPTER TWO

Athena's city

1 Trans. E. D. A. Morshead.

2 'Age of Heroes' is loosely 1500–1100 BC.

3 During the eighth century BC warfare in Greece changed. Rows of soldiers, all armed in a similar way, replaced individual warrior fighters. Usually standing eight deep in a phalanx, these men were named for the armour and equipment which they carried — the *hopla*: a metal breastplate, metal greaves for the legs, a long spear, a large round shield. These men also stood tall thanks to their crested helmets.

4 (*Kolakes*) flatterers, (*parasitoi*) parasites. This belief in self-reliance may even have fostered

an entrenched slave system — very difficult for a 'free' Greek to enter the 'free labour' market.

5 Hesiod, *Works and Days*, 2.349–350. Trans. H. G. Evelyn-White (1914) [LCL].

6 'Balkan' means 'a chain of wooded mountains' in Ottoman Turkish.

7 Still, it is inaccurate to label this period the Greek 'Dark Ages'. The latest excavations (summer 2008) at Lefkandi on the Greek island of Euboea show that culture within the city-states could be vibrant, sophisticated. Here women are buried with fabulous necklaces, their breasts shielded with solid gold breast cups, in communal graves; the eye sockets of their men stare, blind, at heavily decorated pots. But there is still not the gauze-fine craftsmanship, the exquisite palatial culture that fluoresced between 1600 and 1200 BC — the civilisation of the Greek Late Bronze Age. Cf. Irene Lemnos' excellent excavations; work on Lefkandi resumed in 2003. www.lefkandi.classics.ox.ac.uk/ Nb. Through this period Cyprus keeps a syllabic writing system.

8 Operated by a German gunner.

9 Date *c.*510 BC. Akkadian was a common written language of this period, Elamite a spoken lingua franca.

10 Herodotus, 8.100.

11 Socrates served here one year and was elected leader of the council for one day. Xenophon, *Memorabilia*, 1.1.18.

12 The earliest surviving recorded example of the *demos* as a political unit has, just very recently, been made whole. It is carved on a block of stone, the letters each about an inch high. For decades one half of the name languished in the storerooms of the National Epigraphical Museum in Athens — there are so many fragments here and simply not enough scholars to publish them. If you hold up the loose half — not for too long, this is heavy marble and arms will ache after a while — '*mos*' has been reunited with '*de*'. Fragments currently being re-catalogued.

13 Origin of this phrase disputed, but the most likely relation does now seem to be with a Chinese proverb that originates around the fifth century BC.

14 In Homer's magnificent poetry (and in the absence in 1000–700 BC of a renaissance, a new 'Golden Age', a brilliance visible in the archaeological record), there is in the Hellenic diaspora a keen nostalgia, a sense of underlying disappointment.

15 Aristotle, *Athenian Constitution*, 5.3. Trans. P. J. Rhodes (1984).

16 Solon Frag. 6W = Aristotle, *Ath. Pol.*, 12.2. Trans. P. J. Rhodes (2002) [adapt.].

17 Cat. ref. 3477.

18 The Spartans did not like change. Throughout the sixth century, when a city-state was controlled by a tyrant, rather than the traditional dynasties of aristocratic families, the Spartans would intervene. *Tyrannos* (the word originated in Lydia) at this time did not have the monstrous connotations we tar it with today. Tyrants were frequently supporters of the people. In 510 BC the Delphic Oracle had been bribed to persuade Sparta to intervene in Athenian aristocratic affairs. Isagoras' use of Spartan muscle did not necessarily mean he was a confirmed supporter of the Spartans, but that he was simply forming pragmatic alliances to further his own causes during the stasis of the age.

19 Herodotus, 5.66.

20 Quotation taken from Ober, Raaflaub, and Wallace (co-authors) (2007), 54. For an

up-to-date overview of the origins of Athenian democracy this volume is hard to beat.

21 See Hanson (1986); (1991), 69–71.

22 Aeschylus, *Suppliants*, or *Suppliant Women*, 604; 699.

23 An inscription records offerings made to Demokratia, Tyche and Eirene in 331–330 BC (*IG* II 2, 1496. 131, 140–1). Cf. Smith (2003), 7.

24 One hundred years after Solon's reforms those old families with old, entrenched interests, who had climbed to the stony heights of the Areopagus (the hill is a baby brother to the brooding Acropolis, where schoolkids scramble and slip now), who had been invited in as protectors of the people, appeared self-serving; many were banished, ostracised; the council purged. A neo-conservative counter-revolution seemed certain, a true, full-blown, direct democracy too enormous, too scary an idea to take on. These were uncertain times.

25 Because the Spartans did not write about themselves, we rely almost exclusively on perceptions of their society from outsiders. Paul Cartledge deals with the difficulties of this 'Spartan mirage' for the historian in his masterful *Spartan Reflections* (2001).

26 Thucydides, 2.39. Trans. C. F. Smith (1919).

27 Aristophanes, *Lysistrata*, 18, originally from Homer, *Iliad*, 6.492.

28 Sophocles, *Women of Trachis*, 281–3. Trans. R. C. Jebb (1892).

29 Euripides, *Hecuba*, 639–56. Trans. E. P. Coleridge (1938).

CHAPTER THREE

Socrates in the Agora

1 Trans. J. Fogel (2002).

2 See Theophrastus (372–287 BC), *Enquiry into Plants*.

3 Excavations ongoing. See American School at Athens website www.asca.edu.gr. Well dated to *c.*395–375 BC.

4 Xenophon, *Memorabilia*, 4.2.1.

5 Diogenes Laertius, 2.122.

6 Although the historical existence of Simon is debated, recent work does tend towards his identification as a real man. A useful investigation of the problem and of the influence of the 'Simon' tradition is presented by Sellars (2003).

7 Luis E. Navia concludes his scholarly work, *Antisthenes of Athens; Setting the World Aright* (2001), with a pseudo-Dialogue of Simon.

8 Recent scholarship puts his dates at 450–410 BC. See Sellars, n.6, above.

9 Socrates' divine voice is held responsible for this prescient change of tack. The hand of God is questionable; but the local colour is spot-on.

10 In the fifth century BC, chance meetings with friends or strangers were also thought to augur the future. This was a view to which Socrates subscribed – although adding his own idiosyncratic interpretation. *'However, while some name what forewarns them "birds", "voices", "omens" or "prophets", I call this a "divinity" [daimonion], and I think by naming it thus, I speak more truthfully and more piously than those who attribute the power of gods to the birds. Indeed, I have the following proof that I do not speak falsely concerning the god; for, though I told*

the advice of the god to many friends, never once was I shown to have spoken falsely.' Xenophon, *Apology*, 13. Trans. J. A. Martinez (2002). *'And yet most people say that they are "warned away" or "encouraged" by the birds and the chance meetings; and Socrates expressed it in the way he knew: he said that "the divinity signalled".'* Xenophon, *Memorabilia*, 1.1.4. Trans. J. Fogel (2002).

11 Cf. Zaidman, Pantel and Cartledge (1992), 55.

12 Diogenes Laertius, *Lives of Eminent Philosophers*, Democritus, 9.44–5.

13 Plato's aim here was to 'prove', in hindsight, that Socrates was not a sophist.

14 Plato, *Euthyphro*, 3d. Trans. H. N. Fowler (1914) [adapt.] [LCL].

15 Frag. 12 Kock (Giannantoni I A2).

16 The precise location of the prison is still disputed. The marble-chippings on the floor of the 'prison-house' could either be the result of artisans dispatching the culture of Athens or rough flooring for its troublemakers.

17 Plato, *Crito*, 52b.

18 Sophocles died a few months after Euripides in 406 BC (cf. Aristophanes, *Frogs*, 82). In his last competition at the Dionysia he dressed his chorus and actors in mourning for the death of his fellow playwright. Cf. *OCD* (3rd edn.), 1422–3.

19 Only Plato remained, a self-proclaimed member of Socrates' circle (*Apology*, 34a) and listed with Crito, Critobulus and Apollodorus as offering to pay the fine of thirty minas proposed by Socrates in lieu of the death penalty (*Apology*, 38b). Plato himself would be (briefly) sold into slavery, and Aristotle (originally from Stageira) would be driven from Athens to die in exile.

CHAPTER FOUR
The Stoa of the King

1 Plato, *Euthyphro*, 1b–c.

2 This explains why – thanks to translation issues – in some medieval Arabic texts it was asserted that Socrates was killed by a king. The King Archon's role was to hear indictments and set in motion the business of justice.

3 Isocrates, *Address to the Areopagus*, 30.

4 Demosthenes, *First Philippic*, 35.

5 Here too were said to be the pronouncements of the law-giver Draco – the Athenian whom we still commemorate with our word 'draconian'.

6 Again, see the American School at Athens' excellent publications and website on the excavations of the Agora.

7 Plato, *Euthyphro*, 1c.

8 Although Anytus was a relatively well-to-do merchant and does play a minor part in the political history of the period.

9 Zeus replies to Hermes, Plato, *Protagoras*, 322d.

10 Plato, *Euthyphro*, 2d–3a. Trans. Brickhouse and Smith (2002).

11 Diogenes Laertius, *The Lives and Opinions of Eminent Philosophers*, 2.21. Trans. C. D. Yonge (1853).

12 Plato, *Apology*, 29d–30a. Trans. B. Jowett (1953).

13 Plato, *Crito*, 52c.

14 Socrates did not 'plead guilty', but he accepted that within the legal framework of Athens his charges could be brought before a court.

15 Plato, *Theaetetus*, 210d; see also Plato, *Statesman*, which ends with a discussion of courage.

16 See Stroud (1998).

17 See also Aristophanes, *Clouds*, 770; *Wasps*, 349; Isocrates, 15.237; Demosthenes, *Against Midias*, 103. Also Stroud (1998), Sickinger (2004).

18 The monument is mentioned in Aristophanes, *Peace*, 1183–4, which was produced in 421 BC.

19 In 411 BC fear gripped the city as a conspiracy led by Theramenes, Antiphon and Pisandros (among others) carried out a spate of political killings and succeeded in passing a motion that effectively overthrew one hundred years of democracy – replacing the elected governing bodies with a Council of Four Hundred. In 404 BC, democracy, which had been fleetingly restored in 410 BC, was overthrown once more, Theramenes again playing a leading role in its downfall. Pisandros was among those who had benefited from the mutilation of the Herms in 415 BC. Cf. Meier (1999), 558.

20 *Sycophantai* in Greek were originally, oddly, 'tale-tellers about figs'. The phrase arose (possibly) because Athenians were not allowed to export anything other than olives from their largely infertile territory. Figs were sometimes smuggled out. Those who shopped the smugglers were 'tale-tellers of figs'. The journey into the English 'sycophant' is therefore rather a convoluted one.

21 Xenophon, *Apology*, 1.2–4. Trans. J. A. Martinez (2002) [adapt.].

22 Many thanks to James Davidson for his help with this point of fact.

23 Indictment quoted in Diogenes Laertius, *On the Lives and Opinions of Eminent Philosophers*, 2.40, and paraphrased in Plato, *Apology*, 24b; *Euthyphro*, 3b; Xenophon, *Memorabilia*, 1.1.1, 1.2.64; *Apology*, 10. When his charges were first read out it was just Socrates, the Archon and one or two witnesses whom history has forgotten. Nb. Brought a 'public action' can also be translated as 'written a sworn indictment against'.

CHAPTER FIVE

The first blood sacrifice

1 Trans. Brickhouse and Smith (2002).

2 *The Athenian Agora Site Guide*, http://www.attalos.com/cgi-bin/feature?lookup= siteguide:26 and http://www.attalos.com/cgi-bin/image?lookup=1997.01.0512, in *Hesperia*, 40 (1971), plate 50. The block was certainly used by the archons when they stood upon it each year to swear their oath to preserve the laws of the city. The exact location of the animal sacrifice is uncertain, although the worn surface of the stone shows this was much used over the centuries. The sacrifice would certainly have taken place very close at hand.

3 Aristotle, *Ath. Pol.*, 57.2, states that the Archon took his myrtle wreath off when presiding over murder trials outside – indicating that for a trial such as that of Socrates, he possibly kept it on.

4 See Miller (1989), esp. 321.

5 Homer, *Iliad*, 3.299–301.

6 IG13 40 (ML 52), 3–4; Andocides, *On the Mysteries*, 1.97; Lycurgus, *Against Leocrates*, 79.

7 Cf. Ober (1991), 142.

8 Plato, *Apology*, 25a. Trans. B. Jowett (1953).

9 A three-obol stipend was paid to jurors for a day's service from the late fifth century to the later part of the fourth. This figure started at 2 obols under Pericles and was raised to 3 obols in the 430s or 420s. Cf. Ober (1989), 142.

10 For majority vote to decide a man's fate (when those voters sat in the court not by virtue of birth, or wealth, or military prowess, or sporting trophies faded in the home, still burning bright in the memory) was a defining shift in human history. And although the Athenians did not know that, two and a half millennia on, nations, leaders and continents would look back to these pungent, frequent gatherings as the birth of 'the West', they did know that they had responsibility and power. This had been the system in Athens for close on one hundred years.

11 The Athenians also relied on amateurs for the smooth operation of the court. On the day you arrived, your name might or might not be pulled out of a box full of the names (ten boxes, one for each tribe) of those in the courtroom; one might be given the job of keeping his eye on the water-clock, five to sort out payment of jurors (3 obols per day), four to count the voting, etc.

12 See Demosthenes, *Against Neaira* 66, Apollodoros' case against the Corinthian prostitute Neaira; 'If it is determined that the prosecutor is a *moichos* [which loosely translates as a sexual philanderer], his sureties are to hand him over to the man who caught him, and that man is to do to the prosecutor, as he would to a *moichos*, whatever he wishes in the courtroom, only not using a knife.' Also Ps-Dem 59.

13 Xenophon, *Apology*, 14.

14 No barristers, attorneys or QCs here; the defendant had to defend himself. The very fact that Socrates seemed – by all extant accounts – unfazed by the task in hand is a great advert for his idiosyncratic approach to life. What Socrates does not appear to have lacked is self-confidence and his own particular brand of self-belief.

> 'Well I am *certainly wiser than this man. It is only too likely that neither of us has any knowledge to boast of; but he thinks that he knows something which he does not know, whereas I am quite conscious of my ignorance. At any rate it seems that I am wiser than he is to this small extent, that I do not think that I know what I do not know.'* Plato, *Apology*, 21d. Trans. H. Tredennick (1954).

The philosopher's reasoning is charismatic. Once the mind has tussled with, and worked through, the right way of doing things, the soul can act. A life becomes an accretion of right, helpful decisions. Socrates tells us that knowledge brings *arete*, virtue/personal happiness. Virtue is knowledge. If we do everything we can to avoid ignorance, and to do what is good, then peace of mind presents itself. He admits to being odd, but seems genuinely to believe that he has done nothing through his life other than try to find 'the good' in the world. His serenity is axiomatic. By all accounts, this was not a distressed man in the dock.

CHAPTER SIX

Checks, balances and magic-men

1 Trans. G. M. A. Grube (1997).

2 The system of secret ballots had been introduced to prevent cronyism, to banish the nightmare-memories of the years of civil war. There were other ways the Athenians tried to keep things fair – see pp. 51–53.

3 For a full discussion of this aspect of the Athenian legal system, see work by Christopher A. Faraone, University of Chicago, e.g., *Curses and Social Control in the Law Courts of Classical Athens*, first delivered as a lecture at the conference 'Democracy, Law and Social Control' at the Historisches Kolleg, Munich, June 1998.

4 DTA, 107, Attic, late fifth or early fourth century BC (DTA = R. Wunsch [1897], *Defixionum Tabellae Atticae*, Appendix to Inscriptiones Graecae III, Berlin).

5 Plato, *Republic*, 364e–5a. Trans. P. Shorey (1930) [adapt.] [LCL].

6 That is, the gods were showing their divine will by random selection.

7 Athenians were an extremely litigious society, but this was not a society of lawyers. The Athenians had to represent themselves – occasionally with a kind of 'phone a friend' policy, when *synegoroi* (friends and relatives) could speak during some of the time allotted to the disputant.

CHAPTER SEVEN

Persuade or obey

1 Trans. H. Tredennick (1954).

2 Hansen (2006).

3 As Cynthia Farrar points out in 'Power to the People', in Ober, Raaflaub and Wallace (2007).

4 Socrates was in fact anti the brand of *demokratia* found in Athens for sixty out of his seventy years (462–411, 410–404, 403–399). Philosophically he did not accept the infallibility of equality: one of the reasons he had reservations about the selection for high office by lot.

5 Euripides, *The Suppliant Women*, 404–18. Trans. P. Vellacott (1972).

6 In Plato's estimation, Socrates did not believe in allotting absolute power to the many, but in appointing experts to oversee political affairs. His friendship with Simon the Shoemaker was a small example of this attitude; Simon knew what he was good at (making shoes) and so he stuck at it. Socrates approved. Socrates also appeared to be fascinated by the Spartan focus on being a 'perfect' soldier. Again, the philosopher saw the sense in this. Better in his mind to do what you are particularly good at than to be a dilettante, a Jack-of-all-trades. His vision of political power was prophetic – it is the style of democracy that we all live with today. The restricted 'Western-style' democracy – benign dictatorships – where experts are elected to run things for the masses is that which he would best recognise. The democracy that killed Socrates remained unconscionable for well over 1,500 years. Here is Wordsworth in 1794: '*I am of that odious class of men called democrats*'; and here the education minister Robert Lowe,

opposing the Reform Bill of 1867: *'Surely the heroic work of so many centuries, the matchless achievements of so many wise heads and strong hands, deserves a nobler consummation than to be sacrificed at the shrine of revolutionary passion or the maudlin enthusiasm of humanity . . . History may tell of other acts as signally disastrous, but of none more wanton, none more disgraceful.'* Cf. Roberts (1994).

7 Pettifogging was an issue, and many – the *sycophantai*, the sycophants – brought cases purely to make money. Yet Socrates' crimes were far more worrying than the daily grind of rapes, boundary disputes, murders, petty thefts. Mockery of the gods and corruption of youth, those flowers of the great Athenian city, are not accusations you bring lightly.

8 This refers to the episode when large numbers of Athenians had offered Ionian Greeks help (against the Persians) after the Spartan King Cleomenes had rejected their call. Herodotus, 5.97.

9 Only one of Socrates' prosecutors, Anytus, with the evidence we have available to us, can be tracked in documents or contemporary literature. It is possible that Meletus and Lycon were the hired hands of political machinators.

10 Plato, *Apology*, 23e.

11 Plato, *Meno*, 94e. Trans. W. R. M. Lamb (1924) [LCL].

12 A public trial (*graphē*) such as this would have been allotted a full day in court. Cf. Lanni (2006), 37 n.102. Little weight was placed upon the evidence of the witnesses – what mattered were the speeches. The plaintiff would speak first, his speech timed by the water-clock (*klepsydra*), which was allowed to flow during the speech and stopped for the reading of the evidence. The time allocated to a speech was measured in terms of the volume of water that the clocks contained (1 *khous* = approx. 5¼ imperial pints). From the only surviving Athenian *klepsydra* that we have, it seems 2 *khoes* would take approximately six minutes to drain. Based upon these figures, it has been (tentatively) argued that the speeches at public trials could have been roughly two hours long. Cf. Todd (1993), 130–33.

13 Plato, *Apology*, 37a–b. Trans. G. M. A. Grube (1997).

14 In 433 BC, a sundial was set up on the Pnyx by Meton (Munn [2006], 201). On Meton and Socrates, see Plutarch, *Alcibiades*, 17.4–5 Munn (2006).

15 Socrates in Aristophanes, *Clouds*, 743–5. See, as an alternative translation, McLeish (1979): *'Stop wriggling. If you come to a dead end, / Turn your analysis round, and take it back / To the nearest crossroads of thought. Look round, / Get the new direction right, and start again.'*

16 In a landscape that had embraced the measurement of time in a prescriptive and predictable way (*parapegmata* and *klepsydra*), Socrates' apparent random questioning appeared counter-intuitive, anti-progressive. Questions such as his were unsettling; they could stick in the memory like burrs. It was easy answers that were more readily forgotten.

   SOCRATES: Following this I questioned one man after another, always conscious of the anger and hatred that I provoked, which distressed and alarmed me. But necessity drove me on, the word of Apollo, I thought, must be considered first.

   The juror-judges were old hands at this game. Men delighted to take up the 3 obols day pay – not to be sniffed at when the courts sat every third, sometimes every second day. They knew how the system worked, how it was played. And judging from the outcome of this trial, they did not take to unorthodoxy. See Hansen (1999), p.186. Courts sat 175–225 days per year.

17 Diverting to think that modern-day lawyers are the children of the Age of Heroes
   – of Achilles, Ajax and Hector.
18 Plato, *Apology*, 18d. Trans. Brickhouse and Smith (2002) [adapt.].
19 Plato, *Apology*, 28a–b. Trans. Brickhouse and Smith.

CHAPTER EIGHT

Peitho, the power of persuasion

1 Existing temple founded mid-fourth century BC.
2 Isocrates, 5.249a. Trans. G. Norlin (1980); Demosthenes, *Pro.*, 54.
3 Sappho, F 57a. Trans. H. T. Wharton (1885).
4 Sappho, F 96.
5 *Inscriptiones Graecae* III.351.
6 Pausanias, 1.43.5 and 5.11.8.
7 Aeschylus, *The Eumenides*, 970–96. Trans. P. Vellacott (1956).
8 Paraphrased from Sir Edward Bysshe, *The Memorable Thoughts of Socrates* (1747), 49.
9 Plato, *Apology*, 28a–b. Trans. Brickhouse and Smith (2002).

CHAPTER NINE

Alopeke: a philosopher is born

1 Trans. Brickhouse and Smith (2002).
2 An unsourced quotation attributed to Socrates, still cited by scholars today, e.g.,
   Rotberg (2004), viii.
3 The Acropolis is 490 feet above sea level.
4 At this time there were ten tribes and 139 *deme*-districts in Athens.
5 Plato, *Gorgias*, 495d.
6 See Aristotle, *Ath. Pol.*, 21.
7 Aristophanes, *Acharnians*, 247–70.
8 Plato, *Republic*, 475d. For the Rural Dionysia, see Whitehead (1986).
9 C. Meier (1999), 3, cites the Persian advance and flight by Athenians as taking place
   in 'the late summer of 480 BC, most likely towards the end of September'.
10 Herodotus, 7.144.
11 Herodotus, 7.56.
12 Herodotus, 9.1–15.
13 Athens was occupied a second time in 479 BC, and the Persians were defeated at the
   Battles of Plataea and Mycale as they had been in *c*.490 BC at Marathon.
14 We hear from Socrates in the Dialogue *Cratylus* that the philosopher himself did
   believe that names had this inherent power. Amusingly, the nickname of Socrates'
   disciple Plato came from his prowess on the wrestling field. He was Plato (*platus*),
   'broad' or 'brick-built'.
15 Diogenes Laertius, *Lives of Eminent Philosophers*, 2.5.1.
16 The ancient tradition that Socrates carved the statues of the three graces on the

Acropolis is attested in Pausanias, 1.22.3, but disputed by modern scholarship (cf. *Kleine Pauly*, 'Sokrates'); the tradition is most likely a confusion with the sculptor Socrates of Thebes, a contemporary of Pindar and mentioned by Pausanias, 9.25.3. Marble masons today are found serving the First Cemetery in modern Dafnis, close to Alopeke.

17 These fifty men were referred to as being 'in the *prytany*'.

18 Aristides, *Or.*, 34.38. This quotation appears in Aelius Aristides' speech, *Against those who burlesque the mysteries*. Trans. Elsner (2007), 30. Contemporary source material focuses mainly on the amount of gold used to cover the statue (because Pheidias stood accused of embezzlement).

19 Lapatin (2007), 132–3.

20 At the time of writing, the Oxford University Experimental Quantum Computation with Ion Traps project has just managed to photograph atoms. See www.physics.ox.ac.uk/al/people/lucas.htm. Many thanks to Dr David Lucas for his demonstration of this phenomenon.

21 See Diogenes Laertius, 9.54.

22 The Parian Marble records that this took place in 467 BC: Diels-Kranz, 59 A 11; cf. Pliny, *Natural History*, 2.149. Aegospotami will witness Athens' final sea-defeat in the Peloponnesian War in 405 BC.

23 Plato, *Crito*, 50a.

24 Loose brotherhoods of loyalty, joined together by blood-relationships and cult practice.

25 Harris (1989).

26 'Violet-crowned': especially of Athens: Pindar, Frag. 76; (cf. B.5.3); Aristophanes, *Acharnians*, 637; *Knights*, 1323. But also used of others earlier, e.g., Hom. Hym., 6.8; Solon, 19.4; Theognis, 250.

27 Plutarch, *On Socrates' Divine Sign*, 20 (589e).

28 Diogenes Laertius, *Lives of Eminent Philosophers*, 2.31. Trans. R. D. Hicks (1925) [adapt.].

29 Plato, *Apology*, 38a. Trans. G. M. A. Grube (1997).

CHAPTER TEN

Kerameikos – potters and beautiful boys

1 These new walls enclosed an area of nearly 1 square mile (1⅛ square miles inc. Piraeus).

2 Cf. Thucydides, 1.89.3. The Persian commander Mardonius had destroyed virtually all of the original walls by the time of his final withdrawal. Cf. Herodotus, 9.13.2.

3 City walls were built quickly from 479 BC and the Long Walls project ran from the 460s through the 450s, completed *c.*445 BC.

4 Cf. Thucydides, 1.93.1–2. Themistocles also persuaded the Athenians to complete the building of the walls of the Piraeus (Thucydides, 1.93.3).

5 Zephaniah, 3.6. See also 1.7–18. Trans. New Living Translation.

6 Zephaniah, 1.2–6. Trans. New Living Translation.

7 Thucydides, 1.124. Trans. P. Woodruff (1993).

8 Cf. Thucydides, 1.90–2.

9 See also Plutarch, *Moralia* Vol. III

10 In 462 a democratic judicial reform of the Areopagus squared the democratic circle (other landmarks included the institution of pay for juries in the 450s, raised by Cleon in the 420s). See Thucydides, 1.100; Plutarch, *Cimon*, 12–13.

11 Other city-states were conducting political experiments at this time. Sparta's fabled social reforms were thought to have started back in the seventh century BC. India too had been experimenting with democratic forms of government.

12 Vase-paintings from the period tell us that tortoises were a very popular pet in ancient Athens.

13 Aristophanes, *Knights*, 1398–1401. Adapted from LCL 1998.

14 The Kerameikos was the kind of place that attracted scandal. Themistocles – the architect of the naval fleet – was said to have driven through here at dawn in a chariot pulled by four courtesans.

15 Xenarchus, 4 K-A; Eubulus, 67 and 82 K-A.

16 See Aeschines, *Against Timarchos*, *passim*.

17 Plato, *Republic*, 2.357b. Trans. P. Shorey (1930).

18 Diogenes Laertius, *Lives of Eminent Philosophers*, 2.31. Trans. C. D. Yonge (1853).

19 Plato, *Phaedo*, 96a, 98b. Trans. H. N. Fowler (1914).

20 Traditionally, an Athenian boy's education was less to do with learning facts than with developing a moral character. The *kitharistes* taught a musical instrument and lyrical thought; the *paidotribes* worked on the body and sports; and the three basic Rs were down to the *grammatistes*. In our overloaded information age this development of spirit, of character, can seem appealing. But the eager minds of the fledgling democracy wanted more. They wanted new data to juggle with imagination. And perhaps too they wanted, in this city of splendid possibilities, to spread their wings a little. Fragments of Greek thought circulating at this time, when Socrates was a young man, suggest that Athenian education was geared to inciting both *aidos* and *sophrosune* – a sense of shame and a sense of moderation. See Democritus (D-K 68 B179). In other words, education was devised to keep young men in their place.

21 Athens was a city that worked to a regular, languid, predictable biological beat. That insistent dripping water-clock, that marking of hours in the court, was still, in many ways, a spectre of the future. The rise of the moon and the turn of the seasons marked time here. Rituals that celebrated these events dictated when the fields were worked, when harvests were gathered, when wars were started. The ideal rhythm of the city was utterly unsyncopated. Disruption meant *stasis*, and *stasis* meant the disintegration of the body politic. *Stasis* was a Greek's greatest fear.

22 Our source is Plato, *Parmenides*, 127a. Plato's account tells us that Parmenides was about sixty-five when he made the visit in around 450 BC. But if we depend on Apollodorus' *Chronicles*, then Parmenides was born *c*.544/541 BC. Did Parmenides visit Athens as a very old man? Is Plato imagining the encounter? Zeno came from the southern Italian town of Elea. It seems he rarely left his home-town. Plato may indeed have fabricated the meeting between Socrates and these two 'fathers' of philosophy – and yet, if we know that so many did flood to Athens at this time, why not these two?

23 Plato, *Parmenides*, 127b–c. Trans. F. M. Cornford (1973). Cf. *Sophist*, 217c.

24 This event was almost certainly reserved for the elite of society. The fact that we do not hear of Socrates participating is further evidence that he was low-born.

25 See Davidson (2007), *passim.*

26 I have relied here heavily on Davidson (2007).

27 Aristophanes, *Frogs*, 1096.

CHAPTER ELEVEN

Pericles: high society, and democracy as high theatre

1   Trans. Brickhouse and Smith (2002) [adapt.].

2   *PCG* iv *Thrattai* Frag. 73=Plutarch, *Pericles*, 13.16. Trans. Miller (2004), 219.

3   Once an ambitious pretender to Athena's throne, Cylon, had attempted to take Athens by taking the Acropolis. His bid failed, and he and his entourage looked set to starve up on the Acropolis rock. But this would mean pollution. The failed agitators were promised safe passage – but Pericles' ancestors wanted revenge, and even though Cylon et al. clung to the altar of the Furies, they were hacked down. Thus men with blood on their hands, and their families, were exiled.

4   *Rhetor* came to mean professional politician in Athens.

5   Plutarch, *Pericles*, 16.3; Hansen (1999), 38.

6   Thucydides, 2.65.8–9. Trans. R. Warner (1972).

7   During Pericles' rivalry with Cimon (late 460s/early 450s), he introduced payment for juries (in response to Cimon's philanthropy with private funds). Cf. Aristotle, *Ath. Pol.*, 27.3–4; Plato, *Gorgias*, 515e; and Nails (2002), 225.

8   Thucydides, 2.60.5. Trans. D. Kagan (1981).

9   Cf. Meier (1995), 389–90.

10 Cf. Lapatin (2007), 127.

11 The exact appearance of the original Odeion (which was burned down in 86 BC during Sulla's siege of Athens) is unknown; Vitruvius (5.9.1, first century BC) alleges that it had a wooden roof made from the spoils of Persian ships. What is certain is that it was a structure on a colossal scale with a forest of interior columns.

12 Cf. Plutarch, *Pericles*, 13.9–11. And the frieze of the Parthenon was perhaps inspired by decorative work at Persepolis.

13 Cf. Isocrates, *Antidosis*, 235, and Wallace (2007), 225.

14 Olympiodoros, *Commentary on Plato's Alcibiades*, 138.4–11. '*The songs which Perikles learned from Damon through which he harmonized the city.*'

15 Plutarch, *Pericles*, 13. Cf. Wallace (2007), 226, and Kimball and Edgell (2001), 91.

16 *PCG* iv *Thrattai* Frag. 73=Plutarch, *Pericles*, 13.6. Trans. Miller (2004), 219.

17 Anaximander, recorded in Censorinus, *De Die Natali*, 4.7.

18 Simplicius, *In Phys.*, 156, 13ff. [Diels-Kranz 59 B12].

19 Cf. Plato, *Phaedrus*, 270a. Trans. H. Fowler [LCL].

20 Socrates would have been very young when he went to Pericles' house. There is a possibility that he never did, and just met Anaxagoras elsewhere in the city. Plato's use of Aspasia, Pericles' consort, in his dialogue, though, might suggest that Socrates had an early acquaintance with the two in Pericles' own home (which Pericles shared with Aspasia).

21 Aristophanes, *Clouds*, 157–68. See also trans. McLeish (1979): STUDENT: *Chairephon asked him his opinion on gnats: / 'Do they buzz from the front end . . . or the back?' /* STREPSIADES:

And what was his opinion concerning gnats? / STUDENT: *He explained that the guts of a gnat* / *Are hollow, a sort of narrow tube. The air* / *Is sucked in at the front, and forced* / *Under pressure* / *down and out the back.* / *It's the narrowness of the hole that makes the noise.* / STREPSIADES: *It's* / *a kind of trumpet, then, a gnat's behind?* / *What a brilliant man he must be,* / *What an expert on* / *gnat's anatomy!* / *Compared to that, it's child's play to win in court.*

22 Plato, *Protagoras*, 314e–16a.

23 Plato, *Phaedo*, 97c. Trans. H. N. Fowler (1914) [adapt.] [LCL].

24 Socrates advised against going on trying to work out the astronomical properties of the heavens, *'their distances from the earth, their orbits and their sources'*. Xenophon, *Memorabilia*, 4.7.4–5. Trans. J. Fogel (2002). Socrates, it seems, stared up into the night sky, to comprehend its usefulness and its beauty – but not to understand it as a series of scientific facts: *'He said that these things were capable too of filling up a person's lifetime, and of stopping one from pursuing many useful kinds of learning.'* Xenophon, *Memorabilia*, 4.7.5. Trans. J. Fogel (2002).

25 See, e.g., Athens Acropolis Museum, 607. Base for a ritual water-basin dedicated by Smikythe the washerwoman, or Athens National Archaeological Museum, x6837, miniature shield with the face of a Gorgon dedicated by Phrygia the bread-seller.

26 Although most wealthy Athenians had country estates where their food was grown, many managed the running of the estates themselves. Socrates did not fall into this social category.

27 See also current excavations at Vari led by Barbara Tsakrigis.

28 Some sources tell us that Pericles' clever bedmate Aspasia also held salons at the home that she, unofficially, shared with the General. Scandalously Aspasia was allowed to speak; even more shockingly, Pericles invited not just his colleagues, but their wives to hear what she had to say.

29 Herodotus said of Babylon *'the magnificence of this city is not matched anywhere else in the world'*. In Egypt the mighty pyramids at Giza, monuments of polished stone decorated with the carvings of animals, stood as testimony to the powers of human endeavour (Herodotus, 2.124.1–125.7).

30 Herodotus, 3.80.

CHAPTER TWELVE

Delos – and the birth of an empire

1 Trans. W. R. M. Lamb (1925) [LCL].

2 Herodotus, 6.46–7. Trans. A. De Sélincourt (1954).

3 Gold wreath with myrtle, apple and pear blossom, late fourth century BC. Archaeological Museum of Thessaloniki (restored as part of the 'History Lost' exhibition, made up of pieces rescued from the illicit antiquities trade, presented by the Hellenic Foundation for Culture).

4 Cf. Powell (2nd edn., 2001), 20–1.

5 Cf. Meier (1999), 291.

6 Thucydides, 1.100; Plutarch, *Cimon*, 12–13.

7 Eventually, the Peace of Callias came in *c.*449 BC, an agreement between Athens and

Persia to stop hostilities. In theory the League could be disbanded; but everyone guessed that this was no real peace, just an uneasy stand-off.

8 List taken from pp. 125–6 of Beard (2002).

CHAPTER THIRTEEN

Purple ambition

1 Trans. R. Warner (1972).

2 Trans. Brickhouse and Smith (2002).

3 IGI3 259–72 9EM6647 + 13453 + 13454.

4 Meiggs (1972). See Appendix 14 for a wonderfully comprehensive catalogue of all six tribute districts. See also J. Hale (2010).

5 Rhodes (2005), 174.

6 Cf. French (2006), 121–2.

7 Cf. Rhodes (2007), 221–2.

8 Thucydides, 3.82.1–2. Trans. R. Warner (1972).

9 The one building on the Acropolis that would inspire Pausanias to a whole paragraph 700 years later. Construction did not begin on the Erechtheion until 420 BC.

10 Plutarch, *Pericles*, 13.1–3.

11 In this section I have relied heavily on Mary Beard's fine little book *The Parthenon* (2002).

12 Material presented by Dr Alexandros Mantis, Director of the Acropolis Ephorate, Greek Archaeological Committee (UK) Lecture, 22 October 2008, King's College London.

13 Cimon's relative Thucydides, son of Melesias: Plutarch, *Pericles*, 12.2 and 14.2.

14 Thucydides, 2.61.4; 64.5–6. Trans. R. Warner (1972).

15 The pro-Athenian King Evagoras, born in Salamis in 435 BC, worked with the Persians to rout Spartan forces, his ambition to reunite the eastern Mediterranean under Athenian rule, with Cyprus its easternmost outpost. Evagoras was given honorary Athenian citizenship (*c*.407 BC) and honoured with the erection of a statue next to the Stoa of Zeus Eleutherios, in the Athenian Agora. See Karageorghis (1982).

16 Plato, *Alcibiades*, I, 134b. What we do not know is how terrible – or not – he thought it to be *apolis*, cityless or exiled from the city. As Herodotus and Sophocles had already made clear, this was a fate of tragic status. Nb In 399 BC Socrates refused to flee the city.

17 Plato, *Phaedrus*, 279b–c.

18 Thucydides, 1.10.2. Trans. R. Warner (1972).

19 Alcman, *Partheneion*, 3.61.

20 Homer, *Odyssey*, 13.412; *Iliad*, 3.443.

21 See *The River Eurotas Monuments*, Ministry of Culture, 5th Ephorate of Prehistoric and Classical Antiquities, Sparta (2008).

22 King Agesilaus in Plutarch, *Moralia*, 217e (cf. 210e).

23 The historian Xenophon had fought for the Spartans as a mercenary. Perhaps Xenophon exaggerated Socrates' Spartan affiliation in his *Oeconomicus*. But unless he wanted to be laughed out of town, there must have been a kernel of truth in the

historian-general's opinion. These Laconophile tendencies have already been flagged in Aristophanes' *Birds*, 414 BC.

24 Plato, *Crito*, 53b. Trans. G. M. A. Grube.

25 Plato, *Parmenides*, 128c. Trans. M. Gill and P. Ryan (1997).

26 Plato, *Republic*, 8.558a–c. Trans. G. M. A. Grube, rev. C. D. C. Reeve, in Cooper (1997) [adapt.].

27 Authors include Aristophanes, Thucydides, Xenophon, Plato, Plutarch, Andocides, Lysias and Demosthenes.

28 See recent discussion of this mosaic by H. A. Shapiro in *Art in Athens during the Peloponnesian War* ed. Olga Palagia. CUP 2009. Chap 10 *passim*.

CHAPTER FOURTEEN

Paddling in the river, sweating in the gym: Socratic youth

1 Trans. J. Fogel (2002) [adapt.].

2 See Chapter 53 where Socrates bathes before he dies.

3 Plato, *Phaedrus*, 229a. Trans. H. N. Fowler (1954) [LCL].

4 Plato, *Apology*, 40c. Trans. H. Tredennick (1954).

5 Plato, *Phaedrus*, 230b–d. Trans. H. N. Fowler (1954) [LCL].

6 Theognis, 1335–6. See also trans. by T. K. Hubbard (2003).

7 Sarla, Evangelou and Tsimpidis-Pentazos (1973), 26; Plutarch, *Themistocles*, 1.

8 Aristophanes, *The Knights*, 309.

9 Now in Athens' Epigraphical Museum, cat. no. 12553.

10 Pseudo-platonic Axiochus, 364a–5a. Trans. J. P. Hershbell [adapt.].

11 Herodotus describes a sanctuary here in 490/89 BC. The 'white-bitch' or 'swift-dog' was supposed to have stolen a piece of sacrificial meat offered by the wealthy Athenian Diodymous. Suda k2721 e3160

12 Herodotus, 5.63.

CHAPTER FIFTEEN

Gym-hardened fighting men

1 Trans. J. Davidson (2007).

2 Plato, *Lysis*, 203a; *Euthydemus*, 271a.

3 Aristophanes, *Clouds*, 1005–15. Trans. A. H. Sommerstein (1973) [adapt.].

4 Themistocles tried to tempt non-*nothoi* down here, to break class barriers, as it were. And after Socrates' death, a disciple of his, Antisthenes, set up a 'Socratic' school at Kynosarges – but partly because of its sub-prime reputation, the venture never had the lasting impact of the Academy or the Lyceum.

5 The *ephebes* went on to cite as their witnesses an impressive array of gods and goddesses to this oath: '*Aglauros, Hestia, Enyo, Enyalios, Ares and Athena Areia, Zeus, Thallo, Auxo, Hegemone, Herakles, (and) the boundaries of my fatherland, the wheat, the barley, the vines, the olives, the figs.*' If you considered going back on your words, there would have been very few

places to run to, nowhere to hide. Trans. P. Harding, quoted in Loren J. Samons, *What's Wrong with Democracy? From Athenian Practice to American Worship*, Ch. 2.

6 At first it appears that we have opened a window onto a violent society. The literary evidence seems to back up this picture – just think of the gore of Greek tragedy, the chill of Aristotle's words '*revenge is sweet*' (Aristotle, *Rhet.*, 1370b30), or of the *lex talionis* – a tacit understanding that all civilians, Hellenic and Barbarian alike, could be killed or enslaved during warfare (cf. Thucydides, 3.36). But in comparative terms, Athens was an ordered place, focused – particularly in Socrates' youth and middle-age – on trying to achieve some kind of heroic perfection on earth that was not animated by blood-lust.

7 Gabriel Herman discusses this in 'How Violent was Athenian Society?' in Hornblower and Osborne (1994). See also Herman (2006).

8 Thucydides, 1.6.3. Trans. R. Warner (1972) [adapt.].

9 Antiphon, *Tetralogies*, 2.1.1; 2.2.3–7. Translation taken from Davidson (2007), 69. Ch. 3, 'Age-classes, Love-rules and Corrupting the Young' is extremely helpful for anyone interested in the issues of age divisions in Athens.

10 *Theaetetus*, 169bc. Nb Although Plato's background as a wrestler encouraged his overuse of athletic and wrestling metaphors in his Dialogues, his portrayal of Socrates as a keen competitor rings true. This statement is in fact an allegory for the need to wrestle with words. It also echoes Socrates' predilection for the thoughts of, e.g., Hesiod, quoted at Plato, *Republic*, 364d.

> *Vice in abundance is easy to get*
> *The road is smooth and begins beside you,*
> *But the gods have put sweat between us and virtue.*

Trans. G. M. A. Grube, rev. C. D. C. Reeve (1997). See Ch. 35.

11 Plutarch, *Agesilaus*, 34.7. Trans. J. Davidson (2007).

12 Numerous refs. See, e.g., Bacchylides, *Ode* 17.

CHAPTER SIXTEEN

'Golden Age' Athens

1 Trans. E. O'Neill, Jr (1938).

2 Konstam and Hoffman (2004).

3 The new Acropolis Museum does what the Attic landscape once did naturally. The soft, sand-blasted porous concrete inside the Museum building is designed not to fight for the light – it is those lifelike sculptures and cast figures that greedily grab the light-lines.

4 See Rose (2003). See also Aristotle, *History of Animals*, 585b, 586a, and Aristotle, *Generation of Animals*, 721b.

5 Plato, *Crito*, 52e–53a. Trans. H. N. Fowler (1914) [LCL].

6 A lost work by Aristophanes of Byzantium, *The Vocabulary of Age-groups*, explained exactly how this system worked.

7 Aeschines, 1.173, 170. Trans. J. Davidson (2007).

8 The Greeks don't seem to have made a connection with the fact that most Athenians

didn't marry until their early forties (Aristotle thought thirty-seven was the perfect age to get hitched) and so in their middle years were probably in a state of permanent semi-arousal. The roaring trade of those brothels is also explained.

9 Aristophanes, *Peace*, 762–4. Trans. E. O'Neill, Jr (1938).

10 Plato, *Charmides*, 155d.

11 Xenophon, *Apology*, 20.

12 Plato, *Apology*, 23c–d. Trans. Brickhouse and Smith (2002).

13 In Libanius' fourth-century AD *Apology of Socrates*, the aristocratic poets that Socrates is said to have quoted, and therefore used to corrupt the young men of Athens, are Pindar and Theognis.

14 In the fifth century BC the mechanics of the fleet (which meant a big boost to the economy and a massive influx of people to Attica) encouraged the Athenians to define 'metics' (literally someone who has transferred homes) as foreigners, as 'others' (as opposed to citizens). Then in 445/4, the citizenship lists were purged: Philochorus, FGr Hist 328 F119; Plutarch, *Pericles*, 37.4; Stadter (1989), 336–9 (from p.137 of Raaflaub, *The Origins of Democracy*).

CHAPTER SEVENTEEN
Aspasia – *Sophe Kai Politike*

1 Pseudo-Xenophon, *Constitution of the Athenians* 2.2. *See also Xenophon Poroi.*

2 The early history and geology of Miletus are thoroughly documented in Greaves (2002).

3 An extremely useful introduction to Greek philosophy, which details the lives of the thinkers mentioned here, is Brunschwig and Lloyd (2000).

4 See also Hippocratic Corpus, DW ('On Diseases of Women,' 36 of the Hippocratic Corpus) 1.2, L 8.14; DW 1.3, L 8.22.

5 See, e.g., Aristotle PA 650a8 ff.; GA 775a14–20.

6 Aristotle, *Politics*, 1.1260a (quoting Sophocles, *Ajax*, 293).

7 See also the disputations of Demosthenes in the fourth century BC.

8 Free women were alluring, petrifying things. The story of the prostitute Neaira, brought up in the house of Nikarete as her 'daughter', shows that sex with a 'free woman' came at a higher premium than sex with a slave.

9 Xenophon, *Oeconomicus*, 7.30. Trans. S. Blundell (1998).

10 Xenophon, *Oeconomicus*, 7.5. Trans. H. G. Dakyns (1890).

11 Euripides, *Orestes*, 108.

12 Frag. 205, Jensen.

13 Lysias 3 [*Simon*].6. Trans W. R. M. Lamb (1930) [LCL].

14 Cratinus, *Cheirons*, Frags 246 268 K-A.

15 Eupolis, *Demes* (110 K-A) produced 411 BC. Interestingly in his play *Philoi*, produced in 424/3, Aspasia was described, in effect, as a ball-breaker, and in the *Marikas*, which beat Aristophanes' *Clouds* in the drama competition of 423, she was mentioned as a 'bastard' child.

16 Clearchus of Soli, *Erotika*, Frag. 26, Frag. 30.

17 Madeleine Henry's discussion of Aspasia's reception in *Prisoner of History* (1995) is

enormously helpful for anyone interested in Aspasia. Nb. Interesting that the male collective *hetairoi* refers to an aristocratic band of intimate comrades.

18 See Plutarch, *Pericles*, 24 and 32.

19 See Bicknell, (1982) 240–50, and the analysis of this gravestone (*IG* II 2, 7394).

20 An interesting side-effect of this legislation was an increased focus on women in the body politic. Women both became more prominent on vase-paintings and painted frescoes and were mentioned more often in inscriptions. They were also subject to tighter legal controls.

21 Close on Pericles' death in 429 BC, the Assembly, with honorific motives, passed a decree that accepted Pericles Junior as an Athenian citizen.

22 There are rare exceptions. The poet Sappho had a brother who (we are told) bought the freedom of a feisty-sounding girl called Rhodopis. Rhodopis ran businesses in Egypt, made a tidy profit – and dedicated one-tenth (in the form of iron spits, early money) of her fortune to Apollo at Delphi. An anachronistic but useful parallel is to look at the career of Theodora, Empress of Byzantium, who, via increasingly helpful liaisons with increasingly wealthy men, and eventually by marrying the Emperor Justinian, managed in the sixth century AD to access control of the most powerful civilisation in the eastern Mediterranean.

23 Cratinus, *Cheirons*, Frag. 258 K-A and 259 K-A, in Henry (1995).

24 See Plato, *Menexenus*; *Symposium*; Aristophanes, *Archarnians*; Xenophon, *Memorabilia, Oeconomicus*.

25 Aristotle, *Rhetoric*, 1398b. Trans. H. C. Lawson-Tancred (1991).

26 Aspasia suffered particularly at the hands of early Christian scholars and copyists: as a pagan philosopher who was not only female, but overtly sexual, she was prime material for censorship. This goes a long way to explain why we know so much and yet so little about her. Interesting that the Christian neo-Platonist Synesius of Cyrene, a pupil of the female philosopher Hypatia, tried to redeem her reputation a little.

27 Theophrastus, *Characters*, 28.

28 Plutarch, *Pericles*, 24.3; Plato, *Menexenus*, 235e–6b.

29 Plato, *Republic*, 353b.

30 Plato, *Menexenus*, 236d–49c.

31 Xenophon, *Memorabilia*, II, 6.36.

32 Something we accept now, that having power, changing things, gives a rush, a high.

33 Xenophon, *Oeconomicus*, 3.15. Trans. E. C. Marchant (1992) [LCL].

34 Plato, *Menexenus*, 235–6. Of course Socrates himself took a dim view of rhetoric.

35 Interesting that both Cratinus and Eupolis apparently referred to Aspasia as a 'Helen': see *Prospaltians*, 267 K-A. Later in Socrates' lifetime Euripides has Helen call herself a 'bitch-whore' – these were women whose political machinations tempted men to their beds and to untimely deaths.

36 Plato, *Menexenus*, 235e. Trans. B. Jowett (1953).

37 Plato, *Menexenus*, 236b.

38 Josiah Ober, ref. from Gale (2000), 367.

39 The Tektas shipwreck is now on display in the Bodrum Underwater Archaeology Museum, Bodrum.

40 Thucydides, 1.115.2.

41 Plutarch, *Pericles*, 24, and *Duris*, 28.2–3.

42 Herodotus, 6, 19.

CHAPTER EIGHTEEN

Samos

1 *The Spartan Military Spirit* (Tyrtaios, Frag. 9D.21–30 [Bergk]. Trans. R. Lattimore (1955).

2 The city walls are still visible. For most recent excavations see photothek@athen. dainst.org. Many thanks to Dr. Dimitris Grigoropoulos and the Institute at Samos, and Deutsches Archäologisches Institut for their help with this chapter.

3 Thucydides, 1.115–18.

4 Sophocles, *Oedipus the King*, 369–75. Trans. S. Berg and D. Clay (1978).

5 Plutarch, *Pericles*, 8.6. Trans. I. Scott-Kilvert (1960) [adapt.].

6 It was also in the late 440s that Pericles' favourite composer, Damon, was exiled from the city. A number of *ostraka* bearing his name have been excavated; it could be that he was ostracised for interfering with traditional Athenian music – for creating something that was just too, suspiciously, new.

7 Diogenes Laertius, 2.23: '*Ion of Chios relates that in his youth he visited Samos in the company of Archelaus; and Aristotle that he went to Delphi; he went also to the Isthmus, according to Favorinus in the first book of his Memorabilia.*' Although our later, textual reference has Socrates in Samos as a philosopher, it is just as likely that he would have visited the place as a soldier. Trans. R. D. Hicks (1925).

8 See, e.g., Stele 385, Piraeus Museum, memorialising Chairedemos and Lykeas.

9 Estimate taken from p.22 of Waterfield (2009). The other figures he offers are: 1,200 rich enough to fund liturgies, 3,000 with large estates, a further 3,000 not quite as well off but liable for emergency taxation, 9,000 *thetes*.

10 Mark Anderson in his interesting 2005 paper 'Socrates as Hoplite' points out the number of places where Socrates, quite possibly, could have fought. These include: Therme, Pydna, Beroea, Strepsa, Spartolus, Mende, Scione, Torone, Gale, Singus, Mecyera, Thyssus, Cleonae, Acanthos, Olophyxus, Stageira, Bormiscus, Galepsos and Trailus. See Anderson (2005), *passim*.

11 See Graham (2008).

12 Aristophanes, *Clouds*, 225; 227–34.

13 Plato, *Phaedo*, 96a. Trans. H. Tredennick (1954).

14 Aristotle, *Politics*, 7.1333b38–1334a2. Trans. T. A. Sinclair, rev. T. J. Saunders (1981) [adapt.].

15 Trans. Brickhouse and Smith (2002)

16 My thanks for help with this chapter and for access to the Isthmus site go to Prof. Elizabeth Gebhard and the team working on the University of Chicago excavations at the inspiring excavation of the Sanctuary of Poseidon at Isthmia. See http://humanities.uchicago.edu/isthmia and http://isthmia.ohio-state.edu

17 Herodotus tells us that an official Athenian delegation sailed in a 'special' ship to the Isthmus. The fact that Plato omits this detail suggests that Socrates was not perhaps a part of this 'official embassy'.

18 The Isthmian Games are a useful reminder never to think of Socrates as a cartoon philosopher – a quiet white-beard. His purpose was all about understanding and participating in, the grimy, joyful-sorrowful business of being, of living, of sweating out our lifespan in the real world. They also remind us to head-shift; to see fifth-century Greece with fifth-century eyes. They remind us that Socrates had a youth, as well as a middle and old age. That he was not a remote aesthete, but a full-blooded fifth-century Greek.

19 The basins to collect this water have been identified. The site is now open to the public and a visit is highly recommended.

20 The heroic sponsor of the games would have chimed with Socrates' own ambiguous attitude to dying and the afterlife. See Plato, *Phaedo, passim*.

21 Sport, sustenance, politics, culture, competition, international relations – for the Ancient Greeks religion lay at the heart of everything.

22 Plato, *Republic*, 379c. Trans. R. Waterfield (1993).

23 Aristophanes, *Acharnians*, 524. Trans. M. M. Henry (1995).

CHAPTER NINETEEN
Flexing muscles

1 Trans. R. Warner (1972).

2 Thucydides, 1.33.

3 The date of the Megarian decree is the subject of much debate; 'around 432' is as secure as possible. See, e.g., J. McDonald (1994), with extensive bibliography.

4 Aristophanes, *Acharnians*, 528–9. Trans. M. M. Henry (1995).

5 This was a turn in the popular tide that would eventually leave charming, witty, sexy Aspasia stranded. The parallels with the story of Helen of Troy are numerous.

6 Cf. Socrates' fate, see Ch. 50 onwards

7 Potidaea, 432–429 BC (Plato, *Symposium*, 219e–21a); Delium, 424 (Plato, *Apology*, 28e, *Laches*, 181a–b and *Symposium*, 221a–b); Amphipolis, 422 (*Apology*, 28e).

8 The keenest moral template for Socrates' society are Homer's epics and the epics of other epic-cycle poets. The *Iliad* and the *Odyssey* speak of many things, but they recall a long, bloody, seemingly pointless conflict – the Trojan War. Warmongering in antiquity was pragmatic before it was ethical. The poor in the democratic body knew that conflict could be an income generator; a poor soldier could earn from war (booty and payment). Socrates himself, middle-aged, hard-up, might even have volunteered for service – a drachma a day, potentially what a soldier can earn, is not to be sniffed at. As stated before, following Anderson, Socrates almost certainly fought at Therme, Pydna, Beroea, Strepsa, Mende, Scione, Torone, Gale, Singus, Mecygerna, Thyssus, Cleonae, Acanthos, Olophyxus, Stageira, Bormiscus, Galepsos and Trailus.

9 See Morrison (1987) and (1988) and Coates, Platis and Shaw (1990).

10 Plato, *Crito*, 49b. Trans. Brickhouse and Smith (2002).

11 Thucydides, 1.23.6. Trans. R. Warner (1972).

12 Plato, *Apology*, 28d–29b. Trans. H. N. Fowler (1914) [LCL] and Brickhouse and Smith (2002) [adapt.].

CHAPTER TWENTY

Socrates the soldier

1 Trans. W. R. M. Lamb (1925) [LCL].
2 Herodotus, 8.129, mentions a Greek temple to Poseidon in front of the city.
3 One of the scant remains from the site is a spearhead from the Geometric Period, now held by the British Museum. See Forsdyke in the *British Museum Quarterly*, VI (1932), 82f., and viii (1934), 108.
4 IG I³ 279 (cf. Thucydides, 2.70).
5 Diogenes Laertius, 2.23: '*Again he served at Potidaea, whither he had gone by sea, as land communications were interrupted by the war.*' Trans. R. D. Hicks (1925) [LCL].
6 Van Wees (2004) has a vivid description of the conditions of the campaign in this period.
7 Plutarch, *Alcibiades*, 7.2–3.
8 Plato, *Protagoras*, 309a.
9 Plato, *Symposium*, 219d.
10 Plato, *Phaedrus*, 229a.
11 Plutarch, *Alcibiades*, 1.3. Trans. I. Scott-Kilvert (1960). Nb Some sources say Alcibiades was only nineteen, but he would not have been allowed to fight beyond Attica until he was twenty.
12 Xenophon, *Memorabilia*, 1.2.24. Trans. E. C. Marchant (1992) [adapt.] [LCL].
13 Polyaenus, *Strategemata*, 1.40; cited by Kagan (1991), 196; citing Hatzfeld, *Alcibiades*, 164.
14 Plato, *Alcibiades*, I, 105a–c. (Nb Plato's authorship of *Alcibiades* is much disputed.)
15 Pindar, *Nemean Odes*, 3.40. Trans. R. Lattimore (1959).
16 Xenophon, *Memorabilia*, 1.3.13. Trans. H. Tredennick and R. Waterfield (1990) [adapt.].
17 Plato, *Symposium*, 220e.
18 Subconsciously we imagine this apparent humility as the selfless act of an immaterial man – maybe Socrates was riled by the blatant inequality. Perhaps this choice to honour not the virtuous but the great sparked his promotional campaign – you only live a good life if you are good on the inside.

CHAPTER TWENTY-ONE

Demons and virtues

1 Trans. W. R. M. Lamb [LCL].
2 Plato, *Symposium*, 219e–20d.
3 Plato, *Symposium*, 219e–20e. The man from Alopeke's much-discussed *daimonion* is perplexing. Is it perhaps the development of a personal conscience? Does religion, for Socrates, represent a route through to individual morality, rather than morality itself? Is there a more pedestrian argument? It could be that Socrates' catalepsy (protruding eyes are a textbook sign of the condition) generated in him this otherworldly eccentricity. Whatever the cause, his odd behaviour was registered.
4 Plato, *Crito*, 54d. Trans. H. N. Fowler (1914) [LCL].
5 Thucydides, 2.70.1.

6 Xenophon certainly played around with these ideas, see, e.g., *Memorabilia*, 1.

7 See Ch. 13, for discussions of Socrates' keen interest in the Spartan way of life.

8 *The Constitution of the Lacedaemonians*, 8.2.

9 Plato, *Protagoras*, 360e and following.

10 Plato, *Protagoras*, 353a and following.

11 Plato, *Apology*, 21e.

12 Plato, *Apology*, 30a–b. Trans. H. N. Fowler (1914) [LCL].

13 Euripides, *Phoenician Women*, 240–55. Trans. A. Wilson.

CHAPTER TWENTY-TWO

The plague

1 I am still struck by how, even at the beginning of the twenty-first century, in the smaller Greek villages it is men who go to buy food, not women.

2 The teeth of three corpses from the mass grave (discovered during excavations in 1994 for the extension of the metro) were analysed by the Laboratory of Molecular Neurobiology, Medical School of Athens University and the Laboratory of Micro-chemistry, Institute of Technology-Research of Crete in 2005. The bacterium discovered to be present in all samples was *Salmonella enterica serovar Typhi*. Symptoms of infection include: headache, high fever, anorexia, intestinal bleeding, intestinal perforation, septi-caemia, meningitis, osteomyelitis, hepatomegaly and splenomegaly.

3 Thucydides, 2.51.4–5. Trans. R. Warner (1972).

4 Thucydides, 2.50.1. Trans. R. Warner.

5 Thucydides, 2.52.2–3. Trans. R. Warner [adapt.].

6 Thucydides, 2.53.1–2.

7 Socrates operated in a landscape that was distinctly heroic. The words of Homer were at every street corner, images of tales of Troy and of Odysseus' travels were inescapable: on vases, in stone, on colonnades and temples.

8 'Myrtis" skull was presented at the 71st International Thessaloniki Fair in 2006.

9 See www.archaeology.org/online/features/athens/1.html.

10 Hanson (1998), 9–13.

11 Aristophanes, *Acharnians*, 498–512.

12 See Pollard, (1977).

CHAPTER TWENTY-THREE

Silver Owls and a wise owl

1 Trans. B. B. Rogers (1930) [adapt.] [LCL].

2 A very useful reference book for this kind of social detail is Camp (1986).

3 Prehistory seeped from the earth and sang in the air of classical Athens. It is still there in concrete terms: in the Aladdin's Cave storeroom of the Agora Museum where a Late Bronze Age skull peeps from a wooden drawer; newly discovered ritual objects, the latest a female deity relaxing in a striped, curved throne, are carefully wrapped in tissue paper;

in the Acropolis' still-standing blocks of defensive cyclopean walls; in words such as *'pharmakon'*, first scratched on to Greek Linear B tablets 3,500 years ago as PA-MA-KO and now animated neon-green on pharmacy signs throughout the modern city. Athenian priests and priestesses active during Socrates' lifespan mimicked in their dress gods, goddesses, demigods, nymphs and epic rulers from the 'Age of Heroes'. Choruses of maidens sang praises to the deities of old, from a time before time. Bards – professional and amateur – rhapsodised the words of Homer in open spaces across the city; tales from a thousand years ago that felt as though they happened yesterday.

4 The Temple is still a raised landmark in the Agora, although now mainly used for high-society weddings and state occasions.

5 Plato, *Apology*, 26d–e.

6 Site visit to Agora excavations' research laboratory, 2007.

7 Thanks to Dr Morcom. Currently on display in the Agora can be seen, e.g., gold Daric from Persia, electrum stater discs from Kyzikos, silver staters from Aigina, gold staters from Macedonia.

8 Eupolis, Frag. 352E.

9 Thucydides, 2.13.

10 Fragment of lost fifth-century BC comedy. See also Xenophon's story of Socrates' encounter with Antiphon the Sophist. And see Olsen (2007), pp.445–6.

11 Similar to the *banco*, the first banks set up in Renaissance Florence on the Via Rosso. The modern Greek for 'bank' is still *trapeza*, 'table'.

12 Diogenes Laertius, *Lives of Eminent Philosophers*, 2.25. Trans. R. D. Hicks (1925) [adapt.].

13 Whether or not the story told about Socrates' exasperated father praying to *Zeus Agoraios* (Zeus of the Marketplace) was contemporary, or invented with hindsight, either way it shows that the Agora, its chat, its debates, its fervid humanness, was considered a vital part of Socrates' DNA; and when Socrates spoke at his trial, the language of his defence was woven from the very fabric of these conversations at the money-tables (Plato, *Apology*, 17c).

14 Xenophon, *Memorabilia*, 1.2.60. Trans. J. Fogel (2002).

15 Plato, *Charmides*, 167a. Trans. B. Jowett (1953).

16 Cicero, *Academica*, 1.15.

CHAPTER TWENTY-FOUR

Hot air in the Agora

1 See also trans. McLeish (1979): '*Stop wriggling. If you come to a dead end, / Turn your analysis round, and take it back / To the nearest crossroads of thought. Look round, / Get the new direction right, and start again.*'

2 Demosthenes, 19.184.

3 When you travel round Greece today words are earthquake-cracked at Delphi, in Segesta, reused as a doorstep, in the Acropolis Museum, scratched into the scoop of a Corinthian column. And in the National Epigraphical Museum in Athens – a lithrary rather than a library – they line the walls and litter the floors. More than 7,000 other inscribed fragments are waiting here to be deciphered.

4 Cat. EM 6798. The inscription relates to Salamis.

5 See, e.g., EM 6765, 440/39 BC, account of the supervisors for construction of the statue of Athena Parthenos by Pheidias; also EM 6769, 438 BC, EM 5223 + 5378β + 6710α 447/6–433/2 BC, account of the supervisors for the construction of the Parthenon; and EM 7862 401/400 BC – 399 18 BC, accounts of the treasures of the goddess Athena and the other gods.

6 Piraeus Museum, 4628; see also 5352, standard measurements.

7 Over a 2,500-year period it appears that Athenians have not lost their taste for using outsize red letters to register public protest. At the time of writing, students are rioting and covering Athens' Parliament building and National Library (protected by statues of Socrates and Plato) with red graffiti: 'Pigs, Police, Murderers'.

8 Plato, *Phaedrus*, 228d.

9 Dionisius of Halicarnussus, *Treatise on Isocrates*, Chapter 18. Dionisius quotes a lost work of Aristotle. Aristotle Frag. 140. Aristotle comments on the sale and storage of Isocrates' private speeches in 'bundles' on the book stalls of the Agora.

10 See www.papyrology.ox.ac.uk.

11 P. Saqqara inv. 1972 GP 3, *c*.331–323 BC.

12 Another example of words used to malign effect can be found on the thin lead sheets, covered in crude curses, that are upturned each excavating season throughout the city centre and *deme*-districts of fifth-century Athens.

13 Plato, *Phaedrus*, 275d. Trans. B. Jowett [adapt.].

14 When Pindar used the word he was probably referring to poets/educators.

15 Pindar, *Isthmian*, 5.28. Protagoras was one early visitor to Athens.

16 The Agora had, since Solon's day, been a place where populist points were made. For years – until they were stolen away by Xerxes' Persian soldiers – there stood here two bronze statues of Athens' 'tyrant-slayers'. These fine figures of men, copied many times over by Hellenistic and Roman artists (and then spending the whole of antiquity being looted and reclaimed, finally to be dredged up from the sea-bed off the coast of southern Italy in the 1960s and transferred to Naples' Archaeological Museum), commemorated the termination of tyrannical rule in Athens a generation or so before Socrates was born.

17 Natural science, social science, political theory, the art of rhetoric, mathematics, ethics, logic – all these were rolled out into the public spaces of Athena's city. Although more concerned with the nature of virtue than the nature of the universe, Socrates himself stated that the world was round. Plato, *Phaedo*, 108–9.

18 Plato, *Apology*, 17d; *Republic*, 1.350d.

19 See also Plato, *Protagoras*, 334c–d; *Gorgias*, 449b, 461e–2a.

20 Plato, *Republic*, 6.496a. Trans. B. Jowett (1953).

21 We associate fine-speaking with Athens, but in fact we are informed the art of rhetoric was a foreign import. Aristotle tells us that Corax and Tisias developed the form when the tyrants were banished from Sicily (cf. Rhodes [2005], 75–6: '*by the end of the 470s the tyrants were on their way out*'). For sophists travelling to earn money, see Plato, *Greater Hippias*, 282d.

22 It was said Gorgias had won plaudits at the Olympic Games, where his audience was closer to 20,000. He also spoke to the Athenian Council, or Assembly, in 427 BC.

23 Gorgias, *Helen*, 14. Trans. Sprague (2001).

24 This was also devised to prevent Greek-upon-Greek recriminations as a result of the Peloponnesian Wars.

25 Plato, *Phaedrus*, 279b–c.

26 Plato, *Republic*, 4.422a. Trans. B. Jowett (1953).

27 Plato, *Republic*, 7.536e. Trans. B. Jowett.

28 Plato, *Republic*, 8.557b–d. Trans. B. Jowett.

29 Plato, *Symposium*, 221e–2a. Trans. H. N. Fowler (1914) [LCL].

30 Plato, *Apology*, 33a–b. Trans. H. N. Fowler (1914) [LCL].

31 Plato, *Hippias Minor*, 376c. Trans. W. R. M. Lamb (1926) [LCL].

32 Plato, *Euthyphro*, 9c. Trans. Brickhouse and Smith (2002).

33 Plato, *Euthyphro*, 7d. Trans. Brickhouse and Smith.

34 Plato, *Gorgias*, 465a and following.

35 E.g., Plato, *Republic*, 337a. The basic meaning of *eironeia* (straightforward lying) is first found in the plays of Aristophanes (e.g., *Wasps*, 169–74, *Birds*, 1208–11, and *Clouds*, 444–51), but it is Socrates who imbues the word with all its subtleties and controversies. Cicero, writing in the first century BC, says that in his opinion Socrates surpassed all in his use of irony (Cicero, *De Oratore*, 2.67.270). Cf. Colebrook (2004), 22–64; Lear (2006), 442–62; Emlyn-Jones (2007), 151. See Aristotle, *Nicomachean Ethics*, 4.7.3. See also Plato, *Symposium*, 216e: '*ALCIBIADES: He spends his whole life in chaffing and making game of his fellow men. Whether anyone else has caught him in a serious moment and opened him, and seen the images inside, I know not; but I saw them one day, and thought them so divine and golden, so perfectly fair and wondrous, that I simply had to do as Socrates bade me.*' Trans. W. R. M. Lamb (1925) [LCL].

36 Plato, *Republic*, 337a. Trans. P. Shorey (1930) [LCL].

37 Scholars still fervently debate in what way Socrates was ironic, but all agree that irony was a Socratic hallmark. For some, then and now, Socratic irony is also the hallmark of the sophisticated mindset of a true civilisation.

38 Saxonhouse (2006), *passim*, expounds the view that Socrates was in fact executed because he was 'shameless', i.e. he felt completely unrestrained by a general 'tenor' of accepted behaviour.

39 Plato, *Republic*, 350d.

40 Aristophanes, *Frogs*, 1491–9 (performed in 405 BC). Trans. G. Theodoridis [adapt.].

41 Plato, *Gorgias*, 521d.

42 Plato, *Alcibiades I*, 130e. Trans. D. S. Hutchinson (1997).

43 That is, the Agora is not the means to an end; it is not the means, and not the end; it is simply, and vitally, our human home.

44 Plato, *Apology*, 23c–e. Trans. B. Jowett (1953).

45 Plato, *Phaedrus*, 275d–e. Trans. H. N. Fowler (1914).

CHAPTER TWENTY-FIVE

Democracy, liberty and freedom of speech

1 Trans. H. W. Smyth (1973) [LCL].

2 Trans. D. Kovacs (1995) [LCL].

3 IG II² 1624.81.

4 Many thanks to Alec Tilley for his help with this passage. His own, fascinating views on boat design in the fifth and fourth centuries BC can be found in Tilley (2004) and Tilley (1992).

5 *Iliad*, 2.50–2. Trans. S. Butler.

6 *Iliad*, 18.497–508. Trans. S. Butler.

7 Diogenes Laertius, *On the Lives and Opinions of Eminent Philosophers*, 6.69.

8 Plato, *Gorgias*, 487b (and again in *Protagoras*, 319cd, although this is used more to describe the possibility that each man has in the Assembly for *isegoria*, right of equal speech).

9 Parody of the question posed in the male Assembly. Aristophanes, *Thesmophoriazusae*, 379: See also *Ecclesiazusae*, 392.

10 Aeschines, *Against Timarchus*, 1.23. Trans. N. Fisher (2001) [adapt.].

11 Although Socrates does worry about the unbridled impact of a true democracy, recent readings of the works of Plato concur that he was not as critical as previously judged. See, e.g., Saxonhouse (2006), 98, for the opinion that Socrates does not describe *parrhesia* perjoratively in Book 8 of the *Republic.*

12 For a fascinating discussion of the role of *parrhesia* in Socrates' Athens see Saxonhouse (2006), *passim*.

13 *Gorgias*, 486d–8b and *Laches*, passim. Socrates was a practitioner of *parrhesia*.

14 Aristotle, *Politics*, 1317b12.

15 Aeschylus, *Persians*, lines 584–94. Trans. P. Vellacott (1961).

16 Several triremes named *Eleutheria* were built: IG II² 1604 line 49 (377/6 BC); 1607, line 85 (373/2 BC); 1627, line 202 (330/329 BC); 163, line 488 (323/2 BC). All references from Robinson (2004), 80 (cf. also Hansen [1989], 42).

17 The forgers of the 'Socratic' Dialogues *Eryxias* and *Theages* (these were almost certainly invented) have the philosopher filling the Stoa of Zeus Eleutherios with thoughts and words.

18 Plato, *Republic*, 8.562a. Trans. P. Shorey (1930) [LCL].

19 Herodotus, 9.5.

20 Plato, *Republic*, 5.449a. Trans. B. Jowett (1953).

21 Plato, *Republic*, 5.462d–e (see also 462b). Trans. B. Jowett.

CHAPTER TWENTY-SIX

The good life – after dark

1 Trans. P. Shorey (1930) [LCL].

2 Although there is some scholarly argument that Plato includes this information to prove that the Athenians frequently worshipped 'new gods' and therefore Socrates should not be targeted for his own unorthodox spiritual experiences, archaeological evidence shows us that the cult of Bendis was indeed inaugurated in Athens at this time.

3 IG I³ 136 (SEG 10.64).

4 Contrast the acceptance of this 'new god' when it suits the city, with the anxiety about Socrates' new, 'private' god and the manner of its introduction.

5 Plato, *Symposium*, 197dI–e3. cf. Diogenes Laertius, Socrates XIV.

6 Socrates and his contemporaries lived in a landscape where there was much space to think. With their back-up of wives, slaves and the fruits of an empire, the leisured could enjoy afternoons saturated with thought. Socrates might have lived through times when men did abominable things to one another, when women passed by, their faces worn out by tears. But he lived a long life, and there would have been days of watching and waiting – times when the landscape of Athens and its surrounds could be drunk in. Socrates must have considered keen thoughts here, trying to ascertain whether or not goodness had a place in human society, and how to locate and nurture it.

7 On occasion Socrates did speak of one god, in contrast with the gods (Plato, *Laws*, 10.904a, and *Timaeus*, 41a). He challenged the literal veracity of the mythic stories, the tales in Homer and Hesiod that were the Greek's equivalent of a bible.

8 Plato, *Euthyphro*, 6a–b. Trans. H. N. Fowler (1914) [adapt.] [LCL].

9 This and other fundamental aspects of Greek religion are discussed with great élan by Walter Burkert (1985).

10 Demosthenes, 4.35.

CHAPTER TWENTY-SEVEN
Delphi, the Oracle

1 Trans. Brickhouse and Smith (2002).

2 Today just along the esplanade from modern-day Itea.

3 See Plato's *Apology*, 21a. Trans. H. N. Fowler (1914) [adapt.] [LCL]; also Xenophon's *Memorabilia* and Aristophanes' *Clouds*, *Wasps* and *Birds*.

4 The equivalent of walking to church, temple or mosque through the killing fields of Cambodia or the napalm-blasted pathways of Vietnam. Places that we knew had witnessed hideous suffering; images brought to a mass audience by art (tragedies then, now movies).

5 Of course Apollo is a Johnny-come-lately at Delphi. Originally this was the Python's place. A holy zone for a serpentine female spirit: Homer's 'rocky Pytho'. Myth-stories told of this being the home of Ge, or Gaia, mother-earth. The archaeological remains of Bronze Age female figurines, winkled out of the earth by archaeologists and, haply, by farmers, back up the literature. There is no doubt that for 700 years some kind of female spirit was worshipped here. But then, the stories go, Apollo wrestled the snake-goddess-serpent-dragon, the Python, to the ground. Her spirit slithered away into a cave and the holy hot-spot was his. Visiting in the mid-fifth century BC, it would have been Apollo's brash, colonnaded temple built partly with Athenian money and shared with Dionysos, a sturdy canopy to contain spirits that dominated the crowded Delphic skyline. The Athenians were particularly keen to stamp their mark. One family (the Alcmaeonids) funded the completion (in marble) of Apollo's monumental temple started in the sixth century BC.

6 And almost certainly Leto – although there are no extant remains.

7 Pindar, *Pythian*, 7.12.
8 Porphyry, *On Abstinence*, 2.9; HN 4 n.13.
9 See De Boer and Hale (2000), 399–412; De Boer, Hale and Chanton (2001), 707–10. Broad (2006).

CHAPTER TWENTY-EIGHT

Gnothi Seauton – Know Yourself

1 Trans. O. J. Todd (1992). See also Plato, *Apology*, 21a; *Gorgias*, 447a; Xenophon, *Memorabilia*, 1.2.48.
2 Nb Both Chaerephon's visit to Delphi and the date of this putative visit are uncertain.
3 Pausanias, 10.24.1.
4 Scholiast to Plato, *Phaedrus*, 229e.
5 Macrobius, *Dream of Scipio*, 1.9.2.
6 The Hellenic Ministry for Culture claims the *pronaos* (inner portico) was most likely.
7 Aristotle is reported as having said that Socrates, not Chaerephon, went to Delphi, but this is a relatively unstable source. Diogenes, *Laertius*, 2.23.
8 Cf. Herodotus, 7.141.
9 Pindar, *Pythian*, 7.9–13. Trans. B. L. Gildersleeve (1890).

CHAPTER TWENTY-NINE

Aristocrats, democrats and the realities of war

1 See Hatzilambrou, Parsons and Chapa (2007), 15.
2 Deighton (1995), 34.
3 See pg. 15, *The Oxyrhyncus Papyri*, Volume LXXI, ed. R. Hatzilambrou, P. J. Parsons and J. Chapa, Egypt Exploration Society, London, 2007.
4 There were also pretend equids all around: painted and Amazon-mounted on the walls of the *Stoa Poikile*, the Painted Stoa; free-standing in bronze outside the *Stoa of Zeus Eleutherios*, – the Stoa of Zeus of Freedom, in gaudily coloured terracotta on the roof of the Royal Stoa – the place where Socrates had been charged with his crimes, moulded into tiny models to be offered as votives for the gods in sanctuaries and shrines across the heaving market-place. See also, e.g., The Four-Horse Chariot of Helios, ACR. 19052, and the Four-Horse Chariot of Selene, ACR. 19053, 19054.
5 The writer-general was a huge admirer of Socrates' thought, and a former pupil of the philosopher.
6 Xenophon, *The Cavalry Commander*, 3.2. Trans. E. Marchant and G. W. Bowestock (1925) [LCL].
7 Plato, *Republic*, 2.373e. Trans. B. Jowett (1953).
8 Thucydides, 3.48.

9 Spartans captured from the battle on Sphacteria, an island adjacent to Pylos, in 425 BC. Cf. Powell (1988), 165–70; 237–8.

CHAPTER THIRTY

The Peloponnesian War, phase two – a messy siege

1 Trans. H. Tredennick (1954).
2 Trans. B. Jowett (1953).
3 See illustration in *The City Beneath the City. Antiquities from the Metropolitan Railway Excavations*, by Liana Parlama and Nicholas Stampolidis, Harry N. Abrams (2001). *Stele* currently stored in the Benaki Museum in Athens. The stele mentions men from Socrates' tribe who were killed (also at the battles of Megara and Spartolus).
4 The National Archaeological Museum in Athens, the National Museum in Thessaloniki, and the museum at Olympia all have excellent collections of discarded Greek armour and equipment.
5 Lists taken from Van Wees (2004), 104–8.
6 This strategy depended on two separate forces linking up in Boeotia.
7 Plato, *Symposium*, 219e–220e.
8 Plato, *Symposium*, 219e–221a. Trans. W. R. M. Lamb (1925) [LCL].
9 Plato, *Symposium*, 221a–b. Trans. W. R. M. Lamb (1925) [LCL].
10 See also *Laches*.
11 Although some of the campaign had maintained the hallmarks of limited, ritual warfare, much convention was insulted. The Athenian forces barricaded the temple at Delion and soldiers drank from the sacred spring there. The Boeotians used cavalry, driving down the hoplite foot soldiers (who were then only saved by the arrival of night) and the Spartans (initially) refused to allow the Athenians to collect their dead.
12 If Socrates had fought at Scione, the summer after Delion, this is what he would also have seen there.
13 Plato, *Laches*, 181b; *Symposium*, 221a. And even when Aristophanes astringently mocked Socrates the very next year, he never said he was a coward.
14 'Men hesitate to lay hands on those who show such a countenance as Socrates did even in defeat.' Plato, *Symposium*, 221b–c. Trans. W. R. M. Lamb [LCL].

CHAPTER THIRTY-ONE

Brickbats and bouquets

1 Trans. Brickhouse and Smith (2002).
2 Scholion on Pseudo-Lucian, possibly based on Philochorus' *Atthis*.
3 Aeschines, *Against Ktesiphon*, 76; Plato, *Ion*, 535d–e.
4 Xenophon, *Oeconomicus*, 3.7. Trans. S. Pomeroy (1994) [adapt.].
5 See Diogenes Laertius, *Lives of Eminent Philosophers*, 2.18.
6 For a useful visual guide to the development of theatre in Athens, see Connolly and Dodge (2001), 90–101.

7 R. Parker (2005. Reprinted in paperback 2007), 314.

8 Homer, *Iliad*, 6.132.

9 Aristophanes, *Frogs*, 1009–10.

10 Sophocles, *Ajax*, 964–5. Trans. J. Moore (1954); Sophocles, *Acrisius*, F 58; Aeschylus, *Prometheus Bound*, 226–7; Aeschylus, *Prometheus Bound*, 380.

11 Perhaps one of the reasons that Plato was so vehemently opposed to tragedy. He complained that the political statements of the theatre were, by definition, all crowd-pleasers, demagoguery. Plato, *Gorgias*, 502b–c; *Republic*, X, 602b; *Laws*, VII, 817b–d.

12 Plato, *Ion*, 535d–e. Trans. W. R. M. Lamb (1925) [adapt.].

13 See Rehm (2007).

14 Comedy and tragedy mattered. Comedy was believed to have been born when society learned how to be democratic. After all, democracy should be a place where all people have the opportunity to laugh: oligarchs and tyrants have never been very keen on being mocked. This was a time when theatre was not just the canary in the chamber. It was the poisonous gas. Following the Samian revolt of 440 BC restrictions were brought in on comedy: now comedians had to get a licence – the men in power had to keep a tab on who was choosing to amuse, to diffuse, to incite, to offend. This restriction was lifted by 430 BC so Aristophanes was un-constrained. Aristotle, *Poetics*, 1448a, insists that comedy was 'invented' in Megara 'at the time of their democracy'. See also the Parian Marble (FGrHist 239 A39).

15 Sommerstein (1982), 2 – *Clouds* was performed originally at the City Dionysia of 423 BC, where it was placed third (and last) after Cratinus' *The Wine-flask* (a satire and the winner) and Ameipsias' *Konnos*. Aristophanes himself viewed *Clouds* as his best play (*Wasps*, 1047) and he certainly revised it – it is the revised edition we have. Dover (1968), xvii, also has the Dionysia plus 423 for the first performance. He suggests (xxxii) that in 424 BC Socrates fought as a hoplite at Delion. He also suggests (lxxx) the dates of the revision would have been somewhere between 420 and 417 BC and surmises (lxxxi) that we must reject Hypothesis II, which says that the play was performed again in 423/2, because of the dates of the revision. Dover concludes by saying that the revised edition was unlikely to have been performed in Athens, if at all.

16 Aristophanes, *Clouds*, 445–51.

17 Aristophanes, *Birds*, 1280–3. Socrates joins the ranks of Machiavelli, Thatcher, Rasputin, etc. – those whose personal names have become a political catchword. It was not just Aristophanes who lampooned him, but only Aristophanes whose work survived; cf the lost play *Konnos* by the comic poet Ameipsias, plus four others in fragmentary form.

18 Cratinus' *Wine-flask* (Pytinê in Greek) is a comedy. This play was supposed to have defeated Aristophanes' *Clouds* (it also accuses A. of plagiarism) (cf. Thomas K. Hubbard, *The Mask of Comedy: Aristophanes and the intertextual Parabasis* (Ithaca and London, 1991), 75. Aristophanes' *Clouds* was given third place behind Cratinus' *Wine-flask*, (*Pytinê*) (first prize) and Ameipsias' *Konnos* (second prize); see Pauly-Wissowa *Real-Encyclopädie*, vol. I. 2. 1819 (*s.v.*) Ameipsias. See also Kassel & Austin (1991), 200; this was also the year that Sophocles perhaps premiered his *Maidens of Trachis*.

19 Aristophanes, *Clouds*, 358–66. Trans. A. H. Sommerstein (1973).

20 Aristophanes, *Clouds*, 1504–10. Trans. A. H. Sommerstein (1973)

21 Plato, *Apology*, 18a–d, 19c. Trans. Brickhouse and Smith (2002).
22 See Plato, *Gorgias*, 468b–70b; *Phaedrus*, 248d; Xenophon, *Memorabilia*, 2.1.19, 4.5.10.

CHAPTER THIRTY-TWO
Amphipolis

1 In 405 BC we find Alcibiades negotiating to buy Thracian muscle for the Battle of Aegospotami (but he also defends Greek cities on the Hellespont against Thracian attack).
2 Thucydides, 4.102–8.
3 Thucydides, 4.108.1–3. Trans. R. Warner (1972).
4 Thucydides, 5.3.2–4.
5 A friend of aristocrats and cobblers, an also-ran hoplite – what did Socrates make of these campaigns? In some ways he seems, through the battles, skirmishes, and long marches, to be a funny little fellow, mongrel-class in a land that only understood rigid social divisions. Pursuing his own, private, mental world at a time when all that mattered was communal, the explicit, the shared, the public.
6 Years later Socrates would be invited back to those territories beyond the northern frontier. Archelaus, who was the King of Macedonia from 413 to 399 BC, asked Socrates to speak at his court – see Aristotle, *Rhetoric*, 1398a. Socrates turned him down.

CHAPTER THIRTY-THREE
Socrates in the *symposium*

1 Trans. R. Waterfield (1993).
2 Pherekrates, *Persians*, 130e.
3 Although there were *gynaikeion* – specific rooms where women worked (weaving cloth in particular) and spent time together. Nb. 'flute-girl' has come to be an accepted term for performing slave-girls. The *aulos* (previously identified as a flute) was in fact almost certainly more oboe-like.
4 Aristophanes, *Acharnians*, 530.
5 Plutarch also pointed up the theatrical nature of the *symposia*. In his *Moralia*, 10c–d, Socrates says, '*I am teased in the theatre as if I were at a large symposium.*'
6 Athenaeus, *Deipnosophistai*, 5.217a.
7 Aristophanes ridicules Agathon in his comedies, e.g., *Thesmophoriazusae*.
8 Laughter is, of course, one of those experiences that often escapes the historical record. But it was here, Plato talks of it, and Aristophanes' jokes still make us smile. Aristotle describes there being a 'certain sweetness in life itself'. And despite his some-time reputation as a needling curmudgeon, Socrates too seems to taste that sweetness. Recently laughter has been a focus of interest, see, e.g., Halliwell (2008); Sommerstein (2009); Beard, *Roman Laughter*, forthcoming.
9 Plato, *Symposium*, 221e–2a. Trans. W. R. M. Lamb [LCL].

10 See, for example, [Xen] *Ath. Pol*, 10; Plato, *Laws*, 655; Socrates (Xenophon, *Memorabilia*, 3.10.5); *Iliad*, 2, 211.
11 Plato, *Phaedo*, 100e. Trans. B. Jowett [adapt.].
12 Plato, *Symposium*, 210a–12a.
13 Xenophon, *Symposium*, 5.5.
14 Plato, *Gorgias*, 481d.
15 For further discussion see George Rudebusch, author of *Socrates, Pleasure and Value* (1999).
16 Plato, *Symposium*, 222c.
17 See Kahn (2006), *passim*, for a discussion of the place of pleasure and rational action in Plato's *Protagoras*, e.g., '. . . the attempt to do justice to the deep psychological appeal of hedonism is a major theme of his [Plato's] life's work'.

CHAPTER THIRTY-FOUR

The trouble with love

1 Xenophon, *Symposium*, 4.25–6. Trans. O. J. Todd (1992) [LCL].
2 Xenophon, *Memorabilia*, 4.5.11. Trans. E. C. Marchant (1992) [LCL].
3 See Xenophon, *Symposium*, 4.38; *Memorabilia*, 1.3.14 and 2.1.30.
4 Xenophon, *Memorabilia*, 2.2.4. Trans. E. C. Marchant (1992) [LCL].
5 Xenophon, *Symposium* 8.25. Trans. O. J. Todd (1992) [LCL].
6 He happened to be Plato's uncle (possibly his great-uncle or simply his guardian). You get a sense in the *Symposium* of what a small world Athens was – men bumping into one another on street corners, related to one another through blood or marriage.
7 Xenophon, *Memorabilia*, 1.2.30. Trans. E. C. Marchant (1992) [LCL].
8 Critias was killed when the democrats returned in 403 BC – flagging up to us his markedly oligarchic sympathies.
9 Scholium 'B'. See W. Dindorf, *Scholia Graeca in Homeri Odysseam* (Oxford, 1855), 152–4, and G. Stallbaum, *Eustathii Archiepiscopi Thessalonicensis Commentarii ad Homeri Odysseam* (Leipzig, 1825), 130–2. See also E. Kadletz, 1981. www.jstor.org/stable/1509764.

CHAPTER THIRTY-FIVE

Oh, tell me the truth about love

1 Trans. B. Jowett (1953).
2 Plato, *Theages*, 128b.
3 Xenophon, *Symposium*, 8.2. Trans. O. J. Todd (1992).
4 See Plato, *Symposium*, 177d; *Charmides*, 155c; Xenophon, *Symposium*, 8.2.
5 This is something that perhaps we have busied out of our lives; but those Greeks who enjoyed many hours of *schole* each day and whose physical needs and desires were met by others, had time to delight and to wallow in an acute physical and intellectual exploration of Eros' bitter-sweet gift – in love.
6 Plato, *Lysis*, 218a–b. Trans. S. Lombardo (1997).
7 Plato, *Menexenus*, 234c–5b. Trans. R. G. Bury (1929) [LCL].

CHAPTER THIRTY-SIX

Diotima – a very social priestess

1 Trans. T. J. Saunders (1975).
2 Trans. P. Vellacott (1953).
3 There could quite possibly be some wordplay here, as 'Mantinea' does sound a little like the Greek for 'seer'. And 'Dio-tima' means 'she who is honoured by Zeus/honours Zeus'.
4 Special privileges were given to priestesses when addressing the Council or Assembly. See LSCC 102, Lykourgos, *On the Priestesses*, Frag. 6.4. Some priestess-hoods, e.g., Athena Polias and Demeter and Kore, stay within family dynasties for seven hundred years.
5 Plato, *Symposium*, 211d–e. Trans. H. N. Fowler (1914) [LCL].
6 Joan Breton Connelly has estimated that women participated in 85 per cent of religious activity in Athens (cf. Blok), and that they were prominent in at least forty cults in the city.
7 *The Captive Melanippe*, Frag. 494 K. Trans. Helene Foley in Fantham et al. (1994), 95–6. H. van Looy (ed.), *Euripide VIII²*, Fragments (Paris, 2000), 347–96.
8 List taken from p.167 of Connelly (2007).
9 There are fine examples in, e.g., Museum of Kerkyra (Corfu). If you visit this museum do not forget to check out the Archaic pediment that carries what has to be one of the finest and fiercest Gorgon's heads from antiquity.
10 British Museum 2070 (sceptre) and 1952 (necklace).
11 Cf. Xenophon, *Memorabilia*, 3.11.
12 List compiled by Joan Breton Connelly. p.46 of Connelly (2007).
13 Pindar, *Pythian*, 3.31–2, refers to girls singing songs in the evening.
14 Aristophanes, *Birds*, 873; *Wasps*, 9; *Lysistrata*, 387–90.
15 Aristophanes, *Lysistrata*, 387–8.
16 Arisophanes, *Lysistrata*, 641–7.

CHAPTER THIRTY-SEVEN

Little Bears

1 Plato, *Laws*, 833d.
2 Plato, *Laws*, 774e–5a; see also Aristophanes, *Lysistrata*, 645, for the origins of the Brauron myth.
3 See Xenophon, specific examples below.
4 Xenophon, *Oeconomicus*, 3.12–13. Trans. E. C. Marchant (1992) [adapt.] [LCL].
5 Xenophon, *Memorabilia*, 2.7–9.
6 Plato, *Republic*, 452a.
7 Xenophon, *Oeconomicus*, 7.5. Trans. H. G. Dakyns (1890).
8 Xenophon, *Symposium*, 2.9. Trans. O. J. Todd (1992)[LCL].
9 Plato, *Republic*, 5.455d. Trans. P. Shorey (1930) [LCL].
10 Plato, *Republic*, 5.451e–2a. Trans. P. Shorey [LCL].
11 Xenophon, *Memorabilia*, 3.11.

12 See Zahm (1913), 197–9.

13 Plato, *Theaetetus*, 149a–51d.

14 Plato, *Theaetetus*, 149a; *Greater Hippias*, 298b; *Laches*, 180d.

15 There is a possibility that Plato was encouraging the character of Socrates to fantasise about his mother here so that he could engender a vivid analogy between the work of a midwife and the fact that Socrates struggled to bring new beings (ideas) into the world. It seems perverse, though, for Socrates to invent something so precise for his own family. The allegory stands whether or not the midwife was Socrates' own mother. The fact that Phaenarete is described as well-built (genes inherited by her son), and therefore would be well suited to the intensely physical business of pulling healthy children from mothers, is salient.

16 Plato, *Theaetetus*, 150b–c.

17 Plato, *Menexenus*, 236b. Trans. W. R. M. Lamb [LCL].

18 IG II² 1409.14.

19 Antisthenes, Frag. 142, in Giannantoni, 1990: 2.191 (= Athenaeus, *Deipnosophistai*, 220d); see also Antisthenes, *Aspasia*. There is a possibility that this was not an historical incident, but an event fabricated in Attic comedy.

20 See Boston Museum of Fine Arts, 10.223 and Acropolis Museum 1766–67. Payment was for the Sanctuary of Aphrodite Ourania.

CHAPTER THIRTY-EIGHT

Xanthippe

1 Trans. J. C. Rolfe (1927).

2 Sources for Socrates' bigamy: Diogenes Laertius, 2.26; Aulus Gellius, *Attic Nights*, 15.20.6; cf. Plutarch, *Aristides*, 27.

3 *De Matrimonia*, 62 (Haase, 1902, Teubner edition). Text attributed to Seneca the Elder. Fragmentary. Trans. C. A. Stocks (2008) [adapt.].

4 *De Matrimonia*, 62.

5 See Diogenes Laertius, *Lives of Eminent Philosophers*, 2.26. Trans. R. D. Hicks (1925).

6 Both times at Plato, *Phaedo*, 60a.

7 Cicero, *De Inventione*, 31, 52–3.

CHAPTER THIRTY-NINE

Alcibiades: violet-crowned, punch-drunk

1 Trans. A. Nehamas and P. Woodruff (1997).

2 Plato, *Symposium*, 213c.

3 Lysias, *Against Andokides*, 51. See also M. Reinhold's fascinating 'The history of purple' (1970).

4 Plutarch, *Alcibiades*, 11.2. Trans. I. Scott-Kilvert (1960).

5 Aristotle, *Politics*, 1254b.34–6. Trans. T. A. Sinclair, rev. T. J. Saunders (1981).

6 Plato, *Symposium*, 218d. Trans. A. Nehamas and P. Woodruff (1997).

7 Plato, *Symposium*, 215d–e. Trans. C. D. C. Reeve (2006).

8 Xenophon, *Memorabilia*, 1.3.12–13. Trans. J. Fogel (2002) [adapt.].
9 Socrates was carnal as well as cerebral, and it is little surprise that the story of the *Symposium* is given to us by Xenophon and Plato within the modest four walls of an Athenian home; where drinking-games, remedies for hiccups and news of neighbours are as much a part of the search for the truth about love, as is Socrates' definition of what it is to be human.
10 Plato, *Alcibiades* I, 134a–b. Trans. W. R. M. Lamb (1927) [LCL].

CHAPTER FORTY

Melos

1 Trans. Brickhouse and Smith (2002).
2 Cleon in Thucydides, 3.38–39. Trans. J. M. Dent (1910) [adapted].
3 Alcibiades may have considered Melos an opportunity to make a favourable impact on the Athenians. See following chapter; this was perhaps a curtain-raiser for the invasion of Sicily.
4 Thucydides, 5.84.
5 Thucydides, 5.105.2. Trans. J. M. Dent (1910).
6 Recent excavated finds held in the Milos Museum since 1984.
7 There is an ancient tradition that Phaedo (the eponym of one of Plato's Dialogues) was a Melian survivor.

CHAPTER FORTY-ONE

Venus de Milo abused

1 Trans. P. Vellacott (1973).
2 Plutarch, *Life of Alcibiades*, 16.4–5. '*And he picked out a woman from among the prisoners of Melos to be his mistress, and reared a son she bore him. This was an instance of what they called his kindness of heart, but the execution of all the grown men of Melos was chiefly due to him, since he supported the decree.*' Trans. B. Perrin (1916) [LCL].
3 Andocides, *Against Alcibiades*, 22. Trans. K. J. Maidment (1941) [LCL].
4 Hyperides, Frag. 55.

CHAPTER FORTY-TWO

Priest of nonsense: playing with fire

1 Libanius *Apology*, 154–5. This refutes the lost pamphlet *Accusation Against Socrates*, published in 393/2 BC by Polycrates.
2 For a full discussion of the Derveni Manuscript, see Richard Janko, *passim*, in Ahbel-Rappe and Kamtekar (eds.) (2006), Ch.34, 56–7.
3 See Sir Kenneth Dover, *Aristophanes' Frogs* (OUP, 1997) for the suggestion that this story bears relation to Socrates' own trial.

4 Xenophon, *Hellenica*, 2.2.9, and Plutarch, *Lysis*, 14.4.

5 Aristophanes, *Birds*, 1072–5. Trans. J. Henderson (2000).

6 Aristophanes, *Birds*, 1420. Trans. J. Henderson (2000).

7 Rumbles of discontent as early as the invasion of Samos back in 440 BC seemed to suggest that the most stand-out of Pericles' circle of intellectuals were, somehow, creating hardships on the ground for ordinary Athenians. Damon (the composer), Anaxagoras (the natural philosopher) and Pheidias (the architect and sculptor) found themselves under fire throughout the 430s. Aspasia was charged with *asebeia* – impiety. Many more were ostracised and exiled.

8 Diogenes Laertius, *Life of Protagoras*, 9.51. See also trans. C. D. Yonge (1853): '*Concerning the Gods, I am not able to know for certain whether they exist or whether they do not. For there are many things which prevent one from knowing, especially the obscurity of the subject, and the shortness of the life of man*' [adapt.].

9 Euripides, *Bacchae*, 200.

10 Thucydides, 6.31.1. Trans. C. F. Smith (1919) [adapt.].

11 Cat. no. 752.

CHAPTER FORTY-THREE
Sicily

1 Trans. P. Vellacott (1973).

2 My thanks to Dr Moreno for alerting me to unexcavated sites on the high ground of Euboea. See Moreno (2001) and Moreno (2009).

3 Themistocles had pointed the way in his putative campaign.

4 Thucydides, 6.31.4. Trans. R. Warner (1972).

5 Aristophanes, *Lysistrata*, 390–7; Plutarch, *Nicias*, 13.7.

6 Agora I 7307.

7 See Plutarch, *Alcibiades*, 22.4, for impeachment, including confiscation of property and cursing by priests: '. . . *His case went by default, his property was confiscated, and besides that, it was also decreed that his name should be publicly cursed by all priests and priestesses*.' Trans. B. Perrin (1916) [LCL].

8 *Vt. Marc.* 41, in R. Janko, 'Socrates the Freethinker', in Ahbel-Rappe and Kamtekar (eds.) (2006), 60.

CHAPTER FORTY-FOUR
Rivers of blood

1 Trans. R. Warner (1972).

2 Diodorus Siculus, *Universal Library*, 13.19.

3 Euripides, *Phoenician Women*, 1410–15. Trans. G. Murray (1913).

4 Xenophon, *Anabasis* 2.5.33. Trans. C. L. Brownson (1922) [adapt.], [LCL]

5 Samons, *What's Wrong With Democracy*, 53 n. 59. Oaths of Loyalty, IGi³ 39, 40 = Fornara 102, 103; oath 'to love' the *demos*: IG I³ 37 = ML 47 = Fornara 99.

6 The real, awful drama of the moment inspired Plato to set one of his dramatic Socratic Dialogues, *Ion*, before the news hits Athens.

7 Cf Heraclides of Clazomenae: who proposes the increase in assembly pay from 1 obol to 2 obols, *c.*400–395 since there had been a further increase to 3 obols by the time of Aristophanes' *Ecclesiazusae*, in the late 390s (*Ath. Pol.* 41. iii, Ar. *Eccl.* 289–311, 392), so he must have been made an Athenian citizen by then; and at some time he served as general (Plat. *Ion* 541 D 1–4, Ath. XI. 560 A, Ael, V.H. XIV. 5). The surviving part of the inscription (M&L 70=IG i3 227 with addenda) records his being awarded honours less than citizenship, and therefore earlier, probably in connection with the alleged Peace of Epilycus between Athens and Persia *c.*423.

8 Plato, *Ion*, 541c–d. Trans. T. J. Saunders (1987).

9 Aristophanes, *Birds*, 1277–83. Trans. A. H. Sommerstein (1987). Nb *Birds* was presented in 414 BC.

10 Aristophanes, *Birds*, 1553–5. Trans. A. H. Sommerstein.

11 Aristophanes, *Frogs*, 1431–3.

CHAPTER FORTY-FIVE
Decelea – closing down the mines

1 For a full account of this episode, see Hughes (2005), Ch. 6, 'The Rape of "Fair Hellen"', and notes, *passim*.

2 Plutarch, *Alcibiades*, 15.1. Thucydides, 7.91.6.

3 In Athens itself in 411 BC a coup put 400 oligarchs in power – one of the first things they did was approach the Spartan king, holed up in the fort at Decelea, to try to do a deal.

4 Thucydides, 7.27.

5 Xenophon, *Hellenica*, 3.3.6. Trans. C. L. Brownson [LCL].

CHAPTER FORTY-SIX
Time of terror

1 Plutarch, *Alcibiades* 34.6.

2 Plutarch, *Alcibiades*, 23; *Lysander*, 22; *Agesilaus*, 3; Xenophon, *Hellenica*, 3.3.1–2.

3 Plutarch, *Alcibiades*, 24.4. Trans. I. Scott-Kilvert (1960).

4 See Samons (2000), 281–93.

5 A title resurrected by the Greek dictator Metaxas in the 1930s.

6 Thucydides, 8.66.

7 Thucydides, 8.97.

8 Compare with Mark Antony, a Roman exiled from Rome, but a man with the loyalty of the Roman navy.

9 ML 58 = Fornara 119 and Xenophon, *Hellenica*, 1.1.22.

10 Aristophanes, *Frogs*, 735–7. Trans. D. Barrett (1964).

11 Aristophanes, *Frogs*, 695–702. Trans. G. Murray (1908).

12 See Finley (1971), 11–12 for inscription reference.

13 Aristophanes, *Frogs*, 1425. Trans. J. Savage (2010).

14 Plutarch, *Alcibiades*, 34.6.

15 And, curiously, the embattled Athens that Socrates refused to leave was defiantly productive. Aristophanes wrote his *Lysistrata* and the *Women at the Thesmophoria*. Sophocles – the playwright, one of those caught up, reluctantly, in the coup of 411 – was eighty by now, but still he produced the finest of works. His almost unbearably angry play *Philoctetes* deals with the issue of deception – one feels this has to be a comment on the world around him. Cf. Heraclitus' comments on the value of strife.

16 Plato, *Phaedrus*, 259a–b. Trans. H. Fowler (1914) [LCL].

17 Plato, *Lysis*, 204a.

18 Plato, *Lysis*, 205e–6a. Trans. W. R. M. Lamb (1925) [LCL].

19 Plato, *Lysis*, 203a–b.

20 See *City Beneath the City*, p. 249.

21 Plato, *Lysis*, 221d. Trans. B. Jowett (1953) [adapt.].

22 Exhibit 3280–1, found at Moschato.

23 Plato, *Apology*, 23c–e. Trans. Brickhouse and Smith (2002).

CHAPTER FORTY-SEVEN

Arginusae – standing out in the crowd

1 Trans. Brickhouse and Smith (2002).

2 Plato, *Apology*, 32b; *Gorgias*, 473e; Xenophon, *Hellenica*, 1.7.16; *Memorabilia*, 1.1.18, 4.4.2.

3 Plato, *Apology*, 32b; Xenophon, *Hellenica*, 1.7.15. Nb The case first went through the Council, Socrates presided over the second day of the Assembly meeting.

4 See Hansen (1999), 248.

5 Xenophon, *Oeconomicus*, 2.2–4, details Socrates' meagre financial situation.

6 Thompson and Wycherley (1972), 44.

7 Voting was originally calibrated by the deposit of an olive leaf by each councillor, but in Socrates' day voting could also be by show of hands. For details of how the *Boule* functioned, see Rhodes (1972).

8 Xenophon, *Hellenica*, 1.7.16–33.

9 Xenophon, *Hellenica*, 1.7.11 (also 12–13). Trans. C. L. Brownson (1918).

10 Could this perhaps be the coalesced passion of a group, trying to find someone to blame for the tragedy of mortality that Arginusae represents?

11 For further illumination see Brunt (1993); Figuiera (1991).

12 Diodorus of Athens, see Jacoby, FGrH 372 (Diod. Periegetes Frags. 34, 35, 40).

13 Xenophon, *Hellenica*, 1.7.16–33.

14 Plato, *Apology*, 18a. Trans. Brickhouse and Smith (2002).

CHAPTER FORTY-EIGHT

Tall poppies, cut corn

1 Trans. J. Barnes (1996). Herodotus tells the same story at 5.92.
2 A democracy still craves heroes. Homeric paragons were still the touchstone of all Athenians, and 'the people' still wanted visionaries — leaders who seemed somehow 'better', to gleam. But whereas it is tempting to fantasise about the great achievements of literary heroes being, really, our own, with mortal success comes envy. The introduction of ostracism is a tangible reminder of this.
3 Sophocles, *Oedipus Rex*, 380–2; 1524–30.
4 Euripides, *Hecuba*, 154–60. Trans. E. P. Coleridge (1938).
5 Plato, *Apology*, 28a–b. Trans. B. Jowett (1953).
6 Euripides, *Phoenician Women*, 243.
7 Demosthenes, 57.45 and 57.31. Although this statement was made in the 340s BC, reference was made back to the period when wet-nurses were usually slave-women, ribbon-sellers usually metic women.
8 Trans. J. D. Sosin. See also Sosin (2008), 105–8.
9 Aristophanes, *Frogs*, 1497.
10 Robin Waterfield's phrase, in Waterfield (2009), 112. As already mentioned, this publication is an incisive examination of the build-up to the trial of Socrates.
11 Xenophon, *Hellenica*, 2.2.8, and Plutarch, *Lysander*, 14–15.
12 Xenophon, *Hellenica*, 2.2.10–11. Trans. R. Warner (1966).
13 Xenophon, *Apology*, 8. He continues, '*And that while other men furnish themselves with expensive delicacies from the market-place I produce, at no cost, more pleasurable ones from my own soul.*' Trans. J. A. Martinez (2002).
14 Xenophon, *Hellenica*, 2.2.20. Trans. R. Warner (1966).
15 Xenophon, *Hellenica*, 2.2.23.

CHAPTER FORTY-NINE

Thirty Tyrants

1 Lysias, *Against Eratosthenes*, esp. 5–21.
2 References to alternative forms of execution can be found, for instance, in Aristophanes, *Thesmophoriazusae*, 929–1209, and Xenophon, *Hellenica*, 1.7.20.
3 Aristophanes, *Frogs*, 120–7.
4 Andocides, 3.10.
5 Xenophon, *Memorabilia*, 1.2.35.
6 Xenophon, *Memorabilia*, 1.2.12. Trans. J. Fogel (2002).
7 Xenophon, *Memorabilia*, 1.2.18–19. Trans. J. Fogel.
8 The Ancient sources were quick to promote the argument that Socrates abused his position as a teacher. This view has down the years been vigorously maintained by modern-day teachers and tutors.

9 This fact is frequently employed to show that Socrates had sympathies with the Thirty. The question is still open as to why Socrates chose not to leave Athens at this time, as other committed democrats did.

10 A later source, Diodorus Siculus, has it that Socrates and two young companions tried to stop the two Scythian guards who had come to exterminate Theramenes — but he begged the philosopher to hold back. *Universal Library*, 14.5.1–3.

11 Xenophon, *Hellenica*, 2.3.15. Trans. R. Warner (1966).

12 Xenophon, *Hellenica*, 2.4.9. Trans. R. Warner (1966).

13 Xenophon, *Hellenica*, 2.4.3, see also Diodorus Siculus, XIV, 32.

14 Plato, *Apology*, 32c–d. Trans. Brickhouse and Smith (2002).

CHAPTER FIFTY

The scapegoat

1 Words reproduced in a variety of scholia and sources from the second century BC to late Antiquity.

2 Socrates was that difficult thing in society: a maverick at the centre of things. Think of a hermit; an anchorite; a prophet on the hill. These remote radicals are less troubling than the inscrutable, revolutionary boy next door.

3 We know that Socrates gave a thought to how the clothes got onto his back, thanks to a little anecdote in Xenophon's *Memorabilia*, 2.7.1–12. Because of the political turmoil following an oligarchic coup, no fewer than fourteen homeless female relatives had to move in to Aristarchus' household. Socrates' advice was brisk — get them to set up a wool-working business so they could derive both job satisfaction and turn a pretty profit. The exchange gives us a little hint of his view on women — that they should be allowed to be a more productive, perhaps even a more valued, part of the body politic. Another troubling half-suggestion that may have earned him distrust.

4 Xenophon, *Memorabilia*, 1.2.9. Trans. J. Fogel (2002).

5 Plato, *Apology*, 17d–18a.

6 Unlike those citizens who have lived and died to be jurors — just listen to Aristophanes in his play *Wasps*: '*It's this that grieves us most of all, to see men who have never served or held either lance or oar in defence of their country, enriching themselves at our expense without ever raising a blister on their hands. In short, I give it as my deliberate opinion that in future every citizen not possessed of a sting shall not receive the three obols.*' Aristophanes, *Wasps* 1117–21. Trans. E. O'Neill (1938).

7 We should, instead, think of him as an unconventional political activist — understanding *polis* in the Greek sense: as a body of men. See Plato, *Gorgias*, 521d, and *Meno*, 100a.

8 Plato, *Gorgias*, 474a.

9 Indictment quoted in Diogenes Laertius, *On the Lives and Opinions of Eminent Philosophers*, 2.40. See also trans. M. Munn (2000): '*Meletus, son of Meletus of Pitthus, has written a sworn indictment against Socrates, son of Sophroniskos of Alopeke, as follows: Socrates has committed the offence of not acknowledging the gods acknowledged by the state and of introducing other new divinities. He has committed the further offence of corrupting the young. Penalty proposed: capital punishment.*' Also para-

phrased in Plato, *Apology*, 24b; *Euthyphro*, 3b; Xenophon, *Memorabilia*, 1.1.1, 1.2.64; *Apology*, 10. When his charges were first read out they were heard by Meletus, the Archon and one or two witnesses whom history has forgotten (possibly by Anytus and Lycon).

10 Plato, *Apology*, 35d–36d.

CHAPTER FIFTY-ONE

An apology

1 Alternative translation: '*I shall be like a doctor tried by a bench of children on a charge brought by a cook.*' Trans. W. R. M. Lamb (1925) [LCL].

2 Plato, *Phaedo*, 109b: '*We live around the sea like frogs live around a pond.*' But Socrates turned his back on the sea. We hear that apart from his military campaigns and that one trip to the Isthmus of Corinth, Socrates shunned his companions' taste for ocean-travel – for yearning to view, and acquire, what lay beyond each horizon. What drew Socrates were not the international highways of the sea, but the twists and turns of rivers. He fought by the broad banks of the reeded River Strymon in Macedonia, he paddled with his favourite it-boys in the Ilissos and composed his thoughts along the lost river of the Eridanos in Athens. It was the rivers that wind through human existence, rather than the oceans that sit at its edge, that constituted his natural home.

3 Plato, *Symposium*, 213e. Trans. M. Joyce (1935).

4 Plato, *Apology*, 35e–8c.

5 Plato, *Apology*, 17b–c.

6 Socrates in Plato, *Apology*, 36b–7a. Trans. H. N. Fowler (1914) [LCL].

7 Plato, *Apology*, 21a.

8 Plato, *Apology*, 20e. Trans. H. N. Fowler (1914) [LCL].

9 Plato, *Apology*, 21a. Trans. H. N. Fowler [LCL].

10 We also hear from Xenophon that Socrates' friends defended him in court.

11 The amount of time Socrates would have been given for his speech is unclear. The length of Plato's account suggests little more than two *khoes*. (A *khoe* is a pitcher-full. In a recent archaeological experiment this seems to give Socrates only six minutes for his final speech.) Since the jury was given no opportunity to confer when making a decision, the voting process is unlikely to have lasted longer than was practically necessary. Cf. Todd (1993), 132–5.

12 Trans M. J. Levett, rev. M. Burnyeat (1990).

13 Plato, *Apology*, 37a–b. Trans. Brickhouse and Smith (2002).

14 There is still some debate as to whether bronze ballots had been brought in by the time of Socrates' trial or whether pebbles were still being used. As yet the archaeological evidence is inconclusive.

15 Aeschines, *Against Timarchus*, 1.30; Demosthenes, *Against Aristogeiton*, 26.2.

16 Aristocrats engaged in vicious blood-feuds (the year of Socrates' trial prostitutes across the city owned by noble families were tortured and murdered by rival aristocratic houses). Socrates' exhortation to 'turn the other cheek' (not as a philanthropic gesture, but because doing so would ensure your own happiness rather then engendering a sense of hate) was considered dangerous nonsense.

17 Professor Paul Cartledge has quite rightly pointed out in his recent work *Ancient Greek Political Thought in Practice* (CUP, 2009) Chapter 7, that the population of Athens was justified in condemning Socrates according to the laws of the day. This raises the interesting question of the ethics of this decision.

18 Plato, *Phaedo*, 117c.

CHAPTER FIFTY-TWO
Twilight and Delos at dawn

1 'Athoi Proverbia'. See W. Bühler (ed.), *Zenotü Athoi proverbia, vulgari ceteraque memoria acuta edidit et enarravit*. Winfried W. Bühler, vol. 4: *Libri secundi proverbia 1–40* complexum (Göttingen, 1982).

2 Plato, *Phaedo*, 58a–c.

3 There is some debate as to the dating of the trip to Delos – and therefore of Socrates' trial. From extant sources it could be inferred that the Delia took place in the (Delian) month of Hieros, in turn associated with Anthesterion (January/February). See Deubner (1932), 203–4. Others date it to the month of Thargelion (April/May), e.g., Nails (2006), 15. White (2000), 155, suggests 7th Mounichion (March/April) for the date of Socrates' trial. For further discussion see Calame (1997:), 107–8.

4 Hesiod, *Homeric Hymn to Apollo* (HAp 14–126).

5 Plutarch, *Theseus*, 23.1.

6 Plutarch, *Theseus*, 23.1, Walker (1995), 43; and Marshall (2000), 352–3.

7 F. Sokolowski (ed.), *Les Lois Sacrées de Cités Grecques: Supplément* (Paris, 1962),

8 Callimachus, *Hymn to Delos*, 307–15, and Plutarch, *Theseus*, 21.1–2.

9 See Hughes (2005), 231–2.

10 Lonsdale (1995), *passim*, for an excellent discussion of the dance in Minoan religion.

11 Work would not start again on the temple until 314 BC.

CHAPTER FIFTY-THREE
Socrates bound

1 Trans. H. N. Fowler (1914).

2 Excellent work dealing with crime and punishment in Athens: Todd (2000), 31–51, and Allen (2000).

3 See, for example, Antiphon 5, *On the Murder of Herodes*, 17.

4 Herodotus, 9.37.2.

5 Plato, *Republic*, 439e.

6 You can still wander around the perimeter of the prison remains, but at the time of writing (2010) access inside had been indefinitely restricted.

7 Plato, *Crito*, 43a. Trans. J. Savage (2010).

8 For a fuller discussion of the role of the Eleven, see Allen (2000); Hunter (1994); Todd (1993); and Herman (2006).

9 But even here perhaps we are being presented with a truth within a story within a

half-truth. Orphic mythology, often dealing with such lyric pursuits, makes much play of the connection between the pursuits of the body (*soma*) and a tomb (*sema*).

10 Xenophon, *Memorabilia*, 4.8.2–3.

11 Plato, *Crito*, 43b. Trans. H. N. Fowler (1914) [LCL].

12 Plato, *Crito*, 45a–c. Trans. H. N. Fowler [LCL].

13 Plato, *Crito*, 50a–b. Trans. H. N. Fowler [LCL] [adapt.].

14 Xenophon, *Apology*, 7. Trans. O. J. Todd (1992) [LCL].

15 Plato, *Crito*, 49a–b. Trans. H. N. Fowler (1914) [LCL] .

16 This potent little plant could have been imported from Asia Minor or Crete. *To pharmakon*, as Plato calls it – the 'useful little thing', which crops up in the earliest form of Greek on Linear B tablets – grew well on Crete, an island that yielded a constitution, the 'Gortyn Code' which Socrates was said to have admired.

17 Plato refers to children who eat hemlock by accident – so, with its purple-spotted stalk and distinctive leaves, it must have grown in the region. Plato, *Lysis*, 219e.

18 Aristophanes, *Frogs*, 117–27. Trans. J. Henderson (2008) [adapt.].

19 See Allen (2000), 234.

20 Plato, *Symposium*, 174a.

21 Plato, *Phaedo*, 89b. Trans. H. N. Fowler (1914) [adapt.].

22 Edith Bloch's article 'Hemlock Poisoning and the Death of Socrates' is essential reading. Her statements on the matter – following her research – are assertive: 'Socrates suffered a peripheral neuropathy, a toxin-induced condition resembling the Guillain-Barré syndrome, brought about by the alkaloids in *Conium maculatum*, the poison hemlock plant.'

23 Transgressive behaviour worthy of the death penalty was in fact fairly limited. '*Now of all the acts for which the laws have prescribed the death penalty – temple robbery, burglary, enslavement, treason to the state – not even my adversaries themselves charge me with having committed any of these.*' Xenophon, *Apology*, 25. Trans. O. J. Todd (1992) [LCL].

24 Plato, aged twenty-eight, sick to the stomach, we are told could not be there.

25 Plato, *Phaedo*, 118a. Trans. H. N. Fowler (1914) [LCL].

26 Plato, *Phaedo*, 118a. Trans. H. N. Fowler [LCL].

27 See, e.g., votive relief NMA 1388 from 400/399 BC, where Asclepius sits proud on an *omphalos* rock.

28 Plato, *Phaedo*, 118a. Trans. G. M. A. Grube (1997).

29 Plato, *Phaedo* 118a. Trans. H. N. Fowler (1914) [LCL].

30 Cf. the similarity of the *soma* (body) and the *sema* (tomb).

31 Plato, *Phaedo*. 63c. Trans. H. N. Fowler [adapt.] [LCL].

32 Robin Waterfield has recently come to a similar conclusion in *Why Socrates Died – Dispelling the Myths* (2009). Waterfield also suggests that because Socrates had failed in his mission, he readily accepted his own sacrifice, and called to Asclepius with his last breath because he believed his own extinction to be a healing act for the city.

33 Plato, *Apology*, 42a.

CHAPTER FIFTY-FOUR

Flight from the world

1 See a vase by the Sappho painter (Bowdoin College Museum of Art 1984, 023). Lysias, *Against Eratosthenes*, 18; Plato, *Phaedo*, 115c.

2 Shear (1995), 'Bouleuterion, Metroon and the Archives at Athens', in Hansen and Raaflaub (1995), 157–190; S. G. Miller (1995), 'Old Metroon and Old Bouleuterion in the classical Agora of Athens', in M. H. Hansen and K. Raaflaub (1995), 133–56.

3 Alcibiades even managed to force his way into this *locus* of Socrates' life. Guards stood outside the state archive the day Socrates was killed, as they did every day of the week – apparently because Alcibiades had once broken in at dead of night to erad-icate investigations into his financial affairs, which had been stored inside. Athenaeus, *Deipnosophistai*, 9.407b–c, on which see Miller (1995), 137. Cf. Plato, *Alcibiades* I 134b.

4 The following details are as laid out by Diogenes Laertius, 1.5.43. Since this is a later source/tradition it is quite possible that this aspect of Socrates' afterlife was fabri-cated. Still, given the quick turnaround of Athenian attitude exemplified by Mytilene, it is also a possibility.

5 Was it simply because we are deeply uncomfortable with those who break the mould? As Alcibiades asserts in the *Symposium* (Plato, *Symposium*, 221c), what Socrates did again and again and again was to take men out of their comfort zones.

6 Some say that there is a certain blackness in Socrates' philosophy. In Plato's, yes, in Socrates'– who can say? As we live our lives with intelligence agencies investing massively in venture capital in order to keep the toys in their box cutting-edge, one wonders whether Socrates would have heaved a world-weary sigh. Don't put all your energies into spy machines, why not try to stop the need for spying? Don't build walls and ships; try to discover 'the good' in those around us. Instead of creating a pretend world on earth – with pretty, impressive objects such as the Parthenon, the White House, the Kremlin – striving to create, and invent, and battle-building yourself out of trouble, make your heart strong. Nowadays we look anxiously for our enemies; for anarchists, terrorists, capitalists, communists, nihilists. But Socrates reminds us of the uncom-fortable truth, that the enemy is always within. It is down to us. That it is not 'their' fault, but 'ours' has to be his single most important, and hard-to-swallow, philosophy.

7 Plato, *Phaedo*, 69b. Trans. H. N. Fowler (1914) [LCL].

8 Plato continued on to Sicily, southern Italy, Cyrene and Egypt.

9 Syllogism based on Aristotle's system of logic as recounted in the *Organon*.

10 Gold keeps its colour at the highest heat, after many thousands of years in the earth. But bronze – the heroic element of Athens – tarnishes. So many bronze statues from the 'Golden Age' have vanished that we can be fooled into thinking this was a land of stone. But bronze would have been everywhere, some of it painted, some of it left au naturel; coins were made of bronze, as were furniture decorations, ceremonial swords, religious tokens. As it oxidises, raw bronze dulls, greens, its surface complexes over time. As the Athenian democracy was oxygenated, as it breathed in and out over the years, its patina too became more complex.

11 Even a god had to be morally good in Socrates' way of thinking; this was very uncon-ventional, see, e.g., *Euthyphro* 6a–c.

Coda: The tomb of Socrates – the Tower of the Winds

1 Trans. Brickhouse and Smith (2002).
2 Beard (2002), p.71ff.
3 Plutarch, *Moralia, On Banishment*, 600f.
4 Plato, *Apology*, 29a–b. Trans. Brickhouse and Smith (2002).

Afterword

1 Zanker (1995), 58.
2 Plato, *Phaedrus*, 275d–e. Trans. H. N. Fowler [LCL]. Nb. Socrates' mistrust of the written word was particularly out of kilter with Athens towards the end of his life when democracy had been declared restored on stone stelai around the city and on papyrus sheets in the Metroon.

APPENDIX ONE
Honouring Aphrodite

1 Euripides, Frag. 898; see Nauck (1926), p.648; Segal (1965), p.119 – see Rosenzweig (2007), p.80.
2 One day in the future, doubtless, Aphrodite's sanctuary on the banks of the Ilissos, Aphrodite Ourania 'in the gardens' will be discovered, a sanctuary that would have been familiar to Socrates.
3 Dillon (2003), 57–8.
4 Pausanias, 1.27.3.
5 See Rosenzweig (2007), p.18, for a discussion of the likelihood of this nomination. I have relied heavily on Rosenzweig in this Appendix.
6 1980–2, American School at Athens.
7 The inscription continues with the names of the benefactors. '*Archinos, son of Alypetos from Skambonidai, and his mother, Menekrateia, daughter of Dexikrates from Ikaria, priestess of Aphrodite.*' Mid-fourth-century BC. IG II² 4596; Beschi (1967/8), p.522; Hansen (1989), p.186, no. 775.
8 Aphrodite was of course worshipped elsewhere in Attica: at the Bay of Phaleron east of Piraeus, in the Ilissos and in Daphni to the north. And at least eight state-sponsored shrines in Attica.
9 4 of Hecatombaeon and 4 of Munichion.
10 We know from Menander's New Comedy *The Flatterer* how the rites – in this case to Aphrodite on the fourth of the month – were practised. The Athenians, on this occasion a guild of Aphrodite-worshippers called the Tetradistai, hired a professional sacrificer.
11 Plato, *Symposium*, 211b–c. Trans. W. Hamilton (1951).
12 Plato, *Gorgias*, 508a. Trans. D. J. Zeyl (1997) [adapt.].

13 Plato, *Philebus*, 28d–30c.

14 See Rosenzweig (2007), 18, for a discussion of the likelihood of this nomination.

15 Plato, *Phaedrus*, 251b. Trans. H. N. Fowler [LCL]; Plato, *Symposium*, 177e; Xenophon, *Symposium*, 8.2.

APPENDIX TWO

Mysteria – the Eleusinian Mysteries

1 Cat. ref. 4011. My thanks to Professor Cosmopoulos for this reference and for his time spent guiding me around this site.

2 Although slaves, it seemed, could also be involved.

3 Aeschylus' home *deme* was Eleusis.

4 See Parker (2007), 46ff.

5 Plato, *Phaedrus*, 250c; Plutarch, Frag. 178; both cited by Parker (2007), 354–5.

6 Conveniently, Eleusis doubled up as a sanctuary for the body as well as the soul. The complex was surrounded by a fortified wall. Xerxes' men had smashed this down in 479 BC, but it had been re-built with a flourish as part of Pericles' grand PR exercise, and within thirty years it kept Greeks safe once more. Once democracy was re-restored to Athens in 404/3 BC Eleusis was declared a refuge for oligarchs (until 401). If those with a cloudy political past felt unhappy in Athens they were guaranteed safe passage here.

7 By Socrates' day, Eleusis had already been a significant ritual site for well over 1,000 years. See Cosmopoulos (2003) for a fascinating description of Eleusis and the Eleusinian Mysteries. Eleusis exemplified the inescapable rhythm of ritual life in Athens that Socrates threatened to disturb. The timing of his trial did indeed interrupt that calendrical and meterological beat.

BIBLIOGRAPHY

⁓⁓⁓⁓⁓⁓⁓

Ancient Texts and Translations

⁓⁓⁓⁓⁓⁓⁓

ARISTOPHANES, *Birds; Lysistrata; Women at the Thesmophoria*:
Birds, Lysistrata, Women at the Thesmophoria; translated by J. Henderson. Cambridge,
MA: Harvard University Press; London: William Heinemann Ltd. 2000.

ARISTOPHANES, *Clouds*:
Clouds/Aristophanes; edited with translation and notes by A. H.
Sommerstein. Warminster: Aris & Phillips. 1982.

ARISTOPHANES, *Wasps*:
Aristophanes' Wasps; edited with introduction and commentary by Douglas M.
MacDowell. Oxford: Clarendon Press. 1971.

ATHENAEUS, *The Deipnosophists*:
The Learned Banqueters, translated by S. D. Olson. Cambridge, MA: Harvard
University Press. 2007.

AULUS GELLIUS, *The Attic Nights*:
The Attic Nights/Aulus Gellius; translated by J. C. Rolfe. London: W.
Heinemann. 1927.

CALLIMACHUS, *Hymns and Epigrams*:
Hymns and Epigrams/ Callimachus; translated by A. W. Mair. London:
Heinemann. 1955.

CALLIMACHUS, *Hymn to Delos*:
Callimachus, Hymn to Delos; introduction and commentary by W. H.
Mineur. Leiden: E. J. Brill. 1984.

DIOGENES LAERTIUS, *Lives of Eminent Philosophers*:
Lives of Eminent Philosophers/ Diogenes Laertius; translated by R. D. Hicks.
London: W. Heinemann. 1925.

DIOGENES LAERTIUS, *Lives of Eminent Philosophers*:
The Lives and Opinions of Eminent Philosophers; translated by C. D. Yonge.
London: George Bell and Sons. Reprinted in original format by Kessinger
Publishing. 1901.

EURIPIDES, *Selected Fragmentary Plays*:
Euripides: Selected Fragmentary Plays: Philoctetes, Alexandros (with Palamedes and Sisyphus), Oedipus, Andromeda, Hypsipyle, Antiope, Archelaus, volume two; with introductions, translations and commentaries by C. Collard, M. J. Cropp, K. H. Lee. Warminster: Aris & Phillips. 2004.

ISOCRATES:
Isocrates in three volumes; translated by L. V. Hook. Cambridge, MA: Harvard University Press; London: William Heinemann Ltd. 1986.

PANAETIUS:
Panaetii Rhodii Fragmenta; edited by M. van Straaten. Leiden: E. J. Brill. 1952.

PAUSANIAS, *Description of Greece*:
Description of Greece/ Pausanius in four volumes; translated by W. H. S. Jones and H. A. Ormerod. Cambridge, MA: Harvard University Press; London: William Heinemann Ltd. 1918.

PAUSANIAS, *Description of Greece*:
Pausanias's Description of Greece in six volumes; translated with commentary by J. G. Frazer. London: Macmillan. 1898.

PLATO, *Crito*:
Plato: Crito; with introduction and commentary by C. Emlyn-Jones. London: Duckworth/Bristol Classical Press. 1999.

PLATO, *Euthyphro; Apology; Crito; Phaedo; Phaedrus*:
Euthyphro; Apology; Crito; Phaedo; Phaedrus; translated by H. N. Fowler and introduced by W. R. M. Lamb. Cambridge, MA: Harvard University Press; London: Heinemann. 1960.

PLATO, *Laches; Protagoras; Meno; Euthydemus*:
Laches; Protagoras; Meno; Euthydemus/Plato; translated by W. R. M. Lamb. London: William Heinemann Ltd. 1924.

PLATO, *Laws*:
Laws in twelve volumes, vols. 10 & 11 translated by R. G. Bury. Cambridge, MA: Harvard University Press; London: William Heinemann Ltd. 1967 & 1968.

PLATO, *Phaedo*:
Plato: the Phaedo; edited with introduction and notes by W. D. Geddes. London: Macmillan 1863.

PLATO, *Protagoras*:
Protagoras/ Plato; edited by N. Denyer. Cambridge: Cambridge University Press. 2008.

PLATO, *Republic*:
Plato Republic 1–2.368c4; with introduction, translation and commentary by C. Emlyn-Jones. Oxford: Aris and Philips Classical Texts, Oxbow Books. 2007.

PLATO, *The Statesman; Philebus; Ion:*
The Statesman; Philebus; Ion/ Plato; translated by H. N. Fowler. London: W. Heinemann Ltd. 1925.

PLUTARCH, *Lives:*
Lives volumes 1 and 2; translated by B. Perrin. London: W. Heinemann. 1914 and 1948.

PSEUDO-XENOPHON, *Constitution of the Athenians:*
The Old Oligarch: Pseudo-Xenophon's 'Constitution of the Athenians' 2nd ed. with introduction, translation and commentary by R. Osborne. London: London Association of Classical Teachers. 2004.

SCHOLIA ON ARISTOPHANES:
Scholia Graeca in Aristophanem, cum prolegomenis grammaticorum, varietate lectionis optimorum codicum integra, ceterorum selecta, annotatione criticorum item selecta, cui sua quaedam inseruit
edited by F. Dübner. Paris: Firmin Didot. 1842.

SENECA THE ELDER:
L. Annaei Senecae ludus de morte Claudii, Epigrammata super exilio; edited by F. Haase. Lipsiae: in aedibus B.G. Teubneri. 1902.

XENOPHON, *Memorabilia; Oeconomicus; Symposium; Apology:*
Memorabilia; Oeconomicus; Symposium; Apology; translated by E. C. Marchant and O. J. Todd. Cambridge, MA: Harvard University Press; London: Heinemann. 1923.

◈◈◈◈◈

Translations and Commentaries

@@@@@@@@@@@@@@

AESCHINES

Aeschines:
Davidson, J. (2007) *The Greeks and Greek love: a radical reappraisal of homosexuality in Ancient Greece*. London: Weidenfeld and Nicolson.
Aeschines, *Against Timarchus*:
Fisher, N. (2001) *Aeschines. Against Timarchus*. Oxford: Oxford University Press.

AESCHYLUS

Aeschylus, *Eumenides*:
Morshead, E. D. A., from The Internet Classics Archive:
  http://classics.mit.edu/Aeschylus/eumendides.html
Vellacott, P. (1956) *The Oresteian trilogy: Agamemnon, The Choephori, The Eumenides*. Harmondsworth: Penguin.
Aeschylus, *The Persians*:
Smyth, H. W. (1973) *Aeschylus. Vol. I*. Cambridge, MA: Harvard University Press. Loeb Classical Library [LCL].
Vellacott, P. (1961) *Aeschylus. Prometheus bound; The Suppliants; Seven against Thebes; The Persians*. Harmondsworth: Penguin.

ANDOCIDES

Andocides, *Against Alcibiades*:
Maidment, K. J. (1941) *Minor Attic Orators. Vol I*. London: W. Heinemann. LCL.

ARISTOPHANES

Aristophanes, *Acharnians*:
Allen, D. (1996) 'A Schedule of Boundaries: An Exploration, launched from the Water-Clock, of Athenian Time' in *Greece and Rome* 43.
Henry, M. M. (1995) *Prisoner of history: Aspasia of Miletus and her biographical tradition*. Oxford: Oxford University Press.

Aristophanes, *Birds*:

Henderson, J. (2000) *Birds. Lysistrata. Women at the Thesmophoria.* Cambridge, MA: Harvard University Press. LCL.

Rogers, B. B. (1930) *The Birds of Aristophanes: the Greek text revised, with a translation into corresponding metres, introduction and commentary.* London: Bell.

Sommerstein, A. H. (1987) *Aristophanes: Birds.* Warminster: Aris and Phillips.

Aristophanes, *Clouds*:

McLeish, K. (1979) *Aristophanes. Clouds. Women in Power. Knights.* Cambridge: University of Cambridge Press.

Sommerstein, A. H. (1973) *Aristophanes. Lysistrata. The Acharnians. The Clouds.* London: Penguin.

Aristophanes, *Ecclesiazusae, Peace* and *Wasps*:

O'Neill Jr, E. (1938) *Aristophanes. The Complete Greek drama. Vol. 2.* New York: Random House.

Aristophanes, *Frogs*:

Barrett, D. (1964) *Aristophanes. The Frogs and other plays.* Harmondsworth: Penguin.

Henderson, J. (2008) *Aristophanes: Frogs.* Newburyport, MA: Focus Publishing/R Pullins and Co.

Murray, G. (1908) *The Frogs of Aristophanes.* London: George Allen & Unwin.

Theodoridis, G.
http://www.poetryintranslation.com/PITBR/Greek/FrogsActIISceneIII.htm

ARISTOTLE

Aristotle, *Athenian Constitution*:

Rhodes, P. J. (1984) *Aristotle. The Athenian Constitution.* London: Penguin.

Aristotle, *Politics*:

Barnes, J. in S. Everson (ed.) (1996) *Aristotle. The Politics and the Constitution of Athens.* Cambridge: Cambridge University Press.

Sinclair, T. A., revised by T. J. Saunders (1981) *Aristotle. The Politics.* Harmondsworth: Penguin.

Aristotle, *Rhetoric*:

Lawson-Tancred, H. C. (1991) *Aristotle. The Art of Rhetoric.* London: Penguin.

AULUS GELLIUS

Aulus Gellius, *Attic Nights*:
J. C. Rolfe (1927) *The Attic Nights of Aulus Gellius*. London: W. Heinemann; Cambridge, MA: Havard University Press. LCL.

AXIOCHUS

Axiochus:
Hershbell, J. P. in J. M. Cooper (ed.) (1997) *Complete works / Plato*. Indianapolis: Hackett Publishing.

CENSORINUS

Censorinus, *De Die Natali*:
Parker, H. N. (2007) *The Birthday Book; Censorinus*. Chicago: University of Chicago Press.

CRATINUS

Cratinus, *Cheirons*:
Henry, M. M. (1995) *Prisoner of History: Aspasia of Miletus and her Biographical Tradition*. Oxford: Oxford University Press.

DIOGENES LAERTIUS

Diogenes Laertius, *Lives of Eminent Philosophers*:
Hicks, R. D. (1925) *Lives of Eminent Philosophers*. Cambridge, MA: University of Harvard Press. LCL.
Munn, M. (2000) *The School of History. Athens in the Age of Socrates*. Berkeley: University of California Press.
Yonge, C. D. (1853) *The Lives and Opinions of Eminent Philosophers by Diogenes Laertius*. London: Henry G. Bohn.

EURIPIDES

Euripides, *Hecuba*:

Coleridge, E. P. in W. J. Oates and E. O'Neill Jr (eds.) (1938) *Euripides. The Complete Greek Drama in two volumes*. Vol. *I Hecuba*. New York: Random House.

Euripides, *Hippolytus*:

Kovacs, D. (1995) *Children of Heracles. Hippolytus. Andromache. Hecuba*. Cambridge, MA: Harvard University Press. LCL.

Vellacott, P. (1953) *Three plays: Hippolytus, Iphigenia in Tauris, Alcestis. Euripides*. Harmondsworth: Penguin.

Euripides, *Orestes*:

Blundell, S. (1995) *Women in Ancient Greece*. London: British Museum Press.

Euripides, *Phoenician Women*:

Murray, G. (1913) *Euripides. Euripidis Fabulae*. Oxford: Clarendon Press. [Perseus Trans.].

Wilson, A. See website: http://www.users.globalnet.co.uk/~loxias/phoenissae.htm

Euripides, *The Suppliant Women*:

Vellacott, P. (1972) *Euripides. Orestes and Other Plays*. Harmondsworth: Penguin.

Euripides, *Women of Troy*:

Vellacott, P. (1973) *The Bacchae and Other Plays. Euripides*. Harmondsworth: Penguin.

GORGIAS

Gorgias, *Helen*:

Sprague, R. K. (ed.) (2001) *The Older Sophists*. Indianapolis: Hackett Publishing.

HERODOTUS

Herodotus:

De Sélincourt, A. (1954) *The Histories. Herodotus*. Harmondsworth: Penguin.

Godley, A. D. (1920) *The Persian Wars*. Cambridge, MA: Harvard University Press. LCL.

Purvis, A. (2007) in R. B. Strassler, *The Landmark Herodotus: The Histories*. New York: Pantheon.

HESIOD

Hesiod, *Works and Days*:
Evelyn-White, H. G. (1914) *Hesiod, Homeric Hymns and Homerica.* London: Heinemann.
Most, G. W. (2006) *Hesiod. Theogony. Works and Days. Testimonia.* Cambridge, MA: Harvard University Press. LCL.
Tandy, D. W. and Neale, W. C. (1996) *Hesiod's Works and Days.* Berkeley, CA: University of California Press.
Wender, D. (1973) *Hesiod. Theogony. Works and Days. Theognis. Elegies.* London: Penguin.

HOMER

Homer, *Iliad*:
Butler, S. [Perseus edition –
http://www.perseus.tufts.edu/hopper/text?doc=Perseus:text:1999.01.0134].

ISOCRATES

Isocrates, *Address to the Areopagus*:
Mirhady, D. C. and Yun Lee Too (2000) *Isocrates Vol. I.* Austin: University of Texas Press.
Norlin, G. (1980) *Isocrates. Vol. 2.* Cambridge, MA: Havard University Press. LCL.

LYSIAS

Lysias, *Simon*:
Lamb, W. R. M. (1930) *Lysias.* Cambridge, MA: Harvard University Press. LCL.
Todd, L. S. (2000) *Lysias.* Austin: University of Texas Press.

PINDAR

Pindar, *Nemean Odes*:
Lattimore, R. (1959) *The Odes of Pindar.* Chicago: University of Chicago Press.

Pindar, *Pythian Odes*:

Gildersleeve, B. L. (1890) *Pindar. The Olympian and Pythian Odes*. London: Macmillan.

PLATO

Plato, *Alcibiades I*:

Hutchinson, D. S. in J. M. Cooper (ed.) (1997) *Complete works / Plato*. Indianapolis: Hackett Publishing.

Lamb, W. R. M. (1927) *Plato. Charmides. Alcibiades I and II. Hipparchus. The Lovers. Theages. Minos. Epinomis*. Cambridge, MA: Harvard University Press. LCL.

Plato, *Apology*:

Brickhouse, T. C. and N. D. Smith (2002) *The Trial and Execution of Socrates. Sources and Controversies*. Oxford: Oxford University Press.

Fowler, H. N. (1914) *Plato. Euthyphro, Apology, Crito, Phaedo, Phaedrus*. Cambidge, MA: Harvard University Press. LCL.

Grube, G. M. A. in J. M. Cooper (ed.) (1997) *Complete works / Plato*. Indianapolis: Hackett Publishing.

Jowett, B. (1953) *The Dialogues of Plato*. Oxford: Clarendon Press.

Tredennick, H. (1954) *Plato. The Last Days of Socrates*. London: Penguin.

Tredennick, H. in E. Hamilton and H. Cairns (eds.) (1973) *The Collected Dialogues of Plato*. Princeton, NJ: Princeton University Press.

Plato, *Charmides*:

Jowett, B. (1953) *The Dialogues of Plato*. Oxford: Clarendon Press.

Plato, *Crito*:

Fowler, H. N. (1914) *Plato. Euthyphro, Apology, Crito, Phaedo, Phaedrus*. Cambridge, MA: Harvard University Press. LCL.

Grube, G. M. A. in J. M. Cooper (ed.) (1997) *Complete works / Plato*. Indianapolis: Hackett Publishing.

Plato, *Euthyphro*:

Brickhouse, T. C. and Smith, N. D. (2002) *The Trial and Execution of Socrates. Sources and Controversies*. Oxford: Oxford University Press.

Fowler, H. N. (1914) *Plato. Euthyphro, Apology, Crito, Phaedo, Phaedrus*. Cambridge, MA: Harvard University Press. LCL.

Plato, *Gorgias*:

Lamb, W. R. M. (1925) *Plato. Lysis, Symposium, Gorgias*. Cambridge, MA: Harvard University Press. LCL.

Zeyl, D. J. in J. M. Cooper (ed.) (1997) *Complete works / Plato*. Indianapolis: Hackett Publishing.

Plato, *Hippias Minor*:

Lamb, W. R. M. (1926) *Volume IV. Cratylus. Parmenides. Greater Hippias. Lesser Hippias.* Cambridge, MA: Harvard University Press. LCL.

Plato, *Ion*:

Lamb, W. R. M. (1925) *Plato. Statesman. Philebus. Ion.* Cambridge, MA: Harvard University Press. LCL.

Saunders, T. J. (ed.) (1987) *Early Socratic Dialogues.* London: Penguin.

Plato, *Laches*:

Jowett, B. (1953) *The Dialogues of Plato I.* Oxford: Clarendon Press.

Plato, *Laws*:

Saunders, T. J. (1975) *Plato: The Laws.* Harmondsworth: Penguin.

Plato, *Lysis*:

Jowett, B. (1953) *The Dialogues of Plato I.* Oxford: Clarendon Press.

Lamb, W. R. M. (1925) *Plato. Lysis, Symposium, Gorgias.* Cambridge, MA: Harvard University Press. LCL.

Lombardo, S. in J. M. Cooper (ed.) (1997) *Complete works / Plato.* Indianapolis: Hackett Publishing.

Plato, *Menexenus*:

Bury, R. G. (1929) *Plato. Timaeus. Critias. Cleitophon. Menexenus. Epistles.* Cambridge, MA: Harvard University Press. LCL.

Jowett, B. (1953) *The Dialogues of Plato.* Oxford: Clarendon Press.

Plato, *Meno*:

Guthrie, W. K. C. (1956) *Plato. Protagoras and Meno.* London: Penguin.

Lamb, W. R. M. (1924) *Plato. Laches, Protagoras, Meno, Euthydemus.* Cambridge, MA: Harvard University Press. LCL.

Plato, *Parmenides*:

Cornford, F. M. in E. Hamilton and H. Cairns (eds.) (1973) *The Collected Dialogues of Plato.* Princeton, NJ: Princeton University Press.

Gill, M. L. and P. Ryan in J. M. Cooper (ed.) (1997) *Complete works / Plato.* Indianapolis: Hackett Publishing.

Plato, *Phaedo*:

Fowler, H. N. (1914) *Plato. Euthyphro, Apology, Crito, Phaedo, Phaedrus.* Cambridge, MA: Harvard University Press. LCL.

Jowett, B. (1953) *The Dialogues of Plato Vol. I.* Oxford: Clarendon Press.

Tredennick, H. (1954) *Plato. The Last Days of Socrates.* London: Penguin.

Plato, *Phaedrus*:

Fowler, H. N. (1914) *Plato. Euthyphro, Apology, Crito, Phaedo, Phaedrus.* Cambridge, MA: Harvard University Press. LCL.

Jowett, B. (1953) *The Dialogues of Plato I.* Oxford: Clarendon Press.

Plato, *Protagoras*:

Jowett, B. (1953) *The Dialogues of Plato Vol. I.* Oxford: Clarendon Press.

Lamb, W. R. M. (1924) *Plato. Laches. Protagoras. Meno. Euthydemus.* Cambridge, MA: Harvard University Press. LCL.

Plato, *Republic*:

Grube, G. M. A. revised by C. D. C. Reeve in J. M. Cooper (ed.) (1997) *Complete works / Plato.* Indianapolis: Hackett Publishing.

Jowett, B. (1953) *The Dialogues of Plato.* Oxford: Clarendon Press.

Shorey, P. (1930) *Plato's Republic I.* Cambridge, MA: Harvard University Press. LCL.

Waterfield, R. (1993) *Plato. Republic.* New York: Oxford University Press.

Plato, *Sophist*:

Cornford, F. M. in E. Hamilton and H. Cairns (eds.) (1973) *The Collected Dialogues of Plato.* Princeton, NJ: Princeton University Press.

Plato, *Symposium*:

Gill, C. (1999) *Plato. The Symposium.* London: Penguin.

Hamilton, W. (1951) *Plato. The Symposium.* Harmondsworth: Penguin.

Jowett, B. (1953) *The Dialogues of Plato I.* Oxford: Clarendon Press.

Joyce, M. (1935) *Plato's Symposium, or, The Drinking Party.* London: Dent.

Lamb, W. R. M. (1925) *Plato. Lysis, Symposium, Gorgias.* Cambridge, MA: Harvard University Press. LCL.

Nehamas, A. and P. Woodruff in J. M. Cooper (ed.) (1997) *Complete works / Plato.* Indianapolis: Hackett Publishing.

Reeve, C. D. C. (ed. and trans.) (2006) *Plato on Love.* Indianapolis: Hackett Publishing.

Plato, *Theaetetus*:

Levett, M. J., revised by M. Burnyeat (1990) *The Theaetetus of Plato.* Indianapolis: Hackett Publishing.

PLUTARCH

Plutarch, *Agesilaus*:

Davidson, J. (2007) *The Greeks and Greek Love: a radical reappraisal of homosexuality in Ancient Greece.* London: Weidenfeld and Nicolson.

Shipley, D. R. (1997) *A Commentary on Plutarch's life of Agesilaos: response to sources in the presentation of character.* Oxford: Clarendon Press.

Plutarch, *Life of Alcibiades*:

Perrin, B. (1916) *Lives IV.* Cambridge, MA: Harvard University Press. LCL.

Plutarch, *Life of Pericles*:

Scott-Kilvert, I. (1960) *Plutarch. The Rise and Fall of Athens: nine Greek lives.* Harmondsworth: Penguin.

Waterfield, R. (2008) *Greek lives: a selection of nine Greek lives. Plutarch.* Oxford: Oxford University Press.

POLYAENUS

Polyaenus, *Strategemata*:

Joyce, M. in E. Hamilton and H. Cairns (eds.) (1973) *The Collected Dialogues of Plato.* Princeton, NJ: Princeton University Press.

Kagan, D. (1991) *The Peace of Nicias and the Sicilian Expedition.* New York: Cornell University Press.

PORPHYRY

Porphyry, *On Abstinence From Killing Animals*:

Clark, G. (2000) *Porphyry. On Abstinence from Killing Animals.* London: Duckworth.

SAPPHO

Sappho, *Fragments*:

Duffy, C. A. (2009) *Stung with Love: poems and fragments of Sappho.* London: Penguin.

Wharton, H. T. (1885) *Sappho: memoir, text, selected readings and a literal translation.* London: Stott.

SOPHOCLES

Sophocles, *Ajax*:

Moore, J. in D. Grene and R. Lattimore (eds.) (1954) *Sophocles. Vol. II.* London; Chicago: University of Chicago Press.

Sophocles, *Oedipus the King*:

Berg, S. and Clay, D. (1978) *Oedipus the King: The Greek Tragedy in New Translations.* New York: Oxford University Press.

Sophocles, *Women of Trachis*:
Jebb, R. C. (1892) *Sophocles. The Plays and Fragments with critical notes, commentary and translation in English prose. Part V. The Trachinae.* Cambridge: Cambridge University Press.

THEOGNIS

Theognis:
Bing, P. and Cohen, R. (1991) *Games of Venus: an anthology of Greek and Roman erotic verse from Sappho to Ovid.* London: Routledge.
Hubbard, T. K. (ed.) (2003) *Homosexuality in Greece and Rome. A Sourcebook of Basic Documents.* Berkeley: University of California Press.

THUCYDIDES

Thucydides:
Crawley, R. (1910) *Thucydides, The Peloponnesian War.* London: J. M. Dent; New York: E. P. Dutton.
Hammond, M. (2009) *Thucydides. The Peloponnesian War.* New York; Oxford: Oxford University Press.
Kagan, D. (1981) *The Peace of Nicias and the Sicilian Expedition.* New York: Cornell University Press.
Smith, C. F. (1919) *Thucydides. History of the Peloponnesian War.* Cambridge, MA: Harvard University Press. LCL.
Warner, R. (1972) *History of the Peloponnesian War. Thucydides.* Harmondsworth: Penguin.
Woodruff, P. (1993) *On justice, power, and human nature: the essence of Thucydides' History of the Peloponnesian War.* Indianapolis; Cambridge: Hackett Publishing.

TYRTAIOS

Tyrtaios, *Fragment*:
Lattimore, R. (1955). *Greek Lyrics.* Chicago: University of Chicago Press.

XENOPHON

Xenophon:
Bysshe, E. (1747) *The Memorable Thoughts of Socrates.* George Faulkner: Dublin.
H. Tredennick and R. Waterfield (1990) *Xenophon. Conversations of Socrates.* London: Penguin.

Xenophon, *Anabasis*:
Brownson, C. L. (1922, rev. J. Dillery 1998) *Anabasis, Xenophon.* Cambridge, MA: Harvard University Press.

Xenophon *Apology*:
Martinez, J. A. in T. C. Brickhouse and N. D. Smith (2002) *The Trial and Execution of Socrates. Sources and Controversies.* Oxford: Oxford University Press.
Todd, O. J. in E. C. Marchant and O. J. Todd (1992) *Memorabilia, Oeconomicus, Symposium, Apology.* Cambridge, MA: Harvard University Press. LCL.
Tredennick, H. and R. Waterfield, (1990) *Conversations of Socrates. Xenophon.* London: Penguin.

Xenophon, *Hellenica*:
Brownson, C. L. (1918) *Xenophon. Hellenica. Books 1–4.* Cambridge, MA: Harvard University Press. LCL.
Marincola, J. (2009) in R. S. Strassler (ed.) *Landmark Xenophon's Hellenika.* New York: Pantheon.
Warner, R. (1966, rev. G. Cawkwell 1979) *Xenophon. A History of My Times.* Harmondsworth: Penguin.

Xenophon, *Memorabilia*:
Fogel, J. in T. C. Brickhouse and N. D. Smith (2002) *The Trial and Execution of Socrates. Sources and Controversies.* Oxford: Oxford University Press.
Gutenberg Project. 1889 Cassell and Company edition by David Price. (http://www.gutenberg.org/files/17490/17490-h/17490-h.htm)
Marchant, E. C. in E. C. Marchant and O. J. Todd (1992) *Memorabilia, Oeconomicus, Symposium, Apology.* Cambridge, MA: Harvard University Press. LCL.
Tredennick, H. and Waterfield, R. (1990) *Xenophon. Conversations of Socrates.* London: Penguin.

Xenophon, *Oeconomicus*:
Blundell, S. and Williamson, M. (1998) *The Sacred and the Feminine in Ancient Greece.* London: Routledge.
Dakyns, H. G. (1890) *The Works of Xenophon.* London: Macmillan.
Marchant, E. C. in E. C. Marchant and O. J. Todd (1992) *Memorabilia, Oeconomicus, Symposium, Apology.* Cambridge, MA: Harvard University Press. LCL.

Pomeroy, S. (1994) *Xenophon. Oeconomicus: a social and historical commentary.* Oxford: Clarendon Press.

Xenophon *Symposium*:

Todd, O. J. in E. C. Marchant and O. J. Todd (1992) *Memorabilia, Oeconomicus, Symposium, Apology.* Cambridge, MA: Harvard University Press. LCL.

Xenophon, *The Cavalry Commander*:

Marchant, E. and Bowersock, G. W. (1925) *Xenophon. Scripta Minora.* Cambridge, MA: Harvard University Press. LCL.

Waterfield, R. and Cartledge, P. (1997) *Hiero the Tyrant and Other Treatises.* London: Penguin.

ZEPHANIAH

Holy Bible, New Living Translation, copyright 1996. Used by permission of Tyndale House Publishers, Inc., Wheaton, Illinois 60189.

OTHER

Oath of Ephebes:

Rhodes, P. J. and Osborne, R. (2003) *Greek Historical Inscriptions.* New York: Oxford University Press.

Samons, L. J. (2004) *What's Wrong with Democracy? From Athenian Practice to American Worship.* Berkeley: University of California Press.

OTHER WORKS

Ahbel-Rappe, S. and Kamtekar, R. (eds.) (2006) *A Companion to Socrates.* Oxford: Blackwell Publishing.

Alexander, J. A (1963) *Potidaea: Its History and Remains.* Athens: University of Georgia Press.

Allen, D. S. (2000) *The World of Prometheus: The Politics of Punishing in Democratic Athens.* Princeton, NJ: Princeton University Press.

Alon, I (1995) *Socrates Arabus: Life and Teachings.* Jerusalem: The Hebrew University of Jerusalem.

Anderson, M. (2005) 'Socrates as Hoplite' in *Ancient Philosophy* 25: 273–289.

Armstrong, A. H. (1965) *An Introduction to Ancient Philosophy.* London and USA: Methuen.

Arnold, I. R. (1933) 'Local Festivals at Delos' in *American Journal of Archaeology* 37: 452–458.

Atchley, S. C. (1938) *Wild Flowers of Attica*. Oxford: Clarendon Press.

Ault, B. A. (2005) 'Housing the Poor and the Homeless in Ancient Greece' in B. A. Ault and L. C. Nevett (eds.) *Ancient Greek Houses and Households: Chronological, Regional, and Social Diversity*. Philadelphia: University of Pennsylvania Press: 140–159.

Austin, C. and S. D. Olson (2004) *Aristophanes* Thesmophoriazusae (Oxford/New York: OUP).

Aveni, F. A. and Ammerman, A. (2001) 'Early Greek Astronomy in the Oral Tradition and the Search for Archaeological Correlates' in *Archaeoastronomy* 16: 83–97.

Bailey, D. M. (1974) 'A Caricature of Socrates' in *American Journal of Archaeology* 78: 426.

Baumann, H. (1993) *Greek Wild Flowers and Plant Lore in Ancient Greece*; translated and augmented by W. T. Stearn and E. R. Stearn. London: Herbert Press.

Beard, M. (2002) *The Parthenon*. London: Profile Books.

Bell, A. (2004) *Spectacular Power in the Greek and Roman City*. New York: Oxford University Press.

Benson, L. D. (ed.) (3rd edn. 1987) *The Riverside Chaucer*. Boston: Houghton Mifflin.

Bernal, M. (1996) *Black Athena: The Afroasiatic Roots of Classical Civilization. Volume II: The Archaeological Evidence*. New Brunswick, NJ: Rutgers University Press.

Bers, V. (1985) 'Dikastic *Thorubos*' in P. A. Cartledge and F. D. Harvey (eds.) *Crux: Essays in Greek History Presented to G.E.M. de Ste. Croix on His 75th Birthday*. London: Duckworth: 1–15.

Beschi, L. (1967/8) 'Contributi di Topographia Ateniese' ASAtene 45/46: 511–536.

Bicknell, P. J. 'Axiochus Alkibiadou, Aspasia and Aspasios' in *Acta Classica* 51: 240–250.

———— (1982) (1974) 'Sokrates' Mistress Xanthippe' in *Apeiron* 8: 1–5.

Billington, S. and Green, M. (eds.) (1996) *The Concept of the Goddesses*. London and New York: Routledge.

Bloch, E. (2002) 'Hemlock Poisoning and the Death of Socrates. Did Plato tell the truth?' in T. C. Brickhouse and N. D. Smith, *The Trial and Execution of Socrates. Sources and Controversies*. Oxford: Oxford University Press.

Blundell, S. (1995) *Women in Ancient Greece*. London: British Museum Press.

Blundell, S. and Williamson, M. (eds.) (1998) *The Sacred and the Feminine in Ancient Greece*. London and New York: Routledge.

Boardman, J. (1990) '*Symposion* Furniture' in O. Murray (ed.) *Sympotica: A Symposium on the Symposion*. Oxford: Clarendon Press: 122–131.

Boedeker, D. and Raaflaub, K. A. (eds.) (1998) *Democracy, Empire, and the Arts in Fifth-Century Athens.* Cambridge, MA: Harvard University Press.

Boegehold, A. L. (1995) *The Lawcourts at Athens: Sites, Buildings, Equipment, Procedure, and Testimonia; with Contributions by John McK. Camp II.* Princeton, NJ: American School of Classical Studies at Athens.

Boersma, J. S. (1970) *Athenian Building Policy from 561/0 to 405/4 B.C.* Groningen: Wolters-Noordhoff Publishing.

Brickhouse, T. C. and Smith, N. D. (2004) *Routledge Philosophy Guidebook to Plato and the Trial of Socrates.* London: Routledge.

———— (2002) *The Trial and Execution of Socrates: Sources and Controversies.* Oxford: Oxford University Press.

Bringmann, K. (1971) 'Xenophons Hellenika und Agesilaos. Zu ihrer Entstehungsweise und Datierung', *Gymnasium* 78: 224–241.

Broad, W. J. (2006) *The Oracle: The Lost Secrets and Hidden Message of Ancient Delphi.* New York: Penguin.

Broneer, O. T. (1941) *The Lion Monument at Amphipolis.* Cambridge, MA: Harvard University Press.

Bruit Zaidman, L., Schmitt Pantel, P., and Cartledge, P. (1992) *Religion in the Ancient Greek City;* translated by Paul Cartledge. Cambridge: Cambridge University Press.

Bruneau, P. (2006) *Etudes d'archéologie délienne* in *Bulletin de Correspondance Hellénique.* Supplément: 47. Athens: École française d'Athènes.

Brunschwig, J. and Lloyd, G. E. R. with the collaboration of Pierre Pellegrin (eds.) (2000) *Greek Thought: A Guide to Classical Knowledge;* translated under the direction of C. Porter. Cambridge, MA: The Belknap Press of Harvard University Press.

Brunt, P. A. (1993) *Studies in Greek History and Thought.* Oxford: Clarendon Press.

Bryan, W. F. and Dempster, G. (1958) *Sources and Analogues of Chaucer's Canterbury Tales.* New York: Humanities Press.

Bühler, W. (ed.) (1999) *Zenobii Athoi proverbia/vulgari ceteraque memoria aucta edidit et enarravit Winfried Bühler, vol. 5: Libri secundi proverbia 41–108 complexum.* Gottingae [Göttingen]: Vandenhoeck & Ruprecht.

Burger, R. (1999) *The Phaedo: A Platonic Labyrinth.* South Bend, IN: St Augustine's Press. Originally published New Haven, CT: Yale University Press, 1984.

Burkert, W. (1985) *Greek Religion: Archaic and Classical;* translated by J. Raffan. Oxford: Blackwell Publishing.

Burr Thompson, D. (1993) *An Ancient Shopping Centre: The Athenian Agora.* Princeton, NJ: American School of Classical Studies at Athens.

Calame, C. (1997) *Choruses of Young Women in Ancient Greece: Their Morphology, Religious Role and Social Function*; translated by D. Collins and J. Orion. London: Rowman and Littlefield.

——— (1996) *Thésée et l'imaginaire athénien: Légende et culte en Grèce antique*. 2nd edn. with corrections. Lausanne: Editions Payot Lausanne.

Cameron, A. and Kuhrt, A. (eds.) (1993) *Images of Women in Antiquity*. London: Routledge.

Camp, J. Mck. (1986. Revised 1999 and April 2010) *The Athenian Agora: Excavations in the Heart of Classical Athens*. London: Thames and Hudson.

——— (1990) *The Athenian Agora: A Guide to the Excavation and Museum* (4th edn.). Athens: American School of Classical Studies at Athens.

——— (2003) *The Athenian Agora: A Short Guide*. Athens: American School of Classical Studies at Athens.

——— (1998) *Horses and Horsemanship in the Athenian Agora*. Athens: American School of Classical Studies at Athens.

Cantarella, E. (2002) *Bisexuality in the Ancient World*; translated by C. Ó. Cuilleanáin. New Haven, CT: Yale Nota Bene.

Carey, C. (2001) *Democracy in Classical Athens*. London: Bristol Classical Press.

——— (1997) *Trials from Classical Athens*. London and New York: Routledge.

Cartledge, P. (2009) *Ancient Greek Political Thought in Practice*. Cambridge: Cambridge University Press.

——— (2002) *Sparta and Lakonia: A Regional History 1300 to 362 BC*. London: Routledge.

——— (2001) *Spartan Reflections*. London: Duckworth.

——— (2006) 'Spartan Traditions and Receptions' in *Hermathena* 181: 41–49.

——— (2003) *The Spartans: An Epic History*. London: Macmillan.

——— (2006) *Thermopylae: The Battle that Changed the World*. London: Macmillan.

Coates, J. F., Morrison, J. S. and Rankov, N. B. (2000) *The Athenian Trireme: The History and Reconstruction of an Ancient Greek Warship*; rev. 2nd edn. Cambridge: Cambridge University Press.

Coates, J. F., Platis, S. K. and Shaw, J. T. (1990) *The Trireme Trials 1988: Report on the Anglo-Hellenic Sea Trials of Olympias*. Oxford: Oxbow Books.

Colaiaco, J. A (2001) *Socrates Against Athens: Philosophy on Trial*. New York and London: Routledge.

Colebrook, C. (2004) *Irony*. London and New York: Routledge.

Collard, C., Cropp, M. J., and Lee, K.H. (2004) *Euripides: Selected Fragmentary Plays. Vol. 2, Philoctetes, Alexandros* (with *Palamedes and Sisyphus*), *Oedipus,*

Andromeda, Hypsipyle, Antiope, Archelaus; with Introductions, Translations and Commentaries. Warminster: Aris & Phillips.

Conacher, D. J. (1998a) *Euripides and the Sophists: Some Dramatic Treatments of Philosophical Ideas.* London: Duckworth.

Connelly, J. B. (2007) *Portrait of a Priestess: Women and Ritual in Ancient Greece.* Princeton, NJ: Princeton University Press.

Connolly P. and Dodge, H. (2001) *The Ancient City: Life in Classical Athens and Rome.* Oxford: Oxford University Press.

Connor, W. R. (1991) 'The Other 399: Religion and the Trial of Socrates' in M. A. Flower and M. Toher (eds.) *Georgica : Greek Studies in Honour of George Cawkwell.* London: University of London, Institute of Classical Studies: 49–56.

Cosmopoulos, M. B. (ed.) (2003) *Greek Mysteries: The Archaeology and Ritual of Ancient Greek Secret Cults.* London and New York: Routledge.

Csapo, E. and Slater, W. J. (1995) *The Context of Ancient Drama.* Ann Arbor: University of Michigan Press.

Davidson, J. (1998) *Courtesans and Fishcakes: The Consuming Passions of Classical Athens.* London: Fontana Press.

———— (2007) *The Greeks and Greek Love: A Radical Reappraisal of Homosexuality in Ancient Greece.* London: Weidenfeld & Nicolson.

Davies, J. K. (2003) 'Democracy without Theory' in P. Derow and R. Parker (eds.), *Herodotus and his World: Essays from a Conference in Memory of George Forrest.* Oxford: Oxford University Press. 319–366.

De Boer, J. Z. and Hale, J. R. (2000) 'The Geological Origin of the Oracles at Delphi, Greece' in *Geological Society Special Publication* 171: 399–412.

De Boer, J. Z. Hale, J. R. and Chanton, J. (2001) 'New Evidence of the Geological Origins of the Ancient Delphic Oracle (Greece)' in *Geology* 29: 707–710.

Deacy, S. and Pierce, K. F. (eds.) (2002) *Rape in Antiquity: Sexual Violence in the Greek and Roman Worlds.* London: Duckworth.

Dean-Jones, L. (1994) *Women's Bodies in Classical Greek Science.* Oxford: Clarendon.

Deighton, H. J. (1995) *A Day in the Life of Ancient Athens.* Bristol: Bristol Classical Press.

Delebecque, É. (1957) *Essai sur la Vie de Xénophon* (Paris: C. Klincksieck).

Demand, N. (1995) 'Monuments, Midwives and Gynecology' in Ph. J. van der Eijk, H. F. J. Horstmanshoff and P. H. Shrijvers (eds.) *Ancient Medicine in its Socio-Cultural Context.* Amsterdam: Rodopi: 275–291.

Denyer, N. (2008) *Protagoras/ Plato.* Cambridge: Cambridge University Press.

Deubner, L. (1932) *Attische Feste* (Berlin: Verlag Heinrich Keller).

Develin, R. (1989) *Athenian Officials 684–321 B.C.* Cambridge: Cambridge University Press.

Dherbey, G. and Gourinat, J. B. (eds.) (2001) *Socrate et les Socratiques*. Paris: J. Vrin.

Dillon, J. (2006) 'Review: G. Betegh's *The Derveni Papyrus: Cosmology, Theology and Interpretation*, Cambridge University Press, 2004' in *Hermathena* 181.

Dillon, M. (2003) *Girls and Women in Classical Greek Religion*. London and New York: Routledge.

Dohrn-van Rossom, G. (1996) *History of the Hour: Clocks and Modern Temporal Orders*. Trans. T. Dunlap. Chicago: University of Chicago Press.

Dorian, L. (2006) 'Xenophon's Socrates' translated by S. Menn in S. Ahbel-Rappe and R. Kamtekar (eds.) (2006) *A Companion to Socrates*. Oxford: Blackwell: 93–109.

Döring, K. (1998) 'Sokrates, die Sokratiker und die von ihnen begründeten Traditionen' in K. von Döring, H. Flashar, G. B. Kerferd, C. Oser-Grote and H. Waschkies (eds.) *Die Philosophie der Antike 2/1: Sophistik, Sokrates, Sokratik, Mathematik, Medizin*. Basel: Schwabe & Co: 139–364.

Dover, K. J. (1996) 'Aristophanes (1)', *OCD³* (Oxford/New York: OUP): 163–165.

———— (1968) *Aristophanes* Clouds. Oxford: Clarendon.

———— (1993) *Aristophanes* Frogs (Oxford/New York: OUP).

Dowden, K. (1992) *The Uses of Greek Mythology*. London and New York: Routledge.

Dübner, F. (1842) *Scholia Graeca in Aristophanem, cum prolegomenis grammaticorum, varietate lectionis optimorum codicum integra, ceterorum selecta, annotatione criticorum item selecta, cui sua quaedam inseruit*. Paris: Firmin Didot.

duBois, P. (2010) *Out of Athens. The New Ancient Greeks*. Cambridge, MA: Harvard University Press.

Edelstein, L. (1966) *Plato's Seventh Letter* (Leiden: Brill).

Edmonds III, R. G. (2000) 'Socrates the Beautiful: Role Reversal and Midwifery in Plato's *Symposium*' in *TAPA* 130: 261–285.

Edmunds, L. (2006) 'What was Socrates Called?' in *Classical Quarterly* 56: 414–425.

Emerson, M. (2007) *Greek Sanctuaries: An Introduction*. London: Bristol Classical Press.

Emlyn-Jones, C. (1999) *Plato: Crito*. London: Duckworth/Bristol Classical Press.

———— (2007) *Plato Republic 1-2.368c4*. Oxford: Aris and Phillips Classical Texts, Oxbow Books.

Evans, J. C. (1998) *The History and Practice of Ancient Astronomy*. Oxford: Oxford University Press.

Faraone, C. A. (2002) 'Curses and Social Control in the Law Courts of Classical Athens' in D. Cohen and E. Müller-Luckner (eds.) *Demokratie, Recht und soziale Kontrolle im klassischen Athen*. München: Oldenbourg.

Fernández-Armesto, F. (2001) *Civilisations: Culture, Ambition, and the Transformation of Nature*. New York: The Free Press.

Ferrari, G. R. F. (2005) *City and Soul in Plato's Republic*. Chicago and London: University of Chicago Press.

Figueira, T. J. (1991) *Athens and Aegina in the Age of Imperial Colonization*. Baltimore: Johns Hopkins University Press.

Finley, M. (1973) *The Ancient Economy*. Berkeley: University of California Press.

Fitton, J. W. (1970) 'That was no Lady, that was ...' in *Classical Quarterly* 20: 56–66.

Foley, H. P. (2001) *Female Acts in Greek Tragedy*. Princeton, NJ: Princeton University Press.

———— (1994) *Homeric Hymn to Demeter: Translation, Commentary, and Interpretive Essay*. Princeton, NJ: Princeton University Press.

Forstater, M. (2004) *The Living Wisdom of Socrates*. London: Hodder and Stoughton.

Fraser, P. M. and Matthews, E. (eds.) (1987) *A Lexicon of Greek Personal Names*. Vol. 1. Oxford: Clarendon Press.

Frazer, J. G. (1898) *Pausaniass' Description of Greece*, translated with a commentary. (6 vols). London: Macmillan.

French, A. (1964) *The Growth of the Athenian Economy*. London and New York: Routledge, Taylor & Francis.

Frost, F. J. (1980) 'Plutarch and Theseus' reprinted in F. J. Frost (2005) *Politics and the Athenians: Essays on Athenian History and Historiography*. Toronto: E. Kent.

Gabrielsen, V. (1994) *Financing the Athenian Fleet: Public Taxation and Social Relations*. 68–86. Baltimore; London: Johns Hopkins University Press.

Gale, X. L. (2000) 'Historical Studies and Postmodernism: Rereading Aspasia of Miletus' in *College English* 62.3: 361–386.

Garland, R. (1990) *The Greek Way of Life: From Conception to Old Age*. London: Duckworth.

———— (2001, 2nd edn.) *The Piraeus from the Fifth to the First Century B.C.* London: Duckworth.

Gellrich, M. (1994) 'Socratic Magic: Enchantment, Irony, and Persuasion in Plato's Dialogues' in *Classical World* 87.4: 275–309.

Gerolymatos, A. (1986) *Espionage and Treason: A Study of the Proxenia in Political and Military Intelligence Gathering in Classical Greece*. Amsterdam: J. C. Gieben.

Glenn, C. (1994) 'Sex, Lies and Manuscript: Refiguring Aspasia in the History of Rhetoric' in *College Composition and Communication* 45.2: 180–199.

Godwin, J. (2002) *The Pagan Dream of the Renaissance*. Grand Rapids, MI: Phanes Press, Inc.

Golden, M. (1988) 'Did the Ancients Care when Their Children Died?' in *Greece and Rome* 35.2: 152–163.

Goldhill, S. (2004) *Love, Sex and Tragedy: Why Classics Matters*. London: John Murray.

Goodison, L. and Morris, C. (eds.) (1998) *Ancient Goddesses: The Myths and the Evidence*. London: British Museum Press.

Gottlieb, A. (1971) *Socrates*. London: Phoenix.

Graham, D. W. (2006) *Explaining the Cosmos: The Ionian Tradition of Scientific Philosophy*. Princeton, NJ: Princeton University Press.

———— (2008) 'Socrates on Samos' in *Classical Quarterly* 58: 308–313.

Grant, M. (2001) *The Rise of the Greeks*. London: Phoenix.

Gray, V. J. (ed.) (2007) *Xenophon on Government*. Cambridge: Cambridge University Press.

Greaves, A. M. (2002) *Miletos: A History*. London: Routledge.

Green, J. R. (2001) 'Comic Cuts: Snippets of Action on the Greek Comic Stage' in *Bulletin of the Institute of Classical Studies* 45: 37–64.

———— (1994) *Theatre in Ancient Greek Society*. London: Routledge.

Gress, D. (1998) *From Plato to Nato: The Idea of the West and Its Opponents*. New York: The Free Press.

Guthrie, W. K. C. (2000) *Socrates*. Cambridge: Cambridge University Press.

Hale, J. R. (2010) *Lords of the Sea: The Triumph and Tragedy of Ancient Athens*. London: Gibson Square Books Ltd.

Halliwell, S. (2008) *Greek Laughter: A Study of Cultural Psychology from Homer to Early Christianity*. Cambridge: Cambridge University Press.

Hamel, D. (2003) *Trying Neaira: The True Story of a Courtesan's Scandalous Life in Ancient Greece*. New Haven and London: Yale University Press.

Hannah, R. (2005) *Greek and Roman Calendars: Constructions of Time in the Classical World*. London: Duckworth.

Hansen, M. H. (1999) *The Athenian Democracy in the Age of Demosthenes: Structure, Principles and Ideology*. Translated by J. A. Crook. London: Bristol Classical Press.

———— (2006) *Polis: An Introduction to the Ancient Greek City-State*. Oxford: Oxford University Press.

———— (1989) 'Solonian Democracy in Fourth-Century Athens' in *Classica et Mediaevalia* 40: 71–99.

———— (1995) *The Trial of Sokrates – from the Athenian Point of View*. Copenhagen: Det Kongelige Danske Videnskabernes Selskab.

———— (1989) *Was Athens a Democracy?: Popular Rule, Liberty and Equality in*

Ancient and Modern Political Thought. Copenhagen: Royal Danish Academy of Sciences and Letters.

Hanson, A. E. (1991) 'Continuity and Change: Three Case Studies' in S. Pomeroy (ed.) *Women's History and Ancient History.* Chapel Hill; London: University of North Carolina Press: 73–111.

———— (1994) 'A Division of Labor: Roles for Men in Greek and Roman Births' in *Thamyris* 1.2: 157–202.

———— (1975) 'Hippocrates: "Diseases of Women 1"' in *Signs* 1.2: 567–584.

———— (1996) 'Phaenarete: Mother and *Maia*' in R. Wittern and P. Pellegrin (eds.) *Hippokratische Medizin und antike Philosophie: Verhandlungen des VIII. Internationalen Hippokrates-Kolloquiums in Kloster Banz/Staffelstein vom 23.–28. Sept. 1993.* Hildesheim: Olms: 159–181.

Hanson, V. D. (1998) *Warfare and Agriculture in Classical Greece.* Berkeley and Los Angeles: University of California Press.

———— (2005) *A War Like No Other: How the Athenians and the Spartans Fought the Peloponnesian War.* London: Methuen Publishing Ltd.

Harris, W. V. (1989) *Ancient Literacy.* Cambridge, MA: Harvard University Press.

Hatzilambrou R., Parsons P. J., and Chapa J. (eds.) (2007) *The Oxyrhynchus Papyri LXXI.* London: Egypt Exploration Society.

Hawley, R. and Levick, B. (eds.) (1995) *Women in Antiquity: New Assessments.* London and New York: Routledge.

Henrichs, A. (1996) 'Dancing in Athens, Dancing on Delos: Some Patterns of Choral Projection in Euripides.' *Philologus* 140 (1): 48–62.

Henry, M. H. (1995) *Prisoner of History: Aspasia of Miletus and Her Biographical Tradition.* New York: Oxford University Press.

Herman, G. (1994) 'How Violent was Athenian Democracy?' in G. Herman (2006) *Morality and Behaviour in Democratic Athens: A Social History.* Cambridge: Cambridge University Press.

Higgins, M. D. and Higgins, R. (1996) *A Geological Companion to Greece and the Aegean.* London: Duckworth.

Hiscock, M. (2009, forthcoming) 'Socrates, Aegeus and Logoi as "Reasons"'.

Hobbs, A. (2000) *Plato and the Hero. Courage, Manliness and the Impersonal Good.* Cambridge: Cambridge University Press.

Hodge (1981) 'The Mystery of Apollo's E at Delphi' *American Journal of Archaeology* 85: 83–84.

Holland, T. (2005) *Persian Fire: The First World Empire and the Battle for the West.* London: Little, Brown.

Hornblower, S. (2002, 3rd edn.) *The Greek World 479–323 B.C.* London and New York: Routledge.

Hornblower, S. and Osborne, R. (eds.) (1994) *Ritual, Finance, Politics: Athenian democratic accounts presented to David Lewis.* Oxford: Clarendon Press.

Hughes, B. (2005) *Helen of Troy, Goddess, Princess, Whore.* London: Jonathan Cape.

Hughes-Hallett, L. (2004) *Heroes: Saviours, Traitors and Supermen.* London: Fourth Estate.

Hunt, P. (2002) *Slaves, Warfare, and Ideology in the Greek Historians.* Cambridge: Cambridge University Press.

Hunter, V. J. (1994) *Policing Athens: Social Control in the Attic Lawsuits, 420–320 B.C.* Princeton, NJ: Princeton University Press.

Hurwit, J. M. (2004) *The Acropolis in the Age of Pericles.* Cambridge, UK; New York: Cambridge University Press.

——— (1999) *The Athenian Acropolis: History, Mythology, and Archaeology from the Neolithic Era to the Present.* Cambridge: Cambridge University Press.

——— (1995) 'Beautiful Evil: Pandora and the Athena Parthenos' in *AJA* 99.2: 171–186.

Irvine, A. D. (2008) *Socrates on Trial: A Play Based on Aristophanes'* Clouds *and Plato's* Apology, Crito *and* Phaedo *Adapted for Modern Performance.* Toronto: University of Toronto Press.

Irwin, T. H. (1983) 'Euripides and Socrates' in *Classical Philology* 78: 183-197.

Jacoby, F. (1950) *Die Fragmente der griechischen Historiker. Teil 3: Geschichte von Städten und Völkern. Nr. 297–607.* Leiden: E. J. Brill.

Janko, R. (2002–03) 'God, Science and Socrates', in *Bulletin of the Institute of Classical Studies* 46: 1–18.

Johansen, T. (2004) *Plato's Natural Philosophy: A Study of Timaeus-Critias.* Cambridge: Cambridge University Press.

Johnstone, S. (1999) *Disputes and Democracy: The Consequences of Litigation in Ancient Athens.* Austin: University of Texas Press.

Jones, J. E., Graham, A. J., and Sackett, L. H. (1973) *An Attic Country House: Below the Cave of Pan at Vari.* London: British School at Athens: Thames and Hudson.

Jones, W. H. S. (ed.) (1965) *Pausanias: Description of Greece. Vol. I.* New York: Biblo and Tannen.

Joseph, J. E. (2000) *Limiting the Arbitrary: Linguistic Naturalism and Its Opposites in Plato's Cratylus and Modern Theories of Language.* Amsterdam: John Benjamins Publishing.

Joun, F. and Looy, H. (eds.) (2003) *Euripide: Tragédies. Tome VIII, 4e partie. Fragments de drames non identifiés.* Paris: Les Belles Lettres.

Judson, L. and Karasmanis, V. (eds.) (2006) *Remembering Socrates: Philosophical Essays*. Oxford: Clarendon Press.

Just, R. (2000) *Women in Athenian Law and Life*. London and New York: Routledge.

Kadletz, E. (1981) 'The Tongues of Greek Sacrificial Victims' in *Harvard Theological Review* 74.1: 21-29.

Kagan, D. (1981) *The Peace of Nicias and the Sicilian Expedition*. Ithaca, NY: Cornell University Press.

Kahn, H. C. (2006) 'Socrates and Hedonism' in Judson, L. and Karasmanis, V. (eds.) (2006) *Remembering Socrates: Philosophical Essays*. Oxford: Clarendon Press.

Kaltsas, N. and Shapiro, A. (eds.) (2009) *Worshipping Women. Ritual and Reality in Classical Athens*. New York: Alexander S. Onassis Public Benefit Foundation (USA).

Karageorghis, V. (1982) *Cyprus: From the Stone Age to the Romans*. London: Thames and Hudson.

Kendrick Pritchett, W. (1965) *Studies in Ancient Greek Topography. Part I*. Berkeley: University of California Press.

Kerferd, G. B. (1981) *The Sophistic Movement*. Cambridge: Cambridge University Press.

Keuls, E. C. (1993) *The Reign of the Phallus: Sexual Politics in Ancient Athens*. Berkeley and Los Angeles: University of California Press.

King, H. (1998) *Hippocrates' Women: Reading the Female Body in Ancient Greece*. London and New York: Routledge.

Konstam, N. (2002) 'Sculpture: The Art and the Practice' in *Oxford Journal of Archaeology* 21.2: 153-165.

Konstam, N. and Hoffman, H. (2004) 'Casting the Riace Bronzes (2): A Sculptor's Discovery' in *Oxford Journal of Archaeology* 23.4: 397–402.

Laidlaw, W. A. (1933) *A History of Delos*. Oxford: B. Blackwell.

Lane, M. (2006) 'The Evolution of *Eironeia* in Classical Greek Texts: Why Socratic *Eironeia* is not Socratic Irony' in D. Sedley (ed.) *Oxford Studies in Ancient Philosophy* 31. Oxford: Oxford University Press: 49–83.

Lane Fox, R. (2005) *The Classical World: An Epic History from Homer to Hadrian*. London: Penguin.

Lang, M. L. (1978) *Socrates in the Agora*. Princeton, NJ: American School of Classical Studies at Athens.

Lanni, A. (2006) *Law and Justice in the Courts of Classical Athens*. Cambridge: Cambridge University Press.

——— (1997) 'Spectator Sport or Serious Politics? *Hoi periestekotes* and the Athenian Lawcourts' in *Journal of Hellenic Studies* 107: 183–189.

Lapatin, K. D. S. (2007) 'Art and Architecture' in L. J. Samons II (ed.) *The Cambridge Companion to the Age of Pericles*. Cambridge: Cambridge University Press: 125–152.

———— (2001) *Chryselephantine Statuary in the Ancient Mediterranean World*. New York: Oxford University Press.

———— (2006) 'Picturing Socrates' in S. Ahbel-Rappe and R. Kamtekar (eds.) *A Companion to Socrates*. Oxford: Blackwell: 110–159.

Lawton, C. (2006) *Marbleworkers in the Athenian Agora*. Athens: American School of Classical Studies at Athens; Oxford: Oxbow.

Lazenby, J. F. (2003) *Delion* in S. Hornblower and A. Spawforth (eds.) (3rd rev. edn.) *The Oxford Classical Dictionary*. Oxford: Oxford University Press.

Lear, J. (2006) 'The Socratic Method and Psychoanalysis' in Ahbel-Rappe, S. and Kamtekar, R. (eds.) (2006) *A Companion to Socrates*. Oxford: Blackwell: 442–462.

Lefkowitz, M. R. (1979) 'The Euripides *Vita*' in *Greek, Roman and Byzantine Studies* 20: 187–210.

Lendon, J. E. (2005) *Soldiers and Ghosts: A History of Battle in Classical Antiquity*. New Haven and London: Yale University Press.

Ling, R. and Ling, L. (2000) 'Wall and Panel Painting' in R. Ling (ed.) *Making Classical Art: Process and Practice*. Stroud: Tempus.

Llewellyn-Jones, L. (2003) *Aphrodite's Tortoise: The Veiled Woman of Ancient Greece*. Swansea: The Classical Press of Wales.

Lloyd, G. E. R. (1983) *Science, Folklore and Ideology: Studies in the Life Sciences in Ancient Greece*. Cambridge: Cambridge University Press.

Lloyd-Jones, H. (1994) Review of: Woodbury, L. E. (1991) 'Collected Writings', edited by C. G. Brown, R. L. Fowler, E. I. Robbins and P. M. Wallace Matheson. Atlanta, GA: Scholars Press.

Long, C. P. (2003) 'Dancing Naked with Socrates: Pericles, Aspasia, and Socrates at Play with Politics, Rhetoric and Philosophy' in *Ancient Philosophy* 23: 49–69.

Lonsdale, S. H. (1995) 'A Dancing Floor for Ariadne (*Iliad* 18.590–592): Aspects of Ritual Movement in Homer and Minoan Religion' in J. B. Carter and S. P. Morris (eds.) *The Ages of Homer; A Tribute to Emily Townsend Vermeule*. Austin: University of Texas Press: 273–284.

Lowe, N. J. (2007) 'Old Comedy and Aristophanes' in *Greece & Rome* 54: 21–62.

Luckhurst, K. W. (1934) 'Note on Plato *Charmides* 153B' in *Classical Review* 48.6: 207–208.

MacDowell, D. M. (1971) Aristophanes *Wasps*. Edited with introduction and commentary by Douglas M. MacDowell. Oxford: Clarendon Press.

———— (1978) *The Law in Classical Athens*. London: Thames and Hudson.

Macleod, M. D. (2008) *Xenophon:* Apology *and* Memorabilia *I.* Oxford: Aris & Phillips.

McCann, D. R. and Strauss, B. S. (eds.) (2001) *War and Democracy: A Comparative Study of the Korean War and the Peloponnesian War.* Armonk, NY: M. E. Sharpe.

McDonald, J. (1994) 'Supplementing Thucydides' Account of the Megarian Decree' in *Electronic Antiquity* 2.3 (http://scholar.lib.vt.edu/ejournals/ElAnt/V2N3/mcdonald.html).

McDonald, M. and Walton, J. M. (eds.) (2007) *The Cambridge Companion to Greek and Roman Theatre.* Cambridge: Cambridge University Press.

McGovern, P. E. and Michel, R. H. (1990) 'Royal Purple Dye: The Chemical Reconstruction of the Ancient Mediterranean Industry' in *Accounts of Chemical Research* 23.5: 152–158.

McLean, D. R. (2006) 'The Private Life of Socrates in Early Modern France' in S. Ahbel-Rappe and R. Kamtekar (eds.) (2006) *A Companion to Socrates.* Oxford: Blackwell: 353–367.

Marcovich, M. (1996) 'From Ishtar to Aphrodite' in *Journal of Aesthetic Education* 30.2: 43–59.

Marshall, C. W. (2000) 'Rotting Timbers' in *Echos du Monde Classique* 19: 351–357.

May, H. (2000) 'Socrates' in *Wadsworth Philosophers Series.* Belmont, CA: Wadsworth.

Mayor, A. (2003) *Greek Fire, Poison Arrows, and Scorpion Bombs: Biological and Chemical Warfare in the Ancient World.* Woodstock, NY, and New York: Overlook Press.

Meier, C. (1999) *Athens: A Portrait of the City in its Golden Age*; translated by R. Kimber and R. Kimber. London: John Murray.

Meiggs, R. (1972) *The Athenian Empire.* Oxford: Oxford University Press.

Mikalson, J. D. (2005) *Ancient Greek Religion.* Oxford: Blackwell.

——— (1977) 'Religion in the Attic Demes' in *American Journal of Philology* 98.4: 424–435.

Miller, M. C. (1997) *Athens and Persia in the Fifth Century BC: A Study in Cultural Receptivity.* Cambridge: Cambridge University Press.

——— (1989) 'The *Ependytes* in Classical Athens' in *Hesperia* 58.3: 313–329.

Mineur, W. H. (1984) *Callimachus, Hymn to Delos: Introduction and Commentary.* Leiden: E. J. Brill.

Mitchell, L. G. (1997) *Greeks Bearing Gifts. The Public Use of Private Relationships in the Greek World, 435–323 BC.* Cambridge: Cambridge University Press.

Monoson, S. S. (2000) *Plato's Democratic Entanglements: Athenian Politics and the Practice of Philosophy.* Princeton, NJ: Princeton University Press.

Morrison, J. S. (1987) 'The British Sea Trials of the Reconstructed Trireme, 1–15 August 1987' in *Antiquity* 61: 455–459.

——— (1988) 'The Second British Sea Trials of the Reconstructed Trireme, 20 July–5 August 1988' in *Antiquity* 62: 713–714.

Morrison, J. S., Coates, J. F., and Rankov, N. B. (2000) *The Athenian Trireme: The History and Reconstruction of an Ancient Greek Warship.* New York: Cambridge University Press.

Munn, M. (2006) *The Mother of the Gods, Athens, and the Tyranny of Asia: A Study of Sovereignty in Ancient Religion.* Berkeley and Los Angeles: University of California Press.

——— (2000) *The School of History: Athens in the Age of Socrates.* Berkeley: University of California Press.

Murray, O. (1995) 'Liberty and the Ancient Greeks' in J. A. Koumoulides (ed.) *The Good Idea: Democracy and Ancient Greece.* New York: Aristide D. Caratzas: 33–35.

Nails, D. (2002) *The People of Plato: A Prosopography of Plato and Other Sources.* Indianapolis, Cambridge: Hackett Publishing.

——— (2005) 'Socrates', *Stanford Encyclopedia of Philosophy* [http://plato.stanford.edu/entries/socrates/, accessed 4 December 2008].

——— (2006a) 'The Tragedy Off-Stage' in J. H. Lesher, D. Nails and F. C. C. Sheffield *Plato's Symposium: Issues in Interpretation and Reception.* Washington DC: distributed by Harvard University Press. 179–207.

——— (2006b) 'The Trial and Death of Socrates' in S. Ahbel-Rappe and R. Kamtekar (eds.) (2006) *A Companion to Socrates.* Oxford: Blackwell: 5–20.

Nauck, A. (1926) *Tragicorum Graecorum Fragmenta.* 2nd edn. Leipzig.

Navia, L. E. (2001) *Antisthenes of Athens: Setting the World Aright.* Westport, London: Greenwood Press.

Nesselrath, H.-G. (1996) 'Aristophanes (3)', *Der Neue Pauly* I (Stuttgart/Weimar: J.B. Metzler): cols 1122–1130.

——— (2007) *Socrates: A Life Examined.* Amherst, NY: Prometheus Books.

Neugebauer, O. (1975) *A History of Ancient Mathematical Astronomy.* Berlin; New York: Springer-Verlag.

Niku, M. (2007) *The Official Status of the Foreign Residents in Athens, 322–120 B.C.* Helsinki: Suomen Ateenan-instituutin säätiö (Foundation of the Finnish Institute at Athens).

Nutton, V. (2004) *Ancient Medicine.* New York: Routledge.

Ober, J. (1994) 'How to Criticize Democracy in Later Fifth and Fourth Century Athens' in J. P. Euben, J. Wallach, and J. Ober (eds.) *Athenian Political Thought and the Reconstruction of American Democracy.* Ithaca; London: Cornell University Press: 149–171.

Ober, J. and Hedrick, C. W. (eds.) (1993) *The Birth of Democracy. The National Archives, Washington, DC. June 15, 1993–January 2, 1994.* Athens: The American School of Classical Studies at Athens.

Ober, J., Raaflaub, K. A. and Wallace, R. W. (with chapters by P. Cartledge and C. Farrar) (2007) *Origins of Democracy in Ancient Greece.* Berkeley and Los Angeles: University of California Press.

O'Dowd, M. J. and Elliott, P. (1994) *The History of Obstetrics and Gynaecology.* London: Parthenon.

Olson, S. D. (2002) *Aristophanes* Acharnians (Oxford: OUP).

Olson, S. Douglas (2007) *Broken Laughter: Select Fragments of Greek Comedy.* Oxford: Oxford University Press.

Osborne M. J. and Byrne, S. G. (eds.) (1994) *A Lexicon of Greek Personal Names. Vol. II: Attica.* Oxford: Clarendon Press.

Osborne, R. (2004) *The Old Oligarch: Pseudo-Xenophon's Constitution of the Athenians.* London: London Association of Classical Teachers.

Ostwald, M. (1986) *From Popular Sovereignty to the Sovereignty of Law: Law, Society and Politics in Fifth Century Athens.* Berkeley: University of California Press.

Parke, H. W. (1977) *Festivals of the Athenians.* London: Thames and Hudson.

Parker, M. (1986) *Socrates and Athens.* London: Bristol Classical Press.

Parker, R. (1996) *Athenian Religion: A History.* Oxford: Clarendon Press.

————— (2005) *Polytheism and Society in Athens.* Oxford: Oxford University Press.

Parlama, L., Stampolidis, N. and Abrams, H. N. (2000) *The City Beneath the City: Antiquities from the Metropolitan Railway Excavations.* Athens: Greek Ministry of Culture.

Patterson, C. (2007) 'Other Sorts: Slaves, Foreigners, and Women in Periclean Athens' in L. J. Samons II (ed.) *The Cambridge Companion to the Age of Pericles.* Cambridge: Cambridge University Press: 153–178.

Pedley, J. (2006) *Sanctuaries and the Sacred in the Ancient Greek World.* New York: Cambridge University Press.

Pellizer, E. (1990) 'Outlines of a Morphology of Sympotic Entertainment' in O. Murray (ed.) *Sympotica: A Symposium on the Symposion.* Oxford: Clarendon Press: 178–184.

Philips, C. (2007) *Socrates in Love: Philosophy for a Passionate Heart.* New York: W. W. Norton.

Planeaux, C. (1999) 'Socrates, Alcibiades, and Plato's ta Poteideiatika. Does the *Charmides* have an historical setting?' *Mnemosyne* 52: 72–77.

Pollard, J. (1977) *Birds in Greek Life and Myth.* London: Thames and Hudson.

Pomeroy, S. (1994) *Xenophon* Oeconomicus (Oxford: Clarendon).

Pomeroy, S. B. (1994) *Goddesses, Whores, Wives and Slaves: Women in Classical Antiquity.* London: Pimlico, Random House.

———— (2002) *Spartan Women*. New York: Oxford University Press.

Powell, A. (2001) *Athens and Sparta: Constructing Greek Political and Social History from 478 B.C.* 2nd edn. London: Routledge.

Press, G. A. (2007) *Plato: A Guide for the Perplexed*. London/New York: Continuum.

Pritchett, W. K. (1971) *The Greek State at War. I.* Berkeley; London: University of California Press.

Raaflaub K. A., Ober J., and Wallace R. W. co-authors (2007) *Origins of Democracy in Ancient Greece*. Berkeley; London: University of California Press.

Ray, J. (2007) *The Rosetta Stone and the Rebirth of Ancient Egypt*. London: Profile Books.

Rehm, R. (2007) 'Festivals and Audiences in Athens and Rome' in M. McDonald and J. M. Walton (eds.) *The Cambridge Companion to Greek and Roman Theatre*. Cambridge: Cambridge University Press: 184–201.

Reinhold, M. (1970) 'The History of Purple as a Status Symbol in Antiquity' in *Latomus* 116: 1–73.

Reydams-Schils, G. (2005) *The Roman Stoics: Self, Responsibility, and Affection*. Chicago: University of Chicago Press.

Rhodes, P. J. (1972) *The Athenian Boule*. Oxford: Clarendon Press.

———— (2007) *The Greek City States: A Source Book*. Cambridge: Cambridge University Press.

———— (2005) *A History of the Classical Greek World, 478–323 BC*. Oxford: Blackwell.

———— (2003) 'Nothing to do with Democracy: Athenian Drama and the Polis' in *Journal of Hellenic Studies* 123: 104–119.

Roberts, J. T. (1994) *Athens on Trial: The Antidemocratic Tradition in Western Thought*. Princeton, NJ: Princeton University Press.

Roberts, J. W. (1998) *City of Sokrates: An Introduction to Classical Athens*. London: Routledge.

Robertson, N. (1992) *Festivals and Legends: The Formation of Greek Cities in the Light of Public Ritual*. Toronto: University of Toronto Press.

Robertson, W. H. (1990) *An Illustrated History of Contraception: A Concise Account of the Quest for Fertility Control*. Carnforth: Parthenon.

Robinson, E. W. (2004) *Greek Democracy: Readings and Sources*. Oxford: Blackwell.

Robinson, T. M. and Brisson, L. (eds.) (2000) *Plato:* Euthydemus, Lysis, Charmides. *Proceedings of the V Symposium Platonicum Selected Papers*. Sankt Augustin: Academia Verlag.

Romer, F. E. (1996) 'Diagoras the Melian (Diod. Sic. 13.6.7)' in *The Classical World* 89: 393–401.

Rood, T. (2004) *The Sea! The Sea! The Shout of the Ten Thousand in the Modern Imagination.* London: Duckworth.

Rose, M. L. (2003) *The Staff of Oedipus: Transforming Disability in Ancient Greece.* Ann Arbor: University of Michigan Press.

Rosenzweig, R. (2007) *Worshipping Aphrodite: Art and Cult in Classical Athens.* Ann Arbor: University of Michigan Press.

Rotberg, I. C. (ed.) (2004) *Balancing Change and Tradition in Global Education Reform.* Lanham, MD; Oxford: Scarecrow Education.

Rudesbusch, G. (1999) *Socrates, Pleasure, and Value.* New York: Oxford University Press.

Ruschenbusch, E. (1958) 'Patrios Politeia: Theseus, Drakon, Solon und Kleisthenes in Publizistik und Geschichtsschreibung des 5. und 4. Jh.' in *Historia* 7: 398–424.

Rutherford, I. (2000) 'Theoria and Darshan: Pilgrimage and Vision in Greece and India' in *Classical Quarterly* 50: 133–146.

Sage, M. M. (1996) *Warfare in Ancient Greece: A Sourcebook.* London; New York: Routledge.

Sallares, R. (1991) *The Ecology of the Ancient Greek World.* London: Duckworth.

Salza Prina Ricotti E. (2007) *Meals and Recipes from Ancient Greece*; translated by R. A. Lotero. Los Angeles: J. Paul Getty Museum.

Samons, L. J. (2007) 'Conclusion: Pericles and Athens' in Samons II, L.J. (ed.) *The Cambridge Companion to the Age of Pericles.* New York: Cambridge University Press: 282–307.

———— (2001) 'Democracy, Empire and the Search for the Athenian Character', *Arion* 8.3: 128–157.

———— (2000) *Empire of the Owl: Athenian Imperial Finance.* Stuttgart: F. Steiner.

———— (2004) *What's Wrong with Democracy? From Athenian Practice to American Worship.* Berkeley: University of California Press.

Sands, C. (2008) 'Review: C. Phillips, Socrates in Love. Norton' in *TLS* April 25 2008.

Sarla, M., Evangelou, P. and Tsimpidis-Pentazos, E. (1973) *The Temple of Olympian Zeus and the Roman Agora.* Athens: Keramos Guides.

Saxonhouse, A. W. (2006) *Free Speech and Democracy in Ancient Athens.* New York: Cambridge University Press.

Scanlon, T. F. (2002) *Eros and Greek Athletics.* New York: Oxford University Press.

Schütrumpf, E. E. (2002) 'Xenophon (2)', *Der Neue Pauly* XII.2: cols 633–642.

Scott, D. (ed.) (2007) *Maieusis. Essays on Ancient Philosophy in Honour of Myles Burnyeat.* Oxford: Oxford University Press.

Seager, R. (2001) 'Xenophon and Athenian Democratic Ideology' in *Classical Quarterly* 51: 385–397.

Seel, G. (2006) 'If You Know What Is Best, You Do It: Socratic Intellectualism in Xenophon and Plato' in L. Judson and V. Karasmanis (eds.) *Remembering Socrates: Philosophical Essays*. Oxford: Clarendon Press: 20–50.

Segal, C. P. (1965) 'The Tragedy of Hippolytus: The Waters of the Ocean and the Untouched Meadow' in *HSCP* 70: 117–169.

Sekunda, N. V. (2005) *The Ancient Greeks*. Oxford: Osprey Publishing Ltd.

———— (2000) *The Spartans*. Oxford: Osprey Publishing Ltd.

Sellars, J. (2003) 'Simon the Shoemaker and the Problems of Socrates' in *Journal of Classical Philology* 98: 207–216.

Seung, T. K. (1996) *Plato Rediscovered: Human Value and Social Order*. Lanham, MD: Rowman & Littlefield Publishers.

Sharwood Smith, J. (1990) *Greece and the Persians*. Bristol: Bristol Classical Press.

Shear, T. Leslie. (1995) 'Bouleuterion, Metroon and the Archives at Athens' in Hansen and Raaflaub 1995: 157–190.

Sheehan, S. (2007) *Socrates*. London: Haus Publishing.

Sickinger, J. (2004) 'The Laws of Athens: Publication, Preservation, Consultation' in E. M. Harris and L. Rubinstein, *The Law and the Courts in Ancient Greece*. London: Duckworth: 93–109.

Sifakis, G. M. (2001) 'The Function and Significance of Music in Tragedy', *Bulletin of the Institute of Classical Studies* 45: 21–35.

Simon, E. (1983) *Festivals of Attica: An Archaeological Commentary*. Madison: University of Wisconsin Press.

Sissa, G. and Detienne, M. (2000) *The Daily Life of the Greek Gods*; translated by J. Lloyd. Stanford: Stanford University Press.

Skinner, M. B. (2005) *Sexuality in Greek and Roman Culture*. Oxford: Blackwell.

Smith, A. C. (2003) 'Athenian Political Art from the Fifth and Fourth Centuries BCE: Images of Political Personifications' in C. W. Blackwell (ed.) *Demos: Classical Athenian Democracy* (A. Mahoney and R. Scaife, eds., *The Stoa: A Consortium for Electronic Publication in the Humanities* [www.stoa.org]) edition of 18 January 2003. Contact: cwb@stoa.org.

Smith, R. R. (2009) *Breakfast with Socrates. The Philosophy of Everyday Life*. London: Profile.

Smith, W. (ed.) (1844–1849) *Dictionary of Greek and Roman Biography and Mythology*. London: Taylor and Walton.

Smith, W. S. (1997) 'The Wife of Bath Debates Jerome' in *Chaucer Review* 32.2. Pennsylvania State University: 129–145.

Sokolowski, F. (ed.) (1962) *Les Lois Sacrées de Cités Grecques*. Paris: E. de Boccard.

Solmsen, F. (1969), Review of Edelstein (1966), *Gnomon* 41: 29–34.

Sommerstein, A. H. (1982) *Clouds* /Aristophanes; edited with translation and notes by A. H. Sommerstein. Warminster: Aris & Phillips.

——— (2002) *Greek Drama and Dramatists*. London: Routledge.

——— (2009) *Talking about Laughter: And Other Studies in Greek Comedy*. Oxford: Oxford University Press.

Sosin, J. D. (2008) 'The New Letter from Pasion' in *Zeitschrift für Papyrologie und Epigraphik* 165: 105–108.

Souza, de P. (2003) *The Greek and Persian Wars 499–386 B.C.* Oxford: Osprey Publishing Ltd.

Spivey, N. (2004) *The Ancient Olympics. War Minus the Shooting*. New York: Oxford University Press.

Stadter, P. A. (1989) *A Commentary on Plutarch's Pericles*. Chapel Hill: University of North Carolina Press.

Stefani, O. (1990) *I rilievi del Canova*. Milan: Electa.

Stone, I. F. (1988) *The Trial of Socrates*. Toronto: Little, Brown.

Storey, I. C. and Allan, A. (2005) *A Guide to Ancient Greek Drama*. Oxford: Blackwell.

Stroud, R. S. (1998) *The Athenian Grain-Tax Law of 374/3 B.C.*, in *Hesperia Supplements* 29. Princeton, NJ: American School of Classical Studies at Athens.

Szlezák, T. A. (2000) 'Platon (1)', *Der Neue Pauly* IX (Stuttgart/Weimar: J.B. Metzler), cols 1095–1109.

Taylor, C. C. W. (2000b) 'Review: Describing Greek Philosophy' in *Classical Review* 50: 140–142.

——— (2000a) *Socrates: A Very Short Introduction*. Oxford: Oxford University Press.

Thesleff, H. (1982) *Studies in Platonic Chronology*. Helsinki: Societas Scientiarum Fennica.

Thompson, H. A. and Wycherley, R. E. (1972) *The Agora of Athens: History, Shape and Uses of an Ancient City Center (The Athenian Agora* Vol. 14). Princeton: American School of Classical Studies at Athens.

Thorton, B. S. (1997) *Eros: The Myth of Ancient Greek Sexuality*. Oxford: Westview Press.

Tilley, A. F. (2004) *Seafaring on the Ancient Mediterranean*. Oxford: John and Erica Hedges Ltd [British Archaeological Reports 1268].

——— (1992) 'Three Men to a Room – a Completely Different Trireme' in *Antiquity* 66: 599–610.

Todd, S. C. (1996) *Athens and Sparta*. London: Bristol Classical Press.

——— (2000) 'How to Execute People in Fourth-century Athens' in V. Hunter and J. Edmonson (2000) *Law and Social Status in Classical Athens*. Oxford: Oxford University Press: 31–51.

———— (1993) *The Shape of Athenian Law*. Oxford: Clarendon Press.

Travlos, J. (1971) *Pictorial Dictionary of Ancient Athens*. London: Thames and Hudson.

Tucker, T. G. (1907) *Life in Ancient Athens: The Social and Public Life of a Classical Athenian from Day to Day*. London: Macmillan.

Tuplin, C. J. (1996) 'Xenophon (1)', *OCD³* (Oxford/New York: OUP): 1628–1630.

Van Wees, H. (2004) *Greek Warfare. Myths and Realities*. London: Duckworth.

Vander Waerdt, P. A. (1994) 'Socrates in the Clouds' in P. A. Vander Waerdt (ed.), *The Socratic Movement*. London: Cornell University Press: 48–86.

Vernant, J. (2001) *The Universe, the Gods and Mortals: Ancient Greek Myths*; translated by L. Asher. London: Profile Books.

Vickers, M. (2008) *Sophocles and Alcibiades: Athenian Politics in Ancient Greek Literature*. Stocksfield: Acumen.

Vivante, B. (2007) *Daughters of Gaia: Women in the Ancient Mediterranean World*. Westport, CT: Praeger Publishers.

Walker, H. J. (1995) *Theseus and Athens*. New York: Oxford University Press.

Wallace, R. W. (1994) 'Private Lives and Public Enemies: Freedom of Thought in Classical Athens' in A. L. Boegehold and A. C. Scafuro (eds.) *Athenian Identity and Civic Ideology*. Baltimore; London: The Johns Hopkins University Press: 205–238.

Waterfield, R. (2009) *Why Socrates Died. Dispelling the Myths*. London: Faber and Faber.

Whitby, M. (ed.) (2002) *Sparta*. Edinburgh: Edinburgh University Press.

White, F. C. (2008) 'Beauty of the Soul and Speech in Plato's *Symposium*' in *Classical Quarterly* 58: 69–81.

White, S. A. (2000) 'Socrates at Colonus: A Hero for the Academy' in N. D. Smith and P. B. Woodruff (eds.) (2000) *Reason and Religion in Socratic Philosophy*. Oxford: Oxford University Press: 151–175.

Whitehead, D. (1986) *The Demes of Attica, 508/7–ca.250 B.C.* Princeton and Guildford: Princeton University Press.

Wilkins, E. G. (1979) *'Know Thyself' in Greek and Latin Literature*. New York: Garland Pub.

Wilkins, J. (1990) 'The Young of Athens: Religion and Society in *Herakleidai* of Euripides' in *Classical Quarterly* 40: 329–339.

Wilkins, J. and Hill, S. (2006) *Food in the Ancient World*. Malden, MA; Oxford: Blackwell.

Williams, D. (1993) 'Women on Athenian Vases: Problems of Interpretation' in A. Cameron and A. Kuhrt (eds.), *Images of Women in Antiquity*. Detroit: Wayne State University Press: 92–107.

Wilson, E. (2007) *The Death of Socrates: Hero, Villain, Chatterbox, Saint*. London: Profile Books.

Wood, M. (2005) *The Road to Delphi: The Life and Afterlife of Oracles*. London: Pimlico, Random House.

Woodbury, L. (1965) 'The Date and Atheism of Diagoras of Melos' in *Phoenix* 19: 178–211.

———— (1973) 'Socrates and the Daughter of Aristides' in *Phoenix* 27: 7–25.

Woodhead, A. G. (1959) 'The Institution of the Hellenotamiae' in *Journal of Hellenic Studies* 79: 149–153.

Woodruff, P. (2005) *First Democracy: The Challenge of an Ancient Idea*. New York: Oxford University Press.

———— (1993) *On Justice, Power, and Human Nature: The Essence of Thucydides' History of the Peloponnesian War*; edited and translated by Paul Woodruff. Indianapolis and Cambridge: Hackett Publishing.

Young, S. (1939) 'An Athenian Clepsydra' in *Hesperia* 8.3, *The American Excavations in the Athenian Agora: Sixteenth Report*: 274–284.

Zahm, J. A. (1913) *Women in Science*. New York: Appleton.

Zaidman, L. B. and Pantel, P. S. (1992) *Religion in the Ancient Greek City* translated by P. Cartledge. Cambridge: Cambridge University Press.

Zanker, P. (1995) *The Mask of Socrates: The Image of the Intellectual in Antiquity* translated by A. Shapiro. Berkeley: University of California Press.

INDEX

@@@@@@@@@@@@@

473